CliffsNotes®

AP® English Literature and Composition 2021 Exam

by
Barbara V. Swovelin, M.A.

Houghton Mifflin Harcourt
Boston • New York

About the Author

Barbara V. Swovelin taught AP and Honors classes at Torrey Pines High School in Del Mar, California, for 34 years before retiring in 2014. She is an experienced AP English Exam Reader and a College Board Consultant, working both nationally and internationally. Additionally, she prepares new AP English teachers at College Board Institutes and Workshops. She has also taught graduate-level test preparation classes at California universities since 1986, specializing in the GRE, GMAT, and LSAT exams. Swovelin is also the author of *CliffsNotes AP English Language and Composition*.

Acknowledgments

I am forever indebted to Dr. Jerry Bobrow, in memoriam, for believing in me. I would also like to thank Dr. Allan Casson, in memoriam, and Jean Eggenschwiler for their meticulous work in the first three editions of this book.

Dedication

This book is dedicated to my husband, Jerry, who helped and encouraged me in every step of the process. I also dedicate it to the thousands of students I had over the years, who taught and inspired me more than I can express.

Editorial

Executive Editor: Greg Tubach

Senior Editor: Christina Stambaugh

Production Editor: Jennifer Freilach

Copy Editor: Lynn Northrup

Technical Editor: Jane R. Burstein

Proofreader: Susan Moritz

CliffsNotes® AP® English Literature and Composition 2021 Exam

Copyright © 2020 by Houghton Mifflin Harcourt Publishing Company

All rights reserved.

Library of Congress Control Number: 2019950377
ISBN: 978-1-328-48794-0 (pbk)

Printed in the United States of America
DOO 10 9 8 7 6 5 4 3 2 1
4500800618

For information about permission to reproduce selections from this book, write to trade.permissions@hmhco.com or to Permissions, Houghton Mifflin Harcourt Publishing Company, 3 Park Avenue, 19th Floor, New York, New York 10016.

www.hmhbooks.com

Table of Contents

Text Permissions

Introduction

Overview of the AP English Literature and Composition Exam

About the Exam

The AP English Literature and Composition Exam assesses your ability to perform the college-level work of a freshman English literature class. Actual college credit (either for one semester or for an entire year) may be offered by colleges and universities. The Advanced Placement (AP) English Literature and Composition Exam evaluates a student's competence in complex reading while analyzing and interpreting various genres, periods, and cultures of literature. Emphasis is placed on high-quality works of literature, as students look for central themes, meanings, and social/historical values relevant to the literary work. It is through this understanding that students are expected to use their knowledge and skills of critical analysis while considering the structure, style, imagery, symbolism, and tone, as well as the use of figurative language.

The exam lasts 3 hours and consists of two major sections: multiple choice and free response. The multiple-choice section includes 55 questions that address five reading passages (older exams used four passages with more questions per passage). All the questions in this section have equal value, and you will not be penalized for a wrong answer. The second portion of the exam is called the free-response section, frequently referred to as the essay section. You are given three essay topics, and you must write an essay on each of the three topics in 2 hours. The suggested time allotment for each essay is 40 minutes. Each of the essays is of equal value in your final score.

The multiple-choice questions are designed to test your ability in analyzing passages from works of fiction. These passages are drawn from poetry, novels, short stories, and plays that were originally written in English; therefore, the vast majority of passages come from literature of America and the British Isles. All passages will have been written since the late 16th century to the present; expect passages from many different time periods, but most passages will come from the 20th and 21st centuries. You will be asked questions about the passages' style, content, characters, and themes. Expect five reading passages with 8 to 15 questions per passage.

The free-response questions measure your expository and analytical writing skills. In general, expect that the three different essays will give you an opportunity to demonstrate your competency in the following:

1. Analyze how poetic devices in a short poem or an excerpt from a long poem help to create complex effects.
2. Analyze how an author's literary choices create complex meanings, based on a prose passage, excerpted from a novel or short story.
3. Analyze how a novel or play of your choice applies to a generic literary topic. You might be asked to explore such literary issues as character, setting, or conflict. This essay is called the open question (or topic) because you get to choose which novel or play you want to write on.

How the Exam Is Written and Graded

The AP English Literature and Composition Exam is written by a committee composed of three high school teachers, three university English teachers, and a representative from the College Board. The committee is geographically and ethnically representative, and because most of the members serve for only 4 years, its membership is constantly changing. The committee is responsible for selecting the passages used in both sections of the exam. Members of the committee carefully write the multiple-choice questions and free-response essay prompts, which are then screened by the entire committee and the Educational Testing Service (ETS). All of the questions are pretested in college literature or writing classes before they can be selected for use on an AP examination.

In May, the AP English Literature and Composition Development Committee convenes, and, after reading a large number of randomly selected essays, the committee creates additional notes for the scoring guide that differentiates between the numerical scores of 0–6 for each of the three free-response questions. Therefore, the scoring guide is based on the students' *actual performance* in writing the essays, not how the question writers *anticipate* they should perform.

The essay examinations are read and scored during a 7-day period in early June. In 2005, more than 700 Readers representing the United States, Canada, and other foreign countries read AP English Literature Exams from more than 240,000 test-takers; by 2011 approximately 1,000 Readers scored essays from over 360,000 students; 2017 saw 1,018 Readers score essays from 404,137 test-takers. More than half of the AP Readers are college or university instructors; fewer than half are high school teachers. Each Reader is assigned to score only one essay question during the reading session; accordingly, each student's work is read by at least three different Readers. Some essays are read and chosen as samples to be examined by all the Readers, while others are checked by the table leaders and question leaders after an individual Reader has scored the essay. You can trust that the essay scoring is as professional and accurate as possible. All Readers are thoroughly trained and retrained throughout the week of scoring.

Overall, the entire exam is designed to show your awareness of how an author creates meaning through literary devices, language use, genre conventions, and stylistic choices, and how well you can present your awareness in your own writing. A qualifying score demonstrates your ability to perform college-level work.

How Your Overall Score Is Determined

In the multiple-choice section, you earn 1 point for each correct answer. No points are deducted for wrong answers. Unanswered questions do not count for or against your score. The multiple-choice section equals 45 percent of the total exam score.

The three free-response essays are each scored holistically; the scores range from 0 to 6. These scores are then calculated to equal 55 percent of the total exam score. You can read more detailed information on the scoring of the essays in Chapter 4.

The multiple-choice section score is added to the free-response section score to produce a composite (or total) score. Finally, this composite score is translated into a 5-point scale that is reported in July to you, to your secondary school, and to any college you designated. In 2017, 52.6 percent of the test-takers received a score of 3 or above.

AP final scores are reported as follows:

> 5 = extremely well qualified
> 4 = well qualified
> 3 = qualified
> 2 = possibly qualified
> 1 = no recommendation

Exam Format

The multiple-choice section accounts for 45 percent of the final grade, and the free-response section 55 percent. Each of the three free-response questions accounts for the same percentage.

Multiple-Choice Questions	55 questions	1 hour	45 percent of total grade
Free-Response Questions	3 questions	2 hours	55 percent of total grade

The following tables identify the content of two recent exams. You can see which literary works were chosen, the length of each work, the century in which it was written, the author, and the number of multiple-choice questions. This information will help you understand the overall scope of the exam, the variety of the works chosen, and the amount of reading you'll have on your exam.

Format of the 2014 Exam

Section I	Multiple Choice (1 hour)	55 Questions
"Like as the waves make towards the pebbled shore" 14 lines	17th-century British sonnet (William Shakespeare)	11 questions
The Portrait of a Lady 536 words	20th-century American novel (Henry James)	11 questions
"Andrea del Sarto" 50 lines	19th-century British poem (Robert Browning)	13 questions
"The Race" 55 lines	20th-century American poem (Sharon Olds)	9 questions
"Pharmacy" 660 words	21st-century American short story from a "novel in stories" (Elizabeth Strout)	11 questions
Section II	Free Response (suggested essay time: 40 minutes each; total time: 2 hours)	3 Questions
"For That He Looked Not upon Her" 14 lines	Analysis of a 17th-century British sonnet by George Gascoigne	
The Known World 886 words	Analysis of an American prose passage from a 20th-century novel by Edward P. Jones	
25 suggested titles	Open question on how a character's sacrifice enhances a novel or play	

Format of the 2012 Exam

Section I	Multiple Choice (1 hour)	55 Questions
"Remembrance" 32 lines	19th-century British poem (Emily Brontë)	14 questions
Life on the Mississippi 523 words	19th-century American prose (Mark Twain)	9 questions
Paradise Lost 22 lines	17th-century British poem (John Milton)	10 questions
To the Lighthouse 764 words	20th-century British novel (Virginia Woolf)	14 questions
"A Frog in the Swimming Pool" 27 lines	20th-century American poem (Debora Greger)	8 questions
Section II	Free Response (suggested essay time: 40 minutes each; total time: 2 hours)	3 Questions
"Thou Blind Man's Mark" 14 lines	Analysis of a 16th-century British sonnet by Sir Philip Sidney	
Under the Feet of Jesus 695 words	Analysis of an American prose passage from a 20th-century novel by Helena Maria Viramontes	
37 suggested titles	Open question on how cultural, physical, or geographical surroundings shape character	

Frequently Asked Questions

Q. **Who administers the exam?**

A. The Advanced Placement exams are sponsored by the College Board. The exam is administered through the Educational Testing Service (ETS).

Q. **What materials may I bring to the exam?**

A. Bring your identification card, as well as plenty of pens for the free-response questions and pencils for the multiple-choice questions. You may not bring a dictionary, a thesaurus, or any other reference book.

Q. **May I cancel my score following the exam?**

A. Yes. You always have this option. Check the current AP Bulletin for procedures and deadlines.

Q. **How do I register for an AP exam?**

A. See your school counseling office for registration information. Schools must order AP Exams by November 15th.

Q. **Why are there two AP English exams?**

A. Because not all colleges offer the same curriculum for freshman English. The two separate exams—AP English Language and Composition and AP English Literature and Composition—permit each college to designate the exam that best reflects its curriculum.

Q. **What's the difference between the two AP English exams?**

A. The two exams are similar; both test your ability to analyze the written word and to prove that you can communicate intelligent ideas on a given subject. However, the AP English Literature and Composition Exam places greater emphasis on literary analysis; it includes poetry, fiction, and drama. You will be asked to analyze several poems on the literature exam. The AP English Language and Composition Exam asks questions about nonfiction; there is no poetry or fiction on the language exam. The language exam also places more emphasis on rhetorical analysis and the study of *how* language works.

Q. **Which exam should I take?**

A. If getting college credit is your main concern, the best way to decide which exam to take is to ask the college that you plan to attend. A college may offer either one or two semesters of credit depending on its freshman English curriculum. Generally, a school that offers a literary component combined with expository writing skills in its freshman English course gives up to a full year's course credit for the literature exam. Conversely, a school that requires a full year of freshman writing in various rhetorical modes may give up to a full year's credit for the language exam. But it is complicated; some schools give credit for either exam, so again, check with the individual school for its policy. In addition, it helps to consider your own strengths and weaknesses and your likes and dislikes. If you enjoy reading prose and writing argumentative, analytical essays, then the language exam is for you. If you have a strong literary background, especially in American and British literature and poetry analysis, then the literature exam will be a better fit.

Q. **Is one exam easier than the other?**

A. They are equally rigorous.

Q. **What is an average score?**

A. To earn an average reported score of 3, you must answer approximately 50 to 60 percent of the questions correctly on the multiple-choice section and also write three adequate free-response essays.

Q. **Can I take both the literature exam and the language exam in the same school year?**

A. Yes, they are administered on different days.

Q. How can I find out how much college credit I'll get if I pass the exam?

A. Contact the college and ask the admissions office for a clear, written response. Do not be surprised to find that this is a somewhat confusing issue, compounded by the fact that there are two AP English exams. Additionally, some colleges and universities consider an overall score of 3 as passing, while other colleges require a 4 or even a 5. Some colleges require that all freshmen take their freshman English class, which is usually a composition course. In addition, some schools or programs within a college have different requirements.

Q. What if my school does not offer an AP course or I did not enroll in the course? May I take the exam anyway?

A. Sure! Although an AP course is designed to prepare students for the exam, much of that "preparation" consists of reading quality literature—both fiction and nonfiction—and practicing analysis, critical thinking, and close reading in addition to taking practice AP exams and understanding the format of the exam. You can do this on your own, especially if you have disciplined study habits. However, I do strongly recommend that you read this test-preparation book carefully, and, if you can, also explore the College Board website at https://apcentral.collegeboard.org.

Q. When will I receive my AP exam scores?

A. You will receive your scores at about the same time as the colleges do, in early July.

Q. How can I obtain previous exams to use for practice?

A. You may order previously released exams directly from the College Board; the AP section of College Board information can be found at the College Board's online store at https://apcentral.collegeboard.org.

Q. How often are previous exams released to the public?

A. Multiple-choice exams are generally released every 5 years; free-response topics are released every year.

Q. Is paper provided for the essays?

A. Yes. In fact, you'll write all of your free-response essays in a special book that conceals your identity from the Readers who score it.

Q. How can I approximate my score from my practice exams into an AP scaled score of 1 through 5?

A. Approximating your score is a bit more complicated than merely counting the number of right and wrong answers, but follow these directions. Additionally, you will find a sample scoring worksheet located in this text after the answers and explanations for each full-length practice exam.

The total number of points on the exam is 150. Because the free-response and multiple-choice sections are weighted 55 percent to 45 percent, there are 82.5 points for the free-response essays and 67.5 points for the multiple-choice questions. Because the three essays are graded on a 6-point scale, each point on your essay raw score will be multiplied by 4.583. Three 6s would total 18, and 18×4.583 would round up to 82.5. In the multiple-choice section, each point in the raw score will be multiplied by 1.2272 to equal 67.5.

The total number of points required for a final score of 3, 4, or 5 varies each year, but a very reasonable assumption is that you need to accumulate approximately 114 to 150 points for a score of 5, 98 to 113 for a score of 4, and 81 to 97 for a score of 3.

Preparation for the Exam

Q. How can I prepare?

A. Practice! Become comfortable with the exam and its format. Take several practice exams to work on your timing. Learn new or unfamiliar terms that you might be expected to know for the exam. Practice your essay planning and timed writing. Practice paraphrasing what you read so that this skill becomes second nature before the exam.

Q. **When should I study this book?**

A. Browse through it early in the year before you take the AP exam, and read it carefully 6 weeks or so before the May exam. While you should spend time studying this book, do not exclude time that could be spent reading or rereading poetry, fiction, or drama. This book alone is not a substitute for being well read.

Q. **What should I study the night before the exam?**

A. You cannot cram the night before the exam. You will probably perform better on the exam if you relax the night before. Above all, get a good night's sleep. If you feel that you must study, look over the definitions of some technical terms, and browse through the novels and plays you may use to refresh your memory of the names. See Chapter 4 for advice on preparing for the open topic free-response question.

Multiple-Choice Questions

Q. **Is there a penalty for a wrong answer to the multiple-choice questions?**

A. No. As of 2011, no AP exams will deduct any points for wrong answers.

Q. **Can I still pass the exam even if I don't finish all the multiple-choice questions in time?**

A. Yes! Many students don't finish all the questions and still receive a passing score. Naturally, if you don't finish, you need to exhibit good accuracy on the questions you do complete and write three strong essays. However, since you will not be penalized for any wrong answers, you'll want to fill in something for every question if you see yourself running out of time.

Q. **Should I read the multiple-choice passages and answer the accompanying questions in the order they appear on the exam?**

A. Most students choose to answer the multiple-choice questions in the order they appear on the exam, as it is a very systematic and logical approach. However, keep a steady pace and do not let one passage eat up too much of your time, subsequently causing you to slight your time on later passages. Overall, remember that your score is determined by the total number of questions you answer correctly. If you prefer to "browse" the passages first and complete the questions in order of your personal preference, be sure to keep your eye on the clock to avoid running out of time. Also, of course, be very careful to bubble your answer choices next to the accurate question number.

Q. **How many passages and multiple-choice questions should I expect?**

A. Exams since the mid-1990s have used five passages; most exams before that used four. Each passage will have approximately 10–14 questions; expect 55 total questions. Some older exams had as many as 61 questions and as few as 53, but for several years 55 questions has been the norm and will continue to be so.

Q. **The College Board–released exams document the percentage of students who got each question correct. How can this help me?**

A. Use this information to help you recognize the difficulty level of each question and your ability as a test-taker. You'll want to always get the high-probability questions correct, like those that range about 75 percent or higher. Also notice the very low percentage questions, like those in the 30 percent range or lower. These hard questions may be very time-consuming or very complicated. Don't let them eat up too much time; instead, concentrate on the questions you're most likely to get correct. This will build your score. Remember that, in any case, you will want to mark an answer for all questions since you will not be penalized for an incorrect answer.

Q. **What if a multiple-choice question seems too easy or the answer seems too obvious?**

A. Enjoy! Yes, some of the questions are "easy," and quickly accessible. Do not talk yourself out of a correct answer or second-guess yourself; just smile, answer it, and move on to the next question. Let the easy questions buy time for the more difficult ones.

Q. **When should I guess on the multiple-choice section?**

A. Answer as many of the questions as accurately as you can. Avoid mismanaging your time and spending too long on one passage or one question. Don't be afraid to guess if you can eliminate at least two of the five choices. If you are unsure of an answer, mark out the answers in the questions booklet that you know are wrong:

A.

B. ?

C.

D. ?

E.

The question marks indicate possible answers. If you come back to the question later, you will not waste time considering wrong answers you have already eliminated.

Q. **Are there any trick questions in the multiple-choice section?**

A. No. If you read the passage carefully, you should be able to answer the questions.

Q. **Exactly what scores do I get for a right answer and no answer on the multiple-choice section?**

A. A right answer is 1 point, and an omitted answer is 0. The total score is converted to equal 45 percent of 150, or 67.5 points, if you get all the multiple-choice questions right.

Free-Response Essay Questions

Q. **Does the scoring give extra weight to one of the essays?**

A. No, all three essays are counted equally. Because the free-response section of the exam is 55 percent of your total score, each essay equals 18.3 percent of your free-response score.

Q. **Is the format of the essays the same on all exams?**

A. Basically, yes. For decades the poem topic has been Question 1, the prose topic Question 2, and the open topic Question 3. The poetry question will use a short complete poem or part of a longer one. (Students have not been asked to compare two poems since 2008, and in 2017 the College Board officially stated the exam will no longer have paired poems.) The prose question will use an excerpt from a novel, short story, or, rarely, a complete short story. The open essay question will invite you to explore an aspect of literary fiction in a novel or play of your own choice. A list of suggested titles will follow the prompt. You do NOT have to write on one of these works; you may choose to write on a different work as long as it is an appropriate choice. (Older exams occasionally listed appropriate authors instead of titles, and once no suggestions were offered at all.)

Q. **What are the most important qualities of a high-scoring essay?**

A. All scoring guides can be simplified into three key points. Good essays will

- be on topic, using a defensible thesis to address all parts of the question fully and accurately.
- be strongly developed, combining apt and specific references to the text with relevant and insightful commentary.
- present sophisticated thought and complex argumentation.

Q. **Should I plan my essays in advance?**

A. In general, yes, planning your essay in advance is a good strategy. An outline is never required and will never be seen by the Readers anyway, but clear and logical organization is, indeed, an important component of sophisticated thought. You need to at least organize the points you intend to make and the order in which you plan to present them.

Q. **How many paragraphs should I write for each essay? Should I produce five paragraphs?**

A. Write as many paragraphs as you need to fully develop and present your ideas. Although the introduction-body-conclusion format is most frequently used, and entirely appropriate, the number of body paragraphs presented varies from student to student and topic to topic. An introductory paragraph that contains a thesis is understandably an appropriate beginning, but don't worry if you don't get to the conclusion. Try to avoid "forcing" three body paragraphs into a formulaic essay. Read more about essay organization and development in Chapter 4.

Q. **How many pages should each essay be?**

A. No set length is required; however, most high-scoring essays are *at least* two pages long. Naturally, some essays are shorter and some are longer. Instead of worrying about length, concentrate on addressing all of the tasks of the topic and developing your ideas thoroughly. Be aware that very short essays, such as those that are only about half a page in length, are considered "unacceptably brief" and score very low; they simply do not demonstrate enough development of ideas to receive a passing score. You can read sample student essays in Chapter 4 and in all six practice exams to get a feel for length.

Q. **How much should I worry about grammar and spelling?**

A. Good news! You don't have to worry too much about your spelling. If you can spell reasonably well, no Reader will dock your score. The Readers are remarkably tolerant; they want to reward you for what you do well. Grammar and punctuation can be another issue, though. The Readers are always willing to overlook what they call "minor errors" or "honest mistakes" that are made under timed pressure. They understand that what you have produced is a first draft that is likely to have a few flaws. However, if your grammatical errors are persistent and serious, the Reader will have to lower your score.

Q. **Should I write my essays in cursive or should I print?**

A. You need to write as legibly as you can, so use whatever method is easiest to read. The Readers want to be able to reward you for what your essay does well; to do so, they need to read the words. If you know your writing is hard to read, try to separate your words with a little extra space; this helps the Reader. Please don't forget to use a nice black-ink or blue-ink pen; avoid ones that bleed through paper because you'll want to write on the back of the page.

Q. **Do the essays need a title?**

A. Never. It will never affect your score. I can guarantee that Readers are bored by dull titles anyway.

Q. **How much of the passage in the prompt should I quote?**

A. No set, formulaic answer exists. Yes, you do need to refer to the passage appropriately in order to support your ideas, and many of those examples should take the form of quotations. However, a string of irrelevant quotations, glued together with a few of your own words, will not help your score at all. Read the many sample essays in this book to get a feel for what's appropriate.

Q. **Can I pass the exam if I don't finish an essay?**

A. Of course! Understandably, a radically unfinished essay will receive a very low score, so try to pace yourself accordingly, devoting approximately 40 minutes to each free-response question. Doing so should allow you time to finish each essay. Also, practice your pacing many times before the exam. I also advise practicing the planning period over and over. If, within approximately 10 to 12 minutes, you can organize what you're going to say and the order in which you're going to present your points, you should have enough time to actually write the words and sentences. Finally, if you find yourself in a time crunch on test day, remember that body paragraphs are much more important than concluding paragraphs—especially conclusions that merely summarize. You should devote your time to getting your ideas down on paper.

Q. **How should I begin my essay? Should I paraphrase or repeat the question?**

A. Begin your essay in whatever way makes it easiest for you to write. If you simply cannot begin on your own without rephrasing the question, then do so; however, be aware that you will not receive a point for the thesis if you merely restate the prompt.

Q. In the essay part of the exam, do I have to use a pen?

A. Your proctor will instruct you to write your essays with a pen, but every year some exams are written in pencil by students without pens or whose pens break down mid-exam. A Reader will certainly not penalize an exam written in pencil, but, like bad handwriting, pencil is harder to read. Don't make it more difficult for your Reader if you don't have to.

Q. Do the examiners want detail in the essays?

A. If, by detail, you mean specific evidence from the passages on the exam or from the novel or play of your choice, yes. But they don't want long passages quoted from memory or detailed plot summaries. Remember that your Readers have a copy of the passage in front of them and that they have already read the novel or play you're writing about.

Q. What suggestions about style would you make?

A. Avoid clichés. Nine out of ten AP exams written about the imagery of a passage will describe it as "vivid," regardless of how overused the term may be. The remedy for a cliché is to think of fresh new ways to express your ideas. Readers may reward students for extra attention to original style. If the question suggests a proverb to you, try to resist the temptation to quote it, because 50,000 other students will have thought of the same proverb and used it in their first paragraph. Try to vary your sentence lengths, patterns, and beginnings. Use sophisticated vocabulary to the best of your ability, but do not use words you do not know well, and do not try to impress the Reader with erudite phrases.

Q. Should I write about the punctuation of a poem or a prose passage?

A. Only if it is very unusual or remarkably important and you can say something meaningful about it. Every passage on the exam will be punctuated, and the punctuation will almost never be worth discussing. Most students who waste time writing about the punctuation do so because they can't think of anything else to write about. (Just a brief reminder about punctuation: Place poem titles inside quotation marks; only epic poems of great length are underlined.)

Open Topic Questions

Q. On the open question, is it better to write about a book on the list of suggested works or to choose one that is not on the list?

A. You should choose the work that best fits the question and that you know best. Whether or not you choose a work on the list will not affect your score. If the work you choose is not widely known, it will be read only by someone who knows the book. No Reader has read all the works that are used on the open question, and a Reader finding an essay on a work he or she does not know simply passes it on to another Reader who is familiar with it. The important thing is to choose an appropriate work or an appropriate character within that work.

Q. In answering the open essay question, can I write about works in translation?

A. Yes. Many students use works by classical authors as well as those by more modern European, African, Asian, and South American authors. As of 2020, the list of suggested works on the exam will not contain translated works, but you certainly may write on one. Use the work that best fits the question, and the one you can best analyze.

Q. On the open question, what if I don't know any of the books on the list of suggested works?

A. Reread the question very carefully and think about the books you do know to see if one of them is appropriate. You don't have to use a book from the list, but the work you use must fit the question.

Q. On the open question, is it better to use an older author or a modern one?

A. Use the author that you know best that best fits the question. The time period doesn't matter.

Q. On the open question, is it better to write on a long or difficult work (like *Moby Dick*) than a short or easy work (like *Ethan Frome*)?

A. The important thing is to answer the question. You don't get extra credit for using a hard book, and you lose no credit for choosing a short work. You can't use a short story if the question calls for a novel, but if you don't answer the question and write about *Ulysses* or *War and Peace*, you will get a much lower score than if you do answer the question and write about *The Secret Sharer* or *The Catcher in the Rye*.

Q. On the open question, may I write on two works when the question asks for one?

A. You may, but you shouldn't. The exam will be read and scored on the basis of only one of the two works you write about; however, in a technical sense, all of your commentary on a second work can be considered off topic, since the directions explicitly state that you should choose *a work*. But you will probably have written only half as much as the other writers who followed directions and wrote on only one. You can, of course, refer briefly to other works if doing so improves your essay, but focus on one work.

Q. In the open question, may I write on more than one character?

A. Read the directions very carefully; if they ask for character analysis, invariably the directions will specify one character. Understand that they are offering you the opportunity to explore one character in one work in depth. To write on two characters or two works would result in skimming the surface of each.

Q. Can I write on a novel or play that has been made into a film if I've read the book and seen the movie?

A. Yes, but be careful. Most of the classic (and many not-so-classic) novels have been made into films. Be sure what you say in your essay comes from your reading, not from the movie. The old Greer Garson movie of *Pride and Prejudice* changes the gorgon Lady Catherine into an ally who willingly brings Darcy and Elizabeth together, and the Hollywood version of *Wuthering Heights* ends at the halfway point in the novel. Both Laurence Olivier's and Mel Gibson's versions of *Hamlet* leave out about one-third of the play. Be sure what you're remembering is what you've read, not what you've seen.

Q. What if I can't remember a character's name?

A. Do the best you can. You can sometimes use a phrase like "Hamlet's uncle" (if you forget his name is Claudius), or you can explain that you've forgotten and substitute an X. If you make it clear, the Reader will give you the benefit of the doubt. There have been quite good essays written about Hamlet in which he was (inadvertently) called Macbeth. The Readers are aware that the essays must be written quickly and are tolerant of slips of the pen. You should not invent names, and you should try your best to prepare in advance by knowing the character's name. The effect can be unintentionally comic, as in "I can't remember Othello's wife's name, so I'll call her Darlene." If you review a few works before the exam, you will likely remember the characters' names.

Q. Do you have any further suggestions about answering the open essay question?

A. First and foremost, address how your interpretation relates to the work as a whole in every paragraph. Also, be sure to understand whether the exam is asking about the author, the reader, or the characters in the work. There are, obviously, differences between your perception of Gatsby and Nick's, Daisy's, or Fitzgerald's perception. Although you will not be asked to explain if you liked a particular book, ask yourself whether or not the question calls for a discussion of technique—that is, what the author does for specific purposes—or for a discussion of a character as if that character were alive. In *Lord of the Flies*, Piggy doesn't know that he is a symbol, but Golding and the reader do. And in *Hamlet*, Shakespeare and the reader use Horatio in ways that Hamlet doesn't know about. Don't confuse art and life. Remember that a play or a novel is just that, a play or a novel; although Horatio is necessary to Fortinbras to tell him what has happened, or necessary to Shakespeare to say some things he wants to have said at the end of the play, we don't need him to tell us what has happened because we've just seen or read the whole play. Fortinbras, Horatio, and Hamlet are fictional characters, and educated people should recognize the difference between art's imitation of life and the real thing.

Q. How many books should I prepare with for the open question on the exam?

A. There's no single answer, but I personally recommend that three ought to give you enough comfort to answer the topic. However, to narrow down to three titles, follow these steps: First, become familiar with recent open topics. This book has summarized topics in Chapter 4 and the College Board has access to past topics (with scoring guides and sample student essays) since 1999 at https://apcentral.collegeboard.org/courses/ap-english-literature-and-composition/exam. Second, make a list of three titles that would be appropriate for most topics. Then, review those three works. More specific suggestions for all of these steps are explained in Chapter 4, including what to review in any given text.

Be aware that other teachers may feel that the more books you prepare with, the better you'll be, as long as you know them well. They may suggest you cover several periods and several genres. They may recommend that you know one Shakespearean tragedy and at least two 20th- or 21st-century plays. They may think you should also be familiar with at least one 19th-century and two 21st-century novels. I fear that this can be overkill; after all, you can only write on *one* work, and I worry that if you have too many works floating around in your mind on the day of the exam, you might take too long to choose which one is best for you to write on, and you run the risk of forgetting details. This is merely my opinion, but, in any case, choose works you relate to enough to have something important to say. Review the works carefully. Some years ago, a large number of students wrote on *Romeo and Juliet* on the open question on child-parent conflicts. But very few remembered the play well, probably because they had read it 2 or 3 years before and had not reviewed it before taking the exam.

Chapter 1

Introduction to Poetry Analysis

Poetry: the best words in the best order.

—Samuel Taylor Coleridge

Learning how to effectively analyze poetry is a great opportunity! Do not fear; the poetry genre is actually your friend! With its language so condensed and focused, poetry epitomizes the presentation of multifaceted ideas; if you follow the guidelines and do your practice, you will become quite comfortable in understanding and critiquing it. Plus, learning to analyze poetry can be fun, entertaining, and intellectually rewarding. Keep in mind that half of the AP English Literature and Composition Exam requires poetry analysis, so it is to your advantage to gain the skills that will help to make you comfortable. In this chapter, we'll introduce the basics about poetry: how to read it and how to analyze it, along with the terminology you'll want to be familiar with. We'll also explore a 19th-century poem. Chapters 3 and 4 are devoted to the multiple-choice questions and the free-response (essay) questions, and they will offer you specific information and advice for the poetry that you'll encounter on those sections of the exam.

But first, it is useful to acknowledge an underlying philosophical truth, namely that humanity owes a great debt to poetry. Through poetry, we can gain a greater awareness of our very existence, of our desire to understand the world, of our innate yearning to live life fully. Poetry helps us to grasp abstract ideas and to internalize them; it forces us to grapple with finding meaning, both in the poem and in our world. Like an inspiring work of art or a favorite song that speaks to our souls, poetry can enhance our lives and give them deeper meaning. Like art and music, poetry is expressed in many different ways, in many shapes and forms. Similar to the process in which musicians strive to find the best way to communicate their ideas through melody and lyrics, poets combine their imagination with a mastery of language, and they ultimately show us transcendent ideas in a new light.

The poems that are selected as prompts for the AP exam are not simple ones with a single meaning. If they were, you might initially be gleeful at how easy the poems are to understand, but then you'd quickly find yourself without anything significant to say, without any deeper meanings to analyze. For example, take the famous (and silly) ditty that was composed by Gelett Burgess in 1895 for a humorous magazine that he founded, *The Lark*:

> I never saw a purple cow
> I never hope to see one;
> But I can tell you, anyhow,
> I'd rather see than be one!

What does the poem say? The speaker does not want to be a purple cow. And that's about it. While it is cute and easy to understand, one would have very little to analyze. The author himself grew so tired of the poem that he published this "confession" in 1897:

> Ah, yes, I wrote the "Purple Cow"
> I'm Sorry, now, I wrote it;
> But I can tell you Anyhow
> I'll Kill you if you Quote it!

You should be glad that the poems on the AP exam will offer much more fodder for you to analyze. However, don't think that the chosen poems will be completely inaccessible; rather, they are carefully selected to give you lots of ideas to work with. You *will* be able to understand the poems and make sense of their meaning. When the AP English Literature and Composition Development Committee chooses poems, they believe that students should be able to comprehend the gist of the poem (what it says) and analyze many of its features (how it says it). In the multiple-choice section of the exam, you will be asked questions about both aspects; in the free-response section, you will have the opportunity to write about both. The multiple-choice questions will never ask about all of the poem's features (poetic devices, figures of speech, and so forth), and the free-response poetry prompt will never expect you to write about all of them.

How to Read Poetry

Poetry is so condensed and so focused. Every single word counts, every word has meaning, and many words may be used in an unusual fashion. Therefore, it's helpful to know some tips about reading poetry before you begin to work on analyzing it:

- When you read poetry, read it out loud as often as you can. Try to avoid rushing through it; rather, let the poem's punctuation and stanza divisions guide your pace. Don't automatically take a deep breath at the end of a line unless the punctuation tells you to take that pause. As you read the poem, try to feel and recognize the rhythm as it builds. It is this reading out loud, especially at the beginning of your study of poetry, that will help you appreciate poetic nuances.

- Read a poem from beginning to end more than once. The process is similar to the way in which you gain insight after hearing a great song more than once; you'll get much more out of a poem as you read it again and again. Take time to look up any words that you are not familiar with. Be patient with the poem and with yourself.

- Train yourself to hear the words in your mind as you read; on test day, of course, you can't read the poetry out loud, so you must learn to read it as if you were hearing it out loud. Remember, poetry is intended to be read aloud, so it helps to hear how the sounds in the poem help to convey meaning.

- Paraphrase the poem's meaning by restating it in your own words. Initially this takes time, but practice articulating what the poem says line by line, sentence by sentence, or stanza by stanza. At first, force yourself to paraphrase in writing, and you'll find the more you practice this skill, the faster you can find the right words. Ideally, by the time you take the exam, you'll be far ahead of other test-takers, as you paraphrase simultaneously with reading. Also be firmly aware that the free-response section will not prompt you to paraphrase; just use this thinking skill to make sure you get the gist of the poem.

- Pay attention to poetic devices and how they enhance the poem's basic meaning. This skill, like paraphrasing, comes with practice and multiple readings.

How to Analyze Poetry

Answering the following 10 questions about a given poem will help you to better understand it. Sometimes the poem does not provide all of the answers, but with practice, you'll understand how this information helps you work through a poem systematically.

1. Who is the speaker? What kind of person is the speaker? Can we trust the speaker, or is she or he unreliable or mentally unstable? How can you describe any changes the speaker goes through? Think about the speaker's gender, attitude, social status, or anything that will help you understand what motivates the speaker to burst forth in verse. *Be very careful* when the poem is written in first person (as many are), and *do not confuse* the speaker with the poet; *the speaker is not necessarily the poet.* Yes, some poems are autobiographical, such as William Wordsworth's poems celebrating his childhood and nature, but many are not. For example, the first-person speaker in "Porphyria's Lover," a famous dramatic monologue by Robert Browning, is a madman who has murdered his lover. The poet is not a murderer, but the speaker certainly is. Poets frequently adopt a first-person persona to give the poem a voice, but it is not necessarily the poet's own voice.

2. Does the poem have an identifiable audience? Some are addressed to one's lover, one's parent, one's friend, someone specific, or multiple people. If you can identify the intended audience, think about what that tells you about the listener and how it may affect what the speaker says.

3. What is the dramatic situation, or, in other words, what occasion initiates the poem? Is it placed in a certain time, such as a season, time of day, time of year, or major event (such as war or a parade)? Is it placed in a location, such as city or countryside, land or sea, nation or region? A narrative poem will frequently imply or provide answers to these questions, but many others, such as a lyric poem, will not.

4. Does the poem have any action? If so, what occurs? Is the speaker a participant or an observer? Is the speaker involved in any conflict, either internal or external?

5. What is the central purpose of the poem? How is it achieved, and to what degree is it successful?

6. What is the structure, the organization of the poem? This may relate to the stanza form (such as a sonnet), or to punctuation, or just to the logical thought pattern behind the ideas. Also remember that on the exam you may be reading excerpts from longer pieces, so you won't necessarily know the entire poem's organization; however, you can still analyze the structure of what you are given. Think about how the form or structure enhances the meaning. Paraphrasing the progression of ideas, knowing what point the poet makes first, second, third, and so on will help you to understand the structure.

7. What is the poem's tone? How does it evolve? Be careful to notice when the poet's attitude appears to be different from that of the speaker, which often occurs in ironic works. You will find much more information and advice for addressing tone in Chapter 2.

8. What particular words or phrases stand out and how do they contribute to the poem's theme? What syntactic choices, such as inverted sentences, are unusual? Consider multiple connotations of individual words. Look up any words that you are not familiar with.

9. What images and literary devices does the poet utilize and how do they enhance the poem's theme? Poems are frequently chock-full of imagery. While the list of literary devices a poet may use is enormous, the terms you should be most familiar with are simile, metaphor, and personification. Also be aware of paradox, hyperbole, understatement, and irony. Always think about how these devices add to the poem's meaning.

10. What themes does the poem develop? The poetic examples you read on the exam will be rich, deep, and have more than one possible interpretation of the theme. Think about what statement the poet is making about the human condition, what idea the poet is presenting about humanity. Be cautious when formulating the author's theme in your mind; do not confuse the poem's subject matter with the deeper point that the author is making. For example, if the poem's situation presents characters who are coping with death, the subject matter may be stated as "This poem deals with a widow's thoughts about the loss of her husband." But the theme would be better stated as "The grief of losing a loved one never goes away, and periodically one may be reminded of the loss." Let's try another example; imagine a poem that presents the relationship between a father and his son. The subject matter may be stated as "The poem deals with how we feel about our parents." But the theme is "A parent's loving care often goes unnoticed and unappreciated, despite all the effort it demands."

Another piece of advice: When you initially begin to analyze poetry, don't try to examine everything all at once. Start simply and only examine a few elements at a time. As you do so, be sure that you accurately identify the poetic elements, and then examine *how* they help create meaning. For example, begin by just analyzing the imagery in some poems, and then only later analyze simile, metaphor, and personification. Then explore paradox, overstatement, understatement, and irony. Later, analyze symbols, allegory, or allusions. Finally, address tone. If you focus on how to address each small component of poetry, taking small steps, you'll be able to put it all together before the exam.

Finally, let's address an aspect of poetry that intimidates some students: metrics. Yes, poetry does have identifiable feet (iamb, trochee, anapest, dactyl, and spondee) and metered lines (monometer, dimeter, trimeter, tetrameter, pentameter, hexameter, heptameter, and octameter). However, this is not a major aspect on the exam, and at most you will only be asked about these terms in one or two multiple-choice questions. If you do get such a question, you should be able to count how many stressed syllables occur in each line and then match it up with the appropriate word; do not worry about identifying the name of the foot. If you count six stressed syllables, it's a hexameter! Four stressed syllables? Tetrameter! Make it easy on yourself and don't worry. In the end, you may not get a single question that asks about metrics.

The Terminology of Poetry

In poetry you have a form looking for a subject and a subject looking for a form.
When they come together successfully you have a poem.

—W. H. Auden

It is important to use accurate terminology when analyzing poetry. You want to avoid making mistakes like the poor student who once claimed in an AP poetry essay that in the work ". . . written like an epic poem, the author uses a structured meter of stanzas with 8-8-13 syllable patterns, an adaptation of haiku." Well, perhaps this student did know the difference between epic poetry and haiku, but this kind of careless error is quite distracting to the Reader. Therefore, let's begin by looking at the big picture and some basic definitions. Many *types* of poems exist. The broad term is used to help us categorize poems in the same way that we use different terms to categorize music (such as classical, folk, hip-hop, and rap) or art (such as impressionist, cubist, landscape, and surrealist). Some types of poetry will not be necessary to study for the AP English Literature and Composition exam; these include the acrostic, cinquain, haiku, limerick, and rondeau, among many other types that are either too simple or too obscure. Additionally, be aware that you will NOT be asked to identify the type or form of any poem; instead, understand *why* the poet's choice of a particular form is appropriate for the poem's meaning.

But what *types* of poems do you need to know? You should become familiar with the following categories and simple definitions (more detailed definitions are in Chapter 5):

ballad: a narrative poem, often musical, that tells a story

dramatic monologue: one speaker directly addresses a listener or the audience

elegy: a dignified mourning of death

epic (and mock epic): a long narrative that follows certain conventions

lyric: a short expression of personal feelings or emotions, often musical

metaphysical: a highly complex and abstract poem on a philosophical topic

narrative: a poem that tells a story; these can be long or short

ode: a lengthy poem on a serious subject

pastoral: subjects in nature, such as shepherds and their flocks

After you know what *type* of poem you're reading, you can consider the *form* that poem takes. This general term refers to the structure, the architectural conventions that govern or guide some poems. Become familiar with the following *forms* of poetry:

blank verse: unrhymed lines of iambic pentameter

free verse: no regular rhyme, no regular meter

rhyme royale: 7-line stanzas of iambic pentameter

sestina: 39-line poem with a specific formula

sonnet: 14-line poem in iambic pentameter

stanza forms:

- couplet (and heroic couplet)
- triplet (tercet)
- quatrain
- quintet (cinquain)
- sestet
- septet
- octave
- Spenserian
- ottava rima
- envoy
- apostrophe
- terza rima

villanelle: 19-line poem with a specific formula

It is also important to know the *sound devices* that are used in poetry:

alliteration: repetition of initial sounds

assonance: repetition of similar vowel sounds

cacophony: harsh, grating sounds

consonance: repetition of consonant sounds

dissonance: deliberate use of inharmonious words, phrases, or syllables

euphony: pleasant, harmonious sounds

onomatopoeia: words that imitate natural sounds

rhyme: repetition of similar sounds, usually at the end of lines of poetry

slant rhyme: words that are similar but don't exactly rhyme

Finally, let's give a nod to those familiar poetic devices, the figurative language that poets use so well:

imagery	apostrophe	allegory	understatement
simile	metonymy	allusion	irony
metaphor	synecdoche	paradox	
personification	symbol	hyperbole	

Sample Poem

Now, let's examine a famous 19th-century poem. It is commonly taught in schools (in fact, you might already be familiar with it), so it will definitely not be chosen for the AP exam; however, it does exemplify the quality of the works that you'll encounter on the exam. We'll use the 10 suggested questions in the "How to Analyze Poetry" section to thoroughly explore this sonnet.

London, 1802

by William Wordsworth

Milton! thou shouldst be living at this hour:
England hath need of thee: she is a fen
Of stagnant waters: altar, sword, and pen,
Fireside, the heroic wealth of hall and bower,
Have forfeited their ancient English dower   (5)
Of inward happiness. We are selfish men;
Oh! raise us up, return to us again;
And give us manners, virtue, freedom, power.
Thy soul was like a Star, and dwelt apart:
Thou hadst a voice whose sound was like the sea: (10)
Pure as the naked heavens, majestic, free,
So didst thou travel on life's common way,
In cheerful godliness; and yet thy heart
The lowliest duties on herself did lay.

1. Who is the speaker? Although William Wordsworth is the poet, he is not positively identified as the speaker, regardless of how much the speaker's ideas may represent Wordsworth's known opinions. We do know that the speaker begins as a moralistic naysayer, but ends as someone who praises Milton for his poetic prowess and moral fortitude.

2. Does the poem have an identifiable audience? Although Wordsworth uses apostrophe to address Milton directly, the message of the poem appears to actually be addressed to the general public. (Incidentally, Milton died 128 years before Wordsworth composed this poem in 1802.)

3. What is the dramatic situation? Based on the title, we know the year is 1802 and the location is London. However, the speaker is not necessarily standing in a specific London location. These images are mental, internalized visions of England.

4. Does the poem have any action? No; the speaker simply states his opinion on the current state of affairs in England.

5. What is the central purpose of the poem? The poem has two apparent purposes: (1) to lament the problems in present-day England, and (2) to praise Milton for his nobility and virtue, thinking he can save English society. The first purpose is fulfilled, but the second is questionable. It is true that the speaker praises Milton eloquently, but the late, great poet cannot change 19th-century England.

6. What is the structure, the organization of the poem? The form is a Petrarchan (Italian) sonnet. The first eight lines set up the problem: England is currently a stagnant swamp, stripped of her previous virtue and

glory. The following six lines comment on Milton's positive attributes: his writing is stellar and his personal morals are beyond reproach.

7. What is the poem's tone? How does it evolve? The first eight lines are caustic, angry, and disgusted, but the tone shifts in the last six lines to reverential, hopeful, and respectful.

(We'll combine questions 8 and 9 as we explore every line.)

8. What particular words or phrases stand out and how do they contribute to the poem's theme?

9. What images and literary devices does the poet utilize and how do they enhance the poem's theme?
   - Lines 1–2: "Milton! thou shouldst be living at this hour: / England hath need of thee:" The speaker is pleading to the late poet in an *apostrophe*, which implies that the past was better and that someone as inspiring as Milton could save the country.
   - Lines 2–3: "[England] is a fen / Of stagnant waters:" A fen is a swamp, a bog of unhealthy water. This *metaphor* represents what the speaker considers to be the current state of affairs in the land, a completely negative image.
   - Lines 3–6: "altar, sword, and pen, / Fireside, the heroic wealth of hall and bower, / Have forfeited their ancient English dower / Of inward happiness." The altar is a *synecdoche* that refers to the church, the sword is a *metonymy* that refers to the British military, and the pen is a *metonymy* for the all-inclusive British traditions in literature. The fireside is a *synecdoche* for the security of home, one that is encompassed in the *appositive* phrase "the heroic wealth of hall and bower," which *alludes* to the economy. Wordsworth turns "inward happiness" into a *metaphor* for a dowry, the customary gift expected by a new bridegroom of his wife's family. England has metaphorically given up this traditional gift, and all of her institutions have lost their meaning.
   - Lines 6–8: "We are selfish men; / Oh! raise us up, return to us again; / And give us manners, virtue, freedom, power." After the negative word "selfish," which describes his contemporaries, Wordsworth moves into positive *connotations*, listing the constructive things Milton could resupply to the stagnant country.
   - Line 9: "Thy soul was like a Star, and dwelt apart:" This is a *simile* that compares Milton to the cosmos, making him greater than the rest of humanity and separate from the rest of us.
   - Lines 10–11: "Thou hadst a voice whose sound was like the sea: / Pure as the naked heavens, majestic, free," The power of Milton's poetic voice turns into another *simile*, one that contrasts pure water with the stagnant water of line 3. The *image* of the "naked heavens" enforces the star simile of line 9. These lines also invoke the awe-inspiring forces of nature.
   - Lines 12–13: "So didst thou travel on life's common way, / In cheerful godliness;" These lines create a *metaphor* for the journey of life, bringing Milton back down to earth in a humble way, like everyman. But the *connotation* of "cheerful godliness" elevates Milton again.
   - Lines 13–14: ". . . and yet thy heart / The lowliest duties on herself did lay." The *image* of Milton's heart, taking on the "lowliest duties," reinforces his unpretentious humanity.

10. What themes does the poem develop? Remember, all great works have more than one theme:
    - Despite its current sorry state, England could improve if its countrymen regained their virtues. Thus, countries can recapture their splendor.
    - People can gain inspiration from the past.
    - The past always seems better than the present.
    - When citizens are honorable, a country can prosper.
    - A country's success is related to its cultivation of strong ethical traditions.

In chapters 3 and 4, you'll get advice and strategies for the multiple-choice section and the free-response section. Each of those chapters will have sample poems and appropriate multiple-choice questions and explanations, plus essay prompts and student samples with analyses. In addition, each of the six practice exams in this book (chapters 7–12) will offer plenty of samples on which to practice.

Chapter 2

Introduction to Prose Analysis

Great literature is simply language charged with meaning to the utmost possible degree.

—Ezra Pound

Before you even begin your AP English Literature and Composition class, you will no doubt have received instruction in literary analysis; after all, most English classes utilize high-quality works of literature, including novels, plays, and short stories. Thanks to your background in previous English classes, you're likely to already have a degree of comfort analyzing the kind of prose passages that will appear on the AP exam. But since so much of your exam score is based on your skill in prose analysis, it is wise for you to review and refresh the basics of analyzing prose passages. This chapter is designed to remind you of those basics, along with the vocabulary and the terminology you'll encounter in prose analysis.

It's a universal truth that everyone loves a well-told tale, and the prose passages on the exam will explore high-quality literature that presents humanity in all of its diverse manifestations. On the exam, it's likely that you'll encounter excerpts of heroism and of villainy; you might get to analyze stories of true love and of treacherous deceit; you'll see virtuous humankind in its finest hour; and you'll see characters descend into ignominy.

Remember that you will be presented with two to three prose passages in the multiple-choice section and one prose passage in the free-response section; plus, you get the joy of choosing a novel, epic poem, or play to analyze in the open topic free-response question. The prose passages on the AP exam will range from 300 to 800 words. Like the selected poems, they will represent fictional works (excerpts from novels, short stories, and plays) that were written in English from the 16th through the 21st centuries. You will be well-served if you practice reading and analyzing passages from earlier periods until you are comfortable with them, as the vocabulary and syntax of these older works can be challenging for a modern reader.

Do not expect any nonfiction prose on the AP English Literature and Composition Exam; that genre is more appropriate to the AP English Language and Composition Exam. However, one recent AP exam did use one example of nonfiction, but it was a very imaginative autobiographical piece. The prose *genres* that you should expect on the exam are novels (which are most commonly used), short stories, and plays.

Literary Genres

Novels, because of their length, allow more freedom for the author to develop more detailed literary elements such as:

- characters who can change over time
- plot and subplots that can cross and intersect
- multiple conflicts
- changing time and location
- chapter divisions

Short stories, because of their brevity, generally limit the author's development of literary elements to:

- action that centers on only one or two complex characters
- one plotline
- only one major conflict
- one time period
- limited number of divisions; no chapters

Plays use dialogue and are divided into *scenes* (minor divisions) and acts (major divisions):

- One-act plays, like short stories, usually have few or no divisions.
- Drama can be written in prose (sentences), poetry (verse), or a combination of both.

Literary Traditions

Fictional prose consistently contains the following literary traditions (which are further defined in Chapter 5):

Plot

Although very flexible in its organization, the plot usually includes:

- **exposition:** generally establishes the setting and the characters
- **rising action:** launches the conflict and complicates it
- **climax:** the singular or multiple peaks of action
- **falling action:** the unravelling of the conflict
- **denouement:** the final resolution

Of course, the plot does not necessarily evolve chronologically, and it does not necessarily contain all of the elements listed above; it can leave many issues and questions unresolved.

Character

Major characters, like the protagonist and antagonist, are usually well-developed; minor characters may or may not be. Look for the following character types:

- **protagonist:** the main character of a work who centers the conflict
- **antagonist:** the character (or group) that opposes or rivals the protagonist, either mentally, physically, or both
- **foil:** a character who contrasts with a major character, thereby highlighting the traits of the major character

The following questions will help you to analyze the characters:

- What are the essential qualities and attitudes of the protagonist? The antagonist?
- In what ways do the characters change? Are there moments of self-revelation that help to produce these changes? How do ambiguities in character relate to the overall theme?
- How are the characters' traits revealed? What do their speech mannerisms, gestures, attitudes, modes of dress, and other details tell us about the characters?
- Is the main character sympathetic or unsympathetic? Why? What effect does this have on the work as a whole?

Conflict

Conflict is the vehicle that propels the plot and the characters' actions. The following questions will help you to analyze conflict:

- Are the characters' conflicts internal or external?
- To what degree are the conflicts resolved?
- What is the nature of the conflict? Is it one person against another? An internal conflict? A person at odds with society or the natural world? A battle against technology?
- Does the work have a main conflict? Are there any minor conflict(s)?
- What relationship exists between conflicts? To what degree are they resolved and what is the effect or appropriateness of such resolutions?

Point of View

Point of view establishes who is telling the story and how much knowledge that narrator has. An author may sometimes weave in and out of varying points of view in complicated novels. Understanding the pros and cons of each point of view will help you analyze the author's choices.

Point of View	Pro	Con
First person	We believe and trust the narrator. The plot seems real, as it imitates real life. We learn information along with the narrator, and we usually feel the same emotions.	This POV is subjective and restrictive, yet intimate. Sometimes the narrator is not trustworthy. Readers can confuse narrator and author.
Third-person omniscient	Because we get insights into many (or all) of the characters' inner thoughts and emotions, we get to know characters well, to genuinely understand their motivations. The writer has more freedom to tell more about what's happening. This POV can build tension.	This POV can be long-winded, sometimes even boring. It does not imitate real life since we are not all-knowing. It can be confusing and can keep readers from connecting with some characters.
Third-person limited	We become invested in the character that we know best. It distances the reader from the other characters.	Although this POV is more like real life, the reader might not understand the other characters sufficiently.
Objective (dramatic)	This style is easy to read, fast-paced, and action-oriented.	It's hard to know what the author wants us to think, and it can be difficult to interpret. One has to read between the lines carefully. Characters are not fully developed.

These questions will help you when you analyze the point of view:

- Who is telling the story? Can you trust this narrator?
- What do we learn about the narrator?
- What is the effect of the point of view? How would the story be different if it was told from another point of view?
- What effect is gained by being able to read characters' minds?

Setting

Setting includes the time and the location of the story. Both can serve a major purpose in helping to develop the work. Consider the following issues:

- Where does the action take place? What is the significance when there is a change in location?
- What physical details are present about the location(s)? What is its appearance? Its feeling? Its sound?
- In what way does the social environment—the mores, manners, customs, and rituals of a society—affect the plot and characters? For example, do the characters habitually go to church, do they have afternoon tea, go to a club, drink heavily, meet at certain places and times?
- How does the author create atmosphere, the emotional reaction that both the characters and readers have to the setting?
- When does the story take place? What significance does this add?
- How much time passes during the action?
- In what way does the passage of time affect the characters? The plot? The conflict? The theme?
- Is the author manipulating time by slowing it down or speeding it up? If so, what significance does this add to the work?

Theme

Theme reveals the author's point(s) about the human condition. It will serve you well to discuss the theme of the passage as it relates to a universal truth; that is, a general statement about the human condition, not just a specific statement about the characters in this particular story. Common themes tend to fall into several general categories:

- **The nature of humanity:** Are people mostly good or mostly bad? Are they moral or are they flawed? Are they thinking creatures or just mindless machines?
- **The nature of society:** In what way does their society dictate the characters' actions? Is the effect positive or negative? What perpetuates the society? Is the society flawed or is it idealized, and what does each say about humanity's role in this society?
- **The nature of humankind's relationship with the world:** Do the characters have free will over their own actions? Or do larger forces beyond the characters' control drive them? Or does providence play a role?
- **The nature of our ethical responsibilities:** Are the characters' ethics clear-cut or are they ambiguous?

The following is a list of common themes that recur throughout literature, although this list is somewhat stereotypical. The ideas here are deliberately presented as simple phrases, not complete sentences, so that you will focus on each individual idea. As you peruse the list, consider each theme and try to recall if you've encountered it in any specific works that you have already read. Also, try to contemplate the deeper and more meaningful aspects of each theme. Remember, *every* piece of literature on the exam will have *multiple* themes.

- The importance of one's home, homeland, family, nationality, and so on
- The significance of religion or its lack of significance to a character
- The importance of learning about the larger world and how one fits into it
- The changes people experience after traumatic events, such as soldiers after a war or a family after a divorce
- The innate need for balance and security in anyone's life
- The appreciation of beauty or the need for art
- The need to have something we can hold onto, something we hope will never change
- The psychological impulse to feel stronger than others
- The hero's perception of reality, or how society creates the heroes it wants and needs
- The human desire to understand the world we live in to find order out of chaos
- The desire for morality and fairness and justice in the world
- The importance of friendship, trust, honesty, and personal loyalty
- The coming-of-age events that help to change children into adults
- A character's passage from innocence to maturity
- The search for one's identity, for one's place in society, or a search for one's roots
- The need to feel a sense of accomplishment or some degree of success
- The difference between appearances and reality
- The effect of a need to take revenge
- The power of love, the power of hate
- The desire to rebel against unjust authority
- The effect of holding power over others
- The effect of too much ambition
- The effect of overly critical self-guilt
- The effects of war, both on individual characters and on society
- The universal human desire to be free
- The impact on a character of having too much fear or too little fear
- The effect of feeling alienated or isolated in today's society
- The need to accept personal responsibility for one's actions

Tone and Imagery

The most commonly used analytical terms that apply to both poetry and prose, in both the multiple-choice and the free-response sections, are tone and imagery. Let's look at some ways to address each of these terms.

Tone

Tone is the writer's or speaker's attitude toward the subject, the characters, and the theme—the overall emotional coloring or emotional meaning of a work. The tone will usually be multilayered, with more than one attitude being revealed. The best student responses that address tone in a free-response essay will address the work's complexity or how the tone changes. You should not analyze tone or attitude if either is too simple and obvious.

The following chart has many appropriate adjectives that describe tone in poems and prose.

adoring	calm	disgusted	frivolous	ironic	optimistic	resigned	surprised
afraid	caustic	disheartened	frustrated	irrational	outraged	revengeful	surreptitious
aggravated	cautious	disinterested	furious	irritated	overbearing	reverent	suspicious
aggressive	chaotic	dismal	gentle	jealous	overwhelmed	romantic	sweet
agitated	chauvinistic	disturbed	giddy	joyful	pained	rude	sympathetic
agreeable	cheerful	dominating	happy	joyous	paranoid	sad	threatening
alarmed	cheery	domineering	harsh	laconic	passionate	sarcastic	timid
amazed	childish	dramatic	hateful	lethargic	passive	sardonic	tired
ambiguous	coarse	dreamy	haughty	lighthearted	patronizing	seductive	tragic
amiable	complacent	ecstatic	hollow	lonely	peaceful	sensuous	uncertain
angry	concerned	effervescent	hostile	loud	persuasive	serious	uninterested
apathetic	condescending	effusive	humble	loving	perturbed	sharp	upset
apologetic	confident	elated	humorous	majestic	pessimistic	shocked	vexed
appreciative	confused	embarrassed	hurt	malicious	petulant	shrewd	vibrant
arrogant	consoling	encouraging	hypnotic	manipulative	pitiful	sincere	vicious
artificial	content	enthusiastic	hypocritical	meek	playful	skeptical	vituperative
audacious	contradictory	envious	impatient	melancholic	pleading	snooty	whimsical
authoritative	convincing	euphoric	impious	miserable	positive	solemn	witty
baffled	critical	evil	impotent	morbid	presumptuous	somber	wrathful
banal	curious	excited	incredulous	mournful	proud	soothing	zealous
benevolent	cynical	explosive	indecisive	mystical	questioning	spiteful	
bewildered	dejected	exuberant	indifferent	nervous	quizzical	stern	
bitter	depressed	facetious	informative	numb	reflective	strong	
bleak	desperate	fearful	infuriated	obnoxious	regretful	sultry	
bored	disappointed	friendly	instructive	obsessive	rejuvenated	superficial	
boring	discouraged	frightened	inventive	oppressive	remote	superior	

Next, let's examine how a character's attitudes can be organized into various conceptual groupings. These groupings will help you find appropriate adjectives to describe the character's attitudes:

- **rational thought:** explanatory, instructive, didactic, admonitory, condemnatory, indignant, puzzled, curious, wistful, pensive, thoughtful, preoccupied, deliberate, studied, candid, guileless, thoughtless, innocent, frank, sincere, questioning, uncertain, doubting, incredulous, critical, cynical, insinuating, coaxing, pleading, persuasive, argumentative, oracular

- **pleasure:** peaceful, satisfied, contented, happy, cheerful, pleasant, bright, sprightly, joyful, playful, jubilant, elated, enraptured, delighted, gratified

- **pain:** worried, uneasy, troubled, disappointed, regretful, vexed, annoyed, bored, disgusted, miserable, cheerless, mournful, sorrowful, sad, dismal, melancholy, plaintive, fretful, querulous, irritable, sore, sour, sulky, sullen, bitter, crushed, pathetic, tragic

- **obsession/compulsion:** nervous, hysterical, impulsive, impetuous, reckless, desperate, frantic, wild, fierce, furious, savage, enraged, angry, hungry, greedy, jealous, insane

- **self-control:** calm, quiet, solemn, serious, serene, simple, mild, gentle, temperate, imperturbable, nonchalant, cool, wary, cautious

- **friendliness:** cordial, sociable, gracious, kind, sympathetic, compassionate, forgiving, pitying, indulgent, tolerant, comforting, soothing, tender, loving, caressing, solicitous, accommodating, approving, helpful, obliging, courteous, polite, confiding, trusting

- **unfriendliness:** sharp, severe, cutting, hateful, unsocial, spiteful, harsh, boorish, pitiless, disparaging, derisive, scornful, satiric, insolent, insulting, impudent, belittling, contemptuous, accusing, reproving, scolding, suspicious

- **comedy:** facetious, comedic, ironic, satiric, amused, mocking, playful, humorous, hilarious, uproarious, farcical

- **animation:** lively, eager, excited, earnest, energetic, vigorous, hearty, ardent, passionate, rapturous, ecstatic, feverish, inspired, exalted, breathless, hasty, brisk, crisp, hopeful

- **apathy:** inert, sluggish, languid, dispassionate, dull, colorless, indifferent, stoic, resigned, defeated, helpless, hopeless, dry, monotonous, vacant, feeble, dreaming, blasé, callous

- **self-importance:** impressive, profound, proud, dignified, lofty, imperious, confident, egotistical, peremptory, bombastic, sententious, arrogant, pompous, stiff, boastful, exultant, insolent, domineering, flippant, saucy, positive, resolute, haughty, condescending, challenging, bold, defiant, contemptuous, assured, knowing, cocksure

- **submission and timidity:** meek, shy, humble, docile, ashamed, modest, timid, unpretentious, respectful, apologetic, devout, reverent, servile, obsequious, groveling, contrite, obedient, willing, sycophantic, fawning, ingratiating, deprecatory, submissive, frightened, surprised, horrified, aghast, astonished, alarmed, fearful, terrified, trembling, wondering, awed, astounded, shocked, uncomprehending

One well-known strategy that is very useful in examining tone is encompassed in the acronym DIDLS (diction, imagery, details, language, syntax):

- **diction:** Look for especially meaningful or well-chosen words and phrases; think about their connotations. Take note of any surprising or unusual words; think about how they add to the tone. Explain *how* the diction helps to create the tone.

- **imagery:** Be aware of descriptive images and notice which sense they appeal to. Explain how specific images relate to the character, narrator, or speaker. Note any progression in the imagery, such as dark to light, warm to cold, or slow to fast. Explain *how* the imagery helps to create the tone.

- **details:** Examine the facts in the piece, even the tiniest details, and notice what they reveal about the attitude. Also, notice what is *not* included and *how* that helps to develop the tone.

- **language:** Consider the overall level of the language, not just of the individual words associated with the diction. Words that are useful in describing language include informal, pretentious, obtuse, formal, pedantic, etc. Explain *how* the overall language usage contributes to the tone.

- **syntax:** Examine the sentence structure, the sentence length, and also the level of complexity versus simplicity. Explain *how* this relates to the tone and attitude.

Imagery

Imagery involves the use of language that engages our senses and that can represent a multitude of ideas. Imagery is often created by the use of such figurative language as simile, metaphor, personification, and onomatopoeia. When you discuss imagery in any essay, be sure to analyze *how* the imagery enhances the work. Do not merely identify what kind of imagery it is. Let's examine a few examples.

A reader can easily picture Shakespeare's *visual imagery* that evokes lightness and darkness as Romeo praises Juliet's radiance:

> O, she doth teach the torches to burn bright!
> It seems she hangs upon the cheek of night
> Like a rich jewel in an Ethiop's ear
>
> *—Romeo and Juliet, I. v.*

The contrast of the "torches" that "burn bright" against the "cheek of night" emphasizes Juliet's remarkable and unusual beauty. She glows like a "rich jewel," such as an earring, in an "Ethiop's ear." An Ethiop refers to a black person from Ethiopia, so the dark background upon which the jewel shines reinforces the contrasted imagery and emphasizes how Juliet's beauty is unrivaled.

If you listen, you can hear the *auditory imagery* in John Keats' lines:

> And full-grown lambs loud bleat from hilly bourn,
> Hedge-crickets sing; and now with treble soft
> The redbreast whistles from a garden-croft,
> And gathering swallows twitter in the skies.
>
> *—"To Autumn"*

The four lines are full of different sounds, the lambs "bleat" or cry loudly; the crickets "sing"; the redbreast "whistles" with "treble soft"; and the swallows "twitter." Combined, these auditory images make the scene come alive and invoke the reader to be observant of all that autumn offers and let all of the sounds sing to us, enriching the scene.

One can practically feel the *tactile imagery* that Charles Dickens creates:

> It was a rimy morning, and very damp. I had seen the damp lying on the outside of my little window. . . . Now, I saw the damp lying on the bare hedges and spare grass. . . . On every rail and gate, wet lay clammy; and the marsh-mist was so thick, that the wooden finger on the post directing people to our village—a direction which they never accepted, for they never came there—was invisible to me until I was quite close to it.
>
> *—Great Expectations*

This passage is chock-full of cold and clammy images: the word "damp" is used three times; the morning is "rimy," which means frosty; the hedges and grass are "bare" and "spare." Every rail of fencing and gate are "wet . . . clammy." The marsh-mist is so thick that the narrator (Pip) cannot see the directional sign until he "was quite close to it." Overall, the imagery is oppressively cold and threatening. We feel a need to go inside and sit in front of a warm fire to get the chill off. It fits the icy terror Pip feels as he prepares to meet the unknown convict in the marsh, giving the escaped criminal the file and food he had demanded the day before.

Pay attention and you can taste and savor the *gustatory imagery* as Virginia Woolf describes a meal:

> . . . the lunch on this occasion began with soles, sunk in a deep dish, over which the college cook had spread a counterpane of the whitest cream, save that it was branded here and there with brown spots like the spots on the flanks of a doe. After that came the partridges, but if this suggests a couple of bald, brown birds on a plate you are mistaken. The partridges, many and various, came with all their retinue of sauces and salads, the sharp and the sweet, each in its order; the potatoes, thin as coins but not so hard; their sprouts, foliated as rosebuds but more succulent . . . the serving-man set before us . . . a confection which rose all sugar from the waves. To call it pudding and so relate it to rice and tapioca would be an insult.
>
> *—A Room of One's Own*

Woolf piles luxurious image upon image as she describes a lunch, combining visual and gustatory imagery. We can indeed see the beautiful presentation of the food, such as the soles, spread with "a counterpane of the whitest cream" that had been branded "with brown spots like the spots on the flanks of a doe." This visual description makes the reader virtually drool in anticipation, and we understand and appreciate the delicacy of the white cream sauce with its branded brown spots. The description of the partridges that follows, with their "retinue of sauces and salads, the sharp and the sweet," hints at opposing taste sensations. We can imagine the flavor of the thin, soft potatoes and the succulent sprouts. The finale, a sugary confection, overwhelms our taste buds; indeed, we would not insult such a confection as to call it a pudding.

Finally, take a deep breath and hold your nose as Charles Dickens generates intense *olfactory imagery*:

> Such a staircase . . . was vile indeed to unaccustomed and unhardened senses. Every little habitation within the great foul nest of one high building—that is to say, the room or rooms within every door that opened on the general staircase—left its own heap of refuse on its own landing, besides flinging other refuse from its own windows. The uncontrollable and hopeless mass of decomposition so engendered, would have polluted the air, even if poverty and deprivation had not loaded it with their intangible impurities; the two bad sources combined made it almost insupportable. Through such an atmosphere, by a deep dark shaft of dirt and poison, the way lay. Yielding to his own disturbance of mind, and to his young companion's agitation, which became greater every instant, Mr. Jarvis Lorry twice stopped to rest. Each of these stoppages was made at a doleful grating, by which any languishing good airs that were left uncorrupted, seemed to escape, and all spoilt and sickly vapours seemed to crawl in.

> —*A Tale of Two Cities*

Phew! After reading a passage with such an intense and vile stench, we can hardly breathe; we want a breath of fresh air. The "foul nest" in which every habitation "left its own heap of refuse" and flung "other refuse" from the windows is bad enough, but Dickens compounds it by describing it as an "uncontrollable and hopeless mass of decomposition" that pollutes the air that is already loaded with the "intangible impurities" of "poverty and deprivation." The two characters climbing the stairs are forced to stop twice to rest, but they receive no succor; instead, "any languishing good airs" escaped and "all spoilt and sickly vapours seemed to crawl in." By this point, the reader feels suffocated. The intensity of the disgusting odors becomes oppressive, reinforcing the difficulty of the characters' journey. Within the context of the novel, this passage strongly emphasizes the choking, poverty-stricken atmosphere surrounding the peasantry of France, and serves as a precursor to the French Revolution.

Satire and Comedy

Finally, let's consider the essential components of satire and comedy. The AP exam does present passages that contain satirical and/or comedic elements, although the entire passage may not be so. The subtleties and nuances of satire can sometimes go unnoticed, but students who are comfortable and practiced at recognizing the tools of the satirist and understanding how they create successful satire will have an advantage in their analysis. Of course, satirists can employ all of the devices of figurative language, but in particular you'll find they use irony, caricature, hyperbole, understatement, wit, sarcasm, allusion, and juxtaposition.

Satire can be characterized into two categories: One might tend to make you laugh; the other might tend to make you cringe. In both cases, the ultimate goal is to highlight the foibles of humanity, hoping that people might try to correct their own behavior and improve society. Good satire should make us think.

- **Horatian** satire is gentle, urbane, tolerant, and humorous; it aims to correct human peccadillos with broadly sympathetic laughter or chuckles. Based on the works of the Roman lyrical poet Horace, its customary purpose is "to hold up a mirror" so readers can see themselves and their society in an honest light. The vices and follies in Horatian satire are not destructive or vicious. However, they reflect the foolishness of people, the superficiality and meaninglessness of their lives, and the barrenness of their values. It uses a healthy amount of humor and hyperbole. Alexander Pope's mock-epic poem, *The Rape of the Lock*, and Jonathan Swift's *Gulliver's Travels* are prime examples of Horatian satire.
- **Juvenalian** satire is biting, bitter, indignant, and angry; it emphasizes the corruption of human beings and their iniquitous institutions with contempt, using what is called saeva indignatio, a savage outrage based on the style of the Roman poet Juvenal. Sometimes perceived as enraged or downright mean-spirited, Juvenalian satire sees the vices and follies of humanity as intolerable. Juvenalian satire uses heavy doses of sarcasm and irony. Joseph Heller's *Catch-22* and George Orwell's *Animal Farm* are excellent examples of Juvenalian satire.

Comedy versus Tragedy

Students are generally well-prepared to analyze tragedy; it's likely that you have already studied tragic plays, and you are familiar with the traits of the tragic hero and the essential elements of a tragic plotline. However, students are frequently not as experienced in the analysis of comedic works. The following chart summarizes the important ideas behind comedy and its distinct differences from tragedy.

Comedy	Tragedy
Character: Comedies tend to have more down-to-earth, pragmatic characters; they seem more normal, more like all of us. They often are very flexible, willing to change, and forgiving. They may make up rules as they go, rather than following rigid social dictates.	**Character:** Tragedies tend to have rigid, idealistic, super-human, larger-than-life characters. They are frequently inflexible individuals who see the world only in black-and-white terms: good versus evil; just versus unjust. They do not easily forget or forgive.
The comedic world: Human society in comedies tends to be inconsistent, changeable, and ambiguous. Society tolerates loose ends, and everything does not have to make sense. Comedies tend to focus on the larger community and the interactions among many groups.	**The tragic world:** Society in tragedies is rooted in tradition, order, and citizens who play by the rules. Any divergent action should have consequences, and any violation of the norms upsets the world with tragic consequences. Tragedies frequently stress the role of the individual and the results of the individual's actions over the larger community.
The comic vision: Comedies commonly value the imagination, the ability to look for a variety of answers. Comedy allows some people to have a second chance; if they are clever, they may be able to reverse their fate. Frequently more pacifistic, comedy values keeping one's life over maintaining one's dignity. Ultimately, comedy teaches us to laugh at ourselves, to not take the world too seriously.	**The tragic vision:** Tragedies usually stress order and process, following a course of action with commitment and firm action. Frequently more militaristic, traditional tragedies often arise from warrior cultures, and they value the traits of the good soldier: duty, dignity, and honor. Ultimately, tragedy teaches us about the dark forces in humanity and how mankind must fight to overcome evil, no matter the cost.

You can practice addressing past AP prompts that have elements of satire and comedy by looking at the Question 2 Prose prompt for the following years on the AP website:

- 2017: *The Adventures of Peregrine Pickle*
- 2006: *Lady Windemere's Fan*
- 2003: "The Other Paris"
- 2002: *Kiss and Tell*
- 2001: *Tom Jones*
- 2000: *The Spectator*

In chapters 3 and 4, you'll get advice and strategies for the multiple-choice section and the free-response section. Each of those chapters includes samples of prose passages and poetry, as well as appropriate multiple-choice questions and explanations, plus essay prompts and samples of student essays with analyses. In addition, each of the six practice exams (chapters 7–12) will offer plenty of samples on which to practice.

Chapter 3
Section I of the Exam: Multiple-Choice Questions

Introduction

The multiple-choice section of the AP English Literature and Composition Exam is always 1 hour long and typically contains 55 questions based on five different passages. You will be awarded 1 point for each correct answer. You will not be penalized for a wrong answer, and if you do not answer a question, you simply receive no points for that question. Therefore, you should always attempt to answer every question; even if you are not absolutely certain that you have the best answer, use your elimination skills and take an educated guess.

Each of the five passages will be accompanied by 8–14 questions, and each question will have five answer choices. (Exams earlier than the mid-1990s had four passages with 11–15 questions each; the 1-hour time limit has been quite steady, with very few exceptions in exams from the mid-1980s and earlier.) Two of the passages are from fictional prose works; two are poetry; the fifth passage may be a third poem or a third prose piece, occasionally a work of drama. Though the poems are most often complete works, the prose passages are likely to be excerpted from longer works. It is not common, but on rare occasions a short story has been used for a prose passage. Expect that the poems will range from 14 lines (obviously a sonnet) to about 55 lines at most. The prose passage may be as brief as 300 words or as long as 800 words. The overall amount of reading is essentially balanced across all exams.

The five passages most frequently represent a variety of different periods of British and American literature. Why? Because *all* passages must be written originally in English, hence the exam name, *English Literature*, and most works written in English were done so by authors in English-speaking countries. The multiple-choice section of the exam will never include a work that has been translated, not even a translation from Middle English works to Modern English; therefore, expect that all of the passages on your AP exam were written in English sometime after 1575. Occasionally, a passage might represent other cultures or other areas of the world, but British and American passages do dominate the exam. Although most of the passages in the multiple-choice and free-response sections will have been written in the 20th and 21st centuries, you will be more comfortable if you are adept at reading works from many literary movements and time periods within the various English-language genres. A student who only practices with modern-day authors will not be as relaxed or efficient during the exam as one who has been exposed to works from the 16th through 19th centuries. The passages chosen for the exam are not ones that have found their way into most high school textbooks and anthologies; therefore, you are unlikely to be familiar with any of the passages. Consider this an advantage! You, and your fellow test-takers, have the opportunity to read the passage with fresh eyes instead of viewing it with preconceived notions or trying to remember what your teacher or classmates had said about a piece. Additionally, the passages are rarely identified by author, although sometimes the passage's date may be printed. A poem's title may or may not be given. Any passage that requires copyright permission, obviously contemporary pieces, will of course reveal the title, author, and date of publication. In any case, the AP English Literature and Composition Development Committee will always include any necessary introductory information or footnotes that they deem essential to your understanding of the piece. In this book, expect occasional introductory material preceding a passage and/or footnotes following it.

The passages that are chosen for the exam are not simplistic, easily accessible works. They must be complex enough to generate a number of challenging multiple-choice questions, and these questions must be designed to illuminate the differences in performance among the hundreds of thousands of students taking the exam. If the passages are too hard or too easy, they don't accurately differentiate the test-takers.

To answer the multiple-choice questions, you don't need any specific historical or philosophical background knowledge. The passages are self-contained and self-explanatory. However, the exam does expect you to be familiar with the common terms of literary analysis and to have some familiarity with classical mythology and the more well-known parts of the Old and New Testaments. Because so much British and American literature of the earlier periods is religious, it is quite possible that a religious poem by a writer like George Herbert, Edward Taylor, or Anne Bradstreet may be on the exam. But keep in mind that the test-writers are eager to ensure that no one is given any special advantage; if a religious text is used, it should be just as accessible to a nonbeliever as to a devoted follower of any religion. The questions will always be on literary, not doctrinal, issues.

As you probably already know, no quick and easy shortcut exists to master the analysis of literature. If there were, you wouldn't need to spend 4 years in high school English classes. The AP English Literature and Composition Exam gives you the opportunity to demonstrate what you've learned about reading, writing, and analyzing literature throughout middle school and high school. But you can develop a systematic, disciplined method for approaching the literary texts you'll be asked to analyze on the AP exam.

Naturally, it's common to ask, "How many questions do I have to get right to earn a score of 5?" Naturally, no simple answer exists. Remember that the multiple-choice section counts for 45 percent of your overall score and the three free-response essays combined count for the other 55 percent. However, the College Board does publish information on how many test-takers accurately answered each question on released exams. Older exams, from the 1990s and earlier, tended to have more difficult questions, and the scoring breakdown was gentler, but here is approximate data from recent 21st-century exams.

Overall Score	Approximate % of Correct Answers
5	85–100%
4	69–84%
3	50–68%
2	32–49%
1	31% or lower

Remember that these estimates are merely guidelines. However, the bottom line is that students who can get 85 percent or more multiple-choice questions correct AND write three free-response essays that score in the 6–5 range stand a very good chance of getting an overall score of 5. Students who can answer just half of the multiple-choice questions correctly AND write three free-response essays in the 4–3 range (out of a possible 6) are likely to get an overall score of 3. Finally, don't forget the importance of entering an answer for every multiple-choice question; you will not lose any fraction of a point for a wrong answer.

Abilities Tested

The multiple-choice section tests your ability to analyze the linguistic and literary choices of an author. You are expected to show an awareness of the stylistic effects created by specific word choices and syntactic decisions. These questions also test your ability to examine fictional passages critically; to understand the author's meaning and purpose; to comprehend structural organization; to recognize character development; and to analyze syntax, figurative language, style, and tone. The level of difficulty reflects freshman-level college study.

Basic Skills Necessary

In general, you need to be able to glean the gist of a given passage, demonstrate your skills in literary analysis, and prove that you have an adequate background in grammar. Although the questions don't specifically ask for definitions of terms (such as *subordinate clause* or *syntax*), you should be familiar with terms that may show up in the question stems or in the answer choices. For a review of the terms you might encounter in the exam, read "Terms for the Multiple-Choice and Free-Response Sections" in Chapter 5. In addition, you need to have developed some proficiency in careful reading to analyze and interpret the passages.

Analysis of the Directions

The directions you see on the multiple-choice section of the AP English Literature and Composition Exam will read like this:

> **Directions:** This section contains selections from literary works and questions on their content, style, and form. Read each passage or poem carefully. Then choose the best answer to each question. Pay particular attention to questions that contain the word NOT, LEAST, or EXCEPT.

Here are some suggestions for answering multiple-choice questions, based on the directions.

- Use self-discipline to manage your time effectively during the exam. You can develop this skill through practice. You should divide your time for each passage accordingly. Do not let yourself fall further and further behind as the exam progresses.
- Answer all the questions for each set to the best of your ability before going on to the next passage. This strategy prevents you from having to return to any passage at the end of the exam just to answer a few skipped questions. If you put yourself in the position of returning to a passage, you'll have to reread it, and that process is too time-consuming.
- Focus on reading each passage carefully and critically. First, paraphrase the author's ideas as you read; then, concentrate on the author's literary choices. Avoid getting bogged down in diction, whether it's a word you don't know or the structure of a stanza or sentence that's confusing. Simply keep trying to get the main point, and then let the questions guide what you need to know.
- Read all of the answer choices. Remember that the directions ask for the *best* answer choice, which means that more than one choice for each question might seem reasonable. However, never forget that a wrong answer is wrong for a specific reason. The correct response will never have a single inaccurate word in it. Eliminate the wrong answer choices as you go. You can become more efficient at eliminating wrong answers by practicing spotting the wrong word or phrase in the incorrect responses.

Test-Taking Strategies

You can do well on the multiple-choice section of the AP English Literature and Composition Exam by using some proven test-taking strategies.

Skim the Questions

First, before you read the passage, skim the questions to find out what you should concentrate on. Skimming the questions before reading the passage helps you focus on which aspects the test-writers found important. Skimming involves a very fast reading speed—approximately 1,000 words per minute—so be aware that during this skimming, you are really just glancing at the questions. Ignore the few "generic" questions, such as ones that ask you the author's main purpose or main point; instead, try to find approximately three to five specific ideas that you can look for while you read the passage. Do not try to memorize the questions; just glance at them to help you focus on finding the important points while you read.

This technique works well, but you must practice it frequently before the exam for it to become second nature. You should look for the specific key idea of each question. For example, don't merely note that a question asks you to draw an inference; rather, focus upon the specific content related to the inference. Prior practice is essential for you to become comfortable with the strategy of skimming the questions before reading the passage.

Read Each Passage Actively and Visually

Active reading means you should underline and mark key words and ideas (just the few most important ones) as you read. Use your pencil; it's your friend! Don't sit passively and merely let your eyes move across the page. Scientific studies support the idea that active readers gain higher immediate retention than do passive readers, and immediate retention is all you need in this case. You won't be concerned at all with long-term memory on the day of the exam.

Visual reading means you should picture the action of the passage in your mind; create a movie, if you will. Visual reading is a most valuable tool for eliminating distractions while reading. It gives your brain a task to perform and helps keep your mind focused on the content of the passage. In addition, most people are visual learners; they remember more after they have "seen" something, even if it's an image in their imagination. Take advantage of the fact that this exam is composed of poetry and fictional prose, which are full of images. That makes visualizing much more accessible than something like nonfiction technical writing.

Both active reading and visualization enhance your immediate retention and concentration—just what you need the most on this exam. Practice these skills daily, and you'll see your reading effectiveness improve.

Paraphrase While You Read

This technique also helps your immediate retention, and it improves your understanding of the author's ideas. By definition, paraphrasing, like summarizing, means restating the author's ideas in your own words. This is an essential skill for comprehension, and, just like visual reading, it gives your brain something to do that is on task while you read. Every question that asks about a passage's main ideas or an author's point can be answered correctly if you paraphrase accurately.

For any given passage, paraphrase the author's progression of ideas, and then paraphrase the author's overall theme in a brief phrase that covers all of the paragraphs or stanzas. Initially practice by writing down your concise statement of an author's point immediately after reading a paragraph or a whole passage. Later, you can develop this skill to the point that it's internalized, and you can paraphrase very quickly. You'll find that, eventually, you can paraphrase effectively while you're reading.

Read the Questions Carefully

After you have read the passage, be sure to read the questions very carefully. Don't assume from your earlier skimming that you know each question well. You must understand exactly what a question is asking. Students frequently choose a wrong answer because they have misread the question, either by reading it too quickly or by not being sure what is actually being asked.

Remember that questions of all categories can sometimes be worded as a negative, such as "all of the following . . . EXCEPT." Pay close attention to questions that use the word NOT, LEAST, or EXCEPT. These signal words will not affect which category the question falls into, but they will definitely affect the correct response!

Read the Answer Choices Carefully

Eliminate each wrong answer choice as you read it by crossing out that letter in the exam booklet, and then never waste time rereading wrong answer choices. Make sure the answer that you choose is both accurate according to the passage and that it answers the specific question.

By understanding how to eliminate incorrect answer choices efficiently, you'll save time and increase your accuracy. Of course, the incorrect answer choices are always trying to mislead or misdirect you. So, if you understand the tricks embedded in them, you'll spot and eliminate wrong answer choices more quickly, and you'll be less likely to be deceived. When you are trying to eliminate wrong answer choices, it is helpful to think like a test-writer, not a test-taker. Remember to cross out each wrong answer choice in the exam booklet so you don't waste time rereading them. Keep in mind that answer choices can be wrong for many reasons, such as:

- **Contradictory to the passage:** Many wrong answer choices simply misstate information from the passage. If you read the passage carefully and paraphrase it accurately, you won't be tricked into the time-consuming process of rereading it to decide if an answer choice is consistent with the passage or not.

- **Irrelevant to the question:** These incorrect answer choices may sound good, they may correctly restate something from the passage, but they simply do not answer the specific question at hand. Be sure to read the question carefully, know exactly what it is asking, and then select your answer accordingly.
- **Never addressed in the passage:** Again, poor readers are tricked into rereading the passage to look for ideas that weren't there in the first place. Readers who are accurate at paraphrasing can quickly eliminate the answer choices that have no evidence in the passage.
- **Unreasonable:** If the answer choice makes you shake your head and ask, "Where did they get that idea?" you can say that it's simply unreasonable. You should learn to quickly spot and eliminate unreasonable answer choices.
- **Too general or too specific for the question:** You must understand the degree of specificity that you need for a correct answer and then eliminate the wrong answer choices accordingly. For example, if the question asks about the overall point of a passage, you need a general answer, one that encompasses the content of the entire passage. On the other hand, if you're asked about the author's use of a certain quotation, the correct answer is likely to be quite specific.

Finally, never forget that every wrong answer choice is wrong for a specific reason and will *always* contain an inaccurate word or phrase. Practice crossing out the exact word or phrase that makes a choice wrong, and, after time, you'll find that you can perform faster and with greater confidence. Always remember that the correct answer will not have a single word that is inaccurate.

Leave the Most Difficult Questions for Later

A good defensive strategy is to leave the most difficult questions until the end of each passage. You might gain insight to help answer the harder questions as you tackle the more accessible ones. During your practice, you can learn to recognize which questions are harder or more time-consuming for you and which ones you can do accurately and quickly. Use this knowledge as part of your personal strategy to select the correct answer for the most questions in that set that you possibly can. Remember to treat each passage as a unit; answer all the questions for that passage in a timely manner before going on to the next passage. Because you will not be penalized for a wrong answer, be sure to mark an answer for every question.

One good way to increase your score is to analyze the questions you get wrong on the practice exams. Try to identify the specific reason why you selected an incorrect answer choice. Did you misread the question? Did you misread the answer? Did you try to work too quickly? Next, look for trends; for example, you may have lower accuracy on a certain question type. Then you can study the pattern, analyze your misses, and understand *why* the correct answer really is the best choice. This analysis will help you to avoid repeating the same mistakes.

Remember: Nothing beats extensive practice! As you practice, you'll increase your familiarity with the question types and with the purposely misleading wrong answer choices. Thus, you'll begin to think like a test-writer, not like a test-taker, and your score will inevitably improve.

Answering Multiple-Choice Poetry Questions

Question Categories

In Chapter 1, we examined the basics of poetry: how to read and analyze poems, plus specific poetry terminology. Now let's do something similar, explore what kinds of multiple-choice questions you will see on the exam. It's not hard because, in general, the exam questions fall into just a few categories. Once you become familiar with these, you will more quickly understand what you're being asked. Familiarity will also increase your comfort with the exam format, and it will help you work more efficiently. As with all testing strategies, it is essential to practice correctly recognizing question categories *before* the exam. The following categories are presented in the approximate order of frequency that they appear on the exam.

Note: Be aware that these question categories do not constitute a complete list. You will encounter questions that don't seem to fit into these categories. However, by understanding what types of questions are asked most frequently, you will increase your familiarity with the exam and improve your understanding of how to determine the correct answer. Of course, don't be thrown off guard when you encounter questions that don't fall into preset categories.

Questions about the Speaker and the Dramatic Situation

Overall, most questions on the exam fall into this category. These questions test your ability to understand the stated and implied information about the speaker and the speaker's beliefs or conflicts, as well as any identifiable audience and how that audience affects the poem, and also the situation or occasion that centers the poem, such as time of day, season, or event. Here are some of the ways questions of this category may be worded on the exam:

- The speaker is best characterized as doing which of the following?
- The speaker believes _____ because . . .
- The speaker is talking to . . .
- In lines _____, the speaker is reflecting on . . .
- The speaker's description of _____ helps to characterize the action as . . .
- The phrase "_____" suggests the speaker's . . .
- The poem is set in which of the following locations?
- The central event of the poem is understood to be . . .

Questions about the Poem's Theme or Main Idea

These often-used questions are essentially asking if you understand the basic idea or concept of the poem. A question may ask you to interpret the idea in a given line or two, or in a stanza, or in the poem as a whole. Here are some of the possible wordings of questions in this category:

- The poem can best be described as a lament over . . .
- The subject of lines _____ can best be described as . . .
- Line _____ is best paraphrased as . . .
- The phrase "_____" can be paraphrased as . . .
- The poem as a whole depicts a . . .
- The action of lines _____ is best described as . . .
- Which of the following best paraphrases lines _____?

Questions about the Poem's Structure

These questions ask if you understand how the poem is put together. They will ask about the overall organization, the arrangement of ideas. Here are some examples of how this question category may be worded on the exam:

- The end rhymes formally divide the poem into . . .
- Which of the following best defines the role of the second stanza?
- The last two lines comprise a . . .
- The relationship between lines _____ and _____ is best described as . . .

Questions about Tone and Attitude

These questions inquire about your understanding of the nuances of language that create tone and attitude. They frequently ask about the speaker's attitude, but they differ from questions about the speaker's situation. These questions can be answered by understanding *how* the language creates the speaker's tone or attitude. Here are some of the ways that questions of this category may be worded on the exam:

- The speaker's attitude toward _____ is best described as shifting from _____ to which of the following?
- The excerpt ends on a note of . . .
- The tone of the speaker can best be described as . . .
- In the final stanza, the speaker's attitude toward his conflict is best described as . . .

Questions about Images and Other Literary Devices

These questions test your ability to understand the effect of poetic and literary devices, especially the effect of imagery. A few of these questions may ask you to identify which devices the poet uses, but most will address *how* the devices work within the poem. Questions of this category may be worded in a variety of ways on the exam:

- The image of _____ is most closely linked to what other image in the poem?
- The central metaphor of _____ serves to . . .
- The speaker's feeling of _____ is best suggested by the image of . . .
- Lines _____ present an example of . . .
- The image of the _____ in line _____ is both . . .
- The simile "_____" most emphasizes . . .

Questions about Diction

These questions give you the opportunity to demonstrate your understanding of how the poet's choice of words and phrases affects the meaning and enhances the work. Here are some tips about the potential wording of this question category on the exam:

- Which of the following pairs of lines contradict each other?
- The interjection in line _____ serves to . . .
- The use of "_____" indicates . . .
- In context, "_____" in line _____ most likely refers to . . .
- Lines _____ are based on a distinction between . . .

Questions about Grammar and the Meaning of Words

These questions test your knowledge of how words and phrases function grammatically within a sentence or in the passage as a whole. They may ask about the intended meaning of a specific word or phrase, or they may require that you understand sentence structure. Here are some of the various ways this question type may appear on the exam:

- In context, the phrase "_____" is best understood to mean . . .
- The phrase "_____" in line _____ refers to . . .
- The pronoun "it" in line _____ refers to . . .
- The verbs "_____" and "_____" serve to dramatize . . .
- In line _____, the word "_____" functions as which of the following?

Examples of Poetry Selections, Questions, and Answers

Set 1 Questions

The following poem, a sonnet that John Keats wrote in 1818, provides a good example of the level of difficulty of poetry on the literature exam. Of the two or three poems in the multiple-choice section, one may be a sonnet; the other poem(s) will be longer. Read this poem carefully. Then answer the 12 multiple-choice questions that follow by selecting the best answer of the five choices.

On the Sonnet

If by dull rhymes our English must be chained,
And, like Andromeda, the Sonnet sweet
Fettered, in spite of pained loveliness,
Let us find out, if we must be constrained,
Sandals more interwoven and complete   (5)
To fit the naked foot of poesy;
Let us inspect the lyre, and weigh the stress
Of every chord, and see what may be gained
By ear industrious, and attention meet;
Misers of sound and syllable, no less   (10)
Than Midas of his coinage, let us be
Jealous of dead leaves in the bay-wreath crown;
So, if we may not let the Muse be free,
She will be bound with garlands of her own.

1. The speaker's overall point can be clarified as

   A. sonnets are one of the most cumbersome forms to write

   B. older poets wrote well, even within constrictions

   C. mythological allusions can inspire poets

   D. poets who are constrained by form can lose sight of their inspiration

   E. new musical rhythms can improve poetry

2. In line 4, the pronoun "we" is understood as referring to

   A. English people

   B. poets

   C. mythical victims

   D. shoemakers

   E. readers of poetry

3. In the poem, which of the following best exemplifies the speaker's attempt to add something new to the sonnet form?

   A. Parallel construction

   B. Meter

   C. Metaphor

   D. Allusion

   E. Rhyme scheme

4. Which of the following does NOT add to the speaker's attitude about the sonnet form?

   A. "dull rhymes" (line 1)

   B. "chained" (line 1)

   C. "pained loveliness" (line 3)

   D. "ear industrious" (line 9)

   E. "dead leaves" (line 12)

5. Which of the following suggests a possible solution for reinventing poetry?

   A. "And, like Andromeda, the Sonnet sweet" (line 2)

   B. "To fit the naked foot of poesy" (line 6)

   C. "Let us inspect the lyre, and weigh the stress / Of every chord" (lines 7–8)

   D. "Misers of sound and syllable" (line 10)

   E. "let us be / Jealous of dead leaves" (lines 11–12)

6. Lines 7–9, "Let us inspect the lyre . . . and attention meet," add suspense to the sonnet form in that they

   A. employ enjambment

   B. refer to musical instruments

   C. violate the traditional meter

   D. speak directly to others

   E. value sound and form equally

7. The speaker's point in stating "let us be / Jealous of dead leaves in the bay-wreath crown" (lines 11–12) is that

A. modern poets cannot write with constraint and will eliminate all dead phrases from poetry

B. modern poets can acknowledge the greatness of past poets but must create new poetic forms

C. older poets had the advantage of creating new forms, such as the sonnet

D. poetry should not be rewarded with any prize, such as a bay-wreath crown

E. all poets should look for ways to innovate

8. In the final couplet, the speaker resolves to

A. change "the stress / Of every chord" (lines 7–8)

B. seek inspiration from the Muse

C. follow traditional form

D. weave new garlands for future poets

E. combine perfect sound and meter

9. The speaker finally realizes that

A. verse forms do not really matter

B. future poets will thank him for freeing up the imagination

C. poetic conventions provide a template to work with

D. one cannot chain the imagination

E. great poets worked within constricted forms

10. The image of "dull rhymes" being "chained" (line 1) becomes ironic because

A. the constricting chains become garlands by the end

B. Andromeda was chained to a rock but later freed

C. they bring "pained loveliness" (line 3)

D. they can be "constrained" (line 4) into poesy's sandals

E. bay-wreath crowns produced dull rhymes

11. Within context, the speaker's reference to the lyre indicates that he

A. understands poetry was initially sung or accompanied by musical instruments

B. wishes to change the sound of poetry

C. values traditional symbols

D. believes poetry should be musical

E. associates the instrument with older poetry

12. The unusual rhyme scheme has the effect of

A. inspiring a new generation of poets to change tradition

B. mocking traditional sonnets

C. demonstrating how sound should create meaning

D. adding to the poem's tempo

E. breaking down the fetters of "dull rhyme"

Set 1 Answers

1. D. The speaker laments the way that strict poetic forms, such as the sonnet, can inhibit the poet's ability to explore and express that which inspires the poet to write in the first place, choice D. Notice that he claims the sonnet form is "fettered" and "constrained." He also laments that "dull rhymes" are "chained." These negative images suggest the poet's difficulty when attempting to write within such restraints. Choice A is too strong, and it's too limited; the speaker's overall point deals with the constraining nature of the sonnet form, not the fact that it is one of the most cumbersome forms to write. (Some may want to argue that other strict poetic forms, such as the sestina, are more cumbersome to write than a sonnet, but that is irrelevant.) The speaker would likely agree with choice B, that older poets wrote well, even within the constrictions of such forms as the sonnet, but this idea is not the speaker's overall point; it is a minor epiphany. The speaker would presumably also agree with choice C, that mythological allusions can inspire; indeed, the poet uses several in the poem, but that does not address the speaker's overall point. Choice E has no concrete proof in the poem; the speaker does suggest investigating musical sounds, but doing so does not ensure improving poetry.

2. B. The pronoun "we" must refer to poets; after all, they are the ones who write poetry, choice B. To unchain "our English," the speaker three times urges them to "let us . . ." band together to explore new poetic forms and sounds. Although the pronoun antecedent is not explicitly stated in the poem, it is clearly understood. The pronoun does not refer to the English people themselves (A), but to poets who write in English. The remaining answer choices cannot be the antecedent of the pronoun. Andromeda, the mythical victim (C) who is chained to a rock, is not related to the "we." Shoemakers (D) that make sandals "to fit the naked foot of poesy" are also not part of the "we." Finally, the readers of poetry (E), like the English people in choice A, cannot be the antecedent.

3. E. Sonnets traditionally have 14 lines of iambic pentameter and follow one of two rhyme schemes (see Chapter 5). In this poem, which criticizes the strict form of the sonnet, John Keats chooses to ignore tradition and instead uses an unusual rhyme scheme, choice E: *abc abd cab cde de*. It's as if he wants to show how he can indeed toy with tradition while still maintaining the structure. On the other hand, Keats does create some parallel construction (A) in the poem, such as the repetition of "let us . . . ," but that alone does not exemplify his attempt to add something new to the sonnet form. Also, Keats does follow the traditional meter of sonnets (B), which contradicts the idea of trying something new. Keats also develops more than one metaphor (C), such as the "sandals" that are custom fit for "the naked foot of poesy," but metaphor use is not new to any poetic form. Finally, Keats uses multiple allusions (D) to Andromeda, the traditional lyre, and Midas, but including allusions is also common in many sonnets.

4. D. The phrase "ear industrious," choice D, describes how the speaker wishes poets to tune their ear to pay close attention to the sound of their poetry, "weigh[ing] the stress / Of every chord" to see how poetry can be enhanced and improved. This idea does not add to his negative attitude about the sonnet form per se; rather, he is suggesting an improvement. The phrase "dull rhymes" (A) criticizes the way older poets produced bland works under the restrictions of a sonnet because they were "chained" (B); that is, they were limited in expression. The "pained loveliness" (C) identifies another of the negative effects of the sonnet form; the speaker feels the potential beauty is too forced. The "dead leaves" (E) symbolize lifeless, out-of-date, archaic poetry.

5. C. In spite of his criticism of the sonnet form, Keats offers a few suggestions to improve it, one of which is inspecting the sound (hence "the lyre") and weighing the stress of every syllable ("Of every chord") in the hopes of creating something new, choice C. Choice A, the allusion to Andromeda, is not a suggestion for improving poetry; it is merely a simile that Keats uses to establish the chained restrictions of the sonnet form. Choice B, the "foot of poesy" metaphor, does not articulate a potential solution; the idea of a new sandal is the suggestion, not poesy's foot itself. Notice the play on words with "foot," which refers to not only a literal foot for the sandal, but also the metrical feet that compose lines of poetry (poesy). Choice D criticizes how stingy poets have to be in a sonnet form; they are so limited in the number of words they can use, and they cannot afford to elaborate as much as they might in other forms. Choice E that claims "let us be jealous . . ." is not a suggestion for improving poetry; instead it begins the speaker's reconciliation with older poets. The speaker asserts that current poets should be jealous of how well the older poets were able to write.

6. A. Lines of poetry that demonstrate enjambment have no pause or complete stop between the end of one line and another; usually this is achieved by eliminating any punctuation. Keats makes exquisite use of enjambment in lines 7–9 to stretch out the thought and keep us in suspense, choice A. End-stopped lines would not have the same effect. Notice how he begins line 7 by inviting us to "inspect the lyre" and then invites us to "weigh the stress / Of every chord." The line break after the word "stress" keeps us hanging; we want to know what stress he is speaking of and we have to read the next line to find out. He creates the same suspense by inviting us to "see what may be gained / By ear industrious." Think about how different the poem would be if Keats were to place these grammatical units on the same line. We'd read "[Let's] weigh the stress of every chord," and "[Let's] see what may be gained by ear industrious." We'd speed through the lines, and they would lose their effect. The idea in choice B makes little sense for this question; using musical instruments does not particularly add suspense, and the lyre is only mentioned once. Additionally, the lyre was traditionally used to accompany poetry, especially in Ancient Greece, so its mention should not surprise a reader. Choice C incorrectly states that the lines in question violate the traditional meter of a sonnet; they do not, but instead they are written in customary iambic pentameter. Choice D, that the poet speaks directly to others, is not particularly suspenseful; it is a choice used frequently enough. Choice E inaccurately claims that the lines place equal value on sound and form; instead, these lines explore sounds but not form.

7. B. When the speaker calls out to "let us be / Jealous of dead leaves in the bay-wreath crown," he effectively acknowledges that older poets who gained fame and renown did indeed write poems that are worthy of jealousy. However, the key adjective "dead" implies that these older forms may have worked in the past, but modern poets should strive for newer, livelier forms, not mere imitation, choice B. Choice A is too strong and too absolute. The speaker does not think that modern poets cannot write with constraint; after all, he is doing so in this poem, nor can they possibly eliminate all dead phrases from poetry. Choice C is too much of a stretch; while it may be accurate that older poets were inventing the sonnet form, giving them an advantage, it does not mean that modern poets should be jealous of that advantage. Instead, they should be jealous of what great works the older poets did create. Choice D has no evidence in the poem; we should not make the illogical leap of thinking the speaker disdains all rewards or prizes that poets may receive. Choice E is just too simplistic; yes, the speaker urges modern poets to look for new and innovative ways to write, but that idea does not address the speaker's point in these specific lines.

8. **C.** It is interesting that in the final couplet the speaker resolves to follow traditional form, choice C, acknowledging that "we may not let the Muse be free." In traditional sonnets, the conflict or problem is resolved at the close, and Keats chooses to follow this form and also to do it in the more traditional end-stopped lines. He is almost begrudging as he accepts the limitations of the sonnet form, but then he realizes the sonnet will produce "garlands of her own." Choice A misunderstands the resolution; the speaker does not change the stress of any chord in the last lines. Choice B may sound tempting, but it does not articulate the speaker's resolution. He is not resolving to seek inspiration from the Muse, but rather, he is acknowledging that she cannot be free; she will be bound by the conventions of the sonnet. Choice D incorrectly states that the speaker hopes to weave new garlands for future poets, but he really wants them to weave their own new forms. Choice E is not in the final resolution, nor in the poem itself; it seems more likely this speaker would think it near-impossible to combine perfect sound and perfect meter, especially in this restrictive sonnet form.

9. **E.** After criticizing the sonnet form for the first 10 lines of the poem, the speaker recognizes that great poets indeed worked within the constricted form that he criticizes, choice E; apparently they did it and did it well, earning bay-wreath crowns. That does not minimize his criticisms; it just states what is true. Choice A is unreasonable; nothing in the poem hints that the speaker thinks verse forms are irrelevant. Choice B is too much of a stretch; not only is it silly to think that the speaker realizes future poets will thank him, but also the poem offers no such idea. Choice C may be true in the world of writing poetry. Forms like the sonnet do provide a template of sorts, but this does not clarify what the speaker realizes by the end of the poem. Remember that he is objecting to the strictness of such templates in the first place. Choice D does not describe what the speaker realizes; undoubtedly he knows all along that imagination cannot be chained; rather, it is the constraint of certain poetic forms that chain the product of the imagination.

10. **A.** The image of the "dull rhymes" being chained and fettered is ironically changed by the last line when those chains are transformed into garlands, choice A. The chain conjures a metallic, heavy, negative image, while garlands suggest something of beauty. Garlands are generally made of flowers and leaves, and they have a positive connotation, not negative. So, by an ironic shift in imagery, the speaker ultimately verifies that one can create something of beauty, even when forced to follow convention. Choice B is irrelevant to this question; the chaining of the mythological Andromeda to a rock for her boastful behavior does not create irony; it is merely a fitting simile. Choice C does not invite irony. The "pained loveliness" describes the speaker's opinion of the current state of the sonnet; sonnets may have beauty, but their dull rhymes and forced structure make that beauty pained. Choice D confuses the images in the first line, the dull rhymes and chains, with the later suggestion that poets should attempt new poetic forms, "interwoven and complete," that create new sandals for poesy. This suggestion is not ironic. Choice E is another confused answer choice that reverses the images. It claims that bay-wreath crowns produced the dull rhymes, but the poets who wrote those old rhymes are the ones who were rewarded with the wreath. In any case, this idea is not ironic.

11. **B.** Ancient Greek poetry recital was traditionally accompanied by someone strumming a lyre, and the most musical of poetic forms, the lyric poem, gets its name from the instrument. The speaker draws on this classical connection between the musical instrument and poetry to indicate that poets should listen more closely to the sounds of words and weigh their stresses in an attempt to experiment with poetic forms, choice B. Choice A is too weak; the speaker's reference to the lyre is designed to do much more than show the poet's knowledge of ancient poetry and its musical accompaniment. Choice C is equally bland; we can easily understand that the speaker values traditional symbols, but that does not clarify the reason for his use of the lyre. Choice D is too much of a stretch; remember that the speaker's suggestion is that poets should listen to the cadence, the sound of the words; but to claim that means he believes poetry should be musical is too much of a leap in logic. Finally, choice E, that the speaker associates the lyre with older poetry, is true, but it does not clarify *why* he references the instrument; it merely states what he knows.

12. E. It makes sense that, since the speaker complains about the "dull rhyme" in older poetry, he would try to do something different, try to break down those "fettered" restraints, choice E. Indeed, Keats does accomplish this, and his unusual rhyme scheme adds surprise and interest. Traditional sonnets begin with either an *abba* or *abab* rhyme scheme, so when readers arrive at line 3, they expect a word that either rhymes with "chained" (line 1) or "sweet" (line 2). Instead they're startled to hear "loveliness" in line 3. Keats continues to plant such surprises several times. However, we have no idea whether or not the rhyme scheme inspired a new generation of poets (A); this answer choice goes too far. Choice B is too negative; the speaker does criticize the strict form of traditional sonnets, but playing with the rhyme scheme does not mock them. Choice C is too esoteric; we cannot judge if the effect demonstrates how sound should create meaning. Choice D incorrectly uses the word "tempo." The rhyme scheme does not add to the tempo, that is, the speed and the pace of the poem. If anything, this rhyme scheme may slow down the tempo since we so often encounter unexpected changes in the rhymes.

Set 2 Questions

The poem for these questions comes from Edgar Lee Masters' *Spoon River Anthology*, first published in 1915. This anthology is unusual in that all of the 244 poems are supposedly epitaphs written by the dead who are buried in the cemetery of the fictional town, Spoon River. This poem is written by a poet named Petit.

Read the poem carefully and then answer the 11 multiple-choice questions that follow by selecting the best answer of the five choices.

Petit, the Poet

SEEDS in a dry pod, tick, tick, tick,
Tick, tick, tick, like mites in a quarrel—
Faint iambics that the full breeze wakens—
But the pine tree makes a symphony thereof.
Triolets, villanelles, rondels, rondeaus, (5)
Ballades by the score with the same old thought:
The snows and the roses of yesterday are vanished;
And what is love but a rose that fades?
Life all around me here in the village:
Tragedy, comedy, valor and truth, (10)
Courage, constancy, heroism, failure—
All in the loom, and oh what patterns!
Woodlands, meadows, streams and rivers—
Blind to all of it all my life long.
Triolets, villanelles, rondels, rondeaus, (15)
Seeds in a dry pod, tick, tick, tick,
Tick, tick, tick, what little iambics,
While Homer and Whitman roared in the pines?

1. Within the context of the poem, the speaker's use of "Seeds" is ironic because

A. they never take root
B. they are usually associated with growth and birth
C. they are not known for onomatopoeia
D. he failed to plant such "seeds" in his own poetry
E. they will eventually grow into the pine trees mentioned later in the poem

2. Which of the following best describes the effect of the simile "like mites in a quarrel" (line 2)?

A. The simile parallels the poet's quarrels with others during his life.
B. It minimizes the rattling of the seed pods.
C. It increases the underlying tension in the poem.
D. It mimics the insignificance of the sound of the seeds in a dry pod.
E. It underscores the tensions in nature.

3. The phrase "Faint iambics" (line 3) implies that

   A. the sounds offer nothing of importance to hear

   B. the poet will use iambic meter to some effect

   C. the pine trees will make a symphony

   D. the sounds promise "ballades by the score"

   E. the sounds contain only "the same old thought"

4. The irony of the speaker mentioning "Triolets, villanelles, rondels, rondeaus" twice (lines 5 and 15) is that

   A. they are all poetic forms that were popular in an older time

   B. the speaker criticizes those poetic forms

   C. the poem is written in free verse

   D. they are poetic forms that this poet uses in other poems

   E. they are esteemed poetic forms that the poet aspires to perfect

5. The speaker's criticism of poetry is suggested in all of the following EXCEPT

   A. "Faint iambics that the full breeze wakens" (line 3)

   B. "Triolets, villanelles, rondels, rondeaus" (line 5)

   C. "And what is love but a rose that fades?" (line 8)

   D. "All in the loom, and oh what patterns!" (line 12)

   E. "Tick, tick, tick, what little iambics" (line 17)

6. Petit the poet, now looking back on his life from the grave, realizes that life was

   A. actually more monotonous than he thought

   B. surrounded by beautiful poetry

   C. melodious with the sounds of nature

   D. slowly ticking away

   E. full of human drama

7. The metaphor of the loom (line 12) is most effective in that it represents

   A. how many different forms of poetry are actually quite similar

   B. how many poems are "stitched" together

   C. how simple joys have been forgotten

   D. that many different individuals are woven together to form society

   E. the rich tapestry of life

8. The speaker's central conflict in life is best represented in which of the following phrases?

   A. "mites in a quarrel" (line 2)

   B. "Faint iambics" (line 3)

   C. "Triolets, villanelles, rondels, rondeaus" (line 5)

   D. "Blind to all of it all my life long" (line 14)

   E. "While Homer and Whitman roared in the pines" (line 18)

9. Which of the following clarifies why the speaker admires Homer and Whitman?

   A. They successfully utilized standard poetic forms.

   B. They wrote epic-length poems.

   C. They produced more important poetry than the speaker.

   D. They surreptitiously mocked standard poetic forms.

   E. They were financially successful poets.

10. The significance of the title can best be described as

   A. implying that the speaker believes that poems should be very short

   B. reflecting the great significance of the speaker's poetry

   C. spotlighting man's insignificance in the universe

   D. revealing how little regard he has for poetry

   E. mirroring the insignificance of the speaker's poetry

11. The repetition of the pine tree image (lines 4 and 18) serves to

   A. affirm that the speaker prefers pines to other trees

   B. emphasize that the speaker lived in an arboreal setting

   C. reinforce the beauty of significant poetry

   D. imply that pine trees serve as a religious metaphor

   E. provide stability by using an image repeatedly

Set 2 Answers

1. **B.** When they appear in literature, seeds are often a symbol for the potential of new life, new birth, and new hope, choice B; after all, they are necessary for almost all of life. Ironically, however, in the context of this poem, the seeds are in a dry pod, merely making ticking sounds reminiscent of "mites in a quarrel" as the breeze moves the pods. They do not offer any promise of new life. The fact that the seeds never take root (A) is true, but that is not the source of their irony. Choice C offers another observation that is probably true; seeds are not widely known for creating onomatopoeia, but that idea is not particularly ironic, especially within the context of this poem. Choice D tries to connect the seeds to the deceased poet, but it is neither accurate nor the source of irony. Choice E is completely off base; nothing in the poem suggests that these seed pods will grow into pine trees, and this idea is not ironic.

2. **D.** Any sound made by "mites in a quarrel" would be miniscule; mites are very tiny creatures, similar to tiny spiders. Thus, the simile is effective because the imagined sound of quarreling mites imitates and emphasizes the insignificance of the "tick, tick, tick" sound of the seeds in the dry pod, choice D. On the other hand, the poem offers no evidence that Petit the poet quarreled with others in his life, making choice A implausible. The sound of the seed pods is real, it is consistent; the mite simile cannot minimize it (B). Choice C is inaccurate in asserting that the poem has underlying tension; after all, Petit is already dead, and he's reminiscing about his life and what might have been. Even if the poem had underlying tension, the insignificant sound of the mites would not increase it. Choice E is one of those "out there in left field" responses; one cannot deny the existence of tensions in nature, but that is not the subject of this poem and the simile does not underscore it.

3. **A.** The phrase "Faint iambics" is a reference to the sounds made by the seeds rattling in the dry pods, a sound he likens to "mites in a quarrel." This goes along with the other negative words, "dry," "mites," "quarrel," and "faint," all of which collectively suggest that the sounds are unimportant; they are just minor, insignificant noises, choice A. Choice B is unreasonable; just because the word "iambics" appears in the poem does not imply that the poem will include iambic meter and, in fact, it does not. Choice C is a misread of lines 3–4; the pine tree does "make a symphony" when the wind blows, but it is in contrast to the barely audible sound of the pods. Choice D is also unrelated; the ballades are mentioned in line 6 as one of the poetic forms that present "the same old thought," but that is irrelevant to the faint iambics. Choice E is too much of a stretch; the "same old thought" is embodied in strict, repetitive old poetic forms, not necessarily in these faint iambics.

4. **C.** "Petit, the Poet" is written in free verse, choice C, which in itself is an ironic form because our poet Petit, now dead, is free from any poetic restraints. In this poem, it appears that during his life, the poet wrote and/or emulated "triolets, villanelles, rondels, rondeaus." You will probably recognize these terms, even if you are not familiar with all of them, as older poetic forms that have quite static formulas. But it seems that now, after death, the poet is finally able to break away from old forms and express his thoughts in free verse, the form that most imitates spoken language. Although you are not necessarily expected to know all of these poetic forms (especially triolets, rondels, and rondeaus), one interesting fact is that all of the forms mentioned demand a very rigid formula. They all require some form of repetition (usually repeating whole lines a certain number of times), and they all strictly limit the number of rhymes. This helps explain why the speaker thinks they only produce "the same old thought." Meanwhile, it may be true that these old forms were popular in earlier times (A), but that does not make their mention ironic. Choice B also presents a true statement: The speaker does criticize the older forms, but this criticism does not create irony. The poem offers no solid basis for thinking that the poet used these older forms in other poems (D); that may or may not be true. Finally, choice E contradicts the poem; the deceased poet Petit does not revere or try to perfect the older poetic forms.

5. **D.** When the speaker marvels at the patterns created in the loom of life, he is not criticizing poetry; instead, he is retroactively noticing the richness of life that was "all around me here in the village." Therefore, choice D is correct. All of the remaining answer choices do accurately represent his criticisms of poetry. Choice A critiques the "faint" sound of iambs, a metrical foot, which he does not use. Choice B lists the poetic forms he believes only produce trite, pedestrian poetry. Choice C remarks that stereotypical subjects in poetry, like love and roses, will fade and lose effectiveness. In choice E, the repetition of "tick, tick, tick" from the opening of the poem, plus the negative phrase "what little iambics," laments the hackneyed sound of forced and repetitive language.

6. **E.** Speaking from his grave, Petit the poet realizes how oblivious he was to the human drama of life, choice E, how he was "blind to all of it all my life long." Now he knows he should have observed how "woodlands, meadows, streams, and rivers" create "tragedy, comedy, valor and truth / Courage, constancy, heroism, [and] failure." Choice A completely contradicts the poem; he now realizes that life was full, not monotonous. Choice B also contradicts the poem; he does not feel he was surrounded by beautiful poetry; he still thinks that the poetry was trite, full of "the same old thought." Choice C is too exaggerated; the only two sounds mentioned are the dull, droning sounds of the seed pods and the symphony of the pine trees; these two images do not mean that he realizes his life was melodious with the sounds of nature. Likewise, it is an exaggeration to claim that he now realizes his life was slowly ticking away (D); perhaps the only attraction of this inaccurate choice is the play on words, using "ticking" while the poem repeats "tick, tick, tick."

7. **E.** The loom metaphorically represents the richness of life, a tapestry woven of "life all around me here in the village" that encompasses the diversity of all humanity, choice E. It is interesting to note that of the many nouns he lists in lines 10–11, representing human behaviors, only two are negative, and they begin and end the list: the first, "tragedy," and the last, "failure." Of the remaining ideas, comedy is neutral and the rest are positive: valor, truth, courage, constancy, and heroism. Choice A is simply ludicrous; you should quickly eliminate this answer choice, as it tries to equate the loom metaphor with poetic forms. Choice B is also misguided; if the loom were a metaphor for poetry, it might make sense to claim it stitches poems together, but it does not represent poetry in the first place; rather, it represents the web of life. Since a loom is an old-fashioned machine, it may be quaint to think that it is a metaphor for the simple joys of life that have been forgotten (C), but this metaphor is not about the machine; instead, it represents the cornucopia of life itself. Choice D also tries to stretch the metaphor too far; the loom does not merely symbolize the individuals in a society, but the collective human drama of the village.

8. **D.** The speaker's central conflict is related to his life-long blindness, his obliviousness to the richness that was all around him, choice D; when he states that he was "Blind to all of it all my life long," he is referring to all of the inspiration surrounding him that could have been his fodder for writing more authentic poetry. The "mites in a quarrel" (A) only serves as a simile to describe the sound of the seed pods, not the speaker's conflict. The same is true of choice B, the "Faint iambics." The list of older poetic forms in choice C does not relate to the speaker's conflict; the list merely represents the archaic forms that he disdains. The final line of the poem, repeated in choice E, refers to poets the speaker praises, and does not relate to his central conflict.

9. **C.** The speaker implies admiration for both Homer and Whitman for their "roar[ing] in the pines." He believes that these two poets wrote works worthy of a symphony, not hackneyed, predictable, mainstream verses about love or roses. While they were composing verse of importance, the "little iambics" keep ticking in the dry pods around Petit. The speaker makes no hint that either poet used standardized poetic forms (A). Whitman largely wrote in free verse, and Homer's works were meant to be sung, not read. It is true that both poets wrote epic-length works (B), but that fact is irrelevant because the speaker does not allude to it in his praise. Choice D has no evidence in the poem; we simply cannot know if the speaker thinks Homer and Whitman were surreptitiously mocking standard poetry. Choice E is completely unfounded and historically questionable. Whitman's life is fairly well-documented, and we know he had some degree of financial success, albeit not great, but we do not even know if Homer ever actually existed, let alone anything about financial success in his time.

10. **E.** The title of this poem is indeed significant; the word "petit" comes from the Old French, and it refers to something small and inconsequential, and therefore the poet's name, like an aptronym (which refers to a person's name that reflects his or her occupation), reflects the insignificance of his poetry, choice E. Choice A is unreasonable; just because the word "petit" refers to something small does not mean the speaker believes poems should be short in length. Choice B contradicts both the poem's title and content. Choice C is just too much of a stretch; taking the name of our title poet and somehow relating it to man's insignificance in the universe makes no sense. Choice D contradicts the poem's content; the speaker *does* have high regard for good poetry, and this answer choice also fails to address the significance of the title.

11. **C.** The first mention of pine trees occurs as "the full breeze wakens" and stirs the tree into producing an audible symphony, a beautiful image after the dull faint sounds of the dry pods. The poem ends with another auditory image, of poets "roaring in the pines," and it leaves us with an explicit reference to the greatness of Homer's and Whitman's poetry, choice C. Choice A is silly; using pine trees twice in the poem does not remotely suggest the speaker prefers pines to any other trees. Choice B is too weak; the repetition has nothing to do with describing the arboreal setting around the poet. Choice D should make you shake your head and wonder where this idea came from; the poem has no hint of religious symbolism or metaphor. Choice E may sound a bit tempting, since poets and authors repeat an image for a reason, but in this poem, the pines do not provide stability. It's more likely that they refer to poetic inspiration, if they are significant at all.

Answering Multiple-Choice Prose Questions

Question Categories

In Chapter 2, we discussed the basics of prose analysis and the key questions that are used in analyzing imaginative literature. Now let's examine the various question categories that you are likely to encounter for the prose passages. Of course, just like the poetry question categories, the following is not a comprehensive list, but it will help you to anticipate what is most likely to appear on the exam. The question categories are presented in order of approximate frequency. Of course, keep in mind that each individual passage's style and content will dictate what types of questions are asked.

Questions about Character and Situation

These questions are the most common; they will focus on the literary situation and on such content as plot, character, conflict, and setting. Here are some of the many ways this question type may be worded on the exam:

- The passage characterizes _____ as someone who . . .
- The reference to _____'s home life serves mainly to . . .
- Which of the following best describes how _____ regards his own future?
- Which of the following serves as a climax in the passage?
- The narrator is most concerned with providing a sense of . . .
- The description of the "_____" suggests . . .
- The primary purpose of the passage is to . . .
- The persona of _____ is characterized primarily as . . .
- The opinions of the character _____ seem to be based on . . .
- The narrator focuses most on presenting . . .
- The most serious disadvantage the character faces is implied as . . .

Questions about the Implications of Phrases

These questions test your understanding of how individual phrases add meaning to the work as a whole. Many of these questions also relate to character, but the questions will ask what a specific phrase reveals about a character. Here are some of the ways this question type may be worded on the exam:

- In context, lines _____ primarily emphasize the character's . . .
- The reference to "_____" in line _____ implies that the character was . . .
- In the context of the whole passage, the idea that the character was "_____" can be considered to mean . . .
- The phrase "_____" most likely refers to . . .
- Which of the following lines best reveals the character's opinion of herself?

Questions about Diction

These questions test your ability to understand the effect of specific word choices that are used in the passage. Here are some of the ways this question type may be worded on the exam:

- In the context of the paragraph in which it appears, the word "_____" connotes all of the following EXCEPT . . .
- The use of the word "_____" serves to . . .
- The word "_____" has the ironic effect of . . .

Questions about Figurative Language

These questions test your awareness of literary devices and literary techniques, along with your understanding of their effect. Here are some of the ways this question type may be worded on the exam:

- Which of the following literary features is most prominent in the passage?
- The irony of the passage depends on . . .
- The first sentence makes use of which of the following literary devices?
- The description of _____ functions as a central metaphor that effectively . . .
- Which of the following best describes the author's figurative treatment of _____?

Questions about the Structure of the Passage

These questions measure your ability to understand how the passage is constructed, and how its organization helps to achieve the author's purpose. Here are some of the ways this question type may be worded on the exam:

- The first four sentences serve which of the following purposes?
- The collective images in the third paragraph serve primarily to . . .
- The last paragraph reveals that the main character feels . . .
- In the second paragraph, the response of the _____ to the _____ is best described as . . .

Questions about Tone and Attitude

These questions reveal your ability to understand how the passage creates tone and attitude. They may ask about the author's attitude or the intended overall tone. Here are some of the ways this question type may be worded on the exam:

- The author's attitude toward the character is best described as . . .
- The tone of the last paragraph is best described as a shift from . . .
- The two views described in lines _____ can be characterized as . . .
- The passage establishes a mood of . . .
- Which of the following best describes the tone of the passage?

Examples of Prose Selections, Questions, and Answers

Set 1 Questions

The following passage is taken from George Eliot's novel *Adam Bede* (1859). Although Mary Ann Evans published it under her pseudonym, it was widely known that she was the author.

Read the passage very carefully. It is not as easy or straightforward as it may first appear. Then answer the 10 multiple-choice questions that follow by choosing the best answer of the five options.

Leisure is gone—gone where the spinning-wheels are gone, and the pack horses, and the slow waggons, and the pedlars, who brought bargains to the door on sunny afternoons.
(5) Ingenious philosophers tell you, perhaps, that the great work of the steam-engine is to create leisure for mankind. Do not believe them: it only creates a vacuum for eager thought to rush in. Even idleness is eager now—eager for
(10) amusement: prone to excursion-trains, art-museums, periodical literature, and exciting novels: prone even to scientific theorising, and cursory peeps through microscopes. Old Leisure was quite a different personage: he only read one
(15) newspaper, innocent of leaders, and was free from that periodicity of sensations which we call post-time. He was a contemplative, rather stout gentleman, of excellent digestion—of quiet perceptions, undiseased by hypothesis: happy in
(20) his inability to know the causes of things, preferring the things themselves. He lived chiefly in the country, among pleasant seats and homesteads, and was fond of sauntering by the fruit-tree wall, and scenting the apricots when
(25) they were warmed by the morning sunshine, or of sheltering himself under the orchard boughs at noon, when the summer pears were falling. He knew nothing of weekday services, and thought none the worse of the Sunday sermon if it
(30) allowed him to sleep from the text to the blessing—liking the afternoon service best, because the prayers were the shortest, and not ashamed to say so; for he had an easy, jolly conscience, broad-backed like himself, and able
(35) to carry a great deal of beer or port-wine,—not being made squeamish by doubts and qualms and lofty aspirations. Life was not a task to him, but a sinecure: he fingered the guineas in his pocket, and ate his dinners, and slept the sleep of
(40) the irresponsible; for had he not kept up his charter by going to church on the Sunday afternoons?

Fine old Leisure! Do not be severe upon him, and judge him by our modern standard: he never
(45) went to Exeter Hall, or heard a popular preacher, or read Tracts for the *Times* or *Sartor Resartus*.*

---

*Exeter Hall was a London building used for lectures and meetings, especially of a religious nature. Tracts for the *Times* and *Sartor Resartus* are important Victorian religious and philosophical books.

1. The reason that old Leisure is "not . . . made squeamish by doubts and qualms and lofty aspirations" (lines 35–37) is simply because

   A. he never contemplates such matters
   B. he believes that his faith shields him against misgivings
   C. his conscience is clear
   D. he has attended church on Sunday afternoons
   E. he is inebriated by a great deal of beer or port-wine

2. The word "sinecure" (line 38) can be best defined as

   A. a guiding or motivating purpose or principle
   B. a job that is hard work, but not well paid
   C. a minor disappointment
   D. a situation that is undemanding, yet lucrative
   E. a simple, monastic lifestyle

3. Each of the following words or phrases gives a hint to old Leisure's place in the social order EXCEPT

   A. "gentleman" (line 18)
   B. "pleasant seats" (line 22)
   C. "port-wine" (line 35)
   D. "guineas" (line 38)
   E. "Exeter Hall" (line 45)

4. Which of the following best describes old Leisure's adherence to his religious obligations?

   A. Fervent
   B. Mechanical
   C. Feigned
   D. Peremptory
   E. Cerebral

5. Which of the following techniques is utilized most effectively in the characterization of old Leisure?

   A. Caricature
   B. Paradox
   C. Apostrophe
   D. Personification
   E. Simile

6. All of the following contrasts between old Leisure and modern leisure are implied in the passage EXCEPT

- **A.** bucolic calm versus urban hustle
- **B.** corporeal versus cerebral
- **C.** women's roles versus men's roles
- **D.** complacent versus overeager
- **E.** soothing versus stimulating

7. Which of the following best describes the overall tone of the passage?

- **A.** Caustically mocking
- **B.** Cloyingly sentimental
- **C.** Mildly satirical
- **D.** Matter of fact
- **E.** Imprudently nostalgic

8. All of the following serve to make a similar point about old Leisure EXCEPT

- **A.** "contemplative" (line 17)
- **B.** "rather stout" (line 17)
- **C.** "of excellent digestion" (line 18)
- **D.** "able to carry a great deal of beer" (lines 34–35)
- **E.** "ate his dinners" (line 39)

9. According to the passage, all of the following are currently popular leisure activities EXCEPT

- **A.** riding on excursion-trains
- **B.** visiting art museums
- **C.** reading periodical literature
- **D.** enjoying exciting novels
- **E.** sauntering by the fruit-tree wall

10. Which of the following is the most important reason that we should "not be severe" with "Fine old Leisure!"?

- **A.** He had "kept up his charter" (lines 40–41).
- **B.** He had gone "to church on the Sunday afternoons" (lines 41–42).
- **C.** We should not "judge him by our modern standard" (line 44).
- **D.** But "he never went to Exeter Hall" (lines 44–45).
- **E.** He never "read Tracts for the *Times* or *Sartor Resartus*" (line 46).

Set 1 Answers

What is most striking about the passage is the characterization of the idea of old Leisure. George Eliot personifies the leisure of the past and devotes most of the passage to describing this idea as a fictitious character. In the course of the passage, the narrator reveals her views about the leisure of her own era and about old Leisure, and she cautions her contemporaries not to be too quick to judge modern leisure as superior.

1. **A.** According to the passage, old Leisure is not bothered by worrying about doubts, nor by striving to meet his aspirations. But *why?* The answer is that he simply never thinks about such matters, choice A; he has "an easy, jolly conscience," so he doesn't worry about much of anything, apparently. Choice B has no support; no connection between his faith and any supposed doubts is evidenced in the passage. Choice C is half right; his clear conscience will help him to avoid any doubts, but this idea has no relation to his lack of aspirations. The ideas in choices D and E are both mentioned in the passage: He did attend Sunday afternoon church, and he did drink a great deal of beer or port-wine, but those ideas are irrelevant to answering this particular question.

2. **D.** The word "sinecure" literally refers to a position that provides income, yet requires little or no work, and it also has some archaic religious undertones. But even if you are not familiar with the word, you can still understand its meaning in this context. "Life was *not a task* to him, *but a sinecure*; he fingered the *guineas in his pocket.* . . ." Thus, a sinecure must be the opposite of a hard-working job; it's a comfortable position, but it still puts the coins in his pocket, choice D. Choice A is off topic; a guiding principle is not the opposite of a task. Choice B states the opposite of the actual meaning of sinecure, and hard work for low pay does not describe old Leisure's situation. Choice C is contradictory to the passage; old Leisure's life is not one of disappointments. Choice E is far off base; with all that beer and port-wine he consumes, old Leisure certainly does not live a simple, monastic lifestyle.

3. E. In this "except" question, the word or phrase in four of the five answer choices does, indeed, give the reader hints about old Leisure's comfortable social position. He is referred to as a "gentlemen" (A), which certainly gives him some stature. In choice B, the fact that he lives in the country among "pleasant seats and homesteads" (referring to ancestral homes) indicates that he is well-off. That he can afford "a great deal of port-wine" (which must be imported from Portugal, hence the name) also indicates his level in society (C). The idea in choice D is the most direct reference; old Leisure has real cash in his pocket, guineas that he can finger. Even if you are not aware that guineas were a very valuable gold coin, you should be able to discern that guineas refer to money. Choice E is the fairly obvious exception in this question; old Leisure has no relationship at all to Exeter Hall; in fact, he has never been to the location.

4. B. Considering the context of his behavior in church, the term "mechanical," choice B, is an ideal description of old Leisure's religious practices; he conducts them in an unthinking, automatic manner. We're told that he knows nothing of weekday services; he goes to church on Sunday afternoon because it's the shortest service, and then he sleeps through the sermon. Mechanical indeed! Choice A offers the opposite; "fervent," which means ardent or passionate, is hardly a description of old Leisure's lackadaisical attitude. "Feigned" (C) means bogus or faked, but old Leisure is not interested in faking it; he just goes through the motions. Some readers may not be familiar with the word "peremptory" (D), which means authoritarian or dictatorial; in this question it is completely off topic and used simply to distract or confuse some test-takers. Finally, the word "cerebral" (E), meaning intellectual, is far off the mark in describing old Leisure's lazy, unthinking approach to religious practice.

5. D. Personification, that is, an author presenting an abstraction as a person or in human form, is the technique that effectively makes old Leisure virtually come alive for the reader, choice D. Indeed, after learning how content, easygoing, and jolly he is, the reader almost wants to meet him and chat over a beer! On the other hand, old Leisure does not come off as a caricature (A) because he is not distorted by ludicrous exaggeration. Nor does he appear as a paradox (B), someone who is self-contradictory. The technique in old Leisure's characterization is not apostrophe (C), in which a personified thing is addressed rhetorically. Nor is the technique a simile (E), which involves the comparison of two unlike things.

6. C. Choice C is the correct answer, the actual exception; the passage never mentions women's roles at all, let alone comparing women to men. The words and phrases in the remaining four answer choices do, indeed, categorize the comparisons between old Leisure and modern leisure. The passage states that old Leisure "lived chiefly in the country," which draws a contrast between the hustle-bustle of the city and the energetic participants in modern leisure (A). As to choice B, old Leisure is definitely more interested in corporeal pleasures, such as eating, drinking, and sleeping; this contrasts with the more cerebral or intellectual pursuits of modern leisure, such as visiting art museums, reading, and exploring scientific theory. Choice D is well-documented in the passage; the participants in modern leisure are shown to be overly eager, and they are never idle, but old Leisure is quite complacent and nonchalant. The same may be said of the ideas in choice E; modern leisure is seen as frenetic and stimulating, whereas old Leisure is quite content to be soothing and calming.

7. C. This passage has a mildly satirical tone, choice C; it's a parody, but it's not at all mean-spirited. Caustically mocking (A) is far too strong a description of the tone; it indicates cutting, bitter language that is downright malicious. Cloyingly sentimental (B) is not accurate either; the word "cloyingly" indicates something that is so overly sweet or saccharine that it becomes tiresome. Matter-of-fact directness (D) indicates material that is blunt and straightforward; it does not describe a lighthearted spoof, such as this passage. The key word in choice E is "imprudently," which describes a foolish or reckless manner. While the tone of the passage is undeniably nostalgic, it's all in good fun; it is not driven by wrongheaded intent.

8. A. In this question, all of the given quotes from the passage describe old Leisure, and four of the five make a similar point; your job is to identify the one answer choice that refers to a different aspect of old Leisure. Choice A, "contemplative," indicates one who is thoughtful, someone who muses. But choice B identifies a different quality, describing old Leisure physically as "rather stout," so you understand that he's quite heavyset. Now you have to see which way the other answer choices go, mental or physical. Choice C, "of excellent digestion," is definitively another physical description, so it is similar to choice B. Choice D, "able to carry a great deal of beer," is another physical attribute. Choice E rounds out the list of the four similar answer choices; "ate his dinners" is yet another physical description. Thus, choice A is the only answer choice that refers to mental processes, rather than physical ones, so it is the correct exception to answer this question.

9. **E.** To answer this question correctly, simply compare the answer choices to the list of modern leisure activities in the passage; four of the answer choices will be listed there, and the one that is not must be the correct exception. Riding on excursion-trains (A) is listed in line 10; check. Visiting art museums (B) appears in lines 10–11; check. Reading periodical literature (C) is listed in line 11; check. Enjoying exciting novels (D) is in lines 11–12; check. Sauntering by the fruit-tree wall, however, is NOT mentioned in this list of currently popular activities; it comes up later as old Leisure happily strolls the countryside. Thus, choice E is the correct exception; it is in the passage, but it is not a current pastime.

10. **C.** After all of this exposition and description of old Leisure, the narrator finally injects a voice, a distinct opinion, in the last paragraph, praising him ("Fine old Leisure!") and insisting that we "not be severe upon him." The narrator's next phrase appears to be the most important justification for bestowing mercy, insisting that we must not "judge him by our modern standard." That is, old Leisure lived his own way in his own time, and we cannot condemn him for not meeting current standards; thus, choice C is correct. Choice A, he had "kept up his charter," appears in an earlier paragraph; it is not the narrator's justification for mercy. The same is true of choice B; his church attendance is mentioned earlier, but it does not relate to this question. Choice D, on the other hand, does appear in the final entreaty for mercy; however, the fact that old Leisure "never went to Exeter Hall" is only a supporting point; it is not the narrator's most important point. Likewise, choice E is also part of the narrator's plea for mercy, but it is another supporting point, not the main argument for leniency.

Set 2 Questions

The passage for these questions is an excerpt from "The Dulham Ladies," a short story written by Sarah Orne Jewett and published in *The Atlantic Monthly* in April, 1886.

Read the passage carefully and answer the 11 multiple-choice questions that follow by selecting the best answer of the five choices.

To be leaders of society in the town of Dulham was as satisfactory to Miss Dobin and Miss Lucinda Dobin as if Dulham were London itself. Of late years, though they would not (5) allow themselves to suspect such treason, the most ill-bred of the younger people in the village made fun of them behind their backs, and laughed at their treasured summer mantillas, their mincing steps, and the shape of (10) their parasols.

They were always conscious of the fact that they were the daughters of a once eminent Dulham minister; but beside this unanswerable claim to the respect of the parish, they were (15) aware that their mother's social position was one of superior altitude. Madam Dobin's grandmother was a Greenaple of Boston. In her younger days she had often visited her relatives, the Greenaples and Hightrees, and in seasons of (20) festivity she could relate to a select and properly excited audience her delightful experiences of town life. Nothing could be finer than her account of having taken tea at Governor Clovenfoot's on Beacon Street in company with (25) an English lord, who was indulging himself in a brief vacation from his arduous duties at the Court of St. James.

"He exclaimed that he had seldom seen in England so beautiful and intelligent a company (30) of ladies," Madam Dobin would always say in conclusion. "He was decorated with the blue ribbon of the Knights of the Garter." Miss Dobin and Miss Lucinda thought for many years that this famous blue ribbon was tied about the (35) noble gentleman's leg. One day they even discussed the question openly; Miss Dobin placing the decoration at his knee, and Miss Lucinda locating it much lower down, according to the length of the short gray socks with which (40) she was familiar.

"You have no imagination, Lucinda," the elder sister replied impatiently. "Of course, those were the days of small-clothes and long silk stockings!"—whereat Miss Lucinda was rebuked, (45) but not persuaded.

"I wish that my dear girls could have the outlook upon society which fell to my portion," Madam Dobin sighed, after she had set these ignorant minds to rights, and enriched them by (50) communicating the final truth about the blue ribbon. "I must not chide you for the absence of opportunities, but if our cousin Harriet Greenaple were only living, you would not lack enjoyment or social education."

(55)   Madam Dobin had now been dead a great many years. She seemed an elderly woman to her daughters some time before she left them; later they thought she had really died comparatively young, since their own years had come to equal

(60)   the record of hers. To be sure, it was the fashion to appear older in her day,—they could remember the sober effect of really youthful persons in cap and frisette; but whether they owed it to the changed times or to their own qualities, they felt

(65)   no older themselves than they ever had. Beside upholding the ministerial dignity of their father, they were obliged to give a lenient sanction to the ways of the world for their mother's sake; and they combined the two duties with reverence and

(70)   impartiality.

Several of her distinguished relatives attended Mrs. Dobin's funeral, which was long considered the most dignified and elegant pageant of that sort which ever had taken place in Dulham. It

(75)   seemed to mark the close of a famous epoch in Dulham history, and it was increasingly difficult forever afterward to keep the tone of society up to the old standard. Somehow, the distinguished relatives had one by one disappeared, though

(80)   they all had excellent reasons for the discontinuance of their visits. A few had left this world altogether, and the family circle of the Greenaples and Hightrees was greatly reduced in circumference. Sometimes, in summer, a stray

(85)   connection drifted Dulham-ward, and was displayed (not to say paraded) by the gratified hostesses. It was a disappointment if the guest could not be persuaded to remain over Sunday and appear at church. When household

(90)   antiquities became fashionable, the ladies remarked a surprising interest in their corner cupboard and best chairs, and some distant relatives revived their almost forgotten custom of paying a summer visit to Dulham. They were

(95)   not long in finding out with what desperate affection Miss Dobin and Miss Lucinda clung to their mother's wedding china and other inheritances, and were allowed to depart without a single tea-cup. One graceless descendant of the

(100)   Hightrees prowled from garret to cellar, and admired the household belongings diligently, but she was not asked to accept even the dislocated cherry-wood footstool that she had discovered in the far corner of the parsonage pew.

1. Which of the following is the most reasonable inference that can be drawn from the opening line, "To be leaders of society . . . as if Dulham were London itself"?

   A. The town of Dulham has a thriving social scene.
   B. The populace of Dulham is elated to have the Dobin ladies as leaders of society.
   C. The Dobin sisters were formerly leaders of society in London.
   D. The idea that Dulham is equivalent to London greatly enhances the ladies' sense of self-importance.
   E. The Dobin sisters find being leaders of society is somewhat pleasing.

2. Within context, the word "treason" (line 5) best refers to

   A. ". . . they would not allow themselves to suspect . . ." (lines 4–5)
   B. ". . . the younger people in the village made fun of them behind their backs." (lines 6–7)
   C. ". . . they were the daughters of a once eminent Dulham minister . . ." (lines 12–13)
   D. ". . . this unanswerable claim" (lines 13–14)
   E. ". . . their mother's social position was one of superior altitude." (lines 15–16)

3. The second paragraph (lines 11–27) suggests which of the following about the Dobin sisters' social standing?

   A. The ladies flaunt their superior standing.
   B. If the ladies had been born as males, their situation would be far different.
   C. The Dobin family is no longer quite so renowned as it once was.
   D. The ladies fear their claim to high social standing is dubious.
   E. The ladies rely on their upper-class Boston relatives for social favors.

4. The two contrary ideas in the phrase "She seemed an elderly woman to her daughters some time before she left them; later they thought she had really died comparatively young" (lines 56–59) present the thematic idea that

   A. many people appear to become elderly before their time
   B. memories and perceptions fade over time
   C. in some cultures, it is fashionable to appear older
   D. the daughters were mistaken in thinking that she died comparatively young
   E. children always consider their parents to be "old," that is, until they reach the same age

5. According to the sixth paragraph (lines 55–70), the ladies' two duties are specifically to

   A. maintain their father's ministerial dignity and to compassionately approve the ways of the world
   B. always serve the town and the First Parish with reverence and impartiality
   C. keep alive the memories of both their father and mother
   D. always remember the sober effect of distinguished clothing and to maintain their own qualities
   E. provide a dignified and an elegant pageant for their mother's funeral

6. What event specifically precipitated "the close of a famous epoch in Dulham history" (lines 75–76)?

   A. the death of their mother
   B. the funeral of their mother
   C. the attendance of distinguished relatives at the funeral
   D. the death of their father
   E. the discontinuance of visiting relatives

7. All of the following made it "increasingly difficult . . . to keep the tone of society up to the old standard" (lines 76–78) EXCEPT that

   A. Mrs. Dobin, the doyenne of local society, had died
   B. distinguished relatives had one by one disappeared
   C. a few relatives had left this world altogether
   D. the family circle of the Greenaples was greatly reduced in circumference
   E. household antiquities became fashionable

8. Which of the following is NOT implied by the sentence in lines 84–87, "Sometimes . . . a stray connection drifted Dulham-ward, and was displayed (not to say paraded) by the gratified hostesses"?

   A. The Dobin ladies are very interested in keeping up appearances.
   B. It was a disappointment if the guest could not appear at church.
   C. It appears that distant relatives are no longer interested in visiting.
   D. The Dobin ladies are always happy when they have a stray relative whom they can parade around.
   E. The Dobin ladies are shameless in flaunting their visiting relatives before the townsfolk.

9. What was the change that caused some distant relatives to resume their "forgotten custom" of paying a summer visit to the ladies at Dulham?

   A. Families grew ever-larger so there were more relatives who could visit.
   B. People became more interested in reviving family relations.
   C. Household antiquities became fashionable.
   D. People became aware of the health benefits of visiting the countryside.
   E. Travel became more convenient.

10. All of the following adjectives may be used to describe the descendants of the Greenaple family EXCEPT

   A. acquisitive and avaricious
   B. arrogant and self-centered
   C. presumptuous and self-important
   D. fulsome and munificent
   E. aloof and dispassionate

11. What was the one thing for which Miss Dobin and Miss Lucinda did show true "desperate affection" (lines 95–96)?

   A. The china, inheritances, and the other household goods
   B. The respect of the townsfolk
   C. Ensuring cordial relations with their relatives
   D. Being leaders of society in Dulham
   E. Keeping the memories of their mother alive

Set 2 Answers

1. D. The Dobin sisters seem to equate the value of society in the small town of Dulham with that of high society in the city of London itself, and this concept surely boosts their self-esteem, choice D, regardless of the comparison's accuracy. But choice A, which infers that Dulham has a thriving social scene comparable to London's, is misguided. The passage offers scant evidence of Dulham's social scene; we only know that the ladies go to church and receive occasional visits from Boston relatives. The name of the town, Dulham, is of interest. "Ham" is the root of the word "hamlet," as in a small town, so "Dulham" really means "dull town," hardly a thriving social center. Choice B contradicts the passage to some degree; we know that the younger people in town make fun of the ladies' old-fashioned appearance behind their backs. We do not know what the older inhabitants think, but it's doubtful they are elated to have the Dobin ladies as the self-appointed leaders of society. Choice C, which claims the ladies used to lead society in London, has no evidence whatsoever in the passage. Choice E might seem intriguing at first, but it is too weak of an answer. The Dobin sisters feel as satisfied as if they lead society in London; that's a big claim, so it is too subdued to say they find Dulham society "somewhat pleasing." They think much more highly of their position than that phrase implies.

2. B. The word "treason" in the passage specifically refers to the way in which the youth of Dulham make fun of the Dobin sisters' old-fashioned appearance and mannerisms behind their backs, choice B. Choice A is perhaps deceiving, especially with the 19th-century syntax in the passage. The phrase ". . . they would not allow themselves to suspect" leads to the word "treason." In fact, "treason" is the direct object of the verb "suspect." It identifies what the ladies choose to ignore, not what the treasonous act actually is. Choice C identifies the ladies' father, the "once eminent Dulham minister," and it has nothing to do with the idea of treason. Choice D describes the way the ladies feel they have some unexplainable claim to respect in the local church; but this, too, is unrelated to treason. Choice E is also irrelevant to this question; their mother's claim of an elite social position ("superior altitude") long ago has nothing to do with the treasonous laughter from the town's youth.

3. C. The reason we know that the Dobin sisters' social standing is no longer what it used to be, choice C, is that they are "always conscious of the fact that they were the daughters of a *once eminent* Dulham minister." Apparently their father was esteemed, but that eminence has passed; it is no more. Choice A has no evidence in the second paragraph. One may make a case that the sisters flaunt their Boston relatives when they "displayed (not to say paraded)" a "stray" family member that occasionally visited, but that implication is based in the seventh paragraph, not the second. Choice B is unreasonable; nothing in the second paragraph (or the passage) hints at gender issues. Eliminate this answer choice quickly and move on. Choice D might be tricky, but if you read it carefully, along with the question and the passage, you'll see why this response is incorrect. The ladies' acknowledgment that they have an "unanswerable claim" to the respect of the parish does not suggest they fear their claim is dubious. After all, the social position of their mother's family trumps their father's lapsed eminence. Choice E is not supported by the passage; the ladies may have upper-class relatives in Boston, but this paragraph does not suggest that they rely on them for anything.

4. E. The quotation in this question describes the way that the ladies thought their mother to be quite "elderly" some years before her death; however, once they reached the age at which she had died, they felt it was actually quite a young age. This conundrum is fairly universal; most children think their parents are old, but when the kids reach adulthood, they still consider themselves to be young, choice E. Choice A does not address the concept of how children view their parents, so it is irrelevant to this question. Choice B contradicts the quotation; the ladies' memories and perceptions have not faded over time. Choice C may be true in some cultures, and indeed the passage states that Madam Dobin lived when "it was the fashion to appear older," but this does not address the thematic idea underlying this quotation. Choice D cannot be the correct response; the question asks for a thematic idea, and this answer is not worded as a theme. Instead, it merely claims the daughters were wrong.

5. A. The sixth paragraph clarifies the two sisters' obligations in life: to uphold their father's "ministerial dignity" and "to give a lenient sanction to the ways of the world." In other words, they must maintain their father's reputation, and, for their mother's sake, they must show compassion to others, choice A. The duties listed in choice B, serving the town and parish, are not specified, although the phrase "with reverence and impartiality" does appear in the paragraph. Choice C, the idea that the ladies must keep their parents' memories alive, is a kind sentiment, but it is not depicted in the passage. Choice D contains ideas that are alluded to in the sixth paragraph, including the "sober effect" of distinguished clothing and paying attention to their own qualities, but neither of these ideas outlines their specific obligations. Choice E is irrelevant to this question; their mother's funeral occurs in the seventh paragraph, and the ladies were not specifically obligated to provide a dignified or elegant pageant; instead the event was perceived as such by others.

6. B. Their mother's funeral, "the most dignified and elegant pageant of that sort which ever had taken place in Dulham," is so significant that it appears to mark the end "of a famous epoch in Dulham history," choice B. Their mother's death (A) naturally must occur before her funeral, but her demise is not clarified as the end of the epoch; rather, her funeral is. Choice C makes no sense; it is true that distinguished relatives attended the funeral, but that fact does not mark the end of the epoch in *local* history. It may be reasonable to assume that the ladies' father had died (D), but it is never specifically mentioned; it cannot signal the end of an era. Choice E, that the distinguished relatives discontinued their visits, refers to the time after their mother's funeral, after the epoch had ended.

7. E. In this question, you are looking for the one option that does NOT address what made it "increasingly difficult . . . to keep the tone of society up to the old standard," and choice E is the exception. The fact that antiques later became fashionable has nothing to do with maintaining social standards. Madam Dobin's death (A) definitely added to the decline of society in Dulham. The fact that Madam Dobin's distinguished relatives stopped visiting Dulham (B) also detracts from society. Choice C, that some relatives had also died, must diminish the tone of society since they, like Madam Dobin, can no longer contribute to it. Choice D merely restates the idea in choice C, that some relatives had died, which tends to keep them from contributing to society.

8. B. In this question, be sure to notice the key word, the all-caps "NOT." Choice B is correct because the sentence in the question does NOT imply the ladies' disappointment when their visiting relatives declined to appear at church; that is merely a fact that is stated explicitly in the next sentence. On the other hand, the fact that the "gratified hostesses" paraded their relatives around town indicates that they were very much concerned with appearances (A). The idea that distant relatives were increasingly uninterested in visiting (C) is suggested in the opening phrase, "Sometimes a stray connection drifted" into town. Choice D, that the ladies are happy to have company, is supported by the way they paraded relatives in town and were "gratified" to have them. Choice E is also implied in the passage; although we might wish that the ladies were not quite so shameless in displaying their relatives, they do indeed parade them about and display them before the townspeople.

9. C. The distant relatives do not get a positive reputation in this passage. Several of them attend Madam Dobin's funeral, but thereafter they visit less frequently (true, some have died in the intervening years). However, once antiques become fashionable, choice C, the relatives flock to Dulham, apparently hoping to receive a valuable keepsake from the home. Choice A contradicts the passage; it clearly states that some relatives had died in the intervening years and it never hints that any families were growing in size. Choice B has no evidence in the passage; it offers no proof that people had become more interested in familial relations. Choice D is completely unreasonable; do not be tricked into looking for nonexistent evidence that people became interested in the health benefits of visiting the countryside. Choice E is equally unfounded in the text; the text offers no mention of the methods of travel or of any increasing convenience.

10. D. Remember to look for the exception, the one answer that does NOT describe the relatives. The Greenaple family in Boston can hardly be called fulsome (flattering) or munificent (generous), choice D; rather, they appear to be the opposite. The adjectives in choice A, acquisitive and avaricious, both describe people who are greedy, and the Greenaple relatives fit the bill. The relatives may also be considered arrogant and self-centered (B) about their "superior altitude" in Boston, especially as Madam Dobin boasts of having taken tea with an English Lord who "was decorated with the blue ribbon of the Knights of the Garter." Presumptuous and self-important (C) also describe the families' upper-class attitude. The adjectives in choice E, aloof and dispassionate, also seem to aptly describe the Greenaple family; they remain distant and uninterested until their desire for the Dobin antiques comes to the fore.

11. A. The Dobin sisters demonstrate "desperate affection" for their mother's china and other inheritances, choice A, none of which they will share with the Greenaple relatives. The sisters do seem to value the respect of the townsfolk (B), along with cordial relations with their relatives (C), as well as being social leaders in Dulham (D), and also keeping their mother's memory alive (E), but none of these ideas are related in the passage to the phrase "desperate affection."

Chapter 4
Section II of the Exam: Free-Response Questions

Introduction

The free-response section of the AP English Literature and Composition Exam offers you a wonderful opportunity! This section asks you to write three essay responses, giving you the opportunity to use your own voice, demonstrate how you organize your thoughts, show how your logic works, exhibit how you develop your ideas, and choose what you personally see as the most important aspects in specific pieces of literature. You should relish the chance to shine as you analyze the three prompts on this section of the exam.

The free-response section is 2 hours long and presents three free-response questions (prompts). The free-response section always follows the multiple-choice section; it is never the first section of the exam. You will be given an answer booklet in which to write your essays, and it has more pages than you will need. Use your own pen, preferably one with black or blue ink. You may not use a dictionary or thesaurus. You can write the three essays in any order you wish, but the vast majority of students write the essays in the order they are presented. You will identify which prompt you are addressing by writing "1," "2," or "3" at the top of every page of each essay. Since you have 2 hours to write the three essays, the suggested time for each is 40 minutes. While you can adjust your time accordingly, it is common sense to try to finish each essay within its recommended time. If you spend too long on any one essay, you are slighting your time on the other essays.

The format of the three free-response questions is as follows:

- Question 1: Analysis of one full-length poem or an excerpt from a longer poem. The poem's length could range from a 14-line sonnet to about 50 lines. You will be prompted to analyze how the author's use of poetic devices creates complex meaning and effect.

- Question 2: Analysis of an excerpt from a fictional work, such as a novel or short story; very rarely you might be given a complete short story. The Question 2 passage will range from about 300–900 words; most passages are at least 600 words, giving you ample ammunition for your essay response. Most frequently you will be prompted to analyze the complex relationships in the passage, usually relationships between characters, via analysis of literary devices. *Note:* Very rarely the prose question has been placed first and the poem question second; this has not been done since 2002.

- Question 3: You will be given a generic literary analysis topic, such as exploring character, conflict, or setting, and you get to choose a suitable novel, epic poem, or play that you can analyze via the given topic. This is referred to as the open topic question because it gives you an open opportunity to choose whatever work you want to write about.

The poems and prose passages chosen for the free-response section, like the passages in the multiple-choice section, were all originally written in English sometime from the 16th to the 21st centuries. They will be accessible to read; you should have no difficulty in getting the gist of the passages, and they will provide rich opportunities for literary analysis. In other words, they will contain abundant examples of poetic and literary devices that you can analyze. However, the directions will not suggest any specific devices to look for or analyze. Unlike the multiple-choice section, each poem and prose piece will be identified. You will be given the author's name, the work's title, and, most often, the date written. If the date is not given, it will be fairly well-understood, like a work written by Shakespeare.

Abilities Tested

This section tests your ability to analyze poetry and prose in your own words under timed pressure. You will have the opportunity to show your awareness of how literary devices and techniques help create complex effects in fictional pieces. The prompts may test your abilities in many areas: to analyze fictional passages and poems; to understand an author's purpose and meaning; to show awareness of organization and structure; to analyze character development and character relationships; and to analyze style and figurative language. Additionally, in the open topic, you will have the chance to choose a suitable literary work to analyze, based on the specific requirements of the prompt. The level of difficulty reflects freshman-level college study.

Basic Skills Necessary

Like the multiple-choice section, you need to be able to glean the gist of a poem or passage, utilize your skills in literary analysis, and have a keen eye for close reading. Additionally, since you will produce three essays, you need to organize your ideas coherently, present on-topic development of ideas, and present your thoughts in grammatically correct sentences, all while keeping your cool under timed pressure. See Chapter 5 for definitions of terms that you may encounter in the essay prompts and/or use in your essay content.

Analysis of the Directions

The directions for Question 1 (poetry) and Question 2 (prose) vary somewhat from year to year based on the specific passages. But, don't let that worry you; know that you will always be asked to read one poem and one prose piece and then write an essay analyzing how literary elements and devices create complex relationships. The open topic will always ask you to analyze a literary work of your own choice via a specific prompt and explore how the specific idea enhances the importance of the work as a whole. Examples and more specific advice follow.

Scoring of the Free-Response Section

Each of the three essays accounts for one-third of the total essay score, and the entire free-response section accounts for 55 percent of the total exam score. (Remember that the multiple-choice section equals 45 percent of your score.) You will find a sample scoring worksheet at the end of every practice exam in this book.

AP Readers will never know anything about you or your school location. Readers never know what scores your other essays received, nor do they know your multiple-choice score. Each Reader is assigned to read the same question over the entire week of scoring. The Readers do not get to choose which question to read, nor do they change from prompt to prompt.

Each essay is read by an experienced, well-trained Reader who is either a high school AP teacher or a college professor. Prior to 2020, free-response essays were scored on a scale of 1 to 9, using a holistic scoring guide, but as of 2020 the essays will be scored using an analytic rubric with a scale of 0 to 6. The Reader will assign a score based on the essay's claim and thesis, its evidence and commentary, and its sophistication and complexity. The Readers don't look for or count errors. (A student who doesn't even attempt to write an essay will receive the equivalent of a 0 score, but it is noted as a dash [—] on the Reader's scoring sheet.)

Although each essay prompt has its own analytic rubric based on that prompt's specific requirements, on the whole, high-quality essays encompass three essential points that all AP Readers look for in every essay. A well-written essay response should be:

- On topic
- Thoroughly developed
- Correct in mechanics and sophisticated in style and thought

Analytic Rubric and Scoring Guidelines

As of the 2020 exam, the College Board will begin using a 6-point analytic rubric in place of the previous holistic 9-point scoring guide. This change is designed to help give you more precise and explicit information about what will help you earn more points and also what to avoid that would keep you from achieving a higher score. The rubric is also designed to add consistency over the years.

The new rubric for all three free-response essays is divided into three essential areas of composition, labeled Row A, Row B, and Row C:

- **Row A - Thesis: 1 point.** You can earn a point by presenting a defendable thesis; you will not get a point if you do not present a defendable thesis. This is the easiest point to earn; simply include a defendable thesis and you get the point!

- **Row B - Evidence and Commentary: 4 points.** You can earn up to 4 points by analyzing textual evidence and by providing commentary that is relevant to the thesis; you will earn fewer points if your commentary is scant or nonexistent. You will earn at least 2 points in Row B by including textual evidence; read the "**AND**" statement under each point value to understand how to earn additional points.

- **Row C - Sophistication: 1 point.** You can earn a point by demonstrating sophisticated and complex thought and style that is appropriate to the thesis; you will not earn a point if you do not present such sophistication. This may be the hardest point to earn, but you can do so by incorporating at least one of the suggested techniques throughout your essay.

Each row is divided into three sections:

- The **Scoring Criteria** is the actual rubric, and it presents specific information about what will earn or lose point(s). The wording for this section will be consistent throughout the years for all three free-response essay prompts. Question 1 (poetry) and Question 2 (prose) will be identical, while Question 3 (open topic) will also address the need to connect your ideas to the significance of the work as a whole.

- The **Decision Rules and Scoring Notes** present relevant information to the specific prompt each year. This will be adjusted each year as necessary and will indicate how students actually performed on any essay prompt. These ideas describe what typical responses demonstrated at each level.

- The **Additional Notes** present supplemental information that clarifies parameters which apply to the scoring.

Sample Rubric for Question 1 (Poetry)

Row A: Thesis (0–1 point)	
Scoring Criteria	
0 points for any of the following:	**1 point for**
• Having no defendable thesis. • Only restating the prompt in the thesis. • Only summarizing the issue with no claim in the thesis. • Presenting a thesis that does not address the prompt.	• Addressing the prompt with a defendable thesis that presents an interpretation and may establish a line of reasoning.
Decision Rules and Scoring Notes	
Theses that do not earn this point	**Theses that do earn this point**
• Only restate the prompt. • Only offer an irrelevant generalized comment about the poem. • Simply describe the poem's features rather than making a defendable claim.	• Take a position on the prompt and provide a defendable interpretation of how the poet portrays the complex relationship called for in the prompt.
Additional Notes	
• The thesis may be one or more sentences anywhere in the essay. • A thesis that meets the criteria can be awarded the point whether or not the rest of the response successfully conveys that line of reasoning.	

Row B: Evidence AND Commentary (0–4 points)				
Scoring Criteria				
0 points for	**1 point for**	**2 points for**	**3 points for**	**4 points for**
• Simply repeating the thesis (if present). • **OR** restating provided information. • **OR** providing mostly irrelevant and/or incoherent examples.	• Summarizing the poem without reference to a thesis. • **OR** providing vague textual references. • **OR** providing textual references of questionable relevance. • **AND** providing little or no commentary.	• Making relevant textual references (direct quotes or paraphrases). • **AND** providing commentary but repeats, oversimplifies, or misinterprets the cited evidence or text.	• Making relevant textual references (direct quotes or paraphrases). • **AND** providing commentary that explains the logical relationship between textual examples and the thesis; however, commentary is uneven, limited, or incomplete.	• Making relevant textual references (direct quotes or paraphrases). • **AND** providing well-developed commentary that explicitly explains the relationship between the evidence and the thesis.
Decision Rules and Scoring Notes				
Typical responses that earn 0 points:	**Typical responses that earn 1 point:**	**Typical responses that earn 2 points:**	**Typical responses that earn 3 points:**	**Typical responses that earn 4 points:**
• Are unclear or fail to address the prompt. • May present mere opinion with no relevant textual references.	• Mention textual references, devices, or techniques with little or no analysis.	• Contain numerous inaccuracies or repetition in commentary. • Offer only simplistic explanations that do not strengthen the argument.	• Provide commentary that is not sufficiently developed or is too limited. • Assume or imply a connection to the thesis that is not consistently explicit.	• Provide commentary that uses significant details of the text to draw conclusions. • Integrate short excerpts throughout in order to support the thesis' interpretation.
Additional Notes				
• Writing that suffers from grammatical and/or mechanical errors that interfere with communication cannot earn the fourth point in this row.				

Row C: Sophistication (0–1 point)	
Scoring Criteria	
0 points for	**1 point for**
• Not meeting the criteria for 1 point.	• Exhibiting sophistication of thought and/or advancing a complex literary argument.

Decision Rules and Scoring Notes	
Responses that do not earn this point:	**Responses that earn this point demonstrate one (or more) of the following:**
• Try to contextualize an interpretation, but make predominantly sweeping generalizations (*"Throughout all history . . ."* OR *"Everyone believes . . ."*). • Only hint at other possible interpretations (*"Some may think . . ."* OR *"Though the poem might be said to . . ."*). • Write one statement about a thematic interpretation of the poem without consistently maintaining that idea. • Oversimplify complexities in the poem. • Present complicated or complex sentences or language that is ineffective and detracts from the argument.	• Present a thesis that demands nuanced analysis of textual evidence and successfully prove it. • Illuminate the significance or relevance of an interpretation within a broader context. • Discuss alternative interpretations of a text. • Acknowledge and account for contradictions, ambiguities, and/or complexities within the text. • Provide relevant analogies to help better understand an interpretation. • Develop a prose style that is especially vivid, persuasive, resounding, or appropriate to the student's argument.
Additional Notes	
• This point should be awarded only if the demonstration of sophistication or complex understanding is part of the argument, not merely a phrase or brief reference.	

Notice in Row B that IF you present relevant evidence from the work, you will earn 2–4 points. Readers will decide on the point value based on the quality of the commentary/analysis.

You can familiarize yourself with the wording of analytic rubrics by reviewing the many rubrics included in this book for each essay prompt. Finally, if you want additional information about this aspect, the website for the AP English Literature and Composition Exam includes prompts, scoring guides, and a few sample essays with commentary for every exam since 1999. Visit https://apcentral.collegeboard.org/courses/ap-english-literature-and-composition/exam. Remember that 9-point holistic scoring guides were used until 2020, when the scoring changed to a 6-point analytic rubric.

Test-Taking Strategies

When answering the three free-response questions, be sure to:

- Use the exam booklet to plan your essay. An unplanned or poorly planned essay frequently results in problems in organization and development.
- Clearly divide your ideas into separate paragraphs; be sure to clearly indent each paragraph.
- Write as legibly as possible; in order to evaluate your essay, the Reader must be able to read it.

Regardless of what the specific directions tell you to do, you will be well-served to remember the following universal tips; they are embedded in every rubric for every free-response prompt:

- **Always ADDRESS THE PROMPT.** AP teachers love to say that phrase is actually what "AP" stands for in the first place. Read the prompt carefully and actively, noting what specific tasks you have to do and how many tasks you must address. If the prompt mandates that you address something specific, be sure to incorporate it into your analysis. Most poetry and prose topics will ask you to analyze *how* literary elements create complex effects, so you should not merely note or list examples of these elements. The open topic will always ask you to address some common or general aspect of literary fiction AND to explain how that aspect adds to the significance of the work *as a whole*. You should address this deeper meaning in every one of your body paragraphs so your essay will have more thrust, more gravitas, and more sophistication.
- **ORGANIZE before you write.** The directions will invariably instruct you to produce "a well-written essay." To do so, it is logical to use a straightforward three-part organizational scheme, providing a brief introduction, multiple body paragraphs, and a conclusion. More specifically:

- **Your introduction:** Let the prompt directions guide you, but also try to arouse the Reader's interest as you address the prompt. Remember that the introduction should be just one paragraph, but even if it is only a single sentence, it makes sense to include a thesis that specifically addresses the prompt. Readers are aware that the thesis may appear anywhere in the essay, but placing it in the introduction lets the Reader know that you are in control and know what interpretation you plan on defending. The most simplistic introductions merely repeat the prompt and will not earn a point, while the more sophisticated ones, those that do earn a point, engage the Reader's intellect while addressing the prompt with an idea that can be defended. In other words, the thesis that earns a point is not obvious, but instead is arguable. The many sample student essays in this book's practice exams will demonstrate a wide range of introductions.

- **Your body paragraphs:** Again, let the prompt guide your analysis of the poem, passage, or novel. In general, two to three well-developed paragraphs will serve you well, as long as they are on topic. On the poetry and prose topics, some students rely on the comfort of addressing just one literary element in each body paragraph, such as tone, imagery, and diction. Indeed, prompts prior to 2020 frequently suggested which elements were most accessible in the poem or passage. Although no Reader can fault such an organizational scheme, in reality Readers will find this simplistic organization too formulaic or overly predictable, which is the major reason that specific elements will no longer be suggested in any free-response prompt. However, if focusing on just one element at a time gives you comfort and helps you produce your essay, by all means do so. But if you can produce a more sophisticated organizational scheme, you can be rewarded. Consider organizing around the progression of ideas in the piece, or around a character's traits. Again, the many student samples in the practice exams will help you see how to develop with style and panache.

- **Your conclusion:** Like the introduction, your conclusion should only be one paragraph. Even if it is only one sentence, be sure to separate it from the body paragraphs. In other words, do not simply tack your conclusion onto the last body paragraph; this will hurt your organization. When you were taught to write, you were invariably told to "tell them what you're going to do (in the introduction), tell them (in the body paragraphs), and then tell them again what you just explained (in the conclusion)." This is good advice for beginning writers and for straightforward organizational schemes, but now it's time to put that advice into perspective. When the essay is as short as a few pages, a conclusion that is merely a boring summary will insult the Reader's intelligence (believe me, please; they got your point already). How do you improve your conclusion? First, try to rephrase your ideas in the summary so the Reader is not hearing the exact same words again, and then broaden your conclusion by adding some food for thought. Ask yourself "So what? What is it that is *important* about this poem, this passage, this novel?" When you formulate answers to those questions, you'll have something significant to say in your conclusion, something more than just a summary, and your Reader will be pleased.

- **DEVELOP your essay.** This vital element is demonstrated by how many sentences you produce in your paragraphs, how many examples from the text you present, and to what degree you analyze them. Of course, no magic number exists, but I would recommend aiming for at least three examples per body paragraph. Why? That helps ensure that each body paragraph is based on ample evidence from the text. I always tell my students that if they base a body paragraph around only one example, it will not be as convincing as a paragraph that analyzes more numerous examples. Generously use examples from the poem and the prose passage, both explicitly and implicitly. In other words, sometimes weave direct quotations and phrases from the text into your own sentences and sometimes refer to the ideas in your own words Also, *thoroughly* explain the relationship between your examples, your ideas, and the prompt; do not assume the Reader can read your mind. Remember that you can get up to 4 points for your development of examples and analysis. Development also centers on how many words you write, how many pages you produce. Most well-developed essays are at least two pages; strongly developed ones are often about four to five pages (or perhaps even more). Rarely does a one-page essay earn a high score; it simply cannot present enough examples and provide sufficient analysis. Remember that quantity (of words) does not guarantee quality (of the essay), but a lack of quantity (too few words) *does* guarantee a lack of quality (and thus a low score). For comparison purposes, each sample essay in this book has a word count provided.

- **WRITE WITH SOPHISTICATION.** Try to use your most sophisticated vocabulary and complex thinking, and also utilize varied syntax as best you can under timed conditions. Avoid all simple sentences or you will appear to have a simple brain. Do not use words you don't really know, and don't try to impress the Reader with fancy words; they will see right through that and frown. Just use the best, the most appropriate words that you can. The complexity of your language and sentence structure should reinforce the sophistication and complexity of your thoughts. This combination will earn you a point under the "Sophistication" category of the analytic rubric. You'll find many ideas for improvement in the "Style" section of this chapter; just remember to connect sophisticated style to the complexity of your thoughts.

Pacing the Essay

With an average time of only 40 minutes per essay, you need to plan your time management. For each essay, consider dividing your time as follows, and then adjust your pacing appropriately after ample practice.

- **Spend about 7–10 minutes reading the prompt and the passage(s) carefully and planning your essay.** This organizational time is crucial to producing a high-scoring essay. In the first 10 minutes of each essay's time, you need to follow the steps below. Do it systematically, and you'll know what you want to write and the order in which you'll present your ideas.

  1. Read the prompt carefully and underline the specific task(s).
  2. Read the passage(s) carefully, noting what ideas, evidence, and literary devices are relevant to the specific essay prompt. Annotate only what you need as you complete this step; you don't get to turn in your marginalia for extra credit!
  3. Conceive your defendable thesis statement, which will ideally be included in your introductory paragraph.
  4. Organize your body paragraphs, deciding which examples from the poem, passage, or novel you plan to include. Consider what relevant remarks you'll make about the examples you've chosen. Understand your body paragraph divisions—when you'll begin a new paragraph and what unifying idea centers each body paragraph.

  The importance of this planning phase cannot be overemphasized. When your essay has been well planned, your writing should flow faster and your essay should stay focused on the topic; your essay should be well organized and the paragraphs well developed. You must practice this essential planning step many times before you take the actual AP exam. On the day of the exam, you'll complete this planning in your exam booklet; it has ample space for it.

- **Take about 25 minutes to write the essay.** If you've planned well, your writing should be fluent and continuous. Avoid stopping to simply reread what you've already written. Twenty-five minutes is sufficient time to produce all the writing that is needed to earn a good score.

- **Save about 5–8 minutes to proofread your essay.** Reserving a few minutes to proofread allows you time to catch the "honest mistakes" that can be corrected easily, such as a misspelled word or a punctuation error. In addition, this time lets you set the essay to rest, knowing that you've written the best draft you can produce under the timed conditions. Then you can go on to the next essay prompt and give it your full, undivided attention. Don't try to rewrite or heavily edit your essay; don't attempt to move paragraphs around with arrows or numbers; trust your original organizational plan.

Style

On the actual exam, you won't have enough time during your proofreading to make major adjustments to your style. However, during your practice, you can experiment with different stylistic devices and find some that you can easily incorporate into your writing. Remember that the top-scoring essays are stylistically mature and relevant to the essay's content, and that the goal is to produce college-level writing. Carefully consider the following questions and then practice the suggestions, and your writing skills WILL improve. Remember that you can earn a point for sophistication throughout the entire essay, not just one sentence.

- **How long are your sentences?** Try to include some variety in sentence length. Remember that the occasional concise, simple sentence can really pack a punch and grab a Reader's attention when it's placed among a series of longer sentences. If an essay's sentences are all of the same length, none will particularly stand out.
- **What words do you use to begin your sentences?** Again, variety is desirable. Try to avoid trite phrasing such as "there is" or "there are" (or any other dull wording). Also avoid beginning every sentence with the subject. For variety, try inserting such grammatical constructions as a participial phrase, an adverbial clause, and so on.

- **Does every word you use help your essay?** Avoid bland, vague words and phrases, such as "a lot," "a little," "things," "much," and "very." Additionally, it is unnecessary to use phrases like "I think," "I believe," "I feel," "in my opinion," "is what," "is why," "is because," "so as you can see," and "in conclusion." Also, never use slang, and be sure to avoid clichés.

- **How many linking verbs do you use?** A linking verb (usually a form of the verb "to be") has no action, is vastly overused, and produces unimaginative prose. Replace as many of these as possible with action verbs.

- **What sentence patterns do you use?** Again, you should aim for variety; avoid using the same pattern over and over. Also, try inverting the normal order. For example, try putting a direct object before the subject for emphasis. Poets frequently use this to good effect, as illustrated by Edward Taylor's line "A curious knot God made in paradise," which would normally be written as "God made a curious knot in paradise."

- **Are all of your compound sentences joined in the same way?** The usual method is to use a comma and a coordinating conjunction (such as "and," "but," or "yet"). Try experimenting with the semicolon and the dash to add emphasis and variety (but be sure you're using these more sophisticated punctuation devices correctly).

- **How many prepositional phrases do you use?** Eliminate as many as possible, especially possessive prepositional phrases. For example, change "the words of Homer" to "Homer's words."

- **Do you use any parallel construction?** Develop your ability to produce parallelisms and your writing will appear more polished and memorable. Parallel construction also adds a delightful, sophisticated rhythm to your sentences. You can find examples of parallelism in Chapter 5, as well as in many of the high-scoring sample essays in this book.

- **Do you include any figures of speech?** If you practice incorporating the occasional use of alliteration, imagery, and other figures of speech, your writing will be more vivid and engaging.

- **What does your essay sound like?** Have a friend read your essay aloud to you and listen to how it sounds. Your essay should avoid any irrelevant reader response/opinion, such as "I really liked . . ." or "It made me feel . . ." Also, don't comment on the author, such as "Shakespeare does a great job of . . ." Or "Fitzgerald was a well-known 20th-century writer who . . ." Finally, do not repeat yourself.

- **Is the literary title punctuated correctly?** Poem titles are placed inside quotation marks (except epic poetry, which is punctuated like novels). Short story titles are also placed inside quotation marks. Novels, epic poems, and full-length plays are underlined. (Do not try to slant your handwriting to mimic italics; Readers will ruefully smirk when they see it.) One way to remember proper punctuation for literature is the rule: short works get "short" punctuation (quotation marks) and long works get long punctuation (underlining). Also, always place commas and periods *inside* quotation marks in American usage. Only in British English are they placed outside.

- **Do you incorporate quotations smoothly and properly?** Avoid copying entire sentences from the poem and/or passage; instead, for greater sophistication, embed the few essential words you need into your own sentences. Place brackets [ ] around any changes you make in a quotation for grammatical correctness or understanding. You do not need to refer to line numbers parenthetically; this is a timed essay, not a research paper. Do not merely copy or reference line numbers, forcing the Reader to go back and reread the lines that you should have quoted. Avoid using quotations for every example; put some examples in your own words and only use quotations when you cannot say it as well yourself.

- **Do you merely summarize the work?** Please don't. The Readers are already well-acquainted with the poem, passage, or novel you choose.

- **Do you define literary terms?** Again, please don't. The Readers are extremely familiar with technical literary terminology.

- **Do you add a title?** Don't. It's not necessary. AP essays never need a title, and they frequently distract the Reader.

- **Do you correctly identify the work's genre?** Poems are not plays or novels; plays are not novels or poems; novels are not poems or plays. Finally, don't forget that poetry is written in stanzas, not paragraphs.

Vocabulary

Let's add another word about vocabulary. Of course, the use of sophisticated language is one of your goals, but do not use words you're not familiar with. In your practice, look up new words in a dictionary before you use them, especially if you discovered them in a thesaurus. Of course, you are not permitted to use a dictionary or a thesaurus during the actual exam, but they are helpful in your practice. Variety in your word choice is as essential as variety in your sentences, but don't try to overload an essay with fancy, polysyllabic words. It's better to use succinct words that specifically fit your purpose.

Use Strong Verbs

Select your verbs carefully; your choices can help you move toward deeper analysis, or, conversely, they can set you up to merely paraphrase the text. As an experienced Reader, whenever I see strong, analytical verbs, I anticipate that the commentary will be insightful. On the contrary, when I see weak verbs, I expect nothing more than mere summary will follow.

Some strong, analytical verbs include the following:

alludes to	creates	explores	probes
alters	criticizes	exposes	reflects
asserts	depicts	heightens/lessens	refutes
assumes	differentiates	hints at	repudiates
clarifies	dispels	ignites	reveals
conjures	elucidates	illustrates	shifts
conjures up	emphasizes	implies	stirs
connotes	enunciates	inspires	suggests
constrains	evokes	invokes	transcends
construes	examines	juxtaposes	

The following weak verbs merely set up paraphrasing:

basically says	considers	mentions	states
begins	continues	proceeds	tells
claims	ends	saying how	writes
concludes by	expresses	says	

The following weak verbs merely point out what is in the piece:

demonstrates	produces	uses
exhibits	shows	utilizes

The Three Types of Free-Response Questions

In this part of the chapter, we'll explore the tasks that were assigned on recent exams and reveal what ideas some of the perceptive students addressed (or what written works were effective choices in the open topic). Of course, these brief observations of student writing are merely a sample, and they cannot and do not represent the wide range of responses produced by hundreds of thousands of students. The purpose here is just to give you an idea of what some students commonly discussed in high-scoring essays.

You may access all of the prompts on AP Central at https://apcentral.collegeboard.org/courses/ap-english-literature-and-composition/exam, plus read their commentary about student performance and peruse sample essays.

Go to the AP Central website and practice writing essays for the previous topics. Then you can compare what you produced to the observations of high-scoring essays that are summarized below. You can also use this information to help you see greater depth in the literature you read, as well as help you notice literary devices and see how to connect them to deeper meaning.

The Poetry Question

The AP poetry and prose free-response essays are similar. There's no reason for any student to think he or she can do well on one but not on the other. If you can read the prose passage well, you can also read the poem well. And vice versa. Remember, the poem will be accessible; you'll be able to understand the poem's basic meaning and its essence, and then use that knowledge as you analyze how different poetic devices contribute to that meaning. As with the prose prompt, the poem will provide you with plenty of elements, details, and devices; with only 40 minutes to write, you'll never run short of material to analyze. As of 2020, every poetry prompt will use the word "complex." This word tells you that the poem is, indeed, multifaceted, and it invites you to explore the depth of that complexity.

Of course, poetry has fewer words than prose. It is denser. It will likely use more figurative language. Its rhythm and other effects of sound are probably more important. It's likely to appear more private and more personal than the prose passage because poetry is so often written in first person. But remember, do not confuse the poet with the speaker; they are *not necessarily* the same. In general, the prompt will tell you if the poem is autobiographical in nature. If the poem is not identified as autobiographical, write your essay response under the assumption that the speaker is not the poet.

Examining the Task on Poetry Questions

The poetry prompt will customarily ask you to analyze how the use of poetic devices creates complex effects in the poem. Of course, the poems will be rich with different poetic devices, and the effects they create will be multifaceted, offering you the opportunity to analyze the poem's meaning from a variety of perspectives. The most common poetic devices mentioned in pre-2020 prompts were tone, imagery, and the vague but all-encompassing terms figurative language and poetic devices. As of 2020, no specific terms will be named; you get to discover them yourself!

Let's examine recent AP exam prompts and acknowledge some of the ideas produced in high-scoring essays. In the following examples, notice how often the prompt asks you to analyze the relationship between the speaker and an idea or a character in the poem. Frequently the phrase "complex relationship" will show up; after 2020, this phrase will be a part of *every* poetry prompt. Use that idea to your advantage, understanding that it implies the relationship will be complicated; it might change or adjust, or it might be ambiguous or even paradoxical.

Note: The directions will *always* instruct you to read carefully and write an essay. Some prompts will add the phrase "well-organized" or "well-developed," which is more than a bit redundant. The following summaries of recent prompts will not repeat these directions to read carefully and to write an essay.

> **2018:** "Plants," written by Olive Senior in 2015. Students were instructed to examine how the poet reveals the complex relationships among the speaker, the implied audience, and plant life. The literary elements syntax, diction, and figurative language were mentioned as possible techniques to consider. Notice the complexity of the initial task: The poem has three relationships to analyze: (1) the speaker, (2) the implied audience, and (3) the plants; high-scoring essays explored all three relationships. Understand that when the prompt mentions syntax and diction, you should be able to find some unusual examples of each and use them to analyze the relationships. Mentioning that the poem has figurative language does not offer much guidance, since all poetry will have figurative language.
>
> **Some observations from high-scoring essays:** Students who wrote high-scoring essays understood that the speaker is using a condescending and intellectually superior tone when addressing the intended audience, which is the rest of humanity. The speaker, with apparent omniscience, informs the supposedly duped audience of the clever machinations of plants as they quietly try to take over the world. The most commonly discussed figurative language device was personification, which is very accessible and evident in the poem. Astute students explored how seemingly insentient plants are presented as secret malevolent evildoers with insidious strategies and purposes of their own. Students frequently and accurately described the diction as militaristic and sinister. The students who effectively addressed syntax often pointed out the unusual enjambment between stanzas, creating sentences that begin mid-stanza and finish in the next stanza, and they connected it to the poem's meaning, such as the way plants can intertwine.

* * *

2017: "The Myth of Music: for my father," written by Rachel M. Harper and published in 1999. Students were invited to analyze the relationship between music and the speaker's multifaceted remembrances of her family. The elements of imagery, tone, and form were suggested for analysis.

Some observations from high-scoring essays: Many students, understandably, addressed the auditory imagery that describes music; many explored metaphor as an example of figurative language. Students who showed great insight into form addressed how the poem's form is akin to the jazz music described in its stanzas: irregular in number of lines, number of words, and number of rhymes. Most were able to connect a personal understanding of how music has a special effect on memory.

* * *

2016: "Juggler," written by Richard Wilbur in 1949. In this poem, the speaker describes the feeling of awe at watching a traveling juggler; the speaker ultimately understands that during the performance, the audience forgets the weight of the world. Students were asked to explore how the speaker describes the character of the juggler and what that description reveals about the speaker. Poetic elements suggested for analysis were imagery, tone, and figurative language.

Some observations from high-scoring essays: High-scoring essays frequently discussed how the speaker is empowered by the juggler's ability to lift people's spirits as he keeps balls flying in the air, and they did not confuse the literal action with the figurative meaning. Some perceptive students noticed how the tone of the poem is exuberant as the juggler performs, but then it turns dark when the juggler's audience returns to real life; however, many noticed how the poem ends with a degree of hope as the speaker is reminded of the juggler's ability.

* * *

2015: "XIV," written by Derek Walcott and first published in 1984. (***Note:*** The poem comes from an anthology of 54 poems by Walcott, each numbered chronologically with a Roman numeral.) Students were initially informed that the speaker is remembering a youthful experience of visiting a storyteller who is an elderly woman. Students were then invited to examine how the author's use of poetic devices enhances the speaker's memory of the event. No specific devices were suggested, but the poem is rich in natural imagery.

Some observations from high-scoring essays: Many of the students who produced high-scoring essays perceived that the natural surroundings of the poem served as a link to the speaker's childhood and that his memories were fond and tinged with magical undertones. Although the Caribbean culture in the poem was unfamiliar to many students, astute responses recognized the universal experiences of childhood that help create enlightenment and understanding. Many students analyzed imagery (especially the contrasts of shadows and light), metaphor, simile, personification, and setting, among others, as they explored the awe and wonderment the speaker feels.

* * *

2014: "For That He Looked Not upon Her," an English sonnet written by George Gascoigne in 1573. In this poem, the speaker laments how his love has shunned him, and he resolves to "look not upon her" any more. Students were instructed to explore how the intricate attitude of the speaker is conveyed through such devices as form, diction, and imagery.

Some observations from high-scoring essays: Insightful essays discussed how the English sonnet form, with its final couplet, helps to create a resolution for the speaker, who, after three quatrains of conflicted attitude, decides to steadfastly avoid his ex-lover and avoid the pain of rejection a second time. Many students noticed how the diction is contradictory, reflecting the speaker's complex emotions. Many students also noted how the animalistic imagery and metaphors that build throughout the three quatrains reflect the speaker's inner turmoil.

* * *

2013: "The Black Walnut Tree," written by Mary Oliver in 1979. In the poem, the speaker and her mother debate whether or not to cut down the large black walnut tree beside their house; at first, they think of the money they could get for selling its lumber and how it has become a maintenance nuisance for them over the years. However, "something brighter than money" stirs their memories, and causes them to take no action. That night, the speaker dreams of her ancestors who came from foreign lands to cultivate and settle the land, and she knows she and her mother would feel shame if they felled the tree. Students were instructed to analyze how the poet expresses the relationship between the black walnut tree and the family via the use of figurative language and other poetic devices. No specific devices were mentioned.

Some observations from high-scoring essays: Some of the insights revealed in high-scoring essays are that the tree symbolizes the endurance of nature and family, as well as a link between the practical world and the family's emotions. Astute students understood how the poem initially explores the relationship between a mother and her daughter before it broadens its focus to the relationship of the entire family's sacrifice and heritage, as the family cultivated land and developed roots in America. Students frequently explored the use of imagery, simile, diction, and symbolism.

* * *

2012: "Thou Blind Man's Mark," written by Sir Philip Sidney and first published in 1598. The speaker rails against desire, a personified being who has ensnared the speaker's thoughts and kept him from preparing for "higher things." The speaker vows to strive for virtue, even though desire is omnipresent in life. Students were directed to analyze how poetic devices helped convey the speaker's complex attitude toward desire. No specific devices were suggested.

Some observations from high-scoring essays: The students who produced high-scoring essays frequently analyzed how desire is essentially a paradoxical emotion that can be detrimental and keep one from achieving higher things in life, but also one that cannot be avoided. The students generally noticed that the speaker resolves this complexity, choosing to fight against the allure and manipulation of desire by concentrating on and developing inner resources. Students often explored alliteration, repetition, irony, and personification in the poem as they connected technique with meaning.

* * *

2011: "A Story," written by Li-Young Lee and published in 1990. In the poem, a 5-year-old boy has asked his father to tell him a new story, and the father struggles to create something new. He ponders that he will disappoint his son, and he envisions the inevitable day when his son is grown and moves out of the house. Ironically, as they sit in a room full of books filled with stories, the father's fears inhibit him from concocting a new story for his young son. Students were instructed to analyze how the poet conveys the complex relationship between father and son through such devices as point of view and poetic structure.

Some observations from high-scoring essays: Overall, students were touched by this tender poem that relates how this father struggles to create a new story at the request of his young son and how he realizes the intricate bond they share. Many students who presented strong analysis explored the parallel and narrative structure of the poem that changes in its perspective and in time. The first-person point of view allowed students to understand the father's conflict: trying to please his son while also fearing that he will ultimately disappoint and lose him when he grows up and moves out. Distinguished responses frequently provided insight into the complex relationship between father and son, plus the irony of the father's inability to respond to his son's simple request for a new story. Many students analyzed imagery, irony, and the symbolism of storytelling as a bond between father and son.

* * *

2010: "The Century Quilt," written by Marilyn Nelson Waniek and published in 1985. The speaker initially reminisces about the comfort she and her sister felt lying under her grandmother's "Indian blanket." She develops the quilt into a symbol that represents her family's multicultural past, the connections between generations, her dreams for the future, and her developing identity. Students were directed to analyze how the poet uses such techniques as structure, imagery, and tone to develop the complex meanings that the speaker attributes to the quilt.

Some observations from high-scoring essays: Many students were quick to notice the varied colors in the imagery as the speaker describes the quilt; in turn, they frequently examined how the individual picture in each square of the quilt represents a different family member within the speaker's ethnically diverse family ancestry. Many students also noticed how the structure moves in time, with each stanza representing an era, first the past, then the present, and finally the future. Some students noticed how the shift in point of view, from first person to third person, adds a degree of universality to the poem's message. Most students described the tone as peaceful and comforting.

Examples of Poetry Selection and Student Essays

Directions: The following poem, "Foreign," was written by William Carlos Williams in 1917. Read the poem carefully. Then write a well-developed essay in which you analyze how the speaker's literary devices convey his complex attitude about humanity.

Foreign

Artsybashev[1] is a Russian.
I am an American.
Let us wonder, my townspeople,
if Artsybashev tends his own fires
as I do, gets himself cursed   (5)
for the baby's failure to thrive,
loosens windows for the woman
who cleans his parlor—
or has he neat servants
and a quiet library, an   (10)
intellectual wife perhaps and
no children,—an apartment
somewhere in a back street or
lives alone or with his mother
or sister—   (15)

I wonder, my townspeople,
if Artsybashev looks upon
himself the more concernedly
or succeeds any better than I
in laying the world.   (20)

I wonder which is the bigger
fool in his own mind.

These are shining topics
my townspeople but—
hardly of great moment.   (25)

[1]**Artsybashev:** A Russian writer and playwright (1878–1927)

Student Essay 1

History has many examples of voices who spoke up to extol the virtue of inclusiveness, to insist that people of different cultures, different nations, different races all must understand that their commonalities are much more important than their differences; indeed, they are not really "foreign" to one another. Eminent names such as Mahatma Gandhi and Nelson Mandela may come to mind, but to that list we must now add the speaker in William Carlos Williams' eloquent poem "Foreign."

The speaker identifies the Russian writer Artsybashev and then he proceeds with a long list of things that they may have in common; it is notable that these are all everyday, homey references that his audience, the local townspeople, can relate to. The speaker wonders if the far-off Russian "tends his own fires / as I do," and if he "gets himself cursed / for the baby's failure to thrive." Or, he wonders, does he instead have "neat servants / and a quiet library, an / intellectual wife perhaps and / no children." He takes care to include families with children, and those without, he mentions wealthy families with servants and also poor families living in "an apartment / somewhere in a back street," and he includes someone "living alone." Thus, he gives everyone in his audience something that they can relate to, a feeling that they personally have something in common with the Russian. He argues powerfully for inclusiveness, concentrating on our shared humanity.

One rhetorical device that helps this poem to coalesce is the speaker's repeated use of the word "wonder." It first appears in line 3, "Let us wonder" as he invites his audience to be thoughtful, enticing their curiosity, so that they may listen to him with an open mind. To underscore the many options that the speaker invites the townspeople to "wonder," he also repeats the word "or" four times between the possibilities he lists. Then in line 16, he changes the emphasis, stating "I wonder, my townspeople," which appears to make the questioning specifically introspective, as the speaker asks if the Russian is as concerned about his life or if he "succeeds any better than I." The final "I wonder" in line 21 is the most personal of all, asking "which is the bigger / fool in his own mind." The speaker is laying himself bare, surprising the audience while opening up to his own self-doubts, and thereby inviting them to take his message into their hearts.

Another interesting feature of this piece is its unique poetic form. It is composed of four stanzas, but they all have a different number of lines: 15, 5, 2, and 3 lines, respectively. The effect keeps the reader a bit off-balance; it forces one to stay focused and engaged. It is interesting that the largest stanza begins the poem, starting with two simple 1-line sentences, each using a linking verb. Then it develops 13 more lines with its many images of different lifestyles, filling our imagination with possibilities, almost as if the possibilities are endless. The following 5-line stanza shortens the speaker's thought appropriately as he personalizes himself and Artsybashev, essentially wondering who succeeded in "laying out the world" in their respective literary works, a simple personal question. The next 2-line stanza is the shocker: a blunt, unexpected admission: worrying about being a fool while wondering if Artsybashev has an equal worry. Were it not separated into one truncated stanza it would not be as forceful. The 3-line finale takes the reader back to the universal, admitting that these "shining topics" of questioning who was more successful in explaining the world or who was the bigger fool, are actually "hardly of great moment." It completes the poem with a whimper, not with a bang.

In the end, the poem finally makes its overall point, albeit in somewhat circumspect language. The speaker knows that he has captured the audience's attention by listing all of the commonalities, questioning these "shining topics" that they can relate to, so then he concludes that the thoughts are "hardly of great moment;" the commonalities between the townspeople and some far-off foreigner are far more important than any supposed differences in the brotherhood of humanity.
(699 words)

Analysis of Student Essay 1

This thoughtful essay immediately piques the Reader's interest and appeals to his or her sense of humanity. Instead of beginning by simply naming the poem, its author, and repeating the prompt, this student immediately addresses the ultimate theme of the work, that the commonalities that intertwine through humanity are more important than the differences. By claiming that people "are not really 'foreign' to one another," the student effectively addresses the prompt and presents a defendable thesis that will earn a point in Row A.

The first body paragraph aptly notes that the speaker and the Russian writer Artsybashev may have many things in common, and it points out that the list includes "everyday, homey references" that include all types of living circumstances. This is effective because it helps prove the student's point that all of the speaker's townspeople and all of us in the audience can relate to at least one of these situations. The student claims that the speaker "argues powerfully for inclusiveness," which may be a bit of an exaggeration; the speaker doesn't really present an argument at all, but this is a quibbling complaint. The student is entirely accurate in stating that the speaker concentrates "on our shared humanity," and thus correctly establishes the speaker's attitude.

The next body paragraph analyzes the multiple repetitions of the word "wonder," a concept that is central to the poem's meaning. It is very pleasing that the student comprehends how this word works within the poem, articulating that it serves three functions: It "invites his audience to be thoughtful," it entices their curiosity, and it allows them to have an open mind. The student also understands the significance of the speaker's change to questioning his own personal wonder, with the switch to "I wonder" appearing twice more in the poem. It is also interesting to note the student's exploration of the quadruple use of "or" between the first stanza's list of options; this is a detail that many students will gloss over or not notice at all. This student presents a strong interpretation of the speaker's final use of "I wonder," especially since the speaker does surprise the audience, "while opening up to his own self-doubts," and thus, he opens their hearts. The student initially claimed that "wonder" allows the audience to open their minds; now it is also used to open their hearts. A Reader will be pleased by this most effective and sophisticated conclusion of the paragraph.

The following paragraph examines the poem's form, concentrating on the four very different stanzas. The student astutely notes that the poem begins with "two simple 1-line sentences, each using a linking verb." The essay would be stronger if the student were to do more than just note this fact; he or she could explore what is important about the predicate nominative in each sentence, which identifies a nationality, or the way that linking verbs, by definition, merely present a state of being. However, the student does accurately acknowledge that the next 13 lines allow the speaker to imagine many possibilities, "almost as if [they] are endless." The student notices that the 5-line stanza "shortens the speaker's thought" and allows him to personalize himself with Artsybashev, but this would be merely a surface-level observation if the student had left it at that. Instead, the student interprets that the speaker wonders how successful they each were in their writing, "'in laying out the world,'" explaining why it is such a personal question. This is an interpretation that works well. The student is particularly strong as he or she examines the blunt force of the 2-line stanza that surprises the audience with the concept of being a fool, noting that if the idea were not separated as it is, it would lose its force. The paragraph concludes by stating the 3-line finale returns to the universal, reminiscent of the manner in which the essay begins. The student finishes with an entirely apropos allusion to T. S. Eliot, and the student is spot-on saying that the poem ends with a whimper, not with a bang. Indeed, the student comprehends that the speaker dismisses "these 'shining topics.'" The body paragraphs would earn 3 of the possible 4 points in Row B.

The conclusion of this essay does far more than merely summarize. Rather, the conclusion reinforces the essay's thesis about the commonalities that unite humanity, and it again drops in a reference to the title. We are left with the concept of "the brotherhood of humanity" and with a smile. This is the kind of well-written conclusion that will shine above so many other pedestrian essays.

The student's writing and thoughts are sophisticated and complex enough to earn a point for sophistication in Row C. This essay is strong in all elements and it truly deserves a high score of 5.

Student Essay 2

The poem "Foreign" by William Carlos Williams is cryptic, almost inscrutable, but it does contain clues as to the author's attitude about himself and about humanity. To read these clues, you have to look at the literary devices.

The imagery is evocative but it's all over the place, so it's hard to tell what the poet wants us to focus on. The imagery seems to draw parallels between the speaker and a Russian writer. It describes a family man who "tends his own fires," has a baby, loose windows, and "neat servants." But then it goes on and on about a different guy, with "an intellectual wife and no children," or a guy who lives alone or a guy who lives with his mother. This imagery all seems to be meant to try to draw the Russians as just regular guys, because they have a lot in common with the speaker.

The syntax also helps to show the speaker's attitude. If you examine the number of lines in each stanza, and even consider the number of words in each line, you can see how the poet drew a pattern that changes as the poem goes on.

Now you can see how to cryptic the poem is. But by looking at the poetic devices, you can decipher clues to understand that the speaker thinks the Russians are "regular guys," they are just like us Americans.
(234 words)

Analysis of Student Essay 2

This essay does not begin with promise or with insight, especially since the student readily admits to finding the poem "cryptic, almost inscrutable," before claiming that it does provide some clues about the author's attitude. Glaringly, the student appears to confuse the author of the poem with the speaker in the poem; it is possible in this case that Williams is, in fact, the speaker, but one cannot jump to that conclusion. Students will be on safer ground if they refer to the speaker in their essay, unless specifically instructed that the poem is autobiographical. In addition, this student does not clarify what the speaker's attitude is, but merely tells us that we have to look at the literary devices to figure it out. Sadly, a Reader will not be favorably impressed by this introduction. It will not earn a point in Row A for its thesis.

The first body paragraph tries to analyze imagery, but it goes astray. We are told the imagery is "evocative," without any explanation or examples, and then the student makes the scattershot declaration that "it's all over the place." One can try to imagine what the student means, but it is hard to do so. The student appears to be unsure, stating that the imagery "seems to draw parallels" between the two writers; this is actually an accurate statement about the poem, but the idea is not developed at all. Instead of exploring what the imagery reveals about the speaker's attitude, the student merely lists what the poem "describes." But then the essay goes even further astray by claiming "it goes on and on about a different guy." The student apparently misread the poem, not understanding that the speaker is imagining many different possible scenarios of Artsybashev's life. The student tries to salvage the paragraph by explaining, with hesitation, that the imagery "seems" to present all Russians as "regular guys" who have commonalities with the speaker. The student's jumbled thinking and lack of understanding is quite apparent in this jumbled and confused paragraph.

The second body paragraph falls completely flat. The student attempts to discuss syntax and connect it to the speaker's attitude, but does not know how to do so. The student essentially wants the Reader to do the work, counting the number of lines and the number of words and thereby discovering "how the poet drew a pattern that changes." A hard-working Reader will let out a sigh, and not a sigh of relief. These body paragraphs will earn 2 points in Row B.

The essay ends by *helpfully* informing us that, after reading this *informative* essay, we can now see "how to [sic] cryptic the poem is." However, the student also reminds us that the speaker thinks that Russians and Americans are all just "regular guys," which is far from the actual point of the poem.

Overall, this student clearly demonstrates his or her need for another year of studying literature. The student's confusion and misunderstandings, the failure to comprehend the speaker's attitude, and the inability to present adequate literary analysis really do not bode well. Additionally, the student's writing is riddled with entirely avoidable errors, such as using the improper second person "you" several times, and producing run-on sentences. Finally, the unsophisticated language does not impress, and it will not earn a point in Row C. This insubstantial essay should earn a low score of 2.

The Prose Question

The comfort you will feel in addressing the prose question is based on the fact that you're already accustomed to analyzing novels and short stories. In the prose passages, you'll more than likely find characters and conflicts, plus some degree of plot, setting, point of view, and theme. Of course, you'll have more words to read than in the poetry selection, but realize that this frequently gives you more to write about. Like the poem selection, you will be able to get the gist of the passage, and the work will also provide you with plenty of ammunition to respond to the prompt. With just 40 minutes, you certainly won't run short of material to analyze. Another similarity to the poetry question is that as of 2020 you will always be asked to explore complex relationships. This consistency will give you comfort and help you explore the passage.

Examining the Task on Previous Essay Questions

The prose prompt will invariably ask you to analyze character; after all, the characters, with their conflicts and complicated relationships, drive fiction. Sometimes you will be directed to analyze how the surrounding environment impacts character; sometimes you will be directed to analyze how the author establishes complex character; sometimes you will be directed to analyze the complex relationship between characters. Be aware that the characters and passages are rich and multifaceted; they will offer you the opportunity to explore a range of interpretations via the author's figurative language. The most common literary devices mentioned in past prompts were selection of detail, tone, and imagery. Other literary elements that appeared in the prompts include figurative language, narrator's attitude, dialogue, diction, and point of view. As of 2020, the exam will not suggest or direct you to analyze specific elements, but knowing what was most commonly asked in the past will help you see more in the works you do get on the exam.

In prose analysis, refer to the narrator, or the character(s), if appropriate (in poetry analysis, refer to the speaker).

Note: The directions will *always* instruct you to read carefully and write an essay. Some prompts will add the phrase "well-organized" or "well-developed," which is more than a bit redundant. The following summaries of recent prompts will not repeat these directions to read carefully and to write an essay.

2018: Students were presented with an excerpt from Nathaniel Hawthorne's 1852 novel, *The Blithedale Romance*, in which two characters, who had been living in a communal rural society that promoted equality, are about to go their separate ways. Students were instructed to analyze how the author uses literary techniques to portray the first-person narrator's attitude toward Zenobia, the female character he is confronting. In the passage, the narrator has come to Zenobia's opulent home, and he is surprised to discover her wealth, as he had only known her in a communal, classless setting.

Some observations from high-scoring essays: Students who wrote strong essays generally noted that the narrator finds Zenobia to be a confusing and contradictory character; he had known her in a community dedicated to equality, yet in the current scene she is wealthy and accustomed to a high-class lifestyle. The narrator realizes that he cannot trust her entirely. Many students discussed the metaphors and similes that compare her to an actress, one who appears in one persona but has another in real life. Many students also discussed a dominant image in the passage, a mirror in the room that serves as an elegant symbol of her two-faced deception.

* * *

2017: Students read an excerpt from Tobias Smollett's 1751 novel, *The Adventures of Peregrine Pickle.* The prompt informed the students of the two characters' names and their relationship: Godfrey Gauntlet is the brother of Mr. Pickle's beloved Emilia; students were also informed that the two men would "confront their own uncontrolled emotions and yet attempt to abide by their social norms." This type of additional context will be provided when necessary for understanding the text. Use it to your advantage. Students were tasked with exploring the complex interactions between the characters' emotions and the social propriety of the day. The prompt suggested exploring dialogue, narrative pace, and tone. "Narrative pace" may be an unusual term to you, but it is the AP English Literature and Composition Development Committee's way of alerting you to an element in the passage that you can address. In this passage, the pace is quite quick, with the two men swiftly exchanging verbal bon mots as they argue over their honor in the first paragraph. The second paragraph describes the swift action each takes as they battle with swords.

Some observations from high-scoring essays: Overall, students understood that the passage showed how men's emotions can conflict with social norms and how quickly their emotions can escalate and initiate violence. Many students noticed how Mr. Pickle's relationship with Emilia is the source of the confrontation between the two men, but by the end, she is never mentioned; they no longer remember the original cause of their fighting. Astute students recognized and appreciated the humor of the passage, seen both in the men's seemingly polite dialogue and in their adherence to the social customs of dueling that attempt to add a patina of civility to acts of violence. Many students discussed how the repetition in the dialogue ironically attempts to normalize their petty insults, and how their attempts to follow rules of engagement add an illusion of decorum to their violent engagement.

* * *

2016: Students were presented an excerpt from Thomas Hardy's 1886 novel, *The Mayor of Casterbridge.* The prompt informed students that the mayor, Michael Henchard, has recently been reunited with his daughter, Elizabeth-Jane. In the years before this reunification, Henchard rose from being a poor farmworker to becoming the prosperous mayor, while Elizabeth-Jane supported herself as a waitress at a tavern. Students were instructed to analyze Hardy's portrayal of the two characters' complex relationship, paying particular attention to the tone, word choice, and selection of detail. The engaging plot, conflict, character descriptions, and dialogue offered ample opportunities for students to respond to the prompt.

Some observations from high-scoring essays: Students analyzed the characters with insight and only rarely lapsed into plot summary. Strong student responses noted how Henchard is a cold, harsh elitist, while his daughter Elizabeth-Jane is warm, humble, and docile; however, instead of stopping with those fairly obvious comments, the more astute students continued, pointing out how their complex relationship is confusing for both of them and it becomes a relationship without any real communication or understanding. Many students recognized that Henchard inwardly loves his daughter but also feels shame for previously abandoning her. His embarrassment of his past keeps him from accepting her as she is in the present, and he constantly criticizes her every action, her every statement. Elizabeth-Jane's conflict also deals with love and regret; students understood that she inwardly and outwardly loves her father, but she feels chagrin when she constantly disappoints him. Some students went deeper by pointing out the double standard faced by women and how the stereotypes of 19th-century mores continue to this day.

* * *

2015: Students read an excerpt from the 1986 novel *The Beet Queen* by Louise Erdrich, and then were instructed to analyze how the author demonstrates the impact of the surrounding environment on the two children, Karl, age 14, and Mary, age 11. Literary devices such as tone, imagery, selection of detail, and point of view were suggested. In the passage, set in North Dakota on a cold spring day in 1932, Karl and Mary have arrived via train at the town of Argus, where they are to begin living with their aunt. No one meets the train, and they walk through the town, continuing toward houses on the outskirts. Karl spots a blooming tree in someone's front yard and embraces its beauty. However, the owner lets her dog loose to attack Karl; he defends himself with a branch he breaks off the tree and tells his sister to run away toward their aunt's house. He, in turn, runs back to the train.

Some observations from high-scoring essays: Students found the passage quite accessible and those who read carefully discovered many subtleties that were ripe for analysis. They noticed that the environment is very harsh, barren, and dreary, and that the use of a third-person narrator enhances this coldness with a very unsympathetic point of view. However, the imagery of the environment changes as Karl sees the blooming tree in a yard on the outskirts of town. Students noted how Karl is described as delicate and fragile, mirroring the beautiful tree surrounded by a hostile environment. Some high-scoring students also explained how the details are initially simple and factual, but then hints of emotion foreshadow Karl's reaction to the tree. Many astute responses saw the tree as a symbol of Karl's innocence, which must be destroyed. Contrasted with Karl's sensitivity is Mary's steadfast, "square and practical nature," and many students acknowledged the appropriateness of Mary staying in the new harsh environment while Karl runs away.

* * *

2014: Students read an excerpt from the 2003 novel *The Known World* by Edward P. Jones, and they were then directed to analyze how the author reveals the character of Moses, considering such elements as point of view, selection of detail, and imagery. The passage immediately established that Moses is a slave, and that his master had died earlier in the evening. As the sun sets, Moses stands in the fields, alone but for the mule he is harnessed to; all others have gone to prepare supper. Moses unhooks himself from the harness, bends down, and takes a pinch of soil and eats it. Apparently, Moses does this often; the narrator describes how Moses knows the different taste of the soil all throughout the year. He returns the mule to the barn and walks into the woods at the edge of the field. It begins to rain torrentially, and Moses lies down after disrobing and lets the rain flow over his body. He sleeps there until morning.

Some observations from high-scoring essays: Many high-scoring essays focused on well-chosen, concrete examples from the text and tied them to specific literary elements, while weaker essays tried to cover everything in the passage. Overall, the high-scoring students recognized that Moses is a complex character who, although a slave, follows his own path and gains knowledge in unusual ways. Many addressed how the selection of detail separates Moses from others, establishes his self-driven independence and his connection to nature. The students who addressed point of view explored how the third-person omniscient narrator limits a reader's insights into Moses' mind as his ideas occur. One brief mention of his wife's thoughts shows that she understands him well, but the rest of the narrative depicts Moses as a contemplative, calm man who is firmly connected to the land and the earth. The interesting imagery of Moses tasting the soil provided plenty of fodder for students' comments. Strong writers analyzed the symbolism of the imagery, noticing that the soil tasted metallic during summer, intimating industrialism, but tasted moldy in autumn, intimating the mortality of all living things. Students also pointed out how the image of Moses, lying naked on the wet grass as the rain pours on him, becomes a symbol of rebirth, of baptism in nature, freeing him from the daily bonds of his slavery.

* * *

2013: Students were instructed to carefully read an excerpt from D. H. Lawrence's 1915 novel, *The Rainbow*, which chronicles the Brangwen family, a rural English farming family in the late 19th century. Then students were directed to analyze how the author uses literary devices to characterize the woman and her situation. These directions may sound vague, but the main character is only referred to as "the woman," and her situation in the passage becomes apparent. While the men work the land focusing on the harvest and the weather, the woman looks in another direction, wondering about the world outside, wanting to gain knowledge. The narration then introduces the local vicar, who appears to be the opposite of the woman's husband, Tom. The woman contemplates why the vicar has power over others who are physically stronger, and she decides it is a result of his knowledge.

Some observations from high-scoring essays: When the prompt does not suggest any specific literary elements to explore, it gives students the freedom to independently discover what the passage offers. While some students prefer the comfort of being guided in their analysis, others favor freedom. High-scoring students explored imagery, form, parallel structure, repetition, diction, and symbolism as they analyzed the woman and her situation. Most students readily understood that the woman is trapped, caged, and caught between two worlds, while not belonging entirely to either. Some students pointed out that the imagery that describes the Brangwen men is visceral, raw, pulsing, thriving, and carnal, while the woman is depicted as intellectual, disillusioned, and yearning for more than her provincial life offers. Astute students who examined the form of the passage noticed some essential stylistic differences in the three paragraphs. The first paragraph that introduces the men is composed of simple, stark, earth-bound images and actions; the men have no thoughts, only reactions to their physical world. But when the second paragraph introduces the woman, the style shifts to longer, more dynamic sentences that explore her many questions about the world. The third paragraph that adds the character of the vicar is filled with her questions about power and knowledge, and it reflects a shift from the Brangwen men to the woman. Students also noticed that the diction describing the vicar is elevated, propelling him to a position above the men, while the diction describing the men dehumanizes them, comparing them to bulls. Overall, the students found the passage accessible, and they scored higher than in many other years.

* * *

2012: Students were presented with an excerpt from *Under the Feet of Jesus*, a 1995 novel by Helena María Viramontes. Students were instructed to analyze the character of Estrella, considering such elements as selection of detail, figurative language, and tone. The passage begins in the past, when Estrella first discovers a man's toolbox near the door of her home. Then the passage transitions to describing how Estrella, a young schoolgirl, is derided by her teachers for being a minority, a migrant student whom they perceive as dirty. The passage transitions again to describing Perfecto Flores, the owner of the toolbox, who has apparently stayed with the family since Estrella discovered his toolbox at the door. He is known for the good quality of his repair work. Over time, he teaches Estrella the names and functions of his tools, satisfying her desire to understand things. The passage ends as Estrella, in her desire to learn, begins to read.

Some observations from high-scoring essays: Students wrote lengthy essays on this prompt, demonstrating a clear understanding of Estrella's predicament, often personally relating to her troubles. Perceptive students noted how Perfecto kindly instructs Estrella, unlike her teachers who criticize her; he fuels her curiosity, but her teachers inhibit it. Many students explored the figurative language, particularly similes and metaphors that establish a connection between the individual letters on the schoolroom blackboard and the individual tools in Perfecto's box; both become a catalyst for Estrella's understanding of the power of letters and words. The passage offers plentiful description of Perfecto's tools and their practical functions, and students used this detail to explore how Estrella finds meaning in her life as she understands the meaning of the tools. Students who did a good job of addressing tone explained that the tone shifts from initially being stark and solemn with Estrella's confusion to becoming confident and more emotional as she comprehends her world. Other students noticed how Estrella is passive in the beginning but takes action by the end.

* * *

2011: Students read an excerpt from *Middlemarch*, a British novel published in 1871–1872 by George Eliot, the pen name of Mary Ann Evans. The prompt explained that the recently married couple, Rosamond and Tertius Lydgate, clash over financial difficulties. Students were directed to analyze the couple's complex relationship, considering such devices as narrative perspective and selection of detail. The term "narrative perspective" may not be familiar to some, but it simply refers to the perspective, the attitude, that the use of an omniscient narrator adds. In this passage, Rosamond is depicted as naïve, spoiled, and petulant; she wants her husband to either ask her father or friends for money, and if he won't do so, she wants to move away. Tertius tries to both control and appease her by accepting the blame for their extravagant spending.

Some observations from high-scoring essays: Discerning students understood how Eliot's omniscient narrator helps to shape the readers' perception of each character. The narrator is both sympathetic and critical of both characters, but weaker student responses did not understand this and instead tended to take the side of one character over the other. Perceptive students commented that the subject of the couple's argument was not the central problem; they saw the real issue as one of control and the couple's actual stumbling block as their excessive pride. Strong students noticed how the selection of detail demonstrates the vacillation and complexity of both characters, even comparing their manipulative dialogue and movements to a discreet chess game. Other students noticed that each character serves as a literary foil, revealing the other's personality through his or her own actions and thoughts. Many students scored quite well on this topic as long as they did not oversimplify.

* * *

2010: Students were presented with an excerpt from Maria Edgeworth's 1801 British novel, *Belinda*. The prompt provided necessary character exposition: Clarence Hervey is a suitor of Belinda's. Her aunt, Mrs. Stanhope, hoping to improve Belinda's social prospects, has arranged for her niece to stay with the fashionable Lady Delacour. Students were instructed to analyze Clarence Hervey's complex character and how the author develops it through such techniques as tone, point of view, and language (another term for word choice). This passage is only one paragraph, and it is entirely devoted to character description, mostly of Mr. Hervey.

Some observations from high-scoring essays: This passage proved a challenge for many, but the more sophisticated students discerned the complexity of Clarence Hervey's character and how the author effectively uses point of view and language to develop his character. While weak essays tended to present Hervey unfavorably as a one-sided, egotistical jerk, the strong essays commented on his paradoxical contradictions. Some students even suggested that he was stuck between two historical ideals: the Age of Enlightenment and the Age of Romanticism. Students who appreciated the subtle satire of the piece saw how the point of view and language combine to break through Hervey's façade and present him not as a villain but merely as a fool. Many understood that on the surface level, the omniscient narrator is initially critical, but later develops sympathy for Hervey's character as he becomes a symbol of lost potential. Some students noticed how the narrator uses absolutes. Students described the changing tone as skeptical, nonchalant, whimsical, sarcastic, and regretful. Some students observed that the language of the passage was subtle and cunning, analogous to the societal tricks people play when toying with love.

Examples of Prose Passage and Student Essays

Directions: The following excerpt comes from E. M. Forster's 1921 novel, *Howards End*. The passage takes place at Howards End, the ancestral Wilcox country home. Before this excerpt begins, Helen Schlegel and Paul Wilcox have mutually broken off their secret, hasty engagement. In the excerpt, Helen's Aunt Juley, Mrs. Munt, arrives, after being driven from the train station by Charles Wilcox, Paul's older brother.

Read the passage carefully. Then write a well-developed essay in which you analyze how the author explores the complex interplay between the characters' emotions and social propriety in the passage.

So they played the game of Capping Families, a round of which is always played when love would unite two members of our race. But they played it with unusual vigour, stating in so many words that Schlegels were better than Wilcoxes, Wilcoxes better than Schlegels. They flung decency aside. The man was young, the woman deeply stirred; in both a vein of coarseness was latent. Their quarrel was no more surprising than are most quarrels—inevitable at the time, incredible afterwards. But it was more than usually futile. A few
(5)   minutes, and they were enlightened. The motor drew up at Howards End, and Helen, looking very pale, ran out to meet her aunt.

"Aunt Juley, I have just had a telegram from Margaret; I—I meant to stop your coming. It isn't—it's over."
The climax was too much for Mrs. Munt. She burst into tears.
(10)   "Aunt Juley dear, don't. Don't let them know I've been so silly. It wasn't anything. Do bear up for my sake."
"Paul," cried Charles Wilcox, pulling his [driving] gloves off.
"Don't let them know. They are never to know."
"Oh, my darling Helen—"
(15)   "Paul! Paul!"
A very young man came out of the house.
"Paul, is there any truth in this?"
"I didn't—I don't—"
"Yes or no, man; plain question, plain answer. Did or didn't Miss Schlegel—"
(20)   "Charles, dear," said a voice from the garden. "Charles, dear Charles, one doesn't ask plain questions. There aren't such things."
They were all silent. It was Mrs. Wilcox.
She approached just as Helen's letter had described her, trailing noiselessly over the lawn, and there was actually a wisp of hay in her hands. She seemed to belong not to the young people and their motor, but to
(25)   the house, and to the tree that overshadowed it. One knew that she worshipped the past, and that the instinctive wisdom the past can alone bestow had descended upon her—that wisdom to which we give the clumsy name of aristocracy. High born she might not be. But assuredly she cared about her ancestors, and let them help her. When she saw Charles angry, Paul frightened, and Mrs. Munt in tears, she heard her ancestors say, "Separate those human beings who will hurt each other most. The rest can wait." So she did
(30)   not ask questions. Still less did she pretend that nothing had happened, as a competent society hostess would have done. She said: "Miss Schlegel, would you take your aunt up to your room or to my room, whichever you think best. Paul, do find Evie, and tell her lunch for six, but I'm not sure whether we shall all be downstairs for it." And when they had obeyed her, she turned to her elder son, who still stood in the throbbing, stinking car, and smiled at him with tenderness, and without saying a word, turned away from
(35)   him towards her flowers.
"Mother," he called, "are you aware that Paul has been playing the fool again?"
"It is all right, dear. They have broken off the engagement."
"Engagement—!"
"They do not love any longer, if you prefer it put that way," said Mrs. Wilcox, stooping down to smell a
(40)   rose.

Student Essay 1

One theme that recurs throughout British literature is the intricate interplay between the character's actions and dialogue, which usually must conform to the social proprieties of their audience, versus their internal dialogue, which can be forged by their sometimes-extreme emotions. On the inside, a character may be raging or crying or terrified, but they usually cannot admit it out loud, or at least not in so many words. A brilliant example of this internal-versus-public image battle is the great novel <u>Howards End</u>, in which E. M. Forster displays the complexities of human emotions versus societal decorum.

The characters' dialogue is weighted with hidden meaning, laden with unspoken emotional subtext. When Helen says blandly "It isn't—it's over," she is actually dying on the inside, but due to social propriety, she feels that she can't display her raw emotion; she must try to keep up appearances, just as she tells her aunt, "Do bear up for my sake." When Paul responds to Charles' pointed question about the relationship, simply mumbling, "I didn't—I don't," it is clear that he is struggling with his raging emotions, but it is equally clear that he feels he can never enunciate them.

Another aspect of the dialogue communicating carefully-coded messages is Mrs. Wilcox's dialogue, all of which conveys the authority of command, and all of which carefully keeps the other characters' emotions sub-rosa. When she commands Charles, "one doesn't ask plain questions," she is telling him not to force his brother Paul to divulge his raw emotions. It is the same when she tells Helen to take her aunt upstairs to a bedroom; it is the same when she sends Paul to give orders to the maid. In each case she might as well be saying "Shoo, don't say another word about your feelings!" However, even though she comes across as so authoritarian, her purpose is to help others by interceding for the greater good; she knows they are hurting inside, and she ultimately upholds their sense of decorum.

The interplay between the social norms of this high-society crowd versus their hidden emotions is further developed in the detailed description of Mrs. Wilcox. It is implied that she is feeling strong emotions herself; after all, her younger son has just broken off his formal engagement, apparently just the latest of his romantic misadventures. However, she comes across as totally calm, cool, and collected, entering by "trailing noiselessly over the lawn, and there was actually a wisp of hay in her hands," she appears to be the epitome of the society doyenne. If her emotions are aroused by the family ruckus, she allows us no clue, no sign in her actions nor her dialogue.

Lastly, the complex emotional undercurrent is reinforced through skillful moderation in the tone of the passage. During the huge argument between Helen and Paul in the opening paragraph, the narrator lets us know that emotions are raw, and the characters throw invectives at each other like weapons; the tone of this portion is frenetic, as if the characters want to get it over with as quickly as possible. Next, in the scene in the driveway, the tone is still fast-paced, but the effect borders on comedic as the characters talk over one another, some thinking one thing and others thinking something else entirely. Finally the tone changes dramatically with the introduction of Mrs. Wilcox; her voice of authority immediately silences all of the other characters and then her cool silent entrance establishes her gravitas, the tone is almost leisurely, with thoughts left hanging in the air. We are left with the reminder that in this society, above all, proper dignity and respect is essential.

Thus, once again the universal theme of this complex interplay is completed. Their emotions are driving these characters, and driving them hard, but they cannot let it show, for they must keep up appearances, all for the sake of adhering to their all-important norms of social propriety.
(659 words)

Analysis of Student Essay 1

This student opens with a quite impressive introduction. It is true that first impressions are important both in life and in essays, but, of course, one must withhold judgment to see if it lives up to that first impression. Any Reader will be pleased to come across this thought-provoking introduction after reading hundreds of bland ones that merely restate the prompt. This essay begins with an overview of the way British literature frequently exposes the conundrum between expressing emotions versus maintaining social propriety. The introduction then focuses in by introducing *Howards End*, promising that it is a "brilliant example" of the "complexities of human emotion versus societal decorum." The essay will earn a point in Row A for its thesis.

The first body paragraph begins pleasantly, both in substance and in style. The student accurately explains that the characters' dialogue is full of passionate implications, but a Reader will also notice the student's stylistic sophistication, such as demonstrating both assonance and parallel construction in the phrase "weighted with hidden meaning, laden with unspoken emotional subtext." The paragraph presents examples from the two young ex-lovers, both caught in the height of emotion, both struggling to hide the pain of their tempestuous breakup from the other. The paragraph does not delve too deeply into analysis, but it does acknowledge the way the two characters struggle with their intense emotions while feeling a desperate need to appear socially proper.

The next body paragraph skillfully explores Mrs. Wilcox's dialogue, pointing out the "carefully-coded messages" she implies. The student discusses three examples of her directives to her two sons and Helen by explaining that her essential message is the same to all; they simply must constrain their feelings. The student adds some depth by understanding Mrs. Wilcox is not merely being authoritarian because she's power-driven or unkind; instead the student explains that she is "interceding for the greater good" and upholding "their sense of decorum."

While the second body paragraph explores Mrs. Wilcox's dialogue, the third presents a cogent analysis of how her character is described, which is an appropriate focus, given that Forster devotes a healthy paragraph to her personality compared to her sparse dialogue. The student suggests that she experiences intense emotions herself but she successfully hides them under a cool exterior. The paragraph would be stronger if the student offered deeper insight, rather than simply stating that she shows no sign of her emotions, although it is a nice touch to label her as the "epitome of the society doyenne."

The student offers a fourth body paragraph that provides additional interesting analysis, focusing on the changing tone in the passage. The student's idea that the "complex emotional undercurrent is reinforced" by moderating the tone is promising, and the student provides ample text evidence for this idea. The essay accurately describes the initial raw, invective-filled, frenetic tone of Helen and Paul's argument. The student's explanation is very plausible, but it would be more convincing if he or she backed it up with some textual proof. Next the student accurately describes the tone shift as the action moves to the driveway, explaining that even though it is still fast-paced, it becomes almost comical with characters talking over one another and not always understanding what has been said. The tone indeed shifts again as Mrs. Wilcox enters the scene, and once again the student takes note of it, but describing the pace as "almost leisurely" is a not-entirely apt choice of words. However, a Reader will give this student the benefit of the doubt because he or she correctly notes that Mrs. Wilcox truly embodies gravitas. Not many students will explore tone, but this student makes a good choice and then finishes with a nice point about the end of the passage reminding us of the importance of quiet decorum in this very-British society. The body paragraphs will earn 4 points, the maximum possible, in Row B.

The conclusion is acceptable but not stellar. It provides a decent summary without being too obvious about it. However, the student appears to be a bit rushed, and he or she is not thinking through the ideas as well as in the earlier parts of the essay. For example, the student claims the "complex interplay" essentially completes the universal theme, but the student never really specifies what that theme is or how the interplay completes it. Additionally, the second sentence has an antecedent problem, using the pronoun "it" to refer to "their emotions." Remember, though, a Reader will reward the student for what he or she does well, and will tend to overlook these few lapses.

The essay would earn a high score of 5. It displays a logical development of its insights, plus it exhibits clear and coherent organization, on-topic discussion, and pleasing style, thus it merits such distinction. To bring it up to an even higher-scoring essay, the student could add more insightful analysis, include more text evidence, and display more sophisticated thought and style to earn a point in Row C.

Student Essay 2

In this excerpt from <u>Howards End</u>, a novel by E. M. Forster, the characters display a complex interplay between their emotions and their sense of propriety. This means that the characters did not say and do what they actually wanted to say and do because it might upset the social order. This conflict is seen in the various characters dialogue, and in the pace, and in the author's choice of details.

The characters dialogue provides the clearest tip-off that they are all holding back and not saying what they really want to say. The exchange in the driveway is a good example. Charles begins with an honest question, "Paul, is there any truth to this?" but Paul can't seem to answer honestly, saying "I didn't—I don't," not by saying what he really wants to say. Then old Mrs. Wilcox says bluntly, "One doesn't ask plain questions. There aren't such things," which means that everyone must shut up and not talk honestly.

The pace of the action also indicates that there is some kind of conflict going on beneath the surface. The pace starts out very fast, with the heated argument, and it slows down just a little in the driveway scene, with everyone talking over one another. But when Mrs. Wilcox issues her command, the pace slows to a crawl. This shows she must have power over them.

The author's details also show that there is more going on than meets the eye. When she learns about the breakup, Mrs. Munt doesn't just react, no, "She burst into tears." Charles isn't just in the car, no, "her elder son, who stood in the throbbing, stinking car." Mrs. Wilcox didn't just walk in from the garden, no, she "trailed noiselessly over the lawn" and for some reason she had "a wisp of hay in her hand." These details show that there is a lot more going on than what meets the eye, a hidden tension of some sort.

In conclusion, an examination of the author's use of dialogue, pace, and details clearly shows that there is a conflict between what's spoken and what is unspoken. The characters are clearly not saying whatever it is they really want to say.

(369 words)

Analysis of Student Essay 2

This essay deserves credit for what it does well: It adequately addresses the topic, it shows acceptable organization and development, and it uses language with satisfactory clarity. However, it is not a stellar essay, and a Reader will have to work too hard to find the implicit analysis.

The introduction merely repeats the directions of the prompt and then tells the Reader what it "means," declaring that the characters worry too much about maintaining proper social decorum to say what they are really thinking. The introduction ends by stating that this "conflict is seen" in the various literary elements suggested in the prompt. This introduction is not impressive, especially since two of the three sentences simply repeat the prompt, but the Reader can hope the body paragraphs get better. Incidentally, the Reader will forgive the apostrophe error in "characters dialogue." The quality of the thesis will earn a point in Row A.

The first body paragraph is devoted to a discussion of the dialogue and how it supposedly demonstrates that the characters hold back. The student explains that the conversation exchange in the driveway is a "good example," but merely reports the action in a "who said what" fashion. The student does try to delve into some analysis by acknowledging that Paul can't find the words to answer honestly, and then he or she repeats the same notion after Mrs. Wilcox's rejoinder that plain questions are simply not asked. Also a Reader might find it a bit condescending for a student to explain what a character's line means (as if the Reader does not understand), plus this student doesn't offer more than the simplistic idea that "everyone must shut up and not talk honestly." While this informal comment is not terribly insightful, at least it offers some surface-level analysis. However, the analysis would be stronger if the student read between the lines more and understood that Mrs. Wilcox represents something much deeper than a person who tells others "to shut up." As the text points out, she represents wisdom; she understands that she needs to help these people who "will hurt each other."

The following paragraph focuses on the pace of the action in the excerpt. Again, the student provides a hint of analysis, understanding that the pace indicates "some kind of conflict." The student correctly notes that the pace begins "very fast with the heated argument," but then offers a questionable claim that the pace "slows down just a little . . .with everyone talking over one another." However, it seems that the actual effect of such frenetic dialogue would be to speed up the pace of a narrative instead of slowing it down, just as it does in real life, so the Reader would hope for some explanatory logic to make this claim more plausible. The student then accurately acknowledges that the pace "slows to a crawl" when Mrs. Wilcox speaks, but unfortunately only concludes that it shows her power over others. More analysis and more depth would definitely help this paragraph.

Given the formulaic organization thus far, the Reader expects the last body paragraph will concentrate on detail, and the student predictably follows form. We are informed that the detail will show more than meets the eye, a generalization that is likely to always be true. The student presents three examples of compelling details, but in quite an informal way. The student tries to point out that these details make the passage richer, emphasizing how the text's diction does not just state the action, but also embellishes it with descriptive detail. Unfortunately, the student's presentation borders on being giggle-worthy with the insertion of "no" three times. One could argue in the student's defense and say that this at least gives the paragraph a voice; indeed, one can almost hear the exaggerated speaking style of a teenager. The paragraph ends by repeating the topic sentence and adding that details in the text show "a hidden tension of some sort." This does not add insightful analysis. The body paragraphs will earn 2 out of the possible 4 points in Row B.

The conclusion, duly noted with the phrase "In conclusion" (just in case the Reader is not aware of that fact), merely repeats what the body paragraphs discussed, and then it reminds us that the characters are not being honest. This two-sentence conclusion adds nothing to the essay.

This essay should earn a score of 3. It adequately meets the basic goals, but it is entirely formulaic in its organization, and it presents no more than surface-level analysis. However, it does have some analysis, usually implicit, and that saves the essay from a lower score. To improve, this student should explore a more organic organization (perhaps by using the progression of the dialogue and action to focus body paragraphs), try to delve deeper into the characters and how their exchanges imply the importance of propriety to their society, and strive for more sophisticated language. It will not earn a point for sophistication in Row C.

The Open Topic Question

The open topic essay is always the last of the free-response questions; it presents a generic literary idea, very frequently about character and conflict, and allows you to choose a novel, epic poem, or play to analyze vis-à-vis that idea. Theoretically, because students understand and like the work they choose to analyze, most find the open topic to be their favorite of the three free-response essays. Frequently, the open topic question yields the longest essay response because students have more to say about the work they get to choose.

Choosing an Appropriate Work

After the prompt, you will see the following information, in one form or another: "You may choose a work from the list below or another work." The provided list will suggest approximately 30 to 40 appropriate works for the topic. However, it is essential that you remember *you can choose to write on a work that is not on the list*. Do not limit yourself to the list, and don't worry if the work you want to write on is not on the list. Now, let's discuss making an appropriate choice. Many students, teachers, and AP Readers like to debate which works are or are not suitable, but all you have to do is use your common sense. By the time you take the AP English Literature and Composition Exam, you will have undoubtedly read many high-quality works of literature in your high school career. You will be well-served to choose a book you have already read and analyzed in one of your English classes. Books you enjoy for pleasure are always nice, and you may be tempted to choose such a work; however, understand the difference between pleasure reading and academic reading. The former tends to be fun but fleeting; the latter tends to be rigorous and long-lasting.

You might ask if you can write about works that have been translated. YES! You can choose to write on a translated work. Many, like *Crime and Punishment*, are excellent choices for many topics. Prior to 2020, some translated works were always included in the suggested list. Even though translated works will no longer appear on the list, you can still write on a translated work.

Another issue, however, is even more important; it deals with reading the directions carefully and following them. The prompt will *always* state to choose a novel; sometimes, if appropriate, it may also offer the option of choosing a play or epic poem. You must follow the directions explicitly. DO NOT, therefore, write on a short story, a short poem, or a one-act play. To address the open topic essay prompt well, you need to choose from fully developed works of literature. Never write on an epic poem or play unless it is clearly indicated as an option.

The specificity of the task presented in the prompt presents a final issue that deals with the directions. Most often you will be directed to write on *only one* character in a work; sometimes you will be directed to center the essay on *one moment* in the work. Again, follow the directions exactly, and do not analyze more than one character or more than one moment. Of course, your analysis will address how your character interacts with other characters, or relate events that precede or follow the important moment, but the central focus of the essay needs to be as specific as the task requires.

Suggestions for High-Scoring Essays

The prompt will *always* include a phrase that deals with the big picture, the overall importance of the work. We English teachers frequently refer to this as "theme," but because that word has many connotations, you will not likely see that word in the prompt directions. Rather, you will be directed to analyze how the generic topic "enhances the meaning of the work as a whole," or "adds significance to the work as a whole," or "illuminates the work as a whole." This means that you *always* need to tie your ideas and text examples of the specific character (or whatever is asked for) to the bigger, deeper, more universal concepts in the work. I strongly advise you to include this deeper meaning, this universal truth, in every body paragraph. If you wait until your conclusion to finally present your analysis of what's most important, it might well be a case of "too little, too late." If, instead, you explicitly state and consistently analyze throughout your essay how your specific text examples enhance universal ideas, you *will* get a higher score. Period.

The prompt will also always instruct you to avoid plot summary. This is valuable advice from your friendly test-writers! The majority of low-scoring essays lapse into banal plot synopsis and forget to tie in the importance of the topic. If you find yourself writing sentences that state (or imply) something like "And then he . . . , after which he . . . before she . . . " you are simply retelling the plot. High-scoring essays refer to an action or example from the text and then smoothly move into the analysis of its importance. Also remember that the Reader will be familiar with the text you choose and does not need any synopsis. If a Reader is not well-versed in the work you choose, he or she will find another Reader who is. There is no need to "explain" your chosen text to the Reader.

All high-scoring essays have traits in common: They present an appropriate work of literature, they focus squarely on the prompt, and they thoroughly explore all parts of the prompt. In other words, they are well-developed by combining a blend of specific text evidence (also referred to as concrete detail) with insightful commentary that produces a persuasive interpretation of the work.

A word on using quotations: You will never be required or expected to use any memorized quotations. However, the student who can embed an *appropriately* quoted phrase or two will be rewarded. Please also be very wary of using any stock, predictable quotes. You will not impress any Reader by including famous, well-known quotes such as Hamlet's "To be or not to be," or Juliet's "O Romeo, Romeo! wherefore art thou, Romeo?" or Kurtz's dying words, "The horror! The horror!" from *Heart of Darkness*.

Keep in mind that high-scoring essays always present clear, logical organization and structure. The concepts contained within the body paragraphs are relevant to each other, and the ideas and paragraphs move forward with an overall purpose.

Finally, well-written essays are, by definition, well-written. They have a sense of style, a distinct voice. Not all high-scoring essays have truly sophisticated style, but they have few (if any) errors in grammar and mechanics, and the students' language is precise, appropriate, and not repetitive.

Suggestions for Preparing for the Open Topic

First, remember that you have been analyzing high-quality literature for years; you should have the confidence to know that you can do it.

Go to the College Board website at https://apcentral.collegeboard.org/courses/ap-english-literature-and-composition/exam and review past AP prompts (remember that the open topic is always the third prompt). As you read each prompt, make a short list of two to three works that you have read that you know would work well. Do not make a long list of works; after all, on the day of the exam, you only need to write on one.

Then, follow these steps a few weeks before the exam:

- Make a list of the major works you studied in grades 9–12 (e.g., *Great Expectations, Oedipus the King, The Grapes of Wrath, Heart of Darkness*).
- Narrow the list to three to five novels (or full-length plays) that really meant a lot to you, that "spoke" to you clearly, works that you've got a lot to say about, especially good, deep universal truths. In general, avoid works that you read in your early years, especially something you read as far back as middle school. You want the work you select to be an appropriate college-level text. Also, in general, list the books you've analyzed, not just read for pleasure and enjoyed. Consider having at least one older piece on your list, say from the 19th century.

- Next, review your list of works. Go to a reputable online or research source to refresh your memory. You need to know these basics:
  - Title and author (be precisely correct on both, please!)
  - Main characters and their dominant traits (again, correctness is so important! It looks bad when students get the names wrong or write "I don't remember, so I'll call him Joe")
  - Major plot events (to use as your examples; remember, be concrete, specific, and concise)
  - Setting (both time and place and their appropriateness)
  - Point of view
  - Important symbols
  - Important quotations (only about three really key ones, and, IF you use them at all, remember to blend them into your own sentences)
  - Anything else helpful, such as a great motif or a dominant style element
- Make a study sheet of the above elements, but don't go on and on. One page per work is plenty. Review these sheets during the days before the exam.
- Remember that articulating more than one universal truth (theme) per work is important. Great literature has many great ideas for you to share. Mulling over more than one idea will give you the flexibility to write on any topic that appears on the exam.

Which Works Appear Most Often?

Teachers frequently love to analyze which works have been suggested on the exam. While the following works have appeared on the suggested list more than others, do not adjust your preparation based on this list. Just take it for what it's worth—simply a list of suggestions. In reality, it does NOT represent all of the works students choose to write on. Remember that translated works will no longer be listed, but you can still write on one.

In order of frequency, the most often suggested works are:

Invisible Man by Ralph Ellison

Wuthering Heights by Emily Brontë

Great Expectations by Charles Dickens

Heart of Darkness by Joseph Conrad

Jane Eyre by Charlotte Brontë

Crime and Punishment by Fyodor Dostoevsky

King Lear by William Shakespeare

The Adventures of Huckleberry Finn by Mark Twain

Beloved by Toni Morrison

The Scarlet Letter by Nathaniel Hawthorne

The Great Gatsby by F. Scott Fitzgerald

Moby Dick by Herman Melville

A Portrait of the Artist as a Young Man by James Joyce

Their Eyes Were Watching God by Zora Neale Hurston

Examining the Task on Open Topic Questions

Now that you understand the scope of the open topic, let's examine recent topics by pointing out what you should focus on in the prompt and mention some works that worked well for that given topic.

2018: Literary characters have often received some kind of gift, whether literal or figurative, an object or a quality. Sometimes this gift can be both a blessing and a burden. Choose a character from a novel, epic poem, or play who has received a gift that is both advantageous and disadvantageous and analyze the complexity of the gift and how it enhances the meaning of the work as a whole.

What to notice: The prompt requires that you analyze *only one* character who receives *only one* gift. The concept of "the gift" is wide open, since it can apply to something tangible or some character trait that the character is "given." However, notice you *must* address both the advantage *and* the disadvantage of the gift, understanding that gifts are complex.

Some Successful Works

Work	Character	The Gift
Frankenstein	Dr. Frankenstein	high intelligence; love of knowledge; ability to create life
Frankenstein	the monster	life itself; love of knowledge
The Picture of Dorian Gray	Dorian Gray	physical beauty
The Bluest Eye	Pauline	passion for organization
Things Fall Apart	Okonkwo	masculine pride
A Raisin in the Sun	Mama	husband's inheritance
Heart of Darkness	Kurtz	power over others

* * *

2017: Analyze a character from a novel, epic poem, or play who has mysterious origins, exploring how these origins shape the character and that character's relationships with others, and how these mysterious origins contribute to the meaning of the work as a whole.

What to notice: Choose *only one* character whose origins are mysterious or unusual; you have great latitude to define what "origins," "mysterious," and "unusual" mean. Notice the complexity of the tasks; analyze how mysterious origins shape the one character *and* that character's relationships with others, *plus* how these origins (not necessarily just the character) contribute meaning to the overall work.

Some successful works: *Beloved, Song of Solomon, One Flew Over the Cuckoo's Nest, Brave New World, Light in August, Wuthering Heights, Their Eyes Were Watching God*

* * *

2016: Choose a character from a novel or a play who intentionally deceives others, whether the deception was meant to hurt or help the other characters. Analyze that character's motives and how the deception contributes to the meaning of the work as a whole.

What to notice: Analyze *only one* character who deceives others with either the purpose of hurting or helping them. Be sure to analyze *why* the character deceives and what the character's motive is. The prompt does not ask about the consequences of the deception. Do not confuse deception with other negative traits such as greed or cruelty. The Chief AP Reader this year pointed out that many of the high-scoring essays expanded their discussion of deception to include "historical, cultural, and social issues of class, race, gender, and sexuality" that added to the meaning of the work as a whole.

Some successful works: *The Great Gatsby; Frankenstein; Beloved; Bless Me, Ultima; A Doll's House; The Kite Runner; Invisible Man; Heart of Darkness; Hamlet*

* * *

2015: Choose a novel, epic poem, or play in which acts of cruelty are significant to the theme. Analyze how cruelty functions in the work as a whole and what the cruelty reveals about the perpetrator and/or victim.

What to notice: This prompt, instead of asking you to analyze only one character, asks you to explore "acts of cruelty." Notice that the word "acts" is plural. This prompt also differs from others in that it assigns only two tasks; most prompts have three. Some high-scoring essays discussed the ways in which the distinction between the perpetrator and the victim may become blurred. The Chief AP Reader's commentary pointed out how many strong student writers addressed the significance of cruelty by discussing such ideas as "the futility of wars, the pervasiveness of racism, the lingering traces of cultural imperialism, the ongoing struggle of feminism, and the abuse of those who are labeled as different."

Some successful works: *The Bluest Eye, The Great Gatsby, All the Pretty Horses, A Passage to India, The Iliad, Heart of Darkness, Othello, Lord of the Flies, The Aeneid, Invisible Man*

* * *

2014: Choose a character from a novel or a play who has deliberately sacrificed, surrendered, or given up something that highlights the character's values. Analyze how the sacrifice illuminates the character's values and adds significance to the meaning of the work as a whole.

What to notice: Discuss *only one* character who has sacrificed something significant, then analyze how that sacrifice adds insight into the character's values and to the meaning of the work as a whole. The more talented students analyzed the deeper meaning of the text within the context of larger ideas in the real world.

Some successful works: *Song of Solomon, The Poisonwood Bible, To Kill a Mockingbird, Coriolanus, Of Mice and Men, Invisible Man, Crime and Punishment, King Lear*

* * *

2013: The prompt defined the term "bildungsroman," a coming-of-age novel that explores the development of a character who eventually discovers his or her place in the world. Choose one significant moment in the development of the protagonist in a bildungsroman and analyze how that moment shapes the meaning of the work as a whole.

What to notice: This prompt presents a few difficulties; be sure to read it carefully. First, you must choose *only one* character from a novel that fits the concept of a bildungsroman, a coming-of-age novel. Then you must select *only one* significant moment from that text, and you must use it to explore how it develops the character and adds meaning to the work as a whole. This is intended to help you avoid banal plot summary.

Some successful works: *The Adventures of Huckleberry Finn, A Portrait of the Artist as a Young Man, Candide, Song of Solomon, Tess of the d'Urbervilles, Great Expectations*

* * *

2012: Choose a character in a novel or play whose psychological or moral traits are shaped by the surrounding cultural, physical, or geographic environment. Analyze how the surroundings affect the character and illuminate the meaning of the work as a whole.

What to notice: Choose *only one* character and analyze how the setting affects, alters, or forms that character and also explore how the character's surroundings add meaning to the work as a whole. The phrase "psychological or moral traits" helps you avoid mere discussion of how the character's actions are a response to the physical world; instead, the phrase invites you to explore the connection between the character's inner world and his or her outer surroundings. Also notice that the prompt offers the opportunity to address the character's surroundings in terms of cultural milieu, a physical terrain or space, or a geographical or national territory, but it does not mention including any discussion of other characters who "surround" the character you chose.

Some successful works: *Heart of Darkness; 1984; Death of a Salesman; Cry, the Beloved Country; The Great Gatsby; King Lear; Great Expectations; Invisible Man*

* * *

2011: Choose a character from a novel or play who faces and responds in some significant way to justice or injustice. Analyze how well the character comprehends justice, the degree to which the character is successful in the search for justice, and the significance of this search to the work as a whole.

What to notice: Choose *only one* character who confronts either justice or injustice and then address all of the tasks: You must analyze (1) how the character understands justice, (2) how successful the character is in searching for justice, and (3) how it adds significance to the work as a whole. These tasks are designed to steer you away from simplistic plot summary. The discussion of the character's success opens up the complex notion that the search for justice may not be entirely successful.

Some successful works: *Beloved, The Grapes of Wrath, Hamlet, The Scarlet Letter, Catch-22, Native Son, Crime and Punishment, Invisible Man, The Picture of Dorian Gray*

* * *

2010: Choose a character from a novel, epic poem, or play who experiences some degree of exile and becomes cut off from birthplace, family, homeland, or other special place. Analyze how the character's experience with exile is both alienating and enriching and how the experience enhances the meaning of the work as a whole.

What to notice: Choose *only one* appropriate character who experiences some form of exile and then explore how the displaced experience is *both* hurtful and helpful to the character. This allows you to analyze the complexity of exile as you address all parts of the prompt.

Some successful works: *The Odyssey, Oedipus Rex, Invisible Man, Heart of Darkness, The Tempest, The Kite Runner, A Portrait of the Artist as a Young Man*

Overall Suggestions and Observations for All Essays

Teachers and professors involved with the AP English Literature and Composition Exam habitually discuss it. The following suggestions and observations will help you avoid common mistakes and understand how to make your analysis stronger.

- Students need to remember to *address the entire prompt*; too often low-scoring essays ignore the overall significance or importance of the work. Understand how many tasks you have to address.
- Always *read the poem and passage carefully*. A cursory reading will likely result in an unfocused response or a misreading of the work.
- Don't oversimplify! Embrace complexity, ambiguity, paradox, and irony. Know that the works presented on the exam are rich and deep; dig into their multiple meanings.
- Students are well-served by planning the essay before writing. Not only does it help organization of the essay, but it also gives you time to ponder the work before producing sentences.
- Students are generally more adept at analyzing prose than poetry, no matter how accessible the poem may be.
- Students are usually most comfortable with the open topic, and it usually has the highest average score of the three essays in any given year.
- Students who write lower-scoring essays typically have difficulty making the leap from simply listing literary devices to explaining their *significance* or how they *create effect* in poetry and prose.
- Too often poetry and prose essays are "device-driven instead of insight-driven." This means that low-scoring essays organize paragraphs around literary devices but do not take the extra step of analyzing what insight those devices add to the work's significance.
- Students too often forget that "complexity is the opposite of superficiality," and instead of analyzing complex ideas, simply paraphrase the work.
- Students need to incorporate quotations into their essays smoothly and avoid stringing them together without any analysis.
- In the open topic, the vast majority of low-scoring essays lapse into plot summary instead of analysis.
- In the open topic, you will never be asked to choose more than one character or more than one work.
- In the open topic, always choose a work from the genre(s) in the prompt. The directions always ask for a novel, but frequently they also allow you to use a play or an epic poem. Never do they ask for a short story or a shorter poem.
- Please punctuate titles correctly. Poems and short stories are placed inside quotation marks; novels, full-length plays, and epic poems should be underlined.

Chapter 5

Definitions of Terms Used in AP Literature and Composition Exams

Terms for the Multiple-Choice and Free-Response Sections

Some of the following terms may be used specifically in the multiple-choice questions and/or answer explanations, or in the free-response prompt instructions. You might choose to incorporate others into your essay writing to help identify and explain the effect of a literary device used by an author or to help build your analysis. The terms in this list can apply to either prose or poetry, although some are used more often in one genre than the other.

Terms that are marked with an asterisk have shown up on past exams, either in the multiple-choice section or in the free-response section.

Note: Terms that are specific to poetry or grammar follow this list.

*ad hominem argument: From the Latin meaning "to or against the person," this is an argument that attacks the opponent, rather than the issues; it appeals to emotion rather than reason, to feeling rather than intellect.

*allegory: The device of using character and/or story elements to symbolically represent an abstraction in addition to their literal meaning. In some allegories, for example, an author may intend the characters to personify an abstraction such as hope or freedom. The allegorical meaning usually deals with a moral truth or a generalization about human existence. Examples include Bunyan's *Pilgrim's Progress*, Spenser's "The Faerie Queen," and Orwell's *Animal Farm*. Compare with *parable*.

*alliteration: The repetition of sounds, especially initial consonant sounds, in two or more neighboring words (as in "she sells sea shells"). Although the term is not usually used in the multiple-choice section, you may want to analyze any alliteration you find in an essay passage. The repeated sounds can serve to reinforce meaning, to unify ideas, and/or to supply a musical sound.

*allusion: A direct or indirect reference to something that is presumably commonly known, such as an event, book, myth, place, or work of art. Allusions can be historical (such as referring to Hitler), literary (such as referring to Kurtz in *Heart of Darkness*), religious (such as referring to Noah and the flood), or mythical (such as referring to Atlas). There are, of course, many more possibilities, and a single work may use multiple layers of allusion.

ambiguity: This term refers to the multiple meanings, either intentional or unintentional, of a word, phrase, sentence, or passage. Ambiguity also can include a sense of uncertainty or ambivalence that a work presents.

*analogy: Drawing a similarity or making a comparison between two different things or the relationship between them. An analogy can explain something unfamiliar by associating it with, or pointing out its similarity to, something more familiar. Analogies can also make writing more vivid, imaginative, and intellectually engaging.

anaphora: Deliberate repetition of the beginning clauses or phrases in sentences to create an effect. For example, Winston Churchill famously claimed, "We shall not flag or fail. We shall go on to the end. We shall fight in France. We shall fight on the seas and oceans. We shall fight with growing confidence and growing strength in the air. We shall defend our island, whatever the cost shall be." His repetition of "We shall . . ." creates a rhetorical effect of solidarity and determination. See also *epistrophe*, which is the opposite of anaphora.

anecdote: A short narrative account of an event that may be amusing, unusual, revealing, or interesting. A good anecdote has a single, definite point and is used to clarify abstract points, and/or to humanize individuals so that readers can relate to them, or to create a memorable image in the reader's mind.

antagonist: From the Greek word that means "opponent" or "rival," the antagonist is the character or group of characters who stand in opposition, either physically, mentally, or both, to the *protagonist*. For example, in Shakespeare's play *Othello*, Iago serves as Othello's antagonist. Not every piece of literature has an antagonist, and not all antagonists are villains.

antihero: A literary character, sometimes the *protagonist*, who is not a traditional hero. While the stereotypical hero may be dashing, strong, brave, resourceful, and/or attractive, the antihero may be incompetent, unlucky, clumsy, dumb, ugly, or clownish. Examples include the senile protagonist of Cervantes' *Don Quixote*. An antihero brings a certain spice to a script that an ordinary hero-villain format cannot because an antihero is multifaceted. He or she can be used to represent many things at the same time, such as social flaws, human frailties, and political culture; usually the antihero combines good and evil, and thus represents the true nature of humanity.

*antithesis: A figure of speech involving a seeming contradiction of ideas, words, clauses, or sentences within a balanced grammatical structure. The resulting parallelism serves to emphasize opposition of ideas. The familiar phrase "Man proposes, God disposes" is an example of antithesis, as is John Dryden's description in *The Hind and the Panther*: "Too black for heaven, and yet too white for hell."

aphorism: A terse statement of known authorship that expresses a general truth or moral principle. For example, consider Alexander Pope's famous line "To err is human, to forgive divine" from *Essay on Criticism*. (If the authorship is unknown, the statement is generally considered to be a folk proverb.) An aphorism can be used to provide a memorable summation of the author's point. See also *maxim*.

*apostrophe: A figure of speech that directly addresses an absent or imaginary person or a personified abstraction, such as liberty or love, or an inanimate object. The effect may be to add familiarity or to increase the emotional intensity. William Wordsworth addresses John Milton as he writes, "Milton, thou shouldst be living at this hour: England hath need of thee," and John Donne speaks directly to death when he writes, "Death be not proud."

archetype: In literature, an archetype is a typical and recognizable character, action, situation, setting, or theme that seems to represent universal patterns of human nature. Archetypical characters include the hero, the mother figure, the innocent youth, the mentor, the villain, and the scapegoat. Archetypical situations include the journey, the initiation, the fall, and the conflict between good and evil.

aside: In drama, this phrase refers to a few words or a short passage spoken by one character to the audience while the other characters on stage seemingly cannot hear the speaker's words. The aside reveals information about the plot or the other characters. It is a theatrical convention that an aside is never audible to the other characters on stage. Contrast with *soliloquy*.

*assonance: Repetition of internal vowel sounds in words that are close to each other. For example, notice the long "i" sound in the poem "Annabelle Lee" by Edgar Allan Poe: "And so all the night-tide, I lie down by the side / of my darling—my darling—my life and my bride." Compare that with the long "o" sound in William Wordsworth's "Daffodils": "A host of golden daffodils." Assonance accentuates musical effect, develops internal rhythm, and creates mood and flow. See also *consonance* and *dissonance*.

asyndeton: Deliberate choice to eliminate conjunctions that would normally join phrases or clauses. It creates speed and urgency. For example, "I came. I saw. I conquered" has much more force than "I came, and then I saw, and then I conquered." Compare with *polysyndeton*.

atmosphere: The overall emotional mood created by the entirety of a literary work, established partly by the setting and partly by the author's choice of objects that are described. Even such elements as a description of the weather can contribute to the atmosphere. Frequently, the atmosphere foreshadows upcoming events. See also *mood*.

attitude: The disposition toward, or opinion of, a subject by a speaker, author, or character. Attitude usually refers to a writer's intellectual position or emotion regarding the subject of the writing. In the free-response section, you will often be asked what the writer's attitude is and how his or her language conveys that attitude. Also be aware that, although the singular term "attitude" is used in this definition and on the exam, the passage will rarely have only one attitude. More often than not, the author's attitude will be more complex, and the student who presents this complexity—no matter how subtle the differences—will appear to be more astute than the student who only uses one adjective to describe attitude. Of course, don't force an attitude for which there is no evidence in the passage; instead, understand that an accurate statement of an author's attitude is not likely to be a blatantly obvious idea. See also *tone*.

*bathos: Alexander Pope coined this term, mocking the unintentional mishaps of lesser writers who, in the process of trying to appear elevated, lapse into trivial or mundane imagery, phrasing, or ideas. Later comic writers use bathos intentionally for mirthful effects. One common trend of bathos is the amusing arrangement of items so that the listed items descend from grandiosity to absurdity. For example, "The famous gangster was wanted for conspiracy, murder, terrorism, and overdue library books." Famous examples appear in Lord Byron's mock epic *Don Juan* and in Alexander Pope's satires. See also ***pathos***.

cacophony: A combination of words with rough or unharmonious sounds that is used for a noisy or jarring poetic effect. It creates colorful, noisy, loud, and energetic sounds like the beat of a drum or the crash of a cymbal. It uses harsh consonant sounds that require a strong, forced delivery, like *p, d, g,* and *k*. Compare with *euphony*.

caricature: A pictorial or literary representation of a character, in which the subject's distinctive features or peculiarities are deliberately exaggerated to produce a comic or grotesque effect. Sometimes a caricature can be so exaggerated that it becomes a grotesque imitation or misrepresentation. Synonymous words include *burlesque,* **parody,** *travesty,* **satire,** and *lampoon*.

carpe diem: Literally, the phrase is Latin for "seize the day," and refers to a common moral or **theme** in literature that illustrates making the most out of life and enjoying it before it ends. Poetry or literature that illustrates this moral is often said to be of the "carpe diem" tradition. Examples include Marvell's "To His Coy Mistress" and Herrick's "To the Virgins, to Make Much of Time."

catharsis: When a reader or dramatic audience experiences an emotional release that brings about a moral or spiritual renewal or brings welcome relief from tension and anxiety. According to Aristotle's *Poetics* (c. 350 B.C.E.), catharsis is the ultimate end of any tragic artistic work. It is through the reader's or audience's feeling of pity (for the tragic figures) and fear (for themselves) that we effectively release these emotions.

chiasmus: A figure of speech based on inverted parallelism. It is a rhetorical figure in which two clauses are related to one another through a reversal of their terms. The purpose is usually to make a larger point or to provide balance and order. In classical rhetoric, the parallel structures did not repeat words; this structure is seen in Alexander Pope's *Essay on Man:* "His time a moment, and a point his space." However, contemporary standards do allow for such repeated words; a commonly cited example comes from John F. Kennedy's inaugural address: ". . . ask not what your country can do for you—ask what you can do for your country."

climax: The moment in a narrative work at which the crisis reaches its point of greatest intensity and is thereafter resolved. It is also the peak of emotional response from a reader or spectator and usually the turning point in the action. Short works traditionally have one climax; of course, longer works, such as novels, may have many.

*colloquialism: The use of slang or informality in speech or writing. While not generally acceptable for formal writing, colloquialisms give language a conversational, familiar tone. Colloquial expressions in writing can include local or regional dialects.

comic relief: A humorous scene, incident, character, or bit of dialogue that occurs after some serious, tragic, or frightening moment. Comic relief is deliberately designed to relieve emotional intensity and simultaneously heighten and highlight the seriousness or tragedy of the main action. Shakespeare provides many examples, such as most of the scenes with the nurse in *Romeo and Juliet*, the porter scene in *Macbeth*, and the grave-digger scene in *Hamlet*.

coming-of-age story: A work in which an adolescent protagonist moves toward adulthood by a process of experience and, usually, disillusionment. This character loses his or her innocence, discovers that previous preconceptions are false, or has the security of childhood torn away, but usually the character matures during this process. These works are sometimes referred to as a bildungsroman. Examples include Ray Bradbury's *Dandelion Wine*, James Joyce's *A Portrait of the Artist as a Young Man*, and Jane Austen's *Northanger Abbey*.

*conceit: A fanciful expression, usually in the form of an extended metaphor or a surprising analogy between seemingly dissimilar objects. A conceit displays intellectual cleverness due to the unusual comparison being made.

conflict: The engine that drives the plot, conflict involves the antagonism between opposing entities, such as two characters (such as a protagonist and an antagonist), between two large groups of people, or between the protagonist and a larger problem such as the forces of nature, ideas, or social mores. Conflict may also be partially or even completely internal, such as the protagonist struggling with psychological difficulties. Complex works frequently have multiple levels of conflict. To simplify, think of conflict as having these sources:

- *Person vs. Self:* The classic inner conflict occurs as the character battles some kind of inner demons, such as an obsession, or some polar-opposite desires, such as being torn between two alternative options in life. One of the major conflicts in *Hamlet* is the conundrum Hamlet faces: Must he obey his (dead) father whose ghost commands him to murder or should he follow his own conscience?

- *Person vs. Person:* Conflict that pits one person against another is about as classic as a storyline can get. This type of conflict is pretty much self-explanatory, with one person struggling for victory over another. For example, Javert and Jean Valjean in *Les Misérables* clash over their conflicting opinions on justice and mercy.

- *Person vs. Fate/God(s):* This type of conflict occurs when a character is trapped, bound by an inevitable destiny; freedom and free will often seem illusory in these stories. You'll find this recurring theme in Greek mythology. For example, Oedipus is unaware that he is fated to marry his own mother, but Odysseus is all too aware of his predicament as he is stymied on his homeward journey due to Poseidon's anger. What can humans do in the face of the gods and fate? Only endure, it seems.

- *Person vs. Society:* This conflict follows the problems of an individual or a group fighting against injustices in society, sometimes successfully, sometimes not so successfully. Atticus Finch battles injustice and the social mores of a small town in *To Kill a Mockingbird*.

- *Person vs. Nature:* In this scenario, humankind battles for survival against the forces of nature and its awesome power. Herman Melville's *Moby Dick* tells the story of one man's obsession with overcoming nature that is nature embodied as a gigantic, monstrous whale. A shorter example is Stephen Crane's "The Open Boat," in which shipwrecked men in a lifeboat struggle against a hostile nature just to stay alive and get to shore.

- *Person vs. the Unknown:* Often seen in science fiction and fantasy, this conflict pits the protagonist against something unseen and/or unknown. H. G. Wells' novel *The War of the Worlds* is a prime example.

- *Person vs. Technology:* This type of conflict focuses on a person or group of people fighting to overcome unemotional and unsympathetic technology, machines that believe they no longer require humanity. Arthur C. Clarke's *2001: A Space Odyssey* tells the gripping story of a lone astronaut pitted against a supercomputer.

*connotation: The nonliteral meaning of a word; the implied, suggested meanings or feelings that are associated with the word. Connotations may involve ideas, emotions, or attitudes. See also **denotation**.

*consonance: A special type of **alliteration** that has a repeated pattern of identical consonant sounds around different vowels, such as in "linger longer," "flip flop," and "longer languor." See also **assonance** and **dissonance**.

*convention: A common feature that has been used so often, so widely, that it has become traditional or expected in a specific genre, such as drama, novels, short stories, or different forms of poetry. For example, it is a convention for an English sonnet to have 14 lines with a specific rhyme scheme, whereas the villanelle has a different set form. Likewise, the use of a chorus and the unities are standard dramatic conventions of Greek tragedy.

*denotation: The strict, literal, dictionary definition of a word, devoid of any emotion, attitude, or color. See also **connotation**.

*denouement: The events in a narrative that follow the climax and the falling action. Traditionally, it wraps up the loose ends and it resolves any unsettled conflicts. Consider the last line of stereotypical fairy tales: "And they lived happily ever after."

details: This term is likely to show up in the free-response prompts; it refers to the facts, particulars, individual items, or parts that make up a larger picture or story. Look for these details, then address how they come together to create the whole, in the way that jigsaw puzzle pieces are small details but, when joined properly, form a coherent big picture. Notice how that big picture is more nuanced because of how all the individual details fit together.

*deus ex machina: Literally meaning "god from machine," it was originally used in Greek drama when an actor, portraying one of the gods, was lowered onto the stage to solve the humans' problems via divine guidance. It is frequently used mockingly, implying ludicrous and implausible solutions, as if the writer could not think of a better way to resolve the characters' conflicts.

*diction: Related to style, diction refers to the writer's particular word choices, especially with regard to their correctness, clearness, and effectiveness. You should be able to describe an author's diction (for example, formal or informal, ornate or plain) and understand the ways in which diction can be used to complement the author's purpose. Diction, combined with syntax, figurative language, literary devices, and so on, creates an author's own individual style.

didactic: From the Greek, "didactic" literally means "instructive." Didactic works have the primary aim of teaching or instructing, especially teaching moral or ethical principles.

*dissonance: The juxtaposition of jarring sounds. It occurs when sounds are so different that they clash with each other. For example, notice how hard it is to read these lines from Ted Hughes' "Wind": "The wind flung a magpie away and a black- / Back gull bent like an iron bar slowly." See also *assonance* and *consonance*.

epic hero: The main character in an epic work or epic poem—typically one who embodies the treasured values of his or her culture. For example, Odysseus is the epic hero in the Greek epic *The Odyssey*—in which he, being "the man who was never at a loss," embodies the ingenuity and quick thinking that Greek culture admired. Compare with *tragic hero*.

epigram: From the Greek for "to write on, to inscribe," an epigram was originally a brief inscription, frequently a short poem, on a tomb or building. Today, it refers to a short, witty, satirical statement in poetry or prose that is both graceful and ingenious. Oscar Wilde is famous for many epigrams, such as "I can resist everything but temptation."

epilogue: A conclusion that is added on to a literary work. In drama it takes the form of one actor stepping out and speaking directly to the audience, asking for their indulgence and appreciation, such as Puck's famous epilogue in Shakespeare's *A Midsummer Night's Dream*. Its opposite is the *prologue*.

epistolary: Derived from the Greek word *epistolē*, which means "letter," this is a literary genre in which writers use letters, journals, and diary entries in their works, or they tell their stories or deliver messages through a series of letters. In Alice Walker's epistolary novel *The Color Purple*, the impoverished black teenage girl, Celie, tells her story through writing letters to both her sister and God.

epistrophe: Deliberately repeating ending clauses or phrases in sentences to create dramatic effect. For example, President Lyndon B. Johnson used epistrophe that urged people to come together for a common cause when he addressed the U.S. Congress in 1965: "There is no Negro problem. There is no Southern problem. There is no Northern problem. There is only an American problem. And we are met here tonight as Americans—not as Democrats or Republicans—we are met here as Americans to solve that problem." See also its opposite, *anaphora*.

epitaph: Not to be confused with the *epigram*, an epitaph is literally the inscription carved on a gravestone; it is derived from the Greek word *epitaphios*, which means "funeral oration." Many famous literary figures have well-known epitaphs, such as John Keats' "Here lies one whose name was writ in water."

eponymous: In literature, this describes a work that is titled after its lead character, such as *David Copperfield* or *Jane Eyre*. An eponym is a word derived from the proper name of a person or place. For example, the word *stentorian* comes from the loud-mouthed Stentor in Greek legend, and *herculean* comes from the muscle-bound hero Hercules of mythology.

euphemism: From the Greek for "good speech," euphemisms are a more agreeable or less offensive substitute for generally unpleasant words or concepts. The euphemism may be used to adhere to standards of social or political correctness, or to add humor or ironic understatement. Saying "earthly remains" rather than "corpse" is an example of euphemism.

euphony: Derived from the Greek word *euphonos*, meaning "sweet-voiced," euphony involves the use of words and phrases that are distinguished as having a wide range of noteworthy melody or loveliness in the sounds they create. This technique gives pleasing and soothing effects to the ear due to repeated vowels and smooth consonants. It utilizes long vowel sounds and harmonious consonants, such as *l, m, n, r,* and soft *f* and *v* sounds. Contrast with *cacophony*.

exposition: A literary device that introduces background information about events, settings, characters, or other elements of a work to the audience or to the readers.

*extended metaphor: A metaphor developed at great length, occurring frequently or used repeatedly throughout a work. See also *metaphor*.

fable: A short piece of fiction that features animals, mythical creatures, or other inanimate objects as characters and usually includes or illustrates a moral lesson. The distinguishing feature of a fable is the anthropomorphism or *personification* involved that leads to the moral lesson. At times, as in Aesop's Fables, this moral lesson is summed up at the end of the fable in a short *maxim*. The word "fable" comes from the Latin word *fābula*, meaning "a story or tale." A person who writes fables is called a fabulist. A fable is similar to a *parable*.

falling action: The events in a narration that occur after the *climax*, but prior to the *denouement*. Frequently the falling action and denouement are intricately linked, especially in short stories.

*figurative language: Writing or speech that is not intended to carry a literal meaning and is usually meant to be imaginative and vivid. See also *figure of speech*.

*figure of speech: A literary device used to produce *figurative language*. Many figures of speech compare dissimilar things. Figures of speech include apostrophe, hyperbole, irony, metaphor, metonymy, oxymoron, paradox, personification, simile, synecdoche, and understatement.

*flashback: A break in the narration in which present action is temporarily interrupted so that the reader can witness past events—usually in the form of a character's memories, dreams, narration, or so forth. Flashbacks allow an author to inform the reader about a place or a character, or they can be used to delay important details until just before a dramatic moment. Frequently the action resumes right where it was interrupted when the flashback is finished. *The Odyssey* contains a monumental flashback when Odysseus tells of his adventures, and he takes four chapters to do so!

*foil: A character that, by contrast, highlights or emphasizes the opposing traits in another character. Usually the foil is a minor character whose traits shed light on a major character. For example, in Shakespeare's *Hamlet*, the minor character Laertes is the son of Polonius and an unthinking man of quick action, so he acts as a foil to the intelligent but reluctant Hamlet.

*foreshadowing: The use of a suggestive word or phrase or hints that help to set the stage as the story unfolds; this gives the reader a tip-off that something is going to happen, but without revealing it directly or spoiling the suspense.

frame story: Frequently considered "a story within a story," it is a narrative that has an "outer frame" that sets up the telling of another story. Chaucer's *Canterbury Tales* has the outer frame setup of the pilgrims telling tales as they travel to Canterbury; their individual tales are the inner story. *Heart of Darkness* uses the outer frame of passengers waiting for the tide to change as they sit on a ship outside of London; the inner frame occurs when Marlow tells his captive audience of his travels from Brussels to the Congo. When you discuss a frame story, consider what effect the outer frame has on the narrative and how it affects the author's purpose. Most frame stories will have breaks in the storytelling, when the time returns to the present before the speaker continues his story.

genre: The major categories into which various literary works fit. The basic divisions of literature are prose, poetry, and drama. However, "genre" is a flexible term; within these broad boundaries are many subdivisions that are often called genres themselves. For example, prose can be divided into fiction (novels and short stories) or nonfiction (essays, biographies, autobiographies, and so on). Poetry can be divided into such subcategories as lyric, dramatic, narrative, epic, and so on. Drama can be divided into tragedy, comedy, melodrama, farce, and so on. On the AP exam, all of the passages will come from the genres of fiction.

grotesque: A work that is characterized by exaggerated distortions or incongruities, such as the fiction of Edgar Allan Poe or *The Metamorphosis* by Franz Kafka.

hamartia: This term from Greek tragedy, which literally means "missing the mark," originally described an archer who misses the target. As a literary term, hamartia now signifies a tragic flaw that stems from one's positive traits; it's as if the character's positive attribute grows to unmanageable proportions and in so doing becomes a fault, which causes catastrophe. In the classic sense, these catastrophic results follow the tragic hero's failure to recognize that his own downfall (as well as others') could have been avoided had he recognized and tamed his fault earlier. The irony of hamartia is that the character trait that brings down the hero is initially admired, like love, ambition, patriotism, and honor. For example, in the character of Macbeth, the personal ambition that makes him so respected is the same characteristic that also permits Lady Macbeth to bait him to commit murder and treason. Similarly, in *Julius Caesar*, Brutus is ennobled by his unstinting love of the Roman Republic, but this same patriotism causes him to kill his best friend, Julius Caesar. These normally positive traits of self-motivation and patriotism caused these two protagonists to "miss the mark," and they realize too late the ethical and spiritual consequences of their actions. See also **hubris** and **tragic hero**.

hubris: Excessive self-pride that turns into arrogance, a formerly good trait that becomes a **hamartia**. Pride by itself is an admirable trait, but when driven to excess becomes obsessive and all-consuming. It inhibits the character from recognizing his personal limitations and understanding that he needs a modicum of humility. This leads to overwhelming pride, and this in turn leads to the character's downfall.

*hyperbole: A figure of speech using deliberate exaggeration or overstatement. Hyperbole often has a comic effect; however, a serious effect is also possible. Often, hyperbole is intended to produce *irony* at the same time. Compare to **understatement**.

*idyll: A simple descriptive work in poetry or prose that deals with rustic life or pastoral scenes or that suggests a mood of idealized peace and contentment.

*imagery: The sensory details or figurative language an author uses to provide description, arouse emotion, or represent abstractions. On a physical level, imagery uses terms related to the five senses: visual, auditory, tactile, gustatory, or olfactory imagery. On a broader and deeper level, however, one image can represent more than one thing. For example, a rose may present visual imagery while also representing the color in a woman's cheeks. An author, therefore, may use complex imagery while simultaneously employing other figures of speech, especially metaphor and simile. In addition, this term can apply to the total of all the images in a work. On the AP exam, pay attention to *how* an author creates imagery and the effect of that imagery.

infer: To draw a reasonable conclusion from the information presented. When a multiple-choice question asks for an inference to be drawn from the passage, the most direct, most reasonable inference is the safest answer choice. If an inference is implausible, it's unlikely to be the correct answer. Note that if the answer choice is something that is directly stated in the passage, it is *not* an inference and therefore is wrong. In your essays, you will demonstrate inferential thinking as you analyze how literary devices create effects.

*in medias res: Literally, "in the middle of things," this refers to a work in which the action is not presented in chronological order. Usually a work that uses this technique has a significant flashback that explains the earlier actions. Classically used in epic poetry, the technique heightens tension and creates mystery.

invective: An emotionally violent, verbal denunciation or an attack using strong, abusive language.

*irony: The contrast between what is stated explicitly and what is really meant; the difference between what appears to be and what is actually true. Irony is used for many reasons, but frequently, it's used to create poignancy or humor. In general, three major types of irony are used in literature:

1. In *verbal* irony, the words literally state the opposite of the writer's (or speaker's) true meaning.
2. In *situational* irony, events turn out the opposite of what was expected. What the characters and readers think ought to happen actually does not happen.
3. In *dramatic* irony, facts or events are unknown to a character in a play or piece of fiction but known to the reader, audience, or other characters in the work.

maxim: A proverb, a short statement believed to contain wisdom or insight into human nature. The defining characteristic of a maxim is that it's *pithy*—that is, it packs a lot of meaning into just a few words. Very similar to *aphorisms*, maxims are frequently more straightforward. Whereas aphorisms often use *metaphor*, maxims may or may not do this. Examples include "Four legs good, two legs bad" and "All animals are equal, but some animals are more equal than others" from George Orwell's *Animal Farm*. In Shakespeare's *Hamlet*, the inane Polonius speaks ironically when he utters his wisest line in the play, "To thine own self be true."

melodrama: A dramatic form characterized by extreme sentimentality, larger-than-life emotion, and unbelievable and sensationalized action, followed by a hollow happy ending. Melodramas originally referred to romantic plays featuring music, singing, and dancing, but by the 18th century they connoted a work with a simplified and coincidental plot, featuring *bathos* and happy endings. These melodramatic traits are present in many literary and cinematic works today. You are undoubtedly familiar with the use of "melodramatic" as a pejorative description of a person, and of the contemporary phrase "drama queen" that stems from it.

*metaphor: A figure of speech using implied comparison of seemingly unlike things or the substitution of one item for the other, suggesting some similarity. For example, consider Carson McCullers' novel title *The Heart Is a Lonely Hunter*. Also, when Romeo says, "But soft! What light through yonder window breaks? / It is the East, and Juliet is the sun!" he is using metaphor to compare her window to the east and Juliet to the sun. Metaphorical language makes writing more vivid, imaginative, thought-provoking, and meaningful. See also *simile*.

*metonymy: A term from the Greek meaning "changed label" or "substitute name," metonymy is a figure of speech in which the name of one object is substituted for that of another closely associated with it. A news release that claims "the White House declared" rather than "the President declared" is using metonymy.

*mood: The literary definition of mood refers to the prevailing atmosphere or emotional aura of a work. In addition, the setting, tone, and events can affect the mood. In this usage, mood is similar to tone and atmosphere. This term has two distinct technical meanings in English writing; see also *grammatical mood* in the "Grammatical Terms" section later in this chapter.

motif: In a literary work, a motif can be seen as an image, sound, action, or other figure that has a symbolic significance and contributes toward the development of a *theme*. Motif and theme are linked in a literary work, but a motif is a recurring image, idea, or symbol that develops or explains a theme, while the theme itself is the central idea or message. In *A Tale of Two Cities*, Charles Dickens develops water as a motif; it comes in the form of the sea, the tide, and tears, among others. The concept of blood is a dominant motif in *Macbeth*.

muse: In classical Greco-Roman literature, an invocation or address may be made to one of the nine muses of mythology, in which the poet asks for the stimulation, talent, understanding, or appropriate mood to create a worthy poem. The invocation of the muse is the traditional opening of Greco-Roman epics and elegies. The term is not confined to poetry, however. It frequently refers to someone, real or figurative, who inspires another in artistic expression. When used as a verb, it means to think deeply and thoughtfully.

*narrative: The telling of a story or an account of an event or series of events.

*onomatopoeia: A figure of speech in which natural sounds are imitated in the sounds of words. Simple examples include such words as "buzz," "hiss," "hum," "crack," "whinny," and "murmur." This term usually is not used in the multiple-choice section. If you identify examples of onomatopoeia in a poem or essay passage, note the effect in your essay.

*oxymoron: From the Greek for "pointedly foolish," an oxymoron is a figure of speech in which the author groups together apparently contradictory terms to suggest a paradox. Simple examples include "jumbo shrimp" and "cruel kindness." This term rarely appears in multiple-choice questions, but you might see it used by an author in a passage or you might find it useful in your own essay writing.

parable: A story or short narrative designed to reveal a symbolically religious principle, a moral lesson, or a universal truth. A parable teaches by comparison with real or literal occurrences that a wide number of people can relate to rather than by using abstract dialogue. Parables are very similar to *fables* in that both teach a lesson via a short narrative, but parables use human characters, while fables use animals, plants, forces of nature, and other nonhuman objects. Parables are also similar to *allegories* in that both usually use human characters; however, allegories are not necessarily created in order to be didactic. Instead, in an allegory it is the characters, setting, and/or images that stand in as symbols for other people and things. An allegory may teach a lesson (sometimes a much more complicated one than in a simplistic parable), but its general function is symbolic rather than moralistic. Well-known examples of parables include "The Prodigal Son" and "The Good Samaritan" in the Bible, and Melville's *Billy Budd* in literature.

*paradox: A statement that appears to be self-contradictory or not in accordance with common sense but, upon closer inspection, contains some degree of truth or validity. The first scene of *Macbeth*, for example, closes with the witches' cryptic remark "Fair is foul, and foul is fair. . . ."

*parallelism: Also referred to as parallel construction or parallel structure, this term comes from Greek roots meaning "beside one another." It refers to the grammatical or rhetorical framing of words, phrases, sentences, or paragraphs to give structural similarity. This can involve, but is not limited to, repetition of a grammatical element such as a preposition or a verbal phrase. A famous example of parallelism begins Charles Dickens' novel *A Tale of Two Cities*: "It was the best of times, it was the worst of times, it was the age of wisdom, it was the age of foolishness, it was the epoch of belief, it was the epoch of incredulity. . . ." The effects of parallelism are numerous, but frequently, parallelism acts as an organizing force to attract the reader's attention, add emphasis and organization, or simply provide a pleasing, musical rhythm. Another famous example comes from the concluding line of Tennyson's poem "Ulysses," as the speaker claims, "To strive, to seek, to find, and not to yield." Many specific terms identify the various forms of parallelism, such as *anaphora, asyndeton, epistrophe*, and symploce; see also *antithesis* and *chiasmus*.

parallel plotline: Also referred to as a parallel narrative, it is a story structure in which the writer includes two or more separate narratives linked by a common character, event, or theme. The effect of these multiple perspectives may include building tension, creating dramatic irony, unraveling a mystery, or revealing character motivation. The essential characteristic of a novel with parallel stories is that it is *nonlinear*, which means that the plotlines will jump around, skipping between timelines and protagonists. Variations of parallel stories go by many different names and follow a variety of patterns. The simplest of these is a basic two-plot combination in which two separate stories are told in the same novel. These may be told consecutively, one after the other, or they can be woven back and forth in a sort of "braided" structure. Generally, the events of the two narratives will overlap throughout the novel or combine in the novel's climax or resolution. A good example is Mark Twain's *The Prince and the Pauper*.

*parody: A work that closely imitates the style or content of another work with the specific aim of comic effect and/or ridicule. As comedy, parody distorts or exaggerates distinctive features of the original. As ridicule, it mimics the work by repeating and borrowing words, phrases, or characteristics in order to illuminate weaknesses in the original. Well-written parody offers insight into the original, but poorly written parody offers only ineffectual imitation. Usually, an audience must grasp the concept of literary allusion and also understand the work that is being parodied to fully appreciate the nuances of the newer work. Occasionally, however, parodies take on a life of their own, and they don't require knowledge of the original.

pastoral: A poem or prose work that idealizes the simplicity of rural country life. Often dealing with shepherds' lives, the pastoral envisions a peaceful, uncorrupted existence in which characters are kind, charming, and serene as they live in nature.

*pathos: In its literary sense, pathos embodies a scene or passage designed to evoke the feeling of pity or sympathetic sorrow in a reader or viewer. Not necessarily limited to suffering, it can also refer to joy, pride, anger, humor, patriotism, or any other strong emotions. Pathos is the Greek word for both "suffering" and "experience." The words "empathy" and "pathetic" are derived from pathos. (*Note:* Many students who have completed a year of AP English Literature class are familiar with Aristotle's three rhetorical appeals of pathos, ethos, and logos; be aware that those terms are more appropriate to use in the analysis of nonfiction. I advise against using "ethos" or "logos" in any of the free-response essays, and, if you do use "pathos," be sure you are using its literary definition.) See also *bathos*.

*pedantic: Describes words, phrases, or a general tone that suffers from being overly scholarly, academic, or bookish.

*personification: A figure of speech in which the author presents or describes concepts, animals, or inanimate objects by endowing them with human attributes or emotions. Personification is used to make these concepts, animals, or objects appear more vivid to the reader. John Keats personifies the nightingale, the Grecian urn, and autumn in three of his major poems.

*point of view: In fictional literature, this is the perspective from which a story is told. When examining point of view, ask two questions: First, who is the narrator telling the story? And second, how much does the narrator know? There are two general divisions of point of view, first-person narrator and third-person narrator, and many subdivisions within those. It helps to separate the options:

- *First-person point of view:* Many narratives appear in the first person in which the narrator speaks as "I" and the narrator is a character in the story who may or may not influence events within it. Be careful to not confuse the narrator with the author, and be sure to consider the narrator's reliability. *Great Expectations* uses first-person narration: The protagonist Pip tells the story. One variation is the first-person reflective point of view, in which the narrator is retelling events years after they have happened, and the narrator has had time to reflect and learn from the events. The short story "The Scarlet Ibis" by James Hurst clearly uses a reflective point of view.

- *Third-person omniscient point of view:* In the third-person narrative, the narrator seems to be someone standing outside the story who refers to all the characters by name or as "he," "she," "they," and so on, but is privy to their individual thoughts, motivations, and emotions. For the reader, this reveals a great deal about the characters, and it provides a degree of objectivity; on the other hand, omniscient point of view sometimes creates a long text with more information than we feel we need, and it is somewhat unrealistic, since no one can actually read other people's minds all the time. *The Scarlet Letter* by Nathaniel Hawthorne and *Little Women* by Louisa May Alcott both use omniscient point of view.

- *Third-person limited point of view:* This narration is confined to the inner thoughts and emotions of one character or, at most, a small number of characters. It can be more realistic and "cuts the clutter" of the omniscient point of view. *1984* by George Orwell only reveals Winston Smith's thoughts.

- *Objective point of view:* Also a third-person narrator, this point of view never comments on the characters' inner thoughts; it presents only the action. While concise and thrifty in its presentation, the reader must read between the lines and do all of the analysis; we do not have any hints or nudges from the narrator telling us whether a character is actually good or bad. Ernest Hemingway's "Hills like White Elephants," like many of his works, uses an objective point of view.

- *Unreliable narrator:* This point of view can be told in first person or third person, but the key is that readers need to eventually realize that they cannot trust what the narrator tells them. The narrator may be insane, deluded, evil, or a trickster, but for some reason, the narrator chooses to sway the readers' opinion in a dishonest way. An unreliable narrator can create a degree of suspense or terror or even humor. In Edgar Allan Poe's "The Cask of Amontillado," readers initially trust the narrator, thinking he has been wronged, but come to realize he is a murderer, committing the crime right before our eyes.

polysyndeton: Deliberately using a multitude of conjunctions in a sentence to join items and thus create an overwhelming effect. For example, Cormac McCarthy used polysyndeton in this passage from his novel *The Crossing:* "He got the fire going and lifted the wolf from the sheet and took the sheet to the creek and crouched in the dark and washed the blood out of it and brought it back and he cut forked sticks from a mountain hackberry and drove them into the ground with a rock and hung the sheet on a trestlepole. . . ." Notice how joining every action with the conjunction "and" separates and intensifies the actions. Compare with **asyndeton**.

prologue: From the Greek *prologos*, which means "before word," a prologue is the introductory material that establishes character or situation. Shakespeare's *Romeo and Juliet* begins with a famous prologue that describes the conflict that audiences will follow. Chaucer's *Canterbury Tales* begins with a long prologue that describes all of the pilgrims who journey to Canterbury. See also its opposite, **epilogue**.

prose: One of the major divisions of literature, prose refers to fiction and nonfiction, in all their forms, because they are written in ordinary language and most closely resemble everyday speech. Technically, anything that isn't poetry or drama is prose. Of course, prose writers often borrow poetic and dramatic elements. Prose is arranged in sentences and paragraphs, while poetry is arranged in lines and stanzas.

*protagonist: From the Greek for "player of the first part," the protagonist was originally the leader of the chorus; then it morphed into the first actor in order of performance. Today, it refers to the main character in a literary work sometimes called the hero, focal character, or central character. The protagonist is a very important tool used in developing a story; the **conflict** revolves around him or her. Readers often want the protagonist to be fair and virtuous, but that is not always the case. At some point in the plot, it's likely that the protagonist will undergo some personal change, which will probably coincide with the climax of the story. The protagonist functions as an emotional heart of the story, helps the audience connect with the story on a basic level, and lets them relate to the joys, fears, and hopes of the character in the story. See also **antagonist** and **antihero**.

repetition: The repeated duplication, either exactly or approximately, of any element of language, such as a sound, word, phrase, clause, sentence, or grammatical pattern. When repetition is poorly done, it bores, but when it's well done, it links and emphasizes ideas while giving the reader the comfort of recognizing something familiar. See also **parallelism**.

*rhetorical question: A question that is asked merely for effect and that does not elicit a reply; the answer is apparent or assumed. For example, in Shakespeare's *Julius Caesar*, the character Brutus asks, "Who is here so vile that will not love his country?"

sarcasm: From the Greek meaning "to tear flesh," sarcasm involves bitter, caustic language that is meant to hurt or ridicule someone or something. It may use irony as a device, but not all ironic statements are sarcastic (that is, intending to ridicule). When well done, sarcasm can be witty and insightful; when poorly done, it's simply cruel.

*satire: A work that makes light of human vices and follies, or ridicules social institutions and conventions. Regardless of whether or not the work aims to reform humans or their society, satire is best seen as a style of writing rather than a purpose for writing. It can be recognized by the many devices that can be used effectively by the satirist, such as **irony, wit, parody, caricature, hyperbole, understatement**, and **sarcasm**. The effects of satire are varied, depending on the writer's goal, but good satire—often humorous—is thought-provoking and insightful about the human condition. Satire can be classified in two ways: *Horatian satire*, named after Horace, who softly needled Roman politicians of his day, gently and indulgently pokes fun at human foibles; *Juvenalian satire*, named after Juvenal, who contemptuously attacked Roman politicians for their immorality, bitterly condemns human vice and folly. Although distinguishing between the two can be a matter of opinion, one might consider *The Rape of the Lock* by Alexander Pope to be Horatian satire and *Animal Farm* by George Orwell to be Juvenalian satire.

setting: In a simplistic sense, setting normally includes both time and place; however, consider the implications of both. Different locations and time periods can affect characters' actions, the atmosphere, the social environment, and the manners and mores of culture. For any given work, think about how a change in location or time would alter the story.

*simile: An explicit comparison, normally using "like," "as," or "if." For example, consider Robbie Burns' famous lines "O, my love is like a red, red rose / That's newly sprung in June. / O, my love is like a melody, / That's sweetly played in tune." See also **metaphor**.

soliloquy: A monologue spoken by an actor at a point in the play when the character believes himself to be alone. The soliloquy usually reveals a character's innermost thoughts, feelings, state of mind, motives, or intentions. The soliloquy often provides insightful and necessary information that would otherwise be inaccessible to the audience. The dramatic convention is that whatever a character says in a soliloquy to the audience must be true, or at least true in the eyes of the character speaking; a soliloquy is a true reflection of what the speaker believes or feels. Well-known examples include speeches by Macbeth and Hamlet. Contrast with an **aside**.

stream of consciousness: William James coined the phrase "stream of consciousness" in his *Principles of Psychology* (1890); in literature, it is a style of writing in which a character's perceptions, thoughts, and memories are presented in an apparently random form, without regard for logical sequence, chronology, syntax, or punctuation. It attempts to express the flow of a character's thoughts and feelings as they come to the character. Stream of consciousness blurs the distinction between levels of reality—such as dreams, memories, imaginative thoughts, or real sensory perception. The technique, invented in the early 20th century, has been used by such authors as Katherine Anne Porter, James Joyce, Virginia Woolf, T. S. Eliot, and William Faulkner. Although the technique can be a challenge to follow, it gives readers the impression of being inside the minds of the characters and, therefore, provides a great deal of insight on plot developments and character motivation in the work.

subplot: A minor or subordinate secondary plot, often involving a minor character's struggles, which takes place simultaneously with the larger plot. The subplot often mirrors or comments upon the main plot, either directly or obliquely. Sometimes two subplots merge into a single storyline later in a play or narrative. However, some important connection between a subplot and the main plot exists, whether it is through the theme, setting, characters, action, or conflict. Subplots are a smaller part of the story; they happen to and because of supporting characters; they are often quicker and easier to resolve; and they have less impact. Subplots can serve many functions, such as introducing new characters, developing the main theme, heightening or releasing tension, increasing the conflict, providing twists in the action, challenging or teaching a moral lesson, and creating mood. Charles Dickens' novel *Great Expectations* has a series of subplots. One involves Pip's acquaintance with Herbert as he tries to help his friend financially. Another subplot involves Pip's plan to get Abel Magwitch out of the country with the help of Wemmick. In Shakespeare's *Romeo and Juliet*, the ongoing conflict between the Capulets and Montagues serves as a subplot that adds dramatic tension.

*syllogism: From the Greek for "reckoning together," a syllogism (or syllogistic reasoning) is a deductive system of formal logic that presents two premises—the first one called major and the second minor—that inevitably lead to a sound conclusion. A frequently cited example proceeds as follows.

- Major premise: All men are mortal.
- Minor premise: Socrates is a man.
- Conclusion: Therefore, Socrates is mortal.

A syllogism's conclusion is valid only if each of the two premises is valid. Syllogisms may also present the specific idea first ("Socrates") and the general idea second ("All men").

*symbol: Generally, a symbol is anything that represents or stands for something else. Usually, the symbol is something concrete—such as an object, action, character, or scene—that represents something more abstract. However, symbols and symbolism can be much more complex. One system classifies symbols into three categories:

1. *Natural symbols* use objects and occurrences from nature to represent ideas commonly associated with them (such as dawn symbolizing hope or a new beginning, a rose symbolizing love, or a tree symbolizing knowledge).

2. *Conventional symbols* are those that have been invested with meaning by a group (religious symbols, such as a cross or Star of David; national symbols, such as a flag or an eagle; or group symbols, such as a skull and crossbones for pirates or the scales of justice for lawyers).

3. *Literary symbols* are sometimes also conventional in the sense that they are found in a variety of works and are generally recognized. However, an individual work's symbols may be more complicated, such as the whale in *Moby Dick* and the jungle in *Heart of Darkness*. On the AP exam, try to determine what abstract idea an object symbolizes and to what extent it is successful in representing that abstraction.

theme: The central idea or message of a work and the insight it offers into life. Usually, the theme is unstated in fictional works, and, of course, quality literature has many themes. The open topic question in the free-response section of the exam will not state the word "theme," but instead direct you to address the "meaning of the work as a whole" or "significance of the work as a whole"; these phrases equate to theme. Frequently, a theme can be stated as a universal or eternal truth, that is, a general statement about the human condition, society, or humanity's relationship to the natural world that rings true. When discussing theme, try to word it in universal terms about humanity, and not specific terms about only the characters in the text. Notice the difference between writing "Hamlet cannot readily accept what he has to do since it is not in his nature" and "People who are forced to complete actions that they would normally abhor must undergo intense self-scrutiny." The first sentence merely describes character; the second addresses theme.

*tone: Similar to mood, tone describes the author's attitude toward his or her material, the audience, or both. Tone is easier to determine in spoken language than in written language. Considering how a work would sound if it were read aloud can help identify an author's tone. Some words describing tone are "playful," "serious," "businesslike," "sarcastic," "humorous," "formal," "ornate," and "somber." As with attitude, an author's tone in the exam's passages can rarely be described by one word. Expect that an explanation will be more complex. See also *attitude*.

tragedy: The branch of drama that uses a serious and dignified style to relate the sorrowful or terrible events that were encountered or caused by a heroic individual and that lead inevitably to a final, devastating catastrophe. Tragedy probes with high solemnity the fundamental questions concerning the role of man in the universe. According to Aristotle, *catharsis* is the essential end of any tragedy. Traditionally, a tragedy is divided into five acts. The first act introduces the characters in a state of happiness, or at the height of their power, influence, or fame. The second act typically introduces a problem or dilemma, which reaches a point of crisis in the third act, but which can still be successfully averted. But in the fourth act, the main characters fail to avert or avoid the impending crisis or catastrophe, and thus disaster occurs. The fifth act traditionally reveals the grim consequences of their failure. In another context, this term may also be applied to other literary works, such as a novel.

tragic hero: The main character in a Greek or Roman tragedy is always a tragic hero. In contrast with the *epic hero* (who embodies the values of his or her culture and appears in an epic poem), the tragic hero is typically an admirable character who appears as the protagonist in a tragic play, but one who is undone by a *hamartia*—a tragic mistake, misconception, or flaw. This hamartia leads to the downfall of the main character, and sometimes all he or she holds dear. In many cases, the tragic flaw results from the character's *hubris*, but for a tragedy to work, the audience must empathize with the main character. Accordingly, in many of the best tragedies, the tragic flaw grows out of some trait that we initially find admirable. Until the late 19th century, tragic heroes traditionally came from the upper class or those in prestigious positions. Any list of these classic tragic heroes must include characters such as Oedipus, Antigone, Macbeth, and Othello. In his late 19th-century plays, Henrik Ibsen is credited with broadening the role of the tragic hero; by including common people with common problems, he invites the reader to relate to his characters sympathetically.

*understatement: As the ironic minimizing of fact, understatement always presents something as less significant than it actually is. The effect can frequently be humorous and emphatic. Understatement is the opposite of *hyperbole*. Two distinct types of understatement exist:

1. *Litotes* is a figure of speech by which an affirmation is made indirectly by denying its opposite. It uses understatement for emphasis, frequently with a negative assertion. For example, "It was no mean feat" means it was quite hard. "He was not averse to a drink" means he drank a lot.

2. *Meiosis*, the Greek term for "understatement" or "belittling," is a rhetorical device in which something is described or referred to as far less important than it really is. A character misrepresents something that is actually very impressive by stating that they are unimpressed. An example is the sword-fighting scene in *Romeo and Juliet* when Mercutio says that he has received only a mere "scratch," when in fact, he has a mortal wound.

verisimilitude: In a literary work, verisimilitude relates to the appearance of believability, of plausibility, such that readers are likely to "buy into" the plot, even if it seems far-fetched. Verisimilitude ensures that even a fantasy must be rooted in some kind of reality, so that readers consider the events credible enough to be able to relate them to their own experiences in some way. The concept of verisimilitude leads to the idea of "suspension of disbelief," or "willing suspension of disbelief," a term coined in 1817 by Samuel Taylor Coleridge. He assumed that if a writer was able to fill his or her work with a "human interest and a semblance of truth," readers would willingly suspend or at least delay their judgment in relation to the believability of a narrative.

volta: A turn or sudden change in emotion, thought, or direction; used most often in a sonnet, it signals the shift that begins the poem's resolution.

wit: In modern usage, wit refers to intellectually amusing language that surprises and delights. A witty statement is humorous, while also displaying the speaker's verbal prowess in creating such ingenious and perceptive remarks. Wit typically uses brief and pithy language to makes a pointed statement. Historically, wit originally referred to a person's basic understanding, but its meaning evolved to include one's speed of understanding, and then finally (in the early 17th century), it grew to mean having quick perception and being amusing through cleverly apt expression.

Terms for Poetry Analysis

The following terms have been used in the questions and/or answers of the multiple-choice section. Those marked with an asterisk are the more important terms.

anapest: A foot of poetry composed of two unstressed syllables followed by a stressed syllable. A perfect example can be found in the well-known Clement Clark Moore poem, "'Twas the <u>night</u> before <u>Christmas</u>, when <u>all</u> through the <u>house</u>, / Not a <u>creature</u> was <u>stirring</u>, not <u>even</u> a <u>mouse</u>." Its opposite is the *dactyl* foot.

ballad/ballad meter: In literary terminology, a ballad is a narrative poem consisting of quatrains of iambic tetrameter alternating with iambic trimeter with an *abcb* or *abab* rhyme scheme. Ballads commonly begin abruptly, tell a story through dialogue and action, use simple or "folksy" language, present tragic themes, and repeat a refrain. "Sir Patrick Spens" is a famous Scottish ballad.

*blank verse: A poem composed in unrhymed iambic pentameter. Shakespeare used it quite extensively in his plays as did Milton in *Paradise Lost*. When you analyze a work with blank verse, notice that it does have rhythm, but it has no rhyme. Ask yourself what effect this gives the poem. For example, in William Wordsworth's famous "Lines Composed a Few Miles Above Tintern Abbey," the constant meter (rhythm of iambic pentameter) might suggest the things we can count on, like nature's seasons, while the lack of rhyme scheme might suggest the unpredictable things we face in life, like mankind's actions.

caesura: From the Latin for "a cutting" or "a slicing," a caesura is a natural pause in a line that is dictated by rhythm, such as in this line from Alexander Pope: "A little learning / is a dangerous thing."

dactyl: A metrical foot of three syllables, including an accented syllable followed by two unaccented ones, such as in the words "poetry" and "basketball." Tennyson's famous poem "The Charge of the Light Brigade" is written in dactylic verse.

dramatic monologue: A poem in which the speaker directly addresses a specific listener who is present or the reader. Like a *soliloquy*, the speaker will reveal, sometimes inadvertently, inner thoughts and character traits. Because the speaker uses first person, some students confuse the speaker with the poet; dramatic monologues are definitely NOT autobiographical. For example, Percy Bysshe Shelley's haunting "Porphyria's Lover" has a speaker who reveals that, in an insane desire to hold love forever, he has murdered his lover. The speaker is most unhinged, but the poet is not.

elegy: A dignified poem that typically mourns death. The conventional elements of the elegy mirror three stages of loss. The poem begins with a lament in which the poet expresses grief, followed by praise and admiration for the deceased, and finally the poet finds consolation and peace. "Oh Captain! My Captain!" by Walt Whitman and "In Memory of W. B. Yeats" by W. H. Auden are both well-known elegies.

*end-stopped: A line with a pause at the end. Lines that end with a period, comma, colon, semicolon, exclamation point, or question mark are end-stopped lines. See its opposite, *enjambment*.

enjambment: From the French for "straddling," it refers to a line in poetry that has no punctuation that indicates a pause or a complete stop. The sentence continues on the next line. As a rule of thumb, when reading poetry, follow the punctuation just as you do in prose, and don't take a deep breath at the end of every line. See its opposite, *end-stopped*.

epic poetry: In its most specific sense, epic poetry is a genre of classical poetry. Traditionally, epics have many conventions: It is a long narrative about a serious subject, told in elevated style, and focused on the feats of a hero who represents the cultural values of a group or nation in which the hero's success or failure will determine the fate of those people or nation. Usually, the epic covers a wide geographic area; it contains superhuman feats of strength; and the gods or supernatural beings frequently participate in the action. The poem begins with the invocation of a *muse* to inspire the poet, and the narrative starts *in medias res*. Classic epics include the *Iliad* and the *Odyssey*. Compare with *mock epic*.

epic simile: A simile of epic proportions (i.e., very long). It is a formal, sustained comparison that can take many lines to develop and is one of the conventions of epic poetry.

epithet: A short, poetic term used to characterize or identify a person. The epithet is frequently used in epic poetry, such as referring to "fleet-footed Achilles" or "rosy-fingered Dawn."

feminine rhyme: Also called *double rhyme*, this term refers to an end rhyme involving two syllables, as in "motion" and "ocean" or "willow" and "billow." The term *feminine rhyme* is also sometimes applied to triple rhymes (rhymes involving three syllables), such as "exciting" and "inviting." The last syllable is unstressed, allowing for a softer sound. Compare to *masculine rhyme*.

*free verse: Poetry that is not written in a traditional meter but is still rhythmical; it lacks the artificial constraints of a regular meter and rhyme scheme but relies on the natural rhythm of phrases and normal pauses. It can be very liberating because lines do not have to have a specific syllable count or rhyming pattern; stanzas do not require a specific line count. The poetry of Walt Whitman often contains free verse, as does a great deal of modern poetry.

*heroic couplet: Two end-stopped iambic pentameter lines rhymed *aa, bb, cc*, usually containing a complete thought in the two-line unit. Geoffrey Chaucer became the first English poet to make extensive use of the heroic couplet. This example, from The Prologue of *The Canterbury Tales*, describes the Knight:

> There was a Knight, a most distinguished man,
>
> Who from the day on which we first began
>
> To ride abroad had followed chivalry
>
> Truth, honor, generousness, and courtesy.

*iamb: A two-syllable foot with an unaccented syllable followed by an accented syllable. The iamb is the most common foot in English poetry and closest to the rhythms of English speech. All of Shakespeare's plays and poems rely on the iambic foot. Notice the iambic meter in the last two lines of Shakespeare's Sonnet 18: "So <u>long</u> as <u>men</u> can <u>breathe</u> or <u>eyes</u> can <u>see</u> / So <u>long</u> lives <u>this</u> and <u>this</u> gives <u>life</u> to <u>thee</u>."

internal rhyme: Rhyme that occurs within a line rather than at the end. A famous example comes from Edgar Allan Poe's unforgettable poem "The Raven": "Once upon a midnight dreary, while I pondered weak and weary."

kenning: Used most often in Old English, Old Norse, and Germanic poetry, a kenning is a compounded image, frequently two words, that describes something or someone. Examples include "whale-road" to refer to the ocean and "peace-weaver" for women.

lyric: A short poem written with repeating stanza patterns that is often designed to be set to music. Unlike a *ballad*, a lyric does not necessarily tell a story; instead, it dwells on something intensely emotional and personal.

masculine rhyme: Also known as *single rhyme*, this term refers to a monosyllabic rhyme or a rhyme that occurs only in stressed final syllables, such as "claims" and "flames" or "rare" and "despair." It is used more frequently than its opposite, *feminine rhyme*, and ends a line of poetry with a degree of finality because of the stressed sound.

metaphysical poetry: This term, although hard to pin down, refers to highly complex and abstract poetry. Initially invented by English poets such as John Donne, Andrew Marvel, and George Herbert in the early 17th century, the term "metaphysical poetry" was unkindly coined by John Dryden in 1693 and used derisively by many authors of the time period, notably Samuel Johnson. These authors thought the metaphysical poets produced works that were too convoluted and difficult to understand. In general, metaphysical poetry rejects the traditional conventions of verse and imagery, choosing instead to produce wildly original images, puns, metaphors, and conceits. These poets approach philosophical and spiritual subjects with reason, but often conclude in paradox. The speaker often strives to persuade his listener, via a most peculiar rationale, to take a particular action. The speaker in "The Flea" by John Donne, master of metaphysical poetry, tries to seduce his young maiden by explaining how their blood is already comingled in a flea that has bitten both of them. The conceit behind the logic compares sex to a flea bite.

*meter: The recognizable pattern of stressed and unstressed syllables in poetry. Each unit of stressed and unstressed syllables is called a "foot," and the terms for the number of feet per line of poetry are wonderfully logical:

- *Monometer:* one foot
- *Dimeter:* two feet

- *Trimeter:* three feet
- *Tetrameter:* four feet
- *Pentameter:* five feet
- *Hexameter:* six feet
- *Heptameter:* seven feet
- *Octameter:* eight feet
- *Nonameter:* nine feet

mock epic: In contrast with an epic poem, a mock epic is a long comic poem that merely imitates features of the classical epic. The poet often takes an elevated style of language, but incongruously applies that language to mundane or ridiculous objects and situations. The mock epic focuses frequently on the exploits of an *antihero* whose activities illustrate the stupidity of the class or group he or she represents. Various other attributes that are common to the classical epic, such as the invocation of the muse or the intervention of the gods, or the long catalogs of characters, appear in the mock epic as well, only to be spoofed. For example, Alexander Pope's *The Rape of the Lock* uses hyperbolic language to describe a lengthy account of how a 17th-century lord cuts a lady's hair in order to steal a lock of it as a keepsake, leading to all sorts of social backlash when the woman is unhappy with her new hairdo. See also *epic poetry*.

octave: An eight-line stanza or any poem of eight lines. The term also refers to the opening eight lines of an Italian or Petrarchan sonnet in which the speaker sets up an objective problem to be solved; the remaining *sestet* comes to a subjective resolution.

ode: A lyric poem of some length dealing with serious subjects in a dignified style. Conventionally, the ode is dedicated to a specific subject. John Keats is renowned for "Ode on a Grecian Urn" and "To a Nightingale."

ottava rima: Originally an Italian poetic form, ottava rima refers to an eight-line stanza that has 11 syllables and a rhyme scheme of *abababcc*. Lord Byron modified it to 10 syllables in his mock epic *Don Juan*, and W. B. Yeats used it in "Sailing to Byzantium."

quatrain: A stanza form consisting of four lines.

rhyme royal: A seven-line stanza of iambic pentameter rhymed *ababbcc*, which was used by Chaucer and other medieval poets.

sestet: A six-line stanza or any poem of six lines. The term also refers to the last six lines of an Italian or Petrarchan sonnet in which the speaker subjectively resolves or comments on the issue or dilemma of the opening *octave*; it brings the sonnet to a unified end.

sestina: A 39-line poem, originally seen in French verse, that consists of six *sestets* (36 lines total) that are followed by a three-line stanza, called an envoy. The form is very complicated; the end words of the first stanza are repeated in a different order as end words in each of the subsequent five stanzas; the closing envoy contains all six words, two per line, placed in the middle and at the end of the three lines. They are difficult to write! Examples include "Sestina" by Elizabeth Bishop and "Two Lorries" by Seamus Heaney.

slant rhyme: Also called *half rhyme, approximate rhyme, inexact rhyme,* and *near rhyme,* this term refers to words that don't exactly rhyme; the sounds are similar but not identical. Slant rhymes create an unusual range of words to give a variety of rhyming effects. They help poets avoid the typical sing-song chiming effects of full rhymes, and allow for creative freedom. Furthermore, slant rhymes provide a subtle discordant note, which disturbs absolute harmony and offers variation in tone. Philip Larkin employed slant rhyme to great effect in his poem "Toads":

Why should I let the toad work

Squat on my life?

Can't I use my wit as a pitchfork

And drive the brute off?

*sonnet: A poem written in iambic pentameter, normally composed of 14 lines. The conventional Italian, or Petrarchan, sonnet is rhymed *abba, abba, cde, cde*; the English, or Shakespearean, sonnet is rhymed *abab, cdcd, efef, gg*.

spondee: A metrical foot that has two consecutive strong, stressed beats, such as "football," "shortcake," "goof-off," "bathrobe," and "story." The spondee is typically slower and heavier to read than an iamb or dactyl. It creates a heightened feeling and increases interest.

*stanza: A repeated grouping of three or more lines, frequently with the same meter and rhyme scheme.

*tercet: A poetic unit of three lines; they do not have to rhyme, but when they do, the rhyme scheme is frequently *aaa*. They can create a nice flow of words, like rolling waves. Thomas Hardy used the tercet very effectively in "The Convergence of the Twain," the poem chosen for the AP exam essay prompt in 2002.

terza rima: A three-line stanza rhymed *aba, bcb, cdc*. For example, Dante's *Divine Comedy* is written in terza rima.

trochee: A metrical foot of poetry consisting of one stressed syllable followed by one unstressed syllable. "The Tyger" by William Blake uses trochees: "<u>Ty</u>ger, <u>Ty</u>ger, <u>burn</u>ing <u>bright</u> / <u>In</u> the <u>for</u>ests <u>of</u> the <u>night</u>."

villanelle: A French fixed form of verse that has 19 lines: five *tercets* followed by a *quatrain*. Whole lines must be repeated in a specific order, and the entire poem has only two rhyming sounds. Perhaps the most famous villanelle is Dylan Thomas' "Do Not Go Gentle Into That Good Night."

Grammatical Terms

active vs. passive voice: English has two voices: active and passive. Both must have a transitive verb, that is, a verb that requires a direct object. Active voice is preferable to passive; it creates more dynamic and concise sentences. In traditional sentences using active voice, the subject is followed by a verb, which in turn is followed by a direct object. Notice this traditional order in the following simple sentence:

I   made   a   mistake.
subject   *verb*   *direct object*

In a passive-voice sentence, the direct object precedes the verb, the verb tense must be changed, and the subject will either be changed into a prepositional phrase or eliminated entirely. Notice the passive voice in this revised sentence:

A   mistake   was made   by me.
direct object   *verb*   *prepositional phrase*

Passive voice has the effect of lessening the importance of the subject (or eliminating the identity of the subject entirely) while increasing the importance of the direct object and the action of the verb.

Be aware that sometimes a writer will place a direct object before the verb for emphasis or surprise; this construction still uses active voice as long as the subject also precedes the verb. This is referred to as a sentence inversion. Notice the unusual location of the direct object in this active-voice sentence:

These facts   the newspaper editor   should have checked   before publication.
direct object   *subject*   *verb*   *prepositional phrase*

Or notice this unusual poetic sentence inversion from Thomas Gray's "Elegy Written in a Country Churchyard":

And all the air   a solemn stillness   holds.
subject   *direct object*   *verb*

*antecedent: The word that is referred to by a pronoun. The antecedent of a pronoun will be a noun. The multiple-choice section of the AP exam occasionally asks for the antecedent of a given pronoun in a long, complex sentence or in a group of sentences.

*clause: A grammatical unit that contains both a subject and a verb. An independent, or main, clause expresses a complete thought and can stand alone as a sentence. A dependent, or subordinate, clause cannot stand alone as a sentence and must be accompanied by an independent clause. Examine this sample sentence: "Because I practiced hard, my AP scores were high." In this sentence, the independent clause is "my AP scores were high," and the dependent (or subordinate) clause is "Because I practiced hard." See also *subordinate clause*.

grammatical mood: When used in its grammatical sense, mood refers to verbal units and a speaker's attitude. (You can read the literary definition of *mood* under "Terms for the Multiple-Choice and Free-Response Sections," earlier in this chapter.) English has three grammatical moods:

1. The *indicative* mood is used only for factual sentences. For example, "Joe eats too quickly."
2. The *subjunctive* mood is used for a doubtful or conditional attitude. For example, "If I were you, I wouldn't eat so quickly."
3. The *imperative* mood is used for commands. For example, "Don't eat so quickly!"

*loose sentence: A type of sentence in which the main idea (independent clause) comes first, followed by dependent grammatical units such as phrases and clauses. If a period were placed at the end of the independent clause, the clause would be a complete sentence. A work containing many loose sentences often seems informal, relaxed, and conversational. See also *periodic sentence*.

*periodic sentence: A sentence that presents its central meaning in a main clause at the end. This final independent clause is preceded by a phrase or clause that cannot stand alone. For example, "Ecstatic with my AP scores, I let out a loud shout of joy!" The effect of a periodic sentence is to add emphasis and structural variety. See also *loose sentence*.

*predicate adjective: This is one type of subject complement—an adjective, group of adjectives, or adjective clause that follows a linking verb. It is in the predicate of the sentence and modifies or describes the subject. For example, in the sentence "My boyfriend is tall, dark, and handsome," the group of predicate adjectives ("tall, dark, and handsome") describes "boyfriend."

*predicate nominative: A second type of subject complement—a noun, group of nouns, or noun clause that renames the subject. Like the predicate adjective, it follows a linking verb and is located in the predicate of the sentence. For example, in the sentence "Abe Lincoln was a man of integrity," the predicate nominative is "a man of integrity," as it renames Abe Lincoln. Occasionally, this term or the term "predicate adjective" appears in a multiple-choice question on the AP exam.

*subject complement: The word (with any accompanying phrases) or clause that follows a linking verb and complements, or completes, the subject of the sentence by either (1) renaming it or (2) describing it. The former is technically called a predicate nominative, the latter a predicate adjective. See *predicate nominative* and *predicate adjective* for examples of sentences. This term appears occasionally in multiple-choice questions.

*subordinate clause: Like all clauses, this word group contains both a subject and a verb (plus any accompanying phrases or modifiers). But unlike the independent clause, the subordinate clause cannot stand alone; it does not express a complete thought. Also called a dependent clause, the subordinate clause depends on a main clause, which is sometimes referred to as an independent clause, to complete its meaning. Easily recognized key words and phrases usually begin these clauses—for example: "although," "because," "unless," "if," "even though," "since," "as soon as," "while," "who," "when," "where," "how," and "that." See also *clause*.

*syntax: The way an author chooses to join words into phrases, clauses, and sentences forms the syntax. In other words, syntax refers to the arrangement or order of grammatical elements in a sentence. In the multiple-choice section of the AP exam, you might be asked some questions about how an author manipulates syntax. In the free-response section, you might choose to analyze how syntax produces complex effects. When you are analyzing syntax, consider such elements as the length or brevity of sentences; note any unusual sentence constructions, analyze the sentence patterns used, and note the kinds of sentences the author uses. Notice if the author uses questions, declarations, exclamations, or rhetorical questions; notice if the sentences might be classified as periodic or loose, simple, compound, or complex sentences. Syntax can be tricky for students to analyze. First, try to classify *what kind* of sentences the author uses, and then try to determine *how* the author's choices amplify meaning—in other words, *why they work well* for the author's purpose.

Chapter 6
Previous Text Used and Recommended Authors to Study for the Exam

The point of your AP English class is to teach you to read and write well about literature. This, not your exam score, should be your chief concern. Don't become preoccupied with what has been or what will be on the exam. Don't spend too much time on practice exams, especially if doing so simply increases your anxiety. However, be aware that as of 2020, your AP English teacher will have direct electronic access to previous exams and can assign them throughout the year.

Still, you must be aware of what the exam experience is like. Three hours is a long time to devote to intense concentration without a break, and many students find it is more exhausting than they had imagined. You should spend some time practicing using the questions from old exams. You will learn from them the level of difficulty of the texts and exactly what kinds of tasks are set for you to write about. You can order copies of the essay questions on old exams from the Advanced Placement Program, 45 Columbus Avenue, New York, NY 10023–6917 and at https://apcentral.collegeboard.org.

Multiple-Choice Passages

The free-response essay topics on the AP English Literature and Composition Exam are released each year, but the multiple-choice questions are not. A complete exam that includes the multiple-choice passages and questions is made public only once every 4 or 5 years. An additional small selection of previously used multiple-choice questions is included in the annually published AP English Literature and Composition Course Description, and your AP teacher will have access to multiple-choice questions and free-response prompts.

Following are the texts in English and American literature on which the released multiple-choice questions have been based in the past. They will give you an idea of the range and the level of difficulty of the poetry and prose that appear on the exam.

Poetry

16th and 17th Centuries

Sir Robert Ayton: "To an Inconsistent One"

Abraham Cowley: "My Picture"

George Herbert: "The Collar" and "Church Monuments"

Ben Jonson: selection from *Volpone*

Andrew Marvell: "A Dialogue between the Soul and Body"

John Milton: selection from *Paradise Lost*

William Shakespeare: "Like As the Waves" (Sonnet 60), "Then Hate Me When Thou Wilt" (Sonnet 90), and soliloquies from *Richard II* and *Richard III*

Sir Thomas Wyatt: "They Flee from Me"

18th Century

Thomas Gray: "Hymn to Adversity"

Alexander Pope: selection from *Imitations of Horace*

19th Century

Emily Brontë: "Remembrance"

Robert Browning: "Andrea del Sarto"

Samuel Taylor Coleridge: "The Eolian Harp"

Emily Dickinson: "I Dreaded that First Robin So"

Gerard Manley Hopkins: "The Habit of Perfection"

William Wordsworth: "There Was a Boy" and "Elegiac Stanzas"

20th and 21st Centuries

Elizabeth Bishop: "Sestina" and "The Imaginary Iceberg"

Amy Clampitt: "A Whippoorwill in the Woods"

Barbara Crooker: "Patty's Charcoal Drive-in"

Robert Frost: "The Most of It"

Debora Greger: "A Frog in the Swimming Pool"

Yusef Komunyakaa: "Facing It"

Sharon Olds: "The Race"

May Sarton: "Lady with a Falcon"

Richard Wilbur: "Beasts" and "Advice to a Prophet"

Jay Wright: "The Albuquerque Graveyard"

Prose

16th and 17th Centuries

John Donne: selection from *Sermons*

18th Century

Henry Fielding: selection from *Tom Jones*

Edward Gibbon: selection from *The Decline and Fall of the Roman Empire*

Samuel Johnson: selection from *The Idler*

19th Century

Charlotte Brontë: selection from *Shirley*

Charles Dickens: selections from *Hard Times* and *A Tale of Two Cities*

George Eliot: selection from *The Mill on the Floss*

Thomas Hardy: selection from *Jude the Obscure*

John Stuart Mill: selection from *Autobiography*

William Makepeace Thackeray: selection from *Vanity Fair*

Henry David Thoreau: selection from *Walden*

Mark Twain: selection from *Life on the Mississippi*

Oscar Wilde: selection from "The Decay of Lying"

20th and 21st Centuries

James Baldwin: selection from *Go Tell It on the Mountain*

Joseph Conrad: selection from *The Secret Agent*

Don DeLillo: selection from *White Noise*

T. S. Eliot: selection from "Tradition and the Individual Talent"

Mary Wilkins Freeman: selection from "A New England Nun"

Zora Neale Hurston: selection from *Their Eyes Were Watching God*

Henry James: selection from *The Portrait of a Lady*

Alan Lightman: selection from *Einstein's Dreams*

Mary McCarthy: selection from *Cast a Cold Eye*

Elizabeth Strout: selection from "Pharmacy"

Virginia Woolf: selections from *Mrs. Dalloway* and *To the Lighthouse*

Free-Response Passages

The following pages list the authors and the works that have been used as the basis of free-response essay questions on past exams.

Poetry Question

In the 5 years that are missing in the following list, no essay question was based on a poetry passage. It is very unlikely that the exam will repeat the omission of a question based on a verse text. The following poems, or excerpts from the following poems, have appeared on the exams.

1966	Emily Dickinson: "I never lost as much but twice"
1967	No poetry question
1968	Sir Edward Dyer: "The lowest trees have tops"
1969	W. B. Yeats: "The Wild Swans at Coole"
1970	Theodore Roethke: "Elegy for Jane"
1971	W. H. Auden: "The Unknown Citizen"
1972	No poetry question
1973	No poetry question
1974	Thomas Kinsella: from "Prologue: Downstream"
1975	No poetry question
1976	Philip Larkin: "Poetry of Departures"
1977	D. H. Lawrence: "Piano"
1978	W. H. Auden: "Law Like Love"
1979	Louise Gluck: "For Jane Meyers" and William Carlos Williams: "Spring and All"
1980	Elizabeth Bishop: "One Art"
1981	Adrienne Rich: "Storm Warnings"
1982	Richard Eberhart: "The Groundhog"
1983	W. H. Auden: "As I Walked Out One Evening"
1984	No poetry question
1985	William Wordsworth: "There Was a Boy" and Robert Frost: "The Most of It"
1986	E. K. Brathwaite: "Ogun"
1987	Sylvia Plath: "Sow"
1988	John Keats: "Bright Star" and Robert Frost: "Choose Something Like a Star"
1989	John Updike: "The Great Scarf of Birds"

1990	William Shakespeare: "How many of my subjects . . ." from *Henry IV*, Part II, Act III
1991	Emily Dickinson: "The Last Night that She Lived"
1992	William Wordsworth: "One summer evening (led by her)" from *The Prelude*, Book I
1993	May Swenson: "The Centaur"
1994	Edgar Allan Poe: "To Helen" and H. D.: "Helen"
1995	John Donne: "The Broken Heart"
1996	Anne Bradstreet: "The Author to Her Book"
1997	Richard Wilbur: "The Death of a Toad"
1998	Eavan Boland: "It's a Woman's World"
1999	Seamus Heaney: "Blackberry-Picking"
2000	Margaret Atwood: "Siren Song" and a passage from the *Odyssey*
2001	William Wordsworth: "London, 1802" and Paul Laurence Dunbar: "Douglass"
2002	Thomas Hardy: "The Convergence of the Twain"
2003	Robert Bridges: "Eros" and Anne Stevenson: "Eros"
2004	Emily Dickinson: "We Grow Accustomed to the Dark" and Robert Frost: "Acquainted with the Night"
2005	William Blake: "The Chimney Sweeper" (1789) and "The Chimney Sweeper" (1794)
2006	Robert Penn Warren: "Evening Hawk"
2007	Richard Wilbur: "A Barred Owl" and Billy Collins: "The History Teacher"
2008	John Keats: "When I Have Fears" and Henry Wadsworth Longfellow: "Mezzo Cammin"
2009	William Shakespeare: from the play *Henry VIII*
2010	Marilyn Nelson Waniek: "The Century Quilt"
2011	Li-Young Lee: "A Story"
2012	Sir Philip Sidney: "Thou Blind Man's Mark"
2013	Mary Oliver: "The Black Walnut Tree"
2014	George Gascoigne: "For That He Looked Not upon Her"
2015	Derek Walcott: "XIV"
2016	Richard Wilbur: "Juggler"
2017	Rachel M. Harper: "The Myth of Music: for my father"
2018	Olive Senior: "Plants"
2019	P. K. Page: "The Landlady"

Since 1966, 20th-century authors have written most of the poems used on the exam, though nine have been chosen from the 16th, 17th, and 18th centuries, and twelve from 19th-century poets. Since 1980, many of the prose and poetry questions have been based on works by women and minority writers.

Prose Question

1970	George Meredith: from the novel *The Ordeal of Richard Feverel*
1971	George Orwell: from the essay "Some Thoughts on the Common Toad"
1972	James Joyce: "Eveline"—complete short story from *Dubliners*
1973	Charles Dickens: from the novel *Hard Times* and E. M. Forster: from the novel *A Passage to India*
1974	Henry James: from the novel *What Maisie Knew*
1975	Pär Lagerkvist: "Father and I"—complete short story

1976	John Gardner: from the verse novel *Jason and Medeia*
1977	No prose question
1978	Samuel Johnson: from a review of Soame Jenyns' "A Free Enquiry into the Nature and Origin of Evil"
1979	Quentin Bell: from *Virginia Woolf: A Biography*
1980	Ralph Ellison: from the novel *Invisible Man* and Henry James: from an essay in *Lippincott's Magazine*
1981	George Bernard Shaw: from a letter on the death of his mother
1982	Adlai Stevenson: a letter to the Senate of the Illinois General Assembly
1983	Thomas Carlyle: from the political lectures *Past and Present*
1984	Jane Austen: from the novel *Emma*
1985	Ernest Hemingway: from the novel *A Farewell to Arms*
1986	Charles Dickens: from the novel *Dombey and Son*
1987	George Eliot: from the novel *Adam Bede*
1988	John Cheever: "Reunion"—complete short story
1989	Joseph Conrad: from the novella *Typhoon*
1990	Joan Didion: from the essay "On Self-Respect"
1991	James Boswell: from the biography *The Life of Samuel Johnson*
1992	Tillie Olsen: from the short story "I Stand Here Ironing"
1993	Lytton Strachey: from "Florence Nightingale" in *Eminent Victorians*
1994	Sarah Orne Jewett: from the short story "A White Heron"
1995	Sandra Cisneros: "Eleven"—complete short story
1996	Nathaniel Hawthorne: from the novel *The Marble Faun*
1997	Joy Kogawa: from the novel *Obasan*
1998	George Eliot: from the novel *Middlemarch*
1999	Cormac McCarthy: from the novel *The Crossing*
2000	Joseph Addison: from *The Spectator*
2001	Henry Fielding: from the novel *Tom Jones*
2002	Alain de Botton: from the novel *Kiss and Tell*
2003	Mavis Gallant: from the short story "The Other Paris"
2004	Henry James: from the short story "The Pupil"
2005	Katharine Brush: "Birthday Party"—complete short story
2006	Oscar Wilde: from the play *Lady Windermere's Fan*
2007	Dalton Trumbo: from the novel *Johnny Got His Gun*
2008	Anita Desai: from the novel *Fasting, Feasting*
2009	Ann Petry: from the novel *The Street*
2010	Maria Edgeworth: from the novel *Belinda*
2011	George Eliot: from the novel *Middlemarch*
2012	Helena Maria Viramontes: from the novel *Under the Feet of Jesus*
2013	D. H. Lawrence: from the novel *The Rainbow*
2014	Edward P. Jones: from the novel *The Known World*
2015	Louise Erdrich: from the novel *The Beet Queen*
2016	Thomas Hardy: from the novel *The Mayor of Casterbridge*

2017	Tobias Smollett: from the novel *The Adventures of Peregrine Pickle*
2018	Nathaniel Hawthorne: from the novel *The Blithedale Romance*
2019	William Dean Howells: from the novel *The Rise of Silas Lapham*

Twenty-seven of the prose passages have come from 20th-century authors, eighteen from 19th-century authors, and two from 18th-century authors. Five questions have used complete short stories; nonfictional prose has not been used since 1991.

Open Topic Question

In the past, the open topic question called for an essay discussing the following:

1971	(using two works) the technical devices used to reveal the meanings of their titles
1972	the use of the opening scene or chapter to introduce significant themes of the play or novel
1973	no essay on drama or fiction
1974	the relevance to the present of a literary work written before 1900
1975	the use of a stereotyped character
1976	the moral meanings of a work in which an individual opposed his or her society
1977	a character's response to the past as a source of meaning in the work
1978	the relation of an implausible incident or character to the realistic aspects of the work
1979	an ostensibly evil character to whom the reader responds with some sympathy or understanding
1980	a character whose private passion is in conflict with his or her moral obligations
1981	a work in which the use of allusion (to myth or the Bible, for example) is significant
1982	the function in a work of a scene of violence
1983	a villain, the nature of villainy, and the relation of the character to meaning
1984	the relation of a single memorable line of poetry or scene in a play or novel to the whole work (an unusual and unsuccessful question)
1985	the cause of feelings of both pleasure and disquietude in a literary work
1986	the effect of an author's manipulation of time in a novel, epic poem, or play
1987	an author's techniques used to change a reader's attitudes, especially toward social ills
1988	an author's making internal or psychological events exciting
1989	the use of distortion in a literary work
1990	the significance in a work of a parent-child conflict
1991	the significance of two contrasting places in a play or novel
1992	the function of a confidant(e) in a play or novel
1993	a work that evokes "thoughtful laughter," why the laughter is thoughtful, and how it relates to the meaning of the work
1994	the function of a character who appears only briefly or not at all in a work
1995	how an alienated character reveals the assumptions and moral values of a society
1996	the significance in a work of an ending that shows a spiritual reassessment or moral reconciliation
1997	the contribution of a scene of a social occasion (such as a wedding, funeral, or party) to the meaning of a work
1998	how uncivilized, free, and wild thinking is central to the value of a work
1999	how a character's struggle with powerful, conflicting forces is related to the meaning of the work
2000	how the investigation of a mystery in a novel or a play throws light on the meaning of the work

2001	an explanation of how a character's apparent madness or irrational behavior might be judged as reasonable
2002	an explanation of how a morally ambiguous character is significant to the work as a whole
2003	an explanation of how the suffering brought upon others by a tragic figure contributes to the tragic vision of the work as a whole
2004	analysis of a central question a novel or play raises and the extent to which it offers any answers
2005	how the tension between a character's outward conformity and inward questioning contributes to the meaning of the work
2006	how the significant role of a country setting functions in the work
2007	how a character's relationship to the past contributes to the meaning of the work
2008	how the relationship between a minor character and a major character illuminates the meaning of the work
2009	how one important symbol functions in a work, and what it reveals about the characters or themes of the work
2010	how a character who has been cut off from home, birthplace, family, or other special place (exiled) adds significance to the work as a whole
2011	how the search for justice adds meaning to the work
2012	how the cultural, physical, and geographical surroundings that shape character contribute to the significance of the work as a whole
2013	how a character's coming of age illuminates the meaning of the work as a whole
2014	how a character's sacrifice illuminates the value of the work as a whole
2015	how cruelty functions and what it reveals about the perpetrator and/or victim in the work as a whole
2016	how the motives of a character who deceives others adds to the meaning of the work as a whole
2017	how a character with unusual or mysterious origins contributes significance to the work as a whole
2018	how a gift a character has received can be positive and negative and contribute to the meaning of the work as a whole
2019	how a character's idealistic view of the world has positive and negative consequences and illuminates the meaning of the work as a whole

Suggested Authors

The following is a list of most of the authors, plays, and novels that have been suggested for use on the open topic free-response essay question and that a significant number of students have chosen to write about. A handful of other titles have appeared on the lists (Melville's novel *Redburn*, for example) that hardly anyone wrote about, and these names have been omitted.

Over the years, the most frequently chosen novels have been Conrad's *Heart of Darkness*, Hawthorne's *The Scarlet Letter*, Fitzgerald's *The Great Gatsby*, Twain's *The Adventures of Huckleberry Finn*, and Morrison's *Beloved*. The plays that students write about most often are Miller's *Death of a Salesman*, Williams' *The Glass Menagerie*, and Shakespeare's *Hamlet*. There have, of course, also been hundreds of other appropriate novels and plays that were not on the lists of suggested titles. A reading of this tabulation will give you a good idea of the range of the works that are probably the most widely taught in AP literature classes.

Chinua Achebe: *Things Fall Apart*

Aeschylus: *The Oresteia*

Edward Albee: *Who's Afraid of Virginia Woolf?*

Sherman Alexie: *Reservation Blues*

Rudolfo Anaya: *Bless Me, Ultima*

Aristophanes: *Lysistrata*

Margaret Atwood: *Alias Grace, The Blind Assassin*, and *Cat's Eye*

Jane Austen: *Pride and Prejudice, Mansfield Park*, and *Persuasion*

Samuel Beckett: *Waiting for Godot*

Bertolt Brecht: *Mother Courage and Her Children*

Charlotte Brontë: *Jane Eyre*

Emily Brontë: *Wuthering Heights*

Albert Camus: *The Stranger* and *The Plague*

Miguel de Cervantes: *Don Quixote*

Anton Chekhov: *The Cherry Orchard*

Kate Chopin: *The Awakening*

Joseph Conrad: *Heart of Darkness, Lord Jim*, and *Victory*

Daniel Defoe: *Moll Flanders*

Charles Dickens: *David Copperfield, Great Expectations, Hard Times*, and *A Tale of Two Cities*

Fyodor Dostoevsky: *Crime and Punishment*

Theodore Dreiser: *An American Tragedy* and *Sister Carrie*

George Eliot: *Middlemarch* and *The Mill on the Floss*

T. S. Eliot: *Murder in the Cathedral*

Ralph Ellison: *Invisible Man*

Euripides: *Medea*

William Faulkner: *As I Lay Dying, Light in August, The Sound and the Fury*, and *Absalom, Absalom!*

Henry Fielding: *Joseph Andrews* and *The History of Tom Jones: a Foundling*

F. Scott Fitzgerald: *The Great Gatsby*

Gustave Flaubert: *Madame Bovary*

E. M. Forster: *A Passage to India*

Charles Frazier: *Cold Mountain*

William Golding: *Lord of the Flies*

Lorraine Hansberry: *A Raisin in the Sun*

Thomas Hardy: *Jude the Obscure, Tess of the d'Urbervilles*, and *The Mayor of Casterbridge*

Nathaniel Hawthorne: *The Scarlet Letter*

Joseph Heller: *Catch-22*

Lillian Hellman: *The Little Foxes*

Ernest Hemingway: *The Sun Also Rises* and *A Farewell to Arms*

Khaled Hosseini: *The Kite Runner*

Zora Neale Hurston: *Their Eyes Were Watching God*

Aldous Huxley: *Brave New World*

Henrik Ibsen: *A Doll's House, An Enemy of the People, Hedda Gabler*, and *The Wild Duck*

John Irving: *A Prayer for Owen Meany*

Henry James: *The Turn of the Screw, Washington Square*, and *The Portrait of a Lady*

James Joyce: *A Portrait of the Artist as a Young Man*

Franz Kafka: *The Metamorphosis* and *The Trial*

Ken Kesey: *One Flew Over the Cuckoo's Nest*

Joy Kogawa: *Obasan*

D. H. Lawrence: *Sons and Lovers*

Chang-rae Lee: *A Gesture Life*

Sinclair Lewis: *Main Street*

Christopher Marlowe: *Doctor Faustus*

Gabriel García Márquez: *One Hundred Years of Solitude*

Cormac McCarthy: *All the Pretty Horses* and *The Crossing*

Carson McCullers: *The Member of the Wedding*

Ian McEwan: *Atonement*

Herman Melville: *Billy Budd* and *Moby Dick*

Arthur Miller: *All My Sons, The Crucible*, and *Death of a Salesman*

Toni Morrison: *Beloved, Song of Solomon, Sula*, and *The Bluest Eye*

Tim O'Brien: *The Things They Carried* and *Going After Cacciato*

Flannery O'Connor: *Wise Blood*

Eugene O'Neill: *The Hairy Ape* and *Long Day's Journey into Night*

George Orwell: *Animal Farm* and *1984*

Alan Paton: *Cry, the Beloved Country*

Jean Rhys: *Wide Sargasso Sea*

J. D. Salinger: *A Catcher in the Rye*

Jean-Paul Sartre: *No Exit*

Peter Shaffer: *Equus*

William Shakespeare: *Hamlet, Julius Caesar, King Lear, Macbeth, The Merchant of Venice, A Midsummer Night's Dream, Othello, Romeo and Juliet*, and *Twelfth Night*

George Bernard Shaw: *Major Barbara, Man and Superman, Mrs. Warren's Profession*, and *Pygmalion*

Mary Shelley: *Frankenstein*

Sophocles: *Antigone* and *Oedipus Rex*

John Steinbeck: *The Grapes of Wrath* and *Of Mice and Men*

Tom Stoppard: *Rosencrantz and Guildenstern Are Dead*

August Strindberg: *Miss Julie*

Jonathan Swift: *Gulliver's Travels*

Leo Tolstoy: *Anna Karenina*

Mark Twain: *The Adventures of Huckleberry Finn*

Voltaire: *Candide*

Kurt Vonnegut: *Slaughterhouse Five*

Alice Walker: *The Color Purple*

Robert Penn Warren: *All the King's Men*

Evelyn Waugh: *The Loved One*

Edith Wharton: *Ethan Frome, The House of Mirth*, and *The Age of Innocence*

Oscar Wilde: *The Importance of Being Earnest* and *The Picture of Dorian Gray*

Thornton Wilder: *Our Town*

Tennessee Williams: *The Glass Menagerie* and *A Streetcar Named Desire*

August Wilson: *Joe Turner's Come and Gone, The Piano Lesson*, and *Fences*

Virginia Woolf: *To the Lighthouse, Orlando*, and *Mrs. Dalloway*

Richard Wright: *Native Son*

Once in a while, an open topic question allows for the choice of a poem rather than a novel or play. Remember, however, that a short poem is not acceptable unless it is specifically suggested. Epic poems might be considered more acceptable. The following poems have been included in the list of works on the exam:

T. S. Eliot: "The Love Song of J. Alfred Prufrock" and "The Waste Land"

Homer: the *Iliad* and the *Odyssey*

John Milton: *Paradise Lost*

Alexander Pope: "The Rape of the Lock"

Do not write on one of these works if the question specifically calls for a novel or play.

Section I: Multiple-Choice Questions

Time: 1 hour

55 questions

Directions: This section contains selections from two passages of prose and three poems with questions on their content, style, and form. Read each selection carefully. Choose the best answer of the five choices.

For questions 1–10, read the following passage carefully before choosing your answers.

Undine's white and gold bedroom, with sea-green panels and old rose carpet, looked along Seventy-second St. toward the leafless tree-tops of the Central Park.

(5) She went to the window, and drawing back its many layers of lace gazed eastward down this long brownstone perspective. Beyond the Park lay Fifth Avenue—and Fifth Avenue was where she wanted to be!

(10) She turned back into the room, and going to her writing-table laid Mrs. Fairford's note before her, and began to study it minutely. She had read in the "Boudoir Chat" of one of the Sunday papers that the smartest women were using the

(15) new pigeon-blood notepaper with white ink; and rather against her mother's advice she had ordered a large supply, with her monogram in silver. It was a disappointment, therefore, to find out that Mrs. Fairford wrote on this old-fashioned white sheet,

(20) without even a monogram—simply her address and telephone number. It gave Undine rather a poor opinion of Mrs. Fairford's social standing, and for a moment she thought with considerable satisfaction of answering the note on her pigeon-

(25) blood paper. Then she remembered Mrs. Heeny's emphatic commendation of Mrs. Fairford, and her pen wavered. What if white paper were really newer than pigeon-blood? It might be more stylish, anyhow. Well, she didn't care if Mrs.

(30) Fairford didn't like red paper—*she* did! And she wasn't going to truckle to any woman who lived in a small house down beyond Park Avenue . . .

Undine was fiercely independent and yet passionately imitative. She wanted to surprise

(35) every one by her dash and originality, but she could not help modelling herself on the last person she met, and the confusion of ideals thus produced cost her much perturbation when she

had to choose between two courses. She hesitated

(40) a moment longer, and then took from the drawer a plain sheet with the hotel address.

It was amusing to write the note in her mother's name—she giggled as she formed the phrase "I should be happy to permit my daughter

(45) to take dinner with you" ("take dinner" seemed more elegant than Mrs. Fairford's "dine")—but when she came to the signature she was met by a new difficulty. Mrs. Fairford had signed herself "Laura Fairford"—just as one school girl would

(50) write to another. But could this be a proper model for Mrs. Spragg? Undine could not tolerate the thought of her mother's abasing herself to a denizen of regions beyond Park Avenue, and she resolutely formed the signature: "Sincerely, Mrs.

(55) Abner E. Spragg." Then uncertainty overcame her, and she re-wrote her note and copied Mrs. Fairford's formula: "Yours sincerely, Leota B. Spragg." But this struck her as an odd juxtaposition of formality and freedom, and she

(60) made a third attempt: "Yours with love, Leota B. Spragg." This, however, seemed excessive, as the ladies had never met; and after several other experiments she finally decided on a compromise, and ended the note: "Yours sincerely, Mrs. Leota

(65) B. Spragg." That might be conventional, Undine reflected, but it was certainly correct.

This point settled, she flung open her door, calling imperiously down the passage: "Céleste!" and adding, as the French maid appeared: "I

(70) want to look over all my dinner-dresses."

Considering the extent of Miss Spragg's wardrobe her dinner-dresses were not many. She had ordered a number the year before but, vexed at her lack of use for them, had tossed them over

(75) impatiently to the maid. Since then, indeed, she and Mrs. Spragg had succumbed to the abstract pleasure of buying two or three more, simply because they were too exquisite and Undine looked too lovely in them; but she's grown tired

(80) of these also—tired of seeing them hang unworn in her wardrobe, like so many derisive points of interrogation. And now, as Céleste spread them out on the bed, they seemed disgustingly common-place, and as familiar as if she had

(85) danced them to shreds. Nevertheless, she yielded to the maid's persuasions and tried them on.

The first and second did not gain by prolonged inspection: they looked old-fashioned already. "It's something about the sleeves," Undine

(90) grumbled as she threw them aside.

The third was certainly the prettiest; but then it was the one she had worn at the hotel dance the night before, and the impossibility of wearing it again within the week was too obvious for

(95) discussion. Yet she enjoyed looking at herself in it. . . .

1. The "many layers of lace" (line 6) in Undine's window is most symbolic of

   A. the fragility of Undine's housing situation

   B. the dominance of material objects in Undine's life

   C. the many levels of help Undine needs to survive

   D. the multiple layers of conflict that Undine hides behind

   E. the transparency the author intends in Undine's life

2. The fact that Undine studied Mrs. Fairford's note "minutely" (line 12) implies that

   A. Undine hopes to learn how her social superiors communicate

   B. Mrs. Fairford did not want to commit to anything in the note

   C. Mrs. Fairford considers herself above the Spraggs in social stature

   D. Undine plans to imitate Mrs. Fairford's style in her reply

   E. Undine is determined to read more into the note than Mrs. Fairford intended

3. All of the following indicate Undine's penchant for imitation EXCEPT that she

   A. bought new notepaper after reading the "Boudoir Chat" (line 13)

   B. chose to use the hotel stationery

   C. "copied Mrs. Fairford's formula" (lines 56–57)

   D. wrote "the note in her mother's name" (lines 42–43)

   E. followed tradition in the way she signed her mother's name

4. Which of the following identifies the author's intended use of irony regarding Undine's purchase of the pigeon-blood notepaper with her silver monogram?

   A. She purchases the striking paper believing it will help increase her social standing, but instead she chooses to write on plain white paper.

   B. Mrs. Fairford has already decided against the new color for stationery.

   C. The "Boudoir Chat" had always given good advice before.

   D. Her mother argued against the purchase of such a large supply.

   E. She should have added her address and phone, as Mrs. Fairford did.

5. The last sentence of the third paragraph, "And she wasn't going to truckle to any woman who lived. . . down beyond Park Avenue" (lines 30–32) implies that Undine feels

   A. she will not accept the dinner invitation from Mrs. Fairford

   B. she will not ingratiate herself to someone she feels is her social inferior

   C. she will scrutinize Mrs. Fairford's home when she visits

   D. Mrs. Fairford is trying to raise her own social standing by inviting Undine to dinner

   E. Mrs. Heeny's esteem for Mrs. Fairford is questionable

6. Which of the following quotations contradicts at least part of the phrase "fiercely independent and yet passionately imitative" (lines 33–34)?

   A. "many layers of lace" (line 6)

   B. "going to her writing-table laid Mrs. Fairford's note before her, and began to study it minutely" (lines 10–12)

   C. "'I should be happy to permit my daughter to take dinner with you'" (lines 44–45)

   D. "might be conventional . . . but it was certainly correct" (lines 65–66)

   E. "they were too exquisite and Undine looked too lovely in them" (lines 78–79)

7. Which of the following can one infer is the greatest difficulty Undine had in replying to Mrs. Fairford?

A. Choosing which stationery to use

B. Determining whether or not to accept the invitation

C. Deciding how to sign her mother's name

D. Deciding whether or not to use the phrase "take dinner"

E. Choosing whether to be "fiercely independent" or "passionately imitative"

8. One similarity between Undine's pigeon-blood notepaper and her dresses is that

A. both are made in the same shades of red that reflect Undine's temperament

B. both are frequently used to advance others' opinions of Undine

C. both are indicative of Undine's socially superior standing

D. both were passed down to the French maid, Céleste

E. both are symbolic of her conspicuous consumption of unnecessary frills

9. The simile "like so many derisive points of interrogation" (lines 81–82), with its personification, is best meant to convey that

A. the dresses themselves are angry and tired of being unworn

B. the dinner-dresses hanging forlornly in the closet seem to be mocking her, asking why she has no opportunity to wear fine garments

C. each dress is eager to be the one chosen for Undine's next dinner invitation

D. Céleste wonders why Undine needs so many dinner-dresses

E. Mrs. Spragg questions the need for more "abstract pleasure" (lines 76–77)

10. What is the intended effect of the author using third-person, limited omniscient point of view?

A. The narrative would be too cumbersome if we were to also see into Mrs. Fairford's mind.

B. It allows the reader to understand Undine's motivations in writing the note to Mrs. Fairford.

C. By only presenting Undine's thoughts and actions, we clearly grasp her shallow and illogical thinking.

D. It symbolizes how Undine represents all other girls in her social situation.

E. It enhances Undine's independence from her mother.

For questions 11–20, read the following poem carefully before choosing your answers.

On Shakespeare

What needs my Shakespeare for his honoured bones,
The labor of an age in pilèd stones?
Or that his hallowed relics should be hid
Under a stary-pointing pyramid?
Dear son of Memory, great heir of fame,   (5)
What need'st thou such weak witness of thy name?
Thou in our wonder and astonishment
Hast built thyself a livelong monument.
For whilst, to th' shame of slow-endeavouring art,
Thy easy numbers flow, and that each heart   (10)
Hath, from the leaves of thy unvalued book,
Those Delphic lines with deep impression took;
Then thou, our fancy of itself bereaving,
Dost make us marble, with too much conceiving;
And, so sepulchred, in such pomp dost lie,   (15)
That kings for such a tomb would wish to die.

John Milton, 1630

11. What is the intended effect of the speaker's referring to Shakespeare as "my Shakespeare" (line 1)?

   A. It suggests the speaker and Shakespeare are equals.

   B. It enforces Shakespeare's fame in literary circles.

   C. It undermines Shakespeare's achievements by emphasizing the speaker's emotion.

   D. It accentuates Shakespeare's need for more glory.

   E. It separates Shakespeare's public persona from the speaker's personal image of him.

12. Given the context of this poem, the phrase "weak witness" (line 6) refers to

   A. Shakespeare's many fans

   B. Shakespeare's voluminous works

   C. monuments to Shakespeare's honor

   D. "Delphic lines" (line 12)

   E. "marble" (line 14)

13. The phrase "Dear son of Memory" (line 5) serves as

   A. an allusion to Shakespearean actors

   B. a conceit for Shakespeare's works

   C. a metaphor for the author of this poem

   D. a metaphor for Shakespeare

   E. personification of Shakespeare's art

14. Which of the following contrasts is presented in the poem?

   A. The visual difference between stone monuments and pyramids

   B. The relative speed with which Shakespeare wrote compared to other poets

   C. Shakespeare's "honoured bones" (line 1) with "hallowed relics" (line 3)

   D. The "unvalued book" (line 11) to the "Delphic lines" (line 12)

   E. The sepulcher in which Shakespeare is buried to kings' tombs

15. Within context, what is the intended meaning of the phrase "Dost make us marble" (line 14)?

   A. Shakespeare's readers are frozen into statues, in awe of his literary gifts.

   B. Readers should marvel at Shakespeare's works.

   C. Shakespeare's works are too complicated for most to understand.

   D. Marble was dominantly used to carve statues at Delphi.

   E. Kings' tombs were also made of marble.

16. Which of the following is the intended effect of the poem's movement from the first-person singular "my" (line 1) to the plural "our" (line 13) and "us" (line 14)?

   A. It shows the speaker's significant influence on other readers of Shakespeare's works.

   B. It weakens the speaker's position by being too inclusive.

   C. It limits the speaker's idea to his own personal time.

   D. It allows the speaker to evolve from presenting a personal viewpoint to becoming a spokesperson for numerous readers.

   E. It magnifies the need for more glory for Shakespeare.

17. Which of the following identifies the intended irony of the word "monument" in line 8?

   A. Most monuments are made of marble, but Shakespeare's is a pyramid.

   B. This "monument" has evolved out of the "weak witness" (line 6).

   C. The monument of Shakespeare's works is more important than any physical monument.

   D. Shakespeare's monument was built so quickly.

   E. Kings wish they could have such a glorious monument.

18. Within context, which of the following is the author's intended meaning of "unvalued" (line 11)?

   A. Not esteemed

   B. Useless

   C. Out of fashion

   D. Expensive

   E. Priceless

19. All of the following poetic devices are found in the poem EXCEPT

    A. understatement

    B. apostrophe

    C. rhetorical question

    D. metaphor

    E. allusion

20. The speaker's attitude toward his subject can best be described as

    A. wondering

    B. reverent

    C. patronizing

    D. effervescent

    E. overwhelmed

For questions 21–30, read the following passage carefully before choosing your answers.

And, even now, as he paced the streets, and listlessly looked around on the gradually increasing bustle and preparation for the day, everything appeared to yield him some new
(5) occasion for despondency. Last night, the sacrifice of a young, affectionate, and beautiful creature, to such a wretch, and in such a cause, had seemed a thing too monstrous to succeed; and the warmer he grew, the more confident he
(10) felt that some interposition must save her from [Arthur Gride's] clutches. But now, when he thought how regularly things went on, from day to day, in the same unvarying round; how youth and beauty died, and ugly griping age lived
(15) tottering on; how crafty avarice grew rich, and manly honest hearts were poor and sad; how few they were who tenanted the stately houses, and how many those who lay in noisome pens, or rose each day and laid them down each night, and
(20) lived and died, father and son, mother and child, race upon race, generation upon generation, without a home to shelter them or the energies of one single man directed to their aid; how, in seeking, not a luxurious and splendid life, but the
(25) bare means of a most wretched and inadequate subsistence, there were women and children in that one town, divided into classes, numbered and estimated as regularly as the noble families and folks of great degree, and reared from infancy
(30) to drive most criminal and dreadful trades; how ignorance was punished and never taught; how jail-doors gaped and gallows loomed, for thousands urged towards them by circumstances darkly curtaining their very cradles' heads, and

(35) but for which they might have earned their honest bread and lived in peace; how many died in soul, and had no chance of life; how many who could scarcely go astray, be they vicious as they would, turned haughtily from the crushed and stricken
(40) wretch who could scarce do otherwise, and who would have been a greater wonder had he or she done well, than even they, had they done ill; how much injustice, misery, and wrong there was, and yet how the world rolled on, from year to year,
(45) alike careless and indifferent, and no man seeking to remedy or redress it; when he thought of all this, and selected from the mass the one slight case on which his thoughts were bent, he felt, indeed, that there was little ground for hope, and
(50) little reason why it should not form an atom in the huge aggregate of distress and sorrow, and add one small and unimportant unit to swell the great amount.

21. The word "listlessly" in the first sentence most likely signals a contrast with which of the following elements?

    A. The way he paced the streets

    B. The way he looked around as he walked

    C. The idea that preparation for the day is gradual

    D. The growing activity in the streets

    E. The character's despondency

22. In the context of the overall passage, the second sentence serves which of the following purposes?

    A. It juxtaposes the character's self-assured attitude of the previous night with his feeling of hopelessness in the morning.

    B. It clarifies why the character is walking at such an early hour.

    C. It confirms the character's purpose as he walks the streets.

    D. It identifies the protagonist's enemy.

    E. It affirms the character's goal of saving the "young, affectionate, and beautiful creature" (lines 6–7).

23. Considering the context, which of the following most accurately describes the author's intended meaning of "interposition" in line 10?

    A. Trespassing

    B. Intrusion

    C. Prying

    D. Intervention

    E. Reconciliation

24. Which of the following is the subject and verb of the main clause in sentence 3 (lines 11–53)?

    A. "he thought" (lines 11–12)
    B. "youth and beauty died" (lines 13–14)
    C. "ignorance was punished" (line 31)
    D. "world rolled on" (line 44)
    E. "he felt" (line 48)

25. Which of the following best describes the stylistic effect of the lengthy sentence 3 (lines 11–53)?

    A. It enunciates the character's disapproval of Arthur Gride.
    B. Its many images build into a culmination of the protagonist's overwhelming gloom.
    C. It weighs the sentence down with tedious detail.
    D. It distracts the reader from the protagonist's problems.
    E. It allows the reader to see into the character's mind.

26. By the end of the passage, it can be inferred that the main character will

    A. overcome his doubts about success
    B. pursue other ways to thwart Arthur Gride
    C. succumb to his doubt that he can save the girl
    D. investigate how to help the poor families in need that he sees as he walks
    E. request unbiased advice from his friends

27. The third sentence (lines 11–53) is most notable for

    A. repetitive descriptions that establish monotony in the passage
    B. parallel syntax that provides accumulation of detail
    C. phrases that add conflicting imagery to the overall picture
    D. several independent clauses that contrast each other
    E. a series of subordinate clauses that confound the reader

28. The passage as a whole establishes an overall mood of

    A. stoic fortitude
    B. guarded optimism
    C. grim despair
    D. virulent retribution
    E. incomprehensible chaos

29. All of the following are present in the passage EXCEPT

    A. concrete images the character physically observes
    B. subordinate clauses
    C. parallel construction
    D. a defeated tone
    E. complex syntax in each sentence

30. Which of the following identifies the use of situational irony in the passage?

    A. The difference between "honest hearts" (line 16) and "criminal and dreadful trades" (line 30)
    B. The character's realization that his dilemma is just "an atom in the huge aggregate of distress and sorrow" (lines 50–51)
    C. The idea that the character can save the girl from "[Arthur Gride's] clutches" (line 11)
    D. The contrast between the previous night and the character's morning walk
    E. The difference between what the character imagines and "the gradually increasing bustle and preparation for the day" (lines 2–3)

For questions 31–43, read the following poem carefully before choosing your answers.

Poetry

I, too, dislike it: there are things that are important beyond all this fiddle.
  Reading it, however, with a perfect contempt for it, one discovers that there is in
    it after all, a place for the genuine.
      Hands that can grasp, eyes
        that can dilate, hair that can rise   (5)
          if it must, these things are important not because a

high-sounding interpretation can be put upon them but because they are
  useful; when they become so derivative as to become unintelligible, the
    same thing may be said for all of us—that we
      do not admire what   (10)
        we cannot understand. The bat,
          holding on upside down or in quest of something to

eat, elephants pushing, a wild horse taking a roll, a tireless wolf under
  a tree, the immovable critic twinkling his skin like a horse that feels a flea, the base-
    ball fan, the statistician—case after case   (15)
      could be cited did
        one wish it; nor is it valid
          to discriminate against "business documents and

school-books"; all these phenomena are important. One must make a distinction
  however: when dragged into prominence by half poets, the result is not poetry,   (20)
    nor till the autocrats among us can be
      "literalists of
        the imagination"—above
          insolence and triviality and can present

for inspection, imaginary gardens with real toads in them, shall we have   (25)
  it. In the meantime, if you demand on the one hand, in defiance of their opinion—
    the raw material of poetry in
      all its rawness, and
        that which is on the other hand,
          genuine, then you are interested in poetry.   (30)

31. Within context, which of the following is closest in meaning to the speaker's use of "fiddle" in line 1?

A. The obscure musicality of poetry that can be distracting to readers
B. The obvious playfulness that poetry uses
C. The useless drivel that bad poets create
D. The difficult subjects some poets write about
E. The senseless ways some poems rhyme

32. What is an effect of the speaker changing from "dislike" in line 1 to "perfect contempt" in line 2?

A. It reinforces the idea that most readers do not relate to poetry.
B. The second term modifies the passion of the first term.
C. It shifts the focus to new forms of poetry.
D. It enhances the negativity the speaker feels for poorly written poetry.
E. The use of "perfect" creates an oxymoron in the second term.

33. The collective effect produced by the phrase "Hands that can grasp, eyes / that can dilate, hair that can rise . . . " (lines 4–5) can best be described as

   A. metaphorically substituting concrete objects for abstract ideas about poetry

   B. combining these parts into the whole person who reacts to genuine poetry

   C. comparing items that must transform to be useful in genuine poetry

   D. understated images that diminish the purpose of poetry

   E. unrelated references to the subjects poets write about

34. In the first stanza, what surprise is suggested by the effect of "the genuine" (line 3)?

   A. Good poetry can create a physical reaction.

   B. Genuine emotions are hard to read.

   C. Contempt can be well-hidden.

   D. Good poetry is difficult to recognize.

   E. Something can be both disliked and genuine.

35. In context, which of the following is the opposite of "high-sounding interpretation" (line 7)?

   A. "genuine" (line 3)

   B. "important" (line 6)

   C. "useful" (line 8)

   D. "unintelligible" (line 8)

   E. "immovable" (line 14)

36. Which of the following can be inferred as the speaker's meaning in lines 8–11, " . . . when they become . . . we cannot understand"?

   A. The speaker will only admire that which is understandable.

   B. The speaker requests that new poets emulate older, revered poets.

   C. The speaker wishes to see imitative and easy-to-understand poetry.

   D. The speaker knows poetry will not be universally admired.

   E. The speaker wants both clarity and originality in poetry.

37. What analogy can be drawn between reading poetry and the animals' actions described in lines 11–14?

   A. The animals' fruitless behaviors are as difficult as understanding bad poetry.

   B. Both are challenging, but can be accomplished.

   C. Both are admirable because they are perplexing.

   D. Reading poetry appeals to the animalistic nature in all humanity.

   E. The humorous vision of the animals applies to readers who do not appreciate poetry.

38. The poet's use of free verse in this poem is appropriate because it

   A. allows the speaker to make unusual connections

   B. emphasizes the speaker's unconventional attitude about poetry

   C. provides a framework to follow the speaker's thoughts

   D. suggests a reverence for tradition in poetry

   E. encourages the poet to experiment with irregular forms

39. What is the speaker's intended purpose in mentioning baseball fans and statisticians (lines 14–15)?

   A. Like poets, both require intense concentration.

   B. Both depend on reading business documents.

   C. Statisticians are often baseball fans.

   D. Both can get so bogged down in detail that they lose sight of the big picture.

   E. Fans and statisticians can be as inaccurate as bad poets.

40. Which of the following best describes the work of "half poets" (line 20)?

A. "high-sounding interpretation" (line 7)

B. "derivative" (line 8) and "unintelligible" (line 8)

C. "immovable critic" (line 14) and "statistician" (line 15)

D. "imaginary gardens with real toads" (line 25)

E. "raw material of poetry" (line 27)

41. Which of the following clarifies the intended meaning of the phrase "imaginary gardens with real toads in them" (line 25)?

A. Genuine poetry connects the sweet spot of the poet's vision to the actual day-to-day real world.

B. Poets must incorporate both positive and negative imagery in successful poetry.

C. The natural world makes the best subject for genuine poetry.

D. The "immovable critic" (line 14) needs to develop the powers of imagination to appreciate genuine poetry.

E. Real toads are the raw material poets should seek.

42. Which of the following best clarifies the speaker's overall point about "the raw material of poetry" (line 27)?

A. A poet needs to strip the real world to its bare essentials to really understand how to write good poetry.

B. The raw material of poetry is difficult to find, but ultimately, the search can be a rewarding process.

C. Poets should use clear, concise, raw language in their poetry.

D. Interest in poetry only stems from the study of nature in its rawness.

E. A poet who combines the real world with the imaginary world has a chance to create genuine poetry.

43. What is most notable about the speaker's movement from the first line to the last line of the poem?

A. In the first line, the speaker points out what is important in poetry and in the last line notices it is interesting.

B. The speaker's attitude changes from aversion to admiration and back.

C. The speaker's attitude morphs from dislike of poetry to interest in poetry.

D. The speaker moves from the specific to the general.

E. The beginning of the poem raises questions and the end of the poem answers them.

For questions 44–55, read the following poem carefully before choosing your answers.

A Satirical Elegy on the Death of a Late Famous General

His Grace! impossible! what, dead!
Of old age too, and in his bed!
And could that Mighty Warrior fall?
And so inglorious, after all!
Well, since he's gone, no matter how,   (5)
The last loud trump[1] must wake him now;
And, trust me, as the noise grows stronger,
He'd wish to sleep a little longer.
And could he be indeed so old
As by the newspapers we're told?   (10)
Threescore[2], I think, is pretty high;
'Twas time in conscience he should die.
This world he cumbered long enough;
He burnt his candle to the snuff;
And that's the reason, some folks think,   (15)
He left behind so great a stink.[3]
Behold his funeral appears,
Nor widow's sighs, nor orphan's tears,
Wont[4] at such times each heart to pierce,
Attend the progress of his hearse.   (20)
But what of that, his friends may say,
He had those honours in his day.
True to his profit and his pride,
He made them weep before he died.
Come hither, all ye empty things,   (25)
Ye bubbles raised by breath of kings;
Who float upon the tide of state,

  Come hither, and behold your fate.
Let pride be taught by this rebuke,
How very mean a thing's a Duke;   (30)
From all his ill-got honours flung,
Turned to that dirt from whence he sprung.

---

[1] **trump:** trumpet signaling the Last Judgment upon one's death
[2] **threescore:** 60 years
[3] **stink:** the foul smell left by a candle's smoldering wick after the candle had burned all the way down
[4] **wont:** custom, usual habit

44. Which of the following best describes the poet's intended effect of using five exclamation points in the first four lines of the poem?

    A. They distract from the overall meaning.

    B. They collectively create irony.

    C. They add humor to a grim situation.

    D. They enhance the poem's sarcasm.

    E. They emphasize the general's death.

45. The implied irony surrounding the general's death is that

    A. he could have lived longer

    B. he died peacefully in bed of old age instead of in battle

    C. his death spurred such mourning

    D. people were surprised at the news of his death

    E. his long life was well-lived

46. Lines 6–8, "The last loud trump . . . sleep a little longer" can best be inferred as meaning

    A. loud noises can keep one from getting sound sleep

    B. the volume of the sound decreases

    C. people generally want to live longer

    D. all the townspeople tried to ignore the sound

    E. people run away from what they fear

47. Which of the following summarizes the speaker's opinion about the general's age and morality in lines 9–12?

    A. The general lived longer than he deserved to.

    B. The general died peacefully with a clear conscience.

    C. The newspapers were critical of the general's lack of scruples.

    D. The speaker believes that the general should have died during war.

    E. The general had few public supporters by the time he died.

48. Within context, which of the following is closest to the intended meaning of "cumbered" in line 13?

    A. Disrupted

    B. Hindered

    C. Embarrassed

    D. Burdened

    E. Facilitated

49. What is the speaker's suggested overall point about "widow's sighs" and "orphan's tears" in line 18?

    A. They lamented the general's death too much in public.

    B. They sigh and cry as they follow the funeral procession, knowing of the general's greatness.

    C. They had previously mourned their lost husbands and fathers, thus they would not mourn the death of the general whose actions led to these deaths.

    D. Their grief over the general's death is misplaced.

    E. They become overwrought at the news of the general's death.

50. The use of the word "pride" in line 29 is striking because

    A. kings naturally should have pride yet are "empty"

    B. the general's pride brought his demise

    C. it is usually a positive word that is used very negatively in the poem

    D. men who are promoted by kings have too much pride

    E. it describes all military men

51. The speaker suggests that which of the following is the general's worst fault?

    A. His overwhelming presence in life

    B. His ability to hide his errors from the public

    C. His bowing down to the wishes of the king

    D. His lack of sincerity to all

    E. His complete lack of morals

52. The poem utilizes all of the following EXCEPT

    A. allegory
    B. hyperbole
    C. imagery
    D. understatement
    E. metaphor

53. In comparison to the first stanza, the second stanza's tone is more

    A. directly ironic
    B. unabashedly critical
    C. gently mocking
    D. satirically evasive
    E. subtly condemning

54. Which of the following is NOT an example of the speaker's sarcasm?

    A. "His Grace! impossible! what, dead!" (line 1)
    B. "'Twas time in conscience he should die" (line 12)
    C. "He burnt his candle to the snuff" (line 14)
    D. "Nor widow's sighs, nor orphan's tears" (line 18)
    E. "He made them weep before he died" (line 24)

55. The intended effect of the poem's rhyming couplets is that they

    A. enhance the appropriateness of an elegy
    B. demonstrate the poet's skill
    C. belittle the speaker's attitude
    D. determine the rhyme scheme
    E. add a playful tone, hiding the speaker's contempt

IF YOU FINISH BEFORE TIME IS CALLED, CHECK YOUR WORK ON THIS SECTION ONLY. DO NOT WORK ON ANY OTHER SECTION IN THE TEST.

Section II: Free-Response Questions

Time: 2 hours

3 questions

Question 1

(Suggested time—40 minutes. This question counts toward one-third of the total free-response section score.)

Directions: In the following poem, "Joy in the Woods," by Claude McKay (first published 1920), the speaker laments that he cannot enjoy the joys of nature while still a slave. Read the poem carefully. Then, in a well-written essay, analyze how McKay uses poetic elements and techniques to convey the complex relationship between the speaker and nature.

In your response you should do the following:

- Respond to the prompt with a thesis that presents an interpretation and may establish a line of reasoning.
- Select and use evidence to develop and support your line of reasoning.
- Explain the relationship between the evidence and your thesis.
- Use appropriate grammar and punctuation in communicating your argument.

Joy in the Woods

There is joy in the woods just now,
   The leaves are whispers of song,
And the birds make mirth on the bough
   And music the whole day long,
And God! to dwell in the town   (5)
   In these springlike summer days,
On my brow an unfading frown
   And hate in my heart always—

A machine out of gear, aye, tired,
Yet forced to go on—for I'm hired.   (10)

Just forced to go on through fear,
   For every day I must eat
And find ugly clothes to wear,
   And bad shoes to hurt my feet
And a shelter for work-drugged sleep!   (15)
   A mere drudge! but what can one do?
A man that's a man cannot weep!
   Suicide? A quitter? Oh, no!

But a slave should never grow tired,
Whom the masters have kindly hired.   (20)

But oh! for the woods, the flowers
   Of natural, sweet perfume,
The heartening, summer showers
   And the smiling shrubs in bloom,
Dust-free, dew-tinted at morn,   (25)
   The fresh and life-giving air,
The billowing waves of corn
   And the birds' notes rich and clear:—

For a man-machine toil-tired
May crave beauty too—though he's hired.   (30)

Question 2

(Suggested time—40 minutes. This question counts toward one-third of the total free-response section score.)

Directions: The following excerpt is the opening of *Nostromo* (1904), a Joseph Conrad novel that takes place in a fictional South American country. In this passage, the narrator describes the location and the people who live in the area. Read the passage carefully. Then, in a well-written essay, analyze how Conrad uses literary techniques to develop the complex atmosphere of the location and characters in the story.

In your response you should do the following:

- Respond to the prompt with a thesis that presents an interpretation and may establish a line of reasoning.
- Select and use evidence to develop and support your line of reasoning.
- Explain the relationship between the evidence and your thesis.
- Use appropriate grammar and punctuation in communicating your argument.

In the time of Spanish rule, and for many years afterwards, the town of Sulaco—the luxuriant beauty of the orange gardens bears witness to its antiquity—had never been commercially anything more important than a coasting port with a fairly large local trade in ox-hides and indigo. The clumsy deep-sea galleons of the conquerors that, needing a brisk gale to move at all, would lie becalmed, where your modern ship built on

(5) clipper lines forges ahead by the mere flapping of her sails, had been barred out of Sulaco by the prevailing calms of its vast gulf. Some harbours of earth are made difficult of access by the treachery of sunken rocks and the tempests of their shores. Sulaco had found an inviolable sanctuary from the temptations of a trading world in the solemn hush of the deep Golfo Placido as if within an enormous semi-circular and unroofed temple open to the ocean, with its walls of lofty mountains hung with the mourning draperies of cloud.

(10) On one side of this broad curve in the straight seaboard of the Republic of Costaguana, the last spur of the coast range forms an insignificant cape whose name is Punta Mala[1]. From the middle of the gulf the point of the land itself is not visible at all; but the shoulder of a steep hill at the back can be made out faintly like a shadow on the sky.

On the other side, what seems to be an isolated patch of blue mist floats lightly on the glare of the horizon.

(15) This is the peninsula of Azuera, a wild chaos of sharp rocks and stony levels cut about by vertical ravines. It lies far out to sea like a rough head of stone stretched from a green-clad coast at the end of a slender neck of sand covered with thickets of thorny scrub. Utterly waterless, for the rainfall runs off at once on all sides into the sea, it has not soil enough—it is said—to grow a single blade of grass, as if it were blighted by a curse. The poor, associating by an obscure instinct of consolation the ideas of evil and wealth, will tell you that it is

(20) deadly because of its forbidden treasures. The common folk of the neighborhood, peons of the *estancias*[2], *vaqueros*[3] of the seaboard plains, tame Indians coming miles to market with a bundle of sugar-cane or a basket of maize worth about threepence, are well aware that heaps of shining gold lie in the gloom of the deep precipices cleaving the stony levels of Azuera. Tradition has it that many adventurers of olden time had perished in the search. The story goes also that within men's memory two wandering sailors—*Americanos*,

(25) perhaps, but *gringos* of some sort for certain—talked over a gambling, good-for-nothing *mozo*[4], and the three stole a donkey to carry for them a bundle of dry sticks, a water-skin, and provisions enough to last a few days. Thus accompanied, and with revolvers at their belts, they had started to chop their way with machetes to the thorny scrub on the neck of the peninsula.

On the second evening an upright spiral of smoke (it could only have been from their camp-fire) was seen

(30) for the first time within memory of man standing up faintly upon the sky above a razor-backed ridge on the stony head. The crew of a coasting schooner, lying becalmed three miles off the shore, stared at it with amazement till dark. A Negro fisherman, living in a lonely hut in a little bay nearby, had seen the start and was on the lookout for some sign. He called to his wife just as the sun was about to set. They had watched the strange portent with envy, incredulity, and awe.

(35) The impious adventurers gave no other sign. The sailors, the Indian, and the stolen *burro* were never seen again. As to the *mozo*, a Sulaco man—his wife paid for some Masses, and the poor four-footed beast, being

without sin, had been probably permitted to die; but the two *gringos*, spectral and alive, are believed to be dwelling to this day amongst the rocks, under the fatal spell of their success. Their souls cannot tear themselves away from their bodies mounting guard over that discovered treasure. They are now rich and hungry and

(40) thirsty—a strange theory of tenacious *gringo* ghosts suffering in their starved and parched flesh of defiant heretics, where a Christian would have renounced and been released.

---

[1] **Punta Mala:** bad point, i.e., dangerous for shipping
[2] ***estancias:*** landed estates or cattle ranches
[3] ***vaqueros:*** cowboys, herdsmen
[4] ***mozo:*** a servant

Question 3

(Suggested time—40 minutes. This question counts toward one-third of the total free-response section score.)

Directions: Most people move or travel from one location to another at some time in their life. Some move a block away, some move across a country, some move to foreign lands, some of them eventually return to their original home.

Either from your own reading or from the list below, choose a character in a work of fiction who moves or travels at least once to another location. Then, in a well-written essay, analyze how any change in location affects the character and how moving adds to an interpretation of the work as a whole. Do not merely summarize the plot.

In your response you should do the following:

- Respond to the prompt with a thesis that presents an interpretation and may establish a line of reasoning.
- Select and use evidence to develop and support your line of reasoning.
- Explain the relationship between the evidence and your thesis.
- Use appropriate grammar and punctuation in communicating your argument.

All the Pretty Horses	*Oliver Twist*
Atonement	*The Other*
Beloved	*A Passage to India*
Black Boy	*The Poisonwood Bible*
The Crossing	*A Portrait of the Artist as a Young Man*
The God of Small Things	*Pride and Prejudice*
The Goldfinch	*Sag Harbor*
The Grapes of Wrath	*The Story of Edgar Sawtelle*
Great Expectations	*Tess of the D'Urbervilles*
Heart of Darkness	*Things Fall Apart*
Invisible Man	*A Thousand Acres*
Jane Eyre	*A Thousand Splendid Suns*
King Lear	*Waiting to Exhale*
The Kite Runner	*When the Emperor Was Divine*
Middlemarch	*Wuthering Heights*
The Namesake	

IF YOU FINISH BEFORE TIME IS CALLED, CHECK YOUR WORK ON THIS SECTION ONLY. DO NOT WORK ON ANY OTHER SECTION IN THE TEST.

Answer Key

Section I: Multiple-Choice Questions

First Prose Passage	First Poem	Second Prose Passage	Second Poem	Third Poem
1. D	11. E	21. D	31. C	44. D
2. E	12. C	22. A	32. D	45. B
3. D	13. D	23. D	33. B	46. C
4. A	14. B	24. E	34. A	47. A
5. B	15. A	25. B	35. C	48. D
6. D	16. D	26. C	36. E	49. C
7. C	17. C	27. B	37. A	50. C
8. E	18. E	28. C	38. B	51. E
9. B	19. A	29. A	39. D	52. A
10. C	20. B	30. E	40. B	53. B
			41. A	54. D
			42. E	55. E
			43. C	

Answers and Explanations

Section I: Multiple-Choice Questions

First Prose Passage

For questions 1–10, the passage comes from The Custom of the Country, *written in 1913 by Edith Wharton. This scene takes place in Undine Spragg's hotel room on the upper-west side of New York City as the young woman contemplates her position in society.*

1. **D.** Undine is clearly conflicted; she wants to fit in to high society, but apparently has not yet been accepted. She worries about the suitability of her address, her choice of stationery, her clothing; ultimately, she is consumed with doing the right thing in society's eyes. These internal conflicts are symbolized by her hiding behind "many layers of lace," choice D; but the lace that covers her windows is a thin fabric, fragile and easily seen through. Choice A, the fragility of Undine's housing situation, has no support in the passage. The idea in choice B, about the dominance of material objects, is found in the passage, but it is irrelevant to answering this question. Choice C is not supported in the passage; we do know Undine has one maid, Céleste, but we have no other information about any other "levels of help." Finally, there is no evidence that the author intends any transparency in Undine's life (E).

2. **E.** When one writes a note to another, it implies a quick, short message. Mrs. Fairford's note to Mrs. Spragg is apparently only a simple dinner invitation for Undine, but the fact that Undine studies it "minutely" underscores how important the invitation is to her own social ambitions. She examines it carefully, analyzing Mrs. Fairford's stationery choice and valediction, hoping to find clues about Mrs. Fairford's supposed wealth and her personality. She is determined to read more into the note than Mrs. Fairford intended, choice E. Choice A is incorrect because Undine does not seem to consider Mrs. Fairford to be her social superior ("she wasn't going to truckle to any woman who lived in a small house down beyond Park Avenue . . . "). Choice B contradicts the passage. Mrs. Fairford did extend a dinner invitation in the note;

she wasn't noncommittal. The idea presented in choice C, that Mrs. Fairford considers herself above the Spraggs, may possibly be true, but that is not the reason Undine studied the note so closely. Likewise, choice D may perhaps be correct; it's likely that Undine will try to imitate Mrs. Fairford's style, but that is not the real reason for her minute study.

3. D. When the author claims that Undine "wrote the note in her mother's name," it literally means that Undine was replying to Mrs. Fairford's invitation as if her mother were the letter writer. It does not mean that Undine is imitating her mother's voice or style; rather, she is merely answering using her mother's name, choice D. The other answer choices all correctly identify instances wherein Undine demonstrates her penchant for imitation; she imitated the paper style she read about in the "Boudoir Chat" (A), before she imitated Mrs. Fairford's plain white paper (B), onto which she "copied Mrs. Fairford's formula" (C), before finally imitating traditional style with the wording of her mother's signature (E).

4. A. Undine is a girl who wants very much to be accepted in high society and looked up to. Therefore, when she reads in the "Boudoir Chat" column of a Sunday paper that pigeon-blood stationery with white ink is the latest style, she immediately buys a "large supply" of it, even going so far as to have her monogram printed in silver, not white. However, after noticing that Mrs. Fairford's note was written on plain, old-fashioned white paper (gasp!), she ironically decides not to use her fancy, expensive notepaper to reply, choice A. None of the other answer choices identify instances of irony. Choice B misreads the passage; Mrs. Fairford was never mentioned in regard to Undine's stationery purchase. Choice C, that the "Boudoir Chat" has always given good advice before, is not supported in the passage. Choice D is true; Undine's mother had argued again the purchase of the extravagant stationery, but it is not an example of irony. Choice E is unreasonable and irrelevant. Whether or not Undine should have added her address and phone is not ironic and has nothing to do with the actual purchase of the stationery.

5. B. A key phrase in the last sentence of the third paragraph is "she wasn't going to truckle to any woman. . . ." To truckle means to obsequiously yield to someone, to flatter and grovel, something Undine is unwilling to do. Additionally, Undine's idea that Mrs. Fairford lives "in a small house down beyond Park Avenue" implies that Undine believes Mrs. Fairford to be below her in social standing, choice B, regardless of her accuracy. It is unreasonable to think that Undine will decline Mrs. Fairford's invitation (A); this would contradict the passage. The idea in choice C, that Undine will scrutinize the Fairford home when she visits, is highly likely, but it is not implied by the sentence in this question. Additionally, the passage offers no evidence that Mrs. Fairford thinks Undine's attending her dinner party will enhance her own social standing (D); the passage clearly implies the Fairfords are ranked above the Spraggs. Choice E is too much of a stretch; the sentence in this question is not related to Mrs. Heeny's esteem for Mrs. Fairford; in fact, Mrs. Heeny's opinion of Mrs. Fairford is only mentioned as an aside in regard to Undine's dilemma over which stationery she should use to reply to the invitation.

6. D. The quotation in the question has two separate ideas: Undine is (1) "fiercely independent," yet she is also (2) "passionately imitative." She wants to act is if she's a liberated free spirit, but she cannot help but model herself "on the last person she met." Choice D, within context, refers to the fashion in which she signs her mother's name: "Yours sincerely, Mrs. Leota B. Spragg," a very traditional way of signing a letter to someone she has never met. This contradicts the idea of her truly being independent. Most of the other choices cite quotes that are irrelevant to answering this question. The "many layers of lace" in choice A refer to her window curtains, not her personality. Choice B, which describes Undine's careful reading of Mrs. Fairford's letter, does not address either her independence or her imitative nature. The phrase "permit my daughter to take dinner with you" in choice C refers to the wording of Undine's reply (using her mother's persona) to Mrs. Fairford's invitation, so it is irrelevant. Undine's dresses that are referred to in choice E, although "exquisite" and making her look "lovely," do not contradict either that she is independent or imitative.

7. C. It seems that poor Undine cannot easily complete her reply to Mrs. Fairford's invitation. She first grapples with what stationery to use (as in choice A), and then later she is indecisive about using the phrase "take dinner" (as in choice D). But later she struggles with her greatest problem, "a new difficulty," specifically that she cannot make up her mind about how to end the letter. The author chronicles three separate attempts in which Undine had to rewrite the letter because she didn't like the ending, before revealing that "after several other experiments she finally decided on a compromise." Considering the number of times she wrote and rewrote her reply, it is reasonable to infer that choosing how to sign her mother's name gave her the greatest difficulty, making choice C correct. Choice B is never discussed in the passage; Undine has already decided to accept the invitation. The idea in choice E is not logical; this passage shows that Undine is tossed about by her independent-yet-imitative nature, not that she makes a conscious choice between them.

8. **E.** Undine appears to erroneously believe that fancy material objects will guarantee her happiness and open up her access to high society. To that aim she buys a "large supply" of the newest fad in stationery, pigeon-blood-colored paper with white ink of all things, and had "ordered a number" of dinner-dresses; however, when the dresses were unused, she "tossed them over impatiently to the maid," and then bought more, which are still basically unworn. This conspicuous consumption of expensive material goods, items that she does not even use, is a trait that will not serve her well over time; choice E is correct. Choice A compares the color of the stationery and the dresses, but the dresses' color is not mentioned in the passage. All the other choices contradict the passage. The fancy items were not, in fact, used to advance others' opinions (B); some were not used at all. Undine does not have socially superior standing (C); that is a status she desires, but has not yet attained. Undine has not passed both items to Céleste (D); she still has the pigeon-blood notepaper.

9. **B.** Visualize the simile of Undine's lonely dinner dresses hanging "unworn in her wardrobe, like so many derisive points of interrogation." On one hand, the image is almost comical; the shape of a clothes hanger hook even mimics the shape of a question mark. However, the image in the simile is also so sad. The negative word "derisive" emphasizes symbolism of the personified gowns sarcastically mocking Undine, questioning and interrogating her about why she never has occasion to wear them, choice B. Choices A and C both assign incorrect emotions to the dresses themselves; choice A claims that the dresses are angry and tired and choice C claims that each dress is eager to be chosen. These answer choices completely miss the point of the dresses' "derisive interrogation." Finally, there is no support in the passage for the idea in choice D, that Céleste questions the need for so many dresses, nor for choice E, that Mrs. Spragg questions the need for more "abstract pleasure."

10. **C.** This author makes good use of third-person, limited omniscient point of view because the reader is allowed to understand Undine's thoughts, but only Undine's thoughts, choice C. We see her shallow nature revealed, believing that she can buy her way into the high society she so covets by showing off fancy clothes and expensive stationery, assuring herself that "Fifth Avenue was where she wanted to be!" The reader sees how irrational and illogical her young mind is as she tries to impress Mrs. Fairford, whom she has never met, with her well-rehearsed reply to a simple dinner invitation. We see Undine's innermost thoughts as she grapples with opposing instincts, being independent yet imitative, as she tries to work her way into society. Choice A, which claims the narrative would become too cumbersome if the point of view were changed and we could also understand Mrs. Fairford's mind, is irrelevant. The question asks about the effect of the actual point of view; it does not ask one to speculate about the effect of any potential changes in point of view. Choice B is too narrow and is only partially correct; the point of view allows the reader to understand much more than just Undine's motivations in writing the note. Choice D, like choice A, does not properly address the question; the *effect* of a given point of view is not to symbolize anything. Choice E, dealing with Undine's independence from her mother, does not have textual support and again does not address this specific question.

First Poem

Questions 11–20 refer to "On Shakespeare," a laudatory poem written by John Milton in 1630. It was included anonymously in the 1632 Second Folio of Shakespeare's plays.

11. **E.** When the speaker refers to Shakespeare as "my Shakespeare" in the first line, he personalizes the great poet; he indicates that he is referring to the poet he personally thinks of, the poet that he personally understands. This subjective identity separates the public Shakespeare from the speaker's personal image of him, choice E. On the other hand, this poem offers no proof that the speaker considers himself on the same level as Shakespeare (A); instead, the speaker puts Shakespeare on a pedestal above all others. Choice B is irrelevant; the use of "my" does not affect Shakespeare's reputation whatsoever. In choice C, part of the phrasing may seem accurate; indeed, the speaker does exhibit emotion. However, the first phrase of the

answer choice contradicts the meaning of the poem. The speaker does not undermine Shakespeare's achievements; instead, he praises them. The concept in choice D is a complete misread of the poem. Shakespeare himself has no need for more glory, and this idea, even if it were remotely accurate, does not answer this question.

12. C. Line 6 repeats the initial question of the poem, this time asking Shakespeare why he would need such "weak witness" of his name, referring to the monuments that have been built in his honor, the pilèd stones of line 2 and pyramid of line 4, choice C. "Weak witness" does not refer to Shakespeare's many fans (A); this contradicts what the poem says about those who admire Shakespeare, as they venerate him and are hardly "weak." Choice B, which refers to Shakespeare's many works, makes no sense within context. If his works were a "weak witness," why would he have such lasting fame with so many fans? Choice D, "Delphic lines," is unreasonable, just a distractor. "Delphic" actually refers to the Greek oracle at Delphi, which was sacred for Apollo, the Greek god associated with poetry; therefore, the use of this phrase in the poem is favorably comparing Shakespeare's lines to the ancients'. The word "marble" in line 14 (E) refers to the way Shakespeare's readers are frozen into marble in awe of his genius, but, like choice B, these readers are not "weak."

13. D. The phrase "Dear son of Memory" is a metaphor that refers directly to Shakespeare, associating him with memory and fame, choice D. In Greek mythology, the muses who inspired art and poetry were the daughters of memory; thus, this reference enhances Shakespeare's association with timeless greatness. Choice A, an allusion to Shakespearean actors, might seem attractive to readers who merely think about how actors must memorize their part in a play, but it has no support in the poem itself. Choosing this answer likely comes from taking the quote out of context. In choice B, a conceit is too strong. The term refers to an extended metaphor in which the connection is so unusual that the reader has to pause and figure out how it fits. Additionally, this answer addresses Shakespeare's works, and the actual metaphor refers to Shakespeare himself, not his writings. Choice C, a metaphor for the poet himself, might seem likely to some, since Milton, the author of the poem, might also be inspired by the Greek muses, but he is not talking about himself in this line; he's referring directly to Shakespeare. Choice E is inaccurate because the phrase "son of Memory" is simply not personification, and it does not refer to Shakespeare's art, but to the man himself.

14. B. Lines 9–10 explain that Shakespeare wrote with greater ease than other poets: "For whilst, to th' shame of slow-endeavoring art, / Thy easy numbers flow. . . . " In other words, some poets feel shame that their artistic endeavors are completed so slowly, in contrast to the way that Shakespeare's "numbers" (words) flow easily and quickly, choice B. The poem does not present any actual visual differentiation between stone monuments and pyramids (A); any reader who thinks so is imagining the difference, as it is not in the poem. Choice C is incorrect for the same reason; the "honoured bones" and "hallowed relics" are not directly contrasted. Choice D is wrong because the "Delphic lines" are contained within the pages of the "unvalued book," not contrasted with it. Finally, the items in choice E, like in choice B, are not concrete or contrasted images in the poem; they exist only in a reader's imagination.

15. A. The poet and Shakespeare's readers are all amazed at Shakespeare's skill, which is so overpowering that it stops them cold, makes them as immobile as a marble statue, choice A. Choice B might seem to have some potential on first glance, but it does not answer this particular question. While it is true that readers should marvel at Shakespeare's works, the question asks specifically about the meaning of the phrase "Dost make us marble." Choice C misreads the poem; readers are not turned into marble because they cannot understand Shakespeare; if that were the case, they would not have such admiration for him. Choice D is irrelevant; whether or not marble was used for statues at Delphi has nothing to do with the line in the poem about readers being morphed into marble. Choice E is equally irrelevant; the stone used in kings' tombs has no bearing on the question.

16. D. In the first line, as the speaker refers to "my Shakespeare," he is asking a rhetorical question, essentially wondering why the Shakespeare he thinks he knows so well would need monuments to his honor. It begins with a very personal viewpoint. However, by the end of the poem, the speaker has transitioned into a spokesperson for all readers who admire Shakespeare, choice D. Choice A is incorrect because the poem offers no evidence of any influence of the speaker on Shakespeare's readers. Choice B is unreasonable; nothing suggests that the speaker is too inclusive or that his position is weakened. (You should not spend much time on this type of answer choice; when an answer choice makes no sense, eliminate it immediately!) Choice C does not address the question; the poem offers no indication that the speaker's idea is limited to his own personal time. Choice E is inaccurate and irrelevant. Nothing in the poem suggests Shakespeare needs more glory, and this idea does not address the change from a singular pronoun in the opening line to plural pronouns by the end.

17. **C.** In line 8, the word "monument" refers to the way that the collected works of Shakespeare create a lasting monument to his fame and talent. The speaker feels this is much more important than physical monuments, choice C. Choice A does not address the question; plus, it is silly and represents a misread of the poem (the pyramid mentioned in line 4 is not real). Choice B represents another misread of the poem. The "weak witness" of line 6 refers to the physical monuments that Shakespeare does not really need, but the monument in this question refers to Shakespeare's collected writings. Although the speaker claims Shakespeare wrote faster than other poets, the poem does not imply that his collected works were ironically built quickly, eliminating choice D. Similarly, choice E sounds good because of the idea that kings wish they could have as glorious a monument as Shakespeare's fans who were turned to marble, but it does not answer the question.

18. **E.** The word "unvalued" in line 11 does not mean without any value; in fact, it means the exact opposite. Today, the speaker might use a word like "invaluable." The book is so valuable that that it becomes impossible to put a price on its worth; hence it is priceless, choice E. Choices A and B are negative in their connotation, not positive. Choice C, out of fashion, misunderstands the text, and choice D, expensive, does not relate to the meaning of the word "unvalued."

19. **A.** The poem does not contain any understatement, choice A, which would have the effect of minimizing something to make it seem less than it really is. The poem does include more than one example of apostrophe (B), beginning when the speaker addresses the absent (and already dead) Shakespeare as "Dear son of Memory, great heir of fame, / What need'st thou such weak witness of thy name?" (lines 5–6). Also, the poem opens with two rhetorical questions (C), both essentially asking why Shakespeare would need monuments in his honor; we know the answer: He does not. Finally, the poem includes a metaphor (D) when the speaker refers to Shakespeare as "son of Memory" in line 5, and allusion (E) is present in the reference to "Delphic lines" in line 12.

20. **B.** The speaker, John Milton himself, highly venerates and reveres his subject, Shakespeare; his attitude toward this preeminent writer is best described as reverent, choice B; it displays an attitude of solemn admiration. Milton had truly devout respect for Shakespeare, as is apparent in this poem. Choice A is incorrect because a wondering attitude refers to feeling doubtful or questioning, or to a state of curiosity, neither of which accurately describes Milton's attitude. Choice C, patronizing, is a negative word that describes an attitude of condescension and demeaning others. Obviously, you need a positive word to describe this speaker's reverent attitude. Choice D, effervescent, goes too far in the other direction, describing an over-the-top enthusiasm, or someone who is extremely exuberant and energetic. This idea is too strong to be the correct answer. Choice E, overwhelmed, means to be overcome, thunderstruck, flabbergasted; like choice D, it is too extreme, but it also far too negative.

Second Prose Passage

For questions 21–30, the passage is from Nicholas Nickleby *by Charles Dickens (serialized between 1838–1839). Nicholas is the main character in the passage.*

21. **D.** The adverb "listlessly" means to do something in a lethargic, sluggish fashion, which contrasts directly with the "increasing bustle and preparation for the day" that is implied in choice D. Choice A is incorrect because "listlessly" does not contrast the way that Nicholas walks; rather, it describes it. Choice B misreads the passage; we never get any hint about the way Nicholas looks around during his walk. While the author does describe the preparation for the day as "gradually increasing," as in choice C, the fact that it is gradual at all does not provide a contrast with the character's listlessness. Choice E is wrong because Nicholas' despondency does not contrast with his listlessness; rather, these two ideas go hand in hand.

22. **A.** The second sentence stands apart from the rest of the passage in that it is the only sentence that states Nicholas, during the previous evening, had thought he could save the "beautiful creature" from [Arthur

Gride's] clutches. That optimism clearly juxtaposes (contrasts) with Nicholas' feelings of despondency and hopelessness the following morning, choice A, which only increase as he walks the streets. Choice B is a misread of the passage; the second sentence does not clarify why Nicholas is walking early in the morning. Choice C has no evidence in the passage; the second sentence does not confirm Nicholas' purpose; it merely establishes what he had thought the previous evening. Additionally, when considering the context of the overall passage, choice C becomes a contradiction; by the end of the passage, Nicholas has lost all sense of purpose. Choice D may seem appealing on first read; the second sentence does indeed identify Nicholas' enemy: Arthur Gride. However, that is not the purpose of the second sentence and, thus, choice D simply does not answer the question as clearly as choice A. Choice E is incorrect for the same reason; the second sentence does inform the reader how Nicholas had previously thought he could save the girl, but that idea does not address the purpose of the sentence in the overall passage.

23. **D.** Considering the context, the best substitution for the word "interposition" is intervention, choice D, which means to extraneously prevent something from happening, exactly what Nicholas hopes will occur to Arthur Gride's plans. Choices A, B, and C might seem appealing at first, but none is as accurate within context or as specific as choice D. Choice A, trespassing, means to encroach, to invade, wrongfully or illegally. Choice B, intrusion, might be the second-best answer, but it merely refers to getting in the way, to thrust oneself on another without welcome. When a group of people are having a conversation and you walk up and butt in with your own comments, you are intruding; however, it does not necessarily mean you completely stop their conversation. Choice C, prying, deals with inquiring disrespectfully or impolitely. When you pry into another's life, you ask about details they may be uncomfortable discussing. Finally, choice E, reconciliation, means to come together, to come to some agreement, which is the complete opposite of what Nicholas wants in this passage.

24. **E.** The third sentence is syntactically complex, and it is easy to fall into the trap of assuming the subject and verb will be located near the beginning because that's what we usually see. However, after the first two transitional words of the sentence, "But now," notice the next phrase is "when he thought how. . . . " The key word "when" signals an adverb clause, which can easily start a sentence and come before the main clause's subject and verb. What follows that adverb clause is a very long series of other clauses (with their own internal phrases), all separated by a semicolon and beginning with the word "how" (the words "when he thought" are parenthetical, not necessary, but understood). Finally, after this lengthy description composed of adverbial subordinate clauses, we find the true subject and verb of the main clause, "he felt" in line 48, choice E. Let's examine a simpler example. Consider this sentence: "When I woke up this morning, I felt completely rested." Notice it begins with an adverbial subordinate clause, "When I woke up this morning," which, if removed from the sentence, cannot stand alone. The main, independent clause is "I felt completely rested." The subject and verb of the main clause? "I felt." The Dickens passage presents the same pattern, but with many more adverbial clauses before we finally reach the main clause. All other answer choices indeed contain a subject and a verb, but they serve as such within the introductory subordinate clauses, not the main, independent clause that comes at the end of the sentence.

25. **B.** The 12 long and complex subordinate clauses that begin the sentence employ intense imagery to describe the many visual vignettes that Nicholas imagines as he walks the streets. These images, full of the horrible plight of the poor and disadvantaged, compound one upon another until Nicholas (and the reader) becomes overwhelmed with their intensity, and it makes perfect sense that their accumulation makes him feel that his "one slight case" has no chance of success, choice B. Choice A is inaccurate because the sentence has nothing to do with Arthur Gride; it is true that Nicholas disapproves of him, but the third sentence does not allude to Gride at all. Choice C is off base; while it is possible some readers might indeed feel that the sentence contains tedious detail, a reader-response answer choice does not address this question, which asks about stylistic effect. Choice D is incorrect for similar reasons; Nicholas' many imagined images are not stylistically designed to distract the reader, but rather to show how many other problems and injustices he has become aware of. Choice E also deals with the reader's experience; while the sentence may indeed allow us to understand Nicholas' thought patterns, that understanding is not the intended stylistic effect of the sentence. All of these inaccurate choices do not answer this specific question.

26. **C.** The passage ends with Nicholas' belief that his "one slight case" amounts to less than "an atom in the huge aggregate of distress and sorrow," which reinforces choice C. It is most likely that Nicholas will succumb (surrender, yield) to his doubts of saving the girl. Choice A contradicts the passage, which offers

no evidence that Nicholas can overcome his problem. Choice B is also off base; the passage offers no indication that Nicholas will seek other ways to thwart Arthur Gride. Choice D is wrong for two reasons: One, the passage offers no evidence that Nicholas will seek out ways to help families in need, and two, the phrasing of this answer choice is inaccurate; it implies Nicholas actually sees the poor families as he walks, but these images are only in his imagination. Remember that the third sentence begins with the phrase "when he thought." Choice E also has no support; the passage never mentions whether or not Nicholas has any friends or whether or not he would consult with them.

27. **B.** The third sentence—with 354 words!—indeed has parallel syntax with a series of subordinate clauses with the same beginning, and these many clauses do provide an accumulation of detail, choice B, albeit detail that Nicholas imagines. Choice A is inaccurate because the descriptions, although mostly about the poor, are not repetitive and they do not establish monotony. The images are not conflicting, as in choice C; they are consistent. Choice D is wrong on one count for the same reason: The clauses do not contrast each other; however, it is also inaccurate in its claim that the sentence has several independent clauses when it actually has only one. Choice E is wrong for a similar reason to choice A; the several subordinate clauses do not confound the reader, since they all point in the same direction.

28. **C.** Grim despair, choice C, indeed describes the mood of this sad and depressing passage. Both choices A and B have positive connotations (fortitude and optimism, respectively), which make them wrong, no matter what qualifying adjective precedes them. Choice D is completely wrong: "Virulent" means lethal, powerful, destructive, and "retribution" deals with retaliation and revenge. Both of these words are too strong, since Nicholas feels powerless. Choice E is inaccurate because the passage as a whole is not chaotic, nor is it incomprehensible. We may not like the depressing world that Nicholas sees, but we can comprehend it.

29. **A.** The images that Nicholas envisions are only in his mind. The first sentence establishes that the morning streets show "gradually increasing bustle and preparation for the day," but Nicholas thinks "everything appeared to yield him some new occasion for despondency," so we do not get any concrete image, only Nicholas' impressions. The second sentence only serves to remind us of Nicholas' emotions on the previous night. And the third sentence takes place entirely in Nicholas' mind. The other literary devices do appear in this passage. All three sentences have subordinate clauses (B). The third sentence is filled with parallel construction (C). The entire passage has a defeated tone (D), and all three sentences have complex syntax (E).

30. **E.** The passage's opening image depicts the real world, the "increasing bustle and preparation of the day," and connotes a flurry of activity as citizens get ready for their daily actions; the action in this situation provides an ironic contrast with Nicholas' unrelenting negative and futile imaginary visions, choice E. Choice A does not answer the question accurately; the fact that many who had "honest hearts" were poor and were subsequently driven into "criminal and dreadful trades" does not equate to irony. Nicholas' realization at the end of the passage (B) is also not ironic; it is consistent with all that comes before. Similarly, Nicholas' earlier idea that he could save the girl (C) does not demonstrate situational irony. Choice D is too much of a stretch; while it is true that during the previous night Nicholas felt encouraged and then he came to his senses the next morning, his emotional change does not really equate to situational irony.

Second Poem

Questions 31–43 refer to Marianne Moore's poem titled "Poetry." Although she revised and condensed this poem many times during her career, this version is from the original 1919 version.

31. **C.** The speaker's use of the word "fiddle" in line 1 refers to useless, bad poetry that is full of nonsense, choice C. Choice A misunderstands Moore's use of the word, incorrectly assuming that it refers to a musical instrument; additionally, choice A is wrong because of the idea that musicality in poetry can be distracting. Choice B also misreads the use of "fiddle," thinking erroneously that it is like fiddling around. Choice D is completely off base because "fiddle" has nothing to do with the subject matter of poetry, whether it may be difficult or not. Choice E has no evidence in the poem; the poet does not mention rhyme.

32. D. The essential point of the poem is that the speaker finds bad poetry to be useless, derivative, and unintelligible. The shift from the negative word "dislike" in line 1 to the much more derisive phrase "perfect contempt" in line 2 signals the true intensity of the speaker's position, choice D. The speaker is certainly not arguing that most readers do not relate to poetry (A). Choice B is incorrect because the second term ("perfect contempt") is not used to modify the passion of the first term ("dislike"), but rather to intensify it. Choice C is seriously off topic; the quotations refer to reactions to poetry, not to new forms of poetry. Finally, the use of "perfect" in the poem's context does not in any way create an oxymoron; choice E is simply incorrect.

33. B. The specific phrases in the lines "Hands that can grasp, eyes / that can dilate, hair that can rise" all employ the use of synecdoche; each of the three phrases describes a potential physical reaction to genuine and useful poetry and each refers to a part of human anatomy: hands, eyes, hair. Consequently, each of these parts combine to represent the whole person who reacts to genuine human poetry, choice B. The lines in the question are not metaphorical (A); the hands, eyes, and hair do not substitute for another thing, rather, they are literal. Similarly, they are not compared items and they do not transform into anything (C); this answer choice suggests the idea of simile, which is not accurate. Choice D inaccurately claims the images are understated and that they diminish the purpose of poetry. Choice E goes astray by claiming these human body parts (the hands, eyes, and hair) are unrelated, when instead they combine to make the whole human who reads poetry. Additionally, the concept that they become subject matter for poets is unfounded in this poem.

34. A. The idea that genuine poetry can actually cause a reader's hands to grasp something, or their eyes to dilate, or their hair to stand on end, is quite a surprising thought. We do not usually expect good poetry to elicit such intense physical reactions, choice A. Choice B actually contradicts the poem, which states that genuine emotion can be aroused by good poetry. Choice C, that contempt can be well-hidden, and choice D, that good poetry can be difficult to recognize, are both likely true in the real world, but they are both irrelevant to this question. Choice E, that something can be both disliked and genuine, contradicts the intent of the poem; the speaker dislikes bad poetry because it is not genuine, not in spite of it.

35. C. The correct answer must include a contrast to the phrase "high-sounding interpretation," which, in the poem's context, indicates the opposite of something that is useful, choice C. Such highfalutin, bombastic interpretations of poetry basically add nothing of value. The other answer choices all provide parallels, rather than contrasts. Choice A, "genuine," equates to good poetry; choice B, "important," refers to the physical reactions readers have to good poetry; choice D, "unintelligible," is a parallel to "high-sounding," and choice E, "immovable," refers to critics.

36. E. The key phrases within the quotation are as follows: "when they become so derivative as to become unintelligible." Thus, "derivative" refers to something that is unoriginal or copied, like trying to paint a copy of a copy of the *Mona Lisa.* "Unintelligible" refers to something that cannot quite be comprehended. Since the speaker is so derisive of poetry that can be described in these terms, we can infer that she wants good poetry to be original and clear in its meaning, choice E. Choice A is an attractive distractor; however, it is wrong for two reasons. The absolute word "only" is not accurate, and the logic of the answer choice is flawed. As it is written, Choice A claims that anything that can be understood will be admired by the speaker, but this is not necessarily true. Choices B, that new poets should emulate older ones, and C, the desire for imitative and easy-to-understand poetry, both contradict the poem, which argues against such puerile, derivative poetry. There is no support in this poem for the idea in choice D; universal admiration for poetry is not mentioned.

37. A. The animals' actions in the poem all seem to be pointless or unsuccessful, choice A. The bat is " . . . holding on upside down or in quest of something to eat," but its actions seem fruitless; the elephants are pushing, presumably against some object, but we have no idea what it is or to what end; the wild horse is "taking a roll," but again this seems like a frivolous activity; the tireless wolf is under a tree, but we don't know its purpose or expectation. Similarly, one can draw an analogy between these seemingly useless behaviors and the difficulty of reading bad poetry because, according to the speaker, "we do not admire what we cannot understand." All the other choices can be eliminated by a careful reading of the poem. There is no allusion to the behaviors being challenging but accomplished (B), nor of their behaviors being admirable because they are perplexing (C), nor of the animalistic nature of humanity (D). Finally, the inclusion of the animal behaviors is certainly not intended to be humorous (E).

38. **B.** Free verse, by definition, has no set rhyme or meter; it allows the freedom to write poetry without being forced into conventional restraints, such as the number of stressed syllables in each line or a strict rhyme scheme. Its use in this poem is effective because it emphasizes the speaker's unconventional attitude about poetry, choice B; she does not want to write verse that is merely derivative, and free verse provides her the freedom to explore ideas without arbitrary restraints. Choice A claims that free verse is appropriate because it allows the speaker to make unusual connections, but it does not really answer the question; it does not address specifically *why* free verse is appropriate. Poets can make unusual connections in any poetic form they choose; this technique is not limited to free verse. Choice C contradicts the very definition of free verse; it does not have a specific framework. Other poetic forms, such as a sonnet or villanelle have very strict frameworks, but free verse casts aside such constraints. In addition, the idea in this answer choice that the framework helps a reader follow the speaker's thoughts is irrelevant. Choice D also contradicts the very notion of free verse; instead of showing reverence or devotion to poetic traditions, free verse breaks from older traditions and follows no set rules of composition. Choice E may perhaps be true in a vague sense, but it does not address the question of *why* free verse is appropriate for *this poem*; the correct response must address the finished product, namely the poem itself. Instead, this choice addresses the incentive a poet may have for choosing free verse.

39. **D.** Within the poem's context, both baseball fans and statisticians are intended to be examples of people who can lose sight of what's really important in the world as they study their seemingly endless numbers and formulas, choice D. Just like the bat, elephants, horse, and wolf in the preceding lines, these people seem to be aimlessly missing the big picture. Choice A, comparing how poets also need intense concentration, is likely true, but it does not describe the speaker's intended purpose. Similarly, choice B might potentially be true; fans and statisticians depend on business documents, but that does not address the intended effect here. Choice C, claiming that statisticians are often baseball fans, may or may not be true, but it is completely irrelevant to this question. Choice E is a near-miss; however, this metaphor deals with one's losing sight of the big picture, not simple inaccuracies.

40. **B.** The speaker's main point faults poets who produce works that are "derivative" and "unintelligible," choice B. The phrase "high-sounding interpretation" (A) refers to fancy but facile interpretations of poetry. The "immovable critic" and "statistician" (C) both refer to those who waste their time and talents frivolously. Choice D contradicts the poem; half poets are bad poets, while genuine poets produce works that combine their imagination with the real world. Therefore, choice D refers to good poets, not half poets. In a similar vein, good poets use the "raw material of poetry" (E) to create genuine poetry; half poets do not produce such elevated works.

41. **A.** Choice A is the best answer because when poets present "imaginary gardens with real toads in them," they will produce genuine poetry; they successfully combine description of the gardens of their imagination with real toads, juxtaposing fairy castles with the not-so-pretty things that are found in the real world. Choice B misidentifies the idea of real and imagined worlds as positive and negative worlds. Both choices C and E make the same error; they concentrate only on the natural world and fail to include the contributions of the imaginary world. The idea in choice D, that the critic needs to develop imagination to appreciate genuine poetry, is almost certainly true; however, that point is irrelevant to answering this particular question.

42. **E.** The "raw material of poetry" refers first to the daily, real-world events and objects that poets write about, such as the "real toads" of line 25. But the speaker's larger point is that poets must begin in the real world, and then they must apply a genuine artistic imagination to describe that "raw material," choice E. Choice A mentions that understanding the essentials of the real world is essential, but it neglects to mention the other essential ingredient: the contribution of the imaginary world. Choice B misses the point when it asserts that raw material is difficult to find; rather, the poem easily finds authentic raw material in a humble garden, in a common toad. Choice C is completely off topic; using clear, concise language is not the speaker's point. Choice D is incorrect for the same reason as choice A; it mentions studying the real world, but it fails to make the connection to the imaginary world.

43. C. The poet begins by exclaiming that she "too" dislikes it, namely poetry, but we later discover that she is referring to her dislike of poorly written poetry. By the end of the poem, she has clarified what one needs to do to create good poetry, namely combine imagination and the real world; when that is done well, one cannot help but become interested in poetry. As stated in choice C, the poet has moved from the initial negative idea to a positive one. The other answer choices provide various incorrect descriptions of the movement in this poem. The poem does not point out what is important and later interesting (A); nor does the speaker's attitude change from admiration back to aversion (B). The speaker does not move from the specific to the general (D); nor does the end of the poem provide answers to questions that were posed earlier (E).

Third Poem

Questions 44–55 refer to "A Satirical Elegy on the Death of a Late Famous General" written by Jonathan Swift *after the Duke of Marlborough's death. During the War of Spanish Succession, Swift accused the duke of prolonging the war for personal profit. Shortly thereafter, the duke was dismissed. The duke died in 1722 and Swift wrote this "eulogy" that year, although it wasn't published until 1764.*

44. D. The ostentatious use of exclamation points, using five in only four lines, immediately establishes the poem's tone of sarcasm, choice D. Because the title has already alerted the reader to the fact that the poem is a satire, the reader should be prepared for the speaker's irreverent tone. It is as if the speaker, walking the streets of London, had just heard the news of the general's death, and he exclaimed to a friend something like, "I can't believe it! That old fraud of a general finally died peacefully, ingloriously, in bed!" Choice A is contradicted by the tone of the poem; the sarcasm emphasizes the overall meaning of the poem. Choice B is simply wrong; the exclamation points are not an example of the use of irony. The use of so many exclamation points may indeed induce humor in the reader, as in choice C, but that is not the author's main reason for their use. Finally, choice E is simply incorrect; the use of so many exclamation points emphasizes the author's reaction, not the general's death.

45. B. The speaker shows amazement that the general merely died of old age, at home, in his own bed, presumably in comfort. The speaker ironically implies that someone of his military background should have instead died heroically in battle, not peacefully of old age, choice B. On the other hand, there is no support in the poem for the ideas in the other answer choices. There is no suggestion that the general could have lived longer (A), or that his death inspired much mourning (C). The poem offers no evidence that people were surprised when the general died (D). Choice E, that the general's life was well-lived, contradicts the poem's overall meaning, and the idea is hardly ironic.

46. C. The fact that the speaker claims the dying general would "wish to sleep a little longer" intimates that many people really aren't ready for their final judgment when called by the "last loud trump," choice C. Ironically, the call of this trumpet will "wake" the general from the sleep of death and then he will learn his fate; given the speaker's animosity toward the general, it's understandable the general would like to postpone his final judgment. The other answer choices are too facile or off topic. Choice A simply asserts that loud noises can interrupt sleep, an idea that is irrelevant. Choice B, claiming the volume of the sound decreases, contradicts the poem, which asserts that the volume "grows stronger." Choice D misstates that it was the townspeople who heard the sound, when in fact, it was the general. Choice E, people run from what they fear, is off topic for this question.

47. A. Line 12 explicitly states that "'Twas time in conscience he should die," which emphasizes the speaker's position that the general did not morally deserve to live such a long life. The general's guilty conscience for sending young soldiers to die unnecessarily should have killed him, choice A. Choice B contradicts the entire concept of the passage; the general did not die with a clear conscience. The poem offers no support for choice C, that newspapers were critical. Choice D is too far-fetched and absolute. While it may be possible that the speaker maliciously believes the general should have died during war, this idea is too strong. The speaker's point about the general is that he unnecessarily sent young men to battle, not necessarily that he should have died in battle himself. The poem offers insufficient evidence for choice E; while we know widows and orphans did not mourn him or watch the progression of his funeral, line 21 informs us that he did have friends; therefore, we do not know how many public supporters the general had.

48. D. Within context, the closest in meaning to "cumbered," when Swift writes "This world he cumbered long enough," is burdened, choice D, which, as a verb, means to weigh down heavily, oppressively. Indeed the speaker believes the general weighed the world down with a heavy load. Choice A, disrupted, merely means to cause a temporary interruption in the progress of something. Choice B, hindered, is an attractive distractor; however, when one hinders something, one merely causes a delay, an impediment that keeps action from happening. This does not fit the context of the poem; the general was not hindering any action from occurring. Choice C is silly; the poem offers no hint that the general was embarrassed. Choice E, facilitated, is an antonym of cumbered; it refers to helping, assisting in some way.

49. C. The widows and orphans do not mourn the general's death; they do not follow the funeral procession, nor do many others. They have already shed their tears for their own husbands and fathers who were sent to an early grave by the general, choice C. The other answer choices all contradict the poem. The widows and orphans are not mourning the general, so they do not lament too much (A), nor do they follow the funeral procession (B). Since they are not mourning the general, their grief is not misplaced (D), nor do they become overwrought at the news (E).

50. C. The word "pride" by itself is a positive word, synonymous with self-respect, confidence, satisfaction at doing something well. But "pride" gains a negative connotation when one has too much of it, and then it becomes synonymous with arrogance and vanity. At the end of the poem, the normally positive word takes on the negativity of overindulgence, choice C. The other answer choices all misstate the intended meaning of "pride" in the context of this poem. Choice A confuses the word "empty," which refers to the metaphorical bubbles raised by the breath of kings, not to the kings themselves. Choice B contradicts the poem: The general died at home in bed; he was not brought down by his pride. Choices D and E are too vague; the poem's use of "pride" is a reference to the general himself, not to all men who are promoted by kings nor to all military men.

51. E. According to the speaker, the general had no morals, choice E, letting "profit and pride" (line 23) get in the way of effective military decisions, resulting in needless deaths. Choice A, the general's "overwhelming presence in life," does not point to a fault. The other answer choices refer to other perceived faults of the general, but they do not identify his primary fault. Neither his ability to hide his errors (B), nor his bowing down to the wishes of the king (C), nor his lack of sincerity (D) rises to the malevolent level of his complete lack of morals.

52. A. The poem is not an allegory, choice A, a work in which characters and/or story elements represent abstract ideas such as hope or charity. The poem does not present such abstract concepts. The poem does have ample hyperbole (B), such as "impossible! what, dead!" (line 1) and "could that Mighty Warrior fall?" (line 3). Imagery (C) also abounds in such examples as "He left behind so great a stink" (line 16) and "widow's sighs" and "orphan's tears" (line 18). Understatement (D), minimizes something to highlight a point. In the poem, understatement can be seen in lines 9–12, "And could he be indeed so old / As by the newspapers we're told? / Threescore, I think, is pretty high; / 'Twas time in conscience he should die." Finally, metaphor (E) can be found in the second stanza, when the poet calls others like the general "Ye bubbles" (line 26).

53. B. Although the entire poem is critical of the general, the first stanza hides its criticism behind hyperbole and understatement. However, the second stanza is much more unabashedly critical, choice B, as the speaker directly chastises the general and other men like him. Choice A is incorrect, not because of the word "directly," but because of the misuse of the word "ironic." The other answer choices are not nearly strong enough in their descriptions. The second stanza is much more pointedly critical than the first; it is not gently mocking (C), nor satirically evasive (D), nor subtly condemning (E); rather, it is unabashedly critical.

54. D. The speaker feels sympathy for the poor widows and orphans who have lost their loved ones because of the general's poor decisions; his sarcasm is not directed toward them at all, choice D. Conversely, the other answer choices all denote instances of intended sarcasm, including "what, dead!" (A), "'Twas time . . . he should die" (B), "He burnt his candle to the snuff" (C), and "He made them weep before he died" (E).

55. E. The rhyming couplets, combined with the iambic tetrameter, create a sing-song rhythm, almost childlike in its sound. This rhythmic tone helps to effectively mask the speaker's disdain and contempt for the general, choice E. The intended effect of the rhyming couplets is not to enhance the appropriateness of the elegy (A). It is silly to think they are used simply to show off the poet's skill (B). The couplets do not belittle the speaker's attitude (C). Finally, while the rhyming couplets do determine the rhyme scheme (D), that does not address the intended effect of their use in this poem.

Section II: Free-Response Questions

Question 1: "Joy in the Woods" by Claude McKay

The following scoring guide explicitly explains how to earn up to 6 total points for a poetry analysis essay. Row A (thesis) can earn up to 1 point; Row B (evidence and commentary) can earn up to 4 points, and Row C (sophistication) can earn up to 1 point.

Row A: Thesis (0–1 point)	
Scoring Criteria	
0 points for any of the following:	**1 point for**
• Having no defendable thesis. • Only restating the prompt in the thesis. • Only summarizing the issue with no claim in the thesis. • Presenting a thesis that does not address the prompt.	• Addressing the prompt with a defendable thesis that presents an interpretation and may establish a line of reasoning.
Decision Rules and Scoring Notes	
Theses that do not earn this point	**Theses that do earn this point**
• Only restate the prompt. • Only offer an irrelevant generalized comment about the poem. • Simply describe the poem's features rather than making a defendable claim.	• Take a position on the prompt and provide a defendable interpretation of how the poet portrays the complex relationship between the speaker and nature.
Additional Notes	
• The thesis may be one or more sentences anywhere in the essay. • A thesis that meets the criteria can be awarded the point whether or not the rest of the response successfully conveys that line of reasoning.	

Row B: Evidence AND Commentary (0–4 points)				
Scoring Criteria				
0 points for	**1 point for**	**2 points for**	**3 points for**	**4 points for**
• Simply repeating the thesis (if present). • **OR** restating provided information. • **OR** providing mostly irrelevant and/or incoherent examples.	• Summarizing the poem without reference to a thesis. • **OR** providing vague textual references. • **OR** providing textual references of questionable relevance. • **AND** providing little or no commentary.	• Making relevant textual references (direct quotes or paraphrases). • **AND** providing commentary but repeats, oversimplifies, or misinterprets the cited evidence or text.	• Making relevant textual references (direct quotes or paraphrases). • **AND** providing commentary that explains the logical relationship between textual examples and the thesis; however, commentary is uneven, limited, or incomplete.	• Making relevant textual references (direct quotes or paraphrases). • **AND** providing well-developed commentary that explicitly explains the relationship between the evidence and the thesis.

Decision Rules and Scoring Notes				
Typical responses that earn 0 points:	**Typical responses that earn 1 point:**	**Typical responses that earn 2 points:**	**Typical responses that earn 3 points:**	**Typical responses that earn 4 points:**
• Are unclear or fail to address the prompt. • May present mere opinion with no relevant textual references.	• Mention textual references, devices, or techniques with little or no analysis.	• Contain numerous inaccuracies or repetition in commentary. • Offer only simplistic explanations that do not strengthen the argument.	• Provide commentary that is not sufficiently developed or is too limited. • Assume or imply a connection to the thesis that is not consistently explicit.	• Provide commentary that uses significant details of the text to draw conclusions. • Integrate short excerpts throughout in order to support the thesis' interpretation.

Additional Notes
• Writing that suffers from grammatical and/or mechanical errors that interfere with communication cannot earn the fourth point in this row.

Row C: Sophistication (0–1 point)

Scoring Criteria	
0 points for	**1 point for**
• Not meeting the criteria for 1 point.	• Exhibiting sophistication of thought and/or advancing a complex literary argument.

Decision Rules and Scoring Notes	
Responses that do not earn this point:	**Responses that earn this point demonstrate one (or more) of the following:**
• Try to contextualize an interpretation, but make predominantly sweeping generalizations (*"Throughout all history . . ." OR "Everyone believes . . ."*). • Only hint at other possible interpretations (*"Some may think. . ." OR "Though the poem might be said to . . ."*). • Write one statement about a thematic interpretation of the poem without consistently maintaining that idea. • Oversimplify complexities in the poem. • Present complicated or complex sentences or language that is ineffective and detracts from the argument.	• Present a thesis that demands nuanced analysis of textual evidence and successfully prove it. • Illuminate the significance or relevance of an interpretation within a broader context. • Discuss alternative interpretations of a text. • Acknowledge and account for contradictions, ambiguities, and/or complexities within the text. • Provide relevant analogies to help better understand an interpretation. • Develop a prose style that is especially vivid, persuasive, resounding, or appropriate to the student's argument.

Additional Notes
• This point should be awarded only if the demonstration of sophistication or complex understanding is part of the argument, not merely a phrase or brief reference.

High-Scoring Essay

Humans crave beauty, and no matter whether it comes in the form of nature, or art or music, or great literature, we love that which gives us a sense of splendor. Of course, not everyone can dwell in the world of beauty every day; some suffer with medical problems, some suffer with family problems; some suffer under oppression. Claude McKay, in his wistful poem "Joy in the Woods," presents a speaker, a slave, who is denied his love of nature by his master. Using nature as a symbol for all that is serene and free, McKay presents a conflicted speaker who must endure his servitude.

The speaker begins by establishing his love of the woods, knowing that while he must "dwell in the town," the woods lie beyond, vibrant with the sights and sounds of nature. His initial effusive tone about the woods, a place he cannot go, is established as he describes the "joy in the woods," the leaves that are metaphorical "whispers of song," the birds that, with personification, "make mirth . . . and music the whole day long." This view of nature is serene but idealized, almost Disneyesque, and surely paints a picture our speaker wishes he could be a part of. However, the first octave shifts by the seventh line, introducing the speaker's "unfading frown" and informing us that he has "hate in my heart always." The speaker's reason for this change of tone is not revealed until the following couplet, similar to an aside, in which he laments that he, a metaphorical "machine out of gear," is "forced to go on—for I'm hired." At this point we simply think he's busy with his job, but upon closer inspection, the transitional word "yet," placed prominently before the idea of being forced, should cue us into the fact that his conflict is more than merely not having the time to go enjoy nature.

The second octave, centrally placed in the poem's form, focuses on the speaker's bleak existence, repeating the word "forced" and introducing "fear." The tone and imagery turn negative as he lists the reasons he must work: He "must eat," he is forced to wear "ugly clothes" and "bad shoes" and find shelter for some "work-drugged sleep." With strong understatement, the speaker sardonically notes that his life is a "mere drudge!" and wonders rhetorically what he can do. He is too much a man to weep or contemplate suicide; he must go on. His laudatory relationship with the natural world from the first stanza has vanished; he is left with the toil and fear of his daily life with no succor from nature. The following couplet, beginning with another transition, "but," grows even darker as we learn he is a slave. However, the speaker does not confine his comments to himself by now; he manifests himself onto all slaves who "should never grow tired." His sarcastic tone also grows as he claims masters have "kindly hired" men like himself. By now his relationship with nature is merely wishful thinking, an imaginary fantasy of freedom, a dream no slave can hope for. It is also notable that this mid-section of the poem is entirely negative while the surrounding sections have the beautiful imagery of nature; it reflects that beauty is out there, but when one's core existence is black and bleak, that beauty is hard to grasp.

The speaker's imagination cannot be suppressed, and in the third octave, he returns to the comfort of nature, heightening our senses with such images as "the woods, the flowers" with their "sweet perfume" and the "smiling shrubs in bloom." Idealized vision? Yes, again, but by this place in the poem, nature has become more than just woods; it now represents freedom, purity, and the life that the speaker cannot have in his slavish reality. The "dust-free," "fresh and life-giving air" that he so craves will remain only in his mind. The final couplet returns to the image of machinery, but now the speaker clarifies that he, indeed, is the machine, and he juxtaposes this image with the wistful and comforting thought that any man-machine can still crave beauty. Like the second couplet, he is not referring to just himself, but to all men confined.

His relationship with the natural world becomes symbolic of the desire of all humans to escape, to experience that which is beautiful, that which has freedom, and that which sustains us when we face adversity.

(742 words)

Analysis of High-Scoring Essay

This high-scoring essay begins with great promise. The introduction is fairly well developed, and it attempts to immediately engage the reader's attention with two sentences that address the human condition, namely our love of beauty, rather than simply naming the author and title. While this thesis does not explicitly address the prompt, it acknowledges that the speaker is conflicted, and it implies a strong relationship between nature, "a symbol for all that is serene and free," and the speaker's "servitude." A Reader will be pleased to not have yet another thesis that blatantly restates the prompt, and this thesis earns a point in Row A.

The first body paragraph explores the first third of the poem, namely the paired opening octave and subsequent couplet. The student understands that the speaker admires nature and "wishes he could be a part of" it, and accurately describes the poem's opening tone as "effusive." This student shows more depth than many by acknowledging that the initial description of nature is idealized, and most Readers will smile at the student's notion that it is "almost Disneyesque." The student acknowledges metaphor ("whispers of song") and personification ("make mirth . . . and music the whole day long") but fails to analyze their effect or tie them to the prompt. The student accurately notes that the poem shifts its focus in line 7, but does not address or identify the change in tone or imagery. By noticing that the couplets that follow each octave are akin to an aside, the student comments on the "machine out of gear" metaphor and understands the speaker cannot be a part of nature because he is "hired." The student's comment about the transition "yet" being placed before the word "forced" demonstrates strong awareness of how it should "cue us in" to the speaker's conflict that the student introduced in the thesis. The student is becoming aware that the speaker's "job" is more than just a time-consuming occupation.

The next paragraph explores the middle section of the poem, noticing how the placement of this octave-couplet combination enhances the form of the poem and the fact that the middle octave and its accompanying couplet dwell on negativity. The student provides examples of this negativity but does nothing more than mention them. However, the commentary gets stronger as the student explores the uses of understatement and rhetorical question in the poem; the use of the word "sardonically" is an impressive description of the speaker's tone. The student also successfully understands that the speaker has turned into the Everyman of Slaves by the end of the couplet, representing all who must live thus. This paragraph ends with strong style and commentary, analyzing how the mid-section of the poem is like the core of an existence that is "black and bleak" while noting that the surrounding sections are beautiful in their imagery.

The final body paragraph discusses the third octave-couplet combination and accurately acknowledges that the speaker's idealized vision of nature, perfectly beautiful, represents more than just a natural setting. It is pure, but it is only in his imagination; the only comfort this man-machine can get in this life is mentally returning to his symbolic place of peace.

The conclusion, albeit only one sentence, is satisfying. It ends the essay not with mere summary but with stylistic sophistication and global comments about humanity's need for beauty to "sustain us when we face adversity." The evidence and commentary in the essay earn 4 points in Row B.

Overall this essay truly deserves its high score and earns a point in Row C. It is clearly on topic, and it addresses all parts of the prompt as it explores the complex relationship between the speaker and nature. The organization is logical and sophisticated, exploring each octave-couplet combination as a unit. This student weaves poetic elements into the essay effectively. The development of ideas is exemplary; the student sees much more in the poem than most students, and he or she consistently analyzes the poem with great insight. The student also demonstrates sustained sophisticated language and style; while an edit might be appropriate here and there, the writing is stellar for a 40-minute draft. It deserves an overall score of 6.

Low-Scoring Essay

Claude McKay writes a confusing poem, "Joy in the Woods", but by the end it becomes clear. The speaker likes nature but he is a slave and can't go to enjoy it because he has to work so his relationship to nature is not what he wants. Claude McKay conveys this through the poem's form, tone, and imagery.

The poem's form is fairly obvious. It has 3 long stanzas, each followed by a short stanza. In the first stanza he talks about how pretty nature is, except for the last two lines that says he frowns and has hate. Then he explains why he has hate: He's hired to work. After that, he says why he has to work: He has to eat, get clothing, and shelter. If he were a quitter, he'd commit suicide, but he's not and he won't. Then we learn he's a slave, hired by a "kind" master. After that, he thinks about nature again, and finishes by telling us he craves beauty but can't get it because he's a slave.

The tone changes from nice to unpleasant. It begins with pretty descriptions which creates a pleasant tone. Then it gets dreary with too much work. Then it gets nice again.

The poem has lots of imagery and like the tone it goes from good to bad and back again. It is pleasant when it describes leaves, birds, and the woods. But it is unpleasant when it describes fear, ugly clothes, bad shoes, suicide and drudgery. Then it gets pleasant again when it brings up woods, flowers, summer showers, shrubs, corn, and birds. The imagery helps the reader see the woods.

(275 words)

Analysis of Low-Scoring Essay

This student's introduction immediately reveals a lack of analytical skills. It does not bode well when the writer admits to confusion in the very first phrase, but at least the student states "it becomes clear" by the end of the poem. The second sentence, a run-on, does paraphrase the basic essentials of the poem, but its simplistic thinking does not communicate any of the nuances that stronger writers will analyze. The thesis is a bland three-part thesis: Readers are told to expect one paragraph on form, one on tone, and one on imagery, in that order. The prompt does not mention any specific poetic elements to discuss, but perhaps this student feels comfortable in choosing three standard devices to analyze. While this thesis does add to the organization, it is so predictable that Readers will be bored. However, the thesis does qualify for a point in Row A.

The student's strongest paragraph follows, noting ideas about form. However, those ideas are not impressive; as soon as the writer states that the "poem's form is fairly obvious," the Reader is not likely to expect much more than superficial commentary. Instead of actually analyzing the poem's form, the student tells us it has "3 long stanzas, each followed by a short stanza," and then drops all scrutiny of poetic form. The paragraph continues by merely summarizing the poem's thought progression, and it does so in a quite simplistic fashion. As the student merely repeats what the speaker has said, we see that the student gets the basic gist of the poem (which is not terribly hard to do) but no more.

The next short paragraph, anorexic in its development and content, basically only informs us that the tone changes from good to bad and back again. We are offered no text examples, no analysis, no acknowledgment of any relationship between the speaker and nature. A Reader will acknowledge that the student accurately notes tone shifts, but that's all we can reward. At least the student is not wrong.

The last paragraph attempts to discuss the poem's imagery. Again we can reward the student for accurately acknowledging that some images are positive and others negative, but it's hardly insightful to point out that words like "suicide" and "fear" are bad while "flowers" and "birds" are good. One also wishes the student had learned how to properly punctuate quotations; this paragraph repeats many words and phrases from the poem in its second, third, and fourth sentences, but fails to place them inside quotation marks. The student finishes with the comment that imagery helps us "see the woods," which is an all-too-common turn of phrase that students present. The evidence and commentary will only earn 1 point in Row B.

Overall, this essay's content is simply too undeveloped. The student needs to concentrate more on the prompt and try to analyze *how* the poet conveys the relationship between speaker and nature, and use poetic elements to aid in such analysis. Unfortunately, this student's style is as simplistic and undeveloped as his or her presentation of ideas, and it will not earn a point in Row C. It should earn an overall score of 2.

Question 2: *Nostromo* by Joseph Conrad

The following scoring guide explicitly explains how to earn up to 6 total points for a prose analysis essay. Row A (thesis) can earn up to 1 point; Row B (evidence and commentary) can earn up to 4 points, and Row C (sophistication) can earn up to 1 point.

Row A: Thesis (0–1 point)	
Scoring Criteria	
0 points for any of the following:	**1 point for**
• Having no defendable thesis. • Only restating the prompt in the thesis. • Only summarizing the issue with no claim in the thesis. • Presenting a thesis that does not address the prompt.	• Addressing the prompt with a defendable thesis that presents an interpretation and may establish a line of reasoning.
Decision Rules and Scoring Notes	
Theses that do not earn this point	**Theses that do earn this point**
• Only restate the prompt. • Only offer an irrelevant generalized comment about the passage. • Simply describe the passage's features rather than making a defendable claim.	• Take a position on the prompt and provide a defendable interpretation of how Conrad portrays the complex atmosphere of the location and characters.

Additional Notes

- The thesis may be one or more sentences anywhere in the response.
- A thesis that meets the criteria can be awarded the point whether or not the rest of the response successfully conveys that line of reasoning.

Row B: Evidence AND Commentary (0–4 points)

Scoring Criteria

0 points for	1 point for	2 points for	3 points for	4 points for
• Simply repeating the thesis (if present). • **OR** restating provided information. • **OR** providing mostly irrelevant and/or incoherent examples.	• Summarizing the passage without reference to a thesis. • **OR** providing vague textual references. • **OR** providing textual references of questionable relevance. • **AND** providing little or no commentary.	• Making relevant textual references (direct quotes or paraphrases). • **AND** providing commentary but repeats, oversimplifies, or misinterprets the cited evidence or text.	• Making relevant textual references (direct quotes or paraphrases). • **AND** providing commentary that explains the logical relationship between textual examples and the thesis; however, commentary is uneven, limited, or incomplete.	• Making relevant textual references (direct quotes or paraphrases). • **AND** providing well-developed commentary that explicitly explains the relationship between the evidence and the thesis.

Decision Rules and Scoring Notes

Typical responses that earn 0 points:	Typical responses that earn 1 point:	Typical responses that earn 2 points:	Typical responses that earn 3 points:	Typical responses that earn 4 points:
• Are unclear or fail to address the prompt. • May present mere opinion with no relevant textual references.	• Mention textual references, devices, or techniques with little or no analysis.	• Contain numerous inaccuracies or repetition in commentary. • Offer only simplistic explanations that do not strengthen the argument.	• Provide commentary that is not sufficiently developed, or is too limited. • Assume or imply a connection to the thesis that is not consistently explicit.	• Provide commentary that uses significant details of the text to draw conclusions. • Integrate short excerpts throughout in order to support the thesis' interpretation.

Additional Notes

- Writing that suffers from grammatical and/or mechanical errors that interfere with communication cannot earn the fourth point in this row.

Row C: Sophistication (0–1 point)

Scoring Criteria

0 points for	1 point for
• Not meeting the criteria for 1 point.	• Exhibiting sophistication of thought and/or advancing a complex literary argument.

Decision Rules and Scoring Notes	
Responses that do not earn this point:	**Responses that earn this point demonstrate one (or more) of the following:**
• Try to contextualize an interpretation, but make predominantly sweeping generalizations (*"Throughout all history . . ."* OR *"Everyone believes . . ."*). • Only hint at other possible interpretations (*"Some may think . . ."* OR *"Though the passage might be said to . . ."*). • Write one statement about a thematic interpretation of the passage without consistently maintaining that idea. • Oversimplify complexities in the passage. • Present complicated or complex sentences or language that is ineffective and detracts from the argument.	• Present a thesis that demands nuanced analysis of textual evidence and successfully prove it. • Illuminate the significance or relevance of an interpretation within a broader context. • Discuss alternative interpretations of a text. • Acknowledge and account for contradictions, ambiguities, and/or complexities within the text. • Provide relevant analogies to help better understand an interpretation. • Develop a prose style that is especially vivid, persuasive, resounding, or appropriate to the student's argument.
Additional Notes	
• This point should be awarded only if the demonstration of sophistication or complex understanding is part of the argument, not merely a phrase or brief reference.	

High-Scoring Essay

If this passage were made into a movie, we'd first see the calm, serene gulf near the quiet town of Sulaco. Then the camera would pan to one side of the gulf, intimating the unwelcoming scenery of Punta Mala. Next, the camera would focus on the other side of the gulf, showing rocky, barren land. Finally, humanity would be introduced: poor locals, making their way in this world. Joseph Conrad, in his novel <u>Nostromo</u>, guides our vision, paragraph by paragraph, as he starts with a big picture and narrows the focus to individuals. This movement helps create the complex atmosphere of the location and the people who inhabit it.

The opening description is quite idyllic: the town of Sulaco is serenely set in a calm gulf, appropriately named Golfo Placido, a placid body of water. The natural description of "luxuriant beauty" and "orange gardens" in the town is inviting, as is the presence of the "solemn hush" of the calm, vast gulf. Because the gulf is so protected from the outside waters, commercial boats, whether "deep-sea galleons" or "modern . . . clipper lines" cannot operate, enhancing the peaceful atmosphere. Conrad notably changes the tone of the passage while sarcastically describing the man-made ships that cannot penetrate the gulf, protecting it from the "temptations of a trading world." The galleons are "clumsy" and "your modern ship" moves by a "mere flapping of her sails." Moreover, when Conrad describes the natural setting, his diction elevates the location to something spiritual as he describes Sulaco as being "an inviolable sanctuary," and comparing it to an "unroofed temple open to the sea." However, the atmosphere, so tranquil and transcendent, is jarred when Conrad concludes the scene by introducing the "walls of lofty mountains hung with the mourning draperies of cloud." The phrasing "hung" and "mourning draperies" holds the hint of something foreboding; perhaps not all is perfect in Sulaco.

In the following two paragraphs, Conrad juxtaposes the two sides on the gulf. On the seaboard side lies the Republic of Costaguana, creating a sad vision and perhaps even unpleasant smell of, well, manure. The range forms an "insignificant cape" with the menacing name "Punta Mala." Nothing on this side of the gulf is inviting, but Conrad adds an ethereal image that increases our curiosity: a steep hill that is so faintly seen it is "like a shadow on the sky." Conrad continues this type of otherworldly description, so hard to touch or see, as he portrays the other side of the gulf with "what seems to be an isolated patch of blue mist" that "floats lightly" on the horizon. Conrad immediately shifts to more concrete and negative imagery as he describes the Azuera peninsula as uninhabitable and unwelcoming. It has "sharp rocks and stony levels," that form steep ravines. Although waterless, thorny scrub bush somehow grows. To complete the "wild chaos" of this dismal scene, Conrad adds that the soil is so barren it seems "as if it were blighted by a curse." The atmosphere of the soothing gulf is strongly contrasted with the harsh land.

It is not until half way through the passage that Conrad introduces humanity to the scene, moving the description from the natural setting to the world of men. Like the difference between the calm gulf and the unpleasant land, Conrad juxtaposes the local residents with "two wandering sailors." The locals, while not perfect, are poor peons who work on local ranches, and "tame Indians" who come to market to sell goods for a very low price. As Conrad explains, these peoples are also superstitious, believing the rocky inclines of Azuera to be "deadly because of its forbidden treasures." This tidbit of folklore increases the tension; Conrad uses it as a springboard to tell a traditional story that introduces the two sailors, gringos, to the locals. They convince a local mozo to join them; all three steal a donkey and head for the hills in search of the "heaps of shining gold" that "lie in the gloom of the deep precipices." The foreshadowing is obvious.

They were never seen again. However, it is in the concluding paragraph of the passage that Conrad completes the contrast between locals and outsiders, and in the process makes a strong diatribe against greed. The local's theoretically pious wife "paid for some Masses," which presumably paves his way to salvation. However, the "impious adventurers," the two gringo sailors, are believed to be still living, "spectral and alive" because their souls cannot release their bodies from the gold. Conrad's description becomes sardonic as he condemns the men, "suffering in their starved and parched flesh of defiant heretics."

With intense imagery and juxtaposition Conrad transitions from an initially peaceful and natural scene to expose the evil greed that is in the soul of men who do not belong.

(803 words)

Analysis of High-Scoring Essay

This compelling essay shows a strong grasp of how Conrad's literary techniques create the complex atmosphere of location and characters who live there. The essay begins with an interesting idea, that of describing how a movie would pan across the scenery before zeroing in on the residents of Sulaco. This effectively mirrors Conrad's organization in the passage. The introduction is engaging, although the thesis is bland, noting only that the movement from nature to man "helps create complex atmosphere." It will earn a point in Row A.

The essay works through the passage chronologically and devotes the first body paragraph to Conrad's opening paragraph, which describes the gulf surrounding the town of Sulaco. The student's observations are astute, noticing how Conrad "elevates the location to something spiritual" and providing apt examples from the text. While some writers would not notice or comment on Conrad's shifting tone, this student perceptively acknowledges Conrad's understated sarcasm as he describes the ships that cannot enter the gulf. Another important detail that many students will not notice is the negativity in Conrad's phrasing at the end of the first paragraph; however, this student not only comments on the way it jars the reader's senses, but he or she also notes that the effect of the negative phrases is to "hint of something foreboding." Many average essays on this topic might describe the overall tone of the paragraph, emphasizing the seemingly beautiful location, but top-scoring essays, like this one, are likely to also analyze the subtle shifts in tone.

The next body paragraph analyzes the contrary images in Conrad's second and third paragraphs, which juxtapose the two sides of the gulf. Once again, the Reader has evidence that this is a discerning student. While most writers will present the unpleasant images of the seaboard side, this writer also notes the "ethereal image that increases our curiosity," the faint hill that seems more like a shadow than a physical object. Once more the student demonstrates more awareness than most writers as he or she compares that image to a vision in Conrad's following paragraph that presents the lightly floating mist on the other side of the bay. But, correctly, the student notices that Conrad "immediately shifts to more concrete and negative imagery." Proving ample textual evidence that the Azuera peninsula is "uninhabitable and unwelcoming," the student completes the paragraph by noting how the placid atmosphere in the gulf is so very different than that of the land.

The following paragraph shifts to Conrad's presentation of humanity; any AP Reader will reward this writer for noticing how the description of local residents and the two wandering sailors parallels Conrad's earlier contrast between gulf and land. The student also notices how the "tidbit of folklore," the superstitious belief that the Azuera holds hidden gold, increases the tension and becomes a springboard to launch into the story of the sailors and the local servant. Instead of simply restating all the detail in the passage, this student gives us the bare essentials and leaves us with the simple thought that "the foreshadowing is obvious." Indeed, what more needs to be said?

"They were never seen again" begins the last body paragraph, fulfilling the obvious implication in the foreshadowing. The student correctly notices how Conrad's last paragraph also fulfills the "contrast between locals and outsiders" while launching into a "strong diatribe against greed." The student admirably reads between the lines, understanding that the local man's wife may or may not actually be pious, and that her paying for "some Masses" may or may not guarantee his salvation. Conrad's harsh condemnation is used to good effect to complete the writer's paragraph. One wishes that the student had more time to develop Conrad's idea, but after the previous apt development of ideas, it's hard to fault the student on this one point. The evidence and commentary definitely deserve 4 points in Row B.

The overly brief conclusion, basically just a quick summary, seems to indicate that the student is suddenly running out of time. However, the overall essay is so strong that this minimalist conclusion does not hurt. Throughout the entire essay, the writer addresses literary techniques such as imagery, juxtaposition, and foreshadowing, while addressing Conrad's tone, diction, and movement of ideas. The organization of the essay is clear, logical, and coherent. The paragraph development is very strong, fusing textual examples with insightful analysis. Finally, the student's command of language is impressive. This student truly understands the sophisticated skills that a writer must display to earn such a high score, and this essay should be rewarded with a point in Row C and an overall score of 6.

Medium-Scoring Essay

Joseph Conrad paints a dreary picture in the passage from <u>Nostromo</u>, a novel set in South America. Conrad uses several literary techniques to establish atmosphere and character, but imagery is used more than anything.

The town of Sulaco rests on a large and deep gulf, the "Golfo Placido" that brings an image of calmness. It has "luxuriant beauty" in its "orange gardens" that have apparently been there throughout antiquity. Old galleons and modern clipper lines cannot penetrate the gulf because it is so deep and calm, so Sulaco has not had much commercial interference from the outside world. All of the imagery that describes Sulaco is pleasant and soothing, so one can imagine that the characters who live there are also agreeable.

The gulf has two sides. The first is described as "insignificant," but its name, Punta Mala, which means a dangerous or bad place, implies it is the opposite of Sulaco. Its insignificance is enhanced by the fact that "the point of the land itself is not visible at all," because if it was important, it wouldn't be invisible. The imagery in the description here is more ominous than the description of the gulf.

The other side of the gulf is described with even harsher imagery. Conrad uses words such as "chaos" "sharp rocks" "stony" "waterless" and "curse" to create a dismal atmosphere. After all of this description, Conrad finally introduces people to the scene. They are "poor" "common folk" "peons" who superstitiously believe that the "stony levels cut about by vertical ravines" are "deadly" because they contain "forbidden treasures." This imagery paints the people as gullible and naïve. In fact, one local "mozo" gets talked into going with two gringo sailors in search of this treasure, along with a stolen burro. Given the scary imagery, it's not surprising that they were never seen again. If they were to pay attention to their surroundings, (that Conrad paints so vividly) they would have never attempted this impossible feat.

Conrad piles on more imagery to describe the gringos, who were never seen again. He says they are believed to still be alive, but are "spectral" and "under the fatal spell of their success." Because they are now "rich and hungry and thirsty" we understand that they found the lost treasure but cannot leave the mountain to enjoy it.

Conrad's imagery paints the location as both calm and ominous, and he paints the locals as poor and naïve, while the sailors are greedy.

(411 words)

Analysis of Medium-Scoring Essay

This essay has some positive points in its favor: It tries to address the prompt, and it organizes ideas satisfactorily. However, the writer does not look deeply enough into the passage, concentrates solely on the imagery, and then does a less-than-stellar job of analyzing it.

The introduction begins with an inaccurate assertion that Conrad "paints a dreary picture." At this point in the essay's progression, the student is ignoring the peaceful, calm atmosphere in the first paragraph of the passage; however, the student will discuss that positive imagery in his or her next paragraph. Such a lapse cannot be overlooked by an AP Reader. The student's thesis tells us that Conrad "uses several literary techniques," but then narrows the focus to include only imagery. The thesis will earn a point in Row A.

The first body paragraph contradicts the "dreary picture" presented in the introduction by describing the town of Sulaco as "pleasant and soothing." The student provides proof of this by quoting and paraphrasing the passage. The student is not inaccurate, but the paragraph does not lead anywhere, and it does not establish strong analysis; rather, it basically tells us that since the atmosphere is pleasant, the characters who live there must also be pleasant.

The next paragraph continues to merely describe the physical setting, one side of the gulf. The writer has picked up on the idea that this part of the location is "insignificant" and tries to verify that idea with the concept that the farthest point is not visible from the gulf. The logic is questionable, but one can see that a simplistic reading might reach this conclusion. The writer concludes the paragraph by remarking that the imagery is now "more ominous," but offers no more analysis.

The following paragraph relates to the "other side of the gulf," but it basically strings together a series of quotations from the passage and tells us it creates "dismal atmosphere." This may be true, but a stronger essay would analyze *how* the images create atmosphere. Next, the writer notices that humanity is introduced to the scene, but again employs the poor technique of stringing together quotations from the text instead of analyzing *how* they work to create character. While the writer does understand that the residents of the area are superstitious, he or she does no more than merely state that idea, expecting the Reader to agree. The writer also simplistically claims that the characters who search for the lost gold should have paid attention to their surroundings, to the "scary imagery" that "Conrad paints." At this point, the student seems to be running out of steam; the essay is not inaccurate in its claims, but the statements are simplistic and deserve more analytical depth.

The last body paragraph is the weakest of all, insisting that Conrad "piles on more imagery" as if the author is using a shovel. The writer seems to not know what to do with the spectral image of the gringos, and seems unaware that they are long dead, that it's their souls that guard the gold, if indeed there was ever any gold to be found.

The essay's final line is a disappointing single-sentence conclusion that is unnecessary since it adds nothing beyond mere summary. The uneven and limited commentary earns 3 points in Row B.

The writer does read the text accurately and attempts to analyze the imagery that creates atmosphere and character. Unfortunately, it falls short in its lack of insightful connection between literary techniques and meaning; the student too often resorts to simply quoting the text and then telling the Reader what is already obvious about those quotes. Its lack of sophistication will not earn a point in Row C. Overall, it deserves a score of 4.

Question 3: How a Character's Move or Travel Affects the Character

The following scoring guide explicitly explains how to earn up to 6 total points for a literary analysis essay. Row A (thesis) can earn up to 1 point; Row B (evidence and commentary) can earn up to 4 points, and Row C (sophistication) can earn up to 1 point.

Row A: Thesis (0–1 point)	
Scoring Criteria	
0 points for any of the following:	**1 point for**
• Having no defendable thesis. • Only restating the prompt in the thesis. • Only summarizing the issue with no claim in the thesis. • Presenting a thesis that does not address the prompt.	• Addressing the prompt with a defendable thesis that presents an interpretation and may establish a line of reasoning.
Decision Rules and Scoring Notes	
Theses that do not earn this point	**Theses that do earn this point**
• Only restate the prompt. • Only offer an irrelevant generalized comment about the chosen work.	• Take a position on the prompt and provide a defendable interpretation of how a change in location affects a character and adds to an interpretation of the chosen work as a whole.

Additional Notes

- The thesis may be one or more sentences anywhere in the response.
- A thesis that meets the criteria can be awarded the point whether or not the rest of the response successfully conveys that line of reasoning.

Row B: Evidence AND Commentary (0–4 points)

Scoring Criteria

0 points for	1 point for	2 points for	3 points for	4 points for
• Simply repeating the thesis (if present). • **OR** restating provided information. • **OR** providing mostly irrelevant and/or incoherent examples.	• Summarizing the chosen work without reference to a thesis. • **OR** providing vague textual references. • **OR** providing textual references of questionable relevance. • **AND** providing little or no commentary.	• Making relevant textual references (direct quotes or paraphrases). • **AND** providing commentary but repeats, oversimplifies, or misinterprets the cited evidence or text.	• Making relevant textual references (direct quotes or paraphrases). • **AND** providing commentary that explains the logical relationship between textual examples and the thesis; however, commentary is uneven, limited, or incomplete.	• Making relevant textual references (direct quotes or paraphrases). • **AND** providing well-developed commentary that explicitly explains the relationship between the evidence and the thesis.

Decision Rules and Scoring Notes

Typical responses that earn 0 points:	Typical responses that earn 1 point:	Typical responses that earn 2 points:	Typical responses that earn 3 points:	Typical responses that earn 4 points:
• Are unclear or fail to address the prompt. • May present mere opinion with no relevant textual references.	• Mention textual references, devices, or techniques with little or no analysis.	• Contain numerous inaccuracies or repetition in commentary. • Offer only simplistic explanations that do not strengthen the argument.	• Provide commentary that is not sufficiently developed or is too limited. • Assume or imply a connection to the thesis that is not consistently explicit.	• Provide commentary that uses significant details of the text to draw conclusions. • Integrate short excerpts throughout in order to support the thesis' interpretation.

Additional Notes

- Writing that suffers from grammatical and/or mechanical errors that interfere with communication cannot earn the fourth point in this row.

Row C: Sophistication (0–1 point)

Scoring Criteria

0 points for	1 point for
• Not meeting the criteria for 1 point.	• Exhibiting sophistication of thought and/or advancing a complex literary argument.

Decision Rules and Scoring Notes	
Responses that do not earn this point:	**Responses that earn this point demonstrate one (or more) of the following:**
• Try to contextualize an interpretation, but make predominantly sweeping generalizations (*"Throughout all history. . ."* OR *"Everyone believes . . ."*). • Only hint at other possible interpretations (*"Some may think . . ."* OR *"Though the work might be said to . . ."*). • Write one statement about a thematic interpretation of the chosen work without consistently maintaining that idea. • Oversimplify complexities in the chosen work. • Present complicated or complex sentences or language that is ineffective and detracts from the argument.	• Present a thesis that demands nuanced analysis of textual evidence and successfully prove it. • Illuminate the significance or relevance of an interpretation within a broader context. • Discuss alternative interpretations of a text. • Acknowledge and account for contradictions, ambiguities, and/or complexities within the text. • Provide relevant analogies to help better understand an interpretation. • Develop a prose style that is especially vivid, persuasive, resounding, or appropriate to the student's argument.
Additional Notes	
• This point should be awarded only if the demonstration of sophistication or complex understanding is part of the argument, not merely a phrase or brief reference.	

High-Scoring Essay

The famous wanderer who took ten years to return from The Trojan War, Odysseus, moves time and again during his adventures in <u>The Odyssey</u>. With each new location in his epic journey, Odysseus overcomes hardship, although he foolishly loses all of his men in the process. Perhaps he learns during his adventures; indeed he should, but he makes some unbelievably boneheaded blunders that delay his homecoming significantly. It is not until he reaches his symbolic homeland of Ithaca that he finally personifies the mighty and wise ruler we expected him to be; he blunders no more. Odysseus' adventures, a method of self-discovery, signify that travel can help us understand our world and ultimately make order out of chaos.

When we first see Odysseus, the supposed hero is crying, lamenting his inability to return home, having been held "captive" on Calypso's island for the last seven years. Upon the command of the gods, she helps him build a raft, and he is again on his way, landing next on the peaceful shores of the Phaiacian people. Shortly after displaying proper and gracious hospitality to their unidentified guest, King Alcinoos and Queen Arete ask him to tell everyone who he is, where he came from, what he has seen of the world, what he knows of civilized and barbaric peoples. The Phaiacians symbolize people who want to gain knowledge about the world around them, and the unknown traveler, Odysseus, is just the man to open their eyes.

As Odysseus tells his long-winded tale of his adventures to his captive audience, he reveals his constant desire to explore the world and learn of others. Just as people who live in a valley wonder what lies beyond the next hill, or a winsome boy who lives on the plains wonders where that train in the distance is headed, Odysseus seeks that which is unknown. Unfortunately, he and his men frequently suffer when he cannot control this obsession. For instance, when they land on the island of the fearsome cyclops, Polyphemos, Odysseus and a few men go ashore to explore. All feel nervous; the men beg him to return to the ship, but, even though he too senses danger, he replies that he wants to see the strange creature himself. It ends in chaos after Polyphemos eats four of Odysseus' men and the rest barely escape. One's desire to see what's over the next hill does not always work out well. A few adventures later, they land on Aiaia, the land of Circe, who turns the scouting crew into pigs. When Odysseus learns of this, the men again ask him to leave and accept their losses; however, the man who cannot turn down any chance at adventure insists on saving the transformed men, claiming "go I must and go I will." Yes, he does save them, but then stays another year, sleeping with the goddess, until his men remind him that they want to get home. His wanderlust has blinded him.

His further adventures clearly demonstrate the need for the traveler to learn about morality in his world. Notably, in Hades, the land of the dead, Odysseus talks with four important shades, people from his life, each of whom reveals vital lessons the hero must learn, albeit too slowly. Teiresias, the Theban seer, implicitly tells Odysseus that he will only be successful if he can control himself and follow the gods' advice. His mother, Anticleia, informs him of trouble at home and urges him to return immediately; sadly he ignores this advice and does not yet understand the importance of his homeland. Agamemnon, Odysseus' leader in the Trojan War, reminds him not to trust anyone, not even his wife. Achilles, perhaps, reveals the most important moral of all: he explicitly tells Odysseus that there is no glory in being a dead hero; he would rather be a plowman on a small farm than lord of the dead. After hearing these lessons, Odysseus and his men finally arrive at the island of Helios, where Odysseus commits his last big blunder. Instead of telling the men honestly and directly Teiresias' advice, that they would die if they ate the cattle of the sun god, he merely says "they may suffer." Naturally, in this moral universe, once they eat the cattle they will die, and Odysseus is the sole survivor, making his way to Calypso's island. Moving to different locations in the world can always teach us about others and about ourselves, lessons that are sometimes painful; we can only wish Odysseus had learned his lessons quicker.

Finally, symbolically, when Odysseus returns to his homeland, as was fated, he becomes "the man who was never at a loss" and shows his true heroism. Indeed, all of his adventures paved the way for the self-discovery he needed to solve the chaos on his homeland: the 102 suitors who plague Penelope to remarry and who wreak havoc in Ithaca. Disguised and unknown to all, he patiently suffers the suitors' indignities; he watches and observes who is moral and who is not; he tests family and servants to understand their loyalty. Then, when the time is right, he reveals his identity and slaughters the wicked men, sparing those who are good. He even moralizes while he becomes a killing machine, as he tells one man he rightfully saves that, "you shall know and tell other men that doing well is far better than doing ill." Now that he has traveled to many locations and knows the outside world, he can put his own house and kingdom in order. When the outraged families of the dead suitors try to retaliate, he makes peace with them and "ended the strife forever," bringing order to the chaos that threatens. Thus, we are left with a morality tale of travel and adventure, reminding us that we can wander the world to learn of others, but sometimes we just need to return home to find what we were looking for all along.

(996 words)

Analysis of High-Scoring Essay

This lengthy essay shows the degree of development a student can accomplish when he or she knows the text quite well; this student is not grasping for ideas, but writing with purpose. One wonders how much more the student would have to say if given more time. In any case, this stellar essay is clearly on topic, discussing how Odysseus' travels to foreign locations affect him and those around him, and how travel can "help us understand our world and ultimately make order out of chaos." The introduction dives right into the text, and its thesis promises that interesting commentary will follow. It easily earns a point in Row A for its thesis.

The first body paragraph explores Odysseus' first appearance in the epic, on Calypso's island, and shows how he is tearfully pining for home. The writer quickly moves him forward to the next location he visits: the land of the Phaiacians. By listing the types of questions King Alcinoos asks Odysseus, the student reveals how the Phaiacians' curiosity symbolizes all people's desire to understand the wider world. This thematic statement effectively addresses the prompt's direction to discuss the significance to the work as a whole, yet it avoids blatantly using the same words, another sign of sophistication in the writer.

The next paragraph opens with a pair of lovely analogies, comparing Odysseus' curiosity about what's out there to valley residents who want to learn what's over the next hill or a "winsome boy" who dreams of getting on that train in the distance, not knowing where it will lead. The writer then presents two of Odysseus' adventures, those with Polyphemos and Circe. One could not expect any student to include all of the locations Odysseus travels to in a 40-minute essay, and this student selects appropriate ones to analyze. The student does not dwell on plot, instead only discussing relevant information to prove the thesis; less-able writers might fall into the trap of simply recounting all the action of these two adventures. Remembering accurately that Odysseus ignores his men's pleas to leave both Polyphemos' and Circe's islands, and instead seems hell-bent on discovering the world for himself, the student points out the harm he causes in doing so. These observations are well-founded in the text and the thesis.

The following paragraph dwells on two more locations to which Odysseus travels, both dark adventures. The student explains how his excursion to Hades, the land of the dead, should teach him many moral lessons, but he is slow to absorb them. Recalling all four of the important shades Odysseus listens to, the student accurately articulates what the hero should have learned. The student then moves to the penultimate adventure at Helios, land of the sun god. Again, instead of explaining all the plot details, the student presents just the essential information, that Odysseus neglected to tell his men that they would certainly die if they ate the cattle on the island. The student does not need to recount how long they were on the island, why they were there so long, and how the men did avoid killing the cattle at first; however, the student rightfully does point out how the men were destined to die because of their immoral action. The writer ends the paragraph lamenting that Odysseus did not learn lessons as he moved from location to location until it was too late to save his men. This sentiment keeps the essay on topic.

The student concludes by recounting Odysseus' return to Ithaca, condensing the last four books of the epic succinctly. Acknowledging that his homecoming is symbolic, the student summarizes all that the hero endures as he waits to exact justice. Observing that after Odysseus "has traveled to many locations and knows the outside world, he can put his own house and kingdom in order," the student quotes the text effectively, explaining that Odysseus "moralizes" to a man he saved. Fulfilling the promise offered in the introductory thesis, the writer remarks that Odysseus brings order to the chaos as he settles peacefully with the suitors' families. Finally, by finishing the essay with the insightful and discerning comment that "we can wander the world to learn of others, but sometimes we just need to return home to find what we were looking for all along," the student shows a maturity not often seen in timed essays. This essay clearly deserves 4 points in Row C because of its outstanding combination of evidence and commentary.

This essay truly deserves high praise. Its development of ideas, its text examples, and its analysis are sophisticated throughout, superb, and far beyond what most students accomplish. Noteworthy, also, is that the essay stays on track throughout, organizes the paragraphs logically, and presents ideas with clarity. It definitely deserves a point in Row C. What more can a Reader expect in a 40-minute essay? A Reader will happily reward it with an overall score of 6.

Low-Scoring Essay

In The Grapes of Wrath the Joad family moves from Oklahoma to California and it does not go well. It is during the great depression and everyone is poor. When the family experiences a massive dust storm, they decide to move and pack up everything they own onto one truck. The travel from Oklahoma to California is very hard and they barely make it in fact grandpa and grandma both die on the journey. It affects the whole family, especially Tom Joad who always tries to help even though he just got out of jail when the book begins.

Once they get to California, things are not much better. They face hardship, prejudice because they are "oakies" and discrimination. But they endure and somehow survive. They still have to move from camp to camp, so they cannot settle in one place like they hoped. They barely have enough to eat, can't get work and everyone around them is suffering too. One night an old family friend, Jim Casey who used to be a preacher but now seems more like a communist, is killed by men who don't like his politics. This really becomes a hardship for Tom because he beats the men up and then has to hide for the rest of the book. At the end he has to go off alone because he cannot be seen near his family or they might be harmed.

Family is very important in The Grapes of Wrath, and their move to California just about breaks them apart. Without their moving, the novel wouldn't have any plot, and the different locations show how people face hardship wherever they go.

(276 words)

Analysis of Low-Scoring Essay

The Grapes of Wrath is an excellent choice for this topic about how moving to new locations affects character. Unfortunately, this student does not present the ideas in the novel well enough to earn an adequate score. Beginning with the very first sentence, this essay fails to impress the Reader; while it does acknowledge that the Joad family moves, which is the basis for the prompt, it only tells us that "it does not go well." That bland understatement does not bode well for the rest of the essay. The writer seems to remember some facts about the Great Depression from a history class and tries to fit them into the plot of the novel. It is true that dust storms plagued Oklahoma in this time period, but the Joad family did not leave because of a "massive dust storm." They had been "tractored off their land" by "the Bank," a collective word author John Steinbeck employs for the inhumane business conglomerate that forced tenants to move. The student tells us the travel to California is "very hard," which is quite an understatement, considering that the student, in a run-on sentence, informs us that both grandpa and grandma die en route! The student finishes the introduction by claiming this affects Tom Joad particularly and then mentions Tom's past jail time. This intro suffers on multiple counts. While it tries to stay on topic, it does not clearly address the prompt and it fails to engage the Reader; we assume the student will focus on Tom Joad, since the prompt specifies one character, but this essay gives us no idea what effect the Joad family move has on Tom, let alone what significance it has to the work as a whole. Notice also that the student fails to underline the novel's title throughout the essay. It fails to earn a point in Row A.

The next paragraph is filled with plot tidbits, but reads like a weak summary of the novel, instead of well-chosen examples and spirited analysis. Overall the student isn't too factually inaccurate, except for the opinionated comment that Jim Casey "seems more like a communist." It's true that the Joads do move often and they do suffer hardship. It's true that Jim Casey is killed and Tom retaliates with fisticuffs. It's true that Tom has to separate from the family for their safety. However, this student's bare-boned and vague plot summary does not address the prompt clearly. The student needs to provide specific text examples regarding one character and analyze how those examples affect the character and add significance to the text as a whole. Also, the writer's clunky language distracts the Reader; he or she uses redundancies like repeating "hard" and "hardship" far too often, plus telling us the Joads faced "prejudice . . . and discrimination" because they are "oakies" [sic]. The weak development of evidence and dearth of commentary earn only 1 point in Row B.

The essay ends with something resembling a conclusion, but unfortunately it barely addresses the prompt. It repeats that the Joads' move "just about breaks them apart" and then, in a feeble attempt to discuss significance, the student cannot say anything more insightful than "the novel wouldn't have any plot" if the family had not moved. In addition, the idea that "people face hardship wherever they go" might be something this student could work with, if it were true. But, alas, it is not, and students should be careful of making such absolute statements. These weaknesses do not justify a point in Row C. Overall, this student would have been much better served by reviewing the text before the test date, outlining key plot events and mulling over thematic ideas ahead of time. As it is written, it appears that the student did sit in a class that studied this novel; unfortunately, we have little evidence that the student actually gained knowledge as a result of the experience. Its collective errors and its lack of development earn an overall score of 1.

Scoring Worksheet

Use the following worksheet to arrive at a probable final AP score on Practice Exam 1. While it is sometimes difficult to be objective enough to score one's own essay, you can use the sample essay answers to approximate an essay score for yourself. You may also give your essays (along with the sample essays) to a friend or relative to score if you feel confident that the individual has the knowledge necessary to make such a judgment and that he or she will feel comfortable in doing so.

Section I: Multiple-Choice Questions

$$\frac{}{\text{right answers}} = \frac{}{\text{multiple-choice raw score}}$$

$$\frac{}{\text{multiple-choice raw score}} \times 1.25 = \frac{}{\text{multiple-choice converted score}} \text{ (of possible 67.5)}$$

Section II: Free-Response Questions

$$\frac{}{\text{question 1 raw score}} + \frac{}{\text{question 2 raw score}} + \frac{}{\text{question 3 raw score}} = \frac{}{\text{essay raw score}}$$

$$\frac{}{\text{essay raw score}} \times 4.583 = \frac{}{\text{essay converted score}} \text{ (of possible 82.5)}$$

Final Score

$$\frac{}{\text{multiple-choice converted score}} + \frac{}{\text{essay converted score}} = \frac{}{\text{final converted score}} \text{ (of possible 150)}$$

Probable Final AP Score	
Final Converted Score	**Probable AP Score**
150–100	5
99–86	4
85–67	3
66–0	1 or 2

Chapter 8

Practice Exam 2

Section I: Multiple-Choice Questions

Time: 1 hour

55 questions

Directions: This section contains selections from two passages of prose and three poems with questions on their content, style, and form. Read each selection carefully. Choose the best answer of the five choices.

For questions 1–12, read the poem carefully before choosing your answers.

Nani

Sitting at her table, she serves
the sopa de arroz[1] to me
instinctively, and I watch her,
the absolute mamá, and eat words
I might have had to say more   (5)
out of embarrassment. To speak
now-foreign words I used to speak,
too, dribble down her mouth as she serves
me albondigas[2]. No more
than a third are easy to me.   (10)
By the stove she does something with words
and looks at me only with her
back. I am full. I tell her
I taste the mint, and watch her speak
smiles at the stove. All my words   (15)
make her smile. Nani[3] never serves
herself, she only watches me
with her skin, her hair. I ask for more.

I watch the mamá warming more
tortillas for me. I watch her   (20)
fingers in the flame for me.
Near her mouth, I see a wrinkle speak
of a man whose body serves
the ants like she serves me, then more words
from more wrinkles about children, words   (25)
about this and that, flowing more
easily from these other mouths. Each serves
as a tremendous string around her,
holding her together. They speak
Nani was this and that to me   (30)
and I wonder just how much of me
will die with her, what were the words
I could have been, was. Her insides speak
through a hundred wrinkles, now, more

---

[1] **sopa de arroz:** rice soup
[2] **albondigas:** spiced meatballs
[3] **nani:** a variation of "nana," granny

than she can bear, steel around her,   (35)
shouting, then, What is this thing she serves?

She asks me if I want more.
I own no words to stop her.
Even before I speak, she serves.

1. The use of present tense throughout the poem serves the purpose of

   A. emphasizing the importance of fresh food
   B. minimizing the relationship between the two characters
   C. underscoring the need for communication
   D. highlighting the timelessness of familial ties
   E. stressing the urgency for the speaker to understand Nani

2. Which of the following best paraphrases the first sentence of the poem (lines 1–6)?

   A. Knowing that her grandson cannot articulate the right words in Spanish, Nani intuitively serves him soup to avoid embarrassing him.
   B. The speaker passively eats Nani's soup because he does not know how to properly ask her for it.
   C. Nani has absolute control over the family, so the grandson feels forced to eat her soup and compliment it.
   D. The grandson's embarrassment at watching his Nani causes him to follow her unspoken command to eat the soup.
   E. If the speaker had a better command of Spanish, he would have directly asked Nani for soup, but she serves him instinctively.

3. What is the grammatical function of "I might have had to say more / out of embarrassment" (lines 5–6)?

   A. It serves as a participial phrase.
   B. It serves as an adjective clause.
   C. It serves as a noun clause.
   D. It serves as a direct object.
   E. It serves as an adverbial clause.

4. The subsequent repetition throughout the poem of the last word in each of the first six lines ("serves," "me," "her," "words," "more," and "speak") has the effect of

   A. revisiting the affection the characters have for each other
   B. reliving the experience over and over
   C. showing what actions are rituals in the family
   D. reminding the reader of the relationship between Nani and her grandson
   E. emphasizing which ideas are most important to the speaker

5. Within context, the phrase "To speak / now-foreign words I used to speak" (lines 6–7) suggests that

   A. Nani does not understand the speaker's meaning
   B. the speaker and Nani sometimes talk together
   C. the speaker is at a loss for the right words
   D. the two characters need to spend more time together
   E. the speaker has had a bilingual upbringing

6. Which of the following phrases implies sacrifice?

   A. "she serves / the sopa de arroz" (lines 1–2)
   B. "I watch her / . . . and eat words" (lines 3–4)
   C. "looks at me only with her / back" (lines 12–13)
   D. "I watch her / fingers in the flame for me" (lines 20–21)
   E. "Her insides speak / through a hundred wrinkles" (lines 33–34)

7. The sentence "I see a wrinkle speak . . . from these other mouths" (lines 22–27) demonstrates which of the following about Nani?

   A. It contradicts her earlier thoughts about her grandson.
   B. It emphasizes Nani's love of family.
   C. It indicates how Nani is surrounded by memories of loved ones.
   D. It reinforces Nani's love of cooking.
   E. It intimates her renewed zest for life.

8. The metaphor "a tremendous string around her" (line 28) represents

  A. the recipes she has gathered over the years and made for her family

  B. all the words and phrases she shares with her grandson

  C. the wrinkles she has gained over the years

  D. all of the cherished people and events in Nani's past

  E. all the thoughts Nani will remember about her grandson

9. Which of the following clarifies the difference in the focus between the first two stanzas?

  A. The first deals exclusively with food; the second ignores it.

  B. The first examines the grandson's discomfort; the second parallels Nani's displeasure.

  C. The first describes the present actions; the second explores Nani's thoughts about her past.

  D. The first scrutinizes the characters' relationship; the second inspects their emotions.

  E. The first presents a communication difficulty; the second solves it.

10. What is the implied answer to the question in line 36, "What is this thing she serves?"

  A. Authenticity

  B. Endurance

  C. Sincerity

  D. Respect

  E. Love

11. The final tercet enforces which of the following thematic ideas for the poem as a whole?

  A. Food is the language of love that endures and helps to hold a family together.

  B. Grandmothers can be counted on for support, whether one wants it or not.

  C. Some family members frequently have difficulty communicating with each other.

  D. Grandmothers always urge their grandchildren to eat more.

  E. Serving others is an innate trait in humanity.

12. The difference between the speaker's character and Nani's character can best be described as

  A. civil and intemperate vs. faultless and austere

  B. respectful and humble vs. generous and giving

  C. fawning and churlish vs. simple and righteous

  D. courteous and loquacious vs. solemn and candid

  E. complacent and honorable vs. reverent and stoic

For questions 13–24, read the following passage carefully before choosing your answers.

Dombey sat in the corner of the darkened room in the great arm-chair by the bedside, and Son lay tucked up warm in a little basket bedstead, carefully disposed on a low settee
(5) immediately in front of the fire and close to it, as if his constitution were analogous to that of a muffin, and it was essential to toast him brown while he was very new.

Dombey was about eight-and-forty years of
(10) age. Son about eight-and-forty minutes. Dombey was rather bald, rather red, and though a handsome well-made man, too stern and pompous in appearance, to be prepossessing. Son was very bald, and very red, and though (of
(15) course) an undeniably fine infant, somewhat crushed and spotty in his general effect, as yet. On the brow of Dombey, Time and his brother Care had set some marks, as on a tree that was to come down in good time—remorseless twins
(20) they are for striding through their human forests, notching as they go—while the countenance of Son was crossed with a thousand little creases, which the same deceitful Time would take delight in smoothing out and wearing away with the flat
(25) part of his scythe, as a preparation of the surface for his deeper operations.

Dombey, exulting in the long-looked-for event, jingled and jingled the heavy gold watch-chain that depended from below his trim blue
(30) coat, whereof the buttons sparkled phosphorescently in the feeble rays of the distant fire. Son, with his little fists curled up and clenched, seemed, in his feeble way, to be squaring at existence for having come upon him so
(35) unexpectedly.

'The House will once again, Mrs Dombey,' said Mr Dombey, 'be not only in name but in fact Dombey and Son;' and he added, in a tone of luxurious satisfaction, with his eyes

(40) half-closed as if he were reading the name in a device of flowers, and inhaling their fragrance at the same time; 'Dom-bey and Son!'

The words had such a softening influence, that he appended a term of endearment to Mrs (45) Dombey's name (though not without some hesitation, as being a man but little used to that form of address): and said, 'Mrs Dombey, my— my dear.'

A transient flush of faint surprise overspread (50) the sick lady's face as she raised her eyes towards him.

'He will be christened Paul, my—Mrs Dombey—of course.'

She feebly echoed, 'Of course,' or rather (55) expressed it by the motion of her lips, and closed her eyes again.

'His father's name, Mrs Dombey, and his grandfather's! I wish his grandfather were alive this day! There is some inconvenience in the (60) necessity of writing Junior,' said Mr Dombey, making a fictitious autograph on his knee; 'but it is merely of a private and personal complexion. It doesn't enter into the correspondence of the House. Its signature remains the same.' And (65) again he said 'Dombey and Son,' in exactly the same tone as before.

Those three words conveyed the one idea of Mr Dombey's life. The earth was made for Dombey and Son to trade in, and the sun and (70) moon were made to give them light. Rivers and seas were formed to float their ships; rainbows gave them promise of fair weather; winds blew for or against their enterprises; stars and planets circled in their orbits, to preserve inviolate a (75) system of which they were the centre. Common abbreviations took new meanings in his eyes, and had sole reference to them. A. D. had no concern with Anno Domini, but stood for anno Dombei—and Son.

(80) He had risen, as his father had before him, in the course of life and death, from Son to Dombey, and for nearly twenty years had been the sole representative of the Firm. Of those years he had been married, ten—married, as (85) some said, to a lady with no heart to give him; whose happiness was in the past, and who was content to bind her broken spirit to the dutiful and meek endurance of the present. Such idle talk was little likely to reach the ears of Mr (90) Dombey, whom it nearly concerned; and probably no one in the world would have received it with such utter incredulity as he, if it had reached him. Dombey and Son had often dealt in hides, but never in hearts. They left that fancy

(95) ware to boys and girls, and boarding-schools and books. Mr Dombey would have reasoned: That a matrimonial alliance with himself must, in the nature of things, be gratifying and honourable to any woman of common sense. That the hope of (100) giving birth to a new partner in such a House, could not fail to awaken a glorious and stirring ambition in the breast of the least ambitious of her sex. That Mrs Dombey had entered on that social contract of matrimony: almost necessarily (105) part of a genteel and wealthy station, even without reference to the perpetuation of family Firms: with her eyes fully open to these advantages. That Mrs Dombey had had daily practical knowledge of his position in society. (110) That Mrs Dombey had always sat at the head of his table, and done the honours of his house in a remarkably lady-like and becoming manner. That Mrs Dombey must have been happy. That she couldn't help it.

13. The "great arm-chair" (line 2) and the "little basket bedstead" (lines 3–4) serve the role of

A. diminishing Son's importance
B. foreshadowing the juxtaposition of the following paragraph
C. establishing Dombey's dominance
D. intimating the family's prosperity
E. demonstrating Dombey's affection for his new baby

14. A notable aspect of the narrator's descriptions of Dombey and Son in the second paragraph is that

A. Son has more worries than Dombey himself
B. they share the same traits
C. Dombey is pretentious; Son is not
D. the Son's traits are more exaggerated than his father's
E. Time and Care will affect them both

15. The narrator's explanation of "Time and his brother Care" (lines 17–18) includes which of the following literary devices?

A. Allusion, simile, and paradox
B. Metaphor, analogy, and conceit
C. Foreshadowing, apostrophe, and euphemism
D. Simile, personification, and foreshadowing
E. Personification, irony, and flashback

16. In the third paragraph, one specific detail in the description of Dombey's attire symbolizes that he

   A. is tied to his company and to earning money
   B. has a flair for extravagance
   C. knows the importance of good fashion
   D. adheres to the norms of society
   E. is sincere in his desire to conform

17. The narrator's parenthetical remark in the fifth paragraph "though not without . . . that form of address" (lines 45–47) supplies which of the following?

   A. Blunt assessment of Dombey's attitude toward his wife
   B. A facetious aside about Dombey's upbringing
   C. Inappropriate reproach of Dombey's term of endearment to his wife
   D. Apt justification of Dombey's softening mood
   E. A snide comment criticizing Dombey's lack of sensitivity

18. Mrs. Dombey's reaction to being called "my—my dear" (lines 47–48) suggests that she

   A. understands her husband's motives in speaking as he does
   B. is too weak from childbirth to respond
   C. is unaccustomed to any kind words from Dombey
   D. wishes she would hear such compliments more often
   E. blushes with embarrassment at such a term

19. Dombey's statement "He will be christened Paul, my—Mrs Dombey—of course" (lines 52–53) has the subtle effect of intimating that

   A. Dombey is proud to now have a son
   B. Dombey cannot be endearing to his wife twice in a row
   C. Dombey does not care for his wife
   D. Dombey will ask his wife later if she agrees
   E. Dombey had previously discussed the child's name with his wife

20. The underlying significance of Dombey's "exulting" (line 27) in Son's birth is that

   A. now the name of the family firm is accurate
   B. he can train his son to take over the company after he retires
   C. he represents all fathers' pride in having a son
   D. now he has someone endearing to care for
   E. he can focus attention on the boy instead of his wife

21. The paragraph that begins "Those three words conveyed the one idea . . . " (lines 67–79) functions to

   A. confirm that the Dombey and Son enterprises will continue to flourish
   B. remind Dombey of how blessed his life has been
   C. establish that Dombey thinks the entire universe exists to revolve around his firm
   D. suggest the Dombey and Son company is successful worldwide
   E. settle the idea that Son will definitely join the company

22. Dombey's delight at the birth of Son is ironic because

   A. he is unsure of being able to provide for his growing family
   B. he has had to wait so long for a son
   C. it compromises his love for Mrs. Dombey
   D. he will not be satisfied with only one son
   E. he only sees his son as completing his commercial ventures

23. The overall tone of the passage can best be described as

   A. malicious and condescending
   B. arrogant and skeptical
   C. presumptuous and contradictory
   D. witty and mocking
   E. lighthearted and laconic

24. Mr. Dombey's reasoning in the final paragraph is designed to

   A. explain to others how he loves Mrs. Dombey
   B. rationally elucidate what his heart feels
   C. logically convince himself of his wife's happiness
   D. add a tone of legality to his thoughts
   E. enhance Mr. Dombey's self-esteem

For questions 25–33, read the following poem carefully before choosing your answers.

Petals

Life is a stream
On which we strew
Petal by petal the flower of our heart;
The end lost in dream,
They float past our view,   (5)
We only watch their glad, early start.

Freighted with hope,
Crimsoned with joy,
We scatter the leaves of our opening rose;
Their widening scope,   (10)
Their distant employ,
We never shall know. And the stream as it flows
Sweeps them away,
Each one is gone
Ever beyond into infinite ways.   (15)
We alone stay
While years hurry on,
The flower fared forth, though its fragrance still stays.

25. The central metaphor of "the flower of our heart" (line 3) depends on which of the following?

A. The reluctance to take chances
B. The changing nature of the stream
C. The finite possibilities in life
D. The fragility of the heart
E. The fear of the future

26. The first two lines of the second stanza (lines 7–8) can best be described as

A. contradicting the images of the first stanza
B. balancing negative and positive connotations
C. shifting the tone to one of optimism
D. diminishing the effect of the petals in the stream
E. focusing on new subject matter

27. Which of the following is NOT consistent with the movement of the stream?

A. "They float past our view" (line 5)
B. "We scatter the leaves of our opening rose" (line 9)
C. "Their widening scope" (line 10)
D. "And the stream as it flows / Sweeps them away" (lines 12–13)
E. "The flower fared forth" (line 18)

28. The meaning of line 7, "Freighted with hope," is most similar to

A. "Life is a stream" (line 1)
B. "The end lost in dream" (line 4)
C. "Their distant employ" (line 11)
D. "Each one is gone" (line 14)
E. "We alone stay" (line 16)

29. The enjambment in lines 12–13 has the effect of

A. scattering the flower petals systematically
B. clarifying how clear the stream's water is
C. flowing as naturally as a real river does
D. distracting the flow of thought
E. slowing and elongating the flow of the stream

30. In its final line, the poem concludes with heavy use of

A. understatement
B. paradox
C. apostrophe
D. alliteration
E. metaphor

31. As a whole, the poem expresses the

A. courage to bare our heart in conditions we cannot control

B. fear of the unknown that inhibits our imagination

C. sentimentality that weighs down our optimism

D. impeding attitude of nature toward humanity

E. need for taking chances in order to occasionally succeed

32. An irony embedded in the poem is that

A. streams cannot flow quickly enough to sweep away petals

B. flower petals cannot withstand emersion in water

C. one must shed layers in life if one wants to bloom

D. life will hurry on regardless of one's actions

E. those who destroy nature will eventually regret their actions

33. The compound imagery of the last line suggests that

A. flowers will eventually die and we will miss them

B. the flowers will not fare well as they drift down the stream

C. we expect too much comfort from nature

D. natural images dominate human senses

E. the petals symbolize events in life, and the scent symbolizes memories

For questions 34–44, read the following passage carefully before choosing your answers.

Note: Lady Susan Vernon is beautiful and charming, but alas, she is a recent widow. She is visiting Churchill, the country estate of her brother-in-law and her sister-in-law, Mr. and Mrs. Vernon, as she writes the following letter to her confidant, Mrs. Alicia Johnson, who lives in London on Edward Street. Meanwhile, Frederica, Lady Susan's sweet and sensible 16-year-old daughter, is currently a student at Miss Summers' school, a finishing school for well-to-do young ladies of the day. Sir James is a very wealthy but somewhat simple-minded bachelor. Reginald De Courcy is Mrs. Vernon's handsome but gullible brother, who also visits Churchill.

Lady Susan Vernon to Mrs. Johnson
Churchill.

My dear Alicia,—you were very good in taking notice of Frederica, and I am grateful for it as a mark of your friendship; but as I cannot have any doubt of the warmth of your affection,
(5) I am far from exacting so heavy a sacrifice. She is a stupid girl, and has nothing to recommend her. I would not, therefore, on my account, have you encumber one moment of your precious time by sending for her to Edward Street, especially as
(10) every visit is so much deducted from the grand affair of education, which I really wish to have attended to while she remains at Miss Summers's. I want her to play and sing with some portion of taste and a good deal of assurance, as she has my
(15) hand and arm and a tolerable voice. I was so much indulged in my infant years that I was never obliged to attend to anything, and consequently am without the accomplishments which are now necessary to finish a pretty
(20) woman. Not that I am an advocate for the prevailing fashion of acquiring a perfect knowledge of all languages, arts, and sciences. It is throwing time away to be mistress of French, Italian, and German: music, singing, and
(25) drawing etc., will gain a woman some applause, but will not add one lover to her list—grace and manner, after all, are of the greatest importance. I do not mean, therefore, that Frederica's acquirements should be more than superficial,
(30) and I flatter myself that she will not remain long enough at school to understand anything thoroughly. I hope to see her the wife of Sir James within a twelve-month. You know on what I ground my hope, and it is certainly a good
(35) foundation, for school must be very humiliating to a girl of Frederica's age. And, by-the-by, you had better not invite her any more on that account, as I wish her to find her situation as unpleasant as possible. I am sure of Sir James at
(40) any time, and could make him renew his application by a line. I shall trouble you meanwhile to prevent his forming any other attachment when he comes to town. Ask him to your house occasionally, and talk to him of
(45) Frederica, that he may not forget her. Upon the whole, I commend my own conduct in this affair extremely, and regard it as a very happy instance of circumspection and tenderness. Some mothers would have insisted on their daughter's accepting
(50) so good an offer on the first overture; but I could not reconcile it to myself to force Frederica into a marriage from which her heart revolted, and

(55) instead of adopting so harsh a measure merely propose to make it her own choice, by rendering her thoroughly uncomfortable till she does accept him—but enough of this tiresome girl. You may well wonder how I contrive to pass my time here, and for the first week it was insufferably dull. Now, however, we begin to mend, our party

(60) is enlarged by Mrs. Vernon's brother, a handsome young man, who promises me some amusement. There is something about him which rather interests me, a sort of sauciness and familiarity which I shall teach him to correct. He is lively,

(65) and seems clever, and when I have inspired him with greater respect for me than his sister's kind offices have implanted, he may be an agreeable flirt. There is exquisite pleasure in subduing an insolent spirit, in making a person predetermined

(70) to dislike acknowledge one's superiority. I have disconcerted him already by my calm reserve, and it shall be my endeavor to humble the pride of these self important De Courcies still lower, to convince Mrs. Vernon that her sisterly cautions

(75) have been bestowed in vain, and to persuade Reginald that she has scandalously belied me. This project will serve at least to amuse me, and prevent my feeling so acutely this dreadful separation from you and all whom I love.

(80) Yours ever,

S. Vernon

34. Which of the following most clearly expresses Lady Susan's initial message to Mrs. Johnson?

A. With your friendly help, Frederica will improve.

B. Your friendship and assistance to my daughter is most essential.

C. Frederica and I value your friendship and sacrifice.

D. While I enjoy your friendship, Frederica does not.

E. I do appreciate your friendship, but you do not need to help my daughter.

35. Within context, "exacting" in line 5 most directly means

A. yielding

B. requesting

C. challenging

D. extorting

E. claiming

36. Given her attitude in the passage as a whole, when Lady Susan claims, "I was so much indulged . . . to finish a pretty woman" (lines 15–20), one can reasonably infer that she

A. believes she does not need the charms one gets at a finishing school

B. regrets not being allowed to attend finishing school

C. understands Frederica needs finishing school to perfect her artistic abilities

D. supports finishing school for young ladies so they can in turn find suitable husbands

E. resents her indulgent childhood

37. Lady Susan's comment about the necessity for finishing schools is ironic because

A. French, Italian, and German are valid languages for a lady to know

B. she believes some ladies need it more than others

C. ladies can get good husbands without going to finishing school

D. eligible bachelors do not care for ladies with such accomplishments

E. she immediately contradicts the idea

38. According to Lady Susan, what is the most serious disadvantage of a lady's education?

A. It is too superficial to understand anything thoroughly.

B. It requires a perfect knowledge of foreign languages.

C. It does not teach grace and manners.

D. It cannot help one get a lover.

E. It focuses on the arts too much.

39. Lady Susan's ultimate goal for Frederica's education is that

A. Frederica will get enough knowledge to find a husband

B. Frederica will equal her mother in singing talent

C. it be superficial and shallow

D. Sir James will appreciate it enough to propose to Frederica

E. it will enable her to become a governess

40. Lady Susan states that she wants her daughter's situation to be "as unpleasant as possible" (lines 38–39) because it will

A. eventually force Frederica to accept Sir James as a husband

B. teach Frederica a valuable lesson about survival in society

C. ironically reinforce Lady Susan's love for her daughter

D. show Frederica how Lady Susan is not like other mothers

E. keep Mrs. Johnson from spending too much time and money on Frederica

41. Lady Susan's comment "I commend my own conduct . . . of circumspection and tenderness" (lines 46–48) implies that she

A. fears she is not an ideal mother but hopes to improve

B. needs confirmation that she is doing what is best for Frederica

C. knows Mrs. Johnson will agree to help her

D. feels no qualms about manipulating her daughter into an unwanted marriage

E. worries what others will say about her parenting behind her back

42. Which of the following clarifies Lady Susan's attitude about Reginald De Courcy?

A. She intuitively feels he can learn to love Frederica and hopes to encourage their marriage.

B. She appreciates how he adds a positive outlook to the present company.

C. She believes he is a pliable play toy that she can subdue to her wishes.

D. She despises his lofty brashness and thinks she is his superior.

E. She feels he is weak and under the control of his sister's command.

43. Based on the passage as a whole, Lady Susan can best be described as

A. dependable and ingenious

B. iniquitous and ruthless

C. guileless and gregarious

D. groveling and cunning

E. incorrigible and ambitious

44. Which of the following best describes the overall tone of Lady Susan's letter?

A. Ambivalent

B. Skeptical

C. Vituperative

D. Haughty

E. Revengeful

For questions 45–55, read the following poem carefully before choosing your answers.

Smile, Smile, Smile

Head to limp head, the sunk-eyed wounded scanned
Yesterday's *Mail*[1]; the casualties (typed small)
And (large) Vast Booty from our Latest Haul.
Also, they read of Cheap Homes, not yet planned;
"For," said the paper, "when this war is done   (5)
The men's first instinct will be making homes.
Meanwhile their foremost need is aerodromes[2],
It being certain war has just begun.
Peace would do wrong to our undying dead,—
The sons we offered might regret they died   (10)
If we got nothing lasting in their stead.
We must be solidly indemnified.
Though all be worthy Victory which all bought.
We rulers sitting in this ancient spot
Would wrong our very selves if we forgot   (15)
The greatest glory will be theirs who fought,
Who kept this nation in integrity."
Nation?—The half-limbed readers did not chafe
But smiled at one another curiously
Like secret men who know their secret safe.   (20)
(This is the thing they know and never speak,
That England one by one had fled to France
Not many elsewhere now save under France).
Pictures of these broad smiles appear each week,
And people in whose voice real feeling rings   (25)
Say: How they smile! They're happy now, poor things.

---

[1]**Mail:** The London-published *Daily Mail* was the de facto official newspaper of the British Army during World War I and was delivered to soldiers on the Western Front by military motor cars. The soldiers reading "Yesterday's *Mail*" are in France.
[2]**aerodromes:** the landing strips used for aircraft operations

45. Within the context of the poem as a whole, the word "scanned" in line 1 suggests that the

  A. soldiers place so little value in the newspaper's content that they read it quickly
  B. newspapers sensationalized headlines to draw in readers
  C. soldiers are too exhausted from battle to peruse the newspaper
  D. military leaders do not allow ample time for any reading
  E. soldiers wish they had more time and energy to read the newspaper

46. Which of the following addresses an implication of the newspaper's headlines, "the casualties (typed small) / And (large) Vast Booty from our Latest Haul" (lines 2–3)?

  A. The newspaper editors are trying to be sensitive to the soldiers.
  B. The people who read the *Mail* want only uplifting news.
  C. Those in charge value the spoils of war more than they value soldiers.
  D. The newspaper owners decide the size of the headlines.
  E. The country's gains in war should be more important than its losses.

47. Which of the following is an example of the speaker's sarcasm?

    A. "Head to limp head, the sunk-eyed wounded scanned / Yesterday's *Mail*" (lines 1–2)

    B. "when this war is done / The men's first instinct will be making homes." (lines 5–6)

    C. "It being certain war has just begun." (line 8)

    D. "The half-limbed readers did not chafe / But smiled at one another curiously" (lines 18–19)

    E. "Like secret men who know their secret safe." (line 20)

48. The personification in the phrase "said the paper," (line 5) has the effect of

    A. adding a note of authority that cannot be doubted

    B. appealing to the common people who read the newspaper

    C. sympathizing with the soldiers at the front

    D. understating the soldiers' response to the article

    E. humanizing the newspaper's words and giving them more power

49. The newspaper's pronouncement in lines 9–12 ("Peace would do wrong . . . We must be solidly indemnified.") provides an example of

    A. cold reality

    B. sincere pleading

    C. ethical persuasion

    D. barbaric logic

    E. misplaced sympathy

50. The simile "Like secret men who know their secret safe" (line 20) is best understood to represent the

    A. reality soldiers know about the horrors of war that others cannot comprehend

    B. war news that the soldiers surreptitiously send to the newspaper

    C. public's misunderstanding of the soldiers' lives

    D. difference between the soldiers and other newspaper readers

    E. need for discretion about the movement of troops at the front

51. Which of the following identifies an effect of the poem's title?

    A. The capitalization, commas, and repetition distract the reader.

    B. The poem contradicts the concept of the word "smile."

    C. The title reminds us to find joy in the face of adversity.

    D. The title introduces the idea of a smile that is echoed in the poem.

    E. The repetition makes it sound childlike.

52. All of the following are examples of irony in the poem EXCEPT

    A. "they read of Cheap Homes, not yet planned" (line 4)

    B. "Peace would do wrong to our undying dead" (line 9)

    C. "The sons we offered might regret they died" (line 10)

    D. "The greatest glory will be theirs who fought, / Who kept this nation in integrity." (lines 16–17)

    E. "The half-limbed readers did not chafe / But smiled at one another curiously" (lines 18–19)

53. The use of an exclamation mark in "How they smile!" (line 26) emphasizes that the

    A. soldiers have moments of joy at the front

    B. newspaper is condescending to the readers

    C. public is gullible

    D. newspaper's propaganda is ineffective

    E. public is shocked to see soldiers smiling

54. Which of the following is NOT a target of the poet's sarcasm?

    A. Politicians and the government

    B. Naïve readers

    C. Newspaper publishers

    D. Soldiers at the front

    E. National rulers

55. The overall tone of the poem can best be described as

   A.   condescending and skeptical
   B.   temperate and admonishing
   C.   passionate and vituperative
   D.   bitter and resentful
   E.   placating and sardonic

IF YOU FINISH BEFORE TIME IS CALLED, CHECK YOUR WORK ON THIS
SECTION ONLY. DO NOT WORK ON ANY OTHER SECTION IN THE TEST.

Section II: Free-Response Questions

Time: 2 hours

3 questions

Question 1

(Suggested time—40 minutes. This question counts toward one-third of the total free-response section score.)

Directions: In the following poem, "A Girl's Garden," written by Robert Frost in 1916, the speaker relates a neighbor's story of growing a garden when she was a child. Read the poem carefully, and then write a well-written essay that analyzes how Frost's use of figurative language and other poetic devices creates the complex relationship between the girl, her garden, and the grown woman she becomes.

In your response you should do the following:

- Respond to the prompt with a thesis that presents an interpretation and may establish a line of reasoning.
- Select and use evidence to develop and support your line of reasoning.
- Explain the relationship between the evidence and your thesis.
- Use appropriate grammar and punctuation in communicating your argument.

A Girl's Garden

A neighbor of mine in the village
    Likes to tell how one spring
When she was a girl on the farm, she did
    A childlike thing.

One day she asked her father   (5)
    To give her a garden plot
To plant and tend and reap herself,
    And he said, "Why not?"

In casting about for a corner
    He thought of an idle bit   (10)
Of walled-off ground where a shop had stood,
    And he said, "Just it."

And he said, "That ought to make you
    An ideal one-girl farm,
And give you a chance to put some strength   (15)
    On your slim-jim arm."

It was not enough of a garden,
    Her father said, to plough;
So she had to work it all by hand,
    But she don't mind now.   (20)

She wheeled the dung in the wheelbarrow
    Along a stretch of road;
But she always ran away and left
    Her not-nice load.

And hid from anyone passing.   (25)
    And then she begged the seed.
She says she thinks she planted one
    Of all things but weed.

A hill each of potatoes,
   Radishes, lettuce, peas,   (30)
Tomatoes, beets, beans, pumpkins, corn,
   And even fruit trees.

And yes, she has long mistrusted
   That a cider apple tree
In bearing there to-day is hers,   (35)
   Or at least may be.

Her crop was a miscellany
   When all was said and done,
A little bit of everything,
   A great deal of none.   (40)

Now when she sees in the village
   How village things go,
Just when it seems to come in right,
   She says, *"I* know!

It's as when I was a farmer——"   (45)
   Oh, never by way of advice!
And she never sins by telling the tale
   To the same person twice.

Question 2

(Suggested time—40 minutes. This question counts toward one-third of the total free-response section score.)

Directions: In the following passage from *The Spectator* (March 11, 1712), English satirist Joseph Addison creates a female character, a Lady of high society, who keeps a diary. Read the diary entries carefully. Then, in a well-written essay, analyze how the passage characterizes the diarist and her society and how this complex characterization develops the goals of Addison's satire.

In your response you should do the following:

- Respond to the prompt with a thesis that presents an interpretation and may establish a line of reasoning.
- Select and use evidence to develop and support your line of reasoning.
- Explain the relationship between the evidence and your thesis.
- Use appropriate grammar and punctuation in communicating your argument.

TUESDAY *night*. Could not go to sleep till one in the morning for thinking of my journal.

WEDNESDAY. *From eight till ten*. Drank two dishes of chocolate in bed, and fell asleep after them.
From ten to eleven. Eat a slice of bread and butter, drank a cup of bohea[1], read *The Spectator*.
From eleven to one. At my toilette, tried a new [headdress]. Gave orders for [my lap dog] Veny to be combed
(5) and washed. *Mem*. I look best in blue.
From one till half an hour after two. Drove to the change. Cheapened[2] a couple of fans.
Till four. At dinner. *Mem*. Mr. Froth passed by in his new liveries.
From four to six. Dressed, paid a visit to old Lady Blithe and her sister, having before heard they were gone out of town that day.
(10) *From six to eleven*. At basset[3]. *Mem*. Never set again upon the ace of diamonds.

THURSDAY. *From eleven at night to eight in the morning*. Dreamed that I punted[4] to Mr. Froth.
From eight to ten. Chocolate. Read two acts in Aurenzebe[5] a-bed.
From ten to eleven. Tea-table. Sent to borrow Lady Faddle's Cupid[6] for Veny. Read the play-bills. Received a letter from Mr. Froth. Mem. Locked it up in my strong box.
(15) Rest of the morning. Fontange, the tirewoman[7], her account of my Lady Blithe's wash. Broke a tooth in my little tortoise-shell comb. Sent Frank to know how my Lady Hectic rested after her monkey's leaping out at window. Looked pale. Fontange tells me my glass is not true. Dressed by three.
From three to four. Dinner cold before I sat down.
From four to eleven. Saw company. Mr. Froth's opinion of Milton. His account of the Mohocks. His
(20) fancy for a pin-cushion. Picture in the lid of his snuff-box. Old Lady Faddle promises me her woman to cut my hair. Lost five guineas at crimp.
Twelve a clock at night. Went to bed.

FRIDAY. Eight in the morning. A-bed. Read over all Mr. Froth's letters. Cupid and Vinny.
Ten a clock. Stayed within all day. Not at home.
(25) From ten to twelve. In conference with my mantua-maker. Sorted a suit of ribands. Broke my blue china cup.
From twelve to one. Shut myself up at my chamber, practiced Lady Betty Modely's skuttle[8].

---

[1]**bohea:** a kind of tea
[2]**Cheapened:** bargained down the price
[3]**basset:** a game of cards
[4]**punted:** gambled or played cards with
[5]**Aurenzebe:** John Dryden's heroic play (1676)
[6]**Cupid:** a male lap dog, apparently borrowed for studding purposes with Veny
[7]**Fontange, the tirewoman:** Mademoiselle de Fontange was a famous London hairdresser who introduced new highly fashionable headdresses. A tirewoman is a lady's maid.
[8]**skuttle:** scuttle, a way of walking in an affected manner

One in the afternoon. Called for my flowered handkerchief. Worked half a violet leaf in it. Eyes ached and head out of order. Threw by my work, and read over the remaining part of Aurenzebe.

(30)   From three to four. Dined.

From four to twelve. Changed my mind, dressed, went abroad, and played at crimp till midnight. Found Mrs. Spitely at home. Conversation: Mrs. Brilliant's necklace false stones. Old Lady Loveday going to be married to a young fellow that is not worth a groat[9]. Miss Prue going into the country. Tom Towneley has red hair. *Mem.* Mrs. Spitely whispered in my ear that she had something to tell me about Mr. Froth; I am sure it is not true.

(35)   Between twelve and one. Dreamed that Mr. Froth lay at my feet, and called me Indamora[10].

SATURDAY. Rose at eight a clock in the morning. Set down to my toilette.

From eight to nine. Shifted a patch for half an hour before I could determine it[11]. Fixed it above my left eyebrow.

From nine to twelve. Drink my tea and dressed.

(40)   From twelve to two. At chapel. A great deal of good company. *Mem.* The third air in the new opera. Lady Blithe dressed frightfully.

From three to four. Dined. Mrs. Kitty called upon me to go to the opera before I was risen from table.

From dinner to six. Drank tea. Turned off a footman for being rude to Veny.

Six a clock. Went to the opera. I did not see Mr. Froth till the beginning of the second act. Mr. Froth

(45) talked to a gentleman in a black wig. Bowed to a lady in the front box. Mr. Froth and his friend clapped Nicolini in the third act. Mr. Froth cried out and Ancora. Mr. Froth led me to my chair. I think he squeezed my hand.

Eleven at night. Went to bed. Melancholy dreams. Methought Nicolini said he was Mr. Froth.

SUNDAY. Indisposed.

---

[9]**groat:** originally a Dutch coin, only worth a trifle by the 18th century
[10]**Indamora:** the captive queen in Dryden's *Aurenzebe*
[11]**determine it:** She is deciding where to place a decorative birthmark patch.

Question 3

(Suggested time—40 minutes. This question counts toward one-third of the total free-response section score.)

Directions: The growth and development of people is strongly influenced by the location where they live as well as the time period in which they grow up. Literary setting, including both time and place, is frequently used significantly in many works of literature. For example, the setting may incite the action of the plot, it may reflect a change of the state of mind of one or more characters, or it may represent the values held by a character or characters and/or society.

Either from your own reading or from the list below, choose a work of fiction in which the setting is significant. Then, in a well-written essay, analyze how the setting affects character and illuminates an interpretation of the work as a whole. Do not merely summarize the plot.

In your response you should do the following:

- Respond to the prompt with a thesis that presents an interpretation and may establish a line of reasoning.
- Select and use evidence to develop and support your line of reasoning.
- Explain the relationship between the evidence and your thesis.
- Use appropriate grammar and punctuation in communicating your argument.

Absalom, Absalom!

The Age of Innocence

Atonement

Ceremony

The Color Purple

The Corrections

The Crossing

Death of a Salesman

Empire Falls

The Grapes of Wrath

Heart of Darkness

The Importance of Being Earnest

Invisible Man

Jane Eyre

The Kite Runner

The Known World

Little Bee

Maggie: A Girl of the Streets

Middlesex

A Midsummer Night's Dream

My Ántonia

Oliver Twist

A Passage to India

The Piano Lesson

The Poisonwood Bible

A Portrait of the Artist as a Young Man

Pride and Prejudice

A Raisin in the Sun

Snow Falling on Cedars

Sula

The Sun Also Rises

A Tale of Two Cities

Tess of the D'Urbervilles

Things Fall Apart

The Underground Railroad

Waiting for Godot

When the Emperor Was Divine

IF YOU FINISH BEFORE TIME IS CALLED, CHECK YOUR WORK ON THIS SECTION ONLY. DO NOT WORK ON ANY OTHER SECTION IN THE TEST.

Answer Key

Section I: Multiple-Choice Questions

First Poem	First Prose Passage	Second Poem	Second Prose Passage	Third Poem
1. D	13. B	25. D	34. E	45. A
2. A	14. D	26. B	35. B	46. C
3. B	15. D	27. B	36. A	47. B
4. E	16. A	28. B	37. E	48. E
5. E	17. E	29. E	38. D	49. D
6. D	18. C	30. D	39. C	50. A
7. C	19. B	31. A	40. A	51. B
8. D	20. A	32. C	41. D	52. E
9. C	21. C	33. E	42. C	53. C
10. E	22. E		43. B	54. D
11. A	23. D		44. D	55. D
12. B	24. C			

Answers and Explanations

Section I: Multiple-Choice Questions

First Poem

The poem for questions 1–12, "Nani," is an autobiographical work written by Alberto Rios and first published in 1982. The poem is set in his grandmother's kitchen.

1. **D.** The present-tense verbs in the poem help to add immediacy to the action; moreover, they emphasize the timelessness of this family's ties to one another, choice D. The words are all inclusive, as Nani "serves," "speak[s] smiles," "watches me," "asks me if I want more," and finally, "she serves" again. Her grandson "watch[es] her," "eat[s]," tells her how he "tastes the mint," and "ask[s] for more." In the second stanza, the grandson observes Nani's reminiscing about a man (presumably her husband) and her own children. All of these details contribute to the constancy of family, the pervasive need for shared memories. Choice A makes little sense; present-tense verbs do not emphasize the importance of food, and we do not have evidence that the food Nani serves is unusually fresh. Choice B is simply unreasonable; present-tense verbs cannot minimize the characters' relationship. Also, while it may be true that the characters need communication (C), present-tense verbs do not underscore that idea. Choice E seems appealing; the grandson may indeed wish to understand Nani's Spanish, but stop and think about it: His desire is not necessarily urgent, and the present-tense verbs do not particularly stress that desire.

2. **A.** As the poem begins, Nani and her grandson are sitting at her table; she serves him rice soup and meatballs and he eats gratefully. However, at a deeper level, this action introduces two essential ideas in the poem: Nani serves him "instinctively," and he acknowledges that he must symbolically "eat words I might have had to say more out of embarrassment." Why? Because he is painfully aware that he no longer has the fluency in Spanish that he once had; he cannot speak the "now-foreign words I used to speak." Therefore, it makes sense that she *instinctively* serves him, not just because it's what grandmothers do, but because it helps him avoid the embarrassment of not remembering how to properly communicate with her in Spanish,

172

choice A. Choice B is not supported in the poem; it does not indicate that the grandson eats passively because he does not know how to ask for it properly. The opening phrase in choice C marks it as erroneous; the poem offers no hint that Nani maintains absolute control over the family. Choice D is inaccurate in its wording and, similar to choice B, demonstrates flawed cause-and-effect logic. The grandson is not embarrassed at watching Nani; rather, he is embarrassed at his inability to speak and understand her language. Additionally, this is not the reason he eats, nor does Nani command him to do so. Choice E gets the emphasis wrong; the point of the first sentence is not the speaker's ineloquent Spanish, but rather Nani's instinctive mothering, giving him food and protecting him from embarrassment.

3. **B.** To understand the function of this adjective clause, let's look at the subjects, verbs, and direct objects in the entire sentence. First "she serves the sopa de arroz." The second subject-verb-direct object is "I watch her," and the third is "[I] eat words." If you insert a parenthetical adjectival relative pronoun before the words, you'll see "[I] eat words [that] I might have had to say more out of embarrassment." The words in the question function as an adjective clause that modifies "words," choice B. Remember that an adjective clause must follow the noun that it modifies, and, although they are usually preceded by a relative pronoun, the word "that" can sometimes be omitted, as it is in this case. You can immediately recognize that choice A is incorrect because the words in the question are not a phrase of any kind; they form a clause, having both a subject and a verb. It cannot be a noun clause (C) because if it were, the clause would have to function as a subject, a direct object (as in choice D), or an object of a preposition. It fulfills none of these. The clause in question cannot be an adverbial clause (E) because it does not modify a verb, an adjective, or another adverb, and adverbial clauses cannot begin with the word "I."

4. **E.** The background is that this poem is a variation of a sestina, which is a very complicated and strict poetic form that originated in the 12th century. Traditionally, a sestina has six stanzas of six lines each (sestets), followed by a three-line tercet, known as an envoy. (The variation in "Nani" is that the poet joins the first three traditional sestets into one stanza, equaling 18 lines, and does so again, creating a second stanza that also has 18 lines.) Making it even more difficult to write, the last word of each of the first six lines must be repeated in the subsequent stanzas in a specific order, AND all six words must be repeated in the envoy. The repetition must follow a strict pattern: *a, b, c, d, e, f* / *f, a, e, b, d, c* / *c, f, d, a, b, e* / *e, c, b, f, a, d* / *d, e, a, c, f, b* / *b, d, f, e, c, a.* The final envoy can use *e, c, a* or *a, c, e.* Whew! The reader must respect the skills of any poet who conquers this complicated pattern. Fortunately, you do not need to know all of this technical information for the AP exam. For this specific question, however, notice the last word of the first six lines, each of which will be repeated six more times in the poem. Here we see (in order) "serves," "me," "her," "words," "more," and "speak," the ideas that are most important to the speaker; that's why they are repeated over and over at the end of a line. The repeated words do not refer to affection (A); they do not relive the experience (B) or remind us of the characters' relationship (D). Choice C is incorrect because only two of the six repeated words refer to actions in the first place, and we do not know if they are familial rituals.

5. **E.** The quotation "To speak now-foreign words I *used to speak*" strongly suggests that the speaker, in his past, was better able to speak the Spanish dialect that his Nani does. But now that he is unpracticed in Spanish, the words have become "foreign." Therefore, he must have had a bilingual upbringing, choice E. On the other hand, the fact that the grandson cannot find the words to speak to Nani in Spanish does not make it reasonable to claim that she does not understand him at all (A). Choice B contradicts the poem; if the two sometimes talk together, the grandson should better understand his lapsed Spanish. The intent in choice C is inaccurate; the problem in the poem is not that the grandson does not have the right words to say; rather, the issue is that he cannot find the right words in Spanish. While it may be a nice idea to think the two characters should spend more time together (D), this concept does not address what is suggested in the quotation, namely that the grandson previously spoke Nani's Spanish more fluently.

6. **D.** The fact that Nani is directly putting her "fingers in the flame for me" as she heats tortillas implies that she is used to sacrificing herself for those she loves, choice D. Serving him soup (A) is a kind, grandmotherly gesture, but it does not imply sacrifice. When the grandson claims, I "eat words" (B), it means that he has not spoken, not that he has sacrificed anything. The phrase she "looks at me only with her back" (C) merely indicates that Nani does not turn around to face her grandson as she cooks. Choice E might initially seem to suggest some sacrifice because of the phrase "a hundred wrinkles," but the presence of wrinkles could merely attest to her longevity, not necessarily to personal sacrifice.

7. **C.** The grandson "see[s]" Nani's wrinkles speak, and he infers the wrinkles tell of a man in her past, of her children, of "this and that," which indicates that Nani's wrinkles literally surround her with memories of loved ones, choice C. Choice A has no evidence in the poem; it does not present any thoughts Nani previously had about her grandson, so the quote in the question cannot contradict what is not in the poem in the first place. The poem does offer proof that Nani loves her family (B), but this answer choice is too limited because it disregards the phrasing about her imagined idea of words "flowing more easily from these other mouths." Choices D and E are both irrelevant; neither love of cooking nor zest for life answers this particular question. Additionally, the idea in choice E, that Nani has gained a renewed zest for life, has no evidence in the poem.

8. **D.** The grandson's imagining that Nani's wrinkles are speaking of her children and "this and that" becomes a metaphor of a "tremendous string around her, / holding her together." The idea that her relatives hold her together and in turn reflect on how much Nani meant to them reinforces that her memories are of cherished people and events in her life, choice D. Choice A misreads the context of the quotation; the "tremendous string" does not refer to her recipes. Choice B is too strong because of the absolute word "all," and because the grandson imagines what her wrinkles speak of, not what she actually shares. Choice C is too direct when what we are looking for is a metaphor; it is true that Nani is wrinkled, but the wrinkles alone do not develop the metaphor of the string that holds her together. Choice E is too limited, since the string of memories is not limited only to Nani's remembrances of her grandson; this answer choice fails to mention her memories of all the other beloved people in her past.

9. **C.** The first stanza is entirely devoted to actions in the present: Nani serves her grandson sopa de arroz and albondigas, he eats, he compliments the flavor, and she serves him more. In contrast, the second stanza begins in the present as the grandson watches Nani warming tortillas, but after the first sentence, this stanza explores his impression of her thoughts about the past, choice C, including a man (presumably her husband), along with her own children and all that Nani meant to them. The grandson also wonders what he means to Nani. Choice A is an inaccurate description of both stanzas. The phrase "deals exclusively with food" is an imprecise paraphrase of the first stanza, since it discusses much more than just food, such as the grandson's discomfort with Spanish. The description of the second stanza is also incorrect because the second stanza begins with more action built around food, namely the tortillas; thus, the second stanza does not ignore food. Both halves of choice B are also inaccurate. First, it is far too limited to claim that the first stanza is focused only on the grandson's discomfort, and second, Nani never expresses displeasure. The verb choice in the first half of choice D is questionable; to scrutinize means to examine, analyze, or dissect, which is hardly what occurs in the first stanza. The second stanza may inspect the two characters' emotions to some degree, but that is not the real focus of the second stanza. Choice E, like all of the other inaccurate choices, is incorrect for two reasons: The first stanza does present the grandson's difficulty communicating with Nani, but it is not the stanza's focus, and the second stanza does not solve it.

10. **E.** When the speaker asks, "What is this thing she serves?" the simple answer is love, choice E. The other answer choices are genuine aspects of Nani's personality; she appears to be authentic and genuine (A), she has endured much in her life (B), she is quite sincere (C), and she is always respectful (D), but these ideas do not answer the question. What does she serve? She serves love.

11. **A.** The final tercet reinforces the thrust of the poem: The food Nani serves becomes a symbol of holding the family together, of the love she offers them, choice A. Choice B is irrelevant to this question; although it is true that grandmothers stereotypically can be counted on and that grandchildren do not always welcome that support, these ideas do not clarify the theme of this particular poem. Choice C is incorrect for the same reason; it is too narrow an idea for the entire poem. While it may be true that some families have difficulty communicating, that is not the overall theme of this loving poem. Choice D is inaccurate for two reasons: Many grandmothers may urge their grandchildren to eat more, but that alone is too narrow to define the thrust of this poem, and the absolute word "always" is surely not correct. It is quite likely that choice E is a true statement; in general, most people do serve others in their life, but once again, this is irrelevant because it is not the overall thrust of the poem.

12. **B.** The grandson is clearly depicted as respectful and humble; he quietly watches Nani, he compliments her, he understands her, and he hopes he means a lot to her. Nani is obviously generous and giving; she keeps serving more food and giving love. Therefore, choice B is correct. In each of the incorrect answer choices, at least one word incorrectly describes one of the characters. In choice A, the grandson is accurately described as civil, but

he is hardly intemperate, which means unrestrained or uncontrolled; Nani, like all people, is probably not faultless and she certainly does not appear to be austere, which means to be somber and harsh. Both words that describe the grandson in choice C are wrong; he is not fawning (flattering or servile), nor is he churlish (rude and impolite). However, the words that describe Nani in choice C are accurate; she appears simple (serving soup, meatballs, and tortillas) and righteous (morally good). In choice D, the word "loquacious," which means talkative, is an inaccurate description of the grandson; he hardly speaks at all; rather, he passively watches and observes Nani. Because the grandson observes that Nani smiles often, she is not solemn, and we have no evidence that she is candid (frank and blunt). Choice E inaccurately describes the grandson as complacent, which means to be self-satisfied and smug, and describes Nani as stoic, which means to be passively resigned.

First Prose Passage

The passage for questions 13–24 is an excerpt from Dombey and Son, which was written by Charles Dickens in the form of an extended serialized novel and published between 1846–1848. This scene takes place in the Dombey residence, as Mrs. Dombey has just given birth to Mr. Dombey's first son.

13. **B.** The dominant images in the first sentence are of Dombey, sitting in a large, "great" chair, while the new baby is tucked up in a "little basket" by the fire. In the second paragraph, the narrator continues to juxtapose the images of father and son, finding comparisons and contrasts in their ages, their complexions, and their foreheads; therefore, the purpose of the first paragraph is to foreshadow this juxtaposition in the second, choice B. Choice A is incorrect because the fact that Dombey has a larger chair than his son's basket does not diminish Son's importance; it does not even affect it. Rather, it is entirely appropriate that a newborn be placed in a practical little basket instead of a large chair. The idea presented in choice C is irrelevant; although it is true that a father is more dominant than a newborn, the mere fact that Dombey sits in a large chair and Son is placed in a little basket does not establish his dominance. Choice D is too strong; the opening passage does not establish the family's great wealth; they appear to be comfortable, but we do not yet know how prosperous they are. "Affection," in choice E, is not supported in the first paragraph, nor in the passage as a whole; Dombey never demonstrates affection for his son; rather, he is happy only because the boy will fulfill his own commercial ambitions.

14. **D.** The second paragraph offers a series of amusing comparisons of the father and son, but it is notable in that the newborn's traits are always more exaggerated than his father's, choice D. The only precise fact about the son is that he is younger (only "eight-and-forty minutes" instead of "eight-and-forty years"); all of the other descriptions are hyperbolic. Dombey is "rather bald," but Son is "very bald"; Dombey is "rather red," but Son is "very red"; Dombey's brow has "some marks," but Son's is "crossed with a thousand little creases." Meanwhile it is inaccurate to think that Son has more worries than his father (A); after all, the baby is unaware of the world, having just been born and his "thousand little creases" are common in newborns. Choice B might seem plausible because the father and son do share common traits, but that in itself is not notable; what is more intriguing is how Son's features are always exaggerated more than his father's. By the end of the passage, Dombey is surely depicted as pretentious (C), but the second paragraph does not establish this trait; of course, the passage offers no evidence for whether or not the newborn is pretentious. Choice E, like choice B, might seem to have some promise since it is true that Time and Care will affect both of these characters. However, once again, this is not a notable observation; rather, it is something that is true of all humanity. Make sure that the answer you choose is not only accurate, but also addresses the specific particulars of the question.

15. **D.** Dickens' detailed description of "Time and his brother Care" is really quite developed and multifaceted. This complex sentence includes a simile, "as on a tree that was to come down in good time," and it includes personification in presenting the abstract nouns as "remorseless twins" and "deceitful." It also includes foreshadowing when describing how Time will smooth out Son's baby wrinkles but replace them later in life with "deeper operations." Therefore, choice D is correct. The incorrect answer choices all include at least one incorrect term. Choice A inaccurately includes *allusion* and *paradox*. Choice B incorrectly includes *conceit*. Choice C erroneously adds *apostrophe*. Choice E includes the questionable term *irony* and the inaccurate term *flashback*.

16. **A.** The question asks you to focus on a single detail in Dombey's attire; notice the way he "jingled and jingled the heavy gold watch-chain." This is a symbol of how he is chained and bound to his life's work: running the company of Dombey and Son, which in turn provides him with great wealth for gold

watch-chains and much more. He keeps jingling the chain because he cannot let go of what it represents; it "depended" from his blue coat. One may try to argue that Dombey's attire shows a flair for extravagance (B), but this is a debatable term and it is not symbolic. Men of Dombey's stature in society commonly wore attire like his. Choice C is inaccurate for a similar reason; it is unknown whether or not Dombey believes in the importance of good fashion, but once again, this is not symbolic. The same logic applies to choice D; Dombey's attire may adhere to the norms of society, but that makes it practical rather than symbolic. Choice E makes little sense; we do not know how much Dombey wants to conform or whether he is sincere in that desire. Again, remember to always select the answer choice that best addresses the specific question, not just something that was mentioned in the passage.

17. **E.** Many readers cannot help but chortle or chuckle at the narrator's repeated snide comments about Dombey, choice E. In this case, the narrator's parenthetical remark essentially condemns Dombey because he is "little used" to speaking to his wife kindly; indeed, he only does so once, and only after hesitating. Instead, he normally addresses her only as "Mrs Dombey," as if she is just another of his many possessions. Choice A may appear reasonable at first, but the parenthetical remark is not all that blunt, and it is not just about Dombey's attitude toward his wife; rather, it is an assessment of Dombey's lack of sensitivity to the entire world. Choice B is clearly wrong because the remark appears to have no bearing on Dombey's upbringing; indeed, we have no idea if he was raised to be so insensitive. Choice C contradicts the intent of the parenthetical remark; this reproach of Dombey criticizes how seldom he addresses his wife with any term of endearment. Choice D may entice some because of the word "softening," which is also in the passage, but the parenthetical remark does not justify his softer comment; rather, it criticizes how seldom he shows kindness.

18. **C.** Mrs. Dombey's immediate reaction to Dombey's calling her "my dear" is a "transient flush of faint surprise," which suggests that he speaks to her gently only on very rare occasions, so she reacts with momentary disbelief, choice C. On the other hand, the passage offers no evidence to suggest that she truly understands his motives (A). Choice B is unreasonable in claiming she is too weak to respond; it is true that she does not speak and is recovering from childbirth, but her reaction here is one of surprise. Choice D sounds reasonable, but it has no evidence in the passage; one might infer that she would appreciate a kind word now and then from her husband, but we do not actually know for a fact that Mrs. Dombey wishes he would compliment her more often. Choice E misunderstands her "transient flush" as being one of embarrassment; she is not embarrassed, but surprised.

19. **B.** In the fifth paragraph, Dombey, after hesitating, first addresses his wife as "Mrs Dombey, my—my dear." Then, two paragraphs later, he almost calls her "my dear" again, but he simply cannot be so endearing twice in the same evening, choice B; instead, he says, "my—Mrs Dombey—of course." Choice A is incorrect in that Dombey's remark does not intimate that he is proud of having a son; he only mentions what the boy shall be named, without bothering to consult his wife. Choice C is far too strong; readers may not approve of the indifferent way Dombey treats his wife, but that does not imply that he does not care for her at all; remember that he does call her "my dear" at least once. Choice D has no evidence in the passage at all; rather, Dombey is painted as a man who has no interest in his wife's opinion, and he is too self-important to name his son anything but Paul, of course, naming him after himself. Choice E is equally unfounded; nothing in Dombey's character indicates he gives a whit what his wife thinks, so it is highly unlikely that he'd have previously consulted with her about the child's name.

20. **A.** The paragraph following Dombey exulting at his son's birth verifies that his pleasure centers on the fact that now "'The House will once again . . . be not only in name but in fact Dombey and Son.'" He repeats the name with satisfaction and emphasis, "'Dom-bey and Son!'" Before Son was born, the company's name was, in fact, inaccurate. Therefore, choice A is correct. Choice B may be true at some point in the future; Dombey indeed plans on his son entering the business and presumably taking over when Dombey retires, but this is only an assumption, not the underlying focal point of Dombey's exultation. Choice C also does not address the underlying significance that the question asks for; the passage does not indicate that Dombey has the typical father's pride in having a son, but instead he selfishly thinks only of his own gain. Choice D is quite unreasonable; Dombey already has someone endearing to care for, his wife, but it appears he cares for no one so much as himself. Choice E is equally unreasonable; he does not appear to focus any attention on his wife in the first place, so it's unlikely that he'll refocus that attention on his son.

21. C. The paragraph in question presents a summary of "the one idea of Mr Dombey's life," namely that all celestial and earthly entities exist only to support the enterprises of the Dombey and Son firm, choice C. The earth permits their trade; the sun and moon "give them light"; rivers and seas "float their ships"; rainbows promise "fair weather"; winds propel their voyages; stars and planets "circled in their orbits to preserve inviolate a system of which they were the centre." He indeed believes that the firm of Dombey and Son is the center of the universe. The paragraph even finishes with typical Dickensian humor: Dombey thinking that A.D. is named for him, that it stands for "anno Dombei—and Son." Choice A may accurately depict Dombey's hoped-for outcome, that the company will continue to flourish, but this paragraph does not confirm that idea. Choice B is completely unfounded; nothing in Dombey's description indicates he is cognizant that his life has been blessed. Choice D overstates an idea; even though the "earth was made for Dombey and Son to trade in," we have seen no evidence that their success is actually worldwide. Choice E, like choice A, is probably an accurate statement—Dombey hopes that Son will join his company—but this answer choice does not address the function of the whole paragraph.

22. E. The irony underlying Dombey's delight in the birth of his son is that he does not take joy for the usual expected, traditional reasons. Rather than rejoicing in his growing family, his every thought in regard to Son deals with his own commercial ventures, choice E. Dombey's own father had apparently died nearly 20 years earlier and Dombey has been the sole proprietor of Dombey and Son; but now the name will once again be literal and factual, which gives him "luxurious satisfaction." He dismisses the "necessity of writing Junior" simply because it won't "enter into the correspondence of the House." The very words of the company, Dombey and Son, "convey the one idea of Mr Dombey's life." Choice A contradicts the passage; it appears that Dombey is never unsure of anything, let alone his ability to provide for his family. Choice B has some basis in the passage; Dombey has had to wait 10 years for the birth of this son, but that is a mere detail, and even if it is true, this does not make Dombey's joy at the child's birth ironic. Choice C has no basis in the passage; we never observe Mr. Dombey expressing anything like sincere love for Mrs. Dombey; thus, Son's birth cannot ironically compromise what did not exist in the first place. There is no evidence for choice D; it is simply unreasonable to jump to the conclusion that he will not be satisfied with only one son.

23. D. The tone of the passage is both witty (clever and amusing) as well as mocking (sarcastic), choice D. Dickens provides profuse humor, such as comparing the newborn to a muffin that needs toasting, and Dombey's self-important "anno Dombei" comment. Dickens also makes good use of clever phrasing, such as his juxtaposition and parallel constructions in the second paragraph, and his lengthy list of earthly and celestial elements in the tenth paragraph, as well as Dombey's seven remarks all beginning with "That . . ." in the last paragraph. All throughout these humorous elements, though, Dickens is also consistently mocking Dombey, a man who ultimately runs his family like he runs his business: calculatingly, callously, coldly, and commercially. Choice A is just too strong in its negativity; the tone is not quite so vicious as to be truly malicious, nor is it condescending. Choice B inaccurately describes the tone as arrogant; Dombey himself is certainly arrogant, but the tone of the passage is not. Also, we may perhaps be skeptical about Dombey's future, but he is not, and that too does not describe the tone of the passage. Choice C is wrong for the same reason; the word "presumptuous" might describe Dombey, but not the tone of the passage, and nothing in the passage is contradictory. Choice E is completely off base. The tone is neither lighthearted nor laconic. Dickens is far too wordy to ever be labeled as laconic!

24. C. The last paragraph hints that some people talk about Mrs. Dombey as being unhappy, but if such talk were to reach Mr. Dombey, he would be incredulous. Dickens takes the reader inside Dombey's head, and he walks us through Dombey's reasoning, presenting seven statements, all beginning with the word "That." Each successive sentence in his internal monologue builds up the momentum of his imaginary self-argument, in which he is forced to conclude that Mrs. Dombey "must have been happy," and that "she couldn't help it," choice C. It's obvious that poor Mr. Dombey is deluding himself. Since this paragraph presents an interior monologue, it does not explain anything to others, as in choice A. Choice B inaccurately assumes Dombey listens to his heart; remember that "Dombey and Son had often dealt in hides, but never in hearts." Thus, his reasoning in the final paragraph cannot elucidate what was never there in the first place. Choice D may sound plausible at first; the way Dombey's thoughts begin each sentence with "That . . ." over and over almost sounds like a court proceeding, but his reasoning is not logical at all. Choice E is hardly reasonable; Dombey is not trying to enhance his own self-esteem; he already has more than enough self-esteem.

Second Poem

The poem for questions 25–33 is "Petals" written by Amy Lowell in 1912.

25. **D.** The central metaphor, "the flower of our heart," begins on line 3 and develops throughout the poem, establishing how the petals of the heart's flower are strewn into the stream of life, floating off to destinations unknown. The heart's fragility (D) is supported by the ideas that we can only watch the flower petals as they make their "glad, early start" in the stream, "Freighted with hope" as they travel to "Their distant employ." However, "We shall never know" the fate of the heart as it travels through life's stream; we can only watch as the stream "Sweeps them away" and enjoy the memory of their fragrance. The stream of life is also a metaphor, but it is merely a vehicle, a conduit, on which the heart's petals float. Choice A incorrectly claims the metaphor depends on a purported reluctance to take chances, but that actually contradicts the poem; the speaker voluntarily chooses to strew the petals into the stream, taking his or her chances in the process. Choice B is inaccurate in stating that the stream has a changing nature; this idea is not described in the poem. Choice C contradicts the poem, which clearly states that the petals are swept away "into infinite ways"; they are not limited by finite possibilities. Finally, the poem offers no hint of fear for the future (E); indeed, the speaker willingly and intentionally drops the petals into the stream without knowing how they will fare or where fate may take them.

26. **B.** The first two lines of the second stanza each contain words that equally balance negative and positive connotations, choice B. Line 7 begins with negativity, the word "Freighted" connotes something heavy and burdensome; line 8 begins with "Crimsoned," which is not as negative but can connote being flushed or ruddy. Each line is then balanced with a positive word: "hope" completes line 7 and "joy" completes line 8. Choice A wrongly states that these lines contradict the images of the first stanza, when instead, they are consistent. The second stanza does not shift the tone (as claimed in choice C); rather, the poem's tone is stable and unchanging throughout. Choice D makes little sense; the first two lines of the second stanza do not diminish the effect of the petals, but rather intensify it. Choice E is completely unreasonable; the subject matter of the second stanza is the same as the first, not a new idea.

27. **B.** The question asks you to find the quotation that is not consistent with the movement of the stream. The quotation in choice B fits that concept because it refers to the act of "[scattering] the leaves of our opening rose," which has nothing to do with the actual movement of the stream's water. All of the other answer choices are consistent with the stream's movement. Choice A describes the flower petals floating by, which indirectly implies the stream's movement. Choice C also suggests the movement of the stream as it describes the "widening scope" of the flower petals as they float down the stream. The idea in choice D, that the stream flows and sweeps the petals away, is consistent with the stream's movement; it specifically mentions the flow of the water. Choice E describes the flowers continuing down the stream; therefore, it refers to the flow of the water as the flowers move downstream.

28. **B.** The phrase "Freighted with hope" parallels the idea that "The end [is] lost in dream," choice B. Notice how the concept of being freighted (moved from one location to another) is similar to the idea of coming to the end of the line, or perhaps even death. In addition, the word "dream" by itself usually has positive connotations; dreams deal with our aspirations and goals, and this relates to the idea of "hope" that completes line 7. Choice A refers to the first line of the poem, which establishes the metaphor of life being a stream, but this does not relate to the image of the petals as they are carried away with hope. The quotation in choice C, "Their distant employ," relates to the idea that the petals will someday find some purpose in life, a purpose that we cannot know, but this does not parallel the idea of having hope. Choice D, "Each one is gone," does not address this question; it deals with the way we lose sight of the petals and it does not relate to the meaning of hope. Choice E is irrelevant to this question; the quotation deals with the way in which humanity stays behind, alone, after strewing the petals of the heart into the stream; it does not directly reflect the idea in "Freighted with hope."

29. **E.** Notice the flow of the words in lines 12–13. Line 12 begins with a short, abrupt sentence, "We never shall know." And then it draws the reader in by dangling the beginning of the next sentence, "And the stream as it flows," which is not concluded until line 13, when it "Sweeps them away." The enjambment between the lines encourages, even requires, the reader to pause and slow down, mimicking a stream as it meanders, choice E; the enjambment draws out the sentence instead of rushing it all into one line. Choice A is unreasonable; this choice deals with the flower petals, not the stream, and it erroneously claims that the effect of the enjambment is to systematically scatter the flowers. Choice B, stating that the stream's water is clear, has absolutely no evidence in the poem, nor does it address the *effect* of the enjambment. Choice C might sound promising at first glance, but notice that it addresses the flow of a river, a much larger force than this gentle stream. The slowing effect of the enjambment does not relate to the more powerful flow of a river. Choice D is illogical; enjambment does not distract the flow of thought in a poem, it encourages a thoughtful pause before finishing the line. A piece of punctuation such as a dash might be distracting, but simple enjambment is not.

30. **D.** This question asks you to identify figurative language in the final line, so it should be a fast and accessible answer. The final line has four "f" sounds in "flower fared forth . . . fragrance" and two "s" sounds in "still stays," so the alliteration, choice D, should be quite obvious. The last line has no understatement (A), nor does it present a paradox (B), something seemingly contradictory that makes sense only on a deeper level. Apostrophe (C), the technique of addressing someone who is not present or an inanimate object, is not used. Metaphor (E) might be tempting to some because the poem uses metaphor throughout, but, if you read the question carefully, you will realize that the poem does not conclude with heavy use of metaphor in the last line.

31. **A.** The poem as a whole relates to the chances we take in life as we bare our heart and leave it vulnerable in circumstances we cannot control, choice A. Notice the courage that the speaker needs to strew the petals of the heart into the stream, only to let them go their own way, knowing that once they touch the water, one cannot control their path. Choice B does not accurately address the poem's meaning. The speaker acknowledges that the final destination of the heart's petals is unknown, but the speaker does not indicate any fear of it. Additionally, this inputted fear does not inhibit the speaker's imagination; the poem states that the petals will go "beyond into infinite ways." The poem may be described as sentimental to some degree (C), but that emotion does not weigh down the poem's optimism. Many poems may address nature as a force that combats and inhibits humanity, choice D, but this poem does not depict nature negatively. The stream is perhaps indifferent to humanity, but it does not impede it. The beginning of choice E that addresses the need to take chances is attractive, but the answer choice then falls apart; the poem does not support the idea of occasional success. Keep in mind that the final fate of the flower petals is completely unknown.

32. **C.** The poem presents the idea that one needs to relinquish something, to shed layers, to willingly discard the flower petals of the heart, "the leaves of our opening rose," in order to bloom "into infinite ways," and thus leave a "fragrance [that] stays." The irony is that we must let go before we can grow, choice C. Choice A is silly and illogical; of course streams can flow quickly enough to sweep away flower petals, and this idea is not ironic. Choice B is equally unreasonable and not grounded in the poem. The flower petals are never immersed in the stream's waters and even if they were, it would not be ironic. Choice D is not exactly ironic, but it tries. It is true that life, metaphorically represented in the stream, hurries on, the "years hurry on," regardless of one's actions, such as strewing our heart's petals into the stream, but this is not a contradictory idea, which is necessary for the concept of irony. Choice E misreads the poem; nature is not being destroyed, and the poem offers no hint of regret for one's actions.

33. **E.** The last line beautifully compounds visual and olfactory imagery. The flower represents the heart, and each petal suggests the different events the heart faces in life. The "fragrance [that] still stays" suggests the sweet memories that linger after those events. These ideas in choice E fit into the poem's optimistic outlook very well. Choice A may be true in real life, but these ideas do not adequately address the last line; the flowers do not die in the poem, and the concept of missing them is not evident. Instead, we remember their fragrance. Choice B likewise implies negativity that the poem does not support; the flowers will "fare forth," but that does not imply they will not fare well downstream. This answer choice also fails to address the compound imagery; it only mentions the flowers, but not the lingering fragrance. Choice C is far too remote from the poem to be a viable answer; the poem does not suggest that we expect too much of anything from nature. Also, like choice B, this choice ignores the compound imagery of the last line. Choice D may seem possible upon first read, but only for a moment. The poem does have a degree of natural imagery in the flowers, petals, stream, and rose, but the poem never suggests that they dominate human senses. This answer choice also fails to address the last line's compound imagery and instead addresses the imagery of the poem overall.

Second Prose Passage

The passage for questions 34–44 comes from Lady Susan *by Jane Austen. Probably written in 1794, it was not published until 1871. It is a short, epistolary novella consisting of letters between Lady Susan and her close confidant and fellow schemer, Alicia Johnson, plus letters that Lady Susan's sister-in-law (Catherine Vernon) exchanges between her mother (Lady De Courcy), her father (Sir Reginald De Courcy), and her brother (Mr. Reginald De Courcy).*

34. **E.** Lady Susan begins by thanking Alicia for "taking notice" of her daughter, Frederica, mentioning that it demonstrates Alicia's friendship. But then she follows by stating that, although she is certain of Alicia's affection, she does not want her friend to overly exert herself on Frederica's behalf, choice E. On the other hand, Lady Susan never indicates that she thinks Frederica might improve (A), either with or without Alicia's help. Choice B contradicts the passage; Lady Susan does not think Alicia's assistance is essential. Choice C, that both Frederica and Lady Susan value Alicia's friendship, has no evidence in the passage; we never know what Frederica thinks of Alicia. Choice D is wrong for the same reason; we have no evidence to support the idea that Frederica does not enjoy Alicia's friendship.

35. **B.** When Lady Susan states "I am far from exacting so heavy a sacrifice," she is asking, requesting (choice B), that Alicia *not* assist Frederica, and *not* sacrifice anything for her. She repeats this message as she tells Alicia that she doesn't want to burden her friend, to "encumber one moment of your precious time." Choice A makes no sense; the verb "yield," when used with a direct object, means to produce or furnish something or to give up something. One cannot produce or give up a sacrifice. "Challenging" (C) does not fit the context of the sentence; Lady Susan is not disputing, confronting, or questioning her friend. "Extorting" (D) refers to blackmailing or swindling; its negative definition has the wrong connotation for Lady Susan's message. "Claiming" (E) does not fit the context of the sentence nor describe Lady Susan's intended meaning, which is to make a request, not an assertion.

36. **A.** If you only read the sentence in this question and take it at face value, you might be fooled. On a literal level, Lady Susan declares that because she was so pampered and spoiled in her childhood, she was never forced to attend a finishing school; therefore, she claims she does not have the accomplishments, the charms that finishing schools supposedly produce in young ladies. However, when you understand the deeper meaning underlying the passage as a whole, it is clear that Lady Susan believes she has far more charms than others, even without having the benefit of attending finishing school, choice A. She "flatters herself" that she has the power to make Sir James "renew his application" to marry Frederica with a simple letter. Her attitude toward Reginald De Courcy gushes with her supreme confidence that she can use her feminine wiles to manipulate the man. Clearly, Lady Susan is confident that she does not need the charms of finishing school to bend males to her will. The passage offers no evidence that she regrets not attending finishing school (B). Choice C is erroneous for multiple reasons; in the first place, the idea that Frederica needs schooling to "perfect" her abilities is inaccurate because Lady Susan does not advocate "perfect knowledge"; additionally, she does not want Frederica to "understand anything thoroughly." Choice D contradicts the passage. Lady Susan does not support finishing schools; instead, she feels that the refinements a girl attains will merely "gain a woman some applause, but will not add one lover." Choice D is also incorrect in mentioning getting a husband; Lady Susan never mentions marriage for ladies from finishing schools, only getting lovers. Choice E, that she resents her indulgent childhood, has no support in the passage.

37. **E.** Lady Susan's comment is ironic because, just as soon as she states that the "accomplishments" of finishing school are "now necessary to finish a pretty woman," she immediately contradicts herself, choice E, stating "Not that I am an advocate of the prevailing fashion." Choice A is irrelevant: it is inconsequential whether or not foreign languages are valid for a lady to know. Choice B, that some ladies need finishing school more than others, has no evidence in the passage. The idea in choice C, that ladies can get good husbands without finishing school, may be true in the passage, but it is not ironic, although it is irrelevant to Lady Susan's comment. Choice D is unreasonable; the passage has no suggestion about whether or not eligible bachelors care about ladies' finishing school, and this response does not answer the question.

38. **D.** Lady Susan stresses that the knowledge ladies learn at finishing school, such as foreign languages, music, singing, and drawing, might bring some degree of admiration in society, but will not get a lady what she really needs: a lover, choice D. This factual question is answered directly by what is stated in the passage. Lady Susan does not advocate learning anything thoroughly, so choice A does not answer the question. Choice B is incorrect for the same reason; Lady Susan does not believe in getting "perfect knowledge" of anything. Choice C may be a bit tricky; Lady Susan does indeed feel that grace and manners are important, but she does not claim that schools fail to teach these skills. The passage offers no proof for choice E, that schools focus too much on the arts, and this idea is definitely not the most serious disadvantage of ladies' education.

39. **C.** Lady Susan's goals for her daughter are indeed sad. Her declaration "I do not mean, therefore, that Frederica's acquirements should be more than superficial" is actually a double negative; she really does think that her daughter's education should be superficial. Additionally, she claims that she does not want Frederica to be at school long enough to "understand anything thoroughly"; in other words, she advocates a particularly shallow education, choice C. Lady Susan never connects Frederica's education with finding a husband (A), nor to marriage with Sir James (D). Given Lady Susan's self-conceit, it's unlikely that she imagines Frederica's singing talent could ever equal her own, which eliminates choice B, and this idea is hardly Lady Susan's goal for Frederica in the first place. Choice E is completely unreasonable, an "out of left field" answer choice; Lady Susan would likely be aghast that Frederica might become a governess, and she definitely does not advocate that as a goal for her daughter's education. You should be able to eliminate answer choices like this very quickly.

40. **A.** Lady Susan's twisted reasoning is demented logic, and it follows thus: (1) She thinks that Frederica is "stupid" with "nothing to recommend her." (2) Sir James has previously proposed to Frederica, "from which her heart revolted." Therefore (3), she knows Frederica detests Sir James, but (4) she wants Frederica to marry him anyway just because he is rich. And so (5) if Frederica's situation were to be made "as unpleasant as possible" and "thoroughly uncomfortable," the unhappy daughter would (6) be forced to accept Sir James' renewed proposal. Thus, choice A is the correct answer. Choice B is unsupported in the passage; it appears that Lady Susan cares little about Frederica's survival in society; she simply wants to dump her daughter on a husband so that she can pursue her own selfish lifestyle. Choice C contradicts the text; Lady Susan shows no love for her daughter at all, and making her daughter miserable would hardly reinforce her love if it existed in the first place. Choice D is illogical; we hope Lady Susan is unlike other mothers, but her purpose in making Frederica unhappy is not to show this trait. Finally, Lady Susan's purpose seems to have no relation to how much time and money Mrs. Johnson spends on Frederica (E).

41. **D.** Apparently, Lady Susan's delusional self-assessment centers on her belief that her horrible selfish behaviors are actually altruistic and magnanimous. She views her machinations, which are intended to make Frederica so very wretched that she is forced to marry a man she detests, as actually benevolent, "a very happy instance of circumspection and tenderness," choice D. Although she claims she "could not reconcile it to [herself] to force Frederica into a marriage from which her heart revolted," she plans to do exactly that, with no qualms whatsoever. Nothing in the passage suggests that Lady Susan would ever admit to having any maternal faults (A), let alone see any need for personal improvement. Choice B is too strong; nothing in Lady Susan's character suggests that she needs validation for any of her actions. Choice C is incorrect because Lady Susan's comment in the question is not relevant to whether or not Mrs. Johnson will help her, something she is sure of in any case. Choice E is contradicted by Lady Susan's character; she cares not a whit about what others say about her or her parenting.

42. **C.** Lady Susan views Reginald De Courcy as an agreeable but simple conquest. She believes he is interesting enough to provide her with "some amusement"; moreover, she has the power to "teach him to correct" his attitude, to inspire him to respect her, and to humble his pride. In addition, she has already admitted that she takes "exquisite pleasure in subduing an insolent spirit." Therefore, choice C is correct. Choice A clearly misreads the passage; Lady Susan does not want Frederica to marry Reginald, but rather Sir James (who happens to be much wealthier). Lady Susan's remarks never indicate that she thinks Reginald adds a positive outlook (B); she does admit he is "lively and seems clever," but she also finds him saucy and too familiar. Choice D is partially accurate. Lady Susan indeed feels superior to Reginald, but the phrasing that she "despises his lofty brashness" is too strong. Finally, the passage indicates that Mrs. Vernon, Reginald's sister, dislikes Lady Susan and has cautioned him against her friendship, but we have no indication that he is under his sister's control (E).

43. **B.** Whenever the AP exam offers answer choices containing more than one adjective to describe a character, all of the wrong answer choices will have at least one incorrect word. That is the case in this question and it

is helpful in eliminating the incorrect answers. Lady Susan offers no positive traits, although on the surface first-read she may appear reasonable to some readers. In choice B, the correct response, both adjectives are accurate in denotation and connotation; Lady Susan is both iniquitous, which means wicked and immoral, and utterly ruthless, which means callous and heartless. Both adjectives in choice A are inaccurate in their connotation. One might try to make a case for Lady Susan being dependable, but the term has a positive connotation (as in trustworthy and faithful); if anything, she is only dependable in her immorality. Ingenious, which means clever and resourceful, might also initially sound plausible, but it, too, has a positive connotation, and any ingenuity Lady Susan possesses is used for nefarious purposes. The two adjectives in choice C are both incorrect. Guileless refers to someone who is candid and straightforward; gregarious refers to someone who is outgoing and unreserved in social situations. In choice D, the word "groveling," which describes one who is submissive and fawning, is the opposite of Lady Susan, although cunning might have some merit as she is shrewd and calculating. Choice E, incorrigible (or irredeemable) and ambitious (highly motivated), could be considered a plausible second-best answer, but notice how ambition can be a positive trait, and it's very hard to find anything positive in Lady Susan. Thus, choice B offers the most accurate descriptions of her character.

44. D. Lady Susan's letter to Mrs. Johnson is haughty throughout, choice D; although seemingly polite on the surface, it is chock-full of her underlying pride and arrogance. On the other hand, Lady Susan is hardly ambivalent, which means indecisive (A); she's also not skeptical, which means cynical (B). Lady Susan's persona may be vituperative, which means insulting and offensive (C), but the tone of her letter is not this harsh. The same logic makes choice E wrong; while Lady Susan's personality may be revengeful and vindictive, the tone of her letter is not.

Third Poem

Questions 45–55 are based on the poem "Smile, Smile, Smile" by Wilfred Owen. The title comes from a famous World War I marching song that contained the lines "Pack up your troubles in your old kit-bag | And smile, smile, smile," written in 1915. Owen, a British soldier, wrote this poem, possibly his last, in September 1918, while stationed at the Western Front in France. He was killed by machine-gun fire one week before the Armistice of 1918.

45. A. The word "scanned" implies that the limp-headed, "sunk-eyed wounded" soldiers glanced over the newspaper's content quickly, choice A. Lines 18–23 provide additional evidence that they discredit the newspaper as a source of truthful information; their disdain explains their reaction. They smile at each other with a secret kinship, knowing the reality of the war is nothing like what is presented in the paper; this explains why they never speak to outsiders of the horrors of war, or of the many British soldiers who were killed and buried in France. The idea in choice B is irrelevant. Although the newspaper does indeed feature a sensationalized headline about "Vast Booty from our Latest Haul," as if pirates have pillaged large quantities of goods, this fact does not address the point of the question, the word "scanned." Choice C might be an attractive, second-best guess by suggesting the soldiers are simply too tired from their war duties to read the newspaper slowly; their sunken eyes might imply fatigue. However, the poem does not offer any other evidence that they are physically exhausted, while it does offer ample proof that the men do not value the newspaper's content. Thus, choice A is a much stronger answer. Choice D is unreasonable because the poem offers no hint of how much time the military leaders allow for reading. Choice E offers a seemingly reasonable idea that the soldiers wish they had more time to read, but the poem provides no evidence of such a desire. Remember that a correct response has to be directly supported in the work.

46. C. Visualize the newspaper that the soldiers are reading: It has only a small headline about "the casualties" (which is deliberately not capitalized), but it has a large headline grandiosely titled "Vast Booty from our Latest Haul." The difference in size and capitalization between the two headlines strongly implies that the newspaper editors value the spoils of war much more than they value the lives of their own soldiers, choice C. The large headline refers to the land and material that Britain gained in the latest fighting, while the small headline serves to minimize the names and thus devalue the lives that were lost in the fighting. Choice A contradicts the poem; the newspaper editors display their own insensitivity with the large crass headline, which is juxtaposed with the diminutive, dismissive list of the names of dead soldiers. Choice B, that newspaper readers want only uplifting news, is unreasonable, and the absolute word "only" is contradicted by the contents of the paper, which in fact does include the names of the deceased soldiers. Choice D makes little sense for this question; newspaper owners may or may not decide the size of the headlines, but this idea does not relate to the implications of difference between the two headlines. Choice E goes too far, inferring an editorial opinion about what "should be" more important in war: the country's gains or the loss of its soldiers.

47. **B.** The poem is chock-full of sarcasm, but of these five answer choices, only one soundly solidifies the speaker's scorn. The condescending idea in choice B that the soldiers' "first instinct" upon the end of war "will be making homes" disdainfully ignores all that the surviving soldiers will face: Putting their lives back together, overcoming the physical and mental trauma of war, reuniting with loved ones, adjusting to civilized society, and reestablishing their profession or vocation will all trump the primacy of the idea of "making homes." Additionally, the word "instinct" refers to a hunch, an intuition, not to a rationally thought-out plan. Choice A, on the other hand, is not sarcastic; it is quite literal, a physical description of the wounded soldiers who read the *Daily Mail.* To merely depict their woebegone appearance is not sarcastic. Choice C is also not sarcastic; it merely states that "war has just begun," after announcing that the military needs more landing airstrips. Choice D returns to a description of the "half-limbed readers" as they finish scanning the newspaper; but just like choice A, it is not sarcastic to realistically describe wounded men. Choice E, which also describes the soldiers in a simile, is not sarcastic. The men's shared secret is that they truly know the horrors of war, and they do not intend to speak of it to anyone who has never experienced battle.

48. **E.** The personified phrase, "said the paper," serves to humanize the newspaper's words, choice E; after all, that is the basic definition of personification in the first place. However, this particular personification also adds more power to the newspaper's stand by giving it a personality, a human voice. Choice A goes too far when it incorrectly asserts that the newspaper's authority absolutely "cannot be doubted" *because* of the personification, which makes no sense. Choice B does not logically address the question about the *effect* of the personification; it does not necessarily add any appeal to the "common people" who read the paper. Choice C contradicts the intent of the poem and misses the effect of this personification. The fact that the soldiers understand that the paper's stance is completely politicized and contrary to what they experience at the front proves that the paper is *not* sympathetic to them. Choice D is unreasonable because the soldiers' response to the article, their smiling in mockery, is not related to the personification at all.

49. **D.** The twisted logic in lines 9–12 is indeed barbaric and cruel, choice D. The newspaper sadly claims that it would be wrong to attempt to make peace in an effort to save lives because thus far there was nothing to reimburse and enrich the country. It ludicrously claims that the soldiers who had died "might regret" their sacrifice if peace came too quickly; the horrifying extension of this logic is that more blood must be spilled to appease the soldiers who have already fallen, a barbarically sad conclusion. Choice A seems to buy into the newspaper's twisted logic and tries to justify it, asserting that the logic is simply pointing out a cold reality. The overall message of the poem strongly contradicts this idea. In choice B, both words are inaccurate: The newspaper pronouncement is neither sincere and genuine nor pleading and imploring. The word *ethical* in choice C is a contradiction; the newspaper's very idea is unethical, and therefore not persuasive. Choice E is incorrect because the newspaper displays no sympathy, so it cannot be misplaced.

50. **A.** The soldiers who scanned the paper "smiled at one another curiously" after reading the biased propaganda, sharing their secret knowledge of the horrors of war, a knowledge that is so intensely negative they cannot even try to explain it to someone who has not experienced it, choice A. Choice B is completely unreasonable; nothing in the poem indicates that the soldiers are sending war news to the paper, either surreptitiously or not. Choice C may appear tempting because it does bring up an accurate point, how the public misunderstands soldiers' lives, but this answer choice fails to address this specific question about the men's shared secret. Choice D falls flat by comparing the soldiers with other newspaper readers, which is irrelevant to the question. Choice E makes a mistake similar to choice C; it misleads the reader with an accurate statement that does not address the question. While it is true that discretion is necessary regarding the movement of troops in any war, this is not related to the men's shared secret.

51. **B.** The thought of a smile conjures up positive images of joy and happiness; however, this poem contains nothing but negativity, death, and fake news about the war, all of which contradict the very definition of a smile, choice B. Do not be fooled by the fact that in reality a smile can be perceived as hiding something negative (such as a smirk or a sneer), but the title of this poem offers no such negative connotations. As to

the other choices, it is unreasonable to conclude that the poem's title being capitalized, repetitive, and set off by commas is designed to distract the reader (A). In fact, a poem's title should always be capitalized, and items in a series should be separated by commas, and repetition per se does not distract the reader; it usually enhances the effect. Choice C is too much of a stretch; the poem offers no evidence of joy in the face of adversity for the soldiers; they only know misery. Some test-takers might be tempted by choice D because it correctly states that the idea of a smile appears in the title and also in the last line of the poem, but this question asks about the *effect* of the title. In addition, the last line is heavily ironic, as the naïve newspaper readers of the time did not understand the reality behind the soldiers' smiles in the newspaper photos. Choice E is too simplistic in claiming repetition sounds childlike; sometimes this may be true, but that is not the case in this poem.

52. E. The lines in choice E describe the newspaper-reading soldiers honestly; they were not chafed or irritated after reading the paper, but rather, they smiled knowingly at each other, secretly understanding how the paper's presentation of the war is so terribly misleading. Thus, choice E is the correct exception; it not an example of irony. On the other hand, all the other answer choices do present truly ironic lines in the poem. Choice A ironically points to the "Cheap Homes" that soldiers will supposedly crave when they return from the war (if they return, that is), which are actually not yet even planned. Choice B ironically claims that making peace would be a bad thing, as it glorifies the martyrs, those noble "undying dead." Choice C is clearly ironic in stating "The sons . . . *might* regret they died," when obviously they already regret it; they died horrible deaths, many from poison gas, all in the cause of seemingly-pointless trench warfare. Choice D ironically presumes that the soldiers' fighting and dying assures the integrity of the nation, when the soldiers know that is a sham; they reject the idea that their sacrifice is truly to guarantee national unity and integrity.

53. C. The quotation that ends the poem refers to the response of newspaper readers who do not understand the soldiers' brutal reality, the ghastly truth that most smiling faces had been extinguished. When these naïve readers say "How they smile!" the exclamation mark enhances how very gullible they are, choice C; they want to believe that the soldiers are truly happy. Choice A has no support in the poem; the soldiers have no joy and their smiles do not indicate happiness. Although the newspaper may be manipulative, it is unreasonable to think that it is being condescending to the readers (B); the paper does not seem to be supercilious, to regard the readers with a superior attitude. Choice D contradicts the poem; it appears that the newspaper's propaganda is actually quite effective; the readers do believe the soldiers are happy and they are sincere in their misguided exclamation. Choice E goes astray by asserting that the public's exclamation demonstrates shock; this description is too strong and too negative.

54. D. This powerful anti-war poem sarcastically criticizes virtually everyone except, of course, the soldiers at the front who are doing the actual fighting and dying, choice D. The poem acerbically rails against politicians and the government (A), stating that they are the "rulers sitting in this ancient spot" who would "wrong our very selves if we forgot" that soldiers fight to bring the nation integrity. Naïve readers (B) are criticized in the last two lines, as the misled public believes soldiers are smiling in pictures because they are happy; we know the soldiers face misery and death and the survivors only smile to each other to acknowledge this secret. Choice C identifies another obvious target of the poet's sarcasm; the entire quote from the newspaper in lines 5–17 is filled with untruthful propaganda. Choice E, national rulers, is a target of the poem's sarcasm in the same way as are politicians and the government.

55. D. Overall, the tone of the poem is best described as bitter and resentful, choice D. The cynical tone encompasses anger and intense sarcasm directed toward the newspaper, the government, and the well-meaning but gullible public. In the other answer choices, either one or both words are incorrect. In choice A, both words are wrong: A *condescending* attitude is one of being haughty and arrogant, while a *skeptical* attitude is one of being uncertain and disbelieving; neither word describes this poem's tone. The word *temperate* in choice B is completely off base; it means calm and pleasant. The second word, *admonishing*, may have some degree of accuracy, as it refers to a tone of reprimanding or scolding. In choice C, the word *vituperative* has promise, as it refers to being extremely angry and scathing, but the word *passionate* is too strong for the tone of this poem; it refers to feeling ardent or even fanatical. In choice E, the word *sardonic* is quite viable, as it refers to being sarcastic and scornful, but the word *placating* is inaccurate because it refers to being calming and appeasing.

Section II: Free-Response Questions

Question 1: "A Girl's Garden" by Robert Frost

The following scoring guide explicitly explains how to earn up to 6 total points for a poetry analysis essay. Row A (thesis) can earn up to 1 point; Row B (evidence and commentary) can earn up to 4 points, and Row C (sophistication) can earn up to 1 point.

Row A: Thesis (0–1 point)	
Scoring Criteria	
0 points for any of the following: • Having no defendable thesis. • Only restating the prompt in the thesis. • Only summarizing the issue with no claim in the thesis. • Presenting a thesis that does not address the prompt.	**1 point for** • Addressing the prompt with a defendable thesis that presents an interpretation and may establish a line of reasoning.
Decision Rules and Scoring Notes	
Theses that do not earn this point • Only restate the prompt. • Only offer an irrelevant generalized comment about the poem. • Simply describe the poem's features rather than making a defendable claim.	**Theses that do earn this point** • Take a position on the prompt and provide a defendable interpretation of how the poet portrays the complex relationship between the girl, her garden, and the woman she becomes.
Additional Notes	
• The thesis may be one or more sentences anywhere in the essay. • A thesis that meets the criteria can be awarded the point whether or not the rest of the response successfully conveys that line of reasoning.	

Row B: Evidence AND Commentary (0–4 points)				
Scoring Criteria				
0 points for	**1 point for**	**2 points for**	**3 points for**	**4 points for**
• Simply repeating the thesis (if present). • **OR** restating provided information. • **OR** providing mostly irrelevant and/or incoherent examples.	• Summarizing the poem without reference to a thesis. • **OR** providing vague textual references. • **OR** providing textual references of questionable relevance. • **AND** providing little or no commentary.	• Making relevant textual references (direct quotes or paraphrases). • **AND** providing commentary but repeats, oversimplifies, or misinterprets the cited evidence or text.	• Making relevant textual references (direct quotes or paraphrases). • **AND** providing commentary that explains the logical relationship between textual examples and the thesis; however, commentary is uneven, limited, or incomplete.	• Making relevant textual references (direct quotes or paraphrases). • **AND** providing well-developed commentary that explicitly explains the relationship between the evidence and the thesis.

Decision Rules and Scoring Notes				
Typical responses that earn 0 points:	**Typical responses that earn 1 point:**	**Typical responses that earn 2 points:**	**Typical responses that earn 3 points:**	**Typical responses that earn 4 points:**
• Are unclear or fail to address the prompt. • May present mere opinion with no relevant textual references.	• Mention textual references, devices, or techniques with little or no analysis.	• Contain numerous inaccuracies or repetition in commentary. • Offer only simplistic explanations that do not strengthen the argument.	• Provide commentary that is not sufficiently developed or is too limited. • Assume or imply a connection to the thesis that is not consistently explicit.	• Provide commentary that uses significant details of the text to draw conclusions. • Integrate short excerpts throughout in order to support the thesis' interpretation.

Additional Notes
• Writing that suffers from grammatical and/or mechanical errors that interfere with communication cannot earn the fourth point in this row.

Row C: Sophistication (0–1 point)	
Scoring Criteria	
0 points for	**1 point for**
• Not meeting the criteria for 1 point.	• Exhibiting sophistication of thought and/or advancing a complex literary argument.
Decision Rules and Scoring Notes	
Responses that do not earn this point:	**Responses that earn this point demonstrate one (or more) of the following:**
• Try to contextualize an interpretation, but make predominantly sweeping generalizations (*"Throughout all history . . ."* OR *"Everyone believes . . ."*). • Only hint at other possible interpretations (*"Some may think . . ."* OR *"Though the poem might be said to . . ."*). • Write one statement about a thematic interpretation of the poem without consistently maintaining that idea. • Oversimplify complexities in the poem. • Present complicated or complex sentences or language that is ineffective and detracts from the argument.	• Present a thesis that demands nuanced analysis of textual evidence and successfully prove it. • Illuminate the significance or relevance of an interpretation within a broader context. • Discuss alternative interpretations of a text. • Acknowledge and account for contradictions, ambiguities, and/or complexities within the text. • Provide relevant analogies to help better understand an interpretation. • Develop a prose style that is especially vivid, persuasive, resounding, or appropriate to the student's argument.

Additional Notes
• This point should be awarded only if the demonstration of sophistication or complex understanding is part of the argument, not merely a phrase or brief reference.

Medium-Scoring Essay

There seems to be a quintessential part of the process of growing up when a little child sets some lofty goal, a goal which may seem quizzical to their parents, but then they set about to make it a reality. And therein lies the lesson. For some children the grand goal may be building a giant treehouse, for others the goal may be more basic, perhaps learning to read and write. For the little girl in Frost's poem, "A Girl's Garden," the most splendid goal is growing and tending a vegetable garden of her very own. And in her efforts to reach this goal, she learns much about gardening, and she learns much about herself.

The girl is not described in much physical detail; we only know that she has a "slim-jim arm" and her father hopes the garden will give her "a chance to put [on] some strength." We can certainly infer that she is just a skinny little thing. It is telling that Frost gives far more attention to the physical details of her little walled-off garden plot. He begins with her hauling the "not-nice load" of dung in the wheelbarrow "along a stretch of road." Then the garden evolves with the exquisite imagery of her planting seeds and building up "A hill each of potatoes, / Radishes, lettuce, peas, / Tomatoes, beets, beans, pumpkins, corn, / And even fruit trees." The pace of the poem seems to quicken, just to fit in all of these details.

As the poem develops the detailed imagery of the garden, the tone also moves forward. In the initial stanzas, the tone seems to reflect the girl's childlike naiveté, "she did / a childlike thing," and she has no regrets, "But she don't mind now." But the tone seems to evolve as the girl labors and the garden takes shape; when the garden finally produces a harvest, the little girl seems to have a more mature outlook, realizing that "Her crop was a miscellany . . . A little bit of everything, / A great deal of none."

The final two stanzas provide a counterpoint to the rest of the poem; the little girl is now all grown up, perhaps even an old woman, and she lives in the village, no longer on her farm. But she still fondly recalls the lessons from her days in the garden; she understands that little garden plot helped to make her into the person she is, and she still cherishes the memories. It's emblematic that she shares the story with everyone she meets, because it is not really a story about gardening, it is a story about herself.

In the end, this poem is yet another example of what may very well be a universal truth, underlying a nearly universal experience. Little children like to set a goal, usually a very grand and lofty goal. And as they work for their goal, they find challenges and rewards and they learn lessons about themselves that will last their entire lives.

(504 words)

Analysis of Medium-Scoring Essay

This essay does an acceptable job of trying to address the prompt and develop its ideas. The introduction begins with some appropriate universal ideas about how children quintessentially set a lofty goal that puzzles their parents and then they try to reach that goal. The thrust of the sentence "And therein lies the lesson" is quite pleasing, but it is ultimately unfulfilled in the introduction, since we never actually learn what the lesson is. The student tells us the girl "learns much about gardening" and "about herself," but does not tell us what she learns; however, this thesis is acceptable enough to earn 1 point according to the criteria in Row A.

The first body paragraph begins by explaining that the girl's appearance is barely described and that we ultimately can only infer that she is "skinny." But *why* the student brings this up is not clear; one wishes the student would try to make an analytical point about it. Next the student brings up that Frost "gives far more attention" to describing her garden itself and then lists two details about the wheelbarrow full of dung before claiming that "the garden evolves with the exquisite imagery of her planting seeds and building up" her plot. The student does accurately note that the pace picks up as the poem lists the many vegetables, but it does not provide any further analysis; he or she notices the pace and mentions it, but seems unsure about what it adds to the poem. The paragraph as a whole, therefore, comes across as disjointed, random, without a clear purpose.

The opening sentence of the third paragraph states that "the tone moves forward," which is a very odd concept when you think about it; tone can shift, change, alter, but it cannot move forward. While the claim that the tone reflects the "girl's childlike naïveté" is enticing, the student does not adequately prove that idea. Then it claims weakly that the "tone seems to evolve" as the girl gains a more mature outlook, but this is stated without any conviction. The student does include a quotation for each idea, but without explaining *how* they create the tone the student describes, the quotations fall flat and the claim is unconvincing. Concluding a paragraph with a quotation is usually not a wise strategy, as it leaves the quotation hanging there, unanalyzed.

The last body paragraph addresses the final two stanzas, when the grown woman now lives in the village, not on the farm. The student acknowledges that the girl understands the garden helped make her who she is and that she cherishes the memories of it. The student's claim that the girl's sharing her story is "emblematic" sounds good until one thinks about the student's logic; just because the grown girl shares a "story about herself" does not make it emblematic, and the student never informs us what it is emblematic of. The evidence and commentary should earn 3 points in Row B because the student's presentation is relevant but uneven and limited.

The conclusion harkens back to the concept in the introduction that the poem represents a universal experience for growing children, but it does no more than repeat the idea, while repeating the word "universal" twice in the same sentence. The last sentence leaves us with the vague notion that children learn lessons from the challenges they face in life, but we're still not sure what lessons the student has in mind.

Overall, the essay presents a plausible reading of the poem, albeit not a deep nor an analytical one. The analysis is superficial, and, with its lack of detail, it is not terribly convincing. Also, the student too often sounds unsure of his or her ideas, which does not help to persuade the Reader of the plausibility of the student's concepts. Finally, the language is too often vague and generic when it needs to be specific and direct. The lack of sophistication keeps it from earning a point in Row C, making this essay's overall score a 4.

Low-Scoring Essay

There are many things to like about the poem "A Girl's Garden" by Robert Frost, including his use of the gentle, rural imagery and the overall light tone. But the real point of the poem is not about the garden specifically, but what the girl learns about gardening.

The little girl begins her garden as a lark, never suspecting how much work it would turn out to be. Her father secretly knows that "she had to work it all by hand." You can see the huge amount of work she did by looking at the imagery, beginning with hauling stinky dung in the wheelbarrow, then planting seeds of every single type of plant, all planted in neat rows, with "a hill each of potatoes, radishes, lettuce, peas . . . " and on and on. She found out that it really was a lot of work after all.

But the light tone of the poem shows how well the girl adapted to all that hard work. The lighthearted sing-song chorus of each stanza almost sounds like a nursery rhyme, and this light touch shows that this garden turned out to be a positive experience for the girl.

Also, years later, when the little girl is all grown up and she lives in the village, she enjoys telling this story to everyone she meets. This also indicates that this was a positive experience for her, in spite of all that hard work.

So, as you can see, there are many things to like about this poem, including Robert Frost's use of rural imagery and lighthearted tone. It's easy to see that the real value of the garden was not in the vegetables it produced, but in the gardening lessons it taught the little girl.

(293 words)

Analysis of Low-Scoring Essay

This essay begins with a simplistic reader-response comment that "There are many things to like about the poem." This phrasing is neither on topic nor relevant to analysis; whether or not a student "likes" a poem is never appropriate to share in an essay. The student does mention Frost's use of "gentle, rural imagery" and "overall light tone," but he or she fails to address *how* the use of poetic devices creates the relationship between the girl and her garden and with the grown woman she later becomes. Instead, the student blurts out that the "real point of the poem" is "what the girl learns about gardening." This idea may have some potential validity, but the presentation of it here it is too vague to know. The essay never presents a defendable thesis that addresses the prompt and, therefore, does not earn a point for Row A.

The first body paragraph merely describes the action of the poem, and, unfortunately, it misrepresents some of the facts. It is true that the girl had no idea how much work her garden would take, and that she begins the task on a whim. However, it is questionable whether or not her father was secretive about her having to work it by hand. Additionally, the student might be misreading the information about her wheeling dung in a wheelbarrow; the student implies she used the dung in her garden patch, but the poem states that she "always ran away and left / Her not-nice load." The student's claim that she placed her plants "in neat rows" is technically not supported by the poem's imagery of "A hill each," but this is perhaps a minor point to criticize. The point of this paragraph is that the girl did not understand how much work her garden would be; the student tells us that in the first sentence and repeats it again in the last sentence. However, the paragraph does not actually provide any proof for that point, simply stating that "You can see the huge amount of work she did by looking at the imagery," but the essay provides little analysis of imagery. Apparently, the student is trying to address the relationship between the girl and her garden, but he or she does not know how to develop it.

The second body paragraph mentions "the light tone" as the key to understanding how the girl adapted to the hard work, but, unfortunately, it offers no proof from the poem. One needs to supply textual quotations to support any claim about tone; otherwise, the claim will not be convincing. While it may be true that the rhyme and meter provide some degree of a "sing-song" feel, the student does not back this idea up and also incorrectly states that each stanza has a "chorus." The student concludes that "this was a positive experience for the girl," which is a questionable assertion, since the poem, instead, states that "When all was said and done, / A little bit of everything / A great deal of none." This brief paragraph has only two sentences, and both use the same weak verb "shows," a word that promises no analysis.

The last body paragraph attempts to address the relationship between the girl and herself as a grown woman, but the only claim the student makes is that she enjoys telling her story so it must have been a positive experience. The student's logic is flawed and the analysis is questionable. The textual references are vague and simplistic, and some evidence is misinterpreted; these traits deserve a score of 2 points in Row B.

The conclusion sadly begins with a phrase that every Reader dreads, "So, as you can see," and then it repeats the first sentence of the introduction. It finishes with yet another atrociously banal phrase, telling us how it is "easy to see" the importance of the lessons the garden taught the little girl. This vague comment leaves the Reader wondering what lessons the student has in mind, or if she learned anything at all.

Overall, this essay is disappointing because of its lack of depth and its mediocre development. Most paragraphs are just two sentences (only the first body paragraph has three), which is insufficient to present examples, develop analysis, and demonstrate insight. The student's vague claims are not clarified or supported. The diction is simplistic and immature, with too-casual phrasing, such as "you can see . . . " and "this shows . . . " The organization is fairly clear in the first two body paragraphs, which plan to present imagery and tone, respectively, but one is left wondering about the purpose of the last paragraph. The essay does not meet the criteria for a point in Row C. Because of its incomplete understanding of the task, its slight and misconstrued presentation of evidence, and its oversimplistic style, this essay deserves an overall score of just 2.

Question 2: A Lady's Diary from Joseph Addison's *Spectator*

The following scoring guide explicitly explains how to earn up to 6 total points for a prose analysis essay. Row A (thesis) can earn up to 1 point; Row B (evidence and commentary) can earn up to 4 points, and Row C (sophistication) can earn up to 1 point.

Row A: Thesis (0–1 point)	
Scoring Criteria	
0 points for any of the following:	**1 point for**
• Having no defendable thesis. • Only restating the prompt in the thesis. • Only summarizing the issue with no claim in the thesis. • Presenting a thesis that does not address the prompt.	• Addressing the prompt with a defendable thesis that presents an interpretation and may establish a line of reasoning.

Decision Rules and Scoring Notes	
Theses that do not earn this point	**Theses that do earn this point**
• Only restate the prompt. • Only offer an irrelevant generalized comment about the passage. • Simply describe the passage's features rather than making a defendable claim.	• Take a position on the prompt and provide a defendable interpretation of how Addison portrays the complex diarist and her society and how these complexities contribute to Addison's satiric purpose.
Additional Notes	
• The thesis may be one or more sentences anywhere in the response. • A thesis that meets the criteria can be awarded the point whether or not the rest of the response successfully conveys that line of reasoning.	

Row B: Evidence AND Commentary (0–4 points)

Scoring Criteria				
0 points for	**1 point for**	**2 points for**	**3 points for**	**4 points for**
• Simply repeating the thesis (if present). • **OR** restating provided information. • **OR** providing mostly irrelevant and/or incoherent examples.	• Summarizing the passage without reference to a thesis. • **OR** providing vague textual references. • **OR** providing textual references of questionable relevance. • **AND** providing little or no commentary.	• Making relevant textual references (direct quotes or paraphrases). • **AND** providing commentary but repeats, oversimplifies, or misinterprets the cited evidence or text.	• Making relevant textual references (direct quotes or paraphrases). • **AND** providing commentary that explains the logical relationship between textual examples and the thesis; however, commentary is uneven, limited, or incomplete.	• Making relevant textual references (direct quotes or paraphrases). • **AND** providing well-developed commentary that explicitly explains the relationship between the evidence and the thesis.
Decision Rules and Scoring Notes				
Typical responses that earn 0 points:	**Typical responses that earn 1 point:**	**Typical responses that earn 2 points:**	**Typical responses that earn 3 points:**	**Typical responses that earn 4 points:**
• Are unclear or fail to address the prompt. • May present mere opinion with no relevant textual references.	• Mention textual references, devices, or techniques with little or no analysis.	• Contain numerous inaccuracies or repetition in commentary. • Offer only simplistic explanations that do not strengthen the argument.	• Provide commentary that is not sufficiently developed, or is too limited. • Assume or imply a connection to the thesis that is not consistently explicit.	• Provide commentary that uses significant details of the text to draw conclusions. • Integrate short excerpts throughout in order to support the thesis' interpretation.
Additional Notes				
• Writing that suffers from grammatical and/or mechanical errors that interfere with communication cannot earn the fourth point in this row.				

Row C: Sophistication (0–1 point)	
Scoring Criteria	
0 points for	**1 point for**
• Not meeting the criteria for 1 point.	• Exhibiting sophistication of thought and/or advancing a complex literary argument.
Decision Rules and Scoring Notes	
Responses that do not earn this point:	**Responses that earn this point demonstrate one (or more) of the following:**
• Try to contextualize an interpretation, but make predominantly sweeping generalizations (*"Throughout all history . . . "* OR *"Everyone believes . . . "*). • Only hint at other possible interpretations (*"Some may think . . . "* OR *"Though the passage might be said to . . . "*). • Write one statement about a thematic interpretation of the passage without consistently maintaining that idea. • Oversimplify complexities in the passage. • Present complicated or complex sentences or language that is ineffective and detracts from the argument.	• Present a thesis that demands nuanced analysis of textual evidence and successfully prove it. • Illuminate the significance or relevance of an interpretation within a broader context. • Discuss alternative interpretations of a text. • Acknowledge and account for contradictions, ambiguities, and/or complexities within the text. • Provide relevant analogies to help better understand an interpretation. • Develop a prose style that is especially vivid, persuasive, resounding, or appropriate to the student's argument.
Additional Notes	
• This point should be awarded only if the demonstration of sophistication or complex understanding is part of the argument, not merely a phrase or brief reference.	

High-Scoring Essay

The pleasure in reading a well-written piece of satire is watching the author skewer his subjects with his rapier-like wit aimed directly at the subject's own foibles. Joseph Addison has created just such a memorable work of satire in this piece, the diary of a society Lady. Usually, the essential goals of writing a diary deal with exploring one's life and trying to figure out how one fits in the world; however, this Lady, representative of her vapid society, never takes advantage of such an opportunity and instead merely lists the insipid motions she goes through. Indeed, Addison skillfully satirizes not only his leading character, the Lady diarist, but he also exposes the foibles of her contemporaries in the self-obsessed British high-society of the 18th century.

Addison's goal is to make a mockery of the Lady's shallow personality by simply allowing the reader to see her own banal thoughts. This becomes apparent in the very first line, in which the Lady establishes what is most important in her life, namely, she "Could not go to sleep till one in the morning for thinking of my journal." The poor thing can't sleep because she can't stop thinking about herself. It is through details such as this memorable opening line that Addison carefully weaves his web of satire, which in turn, ensnares all who come into the path of the Lady.

In the first full entry, "Wednesday," Addison uses a series of short sentences and rapid-fire sentence fragments to establish the tone of the main character. Addison details how this superficial Lady of luxury takes three hours to merely drink hot chocolate, nap, read the paper and have a light breakfast. Then she requires two more hours to dress, noting that she "looks best in blue." By focusing on the Lady's scatter-shot thoughts and her self-centered personality, he indeed sets the tone of her personality as self-indulgent, superficial, and frivolous.

Next, in "Thursday," we see further examples of the Lady's indulgent and self-centered life; her day is just packed, but packed only with trivialities. Addison begins to introduce additional characters, but it turns out that Mr. Froth is every bit as vacuous as the Lady; perhaps this explains her attraction to him. This interaction also reinforces her lack of empathy for the feelings of anyone but herself. Obviously, she and her circle of friends fulfill no positive function in society; they merely exist for themselves and do nothing to improve those who are not as advantaged.

Friday's entry serves to reinforce the reader's initial distaste for the Lady, but also extend our aversion to the haughty foibles of every member of her society that we encounter, clarifying the target of Addison's satire. The Lady wastes yet another day, alternating frivolity with self-pity. When she attempts to accomplish something, a little embroidery for example, she had just begun and "Worked half a violet leaf in it." Suddenly her "Eyes ached and head out of order. Threw by my work. . . . " Oh the poor dear; a little work is just too much for her. However, she then changes her mind and goes out, playing cards and trading scandalous gossip until Midnight.

In "Saturday," Addison adds more detail, more bold satiric strokes, and he introduces more of his unlikeable upper-crust characters, seemingly useless twits and bullies, one and all. The Lady spends her entire morning getting ready for Chapel, with laborious attention to the placement of her beauty mark, and then she takes three more hours to get dressed. However, she reports absolutely nothing of the chapel service, except the usual cruel gossip and that she was thinking about the opera instead of the service. Addison directly implies his indignation at a society without piety. Then, just to round out her day, this feeble and yet terrible "Lady" fires her Footman for the alleged infraction of being "rude" to her dog! This example is just one of the many details that are hidden in the scathing satiric work; these so-called "high society" personages are really just dangerous poseurs. They appear to be merely silly and facile and superficial and self-indulgent; however in reality, their wealth gives them great power over people and their self-centered sense of entitlement and lack of empathy make them truly dangerous to the livelihood of anyone who might dare to cross them.

Finally, it is fitting that Addison chose to end this satiric essay by circling back to the one-line form of his opening. However, he knows that we now understand the true nature of the Lady and of her contemporaries. Thus the closing line is far more cutting; it shines a light on her lack of honorable aspirations; it reinforces her lack of skills; it reveals her true value to society: the Lady is indeed, "Indisposed."

(799 words)

Analysis of High-Scoring Essay

First impressions are always important; that is true in life and in essay writing. One should always try to put one's best foot forward, and the writer of this essay clearly understands the need to do so. The student's introduction is stellar because it is clearly on topic, it is well developed, and it presents pleasing syntax and diction. A Reader will be impressed to encounter phrases like "skewer his subjects" and "rapier-like wit," plus diction such as "vapid," "insipid," and "foibles," because they are not only accurate but they are also apropos for this prompt. The writer clearly addresses all three tasks that are embedded in the prompt and we already understand the student's stand on the Lady, on her society, and on Addison's purpose in writing this 18th-century satire. It truly deserves a point in Row A.

The first body paragraph jumps right into the issue and clarifies this student's take on one of Addison's goals: mocking the Lady's shallow nature. The student presents the example of her first diary entry, a banal and self-centered one-sentence declaration, to establish how Addison "weaves his web of satire," one that will not only excoriate the Lady herself, but will also "ensnare all who come into the path of the Lady." This writer also displays a mildly sarcastic wit, calling the Lady a "poor thing" in faux pity. Although this first body paragraph develops only one example, it is fittingly succinct, as the Lady's first diary entry develops only one thought.

The second body paragraph explores the Lady's entry for Wednesday. The student correctly notices Addison's style, identifying "a series of short sentences and rapid-fire sentence fragments," but one wonders how this relates to establishing the "tone of the main character" or to clarifying what that tone may be. The paragraph then adds several layers of detail from the diary, all of which are trivial actions that the Lady takes great time in completing. The paragraph concludes with an appropriate observation: that all these details paint her as "self-indulgent, superficial, and frivolous."

The next paragraph parallels the diary's chronology, exploring the Thursday entry. The student continues to build a case for the Lady's shallow selfishness and supports the earlier use of "vapid" by epitomizing how the Lady's day is "just packed, but packed only with trivialities." The student then uses the example of the Lady's interactions with Mr. Froth to demonstrate that both she and the members of her society are "vacuous." The student ends the paragraph with a strong criticism of the Lady's society and includes a comment that addresses one of Addison's satiric goals: that these privileged members of the upper-class could choose to do something productive to benefit all of society, but instead they waste their days pursuing nothing but trivial activities.

The paragraph devoted to Friday continues to demonstrate this student's strengths, both in textual observation and in apt analysis. The student focuses on the Lady's inability to accomplish anything, noticing how she gets eye strain and a headache after embroidering only half of a violet leaf; the student adds a biting remark, "Oh the poor dear; a little work is just too much for her." A Reader will appreciate a student who is not afraid to express an opinionated voice.

The last body paragraph devoted to the Lady's Saturday entry is the strongest yet, combining appropriate text detail, strong character analysis, and insightful analysis of Addison's satiric goals. When the writer claims the "unlikeable upper-crust characters" are "useless twits and bullies, one and all," the Reader will be pleased with the strong and accurate diction; in fact, it brought a chuckle to this Reader. Also astutely pleasing is the way that the student notices how much time the Lady devotes to preparing for chapel, and how little attention she pays once she is there. The bold statement "Addison directly implies his indignation at a society without piety" serves to address yet another target of Addison's satire. The paragraph builds and gets stronger, as if the writer is becoming more indignant when he or she chastises the characters as "dangerous poseurs" who misuse their wealth and power and who lack empathy toward those less advantaged. The high quality of this analysis is not typical of run-of-the-mill AP essays, and it will be rewarded with a high score. The essay's relevant textual references and strong commentary that explains the relationship between the text and Addison's satiric purpose deserve 4 points in Row B.

The conclusion notes that it is fitting for Addison to circle back to the Lady's one-line entry format before commenting that Readers will clearly understand the many faults of the Lady and of her society. But this student cleverly uses the Lady's last entry as the last word in the essay. What more needs to be said then that "the Lady is indeed, 'Indisposed.'"

Overall this excellent essay accomplishes a great deal. Of course, no student can include all of the detail in a passage, but this essay includes more than enough to be convincing. Many students had no difficulty describing the Lady and her society, but unfortunately neglected to also explore Addison's *purpose* in writing such satire; this essay avoids falling into that trap. The organization is logical, following the diary's daily entries, which also avoids the overused formulaic organizational scheme of devoting each paragraph to a different literary device. Finally, it is the quality of the student's insights and clarity of the diction that propel this essay to its high score, earning another point in Row C, and a Reader will happily reward the essay with an overall score of 6 for what it does well.

Low-Scoring Essay

In 1712, an English satirist named Joseph Addison created a female character who keeps a diary. If you read it carefully, you can tell that he wrote this Lady's diary so that he could make fun of the character and make fun of her society too. By making fun of the character and her society, he helped to further his satiric goal in his writing.

It is easy to see that Addison is making fun of his character, the Lady, because he paints her as not-too-bright and also self-absorbed and superficial. You can see this in Addison's selection of details. He shows us that the Lady is preoccupied with her diary-writing. Even in the opening line, she seems to be obsessed about it, "Could not go to sleep till one in the morning for thinking of my journal."

Addison also uses other details to make fun of the Lady. One running gag that Addison uses is her compulsive card playing, which is mentioned several times in the passage. You will notice that she plays cards a lot, and she gambles too, but she never seems to win. She writes in her diary, "Lost five guineas at crimp" which sounds like a lot of money to me.

Addison's choice of details when he refers to the Lady's fellow members of society also shows that he wants to make fun of their society too. When Addison describe a character named Mr. Froth, he mocks "his opinion of Milton" and he mocks "his opinion of the Mohocks" and he mocks "His fancy for a pin-cushion." It is obvious to anyone that Addison's choice to include these details is to make fun of the Lady's society.

Finally, Addison uses the tone of this piece to make fun of the characters even more. The tone around the Lady's house shows how lazy she is, and she is mean to her servants too. Her negative tone is also demonstrated by her insincerity, like when she fakes a visit to old Lady Blithe after she "heard they were gone out of town that day."

These are just some of the ways that Addison uses choice of details and also tone to clarify that he is not praising the Lady, but rather he is making fun of her and her society too.

(385 words)

Analysis of Low-Scoring Essay

This essay demonstrates how a student can produce a fair number of words but say very little. Like a one-trick pony, this student repeats the same concept over and over, adding no analysis in the process. The introduction repeats the concept of "making fun" three times in two sentences. Additionally, the thesis tries to address the prompt by claiming that Addison "helped to further his satiric goal," but we are left with no idea what that might be, hoping the student will address it in the body paragraphs. Additionally, students should always avoid using any second-person pronouns; this writer does so twice, claiming "If you read it carefully, you can tell. . . . " The student eventually produces a thesis in the last paragraph that earns 1 point in Row A when he or she claims "that he is not praising the Lady, but rather he is making fun of her and her society too."

In the first body paragraph, this student immediately repeats that Addison is making fun of his character, just in case the Reader was not yet aware that Addison is creating satire. Once again using the second person "you," the student informs us that Addison's selection of details will help us "see" how the Lady is "not-too-bright and also self-absorbed and superficial." While he or she does accurately notice that the Lady is obsessed with her diary, the student does a poor job incorporating the quotation from the first journal entry.

Then, lest we forget, the writer reminds us yet again that Addison is making fun of the Lady by using "other details." In this second body paragraph, the student focuses on the Lady's penchant for card playing, but repeats the idea twice before commenting that "she never seems to win." Unfortunately, the student does not seize this opportunity to analyze the significance of that detail nor to discuss applying it to Addison's satiric goals. Instead, the student editorializes how five guineas "sounds like a lot of money to me." Sadly unimpressive, this irrelevant comment does not further any analysis.

The student again brings up "Addison's choice of details" in the next paragraph, this time to explore the other members of the Lady's society. The student infers that Addison is mocking Mr. Froth's opinion of Milton, and of the "Mohocks" and of pin-cushions, although the text offers scant support for this inference. The student's writing appears to get more cumbersome in this paragraph; for example, the first sentence seems to be missing a verb as we read "Addison's choice of details . . . also that he. . . . " The next sentence also has a grammatical error, with the subject-verb agreement boo-boo of "Addison describe." While these mistakes are not terribly distracting or persistent, they are noticeable. The paragraph ends with a bland and repetitive statement that Addison is making fun of the Lady's society. The student insists that this "is obvious to anyone," so one begins to wonder why we need such repetition.

The last body paragraph addresses the tone of the passage and, just as we should suspect, the student claims that the tone is used "to make fun of the characters even more." However, this student seems unsure about how to address or discuss tone, notably in the sentence that points out "The tone around the Lady's house shows how lazy she is, and she is mean to her servants too." One also wonders about the student's accuracy in claiming that the Lady "fakes a visit to Old Lady Blithe," when she had, in fact, visited her home. This appears to be due to a misread of the passage, albeit a minor one. Unfortunately, this paragraph is as unconvincing as the preceding ones. The repetition in commentary, plus the simplistic explanations that do not strengthen the argument, earn only 2 points in Row B.

The conclusion is only a single sentence, one that merely repeats the thrust of the essay yet again, so it falls flat even though it supplies the thesis for the essay. It appears that the student felt a conclusion was necessary, but did not know what to do with it. It also appears that this student was running out of time. In any case, the essay as a whole does not develop much depth of thought with its constant repetition of the same idea. Of course, it cannot be denied that Addison is making fun of the Lady and her society, but the student fails to address Addison's satiric purpose in doing so. Therefore, the essay only develops a portion of the assigned topic, and it does so poorly. The organization is fairly acceptable and demonstrates some semblance of preplanning, but the language is clunky, simplistic, and repetitive. Compare the diction in this essay to that of the high-scoring essay to understand how using a style that is impressive and sophisticated can help to improve an essay. While this student presents some valid ideas and tries persistently to discuss them, he or she will be well served experiencing a year of freshman English in college. This essay does not earn a point for sophistication in Row C, and it gets an overall score of 3.

Question 3: How Setting Affects Character

The following scoring guide explicitly explains how to earn up to 6 total points for a literary analysis essay. Row A (thesis) can earn up to 1 point; Row B (evidence and commentary) can earn up to 4 points, and Row C (sophistication) can earn up to 1 point.

Row A: Thesis (0–1 point)	
Scoring Criteria	
0 points for any of the following: • Having no defendable thesis. • Only restating the prompt in the thesis. • Only summarizing the issue with no claim in the thesis. • Presenting a thesis that does not address the prompt.	**1 point for** • Addressing the prompt with a defendable thesis that presents an interpretation and may establish a line of reasoning.
Decision Rules and Scoring Notes	
Theses that do not earn this point • Only restate the prompt. • Only offer an irrelevant generalized comment about the chosen work.	**Theses that do earn this point** • Take a position on the prompt and provide a defendable interpretation of how setting affects a character and adds to an interpretation of the chosen work as a whole.
Additional Notes • The thesis may be one or more sentences anywhere in the response. • A thesis that meets the criteria can be awarded the point whether or not the rest of the response successfully conveys that line of reasoning.	

Row B: Evidence AND Commentary (0–4 points)				
Scoring Criteria				
0 points for	**1 point for**	**2 points for**	**3 points for**	**4 points for**
• Simply repeating the thesis (if present). • **OR** restating provided information. • **OR** providing mostly irrelevant and/or incoherent examples.	• Summarizing the chosen work without reference to a thesis. • **OR** providing vague textual references. • **OR** providing textual references of questionable relevance. • **AND** providing little or no commentary.	• Making relevant textual references (direct quotes or paraphrases). • **AND** providing commentary but repeats, oversimplifies, or misinterprets the cited evidence or text.	• Making relevant textual references (direct quotes or paraphrases). • **AND** providing commentary that explains the logical relationship between textual examples and the thesis; however, commentary is uneven, limited, or incomplete.	• Making relevant textual references (direct quotes or paraphrases). • **AND** providing well-developed commentary that explicitly explains the relationship between the evidence and the thesis.

Decision Rules and Scoring Notes				
Typical responses that earn 0 points:	**Typical responses that earn 1 point:**	**Typical responses that earn 2 points:**	**Typical responses that earn 3 points:**	**Typical responses that earn 4 points:**
• Are unclear or fail to address the prompt. • May present mere opinion with no relevant textual references.	• Mention textual references, devices, or techniques with little or no analysis.	• Contain numerous inaccuracies or repetition in commentary. • Offer only simplistic explanations that do not strengthen the argument.	• Provide commentary that is not sufficiently developed or is too limited. • Assume or imply a connection to the thesis that is not consistently explicit.	• Provide commentary that uses significant details of the text to draw conclusions. • Integrate short excerpts throughout in order to support the thesis' interpretation.

Additional Notes

• Writing that suffers from grammatical and/or mechanical errors that interfere with communication cannot earn the fourth point in this row.

Row C: Sophistication (0–1 point)

Scoring Criteria	
0 points for	**1 point for**
• Not meeting the criteria for 1 point.	• Exhibiting sophistication of thought and/or advancing a complex literary argument.

Decision Rules and Scoring Notes	
Responses that do not earn this point:	**Responses that earn this point demonstrate one (or more) of the following:**
• Try to contextualize an interpretation, but make predominantly sweeping generalizations (*"Throughout all history . . . "* OR *"Everyone believes . . . "*). • Only hint at other possible interpretations (*"Some may think . . . "* OR *"Though the work might be said to . . . "*). • Write one statement about a thematic interpretation of the chosen work without consistently maintaining that idea. • Oversimplify complexities in the chosen work. • Present complicated or complex sentences or language that is ineffective and detracts from the argument.	• Present a thesis that demands nuanced analysis of textual evidence and successfully prove it. • Illuminate the significance or relevance of an interpretation within a broader context. • Discuss alternative interpretations of a text. • Acknowledge and account for contradictions, ambiguities, and/or complexities within the text. • Provide relevant analogies to help better understand an interpretation. • Develop a prose style that is especially vivid, persuasive, resounding, or appropriate to the student's argument.

Additional Notes

• This point should be awarded only if the demonstration of sophistication or complex understanding is part of the argument, not merely a phrase or brief reference.

High-Scoring Essay

Setting, although sometimes overlooked, plays an important role in literature, often becoming the force that dictates the action, and hence, the characters and theme. Historical fiction, like Charles Dickens' A Tale of Two Cities, depends heavily on its setting. Were it not for the French Revolution, the novel would have no plot. However simplistic this may sound, the chaos and the conflict of the revolution provide the opportunity, in the worst of times, to bring out the best in all of the characters. In addition to the time setting, the two locales of the title symbolize the dualities in human nature, of selfishness and of sacrifice, of love and of hate.

The novel's action actually begins in 1775, fourteen years before the storming of the Bastille. However, Dickens demonstrates how revolutions are the result of years of hardship and struggle. In the first chapter he establishes the metaphor of the woodman Fate, who is growing the trees that will years later be cut down to make the guillotine, and the farmer, Death, who has set apart his tumbrils that will eventually carry humans to their death instead of pigs and chickens to market. Evidence of human suffering is clearly established in the famous scene in Saint Antoine in which the wine cask breaks outside of the Defarge's wine shop and all around greedily slurp the contents off the streets. Although it will take years, the intense deprivation of the French citizens will lead to the destruction of the French aristocracy. The stupidity, arrogance, and extravagance of the French aristocracy during the time period, personified in the evil Marquis Evremonde as his carriage runs over a child in Paris and he merely flips a coin to the crowd to pay, after questioning what damage might be done to his horses, also adds to the budding revolution. Once the commoners can take no more and the time comes for the revolution to begin, Dickens paints their vengeance as a metaphorical wave that cannot be stopped. However, as horrific as the Reign of Terror became, the time period also allowed some characters to show their true strength and goodness. Notably, Sydney Carton's sacrificing his life so that the beloved Lucie Manette can be reunited with her husband demonstrates that those whom we thought were incapable of goodness can rise to unimagined heights. Horrific times can inspire honorable deeds.

Placing some of the action in the city of Paris is absolutely necessary, of course, as it is the center of the revolution. It is the city that sucks Charles Darnay into returning to his homeland, naively hoping to save his servant Gabelle and inadvertently putting his whole family in danger. It is the city where the horrific and hateful Madame Defarge helps plot the revolution and where she dies at the hand of the British Miss Pross who is powered by a stronger force, love. It is the city where Sydney Carton, facing the guillotine before his death, utters one of the most tear-jerking famous last lines in literature, "It is a far, far better thing that I do, than I have ever done. . . . " The Paris setting symbolizes how humanity can sink to unimaginable evil depths or rise to create beauty, stability, and love.

London, although no idealistic paradise of peace, provides a contrasting physical and emotional backdrop to Paris. London provides a place of succor where Lucie Manette nurses her father back to health after his Bastille imprisonment and is a place of happiness when she marries Charles Darnay. London is the beloved home base for Mr. Lorry, of Tellson's Bank, and Miss Pross, both of whom serve the Manettes faithfully for decades, providing stability for the family. London also introduces the spiky-haired, comical character Jerry Cruncher, who, late in the novel's action in Paris, provides an absolutely essential piece to help solve the novel's perplexing puzzle, a fact he gleaned in his earlier grave robbing days in London. After escaping the horrors of Paris, Jerry returns to London a reformed man, determined to love and care for his family in socially acceptable ways. In this novel of contrasts, London and Paris serve to reinforce the notion that good can come out of bad.

Naturally, it is easy to dismiss a historical novel such as this and conclude that the characters involved were trapped in the events of a time unlike any other. Dickens, however, makes explicit in his famous first sentence that, although "It was the best of times, [and] it was the worst of times," humanity always believes the time they live in is one of superlatives. Perhaps we would be well served to remember this adage in our age of political and social strife. Like Paris rising from the ashes of the French Revolution, we too shall overcome political adversity.

(804 words)

Analysis of High-Scoring Essay

A Tale of Two Cities is a very appropriate choice for this prompt that invites commentary about the significance of setting in a novel or play. When analyzing setting, it is common for students to focus on the location[s] but to slight or ignore the time period. This essay, although not stellar, does an admirable job of addressing both the time setting and the location in a novel. Part of the difficulty of analyzing *A Tale of Two Cities*, though, is its complicated plot, but this student does a good job of choosing apt examples without lapsing into trite plot summary.

The statements that open the introduction are quite bland, and they do not engender excitement in the Reader; especially banal is the comment that without the French Revolution, "the novel would have no plot." Other students might use this claim as their thesis, which sets up an essay that has nowhere to go. Thankfully, this introduction improves as the student acknowledges that the claim oversimplifies and adds how the revolution possibly "provide[s] the opportunity" for characters to shine. Stylistically, a Reader will find the allusion to the novel's famous first sentence pleasing, especially since the student adjusts the wording to fit the introduction's purpose. The concept that the two locales symbolize dualities is intriguing, and the Reader will be interested to see how well the student develops it. This interpretation clearly earns 1 point for Row A.

The first body paragraph is devoted to an analysis of the time setting of the novel. The student acknowledges that the story actually begins years before the revolution that frames the novel's climax, and uses that information to establish how revolutions are indeed "the result of years of hardship and struggle." Presenting the example of the metaphorical woodman and farmer from the first chapter of the novel proves that the student has studied the text thoroughly; this is but a small detail in the text that most students would quickly forget, especially given the overwhelming scale of the action that follows. The student develops three more text examples that occur before the revolution, effectively paralleling the amount of time covered in the novel before the revolution. The student also adds commentary about examples of the action once the horror begins, notably the most famous Sydney Carton sacrifice. The paragraph overall is full of text examples, indeed providing more than most, and it includes ample analysis. Some of this analysis is implied, but at the end the writer explicitly states that "Horrific times can inspire honorable deeds"; this is a nice play on words that addresses the significance of the time setting to the work as a whole.

The following paragraph explores the significance of many of the actions that occur in the scenes in Paris, the epicenter of the revolution. The student presents three examples (revisiting Sydney Carton's death that was presented in the previous paragraph), but with minimal analysis. The example of Madame Defarge's death at the hands of Miss Pross acknowledges the portion of the thesis that mentions the dualities of love and hate. All three examples would benefit from more in-depth analysis, but, like the first body paragraph, the writer leaves us with a thematic universal truth: that "humanity can sink to unimaginable evil depths or rise to create beauty, stability, and love." The stylistic sophistication of this comment helps the essay avoid coming across as mere plot synopsis.

The third body paragraph explores the action in London, the second location in the physical setting of the novel. The student again brings in textual examples that are accurate and avoids launching into unnecessary plot detail. Many students who choose to write on a novel as complicated as this one fall into a trap; they end up explaining more about the plot than the Reader needs. This writer once again wraps up the paragraph with a simple yet profound thought that "good can come out of bad," an attempt to address the deeper significance of the work as a whole. The evidence and commentary use significant details to draw conclusions and support the thesis' interpretation; this qualifies for 4 points in Row B.

The conclusion is interesting. Instead of merely summarizing the points in the body paragraphs, a pedestrian pattern that easily bores the Reader, this student makes a larger philosophical point. Again, it is impressive that the student displays such an insightful depth of knowledge about the novel; "the famous first sentence" does indeed establish much more than a list of opposites. Dickens implies that humanity always feels the events of their lifetime should be described in extreme terms like "best" and "worst." The student broadens the concept by bringing in "our age of political and social strife," and suggests that such strife will be overcome. This is a pleasing snippet of food for thought for the Reader.

Overall, the essay has a few weaknesses, such as briefly explained examples and some clunky sentences. However, this essay has many more good points to reward: It addresses both time and place in the novel, it is clearly organized, it is well developed, and it usually presents a clear and sophisticated style. Remember that a Reader will always reward the student for what he or she does well. This student could have interjected some more thematic ideas throughout the essay, rather than pointing to a universal truth as the last sentence of each paragraph;

however, this is only a petty criticism that would be more appropriate to suggest for a process paper. For a timed essay, discussing an epic-length novel, it covers a lot of ground and it does so impressively. Because it meets one of the criteria in Row C, presenting a thesis that demands nuanced analysis and successfully probing it, the essay earns 1 point in Row C. Therefore, it earns an overall score of 6.

Low-Scoring Essay

In "The Kite Runner," the author creates memorable and sympathetic characters who live in both Afghanistan and America. These two locations make the novel's plot happen. It's also important that the time period is bad because the Russian invasion of Afghanistan causes the main characters to move to America.

The novel is about a rich boy, Amir who is friends with Hassan, the son of Amir's father's servant. They fly kites together, which is a very big deal in Afghanistan. One day, when Amir is about to win the kite flying competition, Hassan is abused by a very bad boy they all hate. Amir sees Hassan being violated, but does nothing, because he is really a coward. He'll regret this for the rest of his life. He and Hassan are never close again. Amir even sets Hassan up as a thief (a really bad thing in Afghan society) but Amir's father, Baba, forgives Hassan anyway.

When the Russians invade, Amir and Baba are forced to flee, this is when the setting moves to America, where they survive and make-do. Baba eventually dies of cancer after being forced to work in a gas station. Amir goes to college, marries a fellow refugee, and becomes a successful writer. Many years later, Amir has to return to Afghanistan to see an old friend of his father's. That man tells Amir that Hassan died while protecting Amir and Baba's home from the Taliban. Amir eventually makes amends for deserting Hassan by adopting Hassan's son and bringing him to America.

Without the setting of Afghanistan and America, plus the important invasion of Afghanistan, "the Kite Runner" would not have such a gripping story. So, the setting makes the novel better by holding the reader's interest.

(290 words)

Analysis of Low-Scoring Essay

If a Reader could reward students with an "E" for effort, this essay might fare better. Unfortunately, as it is, this essay on *The Kite Runner* fails to impress. The introduction begins with a brief comment about characters and then tries to address the prompt a bit by mentioning the novel's two locations, Afghanistan and America, but it merely concludes that the "time period is bad." A Reader will forgive the student's historical misstatement that Russia invaded Afghanistan when technically it was the Soviet Union that did so. But the concept in the thesis does not bode well; the student merely states that the location "makes . . . plot happen" and that the Soviet invasion was bad without providing any further insight into the importance of the setting to the novel as a whole. Because it does not address the prompt or present a defendable claim, the essay does not earn a point in Row A.

The first body paragraph, regretfully, only provides a banal summary of the novel's early plot, before the lead characters move to America. In addition, the student's diction is not particularly impressive, with its use of simplistic and repetitive phrases, such as pointing out that flying kites "is a very big deal," Hassan is despoiled by a "very bad boy," and theft is "a really bad thing." The paragraph should instead concentrate on *how* the setting adds significance to these characters and events and avoid stringing together plot synopsis.

The next paragraph continues with mere plot explanation. The student tries to tie in how the events of the time period affect characters, but only points out that the invasion of Afghanistan causes Amir and Baba to flee to America. Instead of exploring *how* this changed setting affects the characters, the student tells us what happens to them; the student simply summarizes the plot. The student's writing gets cumbersome with grammatical errors, such as claiming that "Baba eventually dies of cancer after being forced to work in a gas station," as if this employment was the cause of his cancer. The run-on sentence about their move to America does not help to impress the Reader. This essay earns 2 points in Row B because it provides some relevant textual references, but the commentary is overly simplistic and repetitive.

The conclusion is a simple summary of the essay; sadly, it does not address the topic that is assigned in the prompt. The conclusion, indeed the entire essay, never explores how the time and place influence the characters, and it never attempts to address any important relationship to the work as a whole. Remember that the directions for Question 3 will always direct you to not merely summarize the plot, yet this student offers nothing else. The essay cannot earn a point in Row C because it does not meet any of the criteria. The overall score is a 2.

Scoring Worksheet

Use the following worksheet to arrive at a probable final AP score on Practice Exam 2. While it is sometimes difficult to be objective enough to score one's own essay, you can use the sample essays to approximate an essay score for yourself. You may also give your essays (along with the sample essays) to a friend or relative to score if you feel confident that the individual has the knowledge necessary to make such a judgment and that he or she will feel comfortable in doing so.

Section I: Multiple-Choice Questions

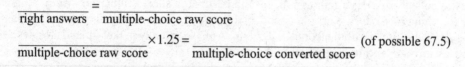

$$\frac{\text{_____}}{\text{right answers}} = \frac{\text{_____}}{\text{multiple-choice raw score}}$$

$$\frac{\text{_____}}{\text{multiple-choice raw score}} \times 1.25 = \frac{\text{_____}}{\text{multiple-choice converted score}} \text{ (of possible 67.5)}$$

Section II: Free-Response Questions

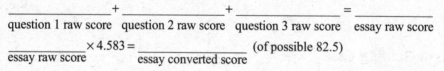

$$\frac{\text{_____}}{\text{question 1 raw score}} + \frac{\text{_____}}{\text{question 2 raw score}} + \frac{\text{_____}}{\text{question 3 raw score}} = \frac{\text{_____}}{\text{essay raw score}}$$

$$\frac{\text{_____}}{\text{essay raw score}} \times 4.583 = \frac{\text{_____}}{\text{essay converted score}} \text{ (of possible 82.5)}$$

Final Score

$$\frac{\text{_____}}{\text{multiple-choice converted score}} + \frac{\text{_____}}{\text{essay converted score}} = \frac{\text{_____}}{\text{final converted score}} \text{ (of possible 150)}$$

Probable Final AP Score	
Final Converted Score	**Probable AP Score**
150–100	5
99–86	4
85–67	3
66–0	1 or 2

Section I: Multiple-Choice Questions

Time: 1 hour

55 questions

Directions: This section contains selections from two passages of prose and three poems with questions on their content, style, and form. Read each selection carefully. Choose the best answer of the five choices.

For questions 1–11, read the passage carefully before choosing your answers.

The Empire Grill was long and low-slung, with windows that ran its entire length, and since the building next door, a Rexall drugstore, had been condemned and razed, it was now possible
(5) to sit at the lunch counter and see straight down Empire Avenue all the way to the old textile mill and its adjacent shirt factory. Both had been abandoned now for the better part of two decades, though their dark, looming shapes at
(10) the foot of the avenue's gentle incline continued to draw the eye. Of course, nothing prevented a person from looking up Empire Avenue in the other direction, but Miles Roby, the proprietor of the restaurant—and its eventual owner, he
(15) hoped—had long noted that his customers rarely did.

No, their natural preference was to gaze down to where the street both literally and figuratively dead-ended at the mill and factory, the
(20) undeniable physical embodiment of the town's past, and it was the magnetic quality of the old, abandoned structures that steeled Miles's resolve to sell the Empire Grill for what little it would bring, just as soon as the restaurant was his.

(25) Just beyond the factory and mill ran the river that long ago had powered them, and Miles often wondered if these old buildings were razed, would the town that had grown up around them be forced to imagine a future? Perhaps not.
(30) Nothing but a chain-link fence had gone up in place of the Rexall, which meant, Miles supposed, that diverting one's attention from the past was not the same as envisioning and embarking upon a future. On the other hand, if
(35) the past were razed, the slate wiped clean, maybe fewer people would confuse it with the future, and that at least would be something. For as long as the mill and factory remained, Miles feared,

many would continue to believe against all
(40) reason that a buyer might be found for one or both, and that consequently Empire Falls would be restored to its old economic viability.

What drew Miles Roby's anxious eye down Empire this particular afternoon in early
(45) September was not the dark, high-windowed shirt factory where his mother had spent most of her adult working life or, just beyond it, the larger, brooding presence of the textile mill, but rather his hope that he'd catch a glimpse of his
(50) daughter, Tick, when she rounded the corner and began her slow, solitary trek up the avenue. Like most of her high school friends, Tick, a rail-thin sophomore, lugged all her books in a canvas L.L. Bean backpack and had to lean forward, as if
(55) into a strong headwind, to balance a weight nearly as great as her own. Oddly, most of the conventions Miles remembered from high school had been subverted. He and his friends had carried their textbooks balanced on their hips,
(60) listing first to the left, then shifting the load and listing to the right. They brought home only the books they would need that night, or the ones they *remembered* needing, leaving the rest crammed in their lockers. Kids today stuffed the
(65) entire contents of their lockers into their seam-stretched backpacks and brought it all home, probably, Miles figured, so they wouldn't have to think through what they'd need and what they could do without, thereby avoiding the kinds of
(70) decisions that might trail consequences. Except that this itself had consequences. A visit to the doctor last spring had revealed the beginnings of scoliosis, a slight curvature of Tick's spine, which worried Miles at several levels. "She's just
(75) carrying too much weight," the doctor explained, unaware, as far as Miles could tell, of the metaphorical implications of her remark. It had taken Tick most of the summer to regain her normal posture, and yesterday, after one day

(80) back at school, she was already hunched over again.

Instead of catching sight of his daughter, the one person in the world he wanted at that moment to see rounding the corner, Miles was (85) instead treated to the sight of Walt Comeau, the person he least wanted to see—the one he could live happily without ever laying eyes on again—pulling into a vacant parking space in front of the Empire Grill. Walt's van was a rolling (90) advertisement for its driver, who'd had THE SILVER FOX stenciled across the hood, just above the grill, and its vanity plates read FOXY 1. The van was tall and Walt short, which meant he had to hop down from the running board, and (95) something about the man's youthful bounce made Miles, who'd seen this both in real life and in his dreams just about every day for the past year, want to grab an ax handle, meet the Silver Fox at the door and stave his head in right there (100) in the entryway.

Instead he turned back to the grill and flipped Horace Weymouth's burger, wondering if he'd already left it on too long. Horace liked his burgers bloody.

(105) "So," Horace closed and folded his *Boston Globe* in anticipation of being fed, his inner clock apparently confirming that Miles had indeed waited too long. "You been out to see Mrs. Whiting yet?"

(110) "Not yet," Miles said. He set up Horace's platter with tomato, lettuce, a slice of Bermuda onion and a pickle, plus the open-faced bun, then pressed down on the burger with his spatula, making it sizzle before slipping it onto the bun. (115) "I usually wait to be summoned."

"I wouldn't," Horace counseled. "Somebody's got to inherit Empire Falls. It might as well be Miles Roby."

1. Describing the Rexall drugstore as "the building next door" (line 3) to the Empire Grill is ironic because

    A.   the Empire Grill benefitted financially once the drugstore closed

    B.   the drugstore went bankrupt

    C.   the building no longer exists

    D.   the customers of the Empire Grill used to patronize the drugstore

    E.   the area no longer needs a drugstore

2. The first two paragraphs imply which of the following about the Empire Grill customers?

    A.   They enjoy the view down Empire Avenue.

    B.   They believe the town will turn around and prosper.

    C.   They assume Miles Roby will remain the manager of the restaurant.

    D.   They work at local factories and come to the Empire Grill for lunch.

    E.   They are pessimistic about the future.

3. The narrator makes which of the following observations about humanity?

    A.   Residents spend too much time living in the past.

    B.   People confuse past successes with future opportunities.

    C.   Citizens always have faith that a bad economy will rebound.

    D.   Older people are more conventional than younger kids.

    E.   People know they need to change with the times.

4. The chain-link fence around the old Rexall drugstore property becomes a symbol of

    A.   the deteriorating economy

    B.   a façade hiding a harsh reality

    C.   restraining any ideas for improvement

    D.   a suggestion of high crime rate in the area

    E.   the need for commercial development

5. Which of the following clarifies Miles' attitude about "Kids today" (line 64)?

    A.   They need more help from their parents than Miles' generation needed.

    B.   They are willing to overload their lives with activity and studies.

    C.   They are disrespectful to adults and authority figures.

    D.   They are averse to making decisions and want no consequences for their actions.

    E.   They are forced to grow up too quickly because of the bad economy.

6. The idea that Miles was "treated to the sight" (line 85) is an example of

   A. paradoxical ambiguity

   B. justifiable confusion

   C. optimistic anticipation

   D. situational irony

   E. exaggerated mockery

7. The narrator's description of Walt Comeau suggests that

   A. both men love the same woman

   B. Miles previously respected Walt

   C. Miles and Walt have had a contentious background

   D. Walt represents a business competitor

   E. Miles envies Walt's higher economic status

8. The difference between what Miles wants to do to Walt Comeau and what he actually does can be considered

   A. a form of bathos

   B. the shift from appearances and reality

   C. the juxtaposition between object and desire

   D. an explanation of Miles' motives

   E. a contradiction of character

9. Horace Weymouth can best be described as being

   A. indifferent, flippant, and impetuous

   B. globally aware, well-intentioned, and serious

   C. demanding, sincere, and self-serving

   D. well-read, temperate, and informative

   E. astute, picky, and supportive

10. Which of the following is the most reasonable inference one can draw about Mrs. Whiting?

   A. She favors Miles Roby.

   B. She commands great obedience.

   C. She controls Empire Falls.

   D. She knows something about Miles' past.

   E. She owns the Empire Grill.

11. Miles' comment "I usually wait to be summoned" (line 115) suggests that he

   A. prefers to avoid Mrs. Whiting

   B. tends to not take risks or to not seize the initiative

   C. wants to ignore Horace's implication

   D. respects Mrs. Whiting inappropriately

   E. values social customs over personal gain

For questions 12–23, read the following poem carefully before choosing your answers.

The following poem was written in 1773 by an African American slave and dedicated to another slave. As the poem begins, the poet is looking at a portrait of herself that the other young slave had drawn for her.

To S. M., a Young African Painter, on Seeing His Works

To show the lab'ring bosom's deep intent,
And thought in living characters to paint,
When first thy pencil did those beauties give,
And breathing figures learnt from thee to live,
How did those prospects give my soul delight,   (5)
A new creation rushing on my sight?
Still, wond'rous youth! each noble path pursue;
On deathless glories fix thine ardent view:
Still may the painter's and the poet's fire,
To aid thy pencil and thy verse conspire!   (10)
And may the charms of each seraphic theme
Conduct thy footsteps to immortal fame!
High to the blissful wonders of the skies
Elate thy soul, and raise thy wishful eyes.
Thrice happy, when exalted to survey   (15)
That splendid city, crown'd with endless day,
Whose twice six gates on radiant hinges ring:
Celestial *Salem*¹ blooms in endless spring.

Calm and serene thy moments glide along,
And may the muse inspire each future song!   (20)
Still, with the sweets of contemplation bless'd,
May peace with balmy wings your soul invest!
But when these shades of time are chas'd away,
And darkness ends in everlasting day,
On what seraphic pinions² shall we move,   (25)
And view the landscapes in the realms above?
There shall thy tongue in heav'nly murmurs flow,
And there my muse with heav'nly transport glow;
No more to tell of *Damon's* tender sighs³,
Or rising radiance of *Aurora's*⁴ eyes;   (30)
For nobler themes demand a nobler strain,
And purer language on th' ethereal plain.
Cease, gentle Muse! the solemn gloom of night
Now seals the fair creation from my sight.

---

¹**Celestial Salem:** possibly an allusion to "Light's Abode, Celestial Salem," a 1400s hymn about the glories of heaven
²**pinions:** wings
³**Damon's tender sighs:** In Virgil's Bucolics, Damon is one of two shepherds who admire the coming dawn and speak of their own friendship.
⁴**Aurora:** the Roman goddess of the dawn

12. The speaker is impressed with the artist's ability to

   A. labor intensely at his artistry

   B. show the subject's delight at the world

   C. bring pleasure to others in the art community

   D. accurately capture the inner feelings of the subject

   E. combine pencil drawings with painted ones

13. Lines 1–6 deal exclusively with

   A. the artist's struggle to depict his subject

   B. the public's opinion of the artist's creation

   C. the speaker seeing her portrait and reacting to it

   D. the speaker explicitly describing the specific details of the portrait

   E. the importance of art in the world

14. The poem includes all of the following devices EXCEPT

   A. heroic couplets

   B. multiple metaphors

   C. classical allusions

   D. sentence inversions

   E. elegiac praise

15. The phrase "breathing figures learnt from thee to live" (line 4) can best be summarized as

   A. acknowledging that art both imitates life and creates life

   B. symbolizing how the artist needs living subjects to paint

   C. emphasizing the role that art plays in the life of the speaker

   D. contrasting an image with the lines that follow

   E. comparing the poet with the artist

16. The use of "fire" (line 9) and "conspire" (line 10) might be interpreted to imply that

   A. the artist and poet might join in subversive behavior

   B. the creative spirit needs to combine words and visual images

   C. all artists need something intense for inspiration

   D. this poet and artist can utilize their art to help overcome oppression

   E. the elements can be used as motivation

17. Lines 13–14 serve as

   A. a command to the artist to search out more celestial subjects

   B. a transition in the thought process of the poem

   C. an instance of the poet's inspiration

   D. a hopeful plea for eternal bliss

   E. a view of what immortal fame will bring

18. The images in lines 15–18 present which of the following ideas?

   A. Inspired artists can achieve spiritual enlightenment.

   B. Gifted artists hope to be rewarded in heaven.

   C. Endless day and endless spring cannot exist together.

   D. The heavenly vision the artist sees will sustain him through life.

   E. Once in heaven, the artist will get new inspiration from the angels.

19. "But when these shades of time are chas'd away" (line 23) shifts the thrust of the poem in that it

   A. suggests an artist needs to find inspiration in worldly matters

   B. proposes an alternative form of stimulation

   C. changes the focus from the upward heavens down to life on earth

   D. begins the speaker's musing about philosophical issues

   E. combines the artist's and the speaker's vision

20. The couplet in lines 25–26 contrasts with what earlier image in the poem?

   A. "A new creation rushing on my sight" (line 6)

   B. "On deathless glories fix thine ardent view" (line 8)

   C. "And may the charms of each seraphic theme / Conduct thy footsteps to immortal fame" (lines 11–12)

   D. ". . . when exalted to survey / That splendid city, crown'd with endless day" (lines 15–16)

   E. "May peace with balmy wings your soul invest" (line 22)

21. The sentence "There shall thy tongue . . . on th' ethereal plain" (lines 27–32) is best paraphrased by which of the following?

    A.   The landscapes of heaven are worthy of classical poets.

    B.   Those who live life purposefully will gain entrance to heaven.

    C.   The speaker should seek spiritual inspiration while still alive.

    D.   In heaven, the poet will focus on nobler topics, using more exalted diction.

    E.   The speaker deserves the rewards of heaven.

22. The irony of the last two lines is that

    A.   the speaker will find inspiration in the future

    B.   the "gloom of night" (line 33) will not end after death

    C.   the speaker cannot achieve the greatness of the artist

    D.   the speaker laments losing her muse

    E.   after the exalted visions of heaven, the poem ends in darkness

23. The speaker's overall evaluation of art is that

    A.   classical art stems from divine inspiration

    B.   quality art is both timeless and a source of spiritual satisfaction

    C.   art can help to ease worldly suffering

    D.   good artists can help others to perfect their skills

    E.   poets and painters both produce worthy art

For questions 24–32, read the following passage carefully before choosing your answers.

It was a Sunday evening in October, and in common with many other young ladies of her class, Katharine Hilbery was pouring out tea. Perhaps a fifth part of her mind was thus
(5) occupied, and the remaining parts leapt over the little barrier of day which interposed between Monday morning and this rather subdued moment, and played with the things one does voluntarily and normally in the daylight. But
(10) although she was silent, she was evidently mistress of a situation which was familiar enough to her, and inclined to let it take its way for the six hundredth time, perhaps, without bringing into play any of her unoccupied faculties. A single
(15) glance was enough to show that Mrs. Hilbery was

so rich in the gifts which make tea-parties of elderly distinguished people successful, that she scarcely needed any help from her daughter, provided that the tiresome business of teacups
(20) and bread and butter was discharged for her.

Considering that the little party had been seated round the tea-table for less than twenty minutes, the animation observable on their faces, and the amount of sound they were producing
(25) collectively, were very creditable to the hostess. It suddenly came into Katharine's mind that if some one opened the door at this moment he would think that they were enjoying themselves; he would think, "What an extremely nice house
(30) to come into!" and instinctively she laughed, and said something to increase the noise, for the credit of the house presumably, since she herself had not been feeling exhilarated. At the very same moment, rather to her amusement, the
(35) door was flung open, and a young man entered the room. Katharine, as she shook hands with him, asked him, in her own mind, "Now, do you think we're enjoying ourselves enormously?" . . . "Mr. Denham, mother," she said aloud, for she
(40) saw that her mother had forgotten his name.

That fact was perceptible to Mr. Denham also, and increased the awkwardness which inevitably attends the entrance of a stranger into a room full of people much at their ease, and all
(45) launched upon sentences. At the same time, it seemed to Mr. Denham as if a thousand softly padded doors had closed between him and the street outside. A fine mist, the etherealized essence of the fog, hung visibly in the wide and
(50) rather empty space of the drawing-room, all silver where the candles were grouped on the tea-table, and ruddy again in the firelight. With the omnibuses and cabs still running in his head, and his body still tingling with his quick walk along
(55) the streets and in and out of traffic and foot-passengers, this drawing-room seemed very remote and still; and the faces of the elderly people were mellowed, at some distance from each other, and had a bloom on them owing to
(60) the fact that the air in the drawing-room was thickened by blue grains of mist. Mr. Denham had come in as Mr. Fortescue, the eminent novelist, reached the middle of a very long sentence. He kept this suspended while the
(65) newcomer sat down, and Mrs. Hilbery deftly joined the severed parts by leaning towards him and remarking:

"Now, what would you do if you were married to an engineer, and had to live in Manchester,
(70) Mr. Denham?"

"Surely she could learn Persian," broke in a thin, elderly gentleman. "Is there no retired schoolmaster or man of letters in Manchester with whom she could read Persian?"

(75) "A cousin of ours has married and gone to live in Manchester," Katharine explained. Mr. Denham muttered something, which was indeed all that was required of him, and the novelist went on where he had left off. Privately, Mr.

(80) Denham cursed himself very sharply for having exchanged the freedom of the street for this sophisticated drawing-room, where, among other disagreeables, he certainly would not appear at his best. He glanced round him, and saw that,

(85) save for Katharine, they were all over forty, the only consolation being that Mr. Fortescue was a considerable celebrity, so that to-morrow one might be glad to have met him.

24. The phrase "Perhaps a fifth part of her mind was thus occupied," (lines 4–5) suggests that Katharine Hilbery

A. carefully watches Mrs. Hilbery for social clues

B. is quite adept at serving others during tea time

C. resents having to pour tea for her old visitors

D. represents the attitude of youthful girls in the time period

E. graciously assists her mother as a hostess

25. The "little barrier of day" (line 6) functions as a

A. minor obstacle that grows over time

B. symbolic reminder of Katharine's duty to family

C. contrast to the pleasant atmosphere of the tea party

D. metaphorical reference to the importance of Sunday tea time

E. representation of the conflict Katharine faces

26. Katharine Hilbery's description in the first paragraph implies that she

A. ignores the needs of her guests

B. rejects the social standards of her class

C. resents her mother's demands for assistance

D. anticipates the day when she will have her mother's social graces

E. performs her social duties in a mechanical manner

27. Which of the following can reasonably be inferred about Mrs. Hilbery's character?

A. She is socially adept and makes her guests comfortable.

B. She relies on Katharine to fulfill all of the duties of a hostess.

C. She feels that Katharine needs further training in the social skills expected of their class.

D. She resents the demands of ladies of their class.

E. She values her guests more than social propriety.

28. Which of the following indicates the irony of Katharine's understanding of the importance of social appearances?

A. " . . . in common with many other young ladies of her class, Katharine Hilbery was pouring out tea." (lines 1–3)

B. " . . . played with the things one does voluntarily and normally in the daylight." (lines 8–9)

C. "But although she was silent, she was evidently mistress of a situation which was familiar enough to her" (lines 9–11)

D. " . . . [Mrs. Hilbery] scarcely needed any help from her daughter, provided that the tiresome business of teacups and bread and butter was discharged for her." (lines 18–20)

E. " . . . instinctively she laughed, and said something to increase the noise" (lines 30–31)

29. The effect of Katharine's mentally asking Mr. Denham's opinion of the gathering "in her own mind" (line 37) is that she

A. wants outside verification of her social class

B. does not really care to hear his potential answer

C. hopes to confirm her previous thoughts about the gathering

D. will do all she can to make him socially acceptable

E. challenges his ability to join in the conversation

30. Mr. Denham's perception upon entering the tea party that "it seemed . . . as if a thousand softly padded doors had closed between him and the street outside" (lines 45–48) suggests that

    A. he feels trapped in the new surroundings

    B. the party-goers are insulated from the real world

    C. he enjoys the comfort of the lush home

    D. the others object to his intrusion

    E. he immediately regrets attending

31. Much of the imagery in the second and third paragraphs of the passage contrasts the

    A. thoughts of Katharine with those of the guests she serves

    B. expensive finery of the guests with Mr. Denham's appearance

    C. human conversation indoors with the industrial noises outdoors

    D. loud chatter of the guests with the silence that follows Mr. Denham's arrival

    E. upper-class attitude of the guests with the lower-class pedestrians on the street

32. Mr. Denham's attitude can best be described as

    A. optimistic

    B. sarcastic

    C. indifferent

    D. opportunistic

    E. charitable

For questions 33–43, read the following poem carefully before choosing your answers.

The Season of Phantasmal Peace

Then all the nations of birds lifted together
the huge net of the shadows of this earth
in multitudinous dialects, twittering tongues,
stitching and crossing it. They lifted up
the shadows of long pines down trackless slopes,   (5)
the shadows of glass-faced towers down evening streets,
the shadow of a frail plant on a city sill—
the net rising soundless at night, the birds' cries soundless, until
there was no longer dusk, or season, decline, or weather,
only this passage of phantasmal light   (10)
that not the narrowest shadow dared to sever.

And men could not see, looking up, what the wild geese drew,
what the ospreys trailed behind them in the silvery ropes
that flashed in the icy sunlight; they could not hear
battalions of starlings waging peaceful cries,   (15)
bearing the net higher, covering this world
like the vines of an orchard, or a mother drawing
the trembling gauze over the trembling eyes
of a child fluttering to sleep;

                        it was the light   (20)
that you will see at evening on the side of a hill
in yellow October, and no one hearing knew
what change had brought into the raven's cawing,
the killdeer's screech, the ember-circling chough[1]
such an immense, soundless, and high concern   (25)
for the fields and cities where the birds belong,
except it was their seasonal passing, Love,
made seasonless, or, from the high privilege of their birth,
something brighter than pity for the wingless ones
below them who shared dark holes in windows and in houses,   (30)
and higher they lifted the net with soundless voices
above all change, betrayals of falling suns,
and this season lasted one moment, like the pause
between dusk and darkness, between fury and peace,
but, for such as our earth is now, it lasted long.   (35)

---

[1]**chough:** a small, crowlike bird, pronounced "chuff"

33. The phrase "all the nations of birds" (line 1) metaphorically represents

  A. the flocking together of like-minded people
  B. the innumerable cultures of earth
  C. the natural ability to fly above conflict
  D. those individuals who see clearly
  E. those who seek a way to join together disparate groups

34. The author's use of alliteration in line 3 has the intended effect of

  A. generating a euphonious murmur from the birds
  B. slowing the pace of the poem
  C. creating harsh sounds that contrast with the birds' normal songs
  D. imitating the sound of birds as they mimic mankind's languages
  E. contradicting the birds' actions

35. The first stanza primarily establishes that

- **A.** the birds will add to mankind's collective sorrows
- **B.** nature will eventually dominate mankind in time
- **C.** the birds fly away with the light of mankind
- **D.** phantasmal light covers the globe
- **E.** the birds fly away with mankind's collective negativity

36. The phrase "phantasmal light" (line 10) relates to the second stanza in that it

- **A.** initiates the idea of knowledge that mankind will eventually comprehend
- **B.** demonstrates the desire for unity that mankind needs
- **C.** circumnavigates the world, bringing ideas of peace to mankind
- **D.** represents the moment between fury and peace that mankind destroys
- **E.** intensifies the darkness that blinds mankind here on earth

37. What was it that "men could not see" (line 12)?

- **A.** "the huge net of the shadows of this earth" (line 2)
- **B.** "the narrowest shadow" (line 11)
- **C.** "the icy sunlight" (line 14)
- **D.** "battalions of starlings" (line 15)
- **E.** "the vines of an orchard" (line 17)

38. What is the intended effect of the placement of the phrase "it was the light" (line 20)?

- **A.** It stands out as a reminder of the need for mankind to open their mind.
- **B.** It emphasizes the ephemeral nature of sunlight.
- **C.** It separates the light of peace from the darkness on earth.
- **D.** It evokes an image of something that cannot be attained.
- **E.** It clashes with the imagery of the rest of the poem.

39. Within context, what is the intended meaning of the phrase "the high privilege of their birth" (line 28)?

- **A.** The animal kingdom is honored more than mankind.
- **B.** Those who are born into high status should help those who are not.
- **C.** Someday everyone will have high status and need no pity.
- **D.** Birds can fly free above the world's problems.
- **E.** Being born into this world is a great privilege.

40. The phrases "cries soundless" (line 8) and "soundless voices" (line 31) most strongly contrast with which of the following?

- **A.** "nations of birds" (line 1)
- **B.** "twittering tongues" (line 3)
- **C.** "soundless at night" (line 8)
- **D.** "fields and cities" (line 26)
- **E.** "dusk and darkness" (line 34)

41. The poem contains all of the following poetic devices EXCEPT

- **A.** metaphor
- **B.** parallel construction
- **C.** simile
- **D.** oxymoron
- **E.** internal rhyme

42. The speaker's overall point may be summarized as

- **A.** mankind can learn compatibility from avian creatures
- **B.** peace is attainable
- **C.** peace will never last more than a moment
- **D.** mankind needs to look to the heavens to glean knowledge
- **E.** darkness and light coexist peacefully on earth

43. The poem implies that mankind is blinded by

- **A.** "the huge net of the shadows" (line 2)
- **B.** "the shadows of glass-faced towers" (line 6)
- **C.** "this passage of phantasmal light" (line 10)
- **D.** "the icy sunlight" (line 14)
- **E.** "something brighter than pity" (line 29)

For questions 44–55, read the following poem carefully before choosing your answers.

Since there's no help, come let us kiss and part

Since there's no help, come let us kiss and part.
Nay, I have done, you get no more of me;
And I am glad, yea glad with all my heart,
That thus so cleanly I myself can free.
Shake hands for ever, cancel all our vows,   (5)
And when we meet at any time again,
Be it not seen in either of our brows
That we one jot of former love retain.
Now at the last gasp of Love's latest breath,
When, his pulse failing, Passion speechless lies;   (10)
When Faith is kneeling by his bed of death,
And Innocence is closing up his eyes—
Now, if thou wouldst, when all have given him over,
From death to life thou might'st him yet recover!

44. The first line of the poem is ironic because

- A.   the couple kiss and part again by the end
- B.   the speaker is culpable for their breakup
- C.   the beloved is also glad to part from the speaker
- D.   the speaker hopes for reunification by the end
- E.   the dramatic situation will reverse by the end

45. Which of the following might explain the repetition of "glad" in line 3?

- A.   It reinforces the speaker's sardonic attitude.
- B.   It moderates the speaker's passion.
- C.   The speaker is trying to convince himself of the emotion.
- D.   The speaker is being facetious to his lover.
- E.   It undermines the fact that the speaker is ending the relationship.

46. The phrase "cancel all our vows" (line 5) suggests that

- A.   the couple's love has religious overtones
- B.   the couple is definitely married
- C.   the simple handshake will negate their previous love
- D.   the couple's love was only verbal
- E.   their vows can easily be renewed at a later time

47. The imagery and personification in lines 9–12 suggest that

- A.   the couple should try harder to revive their love
- B.   passion, faith, and innocence cannot exist without love
- C.   the speaker fears his own death if he cannot be with his beloved
- D.   abstract concepts will help the speaker reconcile his loss
- E.   the couple's relationship is hopeless

48. In line 9, the word "Now" serves as

- A.   a reminder that time has passed
- B.   a volta that transitions the speaker's thoughts
- C.   a conjunction that joins the previous lines
- D.   an ironic shift in the poem's tone
- E.   a subtle urge for the beloved to take action

49. The speaker implies that the logical result of the couple's ignoring their past relationship will be which of the following?

- A.   The beloved will regret losing her lover.
- B.   Their passion will be revived with time.
- C.   The loss of love will be certain.
- D.   Love cannot win against apathy.
- E.   The speaker will renounce his lover.

50. In the poem, which of the following serves as a metaphor?

    A. "glad with all my heart" (line 3)

    B. "Shake hands for ever" (line 5)

    C. "Passion speechless lies" (line 10)

    D. "bed of death" (line 11)

    E. "Innocence is closing up his eyes" (line 12)

51. Within the context of the poem as a whole, which of the following best describes the intended irony of the speaker's statements that he wants to end the relationship?

    A. He knows he wants his beloved to take him back.

    B. He is actually unknowingly taking the first step to encourage reunification.

    C. He trusts that his lover will beg him to reconsider.

    D. He knows that death will follow a loveless life.

    E. He immediately regrets his actions.

52. The speaker's change from the imperative mood (lines 1–8) to the subjunctive (lines 13–14) suggests that

    A. the speaker will be able to seduce his lover to reignite their relationship

    B. the speaker is used to bossing his lover and is surprised at his own weakness

    C. the beloved will become the dominant force in their relationship

    D. the couple will not likely reunite after his harsh words

    E. the speaker is no longer sure of himself and hopes his beloved can restore him

53. The pronoun "him" in lines 13 and 14 refers to

    A. the speaker

    B. Love

    C. Passion

    D. Faith

    E. Innocence

54. The speaker's attitude can best be described as shifting from

    A. gentle chiding to shrewd manipulation

    B. solemn misery to skeptical hope

    C. sincere presumption to uncertain curiosity

    D. dubious confidence to cautious anticipation

    E. arrogant insistence to apologetic pleading

55. The poem implies which of the following about the end of a relationship?

    A. Confusion and uncertainty can follow firm resolve.

    B. Dignity and mutual respect can be salvaged.

    C. A couple can mask their inner emotions when meeting again.

    D. One person of the couple will regret the breakup.

    E. The loss of innocence can never be reversed.

IF YOU FINISH BEFORE TIME IS CALLED, CHECK YOUR WORK ON THIS SECTION ONLY. DO NOT WORK ON ANY OTHER SECTION IN THE TEST.

Section II: Free-Response Questions

Time: 2 hours
3 questions

Question 1

(Suggested time—40 minutes. This question counts toward one-third of the total free-response section score.)

Directions: The following speech, set in the marketplace of Rome, is from Shakespeare's play *Coriolanus* (first performed circa 1608). The title character, previously known as Caius Martius, has just been given the name Coriolanus because of his valor in crushing the city of Corioles. He returns to Rome to run for consul, the highest political office in Rome. In this speech to the plebeians, he is campaigning for their votes.

Read the speech carefully. Then write a well-written essay in which you analyze how Shakespeare uses literary elements to convey Coriolanus' complex attitude toward his audience and public office.

In your response you should do the following:

- Respond to the prompt with a thesis that presents an interpretation and may establish a line of reasoning.
- Select and use evidence to develop and support your line of reasoning.
- Explain the relationship between the evidence and your thesis.
- Use appropriate grammar and punctuation in communicating your argument.

Most sweet voices!
Better it is to die, better to starve,
Than crave the hire[1] which first we do deserve.
Why in this wolvish toge[2] should I stand here,
To beg of Hob[3] and Dick that does appear   (5)
Their needless vouches[4]? Custom calls me to't.
What custom wills, in all things should we do't,
The dust on antique time would lie unswept
And mountainous error be too highly heaped
For truth to o'er-peer[5]. Rather than fool it so,   (10)
Let the high office and the honor go
To one that would do thus. I am half through;
The one part suffered, the other will I do.

Enter three Citizens more

Here come more voices.
Your voices! For your voices I have fought;   (15)
Watched for your voices; for your voices bear
Of wounds two dozen odd; battles thrice six
I have seen and heard of; for your voices have
Done many things, some less, some more. Your voices!
Indeed, I would be consul.   (20)

---

[1]**hire:** reward
[2]**toge:** toga
[3]**Hob:** common, rustic nickname for Robert
[4]**vouches:** attestations, verifications of truth
[5]**o'er-peer:** overtop, overcome

Question 2

(Suggested time—40 minutes. This question counts toward one-third of the total free-response section score.)

Directions: In the following excerpt from *A River Runs through It*, a novella written by Norman Maclean in 1976, two sons are fly-fishing with their father on a river in Montana. Read the excerpt carefully. Then, in a well-written essay, analyze how the author uses figurative language to explore memory and the characters' complex relationships.

In your response you should do the following:

- Respond to the prompt with a thesis that presents an interpretation and may establish a line of reasoning.
- Select and use evidence to develop and support your line of reasoning.
- Explain the relationship between the evidence and your thesis.
- Use appropriate grammar and punctuation in communicating your argument.

"That's his limit," I said to my father.

"He is beautiful," my father said, although my brother had just finished catching his limit in the hole my father had already fished.

(5) This was the last fish we were ever to see Paul catch. My father and I talked about this moment several times later, and whatever our other feelings, we always felt it fitting that, when we saw him catch his last fish, we never saw the fish but only the artistry of the fisherman.

While my father was watching my brother, he reached over to pat me, but he missed, so he had to turn his eyes and look for my knee and try again. He must have thought that I felt neglected and that he should tell me he was proud of me also but for other reasons.

(10) It was a little too deep and fast where Paul was trying to wade the river, and he knew it. He was crouched over the water and his arms were spread wide for balance. If you were a wader of big rivers you could have felt with him even at a distance the power of the water making his legs weak and wavy and ready to swim out from under him. He looked downstream to estimate how far it was to an easier place to wade.

My father said, "He won't take the trouble to walk downstream. He'll swim it." At the same time Paul
(15) thought the same thing, and put his cigarette and matches in his hat.

My father and I sat on the bank and laughed at each other. It never occurred to either of us to hurry to the shore in case he needed help with a rod in his right hand and a basket loaded with fish on his left shoulder. In our family it was no great thing for a fisherman to swim a river with matches in his hair. We laughed at each other because we knew he was getting damn good and wet, and we lived in him, and were swept over the
(20) rocks with him and held his rod high in one of our hands.

As he moved to shore he caught himself on his feet and then was washed off them, and, when he stood again, more of him showed and he staggered to shore. He never stopped to shake himself. He came charging up the bank showering molecules of water and images of himself to show what was sticking out of his basket, and he dripped all over us, like a young duck dog that in its joy forgets to shake itself before getting
(25) close.

"Let's put them all out on the grass and take a picture of them," he said. So we emptied our baskets and arranged them by size and took turns photographing each other admiring them and ourselves. The photographs turned out to be like most amateur snapshots of fishing catches—the fish were white from overexposure and didn't look as big as they actually were and the fishermen looked self-conscious as if some
(30) guide had to catch the fish for them.

However, one closeup picture of him at the end of this day remains in my mind, as if fixed by some chemical bath. Usually, just after he finished fishing he had little to say unless he saw he could have fished better. Otherwise, he merely smiled. Now flies danced around his hatband. Large drops of water ran from under his hat on to his face and then into his lips when he smiled.

(35) At the end of this day, then, I remember him both as a distant abstraction in artistry and as a closeup in water and laughter.

My father always felt shy when compelled to praise one of his family, and his family always felt shy when he praised them. My father said, "You are a fine fisherman."

My brother said, "I'm pretty good with a rod, but I need three more years before I can think like a fish."

(40)   Remembering that he had caught his limit by switching to George's No. 2 Yellow Hackle with a feather wing, I said without knowing how much I said, "You already know how to think like a dead stone fly."

We sat on the bank and the river went by. As always, it was making sounds to itself, and now it made sounds to us. It would be hard to find three men sitting side by side who knew better what a river was saying.

Question 3

(Suggested time—40 minutes. This question counts toward one-third of the total free-response section score.)

Directions: Although most people have a need to fit in, anyone might end up feeling like an outcast, a loner, at some time in life. In many works of literature, a character, for some reason, becomes alienated or isolated from family, friends, some group, or society in general. Some literary characters find a means to reunite and rejoin their group, some change their values, and some strike out on a new solitary path to learn who they truly are.

Either from your own reading or from the list below, choose a character who becomes alienated from others in some way. Then write a well-written essay in which you analyze the source of the character's alienation, how alienation affects the character, and how it adds to an interpretation of the work as a whole. Do not merely summarize the plot.

In your response you should do the following:

- Respond to the prompt with a thesis that presents an interpretation and may establish a line of reasoning.
- Select and use evidence to develop and support your line of reasoning.
- Explain the relationship between the evidence and your thesis.
- Use appropriate grammar and punctuation in communicating your argument.

1984

Atonement

The Awakening

Black Boy

Crime and Punishment

The Crossing

The Crucible

The Curious Incident of the Dog in the Night-Time

Ethan Frome

Family Life

Great Expectations

The Great Gatsby

The Heart Is a Lonely Hunter

Heart of Darkness

Invisible Man

King Lear

The Kite Runner

A Lesson Before Dying

Of Mice and Men

Middlesex

Oliver Twist

The Poisonwood Bible

A Portrait of the Artist as a Young Man

Silas Marner

The Sound and the Fury

The Story of Edgar Sawtelle

The Sun Also Rises

The Tempest

Tess of the D'Urbervilles

A Thousand Acres

When We Were Orphans

White Oleander

IF YOU FINISH BEFORE TIME IS CALLED, CHECK YOUR WORK ON THIS SECTION ONLY. DO NOT WORK ON ANY OTHER SECTION IN THE TEST.

Answer Key

Section I: Multiple-Choice Questions

First Prose Passage	First Poem	Second Prose Passage	Second Poem	Third Poem
1. C	12. D	24. B	33. B	44. D
2. E	13. C	25. D	34. D	45. C
3. B	14. E	26. E	35. E	46. A
4. A	15. A	27. A	36. C	47. E
5. D	16. D	28. E	37. A	48. B
6. D	17. B	29. C	38. C	49. C
7. C	18. A	30. B	39. D	50. D
8. A	19. C	31. C	40. B	51. B
9. E	20. D	32. D	41. E	52. E
10. C	21. D		42. B	53. B
11. B	22. E		43. A	54. D
	23. B			55. A

Answers and Explanations

Section I: Multiple-Choice Questions

First Prose Passage

The excerpt for these questions comes from the novel Empire Falls, *written by Richard Russo in 2001. This scene takes place in the Empire Grill, where Miles Roby is the manager. Empire Falls, a fictional blue-collar town in Maine, has been economically downtrodden for decades.*

1. **C.** Referring to the Rexall drugstore as "the building next door" is ironic because the drugstore "had been condemned and razed," so there is no actual "building" next door, choice C, and thus, customers of the Empire Grill can now see "straight down Empire Avenue." Remember to focus on the specifics of the question, which in this case asks about the intended irony. The incorrect answer choices not only fail to explain any irony, but they are also wrong for other reasons. Choice A, the idea that the Empire Grill became more financially viable after the drugstore closed, has no evidence in the passage; no connection is made between the two establishments. Likewise, no explanation is offered for the demise of the drugstore; we do not know that bankruptcy caused its closure (B). Choice D assumes that the Empire Grill customers used to patronize the drugstore, but that idea, even if true, is irrelevant to this question about irony. Choice E is completely irrelevant to the question; whether or not the area needs a drugstore has nothing to do with the irony of referring to the now nonexistent drugstore as "the building next door."

2. **E.** This question requires that you focus on only the information in the first two paragraphs. They both support the idea that the Empire Grill customers are pessimistic about the future, choice E, because instead of looking up Empire Avenue, they habitually look down, symbolically, past the razed Rexall drugstore, toward the abandoned ruins of the old textile mill and shirt factory. The narrator even mentions that the view is a "dead-end." Notice that no one looks up the street; they only look down at the shells of previous prosperity, which further supports their pessimistic viewpoint. Choice A is incorrect because of the word "enjoy." The passage does not remotely suggest that customers enjoy the view at all. The first two paragraphs do not support that the customers have any faith in an upcoming economic turnaround, which makes choice B incorrect. Choice C, that the customers assume Miles will continue to manage the diner, has no evidence in

the passage. It is true that Miles hopes to buy it and then sell it "for what little it would bring," but that notion does not address this question. Choice D is unreasonable and contradictory. The first two paragraphs indicate no employment opportunities in the area, as the local factories closed decades ago.

3. B. Miles observes that people in Empire Falls seem to hope, against all odds and all reason, that a buyer will purchase the dilapidated mill and factory and eventually restore the town to its previous prosperity. They confuse past success with future prosperity, choice B. Choice A might seem plausible at first glance, but it's only partially correct, at best; it might be possible that some residents live in the past, but this answer fails to include the larger point, that they're also hoping for a better future. In choice C, the absolute word "always" is too strong; we have no indication that the narrator assumes humanity will *always* believe an economic recovery is coming. Choice D is unreasonable and misreads the passage. The narrator does mention that his generation followed certain conventions about carrying their school books that differ from the youth, but that is not the same as being conventional. Choice E is not supported by the narrator's thoughts; if anything, he appears to think that people have not changed with the times.

4. A. The drugstore "had been condemned and razed" and "nothing but a chain-link fence had gone up in place of the Rexall, which . . . divert[ed] one's attention" to the abandoned mill and factory. The physical building that once blocked the view is now gone, but the chain-link fence that now stands serves as a constant symbolic reminder of the deteriorating economy. Choice B is inaccurate because the fence is not a façade and it does not actually hide the reality. One can see through the fence to the abandoned structures down the street. Choice C makes no sense; the fence may physically restrain intruders from the property, but it is hardly a symbol of restraining ideas for improvement. The idea that the fence symbolizes high crime in the area (D) reads too much into the text, which never mentions crime at all. Choice E also reads too much into the image of the fence; it isn't a symbol of need for commercial development. Perhaps one could make a case for the razed building being such a symbol, but not the fence itself.

5. D. Miles believes the reason that today's school kids "stuffed the entire contents of their lockers" into a backpack was to circumvent having to think about what books they actually do need for homework, "thereby avoiding the kinds of decisions that might trail consequences." Therefore, choice D is correct. Miles never indicates that kids need more help from their parents than his generation did (A). Choice B tries to make the overloaded backpacks into a symbol of students' overloaded schedules, but that idea is not intimated in Miles' attitude. Choice C, that today's kids are disrespectful to adults, has no evidence in the passage. Perhaps Miles believes that the bad economy forces kids to grow up too quickly (E), but the text does not offer support for this idea.

6. D. The phrase "treated to the sight," followed shortly by the word "happily," might, in isolation, indicate something positive is coming, but in context, this phrasing is intended to be sarcastic, as Walt Comeau is the last person Miles wants to see; the phrasing is an example of situational irony, choice D. The idea that Miles was "treated to the sight" of Walt is not a paradox, nor is it ambiguous (A). Choice B is inaccurate because Miles is not confused; he knows immediately that Walt is brazenly parking his ostentatious van right in front of the diner. The idea in choice C contradicts the text entirely; Miles clearly dislikes Walt and is not optimistic about Walt's arrival. Choice E is off base; Miles' being "treated to the sight" of Walt's arrival is not exaggerated, nor is it an example of mockery.

7. C. The fact that Miles apparently detests Walt, so much so that Walt has negatively haunted Miles' daily thoughts and his dreams "for the past year," indicates that they have had a contentious background, choice C. But why, we do not know. Because of that uncertainty, choice A is too specific; this passage does not suggest that a romantic triangle is the reason for Miles' enmity toward Walt. Given the intensity of Miles' animosity, it is unreasonable to conclude that Miles previously respected Walt (B). The passage offers no clue about Walt's profession, so we have no reason to think the two men may be business competitors (D). Finally, we have no evidence of whether or not Walt's economic status is superior (E), or if that is the reason for Miles' animosity toward him.

8. A. To understand this question, think about the traditional definition of bathos: It occurs as a sudden shift from high and lofty thoughts and/or language into trivial absurdities. Now, look closely at the text and the question. What Miles *wants* to do to Walt is "grab an axe handle, meet the Silver Fox at the door and stave his head in right there in the entryway." Spur-of-the-moment homicide, how grim! But what actually happens next? Miles "turned back to the grill and flipped Horace Weymouth's burger, wondering if he'd already left it on too long." Although Miles' murderous thoughts cannot be described as lofty, the stark descent into his trivial action of flipping burgers is a form of bathos, choice A. Choice B might entice some students who use the phrase "appearances versus reality" to describe conflict in literature, but it does not apply to this question about the difference between Miles' thoughts and his actions. Choice C makes no sense; the passage has no juxtaposition between any object and any desire. Choice D is equally illogical; explaining Miles' motives cannot address the difference between his thoughts and actions. Choice E is too strong, too absolute; it is not really a contradiction of character to wish one thing but act differently.

9. **E.** Horace Weymouth is astute: He understands Miles cooked his burger too long and also that Miles should go to see Mrs. Whiting. He is also picky: He "liked his burgers bloody" and notices that Miles should have turned it earlier. And he is also supportive: He counsels Miles to go to Mrs. Whiting, believing that he deserves to "inherit Empire Falls." Therefore, choice E is correct. In choice A, all three adjectives are inaccurate; Horace is hardly indifferent (he does care about Miles), he's not flippant (he speaks politely), nor is he impetuous (he is not rash or impulsive). In choice B, the term "globally aware" has no evidence in the text; he reads the *Boston Globe,* but that does not mean he's aware of the wider world. Choice C has two incorrect terms: While Horace does seem sincere, he is not demanding, nor is he self-serving. Choice D is inaccurate because of the terms "well-read" and "informative," neither of which we can verify; it appears Horace is temperate, which means to be calm and mild.

10. **C.** It appears Mrs. Whiting controls Empire Falls, choice C, if not entirely, at least to a large degree, since Horace remarks that Miles should not wait "to be summoned" by her, because if anyone is going to "inherit Empire Falls," Miles Roby is most deserving. It is too much of a stretch to infer that she favors Miles (A); we have no indication of any closeness in their relationship. Choice B is also too strong in claiming she commands great obedience; it appears Miles would go see her if she summoned him, but that is not the same as being commanded to obey. Choice D has no basis in the text; we simply have no idea what Mrs. Whiting may or may not know about Miles' past. Finally, choice E might be true, but we do not know if she actually owns the Empire Grill.

11. **B.** Miles appears to be somewhat passive in nature, observing life from inside the diner and taking no risks, choice B. He does not choose to go directly to Mrs. Whiting unless she summons him. Choice A might be reasonable if taken out of context; perhaps Miles chooses to avoid Mrs. Whiting, but we know he will go if asked, and Horace advises him to take the initiative. Choice C is unreasonable; nothing in Miles' response to Horace suggests that he is choosing to ignore what Horace says. Choice D is inaccurate; the passage offers no evidence that Miles has any inappropriate feelings for Mrs. Whiting. Choice E is another idea that has no real basis in the text. It may be possible that the reason Miles has not gone directly to Mrs. Whiting is that he values social customs over personal gain, but we cannot find any phrasing in the text to specifically support that idea.

First Poem

The poem for these questions is "To S. M., a Young African Painter, on Seeing His Works," written by Phillis Wheatley and published in 1773. Phillis Wheatley was a slave to the Wheatley family in Boston, who were so enlightened that they taught her to read several languages and encouraged her to study the classics and pursue her talent for writing poetry. This poem was inspired by and dedicated to Scipio Moorhead, another slave who was also a poet and an artist. Fortunately, Mr. Moorhead was also "owned" by an enlightened man, a Presbyterian minister, who encouraged his artistic endeavors. Moorhead drew the portrait of Wheatley that is used in her only published book of poems. In this perceptive portrait she is sitting, pen in hand, looking wistfully upward as if she is looking for inspiration. Wheatley's high opinion of the portrait is the opening subject of the poem.

12. **D.** The speaker is impressed with the artist's ability to capture the "deep intent / And thought" of living characters and somehow, through the artistry of his drawing, he transfers those inner thoughts to the figure in his drawing, choice D. Choice A may sound attractive on first read, but the "lab'ring bosom" refers to the subject of the painting, not to how hard the artist worked. Choice B contradicts the description of the portrait; the subject shows deep thoughts, not delight at the world. Choice C has no basis in the poem; it never mentions or alludes to others in the art community. Choice E misunderstands details from the poem. While it is true that paint is mentioned in line 2 and pencils are mentioned in line 3, these two minor details are not what most impress the speaker.

13. **C.** All of the details in lines 1–6 describe the speaker's reaction to seeing her portrait, choice C. The speaker, the subject of the portrait, sees the finished work and she is struck by how lifelike the artist's rendering is, giving breath and capturing her thoughts. As she sees the "new creation," it gives her "soul delight."

The poem never addresses any struggles in the artist, which makes choice A incorrect. Choice B inaccurately assumes the public has seen the artist's work, and they have offered an opinion of it. Choice D is too limited and does not address all six lines in the question. While it is true that the speaker refers to some details in the painting such as the subject's "deep intent / And thought," the descriptions are not really explicit or specific; they refer more to the way the artist had captured the subject's emotions. The first six lines offer so much more than description of specific details in the portrait; most importantly, these lines clarify the speaker's reaction to seeing her portrait. Choice E is a generic response; the poem as a whole alludes to the importance of art in the world, but this poem focuses more attention on the artists who are doing the creating, not so much on the significance of their creations.

14. E. The poem does not include elegiac praise, choice E. Remember that the term "elegy" always refers to a mournful poem that attempts to reconcile someone's death, which is obviously not the subject of this poem. The other poetic devices do appear in this poem. The entire poem is written in heroic couplets (A); every two lines of iambic pentameter do rhyme (a few are slant rhymes) and contain a complete thought. The poem also contains multiple metaphors (B) such as "the shades of time" and "that splendid city." Classical allusions (C) can be found in the references to Damon and Aurora. Finally, the poem has many sentence inversions (D) such as "When first thy pencil did those beauties give" and "May peace with balmy wings your soul invest." Don't miss the fact that the question asks what is *not* used in the poem, so all of the incorrect responses *will* be present in the poem.

15. A. In the process of creating a painting, a gifted artist breathes life into the figures and his art also imitates life by creating realistic portraitures, choice A. Choice B posits an inaccurate idea, claiming that the quotation in the question symbolizes the artist's need for living subjects; rather, this quotation deals with the way the artist paints life into figures on canvas, not his need for live subjects. Choice C is an off-the-wall idea; the quotation refers to the artist's creation, not to the speaker's life or whatever role art plays in it. Choice D misstates the flow of ideas in the poem; the image of artists creating lifelike paintings is consistent with the lines that follow, not contradictory. Choice E is an unreasonable interpretation of the line in question; this quote does not compare the poet and the artist.

16. D. In a poem that is full of ethereal and positive connotations, the words "fire" and "conspire" stand out because of their potentially negative connotations, which might imply that this poet and artist can use their talents to create art that helps to overcome the negative aspects of their lives, choice D. Considering that, in this poem, the poet and the artist are both slaves, it is not unreasonable to think they might have such a motive. Choice A is too strong and goes too far; while suggesting that the artist and the poet might conceivably join forces to fight oppression, there is no hint that they would engage in subversive behavior. Choice B is an odd jumble of ideas; the point that "fire" is a visual image is accurate, but claiming that the artist needs to combine visuals with "words" makes little or no sense. Choice C takes the wrong focus; it is too overarching and too strong. Notice the questionable phrasing; the absolute term "all artists" that, when combined with the idea that artists need "something intense for inspiration," feeds into a stereotype that is not supported in the poem. Choice E is banal and simplistic; "fire" is an element (whether or not it provides motivation), but "conspire" is a verb, not a motivating element.

17. B. To understand how lines 13–14 serve as a transition in the poem's thought process, choice B, you must consider the overall organization of ideas. Lines 1–6 describe the speaker seeing her portrait and the pleasure it brings. In lines 7–12, the speaker encourages the painter and the poet to continue using their artistic gifts to create immortal works of art. Then in lines 13–14, the vision moves to the skies, to the heavens, as the speaker directs "raise thy wishful eyes" and "Elate thy soul." From there, lines 15–22 describe what the poet/artist surveys in heaven, as if it were a first-person point of view of "that splendid city," where their muse will continue to inspire. Line 23 moves from this vision of the heavens back down to an earthly point of view, but the transition is so subtle that it may be overlooked. Whereas lines 15–22 seem to be a first-person view of heaven, lines 23–32 pose many questions: what wings, what landscapes, what tongues? This indicates that the speaker is back on earth, questioning heaven from afar. Choice A incorrectly claims the lines in question form a command. Choice C is clearly incorrect; lines 13–14 are not an instance of the poet's inspiration; rather, the lines urge one to look to the heavens. Choice D is incorrect for a similar reason: These lines do not form a hopeful plea. Choice E might trick some readers because the phrase "immortal fame" immediately precedes the lines in the question; however, lines 13–14 do not envision what immortal fame will bring.

18. **A.** Lines 15–18 illustrate the spirituality that good artists can attain through the act of artistic creation, choice A; they are blessed to survey the heavens that have endless spring, and they glide serenely, inspired by their muse to create future works. Choice B misses the mark because it only deals with the hope for heavenly reward, but in this poem the gifted artists actually achieve such bliss on earth. Choice C posits an unreasonable contradiction; endless day and endless spring *can* both exist together in heaven. Choice D is irrelevant to this question; lines 15–18 do not present the idea that heavenly vision will sustain the artist in life. Choice E may sound attractive—according to the poem, artists will get angelic inspiration in heaven—but that idea is not in lines 15–18; it appears in later lines.

19. **C.** In this transition, the word "But" signals a shift in the poem's focus. The previous visions take place above the earth, up in the heavens, but in line 23, the speaker chases away the "shades of time" and shifts to an earthly perspective, choice C. She then speculates about future inspirations while looking up to "the realms above." Choice A is incorrect because the poem does not imply that the artist needs to find inspiration in worldly matters; instead, the speaker wonders what angels' wings will provide a view to the realms above. Choice B is just plain wrong. You can quickly eliminate this unreasonable answer choice because line 23 does not propose any alternative stimulation. Choice D is too much of a stretch; it may be argued that the speaker addresses philosophical issues, but line 23 certainly does not begin that discussion. Choice E is irrelevant; whether or not the speaker's and artist's visions are united does not answer this question.

20. **D.** In lines 25–26 the speaker wonders what angels' wings will help them "view the landscapes in the realms above." Thus, she must be looking up to the heavens from the earth below. This contrasts with the vision in lines 15–16, in which they are in heaven, surveying the splendid city, choice D. Choice A is incorrect because the "new creation" of line 6 refers to the speaker's portrait and does not contrast with the couplet in the question. Choice B also indicates the wrong subject; in line 8 the speaker suggests the artist focus his "ardent view" on "deathless glories" that will turn into immortal art. This idea does not contrast lines 25–26. Choice C also discusses how the artist's heralded themes will conduct his footsteps to "immortal fame", but, like choice B, these lines do not provide a contrast. Choice E simply references a wish for peace in the artist's soul; it does not contrast looking up to the heavens.

21. **D.** Lines 27–32 discuss how, once in heaven, the poet will no longer need to write on mundane worldly topics, such as Damon's sighs, but instead will explore "nobler themes" with "purer language on th' ethereal plain," choice D. Choice A may sound nice, and it is true that some classical poets explored the landscapes of heaven in their works, but this concept does not answer this question. Choice B also sounds enticing; being rewarded with entrance to heaven is a common theme in Western literature and religion, but it does not address the lines in this question. Choice C misunderstands the sentence in the question, incorrectly thinking that it refers to life on earth when it really refers to the afterlife. Choice E is similar to choice B; one may agree that the speaker deserves the rewards of heaven, but this kind notion is not imbued in lines 27–32.

22. **E.** The last couplet ironically changes the tone of the poem. The first 32 lines are wistful, spiritual, and uplifting, but in the last two lines the speaker urges her muse to "cease" because night's darkness keeps her from seeing "the fair creation," choice E. This change of tone is quite unexpected after such elevated style and exemplary diction. Choice A, the idea that the speaker will find inspiration in the future, misreads these last two lines and, even if the idea in this answer choice were true, it would not be ironic. Choice B is incorrect because the poem does not indicate whether or not the "gloom of night" will continue; as individuals, we may hope not, but that idea is not found in the poem. Choice C reads too much into the poem; there is no support for the idea that the speaker cannot match the artist's greatness. We do have proof of both the poet's and the artist's greatness in the poem, which contradicts choice C. Choice D is another misread of the last lines; although the speaker asks her muse to cease, that does not necessarily mean that she has lost her muse, nor do we know if she laments it.

23. **B.** The poem provides ample evidence that the speaker feels good art will last, bringing "immortal fame" and also the spiritual rewards of "seraphic theme," choice B. Artists will be exalted in life, and they will be serene, even in death. Choice A can be dismissed as irrelevant; whether or not classical art has divine inspiration is immaterial to this question. Choice C may be a common notion in society; we like to think that art can help ease worldly suffering, but this poem does not address that concept. The same objection applies to choice D; the poem does not deal with whether or not good artists help others with their skills. Plus, even if this idea were true, the concept does not answer a question such as this, which asks about the

speaker's evaluation of art, not of artists. Choice E may also be true, but it is also irrelevant; poets and painters do indeed produce worthy art, but that concept does not address this question.

Second Prose Passage

The passage for these questions comes from Night and Day, *written in 1918 by Virginia Woolf. The setting is the upper-class drawing room of the Hilbery family during a Sunday evening social tea party.*

24. B. The fact that Katharine only uses "Perhaps a fifth of her mind" to serve the guests implies that she is quite accustomed to this role, serving tea to the guests in her family's home, choice B; she does not need to focus intense concentration to complete her duties. Remember that in a hidden-level question such as this one, the best answer will be the choice that is most obvious. Choice A, that she carefully watches her mother for social clues, has no support in the passage; indeed, Katharine hardly acknowledges her mother until she reminds her of Mr. Denham's name. Choice C is too strong in implying Katharine resents her social duties; her mind may not be entirely engaged with pouring the tea, but that does not indicate that her attitude is quite so negative. Choice D is too far-fetched; while it may be possible that Katharine represents others of her age, the passage does not suggest any similarities with other girls. In choice E, the word "graciously" is too strong. We only know that Katharine is quite proficient at serving tea; we do not know if her attitude and bearing are gracious.

25. D. The "little barrier of day" is a metaphor for how central this Sunday evening tea time is to Katharine; it's a genteel, civilized moment when she serves her mother's guests, choice D. The rest of the days of the week are merely a minor inconvenience, when she will go about "the things one does voluntarily and normally in the daylight," until Sunday tea time comes again. Choice A begins with an accurate phrase: The "little barrier" is indeed a minor obstacle; however, this barrier does not grow over time. Choice B may seem attractive, but the barrier is not a symbolic reminder of her duty to family; rather it is a metaphor for tea time. She needs no reminder, and instead four-fifths of her brain "leapt over the little barrier of day." Choice C is too strong; the "little barrier" is only in Katharine's mind and it is a minor thought in passing that does not contrast with the tea party's atmosphere. Choice E contradicts the passage, which does not present any conflict for Katharine. Rather, we only know that she helps her mother at tea time.

26. E. Katharine's characterization seems to indicate that she performs her duties in a mechanical manner, choice E, almost like an automaton. Notice how she is labeled in cold, mathematical terms: She only uses "a fifth part of her mind" because she is performing these duties "for the six hundredth time." She lets her mind wander as she goes through the all-too-familiar mechanical and repetitive motions of serving tea. You can use your elimination skills on the other choices. The passage offers no evidence that she ignores her guests (A); in fact, she dutifully fulfills the task of discharging "teacups and bread and butter." Choice B, that Katharine rejects the social standards of her class, likewise has no support in the passage. We simply do not know enough about her social attitudes. In choice C, the word "resents" is too strong. Do not be fooled by the phrase "tiresome business," as it refers to Mrs. Hilbery's attitude toward the mechanics of serving tea, not to Katharine's. Choice D simply has no evidence; we do not know if Katharine hopes to someday have her mother's social graces.

27. A. Mrs. Hilbery is socially adept and makes her guests comfortable, choice A. The proof of Mrs. Hilbery's social poise can be found in the way that her guests converse so easily within just a few minutes of being seated, which is described as "very creditable to the hostess," and it also appears in the manner in which she includes Mr. Denham in the ongoing conversation once he arrives. We also know that a "single glance" is ample to show that she is "so rich in the gifts which make tea-parties . . . successful." Choice B may seem reasonable at first glance, but it is too absolute in claiming that Mrs. Hilbery relegates *all* hostess duties to Katharine; although Mrs. Hilbery has Katharine pour the tea and provide bread and butter, it is the mother who guides the conversation, the primary task of the hostess, and a "single glance" is ample to show that "she scarcely needed any help from her daughter." The passage offers no evidence that Mrs. Hilbery feels Katharine needs more training in social skills than she already has (C); it appears Katharine is already quite proficient in these social graces. Choice D is unreasonable because of the word "resents." According to the passage, Mrs. Hilbery appears to enjoy her social status, and the passage offers no evidence that she resents the demands placed on ladies of their class. Choice E is an unfounded inference and makes little sense. It claims Mrs. Hilbery values her guests more than social propriety, social decorum, but all who are present at the tea party demonstrate proper manners and we see no higher value placed on guests.

28. **E.** To appreciate Katharine's understanding of social mores, pay close attention to her thoughts. She silently performs her duties while musing that if someone were to come into the room, "he would think that they were enjoying themselves" and that he had come into a very agreeable house. As she ponders this idea, "instinctively she laughed, and said something to increase the noise, for the credit of the house presumably." The irony lies in the fact that "she herself had not been feeling exhilarated," making choice E correct. Choice A simply points out that Katharine was pouring tea, as did other young ladies of her class; it does not involve irony. Choice B does not answer the question because this quotation deals with Katharine's wandering thoughts as she serves tea, thinking about the things she will do during the days of the week; this is not ironic, nor is it relevant to social appearances. The quotation in choice C addresses Katharine's proficiency and ease at serving tea, something very familiar to her, but it is not ironic. Choice D is off topic because the quotation refers to Mrs. Hilbery, not Katharine. The fact that Mrs. Hilbery finds the mechanics of serving tea "tiresome" does not indicate irony.

29. **C.** To address this question, look into the details of the second paragraph. The party is established as an amiable one; then Katharine suddenly muses how a newcomer to the room would appreciate how much the guests are enjoying themselves. She next laughs as Mr. Denham simultaneously enters. As she welcomes him, she mentally asks him if he thinks "we're enjoying ourselves enormously," as if she needs verification and confirmation of her previous thoughts, choice C. Choice A begins with a reasonable phrase about Katharine desiring outside verification, but this answer choice is off base, claiming she wants verification of her social class; she instead wants some reassurance of the party's convivial atmosphere. Choice B is unreasonable; although she does not ask the question aloud, it is a stretch to conclude that the reason is because she does not want to hear his potential answer. Choice D is irrelevant because she never asks the question out loud, and her query has nothing to do with making Mr. Denham socially acceptable. It deals with her internal need for confirmation. Choice E is also unreasonable because her imaginary question is completely unrelated to Mr. Denham's ability to join in the ongoing conversation.

30. **B.** As soon as Mr. Denham arrives, he is uncomfortably aware that Mrs. Hilbery does not remember his name. As the lone stranger among the other guests, he feels awkward as they "all launched upon sentences." At that moment, he imagines "a thousand softly padded doors had closed between him and the street outside," which effectively embodies the guests' insulation from the outside world of the city streets, choice B. They are shielded from that reality by the symbolic "thousand softly padded doors." It is unreasonable to infer that Mr. Denham actually feels trapped in the new surroundings (A); if, perhaps, the doors were described as padlocked, dead bolted, or chained shut, he might feel trapped, but rather the soft padding insulates those inside from the noises of the street. Choice C presents too much of a reach; if one looks at the quotation in isolation, it might be possible to think that he enjoys the new surroundings, but within the passage as a whole, he feels uncomfortable and out of place. Choice D is unreasonable; the passage offers no evidence that the other guests object to his presence at the party, and his entrance is barely an intrusion; after all, as soon as he sits down, they all resume talking. The idea that he immediately regrets attending (E) is not justified by his thoughts that occur as he enters (lines 45–47), although it is true that he later "cursed himself very sharply for having exchanged the freedom of the street for this sophisticated drawing-room."

31. **C.** To answer this question about imagery, notice the auditory imagery of the passage; the guests converse easily and collectively produce a quite large "amount of sound." Later they "all launched upon sentences" after Mr. Denham arrives. This imagery of human conversation that dominates the indoor landscape is contrasted with the outdoor auditory imagery as Mr. Denham recalls the industrial sounds of omnibuses, cabs, and traffic, choice C. Inside the drawing room all sounds come from human voices; but outside in the streets all sounds come from machines. Choice A is an odd answer choice because Katharine's thoughts are not an example of imagery, and the guests' thoughts are never mentioned; this answer choice simply does not address the question. Choice B is not supported by the passage, which never describes the appearance of either Mr. Denham or the other guests. Choice D may mislead some readers, but it is ultimately a weak answer choice. While it is true that the guests do produce an "amount of sound," we do not know if it can really be described as loud chatter. Additionally, the passage does not dwell on any silence that follows Mr. Denham's arrival: He enters, some momentary awkwardness ensues, but then the other guests "all launched upon sentences," not continued silence. Choice E is not supported by the passage. While one can assume the guests are of the upper class and perhaps carry an attitude associated with that class, the passage has absolutely no hint of the outdoor pedestrians' attitude or their class. We cannot assume they are of the lower class just because they are walking in the streets.

32. **D.** Mr. Denham's attitude is neatly summed up in the last sentence of the passage when he glances around the room and sees the collective age, excepting Katharine, as "all over forty," but finds consolation in the fact that Mr. Fortescue "was a considerable celebrity" and he "might be glad to have met him." The implication is clearly that Mr. Denham believes he might be able to make some future use of knowing Mr. Fortescue, thus suggesting that he is opportunistic, choice D. On the other hand, the passage does not indicate that Mr. Denham is optimistic (A); instead, he "cursed himself very sharply" for attending and he uncomfortably perceives that Mrs. Hilbery has forgotten his name. He also shows no signs of being sarcastic (B); he appears to be respectful, albeit quiet, and offers only a "muttered" contribution to the conversation, "which was indeed all that was required of him." Choice C, indifferent, is too negative a description; Mr. Denham is not portrayed as apathetic or uninterested. Choice E, charitable, is too positive, as Mr. Denham does not demonstrate generosity or kindness.

Second Poem

The poem for these questions is "The Season of Phantasmal Peace" written by Derek Walcott, a Caribbean writer. Walcott's first poem was published in a local newspaper in 1944 when he was 14. He won the Nobel Prize for Literature in 1992.

33. **B.** In the first line, "all the nations of birds" refers metaphorically to all of the innumerable cultures of the earth, choice B. The poem mentions wild geese, ospreys, starlings, ravens, killdeer, and choughs, which are birds from many disparate locations around the globe. They have "multitudinous dialects" and "twittering tongues," which is a reference to the multiplicity of humanity's languages, and therefore to all of their cultures. This figure of speech is not a metaphor for like-minded people flocking together, as in choice A; the poem never indicates that the birds think alike or have the same mindset. Choice C makes little sense within the context of the poem; it is true that the birds collectively fly above the earth, perhaps even above conflict, but the phrase "all the nations of birds" is not a metaphor for their ability to do so. Choice D claims that the phrase is a metaphor for individuals who see clearly, but it is a stretch with little evidence in the poem; the phrase refers to different cultures, not individuals. Choice E is equally far-fetched, thinking that the phrase represents those who hope to find a way to join together disparate groups.

34. **D.** The alliteration in line 3, "twittering tongues," imitates the sounds that birds make, and in this context, the birds represent the sounds of the "multitudinous dialects," or mankind's many languages, choice D. The repetition of the "t" sound is suggestive of the actual sound of many birds. In choice A, the word "euphonious," which refers to pleasant, mellifluous sounds, is contradicted by the sound the birds make; the sound of twittering is not similar to a murmur. Choice B is inaccurate because the repeated "t" in the alliteration is not a relaxed sound; it cannot slow the pace of the poem. Choice C begins with an accurate idea stating that the alliteration creates harsh sounds, but then the answer choice goes astray by claiming that these sounds contrast the birds' normal songs. Choice E is unreasonable; the sound of the alliteration cannot contradict the birds' actions.

35. **E.** In the first stanza, "all the nations of birds" represent all the cultures of the world, and they collectively lift "the huge net of the shadows of this earth." The shadows, symbolic of darkness and negativity, are bound together in the net as the birds fly the net high into the soundless night until "there was no longer dusk, or season . . . / only this passage of phantasmal light / that not the narrowest shadow dared to sever." The negativity of the earth has been transported away in the net, choice E. Choice A contradicts the first stanza; the birds fly away with mankind's sorrows; they do not add more sorrow. The poem is hopeful for peace, but answer choice A is too strong and absolute. Choice B is unreasonable; the poem offers no hint that nature will come to dominate mankind; the idea of such control is not implied in the first stanza. Choice C falls apart with the last phrase, "the light of mankind." The birds fly away with "the shadows of this earth," not with the light. Choice D, claiming that phantasmal light covers the globe, might seem attractive; however, this is not established in the first stanza. We do not learn that it covers "this world" until the second stanza.

36. **C.** The "soundless" and "seasonless" phantasmal light represents the birds' "seasonal passing, Love" and peace that covers "this world." The phantasmal light originates in the first stanza and expands to cover the globe in the second, choice C. Choice A misinterprets what the phantasmal light means; while the image of light frequently symbolizes knowledge in literature, it is not true in this case. The last phrase of this answer, "that mankind will eventually comprehend," is also questionable because it is too absolute. Choice B is the type of answer that sounds nice philosophically; it is pleasing to think that mankind needs the desire for unity, but that concept is not what the phantasmal light represents. Choice D states that the light represents the moment between fury and peace, but this idea is stated in the third stanza, not the second, and it is not destroyed by mankind. Choice E contradicts the poem; the phantasmal light does not intensify the darkness on earth; rather, the birds fly away with the darkness, allowing mankind to see the light of peace.

37. **A.** "Men could not see . . . what the wild geese drew," which is the gigantic net that holds all of humanity's sorrows being carried high into the sky, choice A. Choice B, "the narrowest shadow," does not identify what men could not see; rather, it represents the shadow that cannot sever the phantasmal light. Choice C might distract some test-takers who read too quickly. They might gloss over the phrasing and see "men could not see" in line 12 and then "the icy sunlight" in line 14. However, the icy sunlight is actual sunlight reflecting off of the "silvery ropes" of the birds' net; these are the ropes that men cannot see, not the sunlight. Choice D is inaccurate because it is the cries of the battalions of starlings that men cannot hear, not something they cannot see. Choice E is incorrect because the vines are part of an elaborate simile for the net that covers the world; it is not something that men cannot see.

38. **C.** The phrase "it was the light" is deliberately set apart from the third stanza, and it separates the peaceful light "that you will see at evening on the side of a hill" in autumn and distinguishes it from the darkness on earth. The line is technically the completion of the previous line that ends stanza two, but this phrase, which begins the third stanza, is rightfully and symbolically separated. Choice A makes little sense; the light in this poem has little to do with mankind having a closed mind that needs opening. Choice B, which claims the placement of the phrase emphasizes the ephemeral nature of sunlight, might be attractive until one studies it more. Sunlight is not necessarily ephemeral or short-lived; after all, the sun shines all day, but this is irrelevant to the placement of the phrase in this question. Choice D contradicts the poem's meaning; the light, "like the pause / between dusk and darkness, between fury and peace," is indeed real for "one moment" that "lasted long." Thus, it is not unattainable. Choice E is simply incorrect; the imagery of the light is consistent with the imagery of the rest of the poem, and the placement of this phrase does not clash with that imagery.

39. **D.** Birds have "the high privilege" of being able to fly free, above the "wingless ones / below them who shared dark holes." They can fly above the problems of the world, choice D. Choice A is unrelated to the poem; it's not about the animal kingdom, nor any supposed hierarchy of honor that places animals over mankind. Choice B might sound attractive philosophically, but it, too, is irrelevant to this poem. It confuses the birds' "high privilege" of flying with people who are born into high status in life. The birds may be trying to help mankind, and we do hope those with status might help others less fortunate, but it simply does not connect to the poem. Also incorrect is the absolute word "should." Choice C is too much of a stretch that bears little significance to the poem and is an incorrect absolute idea; it is ludicrous and contrary to the human condition to think that someday all people will have high status and need no pity. Choice E is too simplistic; it takes the words "privilege" and "birth" from the quotation in the question and tries to apply them inappropriately.

40. **B.** The two oxymoronic phrases in this question, "cries soundless" and "soundless voices," directly contrast the noise of "twittering tongues," choice B. The cries and voices of the birds are soundless because the birds have flown so high that their sounds don't reach the earth. However, the twittering sound the birds make contrasts with the soundless cries and voices. Choice A is incorrect because the birds are described as the "nations of birds," and their sound does not contrast with that. Choice C, "soundless at night," does not indicate a contrast; rather, it reinforces the lack of sound. In choice D, "fields and cities" refers to the location "where the birds belong," and it has no connection to sound. Choice E, "dusk and darkness," refers to the brief moment when the phantasmal light can be seen. It, too, has no relation to sound.

41. **E.** Remember that in this type of question, the correct answer choice will be the only one that is NOT in the poem; all of the incorrect answer choices are somewhere in the poem. This poem does not have any internal rhymes, choice E, which occur when a word in the middle of a line rhymes either with a word at the end of the same line or with a word in the following line. Examples include the witches' famous utterance in *Macbeth*, "Double, double, toil and trouble." But Walcott's poem is written in free verse, so it has no regular meter or rhyme at all. Choice A is incorrect because the poem does include more than one metaphor, such as "the nations of birds" and "the huge net of the shadows." It also contains parallel construction (B) in such phrasing as "the shadows of long pines down trackless slopes / the shadows of glass-faced towers down evening streets /

the shadows of a frail plant on a city sill." Choice C, simile, is evidenced in "like the vines of an orchard, or a mother . . ." and "like the pause / between dusk and darkness." Choice D, oxymoron, shows up in phrases such as "icy sunlight" and "soundless voices." The poem also has ample alliteration and personification.

42. B. The poem as a whole deals with the hope for peace on earth, and the speaker's overall point is that peace is possible, choice B. The birds indeed lift the "shadows of this earth" to reveal "this passage of phantasmal light" that cannot be severed by "the narrowest shadow." Choice A is off base; the poem is not about learning compatibility, harmony, or unity *from* birds; the avian creatures reveal the phantasmal light, but they do not teach us. Choice C misunderstands the end of the poem. While it is true that "this season [of Love] lasted one moment," that moment "lasted long." The absolute idea that peace will never last is incorrect. Choice D wrongly states that mankind needs to look to the heavens to glean knowledge. Although the birds fly high, the speaker is not referring to heaven, and it is not knowledge per se that mankind needs. Choice E contradicts the poem. Darkness and light do not coexist peacefully; there is a fine line between them.

43. A. The poem implies that mankind is metaphorically blinded by "the huge net of the shadows" representing the evil that covers the world, but when the birds carry that net so high that men could no longer see it, they are no longer blinded by the shadows in the net. All that remains is the phantasmal light of peace. Mankind is not blinded by "the shadows of glass-faced towers" (B); instead, man lives among those shadows. Men are also not blinded by the phantasmal light, which represents peace (C); it's their own evil that blinds them to goodness. Choice D is incorrect because "the icy sunlight" does not blind mankind; it reflects the net the birds carry. Notice the "silvery ropes [of the net] . . . flashed in the icy sunlight." Choice E, "something brighter than pity," does not blind mankind; do not be misled by the word "brighter."

Third Poem

The poem for these questions, "Since there's no help, come let us kiss and part," was written by Michael Drayton. Originally published in 1594, it was the 61st sonnet in a progressive group of 64 sonnets, collectively titled Idea's Mirror.

44. D. The first line of the poem is a strong, imperative command as the speaker tells his soon-to-be ex-lover "Since there's no help, come let us kiss and part." It appears that their breakup is certain. However, by the end of the poem, in an ironic twist, the opposite is true; the speaker informs his beloved that their relationship can be saved if she wants to resurrect their love, choice D. He implies he'll be waiting and will run back to her arms if she wishes it. Choice A is completely wrong; it is uncertain if the lovers actually kiss and part in the beginning, and they certainly do not do so at the end. The poem offers no evidence for choice B; the speaker never suggests that he is culpable, blameworthy or at fault, for their breakup. Even if he were to blame himself, no irony is implied. Choice C also fails to identify the irony; we never know what the beloved is thinking, so she may or may not be glad to part from him. Choice E is too absolute, claiming the situation will reverse; we have no evidence that the lady actually tries to revive their love.

45. C. Given that the speaker initially appears to be so very over-confident with his brash and direct language, at least before he suddenly changes his tune later, it is reasonable to infer that he is actually trying to convince himself that he is doing the right thing, that he is actually glad that the relationship is over. Notice that the question asks which answer *might* explain his repetition, and choice C is a plausible idea, not necessarily the only one. The remaining answer choices do not offer reasonable explanations. Choice A incorrectly claims the speaker has a sardonic attitude, but he does not appear to be mocking or scornful toward his beloved. The idea presented in choice B is illogical; repeating an idea does not moderate or temper it; if anything, repeating an idea increases its emphasis. Choice D is unreasonable; we have no cause to doubt the speaker's sincerity, and he is not being facetious or flippant to his love. The idea in choice E may very well be true; it appears that the speaker is the one initiating the breakup, but the repetition of the word "glad" does not undermine this fact.

46. A. The word "vow" often has religious connotations; for example, when a couple is married within a religious institution, they repeat traditional vows that affirm their commitment to each other. The question asks what is suggested by the phrase "cancel our vows," which can easily intimate religious overtones in their relationship, choice A. However, it is too strong to claim that the couple is definitely married, choice B, because we simply do not have any evidence of that fact. Plus, if they can simply "shake hands" to cancel all their vows, it seems unlikely that they are legally wed. Choice C is off base and illogical; their handshake cannot negate or refute the love they previously shared. The idea in choice D makes little sense within the context of this poem; it seems very unlikely that the couple's love was only verbal, and if that were the case, they would not need to kiss and shake hands upon parting. Choice E might be attractive if one focuses only on the last couplet, in which the speaker hopes his lover might try to renew their love; however, that idea is irrelevant to this question, which refers only to the suggestion implied in the phrase "cancel all our vows" in line 5.

47. E. The imagery and personification presented in lines 9–12 suggest that the couple's relationship is bleak and hopeless, choice E. The speaker contemplates Love taking his last breath while his usual supporters can offer no help. Passion, the common companion of Love, lies speechless; Faith, always needed by lovers, is kneeling by his deathbed instead of standing tall; Innocence, often seen in the eyes of young lovers, is closing his own eyes forever. Examining all this compounded imagery, one cannot find any hope for the lover's relationship. Also, considering this unrelenting negativity, it is unreasonable to suggest that the couple simply try harder in their relationship (A). Choice B contradicts the text; Love dies because it cannot exist without Passion, Faith, and Innocence, not the other way around. Choice C is too strong; it seems to make a connection between two ideas, the death of love and the death of the speaker, but the poem never suggests the speaker will die without his love. Choice D is unwarranted; it is true that Love, Passion, Faith, and Innocence are abstract concepts, but they do not help to reconcile or resolve the speaker's loss of his lover.

48. B. In this instance, the word "Now" serves as a volta, a literary transition in thought, which is a traditional turn in the progression of a sonnet. In this poem, the volta "Now" moves the speaker's thoughts from his supposed satisfaction of leaving his lover to the abstract idea of Love dying, which in turn leads the speaker to hoping his lover will help to revive Love, choice B. Choice A makes no sense; this poem does not mention the passage of time, so the word "Now" is not meant to remind us of it. Choice C is incorrect; the word "Now" is not a conjunction and it does not join the previous lines; instead, it signals a transition to a new thought. Also, it is hard to make a case that this one word signals an ironic shift in the poem's tone, as stated in choice D. It is true that lines 9–12 collectively change the poem's tone, but it is not this single word that changes the tone, nor is the word meant to be ironic. Finally, the word "Now" in line 9 does not urge the beloved to take action (E); that occurs in lines 13–14.

49. C. To answer this question, it helps to paraphrase the progression of the speaker's thoughts. To paraphrase lines 1–4, he simply and brusquely states that "Our relationship can't be helped, so let's split up. I'm done with it and am really glad to be free." Lines 5–8 continue with similar thoughts, claiming that "we should just shake hands and ignore any past promises to each other. Whenever we meet again, let's agree to not show 'one jot of [our] former love.'" After the finality of these ideas, the speaker moves from first person into third person in lines 9–12 as he contemplates the death of Love, which no longer has the necessary support of Passion, Faith, or Innocence. At this point in the poem, the speaker offers no hope for their relationship; in other words, he is certain that their love is lost. Thus, choice C is the best answer. Choice A is unfounded; the beloved's feelings are never considered in the poem; instead, it is the speaker who dominates throughout. Choice B, that their passion will be revived with time, is likewise not supported in the poem. Do not be distracted by lines 13–14, in which the speaker suggests his beloved could try to reignite their love, if she wants; these lines do not address this question. Instead, reread the lines that immediately follow the speaker's demand that the parted lovers ignore their past feelings when seen in public. Choice D is fallacious; the concept of apathy is not addressed in the poem; do not confuse the speaker's apparent overconfidence in lines 1–8 with apathy or indifference. Choice E confuses the thought progression of the poem; the speaker renounces his lover in the early lines, only to reverse himself at the end. In any case, choice E is irrelevant because it does not address this specific question.

50. D. In line 11, Faith is personified as "kneeling by his bed of death," choice D, which is a metaphor for the speaker's fading belief in love. Without love, the speaker has nothing to have faith in, nothing to believe in. None of the other answer choices identifies a metaphor. Choice A, "glad with all my heart," is quite literal; the speaker does claim that he is truly happy to be rid of his beloved, although we later understand that he is only deceiving himself at this point. "Shake hands for ever" (B) is also literal; the speaker wants to end their relationship with a handshake. Choice C uses personification, showing how Passion lies (down), as if speechless without love, but this is not metaphorical. Choice E also uses personification; Innocence closes his eyes as Love is lost, but once again, this is not a metaphor.

51. B. The ironic twist in this poem deals with the way the speaker initiates the end of their relationship only to ironically do a turnabout in the last couplet and tell his beloved that she can reunite them, "if thou wouldst." In this interpretation, his demanding a breakup is, in reality, an unexpected, covert first step toward their possibly reuniting, choice B. As it turns out, his apparent desire to be rid of her was not his true desire all along. Choice A is implausible; the speaker's initial statements about the couple's breakup appear to be sincere, regardless of the fact that he reverses his position after envisioning the death of Love in lines 9–12. His statements in lines 1–8 certainly do not indicate that he already knows he wants his lover to take him back. Choice C is not corroborated in the poem; it misreads the speaker's words. He does not believe that she will beg him to reconsider dumping her; instead, he hopes she will choose to woo him to resurrect their love. Choice D is an off-the-wall idea that is irrelevant to this question. Whether or not a loveless life leads to death is unrelated to the speaker's statements about ending the relationship. Choice E is a misreading of the poem; the speaker does not immediately regret his actions; in fact, he technically has taken no action in the poem. He talks to his beloved, but he does not act.

52. E. In the first eight lines, the speaker uses imperative mood verbs more than once. He tells her to "come let us kiss and part" (line 1), "Shake hands [and] cancel all our vows" (line 5), and "Be it not seen . . . " (line 7). However, when he suggests that she revive their love, he changes to the subjunctive mood, saying "if thou wouldst" (line 13) and "thou might'st" (line 14). The subjunctive mood is used for statements that express a wish or for hypothetical comments; this change implies that the speaker is not entirely sure of his commanding imperative language in the first place and perhaps he hopes and wishes that his beloved can restore him, choice E. Choice A is too specific; the shift to subjunctive mood does not suggest he is trying to seduce his lover. Choice B is wrong on two counts; the imperative mood does not suggest that the speaker usually bosses his lover around, and the subjunctive does not remotely suggest that he is surprised or that he has weaknesses. Choice C is simply unreasonable; the shift in verb mood cannot suggest that the beloved will become dominant in their relationship. Choice D has no evidence in the poem; we have no idea whether or not they will reunite, but the verb shifts do not suggest such an idea in the first place. Be sure to understand exactly what a question is asking; the intent of this question is to understand how the verbal imperative mood and subjunctive mood add meaning to the poem.

53. B. The pronoun "him" in lines 13 and 14 refers to Love, choice B. The speaker, now changing to the second person, speaks directly to his beloved, essentially telling her "Don't give up on Love. Even though Passion, Faith, and Innocence have given up, there's still you! 'If thou wouldst,' Love can be saved; you 'might'st' recover him from death back to life." The pronoun "him" does not refer to the speaker (A), nor to Passion (C), Faith (D), or Innocence (E). If you try to substitute any of the wrong answer choices into the paraphrased summary just given, you'll see how they cannot fit.

54. D. When analyzing a character's attitude, consider the poem as a whole and look for changes in attitude. Remember that whenever you are asked a question about attitude and you are given answer choices with more than one word, at least one of the words will be inaccurate in all of the incorrect answers. In this poem, choice D is accurate because the speaker begins with the voice of authority and confidence, but we later realize he is really not all that sure of himself; therefore, his confidence is actually dubious. Also, lines 13–14 shift to cautious anticipation as he suggests his beloved try to revive Love, hoping it can happen. Therefore, choice D is correct. Choice A is inaccurate on all fronts; the speaker is not gently chiding or reprimanding his lover in the beginning, and he is not shrewdly manipulating or controlling her in the end. Choice B also has two inaccurate words; his attitude is not initially one of misery, and his later hope for her to revive their love is not skeptical. Choice C is questionable. The speaker seems sincere at first, but he is not presumptuous (this term is too strong), and uncertain curiosity is not accurate to describe his cautious optimism. Choice E might initially strike one as possibly being accurate. Some readers might consider the speaker arrogant and insistent, but by the end he is definitely not apologetic, nor is he exactly pleading with his lover.

55. A. The speaker initially appears to show firm resolve to end the relationship, but by the end he has weakened his position; this switch demonstrates the confusion and uncertainty that can follow from one's decision to break off a relationship, choice A. The idea that dignity and mutual respect can be salvaged at the end of a relationship (B) may be a wished-for outcome, but the poem offers no evidence for this idea. Choice C may seem reasonable at first glance; after all, the speaker does tell his beloved that they should not show any semblance or hint of their former love if they meet again, but the poem does not conclude that ex-lovers can actually accomplish this. Choice D is too much of a stretch; in real life it may be true that one person may regret a failed relationship more than the other person, but the poem does not imply this to necessarily be true. Choice E is equally detached from the poem's content; whether or not one can ever regain innocence is not this poem's real point about the end of relationships.

Section II: Free-Response Questions

Question 1: *Coriolanus* by William Shakespeare

The following scoring guide explicitly explains how to earn up to 6 total points for a speech analysis essay. Row A (thesis) can earn up to 1 point; Row B (evidence and commentary) can earn up to 4 points, and Row C (sophistication) can earn up to 1 point.

Row A: Thesis (0–1 point)	
Scoring Criteria	
0 points for any of the following:	**1 point for**
• Having no defendable thesis. • Only restating the prompt in the thesis. • Only summarizing the issue with no claim in the thesis. • Presenting a thesis that does not address the prompt.	• Addressing the prompt with a defendable thesis that presents an interpretation and may establish a line of reasoning.
Decision Rules and Scoring Notes	
Theses that do not earn this point	**Theses that do earn this point**
• Only restate the prompt. • Only offer an irrelevant generalized comment about the speech. • Simply describe the speech's features rather than making a defendable claim.	• Take a position on the prompt and provide a defendable interpretation of how Shakespeare portrays Coriolanus' complex attitude toward his audience and public office.
Additional Notes	
• The thesis may be one or more sentences anywhere in the essay. • A thesis that meets the criteria can be awarded the point whether or not the rest of the response successfully conveys that line of reasoning.	

Row B: Evidence AND Commentary (0–4 points)				
Scoring Criteria				
0 points for	**1 point for**	**2 points for**	**3 points for**	**4 points for**
• Simply repeating the thesis (if present). • **OR** restating provided information. • **OR** providing mostly irrelevant and/or incoherent examples.	• Summarizing the speech without reference to a thesis. • **OR** providing vague textual references. • **OR** providing textual references of questionable relevance. • **AND** providing little or no commentary.	• Making relevant textual references (direct quotes or paraphrases). • **AND** providing commentary but repeats, oversimplifies, or misinterprets the cited evidence or text.	• Making relevant textual references (direct quotes or paraphrases). • **AND** providing commentary that explains the logical relationship between textual examples and the thesis; however, commentary is uneven, limited, or incomplete.	• Making relevant textual references (direct quotes or paraphrases). • **AND** providing well-developed commentary that explicitly explains the relationship between the evidence and the thesis.

Decision Rules and Scoring Notes				
Typical responses that earn 0 points:	**Typical responses that earn 1 point:**	**Typical responses that earn 2 points:**	**Typical responses that earn 3 points:**	**Typical responses that earn 4 points:**
• Are unclear or fail to address the prompt. • May present mere opinion with no relevant textual references.	• Mention textual references, devices, or techniques with little or no analysis.	• Contain numerous inaccuracies or repetition in commentary. • Offer only simplistic explanations that do not strengthen the argument.	• Provide commentary that is not sufficiently developed or is too limited. • Assume or imply a connection to the thesis that is not consistently explicit.	• Provide commentary that uses significant details of the text to draw conclusions. • Integrate short excerpts throughout in order to support the thesis' interpretation.

Additional Notes

• Writing that suffers from grammatical and/or mechanical errors that interfere with communication cannot earn the fourth point in this row.

Row C: Sophistication (0–1 point)

Scoring Criteria	
0 points for	**1 point for**
• Not meeting the criteria for 1 point.	• Exhibiting sophistication of thought and/or advancing a complex literary argument.

Decision Rules and Scoring Notes	
Responses that do not earn this point:	**Responses that earn this point demonstrate one (or more) of the following:**
• Try to contextualize an interpretation, but make predominantly sweeping generalizations (*"Throughout all history . . . "* OR *"Everyone believes . . . "*). • Only hint at other possible interpretations (*"Some may think . . . "* OR *"Though the speech might be said to . . . "*). • Write one statement about a thematic interpretation of the speech without consistently maintaining that idea. • Oversimplify complexities in the speech. • Present complicated or complex sentences or language that is ineffective and detracts from the argument.	• Present a thesis that demands nuanced analysis of textual evidence and successfully prove it. • Illuminate the significance or relevance of an interpretation within a broader context. • Discuss alternative interpretations of a text. • Acknowledge and account for contradictions, ambiguities, and/or complexities within the text. • Provide relevant analogies to help better understand an interpretation. • Develop a prose style that is especially vivid, persuasive, resounding, or appropriate to the student's argument.

Additional Notes

• This point should be awarded only if the demonstration of sophistication or complex understanding is part of the argument, not merely a phrase or brief reference.

High-Scoring Essay

A dark threatening tone is established immediately in this excerpt: Coriolanus is struggling; he's torn between his insatiable thirst for power and his revulsion at having to personally grovel before the plebeians. Coriolanus does, indeed, have a complex and conflicted relationship with his audience, the plebeians in the marketplace of Rome. One the one hand he must appear friendly and personable; he must flatter them and beg for their votes, but underneath the surface is a far darker truth: Coriolanus looks down on the plebeians, whom he considers to be far beneath his exalted stature; when you analyze his metaphorical language, it appears that he actually detests them.

It is noteworthy that virtually all of Coriolanus' diction is figurative, beginning with hyperbole in his opening statement which asserts "Better it is to die, better to starve," than to be forced to beg for votes. One might conclude that this statement is not exactly factual. But he continues his over-the-top comments by complaining about the poor, low-class toga that he is forced to wear in an attempt to convince the plebeians that he is just a regular guy, a man of the people. However, the balance of the first portion is concentrated on Coriolanus' foul mood and the underlying dark tone. He makes it clear that his real complaint is with a custom of his society, a custom that forces him to humble himself, to go out in the streets and beg for votes. He believes this custom is stupid and wrong and that he, himself, is a victim, the victim of a "mountainous error."

The scene proceeds with 3 citizens entering, and Coriolanus continues his manipulations with more flowery, figurative language, but the pace seems to pick up, as if his energy is increasing in his power-hungry lust for votes. His next over-the-top verbal manipulation involves laying a guilt trip on the plebeians, claiming that all of his losses and all of his atrocities are actually their fault, not his, because it is only "for your voices I have fought." Thus, Coriolanus entreats the plebeians, you must vote for me, not only because I am the champion who won the victories, but because you bear the guilt and this will help you atone for it.

Throughout this piece, the reader's feelings are manipulated and controlled by masterful word choice and the use of literary devices, the most prominent being the figurative, persuasive language and the unrelenting negative tone like you are being torn in two directions. Coriolanus has a very complex love/hate relationship with the plebeians and it is laid bare for the reader to see. As Coriolanus struggles, the reader is bombarded with his back and forth dialog, one moment he sounds harsh and deadly, but the next moment he is whispering sweet nothings in our collective ear. Ah Coriolanus, has he earned our hatred, or does he deserve our pity?

(482 words)

Analysis of High-Scoring Essay

This student nails it in the first sentence of this essay, immediately demonstrating a clear understanding of the text and of Coriolanus' character. A Reader will be very pleased with such elegant phrasing as "he's torn between his insatiable thirst for power and his revulsion at having to personally grovel before the plebeians." In introducing Coriolanus' "complex and conflicted relationship with his audience," the student explains how he must stoop to flattery while inwardly detesting them. If this essay were a process paper, the introduction would benefit from some more concise language and the elimination of that pesky second-person pronoun, "you." However, the introduction already promises an upper-half essay, and the Reader is hopeful that the essay fulfills that promise. The defendable thesis deserves a point for Row A.

The first body paragraph correctly claims that "virtually all of Coriolanus' diction is figurative," and presents the "Better it is to die, better to starve" hyperbolic sentiment, pointedly noting that it "is not exactly factual." The student paraphrases many of Coriolanus' comments in service of analysis. Students with lesser skills frequently tell the Reader what Coriolanus says, but this student explains how the toga he wears is a deliberate attempt to "convince the plebeians that he is just a regular guy, a man of the people." The student also demonstrates the ability to read between the lines, noticing how the "balance of the first portion" concentrates on Coriolanus' "foul mood and underlying dark tone." Many students do not notice Coriolanus' sarcasm and condescension as he bows to custom; this student understands how he criticizes society and truly thinks himself the victim of a "mountainous error." Perhaps this paragraph could be developed around more concrete examples, but its commentary is admirable.

The second body paragraph explores Coriolanus' speech after more voters have arrived. The first sentence is clunky and would benefit from a rewrite, but the student makes a valid point that Coriolanus' "pace seems to pick up, as if his energy is increasing in his power-hungry lust for votes." Including actual text proof would help establish this insightful idea. The student's point that Coriolanus is manipulating his audience with faulty logic and "a guilt trip" about his many battles is a valid one. However, the student's phrase that "all of his losses and all of his atrocities are actually their fault" is a bit too strong; rather, Coriolanus tells the plebeians that his actions have all been performed on their behalf. The student ends the paragraph essentially paraphrasing Coriolanus' entreaty in first person; some Readers may object to this, but others will see it as adding an implicit underlying analysis. The paraphrasing indeed goes beyond the literal text by adding the idea that the plebeians can "atone" for their guilt by voting for him, a forceful idea.

The concluding paragraph begins with a long sentence that tries to summarize the essay, albeit in far too many words and with some cumbersome phrasing. One wishes the student did not refer to "the reader's feelings" since reader response is never part of an AP essay prompt; what the student means is that it is Coriolanus' audience that is manipulated. Notice the need for editing with the phrasing "the use of literary devices, the most prominent being the figurative, persuasive language and the unrelenting negative tone like you are being torn in two directions." The first problem here is that the student implies one device is "most prominent," but then illogically lists two, figurative language and negative tone. Another problem is that tone is not a literary device in the first place; it is the *result* of language, not a device in itself. Furthermore, the improper second-person pronoun is not appropriate. However, after these perhaps too-harsh observations, a Reader will likely be pleased with the student's finale, which wonders "Ah Coriolanus, has he earned our hatred, or does he deserve our pity?" The evidence and commentary deserve 3 points in Row B; the student presents relevant textual references, but the commentary is too uneven and limited to earn a higher score.

On the whole, this essay is very good in its understanding of the text and its analysis, both explicit and implicit. The organization works well, dividing two body paragraphs into the two sections of the speech. The development is admirable, although a few more examples would be welcome. Finally, the student displays moments of delightful and sophisticated phrasing, which are pleasing to the ear. The criticisms in this evaluation are merely meant as suggestions for improvement, and the few faults in the essay should not really hurt its score. The student should be rewarded with a point in Row C because he or she explores contradictions, ambiguities, and complexities of the text. It earns an overall score of 5.

Low-Scoring Essay

In this excerpt from <u>Coriolanus</u>, the title character displays a complex attitude towards his audience; he can't seem to decide if he loves them or if he hates them. It is easy to see that this character is mixed up in his attitude, because of his use of figurative language.

Coriolanus starts out by saying "Most sweet voices!" but that must be intended to be ironic because it is contradicted by all of his following statements. He shows the negative tone with a series of unpleasant statements like "Better it is to die, better to starve" and "Why in this wolvish toge" and "Their needless vouches." What purpose do these statements serve, other than to show that Coriolanus is angry and conflicted and the mood is dark?

Coriolanus goes on and on with more figurative statements, and they are all negative. He complains about the customs of his country, he calls it a "mountainous error," and he seems to think that he should be immune to obeying custom and, perhaps, even above the law.

In the final part of the excerpt, Coriolanus's statements are no less flowery, but at least they are finally more upbeat. He tries to woo the people into voting for him, so he makes his voice softer and more enticing. He swears to the people that everything he had done, he had done for them. "For your voices I have fought" and I "Watched for your voices" and because of your voices I "bear of wounds two dozen odd." Obviously, he's laying it on pretty thick, but it appears that he'll do anything to get their votes, to attain his ultimate goal, ultimate power!

In conclusion, it's easy to see that Coriolanus is quite a conflicted character. His flowery, figurative language repeatedly demonstrates that he detests all of "the little people" and also that he is miserable at having to meet & mingle and to beg for their votes. That conflict is why the tone is so very dark throughout this piece.

(336 words)

Analysis of Low-Scoring Essay

This student begins poorly by making an incorrect assertion about Coriolanus' attitude toward his audience, stating that Coriolanus "can't seem to decide if he loves them or if he hates them." While the prompt indeed identifies Coriolanus' attitude as complex, this student does not realize that Coriolanus utterly disdains his audience. The complexity of his attitude is embodied in the way he despises having to beg for their votes while playing the phony politician and pretending to be humble. The student's thesis merely repeats the prompt in a simplistic fashion; apparently, he or she intends to prove that "it is easy to see that this character is mixed up in his attitude." As it is written, the thesis seems to claim that the cause of Coriolanus' complex attitude is actually "his use of figurative language," but offers no hint of *how* the student intends to connect the figurative language to the idea of something that "is easy to see." The error in parallelism (" . . . because of his use of figurative language and also by looking . . . ") further distracts the Reader from following the student's train of thought. Unfortunately, this essay is not off to a good start, and it does not deserve a point in Row A.

The first body paragraph attempts to explore the irony in Coriolanus' opening exclamation, as he fawns to his audience, "Most sweet voices!" But the student does not seem to understand the point of Coriolanus' verbal irony, instead claiming that Coriolanus' kind words must be ironic because of the contradictory statements that follow. However, the student apparently misreads the text, not taking him seriously when Coriolanus laments that he really would prefer to die or starve rather than beg for votes, but custom demands it. The paragraph ends by accurately stating that these statements show a "conflicted" and "dark" mood, but one wonders why the student thinks Coriolanus' comments would have no other purpose than to show his anger.

The second body paragraph is all too brief and offers no insights. The Reader will not be impressed to be told that "Coriolanus goes on and on with more figurative statements," even though the student does provide one example. The student's diction and syntax continue to add confusion. Notice the pronoun error, referring to "customs" as "it" and another parallelism error in the phrase " . . . should be immune to obeying custom and, perhaps, even above the law."

The last body paragraph begins by informing us that the "statements are no less flowery, but at least they are finally more upbeat." While this is partially true of the text, it's hard to swallow the logic that Coriolanus' description of fighting for their votes and being wounded numerous times in several battles can be characterized as upbeat. The claim that he "makes his voice softer and more enticing" is also questionable. The paragraph ends with the accurate idea that Coriolanus will "do anything to get their votes," but the inappropriate use of informal phrasing ("he's laying it on pretty thick") and the exaggerated finish ("ultimate power!") do little to redeem the student's credibility. The evidence and commentary are sufficient to earn 2 points in Row B.

Finally, just in case the Reader is not already aware, the student officiously points out that the last paragraph is a conclusion and then repeats the idea from the introduction about how very easy it is to see Coriolanus' conflicted character. The student deserves credit for acknowledging that Coriolanus' figurative language "repeatedly demonstrates that he detests all of 'the little people' and also that he is miserable at having to meet & mingle and to beg for their votes," but this analysis seems like too little, too late. The essay does not meet the criteria to earn a point in Row C.

Overall, this student needs to practice reading complex texts and articulating analytical ideas that specifically relate to the assigned prompt. A Reader would be happy to work with this student, as the essay shows promise, but, unfortunately, the distracting mechanical and grammatical errors, compounded with an overly simplistic development, keep this essay from achieving an adequate score. It deserves an overall score of 2.

Question 2: *A River Runs through It* by Norman Maclean

The following scoring guide explicitly explains how to earn up to 6 total points for a prose analysis essay. Row A (thesis) can earn up to 1 point; Row B (evidence and commentary) can earn up to 4 points, and Row C (sophistication) can earn up to 1 point.

Row A: Thesis (0–1 point)	
Scoring Criteria	
0 points for any of the following:	**1 point for**
• Having no defendable thesis. • Only restating the prompt in the thesis. • Only summarizing the issue with no claim in the thesis. • Presenting a thesis that does not address the prompt.	• Addressing the prompt with a defendable thesis that presents an interpretation and may establish a line of reasoning.

Decision Rules and Scoring Notes	
Theses that do not earn this point	**Theses that do earn this point**
• Only restate the prompt. • Only offer an irrelevant generalized comment about the passage. • Simply describe the passage's features rather than making a defendable claim.	• Take a position on the prompt and provide a defendable interpretation of how Maclean uses figurative language to explore memory and the characters' complex relationships.
Additional Notes	
• The thesis may be one or more sentences anywhere in the response. • A thesis that meets the criteria can be awarded the point whether or not the rest of the response successfully conveys that line of reasoning.	

Row B: Evidence AND Commentary (0–4 points)

Scoring Criteria

0 points for	1 point for	2 points for	3 points for	4 points for
• Simply repeating the thesis (if present). • **OR** restating provided information. • **OR** providing mostly irrelevant and/or incoherent examples.	• Summarizing the passage without reference to a thesis. • **OR** providing vague textual references. • **OR** providing textual references of questionable relevance. • **AND** providing little or no commentary.	• Making relevant textual references (direct quotes or paraphrases). • **AND** providing commentary but repeats, oversimplifies, or misinterprets the cited evidence or text.	• Making relevant textual references (direct quotes or paraphrases). • **AND** providing commentary that explains the logical relationship between textual examples and the thesis; however, commentary is uneven, limited, or incomplete.	• Making relevant textual references (direct quotes or paraphrases). • **AND** providing well-developed commentary that explicitly explains the relationship between the evidence and the thesis.

Decision Rules and Scoring Notes

Typical responses that earn 0 points:	Typical responses that earn 1 point:	Typical responses that earn 2 points:	Typical responses that earn 3 points:	Typical responses that earn 4 points:
• Are unclear or fail to address the prompt. • May present mere opinion with no relevant textual references.	• Mention textual references, devices, or techniques with little or no analysis.	• Contain numerous inaccuracies or repetition in commentary. • Offer only simplistic explanations that do not strengthen the argument.	• Provide commentary that is not sufficiently developed, or is too limited. • Assume or imply a connection to the thesis that is not consistently explicit.	• Provide commentary that uses significant details of the text to draw conclusions. • Integrate short excerpts throughout in order to support the thesis' interpretation.

Additional Notes

• Writing that suffers from grammatical and/or mechanical errors that interfere with communication cannot earn the fourth point in this row.

Row C: Sophistication (0–1 point)	
Scoring Criteria	
0 points for	**1 point for**
• Not meeting the criteria for 1 point.	• Exhibiting sophistication of thought and/or advancing a complex literary argument.
Decision Rules and Scoring Notes	
Responses that do not earn this point:	**Responses that earn this point demonstrate one (or more) of the following:**
• Try to contextualize an interpretation, but make predominantly sweeping generalizations (*"Throughout all history . . . "* OR *"Everyone believes . . . "*). • Only hint at other possible interpretations (*"Some may think . . . "* OR *"Though the passage might be said to . . . "*). • Write one statement about a thematic interpretation of the passage without consistently maintaining that idea. • Oversimplify complexities in the passage. • Present complicated or complex sentences or language that is ineffective and detracts from the argument.	• Present a thesis that demands nuanced analysis of textual evidence and successfully prove it. • Illuminate the significance or relevance of an interpretation within a broader context. • Discuss alternative interpretations of a text. • Acknowledge and account for contradictions, ambiguities, and/or complexities within the text. • Provide relevant analogies to help better understand an interpretation. • Develop a prose style that is especially vivid, persuasive, resounding, or appropriate to the student's argument.
Additional Notes	
• This point should be awarded only if the demonstration of sophistication or complex understanding is part of the argument, not merely a phrase or brief reference.	

High-Scoring Essay

Eugenia Collier, in her short story "Marigolds," noted that "Memory is an abstract painting; it does not present things as they are, but rather as they feel." This concept relates to how memory operates in Norman Maclean's <u>A River Runs through It</u>, which portrays how a father and his two sons cultivate a fond and tender bond while in nature. As the first person narrator presents his detailed memory of one notable afternoon, we discover how memories of a day of fly fishing in a Montana river add to the family's closeness.

The preeminent aspect of the point of view is that it is unidimensional; we only witness the scene from the younger son's perspective. However, he reveals many details about the other characters, as well as their intertwined relationships. Broad hints about their bond appear as early as the opening lines. The younger son speaks to his father, not about himself, but about the success of his older brother, "That's his limit." The father responds, but he does not address his younger son's comment at all; rather, he expresses admiration for his older boy, Paul. The comment, "He is beautiful" pointedly refers not to the fish, but to the fisherman, his older son. Before continuing the action, the narrator inserts a significant detail from his memory: he notes that, "this was the last fish we were ever to see Paul catch," intimating that Paul might die at some time. The narrator mentions how he and his father talked about this moment many times later, and no matter what their other feelings, they "never saw the fish but only the artistry of the fisherman." The narrator's reflection, obviously coined years later, proves that the men had a close relationship and that their recollection of this one incident painted their memory in a positive light, one of mutual admiration. Human memory is a mysterious force in our lives that seems to be overwhelmingly persuasive, and in this case, adds positively to the characters' relationships.

The imagery and detail of the location, particularly the river itself, also provides insight into the characters' relationships. As father and younger son sit on the bank of the swift river, the narrator points out how dad reached over to pat his youngest, while still watching Paul. Dad misses, but takes his eyes away to see his target before trying again to pat his son. The narrator acknowledges that this little gesture shows how dad was proud of him too, "but for other reasons," implying that the boys are not competitive and that father respects both equally. Then the narrator shifts the focus back to Paul out in the river, where it was "a little too deep and fast," before detailing how the current, like a fast-moving baptism, made Paul's "legs weak and wavy." Paul decides to swim ashore instead of floating downstream to a milder landing spot. It is interesting to note that although the imagery highlights the power of the river, the narrator and father feel no need to go to the riverside and help Paul; such is their faith in him. Instead they laugh, vicariously living through Paul as he comically scrambles to the shore with his fishing rod and full basket of fish, even though he is washed off his feet and gets soaked. Any potential danger is diminished as the narrator explains that "in our family it was no great thing for a fisherman to swim a river." Obviously they trust each other and have enjoyed sharing this natural setting before.

After Paul joins them on the bank, they take photographs of all the fish they had caught that day, admiring each other and posing repeatedly with their catch. The narrator acknowledges that the photos cannot capture the majesty of the moment; the fish looked white and overexposed while their poses appeared staged. However, the narrator then finely details one close-up picture of Paul that "remains in [his] mind, as if fixed by some chemical bath." His memory is so touching as he details the photo for the audience: "Now flies danced around his hatband. Large drops of water ran from under his hat on to his face and then into his lips when he smiled." The narrator then crowns the memory with the poignantly sweet comment that "At the end of this day, then, I remember him both as a distant abstraction in artistry and as a close-up in water and laughter." One cannot help but feel the unstated love between the characters, warm and real.

Almost like a camera panning from above, the narrator relates that the three of them stayed by the river bank, which was making sounds to them, as if the river personally spoke only to them. He acknowledges that it would be "hard to find three men sitting side by side who knew better what a river was saying." The unspoken communication, the unstated connection between the characters and the river that runs through their lives combine to reveal men who love each other and who love what nature can offer.

Maclean's eloquent use of point of view, imagery and selection of details, has beautifully captured a significant vignette in the lives of the characters. Instead of noticing his use of devices as he weaves his intricate web to interlace the character's relationships and their memories, both photographic and mental, the reader easily goes along for the ride, quite happy to accept this fictional world.

(909 words)

Analysis of High-Scoring Essay

This student's lengthy essay, at 909 words, explores more than most students do in a 40-minute time period. The student's introduction begins by presenting a thought-provoking quotation from another author, Eugenia Collier. The idea that memory is abstract and only presents feelings is indeed relevant to the Maclean passage. The student does not directly refer to the Collier quotation later in the essay, nor is it necessary to do so, but this is a refreshing opening all the same. The introduction identifies the characters' relationship as "fond and tender" and it notes that the first-person narrator's detailed memory of the vignette helps readers to discover how the characters' "memories of a day . . . add to the family's closeness." The student clearly and subtly addresses all parts of the prompt in this three-sentence introduction and clearly deserves a point in Row A.

The first of four body paragraphs begins by exploring the passage's "unidimensional" point of view, explaining that the narrator will reveal "details about the other characters, as well as their intertwined relationships." Using the interchange between the narrator and his father that opens the passage, the student notices how the first two paragraphs of the excerpt indicate the father's admiration for Paul, perhaps hinting that the father may be partial to his older son. However, the student immediately transitions into an analysis of how the concept of memory works in the passage, explaining that the narrator's phrasing implies the passage of time between the events we're witnessing and the narrator's writing, plus the possibility of tragedy. The student utilizes a significant quotation about how the father and narrator vividly remember "'the artistry of the fisherman,'" to emphasize that the characters' relationship is close and that this positive memory enhances their "mutual admiration." The paragraph ends by stating a universal truth: "Memory is a mysterious force in our lives," which in this story adds yet another positive note to their relationship.

The next paragraph explores some of the imagery and details that are presented in the passage as the student moves forward chronologically. The example of the dad trying to pat his son's knee as they sit on the riverbank is well presented, as it dismisses any previous notion that he may favor Paul over his younger son. The next example shifts, as does the story's action, to Paul standing in the river, detailing how strong the current is with reasonably deep awareness of the imagery. The student provides an interesting insight by suggesting that the river, "like a fast-moving baptism," made it hard for Paul to stand. While this idea could be explored in greater depth, the student notices another interesting detail: the dad and the narrator do not feel any need to help Paul, coupling their "faith in him" to the religious concept of baptism. The student notices that they live vicariously through Paul and they laugh as he "comically scrambles to the shore." The student uses ample detail from the text to convince the Reader that the characters "trust each other" and relish being in nature.

The third body paragraph centers on specific imagery, on the photographs they take that afternoon; the student points out that the pictures "cannot capture the majesty of the moment" by presenting text detail of the less-than-perfect photos. However, as the narrator points out, one close-up photo of Paul stands out and has remained fixed in his memory. The student deftly includes the narrator's observation about how he remembered Paul "'both as a distant abstraction in artistry and as a close-up in water and laughter,'" before acknowledging that the characters have a "warm and real" unstated love.

The last body paragraph explores the end of the passage and compares the image of the three men sitting by the river to "a camera panning from above." This kind of comment is relevant in an abstract way, although it is not clearly explained; the narrative does not visually distance itself, but the narrator's sentiment does. We understand that all three men share a deep tie to the natural world, and the student states it skillfully: "The unspoken communication, the unstated connection between the characters and the river that runs through their lives combine to reveal men who love each other and who love what nature can offer." A Reader will be pleased to encounter a student who can display such sophisticated style. The essay fulfills the criteria for 4 points in Row B; its evidence and commentary are well-developed and support the thesis throughout.

The conclusion once again addresses the prompt and provides an overall summary of the essay's points. As a whole, the essay is on topic throughout. It develops its ideas by utilizing apt text examples and delivers them with panache. The organization is not formulaic; rather, it follows the narration of the excerpt. This student displays a level of style that is stellar for a timed essay. It earns a point in Row C because it presents a nuanced thesis and successfully proves it, plus it accounts for textual complexities. One certainly cannot fault this essay for the few overworked phrases and some wordiness; instead, a Reader will happily reward this student for his or her successes with a score of 6.

Low-Scoring Essay

In his 1976 Novel "A River Runs through It" the author Norman MacLean does an excellent job of using the character's point of view to expand on the meaning of the story.

This emphasis on point of view may seem counter-intuitive at first, because the entire excerpt we read was only in the point of view of the other son, the one who is not named Paul. This is unusual for several reasons. First, it seems odd that the first-person narrator is never named; even though he is essential to the story, we don't even know what to call him. Next, how can the author's use of point of view develop deeper meaning, when the story is only told from one point of view? It is only after careful analysis that it becomes apparent that MacLean wants us to understand the other characters, but only through the lens of the other son; we see them just as he sees them.

This explains why the first part of the action centers on the other son and his interactions with the father figure, and why the story describes Paul's action only from a reserved distance.

Another striking point is how the story concentrates on the other son and the father, even when Paul is crossing the river; the story intimates that Paul could be drowning and the father and the other son might not even notice.

The author uses literary devices such as detailed imagery convey his larger points, his underlying meaning. For example, the visual images of Paul crossing the river are very detailed and the action rises and falls, just like a river, until the reader is practically carried away himself. This imagery continues when Paul goes to the father and the other son and he is soaking wet, he is the only one who is wet, but he shrugs it off like it is nothing.

Another detail that the author uses well is the image of the fish all laid out on the grass. The haul of fish is later reflected in the photographs and memories years later, but those images can't compare to the image our characters see live that day.

Thus, it is through MacLean's effective use of character development through controlling the point of view, as well as his selection of imagery and his selection of great details, establishes why this work "A River Runs through It" is considered by many to be one of the great American novels.

(413 words)

Analysis of Low-Scoring Essay

This well-meaning 413-word essay, unfortunately, fails to offer an adequate analysis of the passage, largely because of irrelevant commentary and some misreading of the text. The essay never presents a defendable thesis and does not earn a point in Row A.

The introduction, one mere sentence, does not address the prompt that asks how the author uses point of view to explore memory and the characters' relationships. The topic's wording is designed to help guide the student's reading of the passage and organization of ideas in the essay itself. However, this student simply offers that the point of view "does an excellent job" of "expand[ing] on the meaning of the story." A Reader will wish that the student addressed the prompt more directly instead of vaguely suggesting something meaningful.

The first body paragraph is perplexing on several counts. The first phrase, "This emphasis on point of view," confounds the Reader because one is not sure what the student means by "This emphasis." Perhaps the student is referring to the prompt. The sentence continues to confuse when it points out that the excerpt's point of view "may seem counter-intuitive at first," since the point of view is of only one character. The Reader is left thinking, "Huh?" That's not what the student wants, surely. Then the student claims that the son's point of view is "unusual" because we never learn the first-person narrator's name and only one person's point of view limits the development of deeper meaning. Again, the Reader is mystified about the student's point. The idea that the narrator's name is not revealed in a first-person excerpt is basically silly, as is the idea that more characters' thoughts are necessary for "deeper meaning." These illogical claims hurt the essay's progression. The student tries to pull it off, claiming that "after careful analysis" (which this student does not exhibit) one realizes that Maclean only wants readers to understand other characters through the narrator's lens. The paragraph still fails to address the prompt.

The next body paragraph, which would be better placed at the end of the previous paragraph, begins with another ambiguous pronoun problem. The phrase "This explains . . . " has no clear antecedent. The student tries to make a case that the point of view is appropriate because the initial action centers on the narrator and his father before describing Paul's action "from a reserved distance." Since the narrative is clearly written years after the events, that phrase may be an attempt to address the prompt that asks students to explore how point of view explores memory, but it could also be literal: that the narrator and his father see Paul in the distance from their vantage on the riverbank. In any case, it does not analyze anything.

The essay continues with some unfortunate misreading of the text. The student erroneously claims that the "story concentrates on the other son and the father, even when Paul is crossing the river." Although the excerpt does have one paragraph that focuses on the narrator and his father as Paul crosses the river, the student misses that they both are living indirectly through Paul and, knowing his ability, apparently see no need to help him ashore. He is not in danger, and the student goes seriously wrong in thinking that "Paul could be drowning" and they "might not even notice." This idea ends the paragraph, and the Reader is still scratching his or her head, trying to figure out what the student thought was so "striking."

The writer again tries to address the prompt in the following paragraph, noting that the "author uses literary devices such as detailed imagery to convey his larger points, his underlying meaning," but the student's point again falls flat. The "example" presented is that the images are "very detailed," without any text support or analysis of specific imagery. Instead, the student exaggerates that the "action rises and falls, just like a river, until the reader is practically carried away himself." It seems harsh to say, but many Readers will giggle at that phrase. The student inserts the specific image of Paul, soaking wet, coming up to his father and brother, but all we learn is that he is wet and they are not. This irrelevant idea does not further any analysis of the prompt.

The student provides a fifth body paragraph that presents the image of the fish "all laid out on the grass." As if grasping for straws, the student notes that the real images of that day cannot compare to the "photographs and memories" the characters see years later. The sentence does contain the word "memories," but that alone is insufficient for the topic. The evidence and commentary, merely superficial, earn 2 points in Row B.

The essay concludes with vacuous and awkward wording. Perhaps the student is trying to play on the novella's title when writing that it is "through MacLean's [sic] effective use of character development through controlling the point of view," but the Reader has trouble getting through the sentiment. Instead of any explanation of how the point of view, imagery, and details help explore memory and the characters' relationships, the student informs us that the work is "considered by many to be one of the great American novels." That phrase typifies students who do not know what to say or how to end an essay. A Reader will also wish that the student would learn to punctuate titles correctly; this novella should be underlined (in a handwritten essay). The fact that the student consistently misspells the author's name is also distracting to the Reader.

Generally, the essay deserves merit for attempting to address the topic. The student can write acceptably (albeit with some grammatical errors like run-on sentences and pronoun problems), but the student does not demonstrate an understanding of *literary* analysis, especially how point of view enhances a text. The student never explores the richness of the text's imagery and detail, and never addresses how the characters' familial relationships are so touching because of the point of view that reflects on a specific day in their past. The narrator's memory of that day is indeed strong and vivid; it is a shame that the student's essay is not. It does not meet the criteria for a point in Row C. It would earn an overall score of 2.

Question 3: An Alienated Character

The following scoring guide explicitly explains how to earn up to 6 total points for a literary analysis essay. Row A (thesis) can earn up to 1 point; Row B (evidence and commentary) can earn up to 4 points, and Row C (sophistication) can earn up to 1 point.

Row A: Thesis (0–1 point)	
Scoring Criteria	
0 points for any of the following:	**1 point for**
• Having no defendable thesis. • Only restating the prompt in the thesis. • Only summarizing the issue with no claim in the thesis. • Presenting a thesis that does not address the prompt.	• Addressing the prompt with a defendable thesis that presents an interpretation and may establish a line of reasoning.
Decision Rules and Scoring Notes	
Theses that do not earn this point	**Theses that do earn this point**
• Only restate the prompt. • Only offer an irrelevant generalized comment about the chosen work.	• Take a position on the prompt and provide a defendable interpretation of the source of a character's alienation and how it affects the character and adds to an interpretation of the chosen work as a whole.
Additional Notes	
• The thesis may be one or more sentences anywhere in the response. • A thesis that meets the criteria can be awarded the point whether or not the rest of the response successfully conveys that line of reasoning.	

Row B: Evidence AND Commentary (0–4 points)

Scoring Criteria

0 points for	1 point for	2 points for	3 points for	4 points for
• Simply repeating the thesis (if present). • **OR** restating provided information. • **OR** providing mostly irrelevant and/or incoherent examples.	• Summarizing the chosen work without reference to a thesis. • **OR** providing vague textual references. • **OR** providing textual references of questionable relevance. • **AND** providing little or no commentary.	• Making relevant textual references (direct quotes or paraphrases). • **AND** providing commentary but repeats, oversimplifies, or misinterprets the cited evidence or text.	• Making relevant textual references (direct quotes or paraphrases). • **AND** providing commentary that explains the logical relationship between textual examples and the thesis; however, commentary is uneven, limited, or incomplete.	• Making relevant textual references (direct quotes or paraphrases). • **AND** providing well-developed commentary that explicitly explains the relationship between the evidence and the thesis.

Decision Rules and Scoring Notes

Typical responses that earn 0 points:	Typical responses that earn 1 point:	Typical responses that earn 2 points:	Typical responses that earn 3 points:	Typical responses that earn 4 points:
• Are unclear or fail to address the prompt. • May present mere opinion with no relevant textual references.	• Mention textual references, devices, or techniques with little or no analysis.	• Contain numerous inaccuracies or repetition in commentary. • Offer only simplistic explanations that do not strengthen the argument.	• Provide commentary that is not sufficiently developed or is too limited. • Assume or imply a connection to the thesis that is not consistently explicit.	• Provide commentary that uses significant details of the text to draw conclusions. • Integrate short excerpts throughout in order to support the thesis' interpretation.

Additional Notes

• Writing that suffers from grammatical and/or mechanical errors that interfere with communication cannot earn the fourth point in this row.

Row C: Sophistication (0–1 point)

Scoring Criteria

0 points for	1 point for
• Not meeting the criteria for 1 point.	• Exhibiting sophistication of thought and/or advancing a complex literary argument.

Decision Rules and Scoring Notes	
Responses that do not earn this point:	**Responses that earn this point demonstrate one (or more) of the following:**
• Try to contextualize an interpretation, but make predominantly sweeping generalizations ("*Throughout all history . . .*" OR "*Everyone believes . . .*"). • Only hint at other possible interpretations ("*Some may think . . .*" OR "*Though the work might be said to . . .*"). • Write one statement about a thematic interpretation of the chosen work without consistently maintaining that idea. • Oversimplify complexities in the chosen work. • Present complicated or complex sentences or language that is ineffective and detracts from the argument.	• Present a thesis that demands nuanced analysis of textual evidence and successfully prove it. • Illuminate the significance or relevance of an interpretation within a broader context. • Discuss alternative interpretations of a text. • Acknowledge and account for contradictions, ambiguities, and/or complexities within the text. • Provide relevant analogies to help better understand an interpretation. • Develop a prose style that is especially vivid, persuasive, resounding, or appropriate to the student's argument.
Additional Notes	
• This point should be awarded only if the demonstration of sophistication or complex understanding is part of the argument, not merely a phrase or brief reference.	

High-Scoring Essay

Many teenagers know how uncomfortable it can be to be torn from their roots and forced to move. They cry, they pout, they complain, but eventually they find a way to fit in. While this scenario is understandably harder when a teen is relocated against her will from a cushy life in Atlanta, Georgia to the African Congo in the 1960s, Rachel Price, of The Poisonwood Bible goes beyond the pale in her reaction. In her massive display of self-absorption, she alienates herself from everyone around her, refusing to see beyond her own personal pity party. Rachel epitomizes how those who reject the opportunity to learn about new cultures will, in their ignorance, ultimately encourage stereotypes and bigotry.

Were it not for her overly-dramatic and selfish responses to all that confronts her, one might be sympathetic to Rachel; the culture shock of such a distant location and such disparate customs would be trying to anyone. However, while the others in the Price family try to adapt to their new surroundings after Reverend Price uproots their life by naively accepting a missionary position in Kilanga, Rachel, the oldest daughter, becomes the pinnacle of isolation from others. After they move to a small Congolese village with dirt roads and no running water, all she worries about is her hair, her appearance, herself. The villagers throw a large party to welcome the newcomers, but instead of trying to understand a new culture, she spits out that she hates sweaty people and is appalled that the local women do not cover their breasts. The opportunity to learn how to accept and learn from others in a new environment is always at her doorstep, but she never opens the door. Although the family stays in the village for a few years, Rachel never tries to understand the villagers, deeming them below her dignity. It is no surprise, then, that she is alienated from the locals and eventually from her own family, who frequently find her intolerable. Her incessant wisecracks and insults personify the Ugly American: unaware of her prejudice and its long-lasting ramifications to society, she carries on, helping only herself, never others.

One climax of Rachel's ability to mentally isolate herself from those around her occurs during a massive, potentially deadly ant attack. Everyone runs for the river in desperation. Rachel, after grabbing her sacred mirror and joining the throng, almost gets stomped by the human stampede. However, to survive, she digs her elbows into those around her and lifts her feet, riding on the wave of humanity. This might be considered a wise choice, except that she is literally and symbolically abusing those she abhors just to save herself. People who act like Rachel will continue to use others for their own benefit, unfortunately never helping others in turn or appreciating them.

Years later, after several failed marriages and now widowed, Rachel inherits The Equatorial, a segregated hotel in South Africa. She is alienated and aloof from the black workers that she depends on, and, as she sits by her hotel pool, a dictator in her little world, she's ironically thinking that the key to life in South Africa lies in understanding the differences between other cultures. This comes from a woman who uses and abuses the black workers who built the pool, while she claims that she put it in "all by herself." What makes Rachel so abhorrent, so isolated, even in her fancy successful surroundings, is that she never realizes she is furthering injustice in the world, contributing to the problem of racism and intolerance. This provides a sad commentary on those who refuse to see others' point of view.

Rachel once claims, "Honestly, there's no sense spending too much time alone in the dark." This is representative of all who isolate themselves in symbolic darkness, the Rachels of the world, who need to learn how much damage they inflict as they sit by their pools, smug and ignorant in their bigotry.

(661 words)

Analysis of High-Scoring Essay

This thought-provoking essay does a quite admirable job, especially since it is tackling such a long and convoluted novel. *The Poisonwood Bible* provides appropriate material for this topic, but it could prove challenging for a student because of its many different narrators. However, this student skillfully selects telling details and uses them well, although not without some relatively minor errors.

The essay begins with a promising introduction. Well developed, relevant, and clearly on topic, this paragraph is impressive. The opening line pulls in the Reader, first with an acknowledgment of the near-universal discomfort that teenagers experience when they are forced to move, and then with the pleasing parallel construction in the second sentence. The focus then narrows to Rachel Price, the misfit eldest daughter who manifests misery when the family moves to a missionary assignment in the Congo. The student accurately points out that Rachel exhibits "a massive display of self-absorption" as she embarks on a "personal pity party" that alienates her from others. Next, the student adds an insightful comment about this character's significance to the work as a whole, noting that Rachel represents "those who reject the opportunity to learn about new cultures" and how they will "encourage stereotypes and bigotry." A Reader will be pleased with the depth of the sentiment that concludes the introduction and will notice that this writer does not ignore that final part of the prompt. It clearly earns a point for Row A.

The first body paragraph explores Rachel's reactions shortly after the family arrives in the Congo. Kindly acknowledging that one could be sympathetic to Rachel were it not for her "overly-dramatic and selfish responses" to the family's move, the writer presents examples from the early portion of the text, relating Rachel's obsession with her hair (which is platinum blonde and long enough to reach her waist) and her disgust at the local villagers' smell and appearance. The student adds an explicit thematic comment about how the opportunity to learn in a new environment is always present, and conveys this idea via a nice turn of phrase, the idea that the opportunity is continually "at her doorstep, but she never opens the door." The paragraph does exhibit some minor exaggeration by claiming that Rachel is alienated from the villagers and her family. The sentiment is true in the big picture, but the student overlooks the fact that the village chief actually tries to negotiate an advantageous marriage to Rachel (which she of course loathes and refuses) and that Rachel does at times try to help the family, such as her feeble attempts to cook when Mrs. Price is bedridden. The Reader will likely forgive this slight misstatement since the essay is true to Rachel's personality as a whole. The paragraph ends with an impressive notion: that Rachel's "wisecracks and insults personify the Ugly American: Unaware of her prejudice and its long-lasting ramifications to society, she carries on, helping only herself, never others." This sentiment acknowledges not just the global significance of one of the novel's major themes, but also the fact that Rachel ultimately survives, nay, she actually thrives, on the African continent, albeit in her own typically selfish way.

The second body paragraph is brief, focusing on one example from the text that is both symbolic and substantial, namely Rachel's surviving the ant attack by hoisting herself upon the fleeing villagers. The student's insight, that she is "literally and symbolically abusing those she abhors just to save herself," is admirable, and this idea is extended to the way those who "act like Rachel will continue to use others" without ever helping them. This short paragraph might be developed more in a process paper, but under the AP exam time restraints it works well.

The final body paragraph explores Rachel's later life, years after the Congo experience, when she is living in apparent luxury as a hotel owner in South Africa. The student's commentary becomes more biting, criticizing Rachel for her blind racial intolerance as she acts like a "dictator in her little world." The example of the pool addition to the hotel is apropos, as it pinpoints Rachel's customary self-centered and egotistical nature. In the text she indeed claims she put the pool in "'all by herself,'" completely ignoring the fact that she is incapable of lifting a finger in physical labor, while also dismissing the local black workers who actually did the work. The student continues on the attack, accusing Rachel of furthering injustice and contributing to racial intolerance. Like the other paragraphs, the student ends this one with a universal truth, one that acknowledges the depth of the prompt. The strong evidence and commentary throughout the essay that supports the thesis' interpretation qualifies for 4 points in Row B.

The conclusion is succinct and strong in its sentiment, as if the student has become more worked up while writing. The well-chosen text quotation illustrates the student's point about people like Rachel "who isolate themselves in symbolic darkness." The essay ends with a remark that is caustic, yet fitting for the essay's content, that "the Rachels of the world [who] need to learn how much damage they inflict as they sit by their pools, smug in their bigotry." Notice how the essay leaves the Reader with the last word "bigotry" just as the introduction did. It is possible that the student did not consciously plan this, but it is nonetheless effective. The last phrase of an essay will be remembered by a Reader, and this one provides more than ample food for thought.

Overall, this essay is well focused and quite persuasive. Particularly impressive is the way the student continually returns to the topic and to the essay's thesis, and it also presents its ideas in a sophisticated writing style. This exceptional essay would easily earn a point in Row C and an overall score of 6.

Medium-Scoring Essay

Stephen Dedalus in <u>A Portrait of the Artist as a Young Man</u> is as alienated as can be, and he seems to like it. When he is quite young he tries to fit in at school, but his bad eyes and weak physical state makes other boys tease him and isolate him. Later he relishes being different and eventually vows to leave his homeland (Ireland).

Stephen eventually becomes alienated from his family, especially his father. Like most kids, he initially looks up to his dad, but when they go on a trip together and his dad gets drunk with old cronies and flirts with old waitresses he used to know, Stephen feels repulsed. He doesn't want to be like his dad the rest of his life and never tries to relate to him or help him. He deliberately alienates himself from his father.

Stephen also becomes isolated from the church. Being an Irish Catholic who falls in line with all of the church's doctrines is expected in Stephen's society. At first he does so and even gets prominent positions at his religious school because of his devotion and intelligence and is offered the opportunity to join the clergy. But when he sees holes in the church's doctrines and realizes the priests are not as holy as he thought, he refuses to follow things like taking communion, further alienating himself from family, friends, religion, and society. He willingly turns his back on religion, refusing to conform to practices he disagrees with.

Ultimately, Stephen leaves his homeland, family, friends, and church. His early alienation by others at school later turns into self-alienation as he chooses to stand up for his own beliefs instead of obeying rules he does not agree with. He shows how important it is to be true to yourself, no matter how much you may be alienated by others.

(310 words)

Analysis of Medium-Scoring Essay

The novel *A Portrait of the Artist as a Young Man* is an excellent choice for this topic about characters who are alienated. Indeed, volumes have been written about Stephen Dedalus' alienation from everything he had initially believed in and how it shapes his character and results in his self-exile. The student who wrote this essay understands the gist of Stephen's character and that his alienation is largely self-imposed, but unfortunately the essay offers only surface-level analysis.

The introductory paragraph appears to begin with the thesis, stating that Stephen is "as alienated as can be" and "seems to like it." While it is generally accurate, this is not a particularly insightful or engaging idea, nor does it relate to the part of the prompt that asks how the character's alienation adds meaning to the work as a whole. The introduction continues with a vague textual example of Stephen's being isolated from other boys at school, incidents that occur in the first chapter of the novel, and then it mentions that he "eventually vows to leave his homeland," jumping to an event that culminates in the last chapter. This is a whirlwind summary of a very complex novel, and ending with the awkward, parenthetical insertion of Ireland just leaves the Reader hanging. The student does show some promise by pointing out that Stephen "relishes being different," and we'll read on to see if this idea gets any development. However, as it is, this introduction does not offer the promise of a high-scoring essay. It does qualify for a point in Row A.

The next paragraph focuses on the idea that Stephen becomes alienated from family, especially his father. The student presents a fairly accurate summarized example from the second chapter, when Stephen and Mr. Dedalus travel to Cork, but unfortunately this student does not develop the example's importance or offer any additional textual evidence. The novel contains several significant scenes with Stephen and his father that are relevant and would help develop the essay, but the student does not mention them. In this paragraph, like the introduction, the student is not wrong in the ideas, but he or she fails to enlarge upon them with sufficient text examples and include an analysis as per the prompt. Although the Reader cannot disagree with the student's points, he or she cannot reward such a simplistic presentation of ideas.

The following paragraph explores Stephen's deteriorating relationship with the church. Similar to the previous paragraphs, the student does not inaccurately represent the text, but rather, fails to explore it in depth. We do understand that Stephen was religiously devout as a child and loses his faith as he grows older, but the student needs to tie this to the prompt much more effectively, instead of merely stating it alienates him. It is true when the student indicates that his alienation is self-willed, and this concept approaches the assignment, exploring the source of his isolation, but the execution here just falls flat.

The final paragraph merely restates the final outcome of the novel: Stephen ultimately decides to leave Ireland and take a solitary path in life. After this summary, the student finally tries to address how Stephen's alienation adds to the meaning of the work as a whole. Sadly, though, the student offers no more than one phrase, that it is "important to be true to yourself, no matter how much you may be alienated by others." Disregarding the inappropriate use of second-person pronouns, this sentiment offers little depth or insight. Unfortunately, it is too little, too late to save the essay. The uneven and limited evidence and commentary in the essay will earn 3 points in Row B.

Overall, this essay tries to address the prompt and is plausible in doing so, but it only explores a portion of it until the very last sentence. The open prompt always asks students to address deeper meaning to the work as a whole, and students who investigate this in every paragraph tend to fare better than those who wait until the conclusion to bring it up. This student demonstrates decent organization, as each paragraph is devoted to a central idea, but the paragraphs fail to develop sufficient text evidence and connect examples to any deeper insights. Many essays suffer from these deficiencies; a lack of rhetorical development equates to a lack of quality. In this case, the writing itself is just okay; it's not stellar, but it's not full of errors. Overall, the essay could be worse, but one wishes it were much better. It does not qualify for a point in Row C, and its overall score will be a 4.

Scoring Worksheet

Use the following worksheet to arrive at a probable final AP score on Practice Exam 3. While it is sometimes difficult to be objective enough to score one's own essay, you can use the sample essay answers to approximate an essay score for yourself. You may also give your essays (along with the sample essays) to a friend or relative to score if you feel confident that the individual has the knowledge necessary to make such a judgment and that he or she will feel comfortable in doing so.

Section I: Multiple-Choice Questions

$$\frac{}{\text{right answers}} = \frac{}{\text{multiple-choice raw score}}$$

$$\frac{}{\text{multiple-choice raw score}} \times 1.25 = \frac{}{\text{multiple-choice converted score}} \text{ (of possible 67.5)}$$

Section II: Free-Response Questions

$$\underline{\hspace{4cm}} + \underline{\hspace{4cm}} + \underline{\hspace{4cm}} = \underline{\hspace{1.5cm}}$$

question 1 raw score   question 2 raw score   question 3 raw score   essay

$$\underline{\hspace{3cm}} \times 4.583 = \underline{\hspace{4cm}} \text{ (of possible 82.5)}$$

essay raw score   essay converted score

Final Score

$$\underline{\hspace{6cm}} + \underline{\hspace{4cm}} = \underline{\hspace{4cm}} \text{ (of possible 150)}$$

multiple-choice converted score   essay converted score   final converted score

Probable Final AP Score	
Final Converted Score	**Probable AP Score**
150–100	5
99–86	4
85–67	3
66–0	1 or 2

Chapter 10

Practice Exam 4

Section I: Multiple-Choice Questions

Time: 1 hour

55 questions

Directions: This section contains selections from three passages of prose and two poems with questions on their content, style, and form. Read each selection carefully. Choose the best answer of the five choices.

For questions 1–11, read the following passage carefully before choosing your answers.

This passage takes place on a late-19th-century steamship as it approaches a cyclone in the South China Sea. When the passage begins, the first mate, Jukes, is on the deck speaking to the engineer who is below deck.

The relations of the "engine-room" and the "deck" of the Nan-Shan were, as is known, of a brotherly nature; therefore Jukes leaned over and begged the other in a restrained tone not to make
(5) a disgusting ass of himself; the skipper was on the other side of the bridge. But the second declared mutinously that he didn't care a rap who was on the other side of the bridge, and Jukes, passing in a flash from lofty disapproval
(10) into a state of exaltation, invited him in unflattering terms to come up and twist the beastly things to please himself, and catch such wind as a donkey of his sort could find. The second rushed up to the fray. He flung himself at
(15) the port ventilator[1] as though he meant to tear it out bodily and toss it overboard. All he did was to move the cowl[2] round a few inches, with an enormous expenditure of force, and seemed spent in the effort. He leaned against the back of
(20) the wheelhouse, and Jukes walked up to him.

"Oh, Heavens!" ejaculated the engineer in a feeble voice. He lifted his eyes to the sky, and then let his glassy stare descend to meet the horizon that, tilting up to an angle of forty
(25) degrees, seemed to hang on a slant for a while and settled down slowly. "Heavens! Phew! What's up, anyhow?"

Jukes, straddling his long legs like a pair of compasses, put on an air of superiority. "We're
(30) going to catch it this time," he said. "The barometer is tumbling down like anything, Harry. And you trying to kick up that silly row. . . ."

The word "barometer" seemed to revive the second engineer's mad animosity. Collecting
(35) afresh all his energies, he directed Jukes in a low and brutal tone to shove the unmentionable instrument down his gory throat. Who cared for his crimson barometer? It was the steam—the steam—that was going down; and what between
(40) the firemen going faint and the chief going silly, it was worse than a dog's life for him; he didn't care a tinker's curse how soon the whole show was blown out of the water. He seemed on the point of having a cry, but after regaining his
(45) breath he muttered darkly, "I'll faint them," and dashed off. He stopped upon the fiddle[3] long enough to shake his fist at the unnatural daylight, and dropped into the dark hole with a whoop.

When Jukes turned, his eyes fell upon the
(50) rounded back and the big red ears of Captain MacWhirr, who had come across. He did not look at his chief officer, but said at once, "That's a very violent man, that second engineer."

"Jolly good second, anyhow," grunted Jukes.
(55) "They can't keep up steam," he added, rapidly, and made a grab at the rail against the coming lurch.

Captain MacWhirr, unprepared, took a run and brought himself up with a jerk by an awning
(60) stanchion.

"A profane man," he said, obstinately. "If this goes on, I'll have to get rid of him the first chance."

"It's the heat," said Jukes. "The weather's
(65) awful. It would make a saint swear. Even up here I feel exactly as if I had my head tied up in a woolen blanket."

Captain MacWhirr looked up. "D'ye mean to say, Mr. Jukes, you ever had your head tied up in
(70) a blanket? What was that for?"

"It's a manner of speaking, sir," said Jukes, stolidly.

"Some of you fellows do go on! What's that about saints swearing? I wish you wouldn't talk (75) so wild. What sort of saint would that be that would swear? No more saint than yourself, I expect. And what's a blanket got to do with it— or the weather either. . . . The heat does not make me swear—does it? It's filthy bad temper. That's (80) what it is. And what's the good of your talking like this?"

Thus Captain MacWhirr expostulated against the use of images in speech, and at the end electrified Jukes by a contemptuous snort, (85) followed by words of passion and resentment: "Damme! I'll fire him out of the ship if he don't look out."

And Jukes, incorrigible, thought: "Goodness me! Somebody's put a new inside to my old man. (90) Here's temper, if you like. Of course it's the weather; what else? It would make an angel quarrelsome—let alone a saint."

---

¹**port ventilator:** one of the curved funnels on the deck that scoops air as the ship moves forward and directs this fresh air below decks
²**cowl:** the hood-shaped top of the ventilator that can be pointed into the wind; it scoops air in and it keeps rain and moisture out
³**fiddle:** the framework around the hatch ladder that leads below deck

1. Within the context of the passage, the phrase "The relations . . . were . . . of a brotherly nature" (lines 1–3) is ironic because it

   A. accentuates the crew's deep camaraderie
   B. emphasizes the stark schism that existed between the officers on the bridge and the sailors working below in the engine room
   C. is immediately followed by an argument with foul language, scuffling, and threats of violence
   D. intimates that there may be other unspoken relations between the men in the engine room and those on deck
   E. emphasizes the good-natured relationship that existed between the sailors working below and those on the deck

2. The action in the first paragraph is best described as a

   A. life-or-death battle between two combatants
   B. group brawl
   C. huge melee
   D. comedic, over-the-top spat
   E. drunken fracas

3. Which of the following is a reasonable inference that can be drawn from the engineer's up-and-down eye movement in the second paragraph?

   A. The eye movements appear to be random and have no pattern.
   B. The engineer has been injured in his tumble.
   C. The engineer is becoming seasick.
   D. The engineer is surveying the bridge.
   E. The ship is rocking violently in the rough sea.

4. The engineer's personality can best be described as

   A. respectful
   B. impulsive
   C. cynical
   D. single-minded
   E. savage

5. In paragraph four, which of the following rejuvenates the engineer's frenzy?

   A. "The word 'barometer' seemed to revive . . . mad animosity" (lines 33–34)
   B. "It was the steam—the steam—that was going down" (lines 38–39)
   C. " . . . between the firemen going faint" (lines 39–40)
   D. " . . . and the chief going silly" (line 40)
   E. "He seemed on the point of having a cry" (lines 43–44)

6. Captain MacWhirr's reaction to the engineer's concern is best described as

   A. oblivious to the engineer's warning
   B. intrigued by the engineer's news
   C. aghast at the engineer's assessment
   D. not at all surprised, as he is prescient about the problem
   E. appreciative of the engineer's timely advice

7. The action of the passage progresses in which of the following manners?

   A. Worrisome peril, comedic misinterpreted dialogue, resolution

   B. Lighthearted action, worrisome peril, comedic misinterpreted dialogue

   C. Worrisome peril, lighthearted action, comedic misinterpreted dialogue

   D. A life-or-death struggle, conflict resolution, comedic misinterpreted dialogue

   E. A comedic struggle, conflict resolution, serious heartfelt dialogue

8. Captain MacWhirr's responses to Jukes' comments "It's the heat . . . tied up in a woolen blanket" (lines 64–67) reveal that

   A. the captain is perceptive in these matters

   B. the captain knows the vessel inside and out

   C. the captain is overly literal and unimaginative

   D. Jukes has tricked the captain

   E. the captain delights in gaining an advantage over Jukes

9. What actually happens in the denouement of the passage?

   A. The characters' conflicts are resolved.

   B. Jukes gains a new insight into Captain MacWhirr.

   C. The sea has calmed and the danger has passed.

   D. The Captain has second thoughts about firing the engineer.

   E. Jukes gains a new insight into the engineer.

10. All of the following add insight into Jukes' character EXCEPT

   A. " . . . leaned over and begged the other in a restrained tone not to make a disgusting ass of himself" (lines 3–5)

   B. " . . . passing in a flash from lofty disapproval into a state of exaltation" (lines 9–10)

   C. " . . . put on an air of superiority" (line 29)

   D. " . . . a contemptuous snort, followed by words of passion and resentment" (lines 84–85)

   E. "'It would make an angel quarrelsome—let alone a saint'" (lines 91–92)

11. The overall tone of the passage can best be described as

   A. reflective yet droll

   B. sarcastic and oppressive

   C. aggressive yet patronizing

   D. mordant and skeptical

   E. witty yet ominous

For questions 12–22, read the following passage carefully before choosing your answers.

In this epistolary novel, Eliza Wharton, a young woman, writes to her friend, Lucy Freeman. Eliza's elderly fiancé recently passed away, after which Eliza stayed with her mother for one month. Eliza is now living with her mother's cousin, Mrs. Richman, and her husband, General Richman, in New Haven.

To Miss Lucy Freeman

My friends, here, are the picture of conjugal felicity. The situation is delightful. The visiting parties perfectly agreeable. Everything tends to facilitate the return of my accustomed vivacity.
(5) I have written to my mother, and received an answer. She praises my fortitude, and admires the philosophy which I have exerted, under, what she calls, my heavy bereavement. Poor woman! She little thinks that my heart was untouched;
(10) and when that is unaffected, other sentiments and passions make but a transient impression. I have been, for a month or two, excluded from the gay world; and, indeed, fancied myself soaring above it. It is now that I begin to descend,
(15) and find my natural propensity for mixing in the busy scenes and active pleasures of life returning. I have received your letter; your moral lecture rather; and be assured, my dear, your monitorial lessons and advice shall be attended to. I believe
(20) I shall never again resume those airs; which you term *coquettish*, but which I think deserve a softer appellation; as they proceed from an innocent heart, and are the effusions of a youthful, and cheerful mind. We are all invited to
(25) spend the day, tomorrow, at Col. Farington's, who has an elegant seat in the neighborhood. Both he and his Lady are strangers to me; but the friends, by whom I am introduced, will procure me a welcome reception. Adieu.

ELIZA WHARTON.

At the Faringtons', Eliza meets Reverend Boyer, and is initially entranced by him, as he is a distraction from her troubles and a well-respected man. After a short acquaintance, Reverend Boyer attempts to profess his admiration for Eliza, and she evades any discussion of his affection. She writes the following letter after she retired to her room.

To Miss Lucy Freeman

(30)   Mrs. Richman came into my chamber as she was passing to her own. Excuse my intrusion, Eliza, said she; I thought I would just step in and ask you if you have passed a pleasant day?

      Perfectly so, madam; and I have now retired
(35) to protract the enjoyment by recollection. What, my dear, is your opinion of our favorite Mr. Boyer? Declaring him your favorite, madam, is sufficient to render me partial to him. But to be frank, independent of that, I think him an
(40) agreeable man. Your heart, I presume, is now free? Yes, and I hope it will long remain so. Your friends, my dear, solicitous for your welfare, wish to see you suitably and agreeably connected. I hope my friends will never again interpose in my
(45) concerns of that nature. You, madam, who have ever known my heart, are sensible, that had the Almighty spared life, in a certain instance, I must have sacrificed my own happiness, or incurred their censure. I am young, gay, volatile. A
(50) melancholy event has lately extricated me from those shackles, which parental authority had imposed on my mind. Let me then enjoy that freedom which I so highly prize. Let me have opportunity, unbiased by opinion, to gratify my
(55) natural disposition in a participation of those pleasures which youth and innocence afford. Of such pleasures, no one, my dear, would wish to deprive you. But beware, Eliza!—Though strewed with flowers, when contemplated by
(60) your lively imagination, it is, after all, a slippery, thorny path. The round of fashionable dissipation is dangerous. A phantom is often pursued, which leaves its deluded votary the real form of wretchedness. She spoke with an
(65) emphasis, and taking up her candle, wished me a good night. I had not power to return the compliment. Something seemingly prophetic in her looks and expressions, cast a momentary gloom upon my mind! But I despise those
(70) contracted ideas which confine virtue to a cell. I have no notion of becoming a recluse. Mrs. Richman has ever been a beloved friend of mine; yet I always thought her rather prudish. Adieu,
                    ELIZA WHARTON.

12. Which of the following addresses an irony of Eliza exclaiming that "Everything tends to facilitate the return of my accustomed vivacity" (lines 3–4)?

   A.   The Richman residence is actually dour and dull.

   B.   The intensity of Eliza's "accustomed vivacity" is not what others believe it should be.

   C.   Eliza is not previously known for being very lively.

   D.   Mrs. Richman warns Eliza against being too gregarious.

   E.   Eliza is invited to the Faringtons' party.

13. The manner in which Eliza relates the contents of her mother's letter implies that

   A.   Mrs. Wharton believes Eliza should continue to mourn as if she had married her fiancé

   B.   Eliza believes her mother needs her support

   C.   Eliza feels sorry for her mother

   D.   Mrs. Wharton thinks Eliza is overcome with grief, but Eliza hardly mourns at all

   E.   Eliza relies on her mother for emotional sustenance

14. An implied irony about Eliza stating that she is beginning "to descend, and find my natural propensity for mixing in the busy scenes and active pleasures of life returning" (lines 14–16) is that

   A.   Eliza had been socially sequestered while she stayed with her mother

   B.   Eliza predicts she will have a moral downfall

   C.   Eliza is returning to her natural character

   D.   Eliza trusts she can maintain a high moral position

   E.   Eliza believed she had soared above the "gay world"

15. Miss Lucy Freeman appears to be

   A.   ethical and principled

   B.   supportive of Eliza's decisions

   C.   seriously worried about Eliza

   D.   judgmental and antisocial

   E.   fawning and impudent

16. Eliza's distaste for the term "*coquettish*" (line 21) suggests that she feels

  A. she will return to her flirtatious ways
  B. it describes her too accurately
  C. it is acceptable to be a coquette if one is young and innocent
  D. she is above such socially unacceptable behavior
  E. Lucy Freeman has exaggerated Eliza's past behavior

17. Given Eliza's comments about coquettish behavior, what is the implication of the last two sentences she writes in her first letter, "We are all invited . . . a welcome reception" (lines 24–29)?

  A. Eliza's immediate transition to her excitement of a pending party implies she will ignore Lucy's advice.
  B. Mrs. Richman thinks Eliza deserves social company, regardless of what Lucy Freeman suggests.
  C. Eliza must believe the Faringtons will not invite any unsavory characters to their soiree.
  D. Mrs. Richman would not put Eliza in an undesirable social situation.
  E. Eliza is quite accustomed to attending parties at strangers' homes.

18. In the second letter, an effect of blending Eliza's and Mrs. Richman's dialogue into one paragraph without any quotation marks to designate the speaker is that

  A. the dialogue becomes so hard to follow that one cannot tell who is speaking
  B. it demonstrates how much the two women have in common in their comments
  C. it slows down the pace of the dialogue throughout their conversation
  D. it muddles the ideas in Eliza's mind and makes it easier for her to dismiss Mrs. Richman's warning
  E. it emphasizes the way Mrs. Richman is advising Eliza to marry suitably

19. When Mrs. Richman reveals that Eliza's friends "wish to see you suitably and agreeably connected" (lines 42–43), Eliza's reply reveals that she

  A. has a guilty conscience about her lack of mourning for her deceased fiancé
  B. had not wanted to marry her fiancé in the first place
  C. appreciates their genuine concern for her well-being
  D. insists she should be able to choose her own husband
  E. never plans on marrying anyone

20. In the second letter, Eliza's comments about her former engagement use all of the following literary devices EXCEPT

  A. metaphor
  B. hyperbole
  C. personification
  D. understatement
  E. allusion

21. Eliza's claim that Mrs. Richman's warning "cast a momentary gloom upon my mind" (lines 68–69) parallels

  A. her partiality to Mr. Boyer because Mrs. Richman favors him
  B. her reaction to her mother's letter
  C. the way Mrs. Richman worries about Eliza's future
  D. the way Eliza dislikes being thought of as a coquette
  E. her quick dismissal of Lucy Freeman's advice

22. Eliza Wharton can best be characterized as

  A. capricious yet transparent
  B. insolent yet contrite
  C. bored yet languid
  D. respectful yet independent
  E. docile yet argumentative

For questions 23–34, read the following poem carefully before choosing your answers.

The Gift

To pull the metal splinter from my palm
my father recited a story in a low voice.
I watched his lovely face and not the blade.
Before the story ended, he'd removed
the iron sliver I thought I'd die from.   (5)

I can't remember the tale,
but hear his voice still, a well
of dark water, a prayer.
And I recall his hands,
two measures of tenderness   (10)
he laid against my face,
the flames of discipline
he raised above my head.

Had you entered that afternoon
you would have thought you saw a man   (15)
planting something in a boy's palm,
a silver tear, a tiny flame.
Had you followed that boy
you would have arrived here,
where I bend over my wife's right hand.   (20)

Look how I shave her thumbnail down
so carefully she feels no pain.
Watch as I lift the splinter out.
I was seven when my father
took my hand like this,   (25)
and I did not hold that shard
between my fingers and think,
Metal that will bury me,
christen it Little Assassin,
Ore Going Deep for My Heart   (30)
And I did not lift up my wound and cry,
Death visited here!
I did what a child does
when he's given something to keep.
I kissed my father.   (35)

23. An effect of the father's reciting a story "in a low voice" (line 2) is that it

   A. makes the story unintelligible
   B. inspires the boy to help his wife years later
   C. shields the father's fears for the boy
   D. calms and soothes the boy
   E. distracts the boy from the story itself

24. The phrase "I watched his lovely face" (line 3) helps to establish

   A. the son's reaction to his father's assistance
   B. the physical resemblance between father and son
   C. the manner in which the son will remove his wife's splinter
   D. a connection between the physical and spiritual world
   E. how much respect the son feels for his father

25. The son exhibits all of the following characteristics EXCEPT

   A.   fear of death
   B.   hyperbolic reactions
   C.   rash decision making
   D.   sentimentality
   E.   sensitivity

26. Within context, the phrase "Before the story ended," (line 4) implies that

   A.   the story itself is insignificant to the father
   B.   the father deliberately made the story last while he removed the splinter
   C.   anything the father made up would have served the same purpose
   D.   the son also told his wife an unfinished story as he removed her splinter
   E.   the father wants his son to supply his own ending

27. The speaker's comment that "I can't remember the tale" (line 6) implies that the

   A.   speaker strives to recollect the details of the tale
   B.   father's tenderness was more significant than the story
   C.   grown son tells a different tale to his wife when she is in pain
   D.   father never finished the tale
   E.   son was not listening to the tale in the first place

28. Lines 9–13, "And I recall his hands . . . he raised above my head" suggest that

   A.   the father was abusive to the son
   B.   parents need to establish their role in children's lives
   C.   the son will become like his father when he has children
   D.   the son reacts negatively to his father's discipline
   E.   the father is both gentle and strict

29. The speaker's claim that "Had you entered that afternoon / you would have thought you saw a man / planting something in a boy's palm" (lines 14–16) is ironic because

   A.   the father is removing something from the boy's palm
   B.   the son fears the metal splinter will kill him
   C.   the wife also needs assistance to remove a splinter from her hand
   D.   the father plants a seed of kindness in his son
   E.   the son understands his father's love at that moment

30. The speaker's use of the imperative mood in lines 21–23 ("Look how I shave her thumbnail down / so carefully she feels no pain. / Watch as I lift the splinter out.") serves the purpose of

   A.   inflating the speaker's sense of purpose
   B.   commanding respect for his consideration to his wife
   C.   speeding up the action
   D.   focusing attention on his actions
   E.   diverting attention from the wife's pain

31. The metal splinter becomes symbolic of

   A.   roadblocks in life we must individually overcome
   B.   the need for parents to care for their children at all times
   C.   industrial encroachment into humanity's lives
   D.   the way in which significant events are repeated in life
   E.   potentially harmful events that transform into something positive

32. Each of the following are examples of metaphor EXCEPT

   A.   "the metal splinter" (line 1)
   B.   "a well / of dark water" (lines 7–8)
   C.   "two measures of tenderness" (line 10)
   D.   "the flames of discipline" (line 12)
   E.   "a silver tear, a tiny flame" (line 17)

33. Which of the following best identifies the significance of the title?

    A. Parents' love for their children takes many forms.

    B. A simple act of kindness can turn into a lifelong gift.

    C. Children never forget the way their parents treated them.

    D. People can transfer gifts to another person.

    E. One should be willing to accept the gifts that others offer.

34. Which of the following is a central idea of the poem?

    A. Children need to follow their parents' examples.

    B. Parental discipline is necessary for a child's growth.

    C. Pain can be deflected with hope and kindness.

    D. A son's relationship with his father mirrors his relationship with his wife.

    E. All people will need help from others in life.

For questions 35–44, read the following passage carefully before choosing your answers.

To help solve a mystery, Gabriel Betteridge, who faithfully worked for Lady Julia Verinder's family for decades, has been tasked with recording what he knows about the events in the house. Instead of getting to the point, he begins to relate his past position as Lady Verinder's land steward.

Well, there I was in clover, you will say. Placed in a position of trust and honour, with a little cottage of my own to live in, with my rounds on the estate to occupy me in the morning, and my
(5) accounts in the afternoon, and my pipe and my *Robinson Crusoe* in the evening—what more could I possibly want to make me happy? Remember what Adam wanted when he was alone in the Garden of Eden; and if you don't
(10) blame it in Adam, don't blame it in me.

The woman I fixed my eye on, was the woman who kept house for me at my cottage. Her name was Selina Goby. I agree with the late William Cobbett about picking a wife. See that she chews
(15) her food well and sets her foot down firmly on the ground when she walks, and you're all right. Selina Goby was all right in both these respects, which was one reason for marrying her. I had another reason, likewise, entirely of my own

(20) discovering. Selina, being a single woman, made me pay so much a week for her board and services. Selina, being my wife, couldn't charge for her board, and would have to give me her services for nothing. That was the point of view I
(25) looked at it from. Economy—with a dash of love. I put it to my mistress, as in duty bound, just as I had put it to myself.

"I have been turning Selina Goby over in my mind," I said, "and I think, my lady, it will be
(30) cheaper to marry her than to keep her."

My lady burst out laughing, and said she didn't know which to be most shocked at—my language or my principles. Some joke tickled her, I suppose, of the sort that you can't take unless
(35) you are a person of quality. Understanding nothing myself but that I was free to put it next to Selina, I went and put it accordingly. And what did Selina say? Lord! how little you must know of women, if you ask that. Of course she
(40) said, Yes.

As my time drew nearer, and there got to be talk of my having a new coat for the ceremony, my mind began to misgive me. I have compared notes with other men as to what they felt while
(45) they were in my interesting situation; and they have all acknowledged that, about a week before it happened, they privately wished themselves out of it. I went a trifle further than that myself; I actually rose up, as it were, and tried to get out
(50) of it. Not for nothing! I was too just a man to expect she would let me off for nothing. Compensation to the woman when the man gets out of it, is one of the laws of England. In obedience to the laws, and after turning it over
(55) carefully in my mind, I offered Selina Goby a feather-bed and fifty shillings to be off the bargain. You will hardly believe it, but it is nevertheless true—she was fool enough to refuse.

After that it was all over with me, of course. I
(60) got the new coat as cheap as I could, and I went through all the rest of it as cheap as I could. We were not a happy couple, and not a miserable couple. We were six of one and half-a-dozen of the other. How it was I don't understand, but we
(65) always seemed to be getting, with the best of motives, in one another's way. When I wanted to go up-stairs, there was my wife coming down; or when my wife wanted to go down, there was I coming up. That is married life, according to my
(70) experience of it.

After five years of misunderstandings on the stairs, it pleased an all-wise Providence to relieve us of each other by taking my wife. I was left with my little girl Penelope, and with no other

(75) child. Shortly afterwards, Sir John died, and my lady was left with her little girl, Miss Rachel, and no other child. I have written to very poor purpose of my lady, if you require to be told that my little Penelope was taken care of, under my
(80) good mistress's own eye, and was sent to school and taught, and made a sharp girl, and prompted, when old enough, to be Miss Rachel's own maid.

35. The narrator's biblical allusion inadvertently informs the reader that

    A. Gabriel thinks his life will be a veritable Garden of Eden in the future

    B. Gabriel thinks that every man must need a woman to complete his life

    C. Gabriel thinks that his own life would feel complete if he had a wife

    D. Gabriel believes that he is a devout man who follows religious teachings

    E. Gabriel believes that the Bible can instruct the common man's life

36. Gabriel's choosing to wed Selina Goby implies all of the following about his character EXCEPT

    A. he is parsimonious

    B. he is vexed about his future

    C. he is not romantic

    D. he is practical

    E. he is not discerning

37. Gabriel takes the most pride in which of the following?

    A. Independently discovering a second reason for marrying Selina Goby

    B. Using the Bible to justify his marital decision

    C. Having such a good relationship with his employer, Lady Verinder

    D. Understanding women so well

    E. Having local men to confide in

38. What does Gabriel imply about the "joke [that] tickled" Lady Verinder (line 33)?

    A. He resents that she laughs at him.

    B. He often amused Lady Verinder.

    C. He worries that he has offended her.

    D. He cannot fathom why she would object to Selina Goby.

    E. He does not understand the joke because he is of a lower class.

39. Gabriel suggests that the trigger for changing his mind about marrying Selina is that he

    A. discovers Selina can easily be bought off

    B. worries Lady Verinder disapproves

    C. ascertains other men wish they had not married

    D. realizes he is expected to buy a new coat for the ceremony

    E. questions his own initial motives

40. Each of the following expresses one of Gabriel's personal principles EXCEPT

    A. "I agree with the late William Cobbett" (lines 13–14)

    B. "Economy—with a dash of love" (lines 25–26)

    C. "I put it to my mistress, as in duty bound" (line 26)

    D. ". . . they privately wished themselves out of it" (lines 47–48)

    E. "Not for nothing!" (line 50)

41. In context, the phrase "off the bargain" (lines 56–57) refers to

    A. bartering the dowry

    B. wheeling-and-dealing with Selina

    C. breaking off their engagement

    D. arguing about the wedding

    E. misunderstandings during their marriage

42. All of the following demonstrate Gabriel's personal method of reasoning EXCEPT

    A. ". . . if you don't blame it in Adam, don't blame it in me" (lines 9–10)

    B. "Selina, being my wife, couldn't charge for her board" (lines 22–23)

    C. "Of course she said, Yes" (lines 39–40)

    D. ". . . she was fool enough to refuse" (line 58)

    E. ". . . it pleased an all-wise Providence to relieve us of each other by taking my wife" (lines 72–73)

43. The point of view most nearly characterizes Gabriel Betteridge as someone who is

   A.   gregarious and imperturbable
   B.   unpretentious and forthright
   C.   disingenuous and deliberate
   D.   cavalier and subtle
   E.   pensive and turbid

44. Which of the following adds humor to the passage?

   A.   "Well, there I was in clover, you will say" (line 1)
   B.   "That was the point of view I looked at it from" (lines 24–25)
   C.   " . . . I went and put it accordingly" (line 37)
   D.   "I went a trifle further than that myself" (line 48)
   E.   "After five years of misunderstandings on the stairs . . . " (lines 71–72)

For questions 45–55, read the following poem carefully before choosing your answers.

Fabrications

As if to prove again
The bright resilience of the frailest form,
A spider has repaired her broken web
Between the palm-trunk and the jasmine tree.

Etched on the clear new light   (5)
Above the still-imponderable ground,
It is a single and gigantic eye
Whose golden pupil, now, the spider is.

Through it you catch the flash
Of steeples brightened as a cloud slips over,   (10)
One loitering star, and off there to the south
Slow vultures kettling in the lofts of air.

Each day men frame and weave
In their own way whatever looms in sight,
Though they must see with human scale and bias,   (15)
And though there is much unseen. The Talmud[1] tells

How dusty travelers once
Came to a river where a roc[2] was wading,
And would have hastened then to strip and bathe,
Had not a booming voice from heaven said,   (20)

"Step not into that water:
Seven years since, a joiner dropped his axe
Therein, and it hath not yet reached the bottom."
Whether beneath our senses or beyond them,

The world is bottomless,   (25)
A drift of star-specks or the Red King's dream,
And fogs our thought, although it is not true
That we grasp nothing till we grasp it all.

Witness this ancient map
Where so much blank and namelessness surround   (30)
A little mushroom-clump of coastal towers
In which we may infer civility,

A harbor-full of spray,
And all those loves which hint of love itself,
Imagining too a pillar at whose top   (35)
A spider's web upholds the architrave.

---

[1]**The Talmud:** the collection of writings that serves as the central text of Judaism and the primary source of Jewish religious law and theology
[2]**roc:** a mythical bird of enormous size and strength that originated in Arabian folktales

45. The first stanza implies which of the following?

   A. Nature is full of surprises.
   B. Spiders are frail creatures.
   C. Some ideas need to be proven on a daily basis.
   D. The natural world is resilient.
   E. Things that appear weak may actually be quite strong.

46. The antecedent of the word "it" in lines 7 and 9 is

   A. "spider" (line 3)
   B. "web" (line 3)
   C. "ground" (line 6)
   D. "eye" (line 7)
   E. "pupil" (line 8)

47. Which of the following lines best initiates the analogy between spiders and mankind?

   A. "A spider has repaired her broken web" (line 3)
   B. "It is a single and gigantic eye" (line 7)
   C. "Through it you catch the flash" (line 9)
   D. "Each day men frame and weave" (line 13)
   E. "That we grasp nothing till we grasp it all" (line 28)

48. The phrase "Above the still-imponderable ground" (line 6) implies that the

   A. web never reaches the ground
   B. morning light makes it hard to see the ground
   C. web will catch airborne insects
   D. spider builds the web close to the ground
   E. spider cannot accurately conceive of the distance from the web to the ground

49. The concept of "A drift of star-specks or the Red King's dream" (line 26) most clearly parallels

   A. "The bright resilience of the frailest form" (line 2)
   B. "Above the still-imponderable ground" (line 6)
   C. "One loitering star" (line 11)
   D. "they must see with human scale and bias" (line 15)
   E. "a booming voice from heaven said" (line 20)

50. The poem contains all of the following literary devices EXCEPT

   A. allusion
   B. analogy
   C. apostrophe
   D. irony
   E. metaphor

51. The speaker implies that

   A. man-made edifices prove mankind's civility
   B. ancient map-makers were accurate
   C. spiders have oversized eyes
   D. people will heed warnings
   E. the spider's web will be broken every day

52. Which of the following serves as the subject of the verb "fogs" in line 27?

   A. "senses" (line 24)
   B. "world" (line 25)
   C. "drift" (line 26)
   D. "dream" (line 26)
   E. "thought" (line 27)

53. The title of the poem suggests that

    A. humanity invents stories for instructional purposes

    B. what is constructed can be destroyed

    C. what is sturdy is also fragile

    D. natural phenomena can represent the world of humanity

    E. it is natural to construct

54. The "ancient map" (line 29) reinforces the speaker's point that

    A. humans cannot fully comprehend the world

    B. humanity is civilized

    C. cartographers can clarify the world's boundaries

    D. steeples and towers can be found along coastlines

    E. humanity is surrounded by water

55. The tone of the speaker can best be described as

    A. remorseful

    B. wistful

    C. confident

    D. anxious

    E. lofty

IF YOU FINISH BEFORE TIME IS CALLED, CHECK YOUR WORK ON THIS SECTION ONLY. DO NOT WORK ON ANY OTHER SECTION IN THE TEST.

Section II: Free-Response Questions

Time: 2 hours

3 questions

Question 1

(Suggested time: 40 minutes. This question counts toward one-third of the total free-response section score.)

Directions: In the following poem, "Snow in the Suburbs," by Thomas Hardy (1925), the speaker watches the impact a snowfall has on outdoor animals. Read the poem carefully. Then, in a well-written essay, analyze how the poetic devices convey the speaker's complex attitude toward nature.

In your response you should do the following:

- Respond to the prompt with a thesis that presents an interpretation and may establish a line of reasoning.
- Select and use evidence to develop and support your line of reasoning.
- Explain the relationship between the evidence and your thesis.
- Use appropriate grammar and punctuation in communicating your argument.

Snow in the Suburbs

Every branch big with it,
Bent every twig with it;
Every fork like a white web-foot;
Every street and pavement mute:
Some flakes have lost their way, and grope back upward when   (5)
Meeting those meandering down they turn and descend again.
The palings[1] are glued together like a wall,
And there is no waft of wind with the fleecy fall.

A sparrow enters the tree,
Whereon immediately   (10)
A snow-lump thrice his own slight size
Descends on him and showers his head and eye
And overturns him,
And near inurns[2] him,
And lights on a nether[3] twig, when its brush   (15)
Starts off a volley of other lodging lumps with a rush.

The steps are a blanched slope,
Up which, with feeble hope,
A black cat comes, wide-eyed and thin;
And we take him in.   (20)

---

[1]**palings:** wooden stakes of a fence
[2]**inurns:** buries
[3]**nether:** lower

Question 2

(Suggested time: 40 minutes. This question counts toward one-third of the total free-response section score.)

Directions: The following passage is an excerpt from Nathaniel Hawthorne's 1843 short story "The Birthmark," which is set in the late 18th century. The passage introduces a recently married couple, Aylmer and Georgiana, who has an unusual birthmark. Read the passage carefully. Then, in a well-written essay, analyze how Hawthorne employs literary devices to characterize the complex relationship between the newlyweds.

In your response you should do the following:

- Respond to the prompt with a thesis that presents an interpretation and may establish a line of reasoning.
- Select and use evidence to develop and support your line of reasoning.
- Explain the relationship between the evidence and your thesis.
- Use appropriate grammar and punctuation in communicating your argument.

In the latter part of the last century there lived a man of science, an eminent proficient in every branch of natural philosophy, who not long before our story opens had made experience of a spiritual affinity more attractive than any chemical one. He had left his laboratory to the care of an assistant, cleared his fine countenance from the furnace smoke, washed the stain of acids from his fingers, and persuaded a beautiful

(5) woman to become his wife. In those days when the comparatively recent discovery of electricity and other kindred mysteries of Nature seemed to open paths into the region of miracle, it was not unusual for the love of science to rival the love of woman in its depth and absorbing energy. The higher intellect, the imagination, the spirit, and even the heart might all find their congenial aliment in pursuits which, as some of their ardent votaries believed, would ascend from one step of powerful intelligence to another, until the philosopher

(10) should lay his hand on the secret of creative force and perhaps make new worlds for himself. We know not whether Aylmer possessed this degree of faith in man's ultimate control over Nature. He had devoted himself, however, too unreservedly to scientific studies ever to be weaned from them by any second passion. His love for his young wife might prove the stronger of the two; but it could only be by intertwining itself with his love of science, and uniting the strength of the latter to his own.

(15) Such a union accordingly took place, and was attended with truly remarkable consequences and a deeply impressive moral. One day, very soon after their marriage, Aylmer sat gazing at his wife with a trouble in his countenance that grew stronger until he spoke.

"Georgiana," said he, "has it never occurred to you that the mark upon your cheek might be removed?"

"No, indeed," said she, smiling; but perceiving the seriousness of his manner, she blushed deeply. "To tell

(20) you the truth it has been so often called a charm that I was simple enough to imagine it might be so."

"Ah, upon another face perhaps it might," replied her husband; "but never on yours. No, dearest Georgiana, you came so nearly perfect from the hand of Nature that this slightest possible defect, which we hesitate whether to term a defect or a beauty, shocks me, as being the visible mark of earthly imperfection."

"Shocks you, my husband!" cried Georgiana, deeply hurt; at first reddening with momentary anger, but

(25) then bursting into tears. "Then why did you take me from my mother's side? You cannot love what shocks you!"

To explain this conversation it must be mentioned that in the centre of Georgiana's left cheek there was a singular mark, deeply interwoven, as it were, with the texture and substance of her face. In the usual state of her complexion—a healthy though delicate bloom—the mark wore a tint of deeper crimson, which imperfectly

(30) defined its shape amid the surrounding rosiness. When she blushed it gradually became more indistinct, and finally vanished amid the triumphant rush of blood that bathed the whole cheek with its brilliant glow. But if any shifting motion caused her to turn pale there was the mark again, a crimson stain upon the snow, in what Aylmer sometimes deemed an almost fearful distinctness. Its shape bore not a little similarity to the human hand, though of the smallest pygmy size. Georgiana's lovers were wont to say that some fairy at her

(35) birth hour had laid her tiny hand upon the infant's cheek, and left this impress there in token of the magic endowments that were to give her such sway over all hearts. Many a desperate swain would have risked life for the privilege of pressing his lips to the mysterious hand. It must not be concealed, however, that the impression wrought by this fairy sign manual varied exceedingly, according to the difference of temperament in the

(40) beholders. Some fastidious persons—but they were exclusively of her own sex—affirmed that the bloody hand, as they chose to call it, quite destroyed the effect of Georgiana's beauty, and rendered her countenance even hideous. But it would be as reasonable to say that one of those small blue stains which sometimes occur in the purest statuary marble would convert the Eve of Powers to a monster. Masculine observers, if the birthmark did not heighten their admiration, contented themselves with wishing it away, that the world might possess one living specimen of ideal loveliness without the semblance of a flaw. After his marriage,—for he

(45) thought little or nothing of the matter before,—Aylmer discovered that this was the case with himself.

Question 3

(Suggested time: 40 minutes. This question counts toward one-third of the total free-response section score.)

Directions: Evil characters in literary works can be complex and reveal more about humanity's choices and motivations than the heroic protagonist.

From your own reading or from the list below, select such an evil character and then write an essay in which you analyze what the character's villainy reveals about humanity and how the character's complexity enhances an interpretation of the work as a whole. Do not merely summarize the plot.

In your response you should do the following:

- Respond to the prompt with a thesis that presents an interpretation and may establish a line of reasoning.
- Select and use evidence to develop and support your line of reasoning.
- Explain the relationship between the evidence and your thesis.
- Use appropriate grammar and punctuation in communicating your argument.

All the Light We Cannot See	*The Merchant of Venice*
Billy Budd	*Night*
Catch-22	*No Country for Old Men*
Cat's Eye	*Oliver Twist*
The Crucible	*One Flew Over the Cuckoo's Nest*
Dracula	*Othello*
East of Eden	*Paradise Lost*
Frankenstein	*Rebecca*
The Goldfinch	*The Scarlet Letter*
Great Expectations	*The Secret Life of Bees*
Heart of Darkness	*Sophie's Choice*
Jane Eyre	*Tess of the D'Urbervilles*
The Kite Runner	*A Thousand Splendid Suns*
The Known World	*To Kill a Mockingbird*
Little Bee	*The Underground Railroad*
Lord of the Flies	*Vanity Fair*
Macbeth	*Who's Afraid of Virginia Woolf?*
Medea	*Wuthering Heights*

IF YOU FINISH BEFORE TIME IS CALLED, CHECK YOUR WORK ON THIS SECTION ONLY. DO NOT WORK ON ANY OTHER SECTION IN THE TEST.

Answer Key

Section I: Multiple-Choice Questions

First Prose Passage	Second Prose Passage	First Poem	Third Prose Passage	Second Poem
1. C	12. B	23. D	35. C	45. D
2. D	13. D	24. A	36. B	46. B
3. E	14. E	25. C	37. A	47. D
4. D	15. A	26. B	38. E	48. E
5. A	16. C	27. B	39. D	49. B
6. A	17. A	28. E	40. D	50. C
7. B	18. D	29. A	41. C	51. A
8. C	19. B	30. D	42. D	52. B
9. B	20. C	31. E	43. B	53. E
10. D	21. E	32. A	44. E	54. A
11. E	22. D	33. B		55. C
		34. C		

Answers and Explanations

Section I: Multiple-Choice Questions

First Prose Passage

The passage for these questions is an excerpt from the novella Typhoon *by Joseph Conrad, which was first published in serial form in 1902. The setting of this excerpt is the storm-tossed Formosa Strait of the South China Sea, as Captain MacWhirr and his first mate, Jukes, command the crew of the newly built steamship, the* Nan-Shan, *but fail to avoid an oncoming typhoon.*

1. **C.** The irony lies in the fact that the phrase promises "relations . . . were . . . of a brotherly nature," yet this supposedly calm and peaceful harmony is immediately proven to be illusory. The true state of affairs is much more contentious; it appears that the engineer is throwing a fit, and Jukes begs him "not to make a disgusting ass of himself," then "the second rushed up to the fray. He flung himself at the port ventilator as though he meant to tear it out bodily and toss it overboard," and the discord goes on and on. It's clear that the crew's interactions on the *Nan-Shan* are far from "brotherly." Therefore, choice C is correct. Choice A gets it backward; this dissonant scene is not indicative of a deep camaraderie among the crew. Choice B is in the right direction, but it goes too far; while it is true that this scene shows friction between the officers on deck and the men working in the engine room, it does not give credence to the notion that there has been long-running strife or a stark schism between the two groups. Choice D is simply off topic; there is nothing to intimate other unspoken relations. Choice E, just like choice A, seems to get it backward; this contentious scene gives no evidence of a good-natured relationship.

2. **D.** The action in the opening scene is intended to be attention-getting, but it is not really violent; while the engineer is later described as displaying "mad animosity," his initial over-the-top antics come across as mostly comedic, choice D. The other answer choices all miss the essential comic aspects of the scene. This quarrel between two characters is not a life-or-death battle (A), nor is it a brawl (B) or a melee, that is, a fight involving a group of people (C). Choice E can easily be eliminated because the passage offers no hint of any alcohol drinking among the men.

3. E. The engineer's eye movements are significant; they fill us in on the background action, that the ship is rocking wildly in violent, rough seas, choice E. Visualize what the engineer sees: First he looks up to the sky, and then, as "he let his glassy stare descend," he sees the watery horizon "tilting up to a [terrifying] angle of forty degrees" and seeming "to hang on a slant for a while" before finally settling down slowly. Whew! The eye movements are certainly not random, so you can eliminate choice A. The passage offers no evidence that the engineer was injured (B); he is merely overwhelmed with what he sees. Choice C is unreasonable; not only does the passage offer no hint that the engineer is seasick, but also it is difficult to believe a seasoned seaman would become seasick so early in the storm. Choice D contradicts the passage. The engineer goes up to the deck to move the ventilator into the wind so it will generate more air below deck; he is not surveying the bridge.

4. D. In order to appreciate a character's personality, be sure you understand the action. The engineer has just one job: to keep the engines running. To do that he needs steam pressure in the boiler to power the engines. What has gone wrong? The steam is dropping because the firemen who are feeding the fuel to the boiler are "going faint." What does he do about it? Upon Jukes' taunting, the engineer rushes onto the deck and tries to twist the port ventilator into the wind, which would provide more fresh air below, so his firemen would be able to do their work and the steam pressure would not fall. Unfortunately, the engineer cannot turn the ventilator more than a few inches, and after his heated exchange with Jukes, he returns below to resume his job. From all this, one can certainly conclude that he is single-minded, choice D; he focuses entirely on performing his job, no matter how much the weather or the crew or anything else tries to thwart him. He is far from respectful (A); he's actually quite impertinent. Choice B, impulsive, is not accurate; the engineer only comes up to the deck because Jukes taunts him to do so. While it is possible the engineer might be cynical (C), the passage does not offer sufficient proof to make this the best choice. Describing the engineer as savage (E) is far too strong; he may have a hot temper and high emotions, but his actions certainly do not go so far as to be savage.

5. A. In this case, the correct answer seems to jump right out; the opening line of paragraph four directly states "The word 'barometer' seemed to revive the second engineer's mad animosity," choice A. Choice B might seem appealing to some as it is in the right direction. It's true that "the steam is going down," referring to the decreasing steam pressure in the engines, which was the original cause of his agitation; however, this question specifically asks what *rejuvenated* his furor, not what initially precipitated it, so choice B is wrong. The other answer choices all identify irrelevant quotes from the paragraph; the engineer's rage was not revived by the firemen going faint (C), nor by the chief going silly (D), nor that he might be about to cry (E).

6. A. Consider that the engineer has come up to the bridge in a near-panic to report a serious problem, the boiler couldn't produce enough steam, which means that the engines will eventually quit, leaving the ship powerless and helpless against the storm. Unfortunately, Captain MacWhirr is oblivious to the significance of the warning, choice A, and he only notes the man's blunt style, saying "'That's a very violent man'" and "'A profane man'" and "'I'll have to get rid of him . . . '" The Captain never actually notices the engineer's message, so he cannot be intrigued by it (B). Similarly, this same logic eliminates choices C and D; Captain MacWhirr cannot be aghast (horrified) or unsurprised at what he never acknowledges. Finally, he is certainly not appreciative of the timely advice (E); instead, he is offended by the engineer's manner.

7. B. Process of elimination works well on this question. Simply put the three plot elements in the right order and you identify choice B as the correct answer. The passage starts with the lighthearted conflict between Jukes and the engineer, then it introduces the background peril of the storm, and it ends with the off-kilter dialogue between Jukes and the Captain. All of the incorrect responses will have at least one inaccurate idea and/or they will list the actions in the wrong chronology. Choice A contains both types of errors: The actions are listed in the wrong order, and it incorrectly asserts that the passage has a resolution. Choice C inaccurately claims that lighthearted action occurs in the middle of the passage. Choice D begins incorrectly; although we may infer that the crew will face life-threatening peril in the oncoming storm, the passage itself has no life-or-death struggle. Choice E wrongly inserts conflict resolution and serious heartfelt dialogue.

8. C. Captain MacWhirr's inane questions about Jukes' head being wrapped in a proverbial woolen blanket and about saints swearing reveal that he is a literalist; he is not capable of comprehending a simple metaphor; in short, he has no imagination, choice C. His pointless questions do not indicate that he is perceptive (A); in fact, his questions seem to prove the opposite. The Captain, as a professional, undoubtedly has knowledge of the vessel (B), but that is irrelevant to this question and his comments have nothing to do with the ship itself. The Captain's questions provide no hint that Jukes has tricked the Captain (D); instead, Jukes was uttering figurative phrases that the Captain took literally. Choice E contradicts the passage; the Captain's questions demonstrate his lack of understanding, plus he is clearly frustrated with Jukes, he feels no delight, and he gains no advantage.

9. **B.** As the passage comes to a close, the Captain's exclamations about the engineer become increasingly heated, finally ending with a threat, "'Damme! I'll fire him out of the ship if he don't look out.'" Thus, Jukes gains a new insight, choice B; the Captain can be quite emotional and volatile after all, and Jukes concludes "'Goodness me! Somebody's put a new inside to my old man. Here's temper, if you like.'" In this denouement, the characters' conflicts are not resolved (A); the Captain, Jukes, and the engineer have settled nothing. Choice C is unreasonable and contradictory; the passage clearly indicates a storm is coming and the ocean will get rougher. Choice D is incorrect in claiming that the Captain is having second thoughts about firing the engineer; rather, he becomes increasingly upset with him. Choice E accurately states that Jukes gains new insight, but it involves the Captain, not the engineer.

10. **D.** All but one of the lines quoted in this question do, indeed, give the reader greater insight into Jukes' character. The correct response, choice D, is a quote that describes the Captain, not Jukes. Choice A shows us that Jukes tries to keep a semblance of decorum on the ship. Choice B demonstrates that Jukes can be both condescending and cruelly eager to let the engineer make a fool of himself. Choice C states explicitly that Jukes thinks himself superior. Choice E lets us know that Jukes is quietly stubborn; without directly saying so to the Captain, he stands by his notion that the heat is responsible for everyone's irritability.

11. **E.** The passage has many witty sections; for example, look at the first paragraph and the implications of the verbal exchanges between Jukes and the engineer, the fourth paragraph that describes the engineer's emotions, and the dialogue between Jukes and Captain MacWhirr that concludes the passage. Although the wording is often humorous, the tone is also ominous, because we know a very serious storm is on the horizon. Therefore, choice E is correct. Choice A is inaccurate in calling the tone reflective, although "droll" may be an acceptable description. Jukes may gain an insight at the very end, but that does not mean the whole passage is reflective. Choice B is too strong in both terms. While Jukes and the engineer are sarcastic in the first paragraph, that tone does not pervade the whole passage, and the term "oppressive" is far too negative. The weather may be oppressive, but the overall tone is not. Choice C is also too extreme in both terms; while some portions may sound aggressive and patronizing, these adjectives do not describe the overall tone. Finally, the word "skeptical" in choice D is inaccurate; the tone is not one of disbelief. Plus, the word "mordant," which is a synonym of sarcastic, only applies to a portion of the passage.

Second Prose Passage

The passage for these questions comes from The Coquette, *an epistolary novel written by Hannah Webster Foster in 1797.*

12. **B.** The introductory material sets the stage for Eliza's situation. Remember that her elderly fiancé had died about 3 months before this letter was written. Eliza had stayed with her mother for 1 month and has been with her relatives, the Richmans, for the last 2 months. In her first letter, Eliza informs Lucy Freeman that living with the Richmans is a "delightful" situation and the "visiting parties perfectly agreeable." She continues to claim that her "accustomed vivacity" is returning, which her relatives apparently encourage. However, we learn Lucy has previously cautioned her from resuming her coquettish airs, and, in her second letter, Eliza reveals that Mrs. Richman warns her against enjoying her freedom too much. Apparently, Eliza's "accustomed vivacity" is a little too much for polite society. Therefore, choice B is correct. Choice A contradicts Eliza's description of the Richman residence; it is very comfortable and affable, not dour and dull. Choice C also contradicts the passage; both Lucy and Mrs. Richman reveal that Eliza has been known for being more than a little lively. Choice D, that Mrs. Richman warns Eliza against being too gregarious, is indeed in the passage, but this warning in itself is not ironic. Choice E is irrelevant to this question; Eliza is invited to a party at the Faringtons' home, but that fact does not address an irony of her regaining her previous liveliness.

13. D. Eliza's description of her mother's letter is a little tricky to read; let's paraphrase her content. Mrs. Wharton believes Eliza has been under "heavy bereavement" and that her heart was in such genuine mourning that when she felt "other sentiments and passions," they were but passing emotions; Mrs. Wharton believes her daughter is indeed experiencing deep grief. However, Eliza reveals that her true reaction is far different. She minimizes any bereavement, explaining that is simply what "[her mother] calls it." She labels her mother as a "Poor woman!" for thinking that Eliza is in mourning, implying she is not. In her second letter, Eliza states explicitly that she did not want to marry her fiancé, that "had the Almighty spared a life," she would have been miserable, and that the "melancholy event" freed her from "those shackles." Therefore, choice D is correct. The idea in choice A, that Mrs. Wharton thinks Eliza should mourn as if she had married, is too strong; it has no specific evidence in the passage. Choice B, that Eliza implies her mother needs her, also has no proof. Choice C, that Eliza feels sorry for her mother, is a misread of her "Poor woman!" phrase; Eliza is not pitying her mother, she is mocking her. Choice E is not implied in Eliza's letters; she apparently relies on no one for emotional support, especially not her mother.

14. E. Notice the irony in Eliza's wording: She informs Lucy that she "fancied herself soaring above" the "gay world" that she had been excluded from while supposedly in mourning for the last 3 months, but then she immediately shifts perspective and "begin[s] to descend" back into her party-filled life. The irony lies in the juxtaposition of her thinking she was "soaring above" and then "descending." Therefore, choice E is correct. Choice A, that Eliza was socially sequestered while staying with her mother, is apparently true, but it does not address the irony of her descent back to her normal personality. Choice B is unreasonable; while it is true that Lucy, Mrs. Richman, and perhaps the readers all fear that Eliza will have a moral downfall, that fear is not why Eliza's statement is ironic. Choice C is true; Eliza is apparently returning to her normal character, but that does not make her descent ironic. Similarly, Eliza likely believes that she can maintain her moral standing in society (D), but it does not address the irony of her descent.

15. A. Everything about Lucy Freeman appears to be socially proper. We understand that she knows Eliza well enough to counsel her friend against immodest behavior, going so far as to label Eliza's actions "coquettish." Although Eliza disdains Lucy's advice as a "moral lecture," Lucy appears to have Eliza's best interests at heart and she is personally ethical and principled, choice A. Choice B is too absolute; Lucy implies she will support her friend's decisions, but only if they are morally proper. It is too much of a stretch to believe that Lucy would support any decision Eliza makes. Choice C is also too much of a stretch; we do understand that Lucy is concerned for her friend, but to say she's *seriously* worried about her is not firmly supported. If we were able to read Lucy's letter, we might know the extent of her worry, but since we only get the information via Eliza's response, we cannot know for sure. Choice D may possibly be accurate in calling Lucy judgmental; after all, she is judging Eliza to some extent, but we have no evidence that she is antisocial. Choice E is flat-out wrong on both counts; Lucy is neither fawning (servile) nor impudent (brazen).

16. C. Eliza takes umbrage at Lucy's term "coquettish," believing it is too harsh a description of her own past behavior. Remember that a coquette is a flirtatious, insincere woman, but Eliza excuses her previous actions as "the effusions of a youthful, and cheerful mind" that were produced by an "innocent heart." Given Eliza's description of her past behavior, it is reasonable to believe Eliza thinks coquettish behavior is acceptable and excusable for an innocent youth, choice C. Choice A may deceive some; although we have plenty of foreshadowing that Eliza may soon return to her flirtatious ways, this does not explain her distaste for the term "coquettish," and it does not answer this question. Choice B is incorrect for a similar reason; although Lucy, Mrs. Richman, and the readers all fear Eliza's coquettish ways, she claims that does not describe her, and that she "shall never again resume those airs." Choice D is too much of a stretch for this specific question. Eliza's distaste for the term "coquettish" deals with her need to defend her past flirtatious behavior; she may claim she won't act that way again, but that does not explain her distaste for the term. Be sure to choose an answer that specifically addresses the question. Finally, it is unreasonable to assume Lucy has exaggerated Eliza's past behavior since Eliza readily admits she innocently flirted in the past (E), plus the idea that Lucy may have exaggerated does not sufficiently explain why Eliza would dislike the term. Choice C is a much stronger answer.

17. A. To understand the implication at the end of Eliza's first letter, it helps to look at the overall progression of her thoughts. She begins by explaining how wonderful her life is at the Richmans' residence. Then she explains how wrong her mother is to believe that Eliza is in mourning. Next she discusses how being "excluded from the gay world" for 2 months initially made her feel above such society, but now she is descending back to her natural propensities. She then addresses Lucy's admonition to avoid returning to her previous coquettish behaviors, which Eliza claims she "shall never again resume." However, she then immediately changes the subject to a party she's looking forward to on the very next day. We therefore have no reason to believe Eliza will follow Lucy's advice, choice A; rather, it appears that she will do the opposite. The errors in choices B, C, and D are all similar. While it is likely that Mrs. Richman thinks Eliza deserves social company (B), and it is also true that the Faringtons would not invite unsavory characters to their party (C), and also that Mrs. Richman would not put Eliza into an undesirable social situation (D), these ideas do not address the connection between Eliza's comments about coquettish behavior and her sudden shift to party anticipation. Choice E, that Eliza is accustomed to attending parties at strangers' homes, has no evidence in the passage, and it is irrelevant to this question.

18. **D.** It is understandable that a reader will have trouble following the conversation between Eliza and Mrs. Richman in the second letter. One has to read carefully while wishing that traditional paragraphs and missing quotation marks were used to separate one speaker from another. Instead, a reader must muddle through it just as Eliza does. The intended effect of this difficulty is that it mirrors Eliza's mindset; it makes it easier for the reader to accept Eliza's quick dismissal of Mrs. Richman's advice, choice D. The nonstop and unpunctuated dialogue keeps Mrs. Richman's ideas from sinking in and changing Eliza's behavior. Choice A would only be attractive to a reader who found the dialogue too frustrating to follow; in fact, with careful reading, one can tell who is speaking. Plus, such a reader-response type of answer would not be appropriate on the AP exam. Choice B misinterprets the dialogue, concluding that Eliza and Mrs. Richman have the same mindset. Choice C is simply inaccurate; the pace of the dialogue is quite speedy, as most comments are single sentences, plus Eliza and Mrs. Richman respond to each other immediately, with no inner contemplation slowing either speaker down. The reader's pace may be slowed because of the need to decipher who is speaking and when she has finished, but that is irrelevant to this question. Choice E is unreasonable; the method of presenting the dialogue has nothing to do with adding emphasis to the way Mrs. Richman advises Eliza to marry. If the author wanted to add such emphasis, Mrs. Richman's advice would be separated into a paragraph of its own.

19. **B.** In the conversation between Eliza and Mrs. Richman, Eliza's longest reply follows Mrs. Richman's comment that Eliza's friends wish to see her "suitably and agreeably connected." Until this point, each woman exchanges one-sentence comments, but now Eliza bursts into a speech with six emotion-laden sentences. Through this process she reveals that, had she married, she would have sacrificed her happiness or done something to incur her friends' "censure." She also infers that marriage would have placed her in "shackles" since she was only marrying out of obedience to her mother. This clearly reveals that she did not want to wed, choice B. Eliza never offers any hint that she feels a speck of remorse over her complete lack of mourning for her deceased fiancé (A). Choice C is similarly incorrect; one might think that Eliza would appreciate her friends' solicitude, but she instead begins by stating "I hope my friends will never again interpose in my concerns of that nature." She does not appreciate their concern, nor their interference. Choice D has no evidence in the passage; in fact, Eliza never actually mentions wanting to get married, let alone insisting she should be allowed to choose a husband. She wants to "enjoy that freedom" that she so highly values. Choice E is too much of an absolute; although Eliza rails against marriage, especially at her age, she does not go so far as to say she will never marry anyone.

20. **C.** Eliza is actually quite eloquent as she angrily responds to Mrs. Richman. She never employs personification, choice C, but she aptly uses other literary devices, such as metaphor (A) while describing her mother's desires as "shackles." This comment is also hyperbolic (B), as is her questionable claim that she must have sacrificed her "own happiness" if she had married. She also uses quite an understatement (D) when she euphemistically and sadly calls her fiancé's death "a melancholy event." Finally, Eliza refers to "the Almighty," an allusion (E) to God.

21. **E.** Remember how quickly Eliza dismissed Lucy's advice in the first letter? She brings the subject up, vows to not be coquettish again, and then immediately revels in her plans for an upcoming party. Similarly, when she laments that Mrs. Richman's unwelcome recommendation "cast a momentary gloom upon my mind," her dismissal of the well-intentioned advice is likewise immediate, commenting that she "always thought [Mrs. Richman] rather prudish." Notice that both instances involve someone close to Eliza offering advice that she promptly ignores. Therefore, choice E is correct. Choice A does not present a parallel situation;

Eliza's comment that Mrs. Richman's favoring of Mr. Boyer is sufficient to make her partial to him is not similar to her quick dismissal of the temporary gloom. Choice B is inaccurate because her mother's letter offers no advice for her to disregard; it is true that Eliza does not agree with her mother, but that does not cast any gloom over her or make it a parallel situation. Choice C is irrelevant; Mrs. Richman's concern for Eliza does not parallel the passing gloom Eliza feels upon hearing her advice. Choice D is not parallel because Eliza experiences no gloom over being thought of as a coquette; she thinks the term is inaccurately harsh and defends her previous behavior.

22. D. While Eliza is definitively independent, valuing her freedom, one cannot deny that she is also dutifully respectful, especially to Mrs. Richman and Lucy. One can also argue that she was respectful to her mother since she was willing to marry her choice of husband even though she did not want to; were it not for the "melancholy event," she would have done so. Therefore, choice D is correct. Choice A incorrectly describes Eliza as capricious; she does not impulsively act on a whim. She may be described as transparent, as we do feel we can see through her motives. Choice B mistakenly describes Eliza as insolent, but she is not so brazen as that. Additionally, she is not contrite and exhibits no remorse for her past. Choice C is completely wrong; we have no indication that Eliza is bored or languid (lethargic) because she comments too often about her many activities. Choice E is incorrect because she is hardly docile (submissive), and her standing up for her own beliefs is not really argumentative. She does not argue with others; she merely expresses her strong opinions.

First Poem

The autobiographical poem for these questions, "The Gift," was written by Li-Young Lee in 1986.

23. D. The father's tale has the effect of soothing his scared son, choice D; his "low voice" helps divert the boy's attention from the splinter in his hand. Notice how the father recites a story "To pull the metal splinter from my palm," and how the son "can't remember the tale," but he still remembers his father's voice as "a prayer." The poem offers no evidence that the father's low voice makes the story unintelligible (A); it appears that the son did hear and understand the words at the time, although he no longer remembers them. Choice B incorrectly draws a connection between the father's low voice and the son's removing a splinter from his wife's hand years later. The father's gift of tenderness and love inspires the son's future actions, not just the father's tone of voice. Choice C, that the father is afraid for his son, also has no evidence in the poem; the boy has a somewhat irrational fear that he could die from the splinter, but the father's low voice exhibits no such fear. Choice E, the idea that the father's low voice distracts the boy from the story, is simply an unreasonable conclusion. The fact that the son does not remember the story years later does not imply that he was distracted from it in the first place.

24. A. The son's comment that he "watched his [father's] lovely face" helps to establish how he will react by the end of the poem, when he realizes he has been "given something to keep" and then kisses his father. The positive phrasing in line 3 predicts the positive ending. The fact that the son focuses on his father's face instead of "the blade" his father uses to extract the splinter ties in with the son's realization that his father gave him a gift, and he in turn kisses his father in thanks. Choice B is not established in the poem; we have no idea if father and son bear any physical resemblance, although they do ultimately share the emotional traits of caring and empathy. Choice C is too much of a stretch; although the son carefully and painlessly removes his wife's splinter years later, the phrase describing his father's "lovely face" does not necessarily establish the son's manner in the future. Choice D is unreasonable; the phrase in this question describes the son's impression of his father's face, but it does not connect it to anything spiritual. Choice E may be a viable idea in the poem; the son indeed respects his father, but the line in question does not necessarily establish that fact.

25. C. The son makes no rash decisions in the poem, choice C. Although he does choose to kiss his father and to gently remove his wife's splinter, neither of these actions is rash. On the other hand, the son *does* exhibit the characteristics in the other answer choices. He has an obvious fear of death (A): He directly states that he "thought I'd die from" the metal splinter and later alludes to the possibility of death when he explains how he did not cry out *Death visited here!* The son is also quite hyperbolic (B) in thinking the splinter could cause his death, although that possibility could occur only in a case of extreme neglect leading to infection. The boy's phrasing to "christen it Little Assassin, / Ore Going Deep for My Heart" is also endearingly hyperbolic. The son also demonstrates sentimentality (D) as he remembers his father's voice and his tender hands, and he kisses his father. His sensitivity (E) is demonstrated as he removes his wife's splinter, gently and painlessly.

26. **B.** The phrase "Before the story ended" indicates that the father removed the splinter prior to completing the story. This idea implies that the story was a ruse the father employed to distract his son from the pain of the metal splinter long enough to remove it; he deliberately makes the story last as long as the distraction is needed to serve its purpose, choice B. Choice A, that the story is insignificant to the father, has no support in the poem; this may possibly be true for the son, since he does not remember the tale, but the father must have remembered the story since he "recited" it, which implies that it has some degree of significance to him. Choice C is an attractive distractor. Remember that the question asks about the phrase within context, and it is immediately followed by the fact that the father had successfully removed the splinter before he could finish the story. The idea that the father could have said anything to serve the same purpose would only work if the father's words were distracting and soothing; however, if his voice was harsh and accusatory, it would not have the same calming effect on his son. Choice D is completely unfounded; the son never hints that he told his wife a story as he removed her splinter. We only see his tender and careful action. Choice E, that the father wants his son to supply his own ending, is unreasonable, especially given that the son does not remember the tale at all.

27. **B.** The speaker dwells on his father's low voice as he removes the splinter and later recalls the tenderness with which he placed his hands on his son's face, but he completely forgets the story itself. These details imply how his father's kindness was more important than the story's content, choice B. Nothing in the poem suggests that the son tries to recollect the details of the tale (A); rather, he completely discounts the tale and only describes his father's voice and gentle touch. Choice C has no evidence in the poem; the son does not tell his wife a tale while she is in pain. Choice D may be deceiving to some; it says that the father never finished his tale, but that fact alone does not suggest why the son cannot remember it. The son tells us that his father's voice and hands are more dominant in his memory. Choice E is unreasonable; nothing in the narrative suggests that the son was not paying attention to the tale at the time. Remember that the comment that he cannot remember the tale is followed with that he still hears his father's voice and recalls his hands.

28. **E.** Lines 9–13 show some contrasts regarding the father. The son refers to his father's hands, which are "two measures of tenderness" but also "the flames of discipline / he raised above my head," so we have evidence that the father is both gentle and strict, choice E. His tenderness is evident throughout the poem, but these lines reveal that the father was also a disciplinarian. Choice A is too strong; some may assume that the father, raising his hands in "flames of discipline," may have actually hit his son, but we have no explicit evidence of that; thus, it is too strong to label the father as abusive. Choice B, that parents need to establish their role in their children's lives, is a viable maxim, but that idea is too general and vague to be the correct response to this question. Choice C draws an unreasonable conclusion: that the son will become like his father when he has children. One can infer he has become somewhat like his father since we see the tenderness with which he removes his wife's splinter years later, but there is no evidence that he has children. Choice D contradicts the poem; the son's every reaction to his father appears positive, not negative.

29. **A.** Notice that the visual imagery pictures the father as "*planting* something in a boy's palm," which is ironic since the father is actually removing the splinter, choice A. To plant something means to insert it, such as seeds in dirt that will in turn grow into plants, but in this case the opposite action occurs. Choice B might sound viable upon first read; it is possibly ironic that the son fears the metal splinter will kill him, when it is not really a deadly threat at all. That fear may possibly be true, but it does not relate to the quotation in this question. Be careful to read each question closely and make sure your answer choice clearly addresses it. Choice C, the idea that the son's wife later needs help getting a splinter out of her hand, is not ironic and it also does not relate to this quotation. Choice D claims that the father planted a seed of kindness in his son, which is symbolically true, but, like the other inaccurate answer choices, it does not address the *irony* in the quotation, so it does not answer the question. Similarly, choice E may be an accurate observation—the son does understand his father's love at that moment—but it is simply not ironic.

30. **D.** The speaker uses imperative verbs as he orders the reader to "Look" as he "shave[s] her thumbnail down," and "Watch" as he "lift[s] the splinter out." These verbs force the reader to focus on his careful actions, and the imperative mood appropriately adds importance to his movements, choice D. Choice A is

off base because the imperative does not inflate the son's sense of purpose; instead, it draws one's attention to what he is doing, to the actual actions he is performing. The first word of choice B, commanding, may appeal to those who understand that the definition of imperative deals with commands. However, the rest of the answer choice does not fit the context: The son is not commanding respect for his consideration to his wife, but instead he is requesting that we pay attention to his actions. Choice C does not accurately address the context of the imperative mood in this poem. In some cases, the imperative may add a degree of speed, since it usually begins a sentence with an action-orientated verb and eliminates the understood subject (you). But in this poem, the action is not swift at all, but slow and careful; thus, this answer choice is a contradiction. Choice E makes no sense for the question; his wife's pain is never described; in fact, he claims that he works so steadily and carefully that "she feels no pain." Therefore, the imperative mood cannot divert attention from something we do not sense in the first place.

31. **E.** The son's splinter is not only painful, it is potentially harmful. The son points out that it was a metal splinter, which in an extreme case might result in a possibly fatal condition, such as tetanus. That is the dire extreme that the son fears when he exclaims, *"Metal that will bury me!"* But this threat is avoided as his father quietly distracts him with a story and gently removes the splinter. The son's reaction proves how the event morphs into something positive, choice E; instead of hysterically crying out how he might have died from the "Little Assassin," he kisses his father and obviously never forgets this example of his father's love. Choice A begins with the alluring idea that the splinter symbolizes roadblocks in life; however, it falls apart with the idea about individually overcoming these obstacles, which contradicts the poem's narrative. Both the son and later his wife need someone else to tenderly help them. Choice B has an interesting idea, but it takes it too far. The splinter might relate to the need for parents to take care of their children, but it is not necessarily symbolic of that need, and parents cannot watch over their children at all times. Choice C takes a small fact, that the splinter is metal, and then exaggerates it into the idea of greater industrial encroachment; this is far too strong and it forces symbolism that does not exist in the first place. Choice D is too weak an answer; the fact that the wife gets a splinter in her thumb years later does not make the child's metal splinter symbolic of repeated significant events. It simply provides the impetus for the poet's recollection.

32. **A.** All of the incorrect answer choices will correctly identify metaphors in the poem; your task is to find the one quotation that is not metaphorical. Choice A is the correct exception; it is literal, naming a real and physical "metal splinter" that the young son has in his palm, and therefore it is not a metaphor. Do not confuse things that are symbolic with things that are metaphorical. Choice B is metaphorical as the son calls his father's voice "a well / of dark water," which establishes the depth and richness of that sound. Choice C is also metaphorical, claiming his father's hands are "two measures of tenderness," describing how the father laid both hands so gently on his son's face. The connotations of this term are deliberate; an action that is *measured* is one that is thoughtful, unhurried, and calculated, which precisely fits the father's actions throughout the poem. "The flames of discipline" (D) is also a metaphor; this refers to the rules and edicts for behavior that are presented to the son by his father's gestures. The "silver tear" and "tiny flame" (E) both stand as metaphors for the metal splinter that the father places in his son's hand after he had removed it from his palm. The image of silver is appropriate because it depicts metal, and the word "tear" fits appropriately both as a noun and a verb. The splinter can take the shape of a tear, the son may shed a tear, and the splinter did literally tear a small hole in his palm. The idea that the splinter is also "a tiny flame" fits the way the splinter must have caused a burning pain in his hand, but it is tiny once removed.

33. **B.** When the father removes his son's splinter, the gift that he offers his son is one of love and tender healing. This kindness serves the son later in life as he in turn acts as tenderly as his father did when he helps his wife; he has not forgotten the gift his father bestowed upon him in his youth, choice B. Choice A is a "second-best" answer choice. It is true that parents' love takes many forms, but this is too vague an answer to be the best response and also it does not address the concept of a gift. Choice C is also too imprecise; the idea that children remember what their parents have done may have some connection to the poem, but it also leaves open the possibility of children also remembering negative actions that their parents may have taken in their lives. Additionally, just like choice A, choice C does not allude to a gift. Choice D does not accurately relate to the poem's title. The father does not transfer his gift to his son; he offers it via his actions and his love. Choice E is irrelevant; one's willingness to accept gifts does not address the significance of this poem's title.

34. **C.** This poem contains a multitude of ideas, but it is only choice C that addresses a central, specific idea of the poem. On a literal level, the father eases his son's physical pain by removing the splinter, but a much deeper point is that, above all else, the son remembers how his father's tenderness and kindness distracted him and eased his childhood trauma. Choice A is far too bland and vague; the poem does not really deal with children's need to follow their parents' examples. Instead, it addresses the son's awareness of his father's gift on a deep emotional level. Choice B is hardly a central idea of the poem. It is true that the father's discipline is mentioned once, but do not confuse this with a central idea, which needs to permeate the poem overall. The idea in choice D makes little sense and is of questionable accuracy. There is no evidence that the son's relationship with his wife parallels his relationship with his father earlier in life, other than the fact that son and wife both needed a splinter to be removed from their hand. This is an analogous situation, but not a mirrored relationship. Choice E, similar to choice A, is just too vague and unspecific to be the best answer. The poem deals specifically with the father's admirable ability to soothe his son's pain through gentle kindness, but choice E merely asserts that all people will need help from others, which can come in many forms.

Third Prose Passage

The passage for these questions comes from The Moonstone, *written by Wilkie Collins and originally published in serial form between January and August 1868. In this excerpt, Gabriel Betteridge, a faithful and long-serving employee of Lady Julia Verinder, describes his engagement and marriage to Selina Goby.*

35. **C.** Gabriel admits that it appears he has everything he could want: a good and respectable job, a little cottage to live in, plus his pipe and *Robinson Crusoe* for evening entertainment. However, his biblical allusion to Adam reveals that he also feels the need for a wife, choice C; he writes, "Remember what Adam wanted when he was alone in the Garden of Eden; and if you don't blame it in Adam, don't blame it in me." Choice A is too much of a stretch; it's unreasonable to think Gabriel believes his life will emulate the Garden of Eden, plus, this answer choice does not address his need for a wife, as in the reference to Adam. Choice B is incorrect because of its absolute phrase that every man must need a wife; Gabriel speaks only for himself. Choice D presents an unwarranted assumption; we do not know Gabriel's degree of religious devotion nor how much he follows religious teachings. We only know that he is aware of the story of Adam and the Garden of Eden. Choice E is unreasonable; the narrator is not preaching about biblical instruction, only this one allusion to a biblical story.

36. **B.** Gabriel exhibits no sense of being irritated or vexed about his future, choice B; rather, he plots a course and logically proceeds to fulfill it. The other answer choices are all inferences that can be properly drawn. Gabriel consistently proves that he is cheap, or parsimonious (A). For example, he chooses Selina so he won't have to pay her as a housekeeper, he balks at buying a new coat for the wedding, then buys the cheapest one he can, and "went through all the rest of it as cheap as I could." Gabriel could hardly be called a romantic, so choice C is logical; he chooses Selina for practical reasons and he does not woo her but instead basically presents marriage as a financial proposition. Gabriel is extremely practical (D); he decides why Selina will be a good wife, presents it to Lady Verinder and then to Selina for approval. He follows a practical step-by-step method. Finally, Gabriel demonstrates his lack of discerning taste (E) when he looks no further than his housekeeper for a wife. He never mentions considering any other potential mates, such as ladies who live nearby.

37. **A.** Gabriel appears particularly pleased with himself when he realizes he can save money by marrying Selina Goby. He claims "I had another reason, likewise, entirely of my own discovering." Notice the wording of this question; it specifically asks what Gabriel is *most* proud of, which means you have to prioritize the answer choices. We can infer that Gabriel is proud to some degree of using his knowledge of the Bible to justify his decision to marry Selina (B); of having a good relationship with Lady Verinder (C); of understanding women, at least in his own opinion (D); and of knowing local men he can confide in before marriage (E). However, he never actually states having pride in these ideas, but he does take credit for discovering a second reason why Selina will make a good wife. Thus, choice A is the strongest answer.

38. **E.** When Lady Verinder "burst out laughing" at Gabriel's rationale for marrying Selina, he is not sure why she is so amused. He believes "some joke tickled her," but that it required being "a person of quality" to understand the joke. Thus, the implied reason he doesn't comprehend her laughter is that he is not of her

class, choice E. Choice A is wrong because Gabriel is too simple and sincere to think that Lady Verinder would be laughing at him, and the verb "resents" is too strong. The passage offers no evidence for choice B, that Gabriel frequently amused Lady Verinder. Choice C is incorrect because, although Gabriel does not understand her laughter, it does not appear that he worries she was offended. Choice D states something that Gabriel probably believes to be true: He cannot imagine why Lady Verinder would object to Selina. However, this idea does not answer the question about the *reason* for her laughter.

39. D. Shortly after Gabriel tells his cute anecdote about Selina accepting his proposal ("Lord! how little you must know of women, if you ask that. Of course she said, Yes"), he soon realizes he will be expected to buy a new coat for the occasion, choice D. That's the precipitating reason his "mind began to misgive [him]." Knowing Gabriel's propensity for parsimony, this sudden doubt should not be unexpected. Choice A contradicts the passage; Selina cannot be bought off, as "she was fool enough to refuse" his offer of a feather-bed and fifty shillings to forgo the engagement, and this fact is not what caused him to have second thoughts. Choice B, that he worries Lady Verinder disapproves of his marriage, has no evidence in the passage. Choice C may sound reasonable at first, but its wording is questionable. When Gabriel talks to other men and asks what they felt while "they were in my interesting situation," they all report getting cold feet about a week before the wedding, NOT that they actually wished they had not married. Choice E is unreasonable; it appears that Gabriel never questions his initial motives; he only balks at spending money on a coat. (As a side note, later in the novel, after his 50 years of service, Lady Verinder presents Gabriel with a "beautiful waistcoat of wool that she had worked herself," a gift that Gabriel tearfully accepts.)

40. D. The correct response must be a quotation that does not suggest Gabriel has principles. When he states " . . . they privately wished themselves out of it," choice D, he is referring to other men who got cold feet, but went through with their marriages, not to himself or his own principles. Choice A shows that he agrees with William Cobbett's principles for choosing a wife: Find a woman who chews her food well and walks firmly. (Incidentally, William Cobbett's popular letters, titled *Advice to Young Men* and published in 1829, suggest that to judge a woman's chewing habits, men should observe how a woman eats a mutton chop or bread and cheese! He also claims "another mark of industry is a quick step . . . that comes down with a hearty will.") In choice B, Gabriel directly states one of his personal principles, that his approach to Selina is "Economy—with a dash of love." While we may wonder how much of a dash of love he actually has, he does seem to value it, at least in principle. Choice C further demonstrates his principles, since he feels "duty bound" to present his marriage wishes to Lady Verinder before asking Selina for her hand. Finally, choice E strongly shows his principles. His exclamation "Not for nothing!" refers to the fact that he will indeed offer Selina some recompense if she agrees to end their engagement, as it is the law.

41. C. When Gabriel offers Selina "a feather-bed and fifty shillings to be *off the bargain*," he is referring to terminating the engagement, choice C; he's offering her a bribe to let him out of his promise of marriage. He is surprised that she declined his offer, "she was fool enough to refuse." He is not bartering or haggling about the dowry (A), nor is he wheeling-and-dealing with her (B). Choice D, arguing about the wedding, has no textual evidence. Although Gabriel admits he and Selina later had "misunderstandings" during their marriage (E), this word does not refer to the phrase "off the bargain" in this context.

42. D. Gabriel has a way of finding self-justifications for his thought process and his actions. Choice D is the only quotation that does not deal with his personal reasoning; the quote "she was fool enough to refuse" actually refers to Selina's action, not Gabriel's. Plus, he was wrong about what she would do; he had expected her to take him up on his offer. Choice A does demonstrate his reasoning, as he draws a parallel between the biblical Adam wanting a wife and his own desire to take a wife. Choice B also reveals Gabriel's reasoning as he realizes Selina cannot charge him for housekeeping if they marry. Gabriel feels soundly justified when he states so directly that Selina, of course, accepted his proposal (C), as if it's the only logical option. Gabriel rationalizes Selina's early death, after only five years of marriage, as an act of Providence, designed to "relieve us of each other" (E).

43. B. The first-person narration gives Gabriel the opportunity to let us see him as he wishes to be seen; we do not have the opportunity to know what others think of him or of his actions. Given that, Gabriel comes across as being quite unpretentious and forthright, choice B; he is down-to-earth and plainspoken. Choice A is incorrect in both traits; one would never describe Gabriel as gregarious (outgoing and social) or imperturbable (stable and unflappable). Notice how he gets discombobulated when Selina refuses his offer to get out of the engagement and when Lady Verinder laughs at his rationale for choosing Selina. In choice C, the word "disingenuous" is incorrect; Gabriel is not insincere or deceitful. The second term in choice C, "deliberate," does apply to Gabriel's way of going about marriage. Choice D is unreasonable; the word "cavalier" refers to someone who is an arrogant cad, and the second term, "subtle," hardly describes the simple Gabriel. Choice E is incorrect because Gabriel is neither pensive (contemplative) nor turbid (confused).

44. E. Gabriel's narrative is frequently humorous, although he probably does not intend for it to be. The news that his wife died is presented as a chuckle-worthy understatement; she was taken by Providence "after five years of misunderstandings on the stairs." But this actually refers to the only fault Gabriel admits in their marriage: that they got in each other's way while passing on the stairway. Many couples might wish that were the only problem they face. Therefore, choice E is correct. The quotation in choice A, that Gabriel "was in clover," is not humorous; it refers to his being in a good position, like a farm animal surrounded by good pasture to eat. Choice B, which lays out Gabriel's logic, does not add humor; it simply states the way he sees his future. Choice C also fails to add humor, as it merely shows how Gabriel methodically goes about his proposal to Selina after getting Lady Verinder's approval. Choice D refers to the way Gabriel extends the logic of other men who all got cold feet, but went through with their marriages. Some may find humor in his "generous" offer to buy out Selina, but his decision to offer her an outright bribe is really not funny.

Second Poem

The poem for these questions is "Fabrications," written by Richard Wilbur and published in 2000.

45. D. The first stanza establishes that the "spider has repaired her broken web," which "prove[s] again / The bright resilience of the frailest form." In other words, the spider's rebuilding implies that nature has the ability to rebound; it is resilient, choice D. Choice A is off base; nature may indeed be full of surprises, but that idea is not implied in the first stanza. Choice B is unreasonable; nothing in the first stanza, or the entire poem for that matter, implies that spiders are frail, although the web that a spider weaves is, indeed, quite fragile. This incorrect answer choice simply tries to connect two disparate ideas, "spiders" and "frailest," from the first stanza. Choice C begins with a fairly reasonable concept, that some ideas need to be proven repeatedly, but the answer then adds the inaccurate word "daily," which is not implied in the poem; it is too strong, too absolute. Choice E makes little sense, claiming that things that appear weak are actually strong. This is a misguided idea, perhaps born in line 2 that states "The bright resilience of the frailest form"; however, this line does not imply strength in things that appear weak.

46. B. The pronoun "it" in lines 7 and 9 refers to the word "web" in line 3, choice B. The web becomes a metaphorical "single and gigantic eye," through which "you can catch the flash / Of steeples . . . / One loitering star . . . / [and] Slow vultures." The pronoun does not refer to the spider (A), but to her web. The ground (C) cannot be the antecedent for this pronoun. The eye (D) is a metaphor for the shape of the whole web, and the pupil (E) metaphorically refers to the spider in the center of the web.

47. D. The first three stanzas describe the spider and her web. The fourth stanza begins the analogy that draws a parallel between spiders and mankind, noting that "Each day men frame and weave," which mirrors the spider's task. Answer choices A, B, and C refer only to the spider and her web, not to mankind. Choice E does not relate to the spider, and it is not the line that initiates the spider/mankind analogy; this analogy was already established before this portion of the poem.

48. E. The line in question states that the ground is "still-imponderable." By definition, something that is imponderable is either difficult or impossible to estimate or to conceive of; therefore, the line suggests that the spider cannot definitively know how far above the ground her web is, choice E. Choice A, that the web never reaches the ground, is silly and irrelevant to this question. Choice B is also unreasonable; nothing in the poem implies that one cannot see the ground because of the morning light. Choice C may be entirely true in nature; spider webs are indeed designed to catch prey such as airborne insects, but that does not relate to this question. Choice D has no evidence whatsoever in the poem, which makes no indication of how high off the ground the web may be.

49. B. The concept of the "drift of star-specks or the Red King's dream" parallels the idea that some things cannot be known conclusively, like the idea of the "still-imponderable ground," choice B. The "bottomless" world cannot be grasped and is akin to drifting stars or the Red King's dream in Lewis Carroll's *Through the Looking Glass,* a fantasy in which we are not sure what to believe. The stars and the dream do not parallel the resilience of the frail web (A). The phrase about the "loitering star" (C) merely refers to a morning star that is visible through the web. Choice D refers to the way humanity has limited vision and scope; it is not parallel to the line in question. The booming voice in choice E introduces the instructive tale from The Talmud, but this is not a parallel to stars and literary fiction.

50. **C.** The poem does not employ apostrophe, a device in which the speaker directly addresses someone or something that is not present, choice C. The poem does contain allusions (A), notably to The Talmud and the fictional Red King. It also establishes an analogy (B) between the spider rebuilding her web and mankind "fram[ing] and weav[ing]." Irony (D) is also evident in the Talmud story, which claims the river is bottomless, yet the travelers observe a roc wading in it. The poem also uses metaphor (E), describing the spider's web as a "gigantic eye" and the spider as the "golden pupil" in that eye.

51. **A.** The speaker implies that man-made "coastal towers" allow us to actually "infer civility," choice A. However, the speaker never implies any judgment about the accuracy of ancient cartographers (B). Choice C is unreasonable; the speaker never mentions the size of a spider's eyes; this answer choice confuses the metaphors of the web, the "gigantic eye," and the spider being the "pupil" of that eye. Choice D is too much of a stretch. It is true that "a booming voice from heaven" did warn the travelers from stepping into the river, but the speaker never goes so far as to suggest that the travelers heeded this warning. Readers may choose to assume they did, but the speaker simply uses the tale as a springboard to his next point. Choice E is too much of an absolute; it is likely that the spider's web will be broken at some point, but to claim that the speaker implies it must be a daily event is unwarranted.

52. **B.** In a more traditional grammatical form, the sentence would read "The world is bottomless . . . and [it] fogs our thought." Thus, the word "world" is the subject, choice B. The word "senses" (A) is the object of the preposition "beneath." In line 26, the "drift" (C) and the "dream" (D) both function as predicate nominatives. The sentence structure is "The world is . . . a drift . . . or dream." Choice E is inaccurate because "thought" functions as the direct object of the verb "fogs."

53. **E.** The word "fabrication," by definition, means to construct, to build, or to invent. One can fabricate a building, an industrial product, or a deceitful story. In this poem, spiders fabricate webs and men fabricate towers; therefore, the poem's title reasonably suggests that building is a natural instinct, both in the insect kingdom and the human kingdom, choice E. While one connotation of fabrication deals with inventing or concocting stories, the intent of such a fabricated story is to deceive, not to instruct (A). Choice B is unreasonable; neither the denotation nor the connotation of the word "fabrication" deals with destruction. Choice C may fool some readers because line 2 states "The bright resilience of the frailest form," which deals with the pliability of the fragile web, but this does not address the title of the poem. Choice D is simply unreasonable because in reality it is true that some natural phenomena do indeed represent the world of humanity, but this idea does not directly relate to the title of the poem.

54. **A.** The ancient map that the speaker describes has "so much blank and namelessness" surrounding the "little mushroom-clump of coastal towers." This idea reinforces the way that mankind cannot grasp the entirety of the world, choice A; after all, it is "bottomless" and "there is much unseen." Choice B is incorrect because the map itself does not make any claim about humanity's civility; rather, it is the speaker who makes this claim. Choice C contradicts the speaker's point, which deals with the vast amount of uncharted territory on the ancient map, with its large areas that are blank and nameless. Choice D is off base; the speaker does mention that man-made towers and steeples are found along coastlines, but his real point is that the maps demonstrate how much is unknown. Choice E draws the unreasonable conclusion that humanity is surrounded by water; the speaker never makes any such point.

55. **C.** The speaker's tone indicates a positive uplifting confidence, choice C. Constructions that can be broken, like spider webs, can always be rebuilt, and ideas like civility and love can still exist. In this question, notice that all of the inaccurate answer choices have negative connotations. The speaker's tone is not remorseful (A), that is, rueful. The word "wistful" (B) refers to a tone of melancholic pensiveness, which is not an accurate description of the tone. The word "anxious" (D) is too strong and too negative to describe the speaker's tone. The word "lofty" (E) has the negative connotation of being condescending, of thinking one is better than others. It, too, does not accurately depict the tone.

Section II: Free-Response Questions

Question 1: "Snow in the Suburbs" by Thomas Hardy

The following scoring guide explicitly explains how to earn up to 6 total points for a poetic analysis essay. Row A (thesis) can earn up to 1 point; Row B (evidence and commentary) can earn up to 4 points, and Row C (sophistication) can earn up to 1 point.

Row A: Thesis (0–1 point)	
Scoring Criteria	
0 points for any of the following:	**1 point for**
• Having no defendable thesis. • Only restating the prompt in the thesis. • Only summarizing the issue with no claim in the thesis. • Presenting a thesis that does not address the prompt.	• Addressing the prompt with a defendable thesis that presents an interpretation and may establish a line of reasoning.
Decision Rules and Scoring Notes	
Theses that do not earn this point	**Theses that do earn this point**
• Only restate the prompt. • Only offer an irrelevant generalized comment about the poem. • Simply describe the poem's features rather than making a defendable claim.	• Take a position on the prompt and provide a defendable interpretation of how the poetic devices convey the speaker's complex attitude toward nature.

Additional Notes

• The thesis may be one or more sentences anywhere in the essay.
• A thesis that meets the criteria can be awarded the point whether or not the rest of the response successfully conveys that line of reasoning.

Row B: Evidence AND Commentary (0–4 points)				
Scoring Criteria				
0 points for	**1 point for**	**2 points for**	**3 points for**	**4 points for**
• Simply repeating the thesis (if present). • **OR** restating provided information. • **OR** providing mostly irrelevant and/or incoherent examples.	• Summarizing the poem without reference to a thesis. • **OR** providing vague textual references. • **OR** providing textual references of questionable relevance. • **AND** providing little or no commentary.	• Making relevant textual references (direct quotes or paraphrases). • **AND** providing commentary but repeats, oversimplifies, or misinterprets the cited evidence or text.	• Making relevant textual references (direct quotes or paraphrases). • **AND** providing commentary that explains the logical relationship between textual examples and the thesis; however, commentary is uneven, limited, or incomplete.	• Making relevant textual references (direct quotes or paraphrases). • **AND** providing well-developed commentary that explicitly explains the relationship between the evidence and the thesis.

Decision Rules and Scoring Notes				
Typical responses that earn 0 points:	**Typical responses that earn 1 point:**	**Typical responses that earn 2 points:**	**Typical responses that earn 3 points:**	**Typical responses that earn 4 points:**
• Are unclear or fail to address the prompt. • May present mere opinion with no relevant textual references.	• Mention textual references, devices, or techniques with little or no analysis.	• Contain numerous inaccuracies or repetition in commentary. • Offer only simplistic explanations that do not strengthen the argument.	• Provide commentary that is not sufficiently developed or is too limited. • Assume or imply a connection to the thesis that is not consistently explicit.	• Provide commentary that uses significant details of the text to draw conclusions. • Integrate short excerpts throughout in order to support the thesis' interpretation.

Additional Notes

• Writing that suffers from grammatical and/or mechanical errors that interfere with communication cannot earn the fourth point in this row.

Row C: Sophistication (0–1 point)

Scoring Criteria	
0 points for	**1 point for**
• Not meeting the criteria for 1 point.	• Exhibiting sophistication of thought and/or advancing a complex literary argument.
Decision Rules and Scoring Notes	
Responses that do not earn this point:	**Responses that earn this point demonstrate one (or more) of the following:**
• Try to contextualize an interpretation, but make predominantly sweeping generalizations (*"Throughout all history . . ."* OR *"Everyone believes . . ."*). • Only hint at other possible interpretations (*"Some may think . . ."* OR *"Though the poem might be said to . . ."*). • Write one statement about a thematic interpretation of the poem without consistently maintaining that idea. • Oversimplify complexities in the poem. • Present complicated or complex sentences or language that is ineffective and detracts from the argument.	• Present a thesis that demands nuanced analysis of textual evidence and successfully prove it. • Illuminate the significance or relevance of an interpretation within a broader context. • Discuss alternative interpretations of a text. • Acknowledge and account for contradictions, ambiguities, and/or complexities within the text. • Provide relevant analogies to help better understand an interpretation. • Develop a prose style that is especially vivid, persuasive, resounding, or appropriate to the student's argument.

Additional Notes

• This point should be awarded only if the demonstration of sophistication or complex understanding is part of the argument, not merely a phrase or brief reference.

High-Scoring Essay

In three stanzas of "Snow in the Suburbs," we get three visual snippets: the speaker first describes the falling snow, then depicts a sparrow struggling in the storm, and finally presents a lone black cat being rescued. Using skillful poetic devices, Hardy transitions from the complexity of the cold and perhaps oppressive atmosphere to the comfort of human kindness.

The first stanza is devoted to describing the snowfall that covers the entire suburban scene in white. Although the word "snow" only appears in the title, the image dominates the first stanza. By repeating the word "every" four times in the first four lines, Hardy establishes the omnipresent force of the snow, the "it" that covers every branch, every twig, every fork in the tree. Hardy personifies "some flakes" with a life of their own, defying the law of gravity as they "lost their way, and grope back upward," as if they could change nature itself. However, after "meeting those meandering down," they reverse course and descend to the earth, which equates to accepting their fate. Interestingly, Hardy mentions three details that establish the suburban setting of the title; without the street, the pavement, or the palings, the location could easily be in the countryside. These details initially appear irrelevant and insignificant because the street and pavement are both "mute," but suburbia takes on greater importance in the last line of the poem when humanity takes action.

The solid white imagery changes in the second stanza, when the speaker notices a spark of color contrast: a sparrow against the backdrop of white snow. The small sparrow, a creature of the natural world, lands on a branch, but "immediately / a snow-lump thrice his own slight size" knocks him on his keister. Hardy's diction and imagery become intriguing: in the first stanza the wayward snowflakes "descend" after they follow their meandering mates; in the second stanza the snow-lump "descends" on the little sparrow. In the first instance, the action is a gentle action, but in the second it appears more harmful. Hence, the speaker's attitude toward nature changes to some degree; that element which was originally a pleasant alliterative "fleecy fall" has become a bully, inadvertently picking on something a fraction of its size. The hapless sparrow falls to the ground. The speed with which the sparrow falls is imitated by the speed of lines 13–14, with three and four short words, respectively. However, just when the bird falls and the reader gasps, inferring that the speaker is hinting at the unpleasantness of nature, the hapless sparrow comes back and "lights on a nether twig," a lower branch, that in turn causes another mini-avalanche below. The bird survives the onslaught of nature.

The final stanza, half the length of the first two, narrows the poem's focus to the world of man, beginning with a description of the steps, presumably of the speaker's domicile. Reminiscent of the completely white imagery in the first stanza, the steps are covered with so much snow that they are no longer visible and become "a blanched slope," another descending image, implying nature's take-over. However, similar to the second stanza, the dominant whiteness is disturbed, this time by a very sad and sympathetic black cat who supplies a complete color contrast to the whiteness. Black cats are so often depicted as frightening and unlucky, but this poor stray creature has "feeble hope," and appears fearful and hungry. We feel for the pitiful feline as it looks up with wide eyes. Finally, the poem ends with the house's inhabitants opening the door and taking the cat inside. We want the cat to be saved; we assume it is. The sparrow can exist in the natural storm without being preyed upon, but this cat needs human kindness.

The speaker understands that nature can be harsh, but all creatures can live in it.

(643 words)

Analysis of High-Scoring Essay

Although the introduction is not stellar, this essay becomes admirable in the development of its body paragraphs. The first paragraph summarizes the three stanzas and then offers the idea that Hardy transitions the atmosphere of the poem. The writing is accurate and adequately addresses the prompt. Its defendable thesis, that "Hardy transitions from the complexity of the cold and perhaps oppressive atmosphere to the comfort of human kindness," deserves a point for Row A.

The student parallels the form of the poem by devoting a body paragraph to each stanza, a logical and accessible organizational scheme. The analysis of the first stanza is insightful and clearly connected to apt textual examples. The student astutely notices that the title uses the word "snow," but it is never mentioned in the poem, even though its image dominates the stanza with an "omnipresent force." The student next makes an interesting observation about the personified snowflakes that drift upward, defying gravity, but must ultimately follow their fate and fall to the ground. Then the student alludes to the title again by pointing out three details that prove the suburban setting, and notes that although they seem insignificant now, they will take on greater meaning in the last stanza. A Reader might wish the student would develop this idea in greater depth, but the paragraph is still quite good in its insights.

The second body paragraph discusses the vignette of the sparrow by introducing the change in Hardy's imagery; specifically, the sparrow adds a spark of contrast to the snow. The student aptly notices Hardy's repeated idea of something descending in the first two stanzas, and also adds the interesting idea that the first instance is gentle, but the second is harmful. The student also fittingly ties this to a shift in the speaker's attitude from recognizing what is pleasant to acknowledging what is an undesirable aspect of the snow. The Reader will also find it amusing when the student claims the snow-lump "knocks [the sparrow] on his keister"; this sudden informality jumps out and helps give the student a voice of his or her own. Another interesting insight is that "the speed with which the sparrow falls is imitated by the speed of lines 13–14" in the poem. The student does not venture into a study of meter, but acknowledges the significance of the shorter lines; many students will not notice this detail. Similar to the informality of the "keister" comment, the student points out how the "reader gasps" when the sparrow falls to the ground and ties this action to a change in the speaker's attitude. Fortunately, the sparrow comes right back and "survives the onslaught of nature."

The last body paragraph studies the third stanza, noting its truncated length but offering no insight about its significance. The student notices the continuation of descending imagery, in this case the steps of the speaker's home that are covered in snow, implying the power of nature. Analogous to the contrasting imagery of the sparrow in the second stanza, the student notices the even greater contrast of the black cat against the snowy backdrop. Mentioning the evil reputation of black cats only to dismiss it, the student shifts to the sympathy we feel for this scared and hungry feline and our relief when the humans take the cat indoors. It is pleasing to the Reader that the writer implicitly understands that the starved cat might have attacked the little sparrow, but we are comforted when all creatures can live. Human kindness indeed saves the day. The evidence and commentary are well-developed and support the thesis' interpretation; the essay earns 4 points in Row B.

The conclusion comes across as rushed and unnecessary. Additionally, its facts might be arguable; since the humans take the cat indoors, only the sparrow is left living in harsh nature. However, given the excellent development of the essay as a whole, one cannot fault it too much for having this slim conclusion.

The essay earns its high score. Although the introduction and conclusion do not impress, the essay overall has admirable body paragraph development, provides insightful analysis of the poem, includes appropriate use of quotations, and displays sophisticated style. Although it is not strong enough to earn a point in Row C, a Reader will be happy to read an essay such as this and reward it with an overall score of 5.

Low-Scoring Essay

The poem "Snow In The Suburbs" by Thomas Hardy provides an excellent overview of a variety of poetic devices, as well as an enjoyable exploration of the speaker's attitude towards nature. After reading this poem, it is obvious that the speaker loves nature.

Examples of his fond, loving descriptions of nature appear throughout the poem. In the first stanza, he goes on and on about nature after a fresh snowfall. All of the descriptions in this stanza are like still-life black and white images, each one a moment frozen in time.

In the next two stanzas, the speaker introduces adorable animals to the winter-wonderland. Stanza two is focused entirely on a comical little sparrow trying to land in a snow-covered tree. Stanza three includes a black cat walking up the steps in the snow. It is obvious that the speaker loves nature, because every image he presents is upbeat.

The poetic devises that the author employs are many and varied, but he makes good use of them. For example, the poem is written in rhyming couplets, and some of them are quite clever, such as rhyming "when" with "again" and rhyming "brush" with "rush." However, some of the rhymed coupled seem to be a bit too strained, such as rhyming "foot" with "mute" and "size" with "eye" when they don't really rhyme.

Another poetic device the author uses is to vary the number of lines in each stanza to increase the dramatic effect. The first and second stanzas each have eight lines, but the final stanza has just four lines. This helps to make those last lines stand out more.

Finally, don't overlook the most important poetic device of all, it's hidden in plain sight: the title of the poem is a big key to the speaker's attitude towards nature. If he lives in the suburbs, he doesn't get to see much wide natural stuff. So when it snows and he gets to see the trees and the sparrow and the cat, and he rejoices in nature, even in the suburbs.

(341 words)

Analysis of Low-Scoring Essay

This student-writer tries to discuss the prompt, but the essay ultimately fails to present any real analysis of what is, after all, a fairly straightforward poem.

The introduction asserts that the speaker "loves nature," perhaps an overstatement, and that Hardy utilizes "a variety of poetic devices." We can reward the student for trying to address the prompt, but the introduction reads more like a simple restatement of the prompt, with little style or substance to entice the Reader's attention. Additionally, a Reader will notice the student's incorrect capitalization of the poem's title. The student does not produce a defendable thesis on the prompt and does not earn a point in Row A.

The first body paragraph says little in just three brief sentences. It promises examples of "his fond, loving descriptions of nature," but it disappoints by merely stating that "he goes on and on about nature after a fresh snowfall." This student needs to learn how to provide specific, concrete examples and then analyze how they work together to create the speaker's attitude. The last sentence shows promise when the student claims that the first stanza's descriptions are like "still-life black and white images . . . frozen in time." This comparison to black and white photos is, of course, an implied analogy; the images in the poem are not literally black and white. However, this sentence is perhaps the best one in the entire essay, and the Reader may be intrigued, but eventually will be let down as this observation is not accompanied with textual evidence and more developed analysis.

The second body paragraph attempts to explore two stanzas, but it merely paraphrases them poorly, even inaccurately. It is hard to agree that the little sparrow and stray black cat are "adorable" considering the details of Hardy's text, and claiming the scene is a "winter-wonderland" certainly exaggerates Hardy's imagery. The student also ignores that, although the bird survives, the poor little creature is battered about because of the storm; additionally, the cat, apprehensive, cold, and lean, hardly presents an "upbeat" cute image. Once again the Reader suspects that this student is grasping for ideas after a perfunctory, speedy reading of the poem.

The third body paragraph attempts to discuss Hardy's "many and varied" poetic devices, but it only manages to explain that the poem has rhyming couplets. But instead of analyzing how the couplets affect the poem and help develop the speaker's attitude, the student merely lists some of them. When the student claims that a few rhymes "seem . . . strained," the Reader immediately knows that the student is not familiar with the term "slant rhyme." The Reader can easily overlook that the student writes "devises" instead of "devices" and "coupled" instead of "couplets," as these are simple mistakes made under timed pressure, but the reasons that this paragraph falls flat are its overly simplistic observations and its lack of any real analysis.

A Reader will be sorry to note that the fourth body paragraph likewise says nothing. The writer tries to make a point about stanza length, but contradicts him- or herself by stating that each stanza has a different number of lines before correcting that misstatement. Unfortunately, this student offers no insights about the effect of the last stanza being half the length of the first two, except for the simplistic observation that it "makes those last lines stand out more."

The concluding paragraph seems rushed; in a silly and inaccurate phrase, this student informs the Reader that the title is the "most important poetic device of all . . . hidden in plain sight." The student's idea is illogical and poorly presented, trying to draw a cause-and-effect connection between the snowfall and the things the speaker sees. The first sentence of this paragraph is a run-on, and the entire paragraph feels forced. A Reader will try once again to ignore the student's mistake of writing "wide" instead of "wild," but the cumulative effect of the errors in this essay can be distracting. The Reader will hope that the student would have spotted and corrected these mistakes if he or she had taken time to proofread. The body paragraphs earn 2 points in Row B; they do present some relevant textual references, but the commentary is too often misinterpreted or oversimplified.

Overall this essay tries to present on-topic ideas, but the main reason it falls apart is the lack of development of any substantial ideas based on solid textual evidence. While the organization is clear, the student's style is simplistic. It cannot earn a point in Row C, and deserves an overall score of 2.

Question 2: "The Birthmark" by Nathaniel Hawthorne

The following scoring guide explicitly explains how to earn up to 6 total points for a prose analysis essay. Row A (thesis) can earn up to 1 point; Row B (evidence and commentary) can earn up to 4 points, and Row C (sophistication) can earn up to 1 point.

Row A: Thesis (0–1 point)	
Scoring Criteria	
0 points for any of the following: • Having no defendable thesis. • Only restating the prompt in the thesis. • Only summarizing the issue with no claim in the thesis. • Presenting a thesis that does not address the prompt.	**1 point for** • Addressing the prompt with a defendable thesis that presents an interpretation and may establish a line of reasoning.
Decision Rules and Scoring Notes	
Theses that do not earn this point • Only restate the prompt. • Only offer an irrelevant generalized comment about the passage. • Simply describe the passage's features rather than making a defendable claim.	**Theses that do earn this point** • Take a position on the prompt and provide a defendable interpretation of how Hawthorne employs literary devices to present the complex relationship between the newlyweds.
Additional Notes	
• The thesis may be one or more sentences anywhere in the response. • A thesis that meets the criteria can be awarded the point whether or not the rest of the response successfully conveys that line of reasoning.	

Row B: Evidence AND Commentary (0–4 points)				
Scoring Criteria				
0 points for	**1 point for**	**2 points for**	**3 points for**	**4 points for**
• Simply repeating the thesis (if present). • **OR** restating provided information. • **OR** providing mostly irrelevant and/or incoherent examples.	• Summarizing the passage without reference to a thesis. • **OR** providing vague textual references. • **OR** providing textual references of questionable relevance. • **AND** providing little or no commentary.	• Making relevant textual references (direct quotes or paraphrases). • **AND** providing commentary but repeats, oversimplifies, or misinterprets the cited evidence or text.	• Making relevant textual references (direct quotes or paraphrases). • **AND** providing commentary that explains the logical relationship between textual examples and the thesis; however, commentary is uneven, limited, or incomplete.	• Making relevant textual references (direct quotes or paraphrases). • **AND** providing well-developed commentary that explicitly explains the relationship between the evidence and the thesis.

Decision Rules and Scoring Notes				
Typical responses that earn 0 points:	**Typical responses that earn 1 point:**	**Typical responses that earn 2 points:**	**Typical responses that earn 3 points:**	**Typical responses that earn 4 points:**
• Are unclear or fail to address the prompt. • May present mere opinion with no relevant textual references.	• Mention textual references, devices, or techniques with little or no analysis.	• Contain numerous inaccuracies or repetition in commentary. • Offer only simplistic explanations that do not strengthen the argument.	• Provide commentary that is not sufficiently developed, or is too limited. • Assume or imply a connection to the thesis that is not consistently explicit.	• Provide commentary that uses significant details of the text to draw conclusions. • Integrate short excerpts throughout in order to support the thesis' interpretation.

Additional Notes

• Writing that suffers from grammatical and/or mechanical errors that interfere with communication cannot earn the fourth point in this row.

Row C: Sophistication (0–1 point)

Scoring Criteria	
0 points for	**1 point for**
• Not meeting the criteria for 1 point.	• Exhibiting sophistication of thought and/or advancing a complex literary argument.

Decision Rules and Scoring Notes	
Responses that do not earn this point:	**Responses that earn this point demonstrate one (or more) of the following:**
• Try to contextualize an interpretation, but make predominantly sweeping generalizations (*"Throughout all history . . . "* OR *"Everyone believes . . . "*). • Only hint at other possible interpretations (*"Some may think . . . "* OR *"Though the passage might be said to . . . "*). • Write one statement about a thematic interpretation of the passage without consistently maintaining that idea. • Oversimplify complexities in the passage. • Present complicated or complex sentences or language that is ineffective and detracts from the argument.	• Present a thesis that demands nuanced analysis of textual evidence and successfully prove it. • Illuminate the significance or relevance of an interpretation within a broader context. • Discuss alternative interpretations of a text. • Acknowledge and account for contradictions, ambiguities, and/or complexities within the text. • Provide relevant analogies to help better understand an interpretation. • Develop a prose style that is especially vivid, persuasive, resounding, or appropriate to the student's argument.

Additional Notes

• This point should be awarded only if the demonstration of sophistication or complex understanding is part of the argument, not merely a phrase or brief reference.

High-Scoring Essay

To be successful, a marriage supposedly takes effort from both husband and wife. If both do not contribute in a positive fashion, the marriage will find itself on thin ice. In "The Birthmark," Hawthorne dives right through that thin ice into the depths of frigid water, using unbalanced point of view, meticulously manipulative diction, and vivid symbolism to suggest that Aylmer and Georgiana's relationship is unhealthy and cold.

Hawthorne's limited omniscient point of view presents a negative portrayal of Aylmer, although his mindset dominates the passage. The long first paragraph sets up Aylmer as a man who values scientific knowledge more than personal relationships. The first sentence interestingly implies that Aylmer's devotion for his wife will be a "spiritual affinity more attractive than any chemical one." However, we immediately find that he "left his laboratory . . . cleared . . . the furnace smoke [from his face], washed the stain of acids from his fingers, and persuaded [Georgiana] to become his wife," to become a mere possession. Hawthorne implicitly emphasizes that during time period, in the Age of Enlightenment when belief in science became dominant, "it was not unusual for the love of science to rival the love of a woman. . . . " At this point, the reader might still be hoping for a happy marriage. However, Hawthorne has misled us with his diction. The mere fact that Aylmer had to <u>persuade</u> Georgiana to marry should send up red flags, and then later, the hint that Aylmer will never "be weaned" of his love for science "by any second passion" should convince us that he is a man obsessed, believing that his love for his wife can only be, at most, "intertwined" with his love of science. By the end of the opening paragraph, the point of view establishes that Aylmer is the dominant partner, the alpha-male of this relationship. Dominate, he will.

As the point of view broadens, the reader understands Georgiana's thoughts that lend immediate sympathy for her. After Aylmer asks her a graceless question about removing her birthmark, she smiles, but she perceives that he is very serious. Hawthorne points out that his query makes her blush deeply; this diction choice is interesting because it is not until later that the reader discovers how her blushing hides the symbolic birthmark. Ironically, just as the reader does not yet see it, the birthmark disappears from view as she blushingly explains how she naively believed those who called it a charm. As Aylmer continues his assault on her facial flaw, "this slightest possible defect . . . of earthly imperfection," she becomes angry, hurt and defensive before she bursts into tears. We cannot help but conclude that she will remain submissive in the face of Aylmer's onslaught and that their marital relationship will never be one of mutual respect.

Hawthorne then launches into a lengthy description of the birthmark and her complexion, wherein he juxtaposes its appearance. For example, when she blushes, the birthmark vanishes amid the alliterative "blood that bathed the whole cheek with its brilliant glow." The diction is decently positive, leading the reader to ignore her birthmark. However, when she becomes pale, the mark becomes a metaphorical and symbolic "crimson stain upon the snow." The two descriptions could not be further apart. Equally distinct are the reactions she gets from the public, which Hawthorne presents as he again expands the point of view to include those around Georgiana. With positive diction, some of her many suitors liken the birthmark to the hand of a fairy, a "token of the magic endowments"; others, notably women, find that it negatively "destroyed the effect of [her] beauty," becoming "hideous." Hawthorne so far presents two opposite viewpoints before mentioning that "masculine observers," not her previous suitors, might wish the mark were gone so that the world would have one instance of perfect beauty. These contrasting viewpoints add depth to the birthmark's symbolism, showing that human appearance cannot be perfect, and humanity cannot be unbiased. Hawthorne returns to Aylmer, who, like these masculine observers, cannot ignore her "semblance of a flaw." His combination of callousness and prideful nature do not bode well for the newlywed's relationship.

Finally, it is interesting that Hawthorne holds back; he chooses to not explain or describe or even mention her birthmark until after Aylmer confronts Georgiana about it. This adds suspense and emphasizes the one-sided nature of their relationship; the narrative is off-balanced, centering almost entirely on Aylmer and hardly detailing Georgiana until the end. By then, it is too late. It appears Aylmer will win.

(763 words)

Analysis of High-Scoring Essay

The excerpt from "The Birthmark" gives students ample opportunity to examine how Nathaniel Hawthorne uses literary devices to characterize the newlywed couple, Aylmer and Georgiana. The prompt allows students to explore whatever they find accessible and appropriate. Most students will easily understand that the couple's relationship is not a mutually respectful one, and that Aylmer dominates his wife. Many students will likely make a connection to the time period of the story, which is set in the late 18th century.

This high-scoring essay does an admirable job of analyzing various literary devices that help to establish the couple's relationship, but it does so without hitting the Reader over the head with them. The student's introduction includes a pleasing turn of phrase; the second sentence states that both partners must contribute to a successful marriage, otherwise "the marriage will find itself on thin ice." A Reader may initially grimace at this overused, trite phrase, but will immediately smile as the student shatters the cliché, exclaiming how " . . . Hawthorne dives right through that thin ice into the depths of frigid water" to "suggest that [the] relationship is unhealthy and cold." The student correctly acknowledges three literary devices that Hawthorne uses: "unbalanced point of view, meticulously manipulative diction, and vivid symbolism." Notice that this student chose appropriate adjectives to describe the point of view and diction rather than merely identifying them; a Reader will be intrigued by these choices, and want to know how the student is going to develop them. Finally, a Reader who sees three devices in a list such as this might be apprehensive that the student will simply use them to organize three body paragraphs; thankfully, this student does not follow such a predictable, potentially trite organizational scheme. The quality of the thesis deserves a point in Row A.

The first body paragraph explores the introductory paragraph of the excerpt, which focuses primarily on Aylmer. The student misidentifies the point of view as limited omniscient, but the Reader will tend to give the benefit of the doubt; indeed, this term is accurate for the introductory paragraph, which is limited to Aylmer's thoughts and background. This minor mistake is seemingly resolved in the later paragraphs, as the student acknowledges Hawthorne "broadens" and "expands" the point of view to include others' thoughts. The student's presentation implicitly supports the thesis claim that Hawthorne's diction is "meticulously manipulative" by noticing that, although Hawthorne initially implies Aylmer will have a stronger "affinity" for his wife than science, and he "immediately" leaves his scientific pursuits after persuading Georgiana to marry him. The student continues with brief commentary about the time period, with its devotion to science, and mentions how a reader "might still" hope for a happy marriage. But then the student asserts a new idea, that "Hawthorne has misled us with his diction," and he or she provides ample text evidence to support the claim. The paragraph concludes by acknowledging that the point of view establishes Aylmer's "alpha-male" personality, and it reinforces it with masterful authority in a precise, forceful, three-word sentence: "Dominate, he will." And just like Aylmer, this student writer dominates at will.

The second body paragraph analyzes how the point of view broadens to include Georgiana's thoughts, and the student notes appropriately this "lend[s] immediate sympathy for her." The student accurately chronicles the changes in her emotions as she reacts to Aylmer's graceless question about removing her birthmark. Making a thought-provoking point about her blushing, the student mentions how Hawthorne has not yet explained that the symbolic birthmark becomes unnoticeable when she blushes. Some may quibble with the student's labeling Hawthorne's delay in explaining the birthmark as a "diction choice," but the student should still be rewarded for noticing the connection between Georgiana's first deep blush and Hawthorne's later description of how that blush will hide the birthmark. The paragraph concludes with an appropriate claim: that Georgiana will likely "remain submissive" and their "marital relationship will never be one of mutual respect."

The third body paragraph explores the final paragraph of the excerpt. The student analyzes Hawthorne's use of juxtaposition as he describes the birthmark's disappearance while Georgiana blushes, contrasting it with the imagery of it being a "'crimson stain upon the snow'" when she pales. The student expands this idea, noticing the parallels between the birthmark's appearance and the reactions Georgiana gets from the public. When commenting that this section expands the point of view to include members of the community, the student parallels Hawthorne by contrasting how Georgiana's past suitors thought of her birthmark with a positive connotation, while the ladies of society viewed it negatively. After noticing that those "masculine observers" who see the birthmark as an imperfection are not Georgiana's previous suitors, the student briefly explores the symbolism of the birthmark, explaining that "human appearance cannot be perfect, and humanity cannot be unbiased." A Reader might wish the student had more time to develop this idea, but it is rewarding all the same. This paragraph finishes by returning to Aylmer, who agrees with those masculine observers who think her birthmark is an impediment, one that he cannot ignore. Calling him callous and prideful, the student predicts that his insensitive nature does not "bode well" for the couple's future.

The last paragraph continues to explore the excerpt and provides yet another interesting observation. The student explains that Hawthorne's choice to not introduce the birthmark until after the couple's confrontation adds to the suspense and also contributes to the off-balanced aspect of this narrative that focuses more on Aylmer than Georgiana. The student ends the essay with a notable idea, claiming that the very organization of Hawthorne's writing predicts that "Aylmer will win" in the marriage. This is certainly not a traditional conclusion, and is refreshing for that fact. At this point, the Reader does not need a summary of the points in the essay, which have already been made quite succinctly. For its significant commentary and well-developed textual evidence, the essay earns 4 points in Row B.

This essay deserves a high score because it is sophisticated and subtle, both in its ideas and in its language. The essay skillfully weaves textual examples and analysis together to provide an insightful investigation of the topic, developing these ideas with pleasing clarity and style that is appropriate to the student's argument; for this, it earns a point in Row C. It should score an overall 6.

Low-Scoring Essay

"The Birthmark" seems to be about a crazy scientist and his new wife. They have not been married long, so their relationship is not yet developed. Because the story takes place in the 1700's, the couple would not have been allowed to spend time together before marriage, and that's why they don't know each other. Maybe the husband, Almer, had never even seen her birthmark before marriage, but he sure doesn't like it now.

Alymer is very smart when it comes to science, but he's not very smart when it comes to being a nice husband. The author shows us that when he picks on Georgiana and suggests she should have her birthmark removed. Apparently he thinks it's a flaw, and if she did not have this flaw, she'd be perfect.

It's hard to know what Georgiana seems to think because she does not get many lines in the story, but she seems feisty. She shows her feistiness when she responds to Alymer's question by saying she thinks her birthmark is a charm.

Their relationship does not look like it will be very successful. Alymer picks on her and will probably not stop until she is dead. That's not a good way to have a good relationship in marriage.

(209 words)

Analysis of Low-Scoring Essay

This student demonstrates how an overly simplistic reading of the passage produces a simplistic essay with scant analysis. The use of the verb "seems" in the first sentence indicates that the student is unsure about his or her assertion, and this opening statement says nothing more than what the story is "about." Immediately labeling the scientist as "crazy" is unnecessarily hyperbolic and comes off as a bit immature. The student then tries to address the prompt by noting that the couple's relationship is "not yet developed," which is a reasonable comment, given the facts in the text. However, the student struggles to establish some kind of causal relationship between the novel's time setting and the character's relationship. The Reader will disregard the erroneous apostrophe in "the 1700's" and focus on the student's claim that this time period, when "the couple would not have been allowed to spend time together before marriage," is the direct cause of their undeveloped relationship. This idea is quite possibly correct, given social mores of the time, but the text does not explicitly make any such connection. The student's introduction ends with another questionable claim that perhaps "Almer [sic] had never even seen [Georgiana's] birthmark before marriage" and then simply states that "he sure doesn't like it now." While that point may be true, this obvious comment does not portend much insight or analysis to come. This introduction has merely skimmed the surface of the characters' relationship and failed to mention any of the literary techniques that Hawthorne uses to characterize the newlyweds' relationship. It fails to earn a point in Row A.

The next short paragraph tries to explore Aylmer's character (continuously misspelling his name throughout the essay). Unfortunately, the student's basic premise is bland, both in its concept and in its expression: Aylmer "is very smart [about science] . . . but he's not very smart [about being] a nice husband." The student correctly identifies ideas about Aylmer's being a scientist and a husband, but then he or she confuses the Reader with an ambiguous pronoun, declaring, "The author shows us that." The paragraph is developed around only a single text example, and instead of analyzing how it characterizes their relationship, the student lapses into a pedestrian character summary.

The following paragraph, which attempts to analyze Georgiana's character, is even more brief and inadequate, with only two sentences. Unfortunately, the student doesn't offer any insight more substantial than that "she seems feisty" in the way she responds to Aylmer, which demonstrates a most superficial analysis.

In the concluding paragraph, the student asserts that the couple's future success looks unlikely and that "Alymer [sic] picks on her and will probably not stop until she is dead." Regardless of whether or not this may be true based on the story, such speculation is really not necessary. The student, perhaps inadvertently, leaves the Reader with some sage advice: "That's not a good way to have a good relationship in marriage." (I can almost hear the Reader sniggering when they read that line of fluff.) The essay will earn 1 point in Row B; it does provide vague references to the text that are questionably relevant.

Ultimately this essay suffers on multiple fronts. Overall, it is not on topic, and instead of analyzing how Hawthorne employs literary devices to characterize the newlyweds' relationship, the student merely presents surface-level analysis about the characters. No literary devices are actually specified or even alluded to, let alone any analyses of how such devices are used to create the characters' relationship. The paragraph development is weak, anorexic even; it provides only one faint example in each body paragraph and offers simplistic ideas at best. Finally, the essay's diction and style are unsophisticated and repetitive. For example, the second paragraph presents "Alymer [sic] is very smart . . . but he's not very smart . . . " and " . . . he thinks it's a flaw, and . . . this flaw." Then the third paragraph claims " . . . she seems feisty. She shows her feistiness . . . " The weak verb choices, such as "seems" and "shows," are used far too often, and they do not lend themselves to thoughtful analysis. The student can be rewarded for having acceptable organization and for not being too inaccurate in ideas per se, but he or she needs to read the prompt much more carefully, think about the clues it provides, and then use those clues to garner insights and examples to develop a successful essay. These traits do not meet the criteria for a point in Row C. This essay will earn an overall score of 1 because it fails to offer adequate analysis, ignores Hawthorne's literary techniques, is repetitive in its presentation, and lacks textual support.

Question 3: An Evil Character's Complexity

The following scoring guide explicitly explains how to earn up to 6 total points for a literary analysis essay. Row A (thesis) can earn up to 1 point; Row B (evidence and commentary) can earn up to 4 points, and Row C (sophistication) can earn up to 1 point.

Row A: Thesis (0–1 point)	
Scoring Criteria	
0 points for any of the following:	**1 point for**
• Having no defendable thesis. • Only restating the prompt in the thesis. • Only summarizing the issue with no claim in the thesis. • Presenting a thesis that does not address the prompt.	• Addressing the prompt with a defendable thesis that presents an interpretation and may establish a line of reasoning.
Decision Rules and Scoring Notes	
Theses that do not earn this point	**Theses that do earn this point**
• Only restate the prompt. • Only offer an irrelevant generalized comment about the chosen work.	• Take a position on the prompt and provide a defendable interpretation of what a character's villainy reveals about humanity and how the character's complexity adds to an interpretation of the chosen work as a whole.
Additional Notes	
• The thesis may be one or more sentences anywhere in the response. • A thesis that meets the criteria can be awarded the point whether or not the rest of the response successfully conveys that line of reasoning.	

Row B: Evidence AND Commentary (0–4 points)

Scoring Criteria

0 points for	1 point for	2 points for	3 points for	4 points for
• Simply repeating the thesis (if present). • **OR** restating provided information. • **OR** providing mostly irrelevant and/or incoherent examples.	• Summarizing the chosen work without reference to a thesis. • **OR** providing vague textual references. • **OR** providing textual references of questionable relevance. • **AND** providing little or no commentary.	• Making relevant textual references (direct quotes or paraphrases). • **AND** providing commentary but repeats, oversimplifies, or misinterprets the cited evidence or text.	• Making relevant textual references (direct quotes or paraphrases). • **AND** providing commentary that explains the logical relationship between textual examples and the thesis; however, commentary is uneven, limited, or incomplete.	• Making relevant textual references (direct quotes or paraphrases). • **AND** providing well-developed commentary that explicitly explains the relationship between the evidence and the thesis.

Decision Rules and Scoring Notes

Typical responses that earn 0 points:	Typical responses that earn 1 point:	Typical responses that earn 2 points:	Typical responses that earn 3 points:	Typical responses that earn 4 points:
• Are unclear or fail to address the prompt. • May present mere opinion with no relevant textual references.	• Mention textual references, devices, or techniques with little or no analysis.	• Contain numerous inaccuracies or repetition in commentary. • Offer only simplistic explanations that do not strengthen the argument.	• Provide commentary that is not sufficiently developed or is too limited. • Assume or imply a connection to the thesis that is not consistently explicit.	• Provide commentary that uses significant details of the text to draw conclusions. • Integrate short excerpts throughout in order to support the thesis' interpretation.

Additional Notes

• Writing that suffers from grammatical and/or mechanical errors that interfere with communication cannot earn the fourth point in this row.

Row C: Sophistication (0–1 point)

Scoring Criteria

0 points for	1 point for
• Not meeting the criteria for 1 point.	• Exhibiting sophistication of thought and/or advancing a complex literary argument.

Decision Rules and Scoring Notes	
Responses that do not earn this point:	**Responses that earn this point demonstrate one (or more) of the following:**
• Try to contextualize an interpretation, but make predominantly sweeping generalizations (*"Throughout all history . . . "* OR *"Everyone believes . . . "*). • Only hint at other possible interpretations (*"Some may think . . . "* OR *"Though the work might be said to . . . "*). • Write one statement about a thematic interpretation of the chosen work without consistently maintaining that idea. • Oversimplify complexities in the chosen work. • Present complicated or complex sentences or language that is ineffective and detracts from the argument.	• Present a thesis that demands nuanced analysis of textual evidence and successfully prove it. • Illuminate the significance or relevance of an interpretation within a broader context. • Discuss alternative interpretations of a text. • Acknowledge and account for contradictions, ambiguities, and/or complexities within the text. • Provide relevant analogies to help better understand an interpretation. • Develop a prose style that is especially vivid, persuasive, resounding, or appropriate to the student's argument.
Additional Notes	
• This point should be awarded only if the demonstration of sophistication or complex understanding is part of the argument, not merely a phrase or brief reference.	

High-Scoring Essay

The desire for power is a most complicated emotion; some people crave power insatiably; some don't want power at all. Some use it to help make the world a better place; some abuse it for their own satisfaction. Nurse Ratched, in Ken Kesey's One Flew Over the Cuckoo's Nest, is a case study of the absolute fanaticism that a thirst for power holds over this evil nurse. Anyone hired as the head nurse in a mental institution should have compassion, patience, plus medical and psychological knowledge, but Nurse Ratched has no redeeming attributes. Set in a psychiatric institution in Oregon in the late 1950s or early 1960s, the men's ward becomes Nurse Ratched's personal little dominion where she dictates, demands, and demeans the vulnerable men into submission. Her obsession for power is fed by ruling and ruining others, symbolizing the ferocious battle going on in her mind; she must prove to herself that she really is in control, but she fears losing control so badly that she must prove it to herself again and again, and it is the patients who pay the terrible price.

Nurse Ratched's evil is so pervasive, so complete, that the reader wonders why; what has drained every last shred of her humanity? A psychiatrist would have a field day analyzing her inner demons, but all we see are her actions, her incessant drive to control everything inside her ward; the outside world cannot intrude into her domain. Kesey establishes a simple-yet-complex metaphor for the tyrannical dehumanization and mechanization of society, labeling it the Combine. Nurse Ratched becomes the core character, the mother board, if you will, and she comes to symbolize all of the evil in the larger Combine, and she is determined to keep this inhumane machine operating efficiently, using her evil nature as the power source. She dictates the men's every move, every medication, every horrific medical treatment. The men have been so beaten down by her that they submit to her machinations and manipulations. For example, they must attend Group Meetings, theoretically for their psychological benefit, but Nurse Ratched slyly eggs the men into airing their deepest secrets and turning on each other, then feeling shame for having done so. They leave the meetings battered and confused, more under her control than ever. She reveals the terrifying implications of the abuse of power; instead of receiving compassionate care and any smidgen of tenderness in their treatments, the vulnerable men are emasculated by a woman who cares not a whit for their well-being.

Of course, the outside world must eventually come into conflict with this powerful woman, and it comes in the form of Randle McMurphy, a ne'er-do-well who, after being convicted of battery and gambling, fakes insanity, thinking that a little time in the mental ward would be better than a stint on a prison work farm. He is rebellious, intelligent, and mischievous enough to want to upset Nurse Ratched's empire. He bets the inmates that he can do so without negative repercussions. They begin a cat-and-mouse game, with McMurphy supposedly wining minor skirmishes such as getting a room where the men can play cards, and disturbing the afternoon Group Meetings. However, the evil of the Combine is all-powerful and Nurse Ratched plays her hand until McMurphy is forced to submit. He becomes aware that his being involuntarily committed means that he cannot be released without her approval, and that she therefore controls his fate. She has horrifying power; she can send him to the Disturbed Ward, order electroshock therapy, and have him lobotomized, all of which she does in her mechanical, methodical, manipulative way. She basically allows McMurphy to upset the smooth running machine she has established, but only enough to warrant ordering medical punishment. After sending him to the Disturbed Ward for fighting with the orderlies, she demands he admit he was wrong; when McMurphy continually refuses, she sends him to electroshock therapy multiple times. After McMurphy organizes a secret ward party that turns wild with drinking and prostitutes, Nurse Ratched humiliates and threatens one of the inmates so severely that he commits suicide. This becomes the final straw for McMurphy, who attacks Ratched, ripping open her uniform to expose her Rubenesque breasts, and choking her. She retaliates by having him lobotomized. She wins. Evil wins. She regains her power.

Ultimately, Nurse Ratched symbolizes how controlling and destroying others, especially those who are more vulnerable, can completely destroy any ounce of humanity one might have once had. She truly embodies the idea of a new Combine, one that threatens our modern society, a mindless, relentless machine that, in its search for power, will stop at nothing.

(776 words)

Analysis of High-Scoring Essay

This essay clearly demonstrates how much a skilled writer can accomplish, even in a timed essay. It begins with a universal truth, the idea that power is a complicated emotion that can be used for improvement of the world or abused for personal satisfaction. Nurse Ratched, the evil and domineering antagonist of *One Flew Over the Cuckoo's Nest,* is a good choice for this prompt, but before examining how she has absolutely no redeeming attributes, the student sensitively describes the positive and caring competence that healthcare professionals in mental institutions should have. This makes for a most effective contrast. The student introduces the essentials of the novel, relating its setting and basic conflict, before clarifying that Nurse Ratched has a symbolic inner battle that causes her to abuse her power, while "it is the patients who pay the terrible price." This introduction does not explicitly address how her evil enhances the work as a whole, but it implies the horrific repercussions of one individual's craving for power. It clearly earns a point for Row A.

The first body paragraph establishes the pervasive extent of her evil nature and the way that she controls every aspect of the men's lives. It is an amusing turn of phrase to read how "a psychiatrist would have a field day analyzing her inner demons," given that she works in a psychiatric ward. The student explains Kesey's mechanical metaphor for control, the Combine, and calls Ratched the mother board of its core, an apt description given her gender and her total control of the ward. The paragraph offers ample examples of her manipulation of the inmates and it accurately comments on the results: "the vulnerable men are emasculated by a woman who cares not a whit for their well-being." Overall, the paragraph is well written and well developed.

The following body paragraph explores the kink in Nurse Ratched's world, the knot in her knickers: a new patient named Randle McMurphy, who refuses to submit to her domination. The student describes his character competently before exploring the "cat-and-mouse game" the two enemies play as they battle for dominance. The novel has plenty of action to choose from, and the student borders on presenting too much plot summary; however, this plot description is used in the effort of analysis as the student explores the way in which Nurse Ratched proceeds in a "mechanical, methodical, manipulative way" to destroy McMurphy, finally ordering him to be lobotomized. The student's brusque ending to the paragraph, "She wins. Evil wins. She regains her power," effectively mirrors the intensity of the struggle and the comprehensive evil of her power-hungry character. The ample textual evidence and well-developed commentary that supports the thesis' interpretation earns 4 points in Row B.

The conclusion is a bit brief, but it is effective. It addresses Nurse Ratched's greater significance, that she symbolizes how those who dominate others can destroy their own humanity. We are left with the terrifying idea that she embodies the Combine, something that portends ominous results in our current society. We need no more.

The essay as a whole deserves its high score. It is eloquent, on topic, well organized, and clearly developed. Its style is vivid and appropriate to the student's argument, earning a point in Row C. Since this is a timed essay, it is hard to find fault with it. However, some Readers might wish that the student had acknowledged how Kesey ultimately supplies a degree of antidote to Nurse Ratched's evil. The student never mentions Chief Bromden, the complex narrator who ultimately euthanizes McMurphy after he is left in a vegetative state, and who escapes by bashing a window open, running away presumably to find his freedom and regain his identity. Keep in mind, though, that a student must focus on the prompt, and this one in particular asks for examination of only one evil character. It might be too much to try to explain Chief Bromden's role, and in doing so, the student might veer away from the topic. Remember that the Reader will always reward a student for what he or she does well, and this particular student does many things very well; this essay deserves its overall score of 6.

Low-Scoring Essay

Lady Macbeth is an evil character who reveals a lot about humanity. She is greedy, ambitious (even more than her famous husband), and complex.

Lady Macbeth is obviously the dominant partner in this marriage. When she reads Macbeth's letter about the witches' prophecy, she doesn't think twice and immediately shows her evil side. She wants her husband to immediately act, committing murder, so they can be powerful. She proves her evil side when she asks the spirits to fill her with cruelty. What humane person would do that?

To convince Macbeth to commit murder, she attacks his masculinity and tells him he'll be more of a man if he does the evil deed. This is an evil act by her, brought by her huge ambition. What's interesting though, is that she wimps out once she realizes that people have actually died. It drives her crazy and she commits suicide in the end.

Without Lady Macbeth, the play would not have much force. As a whole, it is better because of the way she directs her husband to act in the beginning but becomes passive in the end.

(187 words)

Analysis of Low-Scoring Essay

This essay about Lady Macbeth proves that the student is somewhat familiar with the play, but the essay itself fails to impress. The introduction is overly short and it's simplistic, just two uninteresting sentences. It begins by telling us something very basic, that Lady Macbeth is evil, and then it asserts that she "reveals a lot about humanity," a quite vague and vacuous phrase. The second sentence merely lists her characteristics: greedy, ambitious, and complex. The parenthetical comparison to her husband seems to be an attempt at analysis, but it falls flat. This introduction is characteristic of a student who inserts words and phrases from the prompt here and there, such as "evil character," "humanity," and "complex," but without truly addressing the depth of the prompt. What Lady Macbeth may reveal about humanity or how her complexity adds to the work as a whole is still a mystery, both to the Reader and apparently to the student. The essay does not meet the criteria for a point in Row A.

The first body paragraph indicates it will present her dominance in the Macbeths' marriage; however, that idea is not substantiated. Instead, the student discusses how Lady Macbeth "immediately shows her evil side" by urging Macbeth to murder "so they can be powerful." This student does deserve some credit for adding accurate textual detail, such as Lady Macbeth's failure to "think twice" after receiving Macbeth's letter, and her asking "the spirits to fill her with cruelty." Unfortunately, the student goes no deeper and merely tells us this "proves her evil side." Also, concluding the paragraph with a rhetorical question doesn't work terribly well, particularly since the question comes off as a bit inane and immature.

The second body paragraph begins with plot information that would have been more appropriate in the previous paragraph; presenting how Lady Macbeth convinces Macbeth to commit murder supports the student's initial claim that she is the dominant partner. The student then tells us again that she is evil and that ambition was her motive. Then, perhaps in an attempt to explore her complexity, the student jumps to her becoming completely disheveled later in the play, informing us that "she wimps out once she realizes that people have actually died," which, in turn, "drives her crazy and she commits suicide in the end." This informal language and simplistic logic limit the essay's effectiveness. The superficial idea that she becomes crazy is too one-dimensional, and her supposed suicide actually takes place offstage. Just like the first body paragraph, this paragraph needs much more development and analysis. The student does present some relevant textual evidence, but the commentary is simplistic and oversimplified; it earns 2 points in Row B.

The conclusion is frivolous and offers no insights. It appears that the student is trying to address the prompt, which asks how the character's complexity enhances the meaning of the work as a whole, but the student's commentary does not address that. Instead, the conclusion simply tells us that the play is better because she changes from aggressive to passive.

We can reward this student for trying to address the topic, for using a few textual examples, and for writing grammatically correct, complete sentences. However, the essay is clearly flawed in both organization and development. It does not take advantage of the opportunity to explore how Lady Macbeth's complex character enhances the meaning of the entire work. It does not develop ideas satisfactorily, using just a few examples and offering only obvious commentary about them. The organization is weak and rambling; it does not cohere. The language is acceptable, albeit a bit too informal at times. It does not meet the criteria for a point in Row C. These deficiencies show an incomplete or oversimplified understanding of the work and of the prompt, and they hold this essay to an overall score of 2.

Scoring Worksheet

Use the following worksheet to arrive at a probable final AP score on Practice Exam 4. While it is sometimes difficult to be objective enough to score one's own essay, you can use the sample essay answers to approximate an essay score for yourself. Better yet, give your essays (along with the sample scored essays) to a friend or relative who you think is competent to score the essays.

Section I: Multiple-Choice Questions

$$\frac{}{\text{right answers}} = \frac{}{\text{multiple-choice raw score}}$$

$$\frac{}{\text{multiple-choice raw score}} \times 1.25 = \frac{}{\text{multiple-choice converted score}} \text{ (of possible 67.5)}$$

Section II: Free-Response Questions

$$\frac{}{\text{question 1 raw score}} + \frac{}{\text{question 2 raw score}} + \frac{}{\text{question 3 raw score}} = \frac{}{\text{essay raw score}}$$

$$\frac{}{\text{essay raw score}} \times 4.583 = \frac{}{\text{essay converted score}} \text{ (of possible 82.5)}$$

Final Score

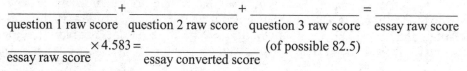

$$\frac{}{\text{multiple-choice converted score}} + \frac{}{\text{essay converted score}} = \frac{}{\text{final converted score}} \text{ (of possible 150)}$$

Probable Final AP Score	
Final Converted Score	**Probable AP Score**
150–100	5
99–86	4
85–67	3
66–0	1 or 2

Chapter 11

Practice Exam 5

Section I: Multiple-Choice Questions

Time: 1 hour
55 questions

Directions: This section contains selections from two passages of prose and three poems, with questions on their content, style, and form. Read each selection carefully. Choose the best answer of the five choices.

For questions 1–13, read the following poem carefully before choosing your answers.

To John Keats, Poet, At Spring Time

I cannot hold my peace, John Keats;
There never was a spring like this;
It is an echo, that repeats
My last year's song and next year's bliss.
I know, in spite of all men say   (5)
Of Beauty, you have felt her most.
Yea, even in your grave her way
Is laid. Poor, troubled, lyric ghost,
Spring never was so fair and dear
As Beauty makes her seem this year.   (10)

I cannot hold my peace, John Keats,
I am as helpless in the toil
Of Spring as any lamb that bleats
To feel the solid earth recoil
Beneath his puny legs. Spring beats   (15)
Her tocsin[1] call to those who love her,
And lo! the dogwood petals cover
Her breast with drifts of snow, and sleek
White gulls fly screaming to her, and hover
About her shoulders, and kiss her cheek,   (20)
While white and purple lilacs muster
A strength that bears them to a cluster
Of color and odor; for her sake
All things that slept are now awake.

And you and I, shall we lie still,   (25)
John Keats, while Beauty summons us?
Somehow I feel your sensitive will
Is pulsing up some tremulous
Sap road of a maple tree, whose leaves
Grow music as they grow, since your   (30)
Wild voice is in them, a harp that grieves
For life that opens death's dark door.
Though dust, your fingers still can push
The Vision Splendid to a birth,
Though now they work as grass in the hush   (35)
Of the night on the broad sweet page of the earth.

'John Keats is dead,' they say, but I
Who hear your full insistent cry
In bud and blossom, leaf and tree,
Know John Keats still writes poetry.   (40)
And while my head is earthward bowed
To read new life sprung from your shroud,
Folks seeing me must think it strange
That merely spring should so derange
My mind. They do not know that you,   (45)
John Keats, keep revel with me, too.

---

[1]tocsin: an alarm bell or warning signal

1. The repetition of "I cannot hold my peace, John Keats" (lines 1 and 11) implies that the speaker

    A. has a lasting grudge with John Keats
    B. is compelled to be heard
    C. will brusquely speak his mind
    D. cannot continue to endure silence
    E. must publicly voice his grief

2. Lines 7–10, "Yea, even in your grave . . . makes her seem this year," have the effect of

    A. expressing the speaker's sadness at Keats' death
    B. connecting the speaker and Keats directly
    C. eulogizing Keats to those who mourn him
    D. contrasting Keats' death with this beautiful, vibrant spring
    E. reiterating that Keats knew nature better than anyone

3. Which of the following does the speaker NOT use for inspiration?

    A. His own past
    B. Keats' sensitivity
    C. Keats' poetry
    D. Keats' actual gravesite
    E. The current beauty of spring

4. Stanza two can best be described as presenting

    A. an elegiac portrayal
    B. lyric overindulgence
    C. a detailed narrative
    D. a dramatic monologue
    E. a pastoral description

5. Stanza two contains all of the following types of imagery EXCEPT

    A. visual
    B. olfactory
    C. kinesthetic
    D. gustatory
    E. auditory

6. The lamb cries out primarily because

    A. he is ecstatic at the beauty of spring
    B. his young legs are practically bouncing on the soft, spongy earth
    C. he feels as helpless as the speaker
    D. his fear of spring's "tocsin call" is overwhelming
    E. he is astounded at the sudden snow drifts he comes upon

7. The last line of the second stanza, "All things that slept are now awake" (line 24), functions as which of the following?

    A. It serves as a transition to the third stanza in which the speaker awakens Keats' spirit.
    B. It summarizes the descriptions of nature in the first two stanzas.
    C. It restates the overall point that all of nature is now awake and growing.
    D. It reiterates the closing lines in the other three stanzas.
    E. It is the counterpoint to the idea stated in the last line of the poem.

8. Which of the following contrasting images are contained in the fourth stanza?

    A. Death and renewal

    B. Spring and winter

    C. Beauty and ugliness

    D. Fear and acceptance

    E. Music and silence

9. What is a logical implication of the speaker's use of "Folks" in line 43?

    A. It implies the common people in the town think him strange because his "head is earthward bowed" (line 41).

    B. It suggests that the speaker separates himself from those who do not appreciate his passion.

    C. It provides a common link between the speaker and others as they pass by.

    D. It reduces the speaker's emotions about Keats and spring to colloquial language.

    E. It magnifies the speaker's disdain of others in the town.

10. The poem contains all of the following poetic devices EXCEPT

    A. apostrophe

    B. personification

    C. aphorism

    D. metaphor

    E. simile

11. Within context, which of the following has an ambiguous implication?

    A. "repeats" (line 3)

    B. "recoil" (line 14)

    C. "muster" (line 21)

    D. "sprung" (line 42)

    E. "derange" (line 44)

12. To the speaker, John Keats embodies which of the following?

    A. The combining of simple thoughts with clear diction

    B. The coupling of a scientific eye with poetic prowess

    C. The melding of lyric creativity and beauty of nature

    D. The merging of life and death

    E. The synthesis of sound and vision

13. All of the following quotations contribute to the poem's motif of natural imagery that describes vibrant, recurring spring growth EXCEPT

    A. "There never was a spring like this" (line 2)

    B. "Spring never was so fair and dear" (line 9)

    C. "I cannot hold my peace, John Keats" (line 11)

    D. "While white and purple lilacs muster" (line 21)

    E. "In bud and blossom, leaf and tree" (line 39)

For questions 14–22, read the following passage carefully before choosing your answers.

It was one of their happy mornings. They trotted along and sat down together, with no thought that life would ever change much for them: they would only get bigger and not go to
(5) school, and it would always be like the holidays; they would always live together and be fond of each other. And the mill with its blooming; the great chestnut-tree under which they played at houses; their own little river, the Ripple, where
(10) the banks seemed like home, and Tom was always seeing the water-rats, while Maggie gathered the purple plumy tops of the reeds, which she forgot and dropped afterwards; above all, the great Floss, along which they wandered with a sense of
(15) travel to see the rushing spring-tide, the awful Eagre[1], come up like a hungry monster, or to see the Great Ash, which had once wailed and groaned like a man—these things would always be just the same to them. Tom thought people
(20) were at a disadvantage who lived on any other spot of the globe; and Maggie, when she read about Christiana passing "the river over which there is no bridge," always saw the Floss between the green pastures by the Great Ash.

(25) Life did change for Tom and Maggie, and yet they were not wrong in believing that the thoughts and loves of those first years would always make part of their lives. We could never have loved the earth so well if we had had no
(30) childhood in it—if it were not the earth where the same flowers come up again every spring that we used to gather with our tiny fingers as we sat lisping to ourselves on the grass, the same hips and haws on the autumn hedgerows, the same
(35) redbreasts that we used to call "God's birds," because they did no harm to the precious crops. What novelty is worth that sweet monotony where everything is known, and *loved* because it is known?

(40)　　The wood I walk in on this mild May day, with the young yellow-brown foliage of the oaks between me and the blue sky, the white star-flowers and the blue-eyed speedwell and the ground ivy at my feet—what grove of tropic
(45) palms, what strange ferns or splendid broad-petalled blossoms, could ever thrill such deep and delicate fibers within me as this home-scene? These familiar flowers, these well-remembered bird notes, this sky, with its fitful brightness,
(50) these furrowed and grassy fields, each with a sort of personality given to it by the capricious hedgerows—such things as these are the mother tongue of our imagination, the language that is laden with all the subtle inextricable associations
(55) the fleeting hours of our childhood left behind them. Our delight in the sunshine on the deep-bladed grass today might be no more than the faint perception of wearied souls if it were not for the sunshine and the grass in the far-off years
(60) which still live in us and transform our perception into love.

---

[1]**Eagre:** (British) a powerful single wave that flows up a river as a result of an especially high tide

14. Which of the following does NOT hint at Tom and Maggie's childhood idealism?

A. " . . . no thought that life would ever change . . . " (lines 2–3)
B. " . . . it would always be like the holidays . . . " (line 5)
C. " . . . their own little river . . . " (line 9)
D. "Tom thought people were at a disadvantage who lived on any other spot of the globe . . . " (lines 19–21)
E. " . . . the white star-flowers and the blue-eyed speedwell and the ground ivy at my feet . . . " (lines 42–44)

15. Which of the following identifies the literary device that is used to describe the Eagre and the Great Ash (lines 15–18)?

A. Onomatopoeia
B. Allegory
C. Foreshadowing
D. Personification
E. Apostrophe

16. The river Floss is associated with which of the following ideas?

A. It is portrayed as an impenetrable barrier, a symbol of the future that Tom and Maggie will never share.
B. It is a literal border, preventing the children from entering greener pastures on the far side.
C. It is a symbol for the inexorable passage of time, always flowing in one direction.
D. It evokes an image of a hungry monster, an Eagre, which scares the children.
E. It serves as an ominous vision of crossing over from the world of the living to the world of the dead.

17. The first sentence of the second paragraph contradicts which of the following?

A. "It was one of their happy mornings" (line 1)
B. "They trotted along and sat down together . . . " (lines 1–2)
C. " . . . with no thought that life would ever change much for them . . . " (lines 2–4)
D. " . . . the awful Eagre, come up like a hungry monster . . . " (lines 15–16)
E. "Tom thought people were at a disadvantage who lived on any other spot on the globe . . . " (lines 19–21)

18. In the second paragraph, what is the effect of the plural pronouns "we," "our," and "ourselves"?

A. It generalizes the sentiments to include all mankind.
B. It proves the close relationship between Tom and Maggie.
C. It broadens the scope to all who live in the area.
D. It individualizes the narrator's comments.
E. It acknowledges the beauty of the natural world.

19. The interjection in lines 44–46, " . . . what grove of tropic palms, what strange ferns or splendid broad-petalled blossoms . . . " serves primarily to

   A. juxtapose an image of beautiful tropical vegetation with the dreary forest in which the narrator walks

   B. allow the narrator to reminisce about visiting a vibrant, tropical paradise

   C. painfully remind the narrator of a long-ago trip with his lost love

   D. allow the narrator to reaffirm devotion to the beloved fields of childhood

   E. foreshadow an inexorable decline

20. What is the author's intended effect of phrases such as " . . . with no thought that life would ever change much for them . . . " (lines 2–4), " . . . where the same flowers come up again every spring . . . " (lines 30–31), and "These familiar flowers, these well-remembered bird notes . . . " (lines 48–49)?

   A. They introduce an image of entropy in the local environment.

   B. They imbue the world with a sense of permanence and stability.

   C. They emphasize the rural setting of the piece.

   D. They serve as an aphorism for a larger picture.

   E. They function as hyperbole, by overstating the obvious.

21. Which of the following best articulates the narrator's intended point about the relationship between nature and childhood in the sentence "These familiar flowers . . . childhood left behind them" (lines 48–56)?

   A. Nature and childhood are integral to each other, but as one grows those connections are lost.

   B. Children learn life-long lessons best when they are exposed to nature.

   C. Children's experiences in the natural world fuel their imagination and imbue them with understated and complex memories that will linger long after childhood is gone.

   D. Nature, while capricious, presents many images that one never forgets as one grows older.

   E. Children can have a scary relationship with nature, but ultimately it is one that fulfills their need for adventure.

22. The tone of the last paragraph can best be described as

   A. reflective and exuberant

   B. nostalgic and appreciative

   C. solemn and instructive

   D. effervescent and passionate

   E. childish and benevolent

For questions 23–33, read the following poem carefully before choosing your answers.

Ode on the Death of a Favourite Cat Drowned in a Tub of Goldfishes

'Twas on a lofty vase's side,
Where China's gayest art had dyed
The azure flowers that blow;
Demurest of the tabby kind,
The pensive Selima, reclined,   (5)
Gazed on the lake below.

Her conscious tail her joy declared;
The fair round face, the snowy beard,
The velvet of her paws,
Her coat, that with the tortoise vies,   (10)
Her ears of jet, and emerald eyes,
She saw; and purred applause.

Still had she gazed; but 'midst the tide
Two angel forms were seen to glide,
The genii of the stream;   (15)
Their scaly armour's Tyrian[1] hue
Through richest purple to the view
Betrayed a golden gleam.

The hapless nymph with wonder saw;
A whisker first and then a claw,   (20)
With many an ardent wish,
She stretched in vain to reach the prize.
What female heart can gold despise?
What cat's averse to fish?

Presumptuous maid! with looks intent   (25)
Again she stretch'd, again she bent,
Nor knew the gulf between.
(Malignant Fate sat by, and smiled)
The slippery verge her feet beguiled,
She tumbled headlong in.   (30)

Eight times emerging from the flood
She mewed to every watery god,
Some speedy aid to send.
No dolphin came, no Nereid[2] stirred;
Nor cruel Tom, nor Susan heard;   (35)
A Favourite has no friend!

From hence, ye beauties, undeceived,
Know, one false step is ne'er retrieved,
And be with caution bold.
Not all that tempts your wandering eyes   (40)
And heedless hearts, is lawful prize;
Nor all that glisters, gold.

---

[1]**Tyrian:** a crimson or purple dye, originally obtained by ancient Greeks and Romans from mollusks
[2]**Nereid:** in Greek mythology, any one of the 50 sea nymph daughters of Nereus and Doris

23. All of the following can be considered examples of exaggerated, inflated language EXCEPT

   A. "lofty vase" (line 1)
   B. "lake" (line 6)
   C. "genii of the stream" (line 15)
   D. "scaly armour" (line 16)
   E. "whisker" (line 20)

24. Selima's instinctual greed can best be exemplified in which of the following quotations?

   A. "Demurest of the tabby kind" (line 4)
   B. "pensive Selima" (line 5)
   C. "What cat's averse to fish?" (line 24)
   D. "Nor knew the gulf between" (line 27)
   E. "A Favourite has no friend!" (line 36)

25. The repetition of the word "her" in stanza two emphasizes which of Selima's characteristics?

   A. The beauty of her coat
   B. Her vanity at seeing her reflection
   C. Her satisfaction at being in charge of her life
   D. Her natural inquisitiveness
   E. Her ability to be easily distracted

26. In regard to the poem's overall narration, the function of the third stanza is to

   A. introduce what will distract Selima and change her fate
   B. enhance the description of Selima's beauty
   C. continue the description of the goldfish
   D. disrupt the flow of the action
   E. contrast Selima's description with the goldfish

27. The speaker uses Selima's unfortunate demise primarily to illustrate which of the following?

   A. The need to avoid all temptation
   B. The failure of Selima's owners to care for her properly
   C. The idea that curiosity can kill a cat
   D. The potential consequences of vanity
   E. The similarities between owners and their pets

28. The subject of the verb "beguiled" in line 29 is

   A. "Fate" (line 28)
   B. "verge" (line 29)
   C. "feet" (line 29)
   D. "She" (line 30)
   E. "flood" (line 31)

29. The poem contains all of the following devices EXCEPT

   A. allusion
   B. personification
   C. sentence inversion
   D. metaphorical conceit
   E. alliteration

30. Which of the following lines in the final stanza moralizes most strongly?

   A. "From hence, ye beauties, undeceived" (line 37)
   B. "Know, one false step is ne'er retrieved" (line 38)
   C. "Not all that tempts your wandering eyes" (line 40)
   D. "And heedless hearts, is lawful prize" (line 41)
   E. "Nor all that glisters, gold" (line 42)

31. Which of the following aphorisms best describes Selima's plight?

   A. Life consists of what a man is thinking of all day. (Emerson)
   B. Be content with your lot; one cannot be first in everything. (Aesop)
   C. Mistrust first impulses; they are nearly always noble. (de Talleyrand)
   D. Never go to excess but let moderation be your guide. (Cicero)
   E. Pride goes before destruction and a haughty spirit before a fall. (Proverbs 16:18)

32. The poem's mock heroic tone is NOT supported by which of the following?

   A. "Her conscious tail her joy declared" (line 7)

   B. "Their scaly armour's Tyrian hue" (line 16)

   C. "The hapless nymph with wonder saw" (line 19)

   D. "Eight times emerging from the flood" (line 31)

   E. "And be with caution bold" (line 39)

33. Which of the following ideas does the poem suggest?

   A. Those who get preferential treatment might not receive help when in need.

   B. Fate is always malignant.

   C. Unattended household pets create chaos in the home.

   D. One cannot swim against a flood.

   E. If appropriately cautious, one will not stumble and fall.

For questions 34–45, read the following passage carefully before choosing your answers.

In this passage, Quoyle, a newly arrived reporter for the local newspaper, the Gammy Bird, is given the task of reporting on the shipping news at a Newfoundland harbor.

He dodged through the rattle of lift trucks and winches on Wharf Road. Boats varnished with rain. Down along he saw the black coastal ferry with its red rails taking on cars, and the
(5) Labrador hospital ship. At the government dock orange flank of the Search and Rescue cutter. A dragger coming in to the fish plant.

Wharf Road was paved with worn, blue stone carried as ballast from some distant place. A
(10) marine stink of oil, fish and dirty water. Beyond the dives and bars a few provisioners. In one window he noticed an immense pyramid of packaged dates of the kind Nutbeem liked— *Desert Jujubes*—red camels, shooting stars on
(15) the label.

The harbormaster's office was at the top of a gritty wooden stair.

Diddy Shovel, the harbormaster, watched Quoyle's yellow slicker emerge from the station
(20) wagon, watched him drop his notepad on the wet cobbles. Sized him up as strong and clumsy. Shovel had been renowned once for his great physical strength. When he was twenty he started

a curious brotherhood called "The Finger Club."
(25) The seven members were all men who could suspend themselves from a beam in Eddie Blunt's cellar by a single little finger. Powerful men in those days. As he grew older, he complemented, then replaced, his physical strength with a
(30) stentorian voice. Was now the only living member of the Finger Club. His thoughts often stopped at that point.

In a minute Quoyle opened the door, looked through the windows twelve feet high, a glass
(35) wall into the drizzled slant of harbor, the public docks and piers in the foreground, and beyond, the sullen bay rubbed with thumbs of fog.

A squeaking sound. Wooden swivel chair spun and the terrible face of the harbormaster
(40) aimed at Quoyle.

"You ought to see it in a storm, the great clouds rolling off the shoulders of the mountains. Or the sunset like a flock of birds on fire. 'Tis the most outrageous set of windows in Newfoundland." A
(45) voice as deep as a shout in a cave.

"I believe that," said Quoyle. Dripping on the floor. Found the coat hook in the corner.

Diddy Shovel's skin was like asphalt, fissured and cracked, thickened by a lifetime of weather,
(50) the scurf of age. Stubble worked through the craquelured[1] surface. His eyelids collapsed in protective folds at the outer corners. Bristled eyebrows; enlarged pores gave the nose a sandy appearance. Jacket split at the shoulder seams.

(55) "I'm Quoyle. New at the *Gammy Bird*. Come to get the shipping news. I'd appreciate suggestions. About the shipping news. Or anything else."

Harbormaster cleared his throat. Man
(60) Imitates Alligator, thought Quoyle. Got up and limped behind the counter. The cool high light from the windows fell on a painting the size of a bed sheet. A ship roared down a wave, and in the trough of the wave, broadside, a smaller boat,
(65) already lost. Men ran along the decks, their mouths open in shrieks.

The harbormaster pulled up a loose-leaf notebook, riffled the pages with his thumb, then handed the book to Quoyle. ARRIVALS on the
(70) cover; a sense of the money gain and loss, cargoes, distance traveled, the smell of the tropics.

Followed Quoyle's gaze.

---

[1]**craquelured:** a network of fine cracks or crackles on the surface of a painting, caused chiefly by shrinkage of paint film or varnish

"Fine picture! That's the *Queen Mary* running (75) down her escort, the *Curacoa*. Back in 1942. Twenty miles off the Irish coast in clear sunlight and crystal visibility. The *queen*, eighty-one thousand ton, converted from passenger liner to troopship, and the cruiser a mere forty-five (80) hundred. Cut her in half like a boiled carrot."

Quoyle wrote until his hand cramped and he discovered he had taken down the names of ships that had called weeks ago.

"How can I tell if the ships are still here?"

(85) The harbormaster pulled up another book. Plywood cover, the word DEPARTURES burned in wavering letters.

"Ha-ha," said Quoyle. "I'd think they'd get you a computer. These logbooks look like a lot of work."

(90) The harbormaster pointed to an alcove behind the counter. Computer screen like boiling milk. The harbormaster punched keys, the names of ships leaped in royal blue letters, their tonnages, owners, country of registration, cargoes, arrival and (95) departure dates, last port of call, next port of call, days out from home port, crew number, captain's name, birthdate and social insurance number. The harbormaster tapped again and a printer hummed, the paper rolled out into a plastic bin. He tore off (100) pages, handed them to Quoyle. The shipping news.

Cracking grin that showed false teeth to the roots. "Now you'll remember that we do it two ways," he said. "So when the storm roars and the power's out you'll look in the old books and it'll all be there. (105) Have a cup of tea. Nothing like it on a wet day."

"I will," said Quoyle.

34. The phrase "the harbormaster, watched Quoyle's yellow slicker emerge from the station wagon" (lines 18–20) might suggest an image of

 A. school children in the rain
 B. the degree to which Quoyle works hard
 C. the contrast between the slicker and the weather
 D. a ghostlike shape with no substance, a slicker inhabited by no one
 E. Quoyle's protective covering

35. Diddy Shovel's memories of his youth suggest he might admire which of the following qualities in the reporter, Quoyle?

 A. The fact that he comes to the wharf for information
 B. The fact that he carries a notebook
 C. The fact that he is strong
 D. The fact that he drives a station wagon
 E. The fact that he has an eye for detail

36. The sentence "His thoughts often stopped at that point" (lines 31–32) implies which of the following about the harbormaster?

 A. He fondly remembers his friends from the past.
 B. He dislikes being reminded of the past.
 C. He cherishes his ability to conjure up pleasant memories.
 D. He laments his lost youth, his lost strength, and his lost friends.
 E. He becomes maudlin and overly emotional when he thinks of the past.

37. The harbormaster's character can best be described as

 A. fastidious and discreet
 B. coarse and taciturn
 C. eccentric and scurrilous
 D. docile and slothful
 E. phlegmatic and munificent

38. The author frequently uses sentence fragments to create the effect of

 A. distracting the flow of the narration
 B. leaving thoughts hanging in the air
 C. befuddling the description of the setting
 D. increasing dramatic tension between the characters
 E. reducing the images and actions to their bare necessities

39. The fact that the painting hanging on the wall is "the size of a bed sheet" (lines 62–63) becomes ironic because

 A. the wall the painting hangs on is not much larger than the bedsheet itself
 B. the painting depicts men who wish they had a bed with clean, dry sheets
 C. a bedsheet is associated with comfort and rest, but the painting depicts death and chaos
 D. the harbormaster appreciates things that are large in size, like himself
 E. a painting of this large size would appear to cost more than the harbor office could afford

40. The harbormaster's claim that the painting is a "Fine picture!" (line 74) is juxtaposed by the fact that

A. the harbormaster has no basis to make such a comment

B. the painting is old and decrepit

C. the painting depicts the horror of mass death at sea

D. the harbormaster clearly knows quality art

E. the painting portrays seafaring men

41. What action must have occurred between the harbormaster's statement "Cut her in half like a boiled carrot" (line 80) and "Quoyle wrote . . ." (line 81)?

A. The harbormaster takes pity on Quoyle and, instead of making him hand copy the next ledger, gives him the computer copy.

B. The harbormaster offers Quoyle a cup of tea to warm him up.

C. Quoyle comments on the painting's quality.

D. Much time has passed and Quoyle has handwritten so much data that his hand cramps up.

E. Both men complete their respective tasks.

42. The passage contains all of the following literary elements EXCEPT

A. simile

B. personification

C. olfactory imagery

D. industrial imagery

E. omniscient point of view

43. Given Quoyle's job, what is ironic about the entries from the arrivals ledger that he copies into his notebook?

A. He wasted his time when he could have printed them from the computer.

B. His job is to get the current news, but the ledger entries he copies are actually weeks old.

C. He could have gotten the same information from another source.

D. His work can easily get smudged in the rain.

E. He knows the newspaper won't print the information anyway.

44. The tone of Quoyle's dialogue can best be described as

A. understated

B. hyperbolic

C. beseeching

D. acerbic

E. patronizing

45. The vignette about his interactions with the old harbormaster should teach Quoyle all of the following lessons EXCEPT

A. one cannot count on the accuracy of computer data

B. being upfront and honest is the best policy

C. some people force others to learn for themselves

D. the fastest route may not always be reliable

E. one should seek information from many sources

For questions 46–55, read the following poem carefully before choosing your answers.

And If I Did, What Then?

"And if I did, what then?
Are you aggriev'd therefore?
The sea hath fish for every man,
And what would you have more?"

Thus did my mistress once,   (5)
Amaze my mind with doubt;
And popp'd a question for the nonce
To beat my brains about.

Whereto I thus replied:
"Each fisherman can wish   (10)
That all the seas at every tide
Were his alone to fish.

"And so did I (in vain)
But since it may not be,
Let such fish there as find the gain,   (15)
And leave the loss for me.

"And with such luck and loss
I will content myself,
Till tides of turning time may toss
Such fishers on the shelf.   (20)

"And when they stick on sands,
That every man may see,
Then will I laugh and clap my hands,
As they do now at me."

46. The mistress' attitude in the first stanza can best be described as

   A. pensive and demure
   B. aggrieved and aggressive
   C. demanding and dismissive
   D. diffident and confident
   E. sincere and contemplative

47. The mistress' first question might imply that

   A. there can be doubt about her confession
   B. she is taken by surprise
   C. she suggests she will amend her ways
   D. she questions her past actions
   E. she is willing to succumb to her lover

48. What point is the mistress making as she exclaims, "The sea hath fish for every man, / And what would you have more?" (lines 3–4)?

   A. Every man deserves the chance to fish for more.
   B. All men are materialistic.
   C. Fishing is not for every man.
   D. Men need to focus on what they really want in life.
   E. Demanding fidelity in a relationship is akin to greed.

49. The speaker's reaction to his mistress in the second stanza can be characterized as

   A. accusatory and spiteful
   B. amused and charmed
   C. angry and malicious
   D. befuddled and bitter
   E. vindictive and flummoxed

50. Once the speaker gathers his thoughts and replies to his mistress, his first point in the third stanza is that

    A. it is futile to expect faithfulness in a relationship

    B. men will have as many mistresses as they want

    C. it is not unreasonable to want fidelity in a relationship

    D. the tide will dictate how many fish a man can catch

    E. men fish best when they fish alone

51. A comparison of the mistress' tone versus the narrator's tone suggests which of the following contrasts?

    A. Biting vs. logical

    B. Mocking vs. pleading

    C. Spiteful vs. forgiving

    D. Unconcerned vs. overwhelmed

    E. Direct vs. philosophical

52. The predominant effect of the poem being composed almost entirely of monosyllabic words is that it

    A. creates a rhythmic, staccato beat

    B. distracts from the speaker's content

    C. streamlines the meaning of the poem

    D. generates a sincere tone of regret

    E. rushes the reader's judgment of the speakers

53. The concept of fish and fishing serves as which of the following?

    A. A sustained parody

    B. A governing metaphor

    C. An allegorical message

    D. A simple fable

    E. A personification of the lovers

54. The poem utilizes which of the following poetic conventions?

    A. Extended syllogism

    B. An *abab* rhyme scheme

    C. Iambic trimeter and tetrameter

    D. In medias res

    E. Abundant imagery

55. The last stanza implies which of the following about the narrator?

    A. He takes pride in getting the last word.

    B. He seeks a way to accept his mistress' infidelity.

    C. He will gloat when others are humiliated as he has been.

    D. He will relish seeing his mistress wronged.

    E. He plots revenge against those who laughed at him.

IF YOU FINISH BEFORE TIME IS CALLED, CHECK YOUR WORK ON THIS SECTION ONLY. DO NOT WORK ON ANY OTHER SECTION IN THE TEST.

Section II: Free-Response Questions

Time: 2 hours

3 questions

Question 1

(Suggested time: 40 minutes. This question counts toward one-third of the total free-response section score.)

Directions: In the following poem, "The Trees are Down," by Charlotte Mew (1929), the speaker decries that local trees are being cut down. Read the poem carefully. Then, in a well-written essay, analyze how Mew conveys the complex relationship between the speaker and the trees through the use of poetic devices.

In your response you should do the following:

- Respond to the prompt with a thesis that presents an interpretation and may establish a line of reasoning.
- Select and use evidence to develop and support your line of reasoning.
- Explain the relationship between the evidence and your thesis.
- Use appropriate grammar and punctuation in communicating your argument.

The Trees are Down

—and he cried with a loud voice:
Hurt not the earth, neither the sea, nor the trees—
(Revelation)

They are cutting down the great plane-trees at the end of the gardens.
For days there has been the grate of the saw, the swish of the branches as they fall,   (5)
The crash of the trunks, the rustle of trodden leaves,
With the 'Whoops' and the 'Whoas,' the loud common talk, the loud common laughs of the men,
    above it all.

I remember one evening of a long past Spring
Turning in at a gate, getting out of a cart, and finding a large dead rat in the mud of the drive.
I remember thinking: alive or dead, a rat was a god-forsaken thing,   (10)
But at least, in May, that even a rat should be alive.

The week's work here is as good as done. There is just one bough
  On the roped bole, in the fine grey rain,
    Green and high
    And lonely against the sky.   (15)
      (Down now!—)
    And but for that,
    If an old dead rat
Did once, for a moment, unmake the Spring, I might never have thought of him again.

It is not for a moment the Spring is unmade to-day;   (20)
These were great trees, it was in them from root to stem:
When the men with the 'Whoops' and the 'Whoas' have carted the whole of the whispering
    loveliness away
Half the Spring, for me, will have gone with them.

It is going now, and my heart has been struck with the hearts of the planes;
Half my life it has beat with these, in the sun, in the rains,   (25)
   In the March wind, the May breeze,
In the great gales that came over to them across the roofs from the great seas.
   There was only a quiet rain when they were dying;
   They must have heard the sparrows flying,
And the small creeping creatures in the earth where they were lying—   (30)
   But I, all day, I heard an angel crying:
   'Hurt not the trees.'

Question 2

(Suggested time: 40 minutes. This question counts toward one-third of the total free-response score.)

Directions: The following excerpt is from Thomas Wolfe's *Look Homeward, Angel* (1929). In the passage, Oliver Gant is resting in his office when he is interrupted by a woman, Eliza Pentland, who is selling books. Read the passage carefully. Then, in a well-written essay, analyze how Wolfe uses literary elements and techniques to develop the complex relationship between the two characters.

In your response you should do the following:

- Respond to the prompt with a thesis that presents an interpretation and may establish a line of reasoning.
- Select and use evidence to develop and support your line of reasoning.
- Explain the relationship between the evidence and your thesis.
- Use appropriate grammar and punctuation in communicating your argument.

Then Oliver met Eliza. He lay one afternoon in Spring upon the smooth leather sofa of his little office, listening to the bright piping noises in the Square. A restoring peace brooded over his great extended body. He thought of the loamy black earth with its sudden young light of flowers, of the beaded chill of beer, and of the plumtree's dropping blossoms. Then he heard the brisk heel-taps of a woman coming down among the

(5) marbles, and he got hastily to his feet. He was drawing on his well brushed coat of heavy black just as she entered.

"I tell you what," said Eliza, pursing her lips in reproachful banter, "I wish I was a man and had nothing to do but lie around all day on a good easy sofa."

"Good afternoon, madam," said Oliver with a flourishing bow. "Yes," he said, as a faint sly grin bent the

(10) corners of his thin mouth, "I reckon you've caught me taking my constitutional. As a matter of fact I very rarely lie down in the daytime, but I've been in bad health for the last year now, and I'm not able to do the work I used to."

He was silent a moment; his face drooped in an expression of hangdog dejection. "Ah, Lord! I don't know what's to become of me!"

(15) "Pshaw!" said Eliza briskly and contemptuously. "There's nothing wrong with you in my opinion. You're a big strapping fellow, in the prime of life. Half of it's only imagination. Most of the time we think we're sick it's all in the mind. I remember three years ago I was teaching school in Hominy Township when I was taken down with pneumonia. Nobody ever expected to see me come out of it alive but I got through it somehow; I well remember one day I was sitting down—as the fellow says, I reckon I was convalescin'; the reason I

(20) remember is Old Doctor Fletcher had just been and when he went out I saw him shake his head at my cousin Sally. 'Why Eliza, what on earth,' she said, just as soon as he had gone, 'he tells me you're spitting up blood every time you cough; you've got consumption as sure as you live.' 'Pshaw,' I said. I remember I laughed just as big as you please, determined to make a big joke of it all; I just thought to myself, I'm not going to give into it, I'll fool them all yet; 'I don't believe a word of it' (I said)," she nodded her head smartly at him, and

(25) pursed her lips, "'and besides, Sally' (I said) 'we've all got to go sometime, and there's no use worrying about wha's going to happen. It may come tomorrow, or it may come later, but it's bound to come to all in the end.'"

"Ah Lord!" said Oliver, shaking his head sadly. "You hit the nail on the head that time. A truer word was never spoken."

Merciful God! He thought, with an anguished inner grin. How long is this going to keep up? But she's a

(30) pippin as surely as you're born. He looked appreciatively at her trim erect figure, noting her milky white skin, her black-brown eyes, with their quaint child's stare, and her jet black hair drawn back tightly from her high white forehead. She had a curious trick of pursing her lips reflectively before she spoke; she liked to take her time, and came to the point after interminable divagations down all the lane-ends of memory and overtone, feasting upon the golden pageant of all she had ever said, done, felt, thought, seen, or replied, with egocentric

(35) delight.

Then, while he looked, she ceased speaking abruptly, put her neat gloved hand to her chin, and stared off with a thoughtful pursed mouth.

"Well," she said after a moment, "if you're getting your health back and spend a good part of your time lying around you ought to have something to occupy your mind." She opened a leather portmanteau she was

(40)   carrying and produced a visiting card and two fat volumes. "My name," she said portentously, with slow emphasis, "is Eliza Pentland, and I represent the Larkin Publishing Company."

    She spoke the words proudly, with dignified gusto. Merciful God! A book-agent! thought Gant.

    "We are offering," said Eliza, opening a huge yellow book with a fancy design of spears and flags and laurel wreaths, "a book of poems called *Gems of Verse for Hearth and Fireside* as well as *Larkin's Domestic*
(45)   *Doctor and Book of Household Remedies*, giving directions for the cure and prevention of over 500 diseases."

    "Well," said Gant, with a faint grin, wetting his big thumb briefly, "I ought to find one that I've got out of that."

    "Why yes," said Eliza nodding smartly, "as the fellow says, you can read poetry for the good of your soul and Larkin for the good of your body."
(50)   He bought the books.

Question 3

(Suggested time: 40 minutes. This question counts toward one-third of the total free-response section score.)

Directions: Many characters in literature face some form of danger, whether it is physical or psychological in nature. Some characters face several dangerous events; some face only a single monumental peril.

Either from your own reading or from the list below, choose a character in a work of fiction who confronts danger. Then, in a well-written essay, analyze how the character responds to danger, what that response reveals about the character, and how it adds to an interpretation of the work as a whole. Do not merely summarize the plot.

In your response you should do the following:

- Respond to the prompt with a thesis that presents an interpretation and may establish a line of reasoning.
- Select and use evidence to develop and support your line of reasoning.
- Explain the relationship between the evidence and your thesis.
- Use appropriate grammar and punctuation in communicating your argument.

Beloved	*No Country for Old Men*
Black Boy	*Obasan*
The Crossing	*Oliver Twist*
The Curious Incident of the Dog in the Night-Time	*Oryx and Crake*
Extremely Loud and Incredibly Close	*The Other*
A Farewell to Arms	*A Passage to India*
Frankenstein	*The Poisonwood Bible*
The Goldfinch	*A Portrait of the Artist as a Young Man*
The Grapes of Wrath	*The Sound and the Fury*
Great Expectations	*The Story of Edgar Sawtelle*
Hamlet	*A Tale of Two Cities*
The Handmaid's Tale	*Tess of the D'Urbervilles*
Heart of Darkness	*Things Fall Apart*
Invisible Man	*The Things They Carried*
Julius Caesar	*A Thousand Acres*
Lord of the Flies	*A Thousand Splendid Suns*
Middlesex	*The Underground Railroad*
The Mill on the Floss	*Wuthering Heights*

IF YOU FINISH BEFORE TIME IS CALLED, CHECK YOUR WORK ON THIS SECTION ONLY. DO NOT WORK ON ANY OTHER SECTION IN THE TEST.

Answer Key

Section I: Multiple-Choice Questions

First Poem	First Prose Passage	Second Poem	Second Prose Passage	Third Poem
1. B	14. E	23. E	34. D	46. C
2. D	15. D	24. C	35. C	47. A
3. D	16. E	25. B	36. D	48. E
4. E	17. C	26. A	37. B	49. D
5. D	18. A	27. D	38. E	50. C
6. B	19. D	28. B	39. C	51. E
7. A	20. B	29. D	40. C	52. A
8. A	21. C	30. B	41. D	53. B
9. B	22. B	31. E	42. E	54. D
10. C		32. E	43. B	55. C
11. E		33. A	44. A	
12. C			45. B	
13. C				

Answers and Explanations

Section I: Multiple-Choice Questions

First Poem

The poem used for questions 1–13, "To John Keats, Poet, At Spring Time," was written by the African American poet of the Harlem Renaissance Countee Cullen in 1924.

1. **B.** John Keats, the darling of the British Romantic literary movement who tragically died at only age 25, became known for his beautifully crafted poems, many of them odes, glorifying the dignity and beauty of nature. Many of his works revel in the moment, the instant when he absorbs all that is around him, and he expresses a sensory awareness that few other poets can match. The speaker in "To John Keats" clearly reveres Keats, and he cannot hold back this emotion as he soaks up the intense beauty of a spring day. He is compelled to speak to the poet he admires so much, choice B. Choice A contradicts the poem; the speaker is certainly not expressing any grudge against Keats. Choice C uses the incorrect adverb "brusquely," which does not describe the speaker's language. Choice D may seem plausible on a cursory read, but the poem offers no indication that the speaker was "enduring silence" and cannot continue to do so; he instead bursts forth with uncontained emotion. Choice E misreads the poem, thinking the speaker grieves, when in fact, he rejoices.

2. **D.** The speaker acknowledges that even Keats' grave bears the beauty of nature, that "Spring never was so fair and dear," making choice D correct. Choice A erroneously assumes that the speaker is expressing sadness at Keats' death, which he is not; instead, he is connecting Keats as a poetic muse to the glory of the current spring. Choice B is not supported by the poem; it has no direct connection between the speaker and Keats, even though the speaker obviously feels a spiritual connection to him; also, any connection they have is not the thrust of the quotation in this question. Choice C misreads the poem in two ways. First, the poem is not technically a eulogy, which would be written in honor of Keats, to extol his talent after his death; rather, Cullen, who highly admired Keats, uses the late poet as his inspiration. Second, the poem is not directed to those who mourn Keats; Cullen is not directing his comments to the public. Choice E is too much of a stretch; no doubt exists that Keats "knew nature" very well, but to claim he was better at it than anyone is implausible.

3. D. The speaker does not refer to Keats' actual burial site (which is in Rome) and, although he refers to Keats' grave metaphorically, he does not use the gravesite for inspiration, choice D. Of course, you are not expected to know that Keats is buried in Rome, nor do you need to know that fact to answer this question; Keats' actual gravesite is simply not in the poem. Also, do not be misled by the lines "my head is earthward bound / To read new life sprung from your shroud." A shroud is a cloth in which a body is covered for burial; it is not a gravesite. All other answer choices have evidence in the poem. The speaker calls on his own past (A) in lines 3–4, "that repeats / My last year's song." Choice B, Keats' sensitivity, can be seen as early as line 6, when the speaker acknowledges that "Of Beauty, you have felt her most," and in lines 27–28 as he claims, "Somehow I feel your sensitive will / Is pulsing up. . . ." The entire poem pays homage to Keats' poetry (C), and specifically the speaker states that, even though the famous poet has died, "Know John Keats still writes poetry" (line 40). The current beauty of spring (E) is evident throughout the poem, beginning with line 2, "There never was a spring like this" and continuing throughout the following stanzas, with lush description.

4. E. A pastoral poem describes simple rural life as romanticized and bucolic. Stanza two fulfills that with its references to lambs playing, flowering dogwood trees, flying gulls, and blooming lilacs, all of which are presented in positive imagery, choice E. Choice A erroneously thinks the poem is an elegy; this work is certainly not a mournful poem about death. Choice B may seem attractive at first; the word "lyric," when used as an adjective, refers to a poetical spontaneous outburst of emotion, which might be accurate, but the stanza does not present overindulgence, which refers to overdone schmaltzy emotion. Stanza two does not present a narrative, detailed or not, which makes choice C incorrect. Neither stanza two nor anything in the poem can be classified as a dramatic monologue (D). That term identifies a poem, similar to a soliloquy, in which a poetic speaker directly addresses the reader or an internal listener at length, revealing personality traits in the process.

5. D. Stanza two entices all of our senses except the sense of taste; it does not include gustatory imagery, choice D. It presents abundant visual imagery (A); one can easily see the lamb, the dogwood, the white gulls, the white and purple lilacs. Olfactory imagery (B) is evidenced by the "odor" of the lilacs, which really do have a lovely aroma. Kinesthetic imagery (C) is present in the way that the lamb "feel[s] the solid earth recoil." Auditory imagery (E) can be heard in the lamb's bleat, the tocsin call, the gull's screaming.

6. B. The lamb bleats "To feel the solid earth recoil / Beneath his puny legs." This calls to mind a young lamb as he bounces in a spongy meadow, choice B. Do not be deceived by the word "solid"; of course the earth is solid, but that does not mean it is not pliable. Choice A mistakenly attributes ecstasy to the lamb, an emotion that has no evidence in the poem; the speaker may be ecstatic, but we can't assume the lamb is also. Choice C is unreasonable; neither the speaker nor the lamb appears helpless. This answer choice misreads the speaker's emotion and imputes unwarranted feelings to the lamb. Choice D is incorrect because the description of the lamb is not connected to the description of the tocsin call; the latter just happens to follow the former, but no evidence exists that the lamb is fearful or overwhelmed by the sounds of spring. Choice E is a complete misread of the stanza; the lamb does not come upon "drifts of snow," first, because they do not exist (the snow drifts are a metaphor for the dogwood flowers that cover the ground), and second, the lamb never appears near them.

7. A. The second stanza concludes with the line "All things that slept are now awake." On the surface, this line seems to refer to the coming of spring, which has awakened all things after the winter. However, notice how it also transitions to the third stanza, choice A, in which the speaker symbolically awakens Keats from the dead as he claims "And you and I, shall we lie still, / John Keats, while Beauty summons us? / Somehow I feel your sensitive will / Is pulsing up. . . ." Choice B is inaccurate because of the word "summarizes"; the line in question does not summarize the first two stanzas; it may apply to stanza two, but certainly not stanza one. Choice C looks appealing at first glance, but the "overall point" of this poem is not that "nature is now awake and growing." Choice D is unreasonable; when one reads the closing line of each stanza, one sees that the last line of stanza two does not reiterate or echo the other stanzas' closing. Choice E is off base because of the word "counterpoint," which refers to some form of contrast or juxtaposition. The ending line of stanza two does not juxtapose the last line of the poem.

8. A. The last stanza clearly provides contrasting images of death and renewal, choice A, in the phrases "'John Keats is dead,'" which is juxtaposed with " . . . new life sprung from your shroud." Choice B is only partially correct; the last stanza refers to spring, but not winter. Choice C is wrong for the same reason; the stanza describes beauty with "In bud and blossom, leaf and tree," but it has no hint of ugliness. Fear and acceptance (D) simply makes no sense; this is too much of a stretch and has no evidence in the stanza. Likewise, the images in choice E, music and silence, have no support in the stanza.

9. **B.** The word "folks" stands out due to its everyday informality, and, when set against the reverential tone the speaker uses for Keats, suggests he separates himself from those who do not understand or appreciate his passion for the coming of spring and for Keats' glory, choice B. Choice A is irrelevant; while it is true that the townspeople think the speaker strange, it does not answer this question about his use of the word "folks." No common link is established between the speaker and others who pass by (C); he is separated both visibly and emotionally. Choice D contradicts the poem; nothing reduces the speaker's emotion about Keats and spring. Choice E inappropriately claims that the word "folks" in the poem somehow "magnifies" the speaker's disdain of others, but he is not really critical of others.

10. **C.** An aphorism is a short, succinct statement that states a general truth or moral principle. The poem "To John Keats" has no such statements, making choice C correct. The entire poem is an apostrophe (A); the speaker expresses his thoughts to the long-dead John Keats. Personification (B) is evidenced in such examples as "Spring beats / her tocsin call." Metaphor (D) can be seen in "a harp that grieves / For life. . . ." The speaker uses simile (E) as he compares himself to a lamb, "I am as helpless . . . as any lamb."

11. **E.** The lines "Folks seeing me must think it strange / That merely spring should so derange / My mind" clearly embody ambiguity. Does the word "derange," choice E, describe what the speaker thinks of himself, hinting at the connotation of a kind of romanticized divine madness that brings insight? Or, conversely, does "derange" refer to the negative judgments of the townspeople? Both views are defensible, which makes this ambiguity an interpretative puzzle for the reader. No other answer choices are ambiguous; each word is used with one clear intent.

12. **C.** The speaker clearly admires John Keats' ability to create lyrical poetry that conveys the awe-inspiring beauty of nature, choice C. He claims, "I know . . . / Of Beauty, you have felt her most," and acknowledges that "I / Who hear your full insistent cry / In bud and blossom, leaf and tree / Know John Keats still writes poetry." On the other hand, choice A is clearly inaccurate. John Keats did not combine simple thoughts with clear diction, and the speaker does not hint at any such idea. Choice B is wrong for the same reason; the speaker does not suggest that Keats had a "scientific eye." Choice D is an illogical extension of the speaker's thoughts; it is true that the poem addresses life and death and renewal, but you should not conclude that the speaker thinks Keats embodies the merging of those two ideas. Choice E is equally unreasonable. The speaker offers no evidence that he thinks Keats embodies the synthesis of sound and vision.

13. **C.** All of the quotations in the inaccurate answer choices describe the vitality of spring in one form or another. Choice A extolls "There never was a spring like this," choice B asserts "Spring never was so fair and dear," choice D lauds the "white and purple lilacs," and choice E celebrates "bud and blossom, leaf and tree." The only exception is choice C, "I cannot hold my peace, John Keats"; this line does not describe spring, but rather, it serves as a springboard for the poet to exclaim his reaction, his awe of the beauty of the season, just as his muse, John Keats, had so glorified the season.

First Prose Passage

The passage used for questions 14–22 is an excerpt from <u>The Mill on the Floss</u> (1860) written by George Eliot, the pen name of Mary Ann Evans. This novel follows the complex relationship between Maggie and Tom, sister and brother, from childhood to adulthood.

14. **E.** Tom and Maggie's childhood idealism is detailed throughout the first paragraph. They naively think their life would never change (A), that life would always be like the holidays (B), and that they would always have "their own little river" (C). In addition, Tom innocently believes that people who live anywhere else in the world are at a disadvantage (D); their home environs must be the best place possible. However, the exception, choice E, which describes flowers and ivy, does not occur when Tom and Maggie are children; instead, it takes place as the adult narrator walks "on this mild May day" (line 40). Thus, this description is not a testament to their youthful idealism.

15. **D.** The "awful Eagre" (a strong wave of water surging up a river) comes "like a hungry monster" and the Great Ash (a large, old tree) once "wailed and groaned like a man." Both phrases demonstrate personification, giving the objects human characteristics. Choice A is incorrect because, although we can imagine the tree wailing and groaning, the text does not use onomatopoeia to refer to those noises. The quote is not allegorical (B); the descriptive phrasing does not represent some abstract idea. Choice C might seem inviting to someone who has read the entire text, knowing that Tom and Maggie will eventually be caught in a flood; however, the quotation in this question, by itself, is not an example of foreshadowing. Apostrophe, choice E, is the device of addressing someone or something that is not present; it cannot be the correct response because the text is simply describing the location, not addressing anything or anyone.

16. **E.** The last sentence of the first paragraph clarifies that the river Floss is associated with crossing over from life to death, choice E, because when Maggie "read about Christiana passing 'the river over which there is no bridge,' [she] always saw the Floss between the green pastures." Choice A has no basis in the passage; while one might hazard a guess that the Floss is a symbol of the future, the text does not portray it as "an impenetrable barrier," and we do not know whether or not Tom and Maggie share a future together. Choice B is a bit silly; the river is not a literal border and it does not prevent the children from doing anything. Choice C may sound inviting, because rivers can easily be presented as an abstract symbol for the passage of time; however, the Floss is not associated with this idea in the passage. Choice D is incorrect because it assumes the Eagre scares the children. It is true that the Eagre is associated with the Floss, but it is not related to fear in Tom and Maggie.

17. **C.** The second paragraph begins with the simple phrase "Life did change for Tom and Maggie . . . ," which directly contradicts the statement that they had "no thought that life would ever change much for them," choice C. It does not contradict that they had happy mornings (A) or that they played together (B). Choice D, referring to the Eagre, is irrelevant to the idea that their lives will change. Choice E is also irrelevant; Tom's notion that others who don't live in this perfect place are disadvantaged has nothing to do with the changes the future holds for them.

18. **A.** After the opening of the second paragraph, the author steps out of the narrative to contemplate universal truths about childhood experiences, articulating that those who grow up engaging with nature come to count on it for comfort. Those who do so tend to appreciate and look forward to "the same flowers . . . the same hips and haws on the autumn hedgerows, the same redbreasts . . . " Eliot uses these plural pronouns to generalize the statements to encompass all those who relate to the natural world in this way, choice A. Choice B makes no sense within context; Tom and Maggie do have a close relationship in the passage, but the plural pronouns do nothing to prove it. Choice C is in the right direction, but it is too limited; the plural pronouns are not restricted to only those who live in the area. Choice D is unreasonable; the narrator's comments are not individualized, and these pronouns have nothing to do with that concept. Choice E also makes no sense; the pronouns do not merely acknowledge the natural world; rather, they refer to those individuals who find lasting beauty in it.

19. **D.** After the narrator muses about tropical palms and strange ferns, apparently in some exotic foreign locale, the focus comes back to the thrill of "this home-scene." It allows the narrator to return to the love of the fields of childhood, choice D. Choice A is initially tempting; the tropics do juxtapose with the English countryside, but the setting in which the narrator walks is certainly not painted as dreary. Be sure to read all of the words in an answer choice and consider their accuracy. The narrator does not reminisce fondly about the tropical foliage (B), but, rather, merely contrasts the tropics with the current setting. Choice C is completely unreasonable; the passage offers no hint whatsoever that the narrator has experienced mature love, let alone the loss of a lover long ago. Choice E is another head-scratcher; the remembrance of a tropical scene does not foreshadow anything, let alone an "inexorable decline."

20. **B.** Each phrase in the question is located in a separate paragraph of the passage, and yet all point to the same effect: the universal desire for permanence and stability in our world, choice B. In choice A, the word "entropy" is the key word that makes this answer choice incorrect; entropy refers to the inexorable process of increasing disorder, breaking down into randomness, which contradicts the intent of the passage. Choice C is too weak, too bland; the phrases in this question do indeed refer to a rural setting, but their intended effect is not simply to emphasize it. The word "aphorism" in choice D is inaccurate; the phrases are not pithy statements of a larger truth. The phrases are not hyperbolic (E); they are not overstating anything obvious.

21. **C.** The sentence in question is a long and complex one; let's paraphrase its many ideas first. It begins by listing the sundry elements of nature such as flowers, birdsong, sky, and fields, and claims these create "the mother tongue of our imagination." In turn, the language of that tongue is "laden with all the subtle inextricable associations the fleeting hours of our childhood left behind them." In other words, the language is overloaded with the understated and complex memories that were left behind by our fleeting childhood. Choice C articulates this precept well. Choice A starts well, but it falls apart at the end of the sentence; the idea that connections between nature and childhood are lost with age contradicts the ideas in the passage. Choice B is very enticing, but it does not pinpoint the purpose of the passage's sentence as well as does choice C; also, it is based on the assumption that the "best" way to learn life-long lessons comes from growing up in nature. Make sure any absolutes that are stated in answer choices are accurate; this one is not. Choice D misreads the passage somewhat; nature is not presented as "capricious"; rather, that term is used to refer to the hedgerows, which are the rows of shrubs that line farmers' fields. Choice E is completely off base for this passage; the children do seek adventure, but their relationship with nature is not scary.

22. **B.** The passage's tone is nostalgic and appreciative, choice B, as the narrator looks back at childhood fondly, grateful for having had a natural upbringing. Each incorrect answer choice includes at least one wrong word. In choice A, "exuberant" is too strong; in choice C, "instructive" goes too far; "effervescent" in choice D is inaccurate. "Childish" and "benevolent" are off base in choice E; the passage is about childhood, but that does not mean its overall tone is childish.

Second Poem

The poem for questions 23–33 comes from "The Death of a Favourite Cat, Drowned in a Tub of Goldfishes," written in 1774 by Thomas Gray. It is based on a true story of a good friend's unfortunate feline.

23. **E.** This poem parodies the tone and language employed in most odes, which are serious and use elevated and lofty language. Gray makes good use of such exaggerated language to describe the sad but humorous story of a lowly housecat, who accidently drowns while trying to catch goldfish in a fishbowl. Notice that the word "whisker" in line 20, choice E, is not an example of exaggerated language; it literally refers to Selima's whisker that the fish first sees. The other answer choices do provide examples of embellished descriptions. Calling a vase "lofty" (A) certainly exaggerates its appearance. The "lake" (B) is an exaggerated way of referring to the water in the fishbowl. The "genii of the stream" is a fanciful term for simple goldfish (C). The "scaly armour" (D) is an extravagant way of describing the appearance of the fish.

24. **C.** The poem's question, "What cat's averse to fish?" is the rhetorical equivalent of asking, "What cat doesn't like to feast on fish?" The obvious answer? None! This quotation exemplifies Selima's innate greed; her feline instincts cannot resist the temptation of the goldfish in the bowl. Therefore, choice C is correct. None of the other answer choices focus on her greed; the correct answer cannot describe positive attributes, such as demure (A) or pensive (B). Choices D ("nor knew the gulf") and E ("has no friend") are off topic; they do not address the idea of "greed" in this question.

25. **B.** Selima gazes into the water and sees her reflection; she "purred applause" and joyfully wagged her tail at the sight of her own face; she admired her whiskers, her fur coat, her ears, and her eyes. Basically, she admires everything about her own reflection, choice B. Choice A is the right direction, but "the beauty of her coat" is only one aspect of her vanity. There is no support in the poem for the ideas in the other answer choices; the poem does not mention "being in charge of her life" (C), nor does it describe Selima as either inquisitive (D) or easily distracted (E).

26. **A.** The first two stanzas describe details of Selima's vanity. Stanzas three and four introduce the fish that she sees as they glide by in the water; they provide the temptation that will cause her ultimate demise, choice A. Stanzas five and six describe her attempt to catch the fish and her disastrous fall into the bowl. Stanza seven leaves the narration and clarifies the moral of the story. The other answer choices do not properly describe the third stanza. It does not mention Selima's beauty (B); that was in stanzas one and two. It does not "continue the description of the goldfish" (C); rather, it begins the description. It certainly does not "disrupt the flow of the action" (D); it introduces the cat's antagonists. The third stanza does not contrast the animals' descriptions (E); rather, the cat had been described as beautiful and so are the fish.

27. **D.** Had Selima not been gazing so approvingly at her own reflection in the water, she might not have noticed the goldfish at all, then she would not have "stretched in vain to reach the prize" (line 22) and fallen into the fishbowl. The poet's message is specific: Unbridled vanity can have unforeseen, dire consequences, choice D. The intended meaning is not simply to avoid all temptation (A); that is too vague. There is no intimation that Selima's death was due to her owner's negligence (B). The statement in choice C, that "curiosity can kill a cat," is far too facile; it merely restates the old wives' tale, and Selima did not die from curiosity. The idea in choice E, similarities between owners and their pets, comes from out of the blue; the poem never mentions anything of the kind.

28. **B.** Gray uses many sentence inversions in this poem to good effect. An excellent example is this sentence, which, if it were composed in the normal subject-verb construction, would read "The slippery verge beguiled her feet." The verge, choice B, is the slippery edge of the fishbowl, which beguiled, or deceived, the cat's feet, and thus, she fell. Grammatically, no other answer choices serve as the subject of the verb in question.

29. **D.** A metaphorical conceit compares two things that are vastly different; to follow the comparison engages intellectual imagination. It frequently dominates a large portion of the work. This poem has no such device, making choice D correct. Choice A, allusion, can be seen in such references as "genii" (the plural of "genie," the supernatural creatures of Middle Eastern folklore); "Tyrian hue" (a very expensive and long-lasting purple dye); and "Nereid" (a minor sea nymph of Greek mythology). The poet uses personification (B) in the phrase "Malignant Fate." The poem has several examples of sentence inversions (C), such as in line 7, "Her conscious tail her joy declared." Alliteration (E) can be found in the phrase "heedless hearts" (line 41).

30. **B.** In the last stanza, the poet steps out of the narrative and proceeds to convey the larger moral of the story. The line in this stanza that moralizes the most is its second line, "Know, one false step is ne'er retrieved," choice B. This directly warns against making one small error in life that might come back to haunt you, or, as in Selima's case, prove deadly. That you can never take back an action, that you must live with the consequences, is the strongest moral statement in the final stanza. The remaining answer choices do not moralize, which means to preach or sermonize. Choice E, "Nor all that glisters, gold," may seem like a possible answer, but it articulates a truth, not a moral. Incidentally, in this last line, Thomas Gray modified the Shakespearean quotation from *The Merchant of Venice* that originally stated, "All that glisters is not gold."

31. **E.** It was Selima's pride and vanity, emboldening her haughty spirit, which caused her destruction and fall, a literal fall into the fishbowl; therefore, choice E is correct. The other answer choices are not supported in the poem. The poem does not dwell on Selima's thoughts (A), nor does it mention her desiring to "be first in everything" (B). There is no mention of mistrusting first impulses (C), nor of letting "moderation be your guide" (D).

32. **E.** A mock heroic poem satirizes and parodies the typical elements of an epic poem or myth. Typically, epics employ a lofty and exaggerated tone; their descriptions are larger than life; their actions are beyond the realm of normal human beings. In this poem, the line "And be with caution bold," choice E, does not display such exaggeration; rather, it is straightforward articulation of a cautionary note. The other answer choices all evince a mock heroic tone. Choice A asserts that Selima's tail is actually conscious, or self-aware. Choice B is likewise over the top; the goldfish do have scales, but they are not "armour," nor are goldfish actually purple ("Tyrian hue"). Choice C personifies a goldfish as a "hapless nymph" and asserts that a fish is capable of experiencing "wonder." Choice D refers to yet another exaggerated description from the poem; Selima does not merely try to jump out of a fishbowl and fail; rather, she strains heroically, jumping not just once, but "eight times emerging," and she is not just trapped in a humble fishbowl, but rather "emerging from the flood" itself. The poem becomes an epic tale of a dire situation, leading to the tragic end of a most heroic cat, thus deserving of this (mock) heroic poem in eulogy.

33. **A.** Selima is identified as the "Favourite Cat" in the title, and again in line 36. However, when the poor feline falls into the tub of goldfish, no one comes to her aid. She cries out, but no mythical creature, "no Nereid," and no "cruel Tom nor Susan" come to help, leaving us with the point that "A Favourite has no friend!" Therefore, choice A is correct. Choice B is too strong and absolute; in this poem Fate is indeed malignant, but that does not mean Fate is always so. Choice C begins with a somewhat relevant phrase about unattended

household pets, but falls apart by claiming they create chaos. Had someone been in the room at the time, it is unlikely she would have met her wet doom, but her demise does not exactly create chaos in the home, and the answer choice broadly applies to all household pets, not just cats. The idea that one cannot swim against a flood (D) makes sense in the real world, but in the poem the flood is used hyperbolically, and Selima is not "swimming against" it; she's trying to climb out of the tub. Choice E, that one will not stumble and fall if appropriately cautious, may in fact be sage advice, but it is not suggested in this poem.

Second Prose Passage

The passage for questions 34–45 comes from the novel The Shipping News, *written by American author Annie Proulx in 1993. Quoyle, the protagonist, has moved with his two daughters and his aunt to Newfoundland, his ancestral home. Prior to this passage, he has gotten a job as a reporter for the* Gammy Bird, *the local newspaper, and part of his beat is getting news on the shipping industry at the harbor.*

34. D. This phrase is notable for what it doesn't say. The harbormaster watched Quoyle's "yellow slicker emerge from the station wagon," but it never mentions if he was cognizant of a person inside that yellow slicker. This conjures up the image of an empty, ghostlike apparition, a yellow slicker that emerges into the rain on its own accord, choice D. The ideas in choices A and B have no support in the passage; there is no reference to school children, either in the rain or not (A), and this quote has no relationship to Quoyle's work ethic (B). Choice C misstates the facts. The yellow slicker *is* appropriate outerwear in the rain; it does not contrast with the weather. Choice E misreads the question and simply restates the obvious; the yellow slicker is, indeed, Quoyle's protective clothing, but this question asks about the image it *suggests*, not the literal meaning.

35. C. The harbormaster looks favorably on Quoyle's physical strength, choice C. Notice that immediately after he remarks on his first impression of Quoyle ("strong and clumsy"), the harbormaster launches into an extended reminiscence of being renowned for his own great strength in his youth. The connotations of these memories are fond and nostalgic, thus revealing that the harbormaster still values physical strength. However, the passage does NOT give any indication of a favorable reaction by the harbormaster to the ideas in the other answer choices; there is no mention of his reaction to Quoyle's gathering information (A), nor of his reaction to Quoyle's carrying a notebook (B). Likewise, there is no mention of his reaction to the station wagon (D), or that Quoyle has an eye for detail (E).

36. D. The statement "His thoughts often stopped at that point" directly follows a poignant phrase, a sad admission that he is "now the only living member of the Finger Club"; all his old friends are long gone, as is his own youth and vigor. He laments these losses so deeply that he must stop his train of thought at that point, choice D. Choice A is true to the passage in that the harbormaster does fondly remember his friends from the past; however, that fact does not answer this particular question. It is not his fond memories that stop his thoughts, but the realization of his many losses. Choice B contradicts the text; he has fond memories of the past, so he does not dislike being reminded of it. Choice C is irrelevant; his ability to conjure up pleasant memories is not related to "his thoughts often stopped at that point." Choice E is tempting; one can infer that the harbormaster does stop his train of thought to avoid becoming overly emotional, but the strong word "maudlin" makes this answer choice incorrect; he is not weepy or mushy.

37. B. "Coarse" is indeed an apt description of the harbormaster, as he is portrayed as quite a rough-looking and well-worn character. The author makes good use of phrases emphasizing that his "skin was like asphalt, fissured and cracked," and yet "Stubble worked through the craquelured surface," and also his "Jacket split at the shoulder seams." In addition, the second part of choice B, "taciturn," accurately describes the harbormaster; he is a man of few words and speaks only when he wants to. Therefore, choice B is correct. The other answer choices all have at least one incorrect word. Choice A asserts that he is discreet, but the passage never hints that he can keep secrets of a delicate nature. Choice C claims that the harbormaster is scurrilous, but he is not described as insulting or offensive. Likewise, he is neither docile (easily managed) as in choice D, nor is he phlegmatic (apathetic) or munificent (overly generous), as in choice E.

38. E. The author's frequent use of sentence fragments serves to break down the images and actions into distinctive individual fragments, almost breaking them into their essential elements, so that every single image makes a stark impression on the reader, choice E. This technique enhances the emotional impact of the words and images; it leverages and increases their intended effect on the reader. This is the opposite of the idea in choice A, that it somehow distracts the reader from the flow of the narration. Also, the author would never intend to have the effect in choice B, to leave thoughts hanging in air, nor the effect in choice C, befuddling the setting. While there is a rising dramatic tension between the characters, as stated in choice D, that is not the purpose of the short sentence fragments.

39. C. A reader's initial reaction to the painting being described as "the size of a bed sheet" might be mild surprise (i.e., a very large painting in a small office), but the deeper meaning, the intended ironic effect, soon becomes apparent. Immediately following this benign reference to a cozy bedsheet, the next two sentences detail the horrifying subject of the painting: the imminent death of hundreds of British sailors due to the accidental collision of their two ships. Therefore, choice C is correct. Choice A merely restates the obvious fact, a large painting is on a small wall; this is not ironic. Choice B is too trite to equate to irony; it is far too simplistic to conclude that those doomed sailors wish they were home in bed. The idea in choice D, that the harbormaster likes larger-than-life things, might be true, but that does not identify the irony here. Choice E may or may not be true, but the affordability of the painting is irrelevant to a question about intended irony in this passage.

40. C. It is jarring to hear the harbormaster proclaim it to be a "fine picture," because the reader has already been tipped off that it depicts a maritime disaster. It is difficult to understand why he likes it so much; even though the painting is large and imposing and depicts ships at sea, all of which he might appreciate, this is juxtaposed with the horrific subject matter, choice C. The other answer choices do not address this jarring juxtaposition. The answer is not related to his knowledge of quality art (D), or to his lack of knowledge (A). There is no description of the painting as "old and decrepit" (B). The idea in answer choice E, the portrayal of seafaring men, is probably the reason the harbormaster likes the painting; it does not juxtapose that thought.

41. D. This question focuses on the basic flow of the action in the passage. Between lines 80 and 81, Quoyle must have been doing a lot of writing, because his hand had cramped up, and thus, choice D is correct. The other answer choices either identify actions that happen outside of the specific time period in the question (A and B), or actions that do not happen at all (C and E).

42. E. The point of view in the passage is objective, not omniscient, choice E. We witness action; we hear dialogue; we see the setting. However, we do not get to understand the characters' inner thoughts. The passage does have similes (A), such as "the sunset like a flock of birds" and "Diddy Shovel's skin was like asphalt." Personification (B) is evident in the phrase "the sullen bay rubbed with thumbs of fog." "A marine stink of oil, fish and dirty water" provides olfactory imagery (C). The first paragraph has ample industrial imagery (D), describing lift trucks, winches, the ferry taking on cars, and the government Search and Rescue cutter.

43. B. The author's intended irony is that Quoyle's job is to get the *news,* but instead, he copies irrelevant, weeks-old listings, choice B. The idea that he could have easily printed them from the computer instead (A) is not ironic; the harbormaster intentionally did not tell Quoyle about the computer to teach him a lesson. This idea is mimicked in choice C; he could have gotten them from another source (i.e., the computer), but that is not ironic. The other answer choices are irrelevant to this question; it does not matter if his work might get smudged in the rain (D) or if he knows that the newspaper won't run the information in any case (E).

44. A. Almost every line of dialogue spoken by Quoyle is understated, restrained, low-key, choice A. Quoyle states, "Come to get the shipping news. I'd appreciate suggestions," but then he adds, "About the shipping news. Or anything else," not elaborating on his inquiry, but intimating that there is a deeper, hidden subtext. On the contrary, Quoyle's dialogue is definitely not hyperbolic or exaggerated (B), nor is it beseeching (C), which describes an urgent appeal. His speech does not sound acerbic, harsh or severe in expression (D), nor is he patronizing or offensively condescending (E).

45. B. This question requires an understanding of the lessons Quoyle should have learned from his interaction with the harbormaster, so you can then decide what lesson he did *not* learn. The incorrect responses *are* valid lessons; the correct response *is not* a valid lesson. The idea in choice A makes sense; Quoyle should learn that he cannot trust the computer data because the harbormaster warns him specifically that the computer is useless when the power is out. Choice D is logical for the same reason; the fastest route for Quoyle would be to get the computer printout, but that would not be available in a storm. Choice C is another little life lesson for Quoyle; the harbormaster could have told him about the computer list first instead of making Quoyle handwrite the information, but in doing so he forced the reporter to learn for himself. Choice E is another little lesson Quoyle should learn; he needs to seek information from several sources, such as the ledgers, the computer, and the harbormaster himself. The exception is the lesson in choice B, the idea that honesty is the best policy. This issue never comes up in the passage; Quoyle is entirely honest when says to the harbormaster "I'd appreciate suggestions. About the shipping news. Or anything else." And when the harbormaster finally provides the current data to Quoyle, that information is entirely accurate also.

Third Poem

The poem presented for questions 46–55 is "And If I Did, What Then?" written by George Gascoigne in 1573.

46. C. The mistress shows her confrontational attitude immediately; indeed, the poet only gives her four lines of dialogue, but that is enough to expose her character. Openly demanding and dismissive, choice C, she sneeringly asks the rhetorical equivalent of "So what?" Her in-your-face posture is the opposite of the idea in choice A, pensive and demure. Choice B is partially correct; the mistress is aggressive, but she is certainly not the aggrieved party. Choice D is self-contradictory; one cannot be both diffident, meaning insecure, and confident at the same time. Choice E is also contradictory; this brazen mistress may be described as sincere, meaning honest and candid, but she is far from contemplative.

47. A. The mistress intentionally sows doubt, choice A, about her veracity by inserting the word "if" (line 1). She hints at her guilt, but she is not actually admitting anything; rather, she is testing the waters to see how her lover will react. Conversely, her initial question does not indicate that she is taken by surprise (B), nor is there any hint that she "will amend her ways" (C). Choices D and E both contradict the mistress' personality. Her aggressive "So what?" question does not indicate that she questions her past actions (D), nor is it a signal of her intention to succumb to her lover (E).

48. E. When the mistress exclaims "The sea hath fish for every man, / And what would you have more?" she is all but admitting that she cannot be faithful to just one man. However, she does not say this out of a sense of guilt; rather, she implies that her lover is being greedy by wanting to have her all to himself, choice E. The other answer choices all reflect a serious misreading of the poem. This line of dialogue is not literally referring to fishing, as in choices A and C. She is, indeed, implying that her lover is greedy in wanting her fidelity, but this is not a lust for material goods, as in choice B. Choice D is confoundingly vague and off topic; the poem contains no mention of what men really want in life.

49. D. The second stanza provides a description of the lover's first reaction to his mistress' surprising and unnerving statement. He feels befuddled as he laments "Amaze my mind with doubt," and also somewhat bitter as he claims "To beat my brains about." Therefore, choice D is correct. Choice E is only partially correct; in the second stanza, the lover is flummoxed (bewildered), but he is not yet vindictive. On the other hand, his reaction in this second stanza is the opposite of the idea in choice B; he is neither amused nor charmed. The descriptions in the other answer choices reflect some of the lover's reactions in the later stanzas; as the poem progresses, he does become more accusatory and perhaps spiteful (A), and he might also be getting more angry and malicious (C), but these do not describe his reaction in the second stanza.

50. C. The speaker's point in the third stanza is a rebuttal to his mistress' startling assertion that he should not be aggrieved if she is unfaithful. He adopts her metaphor of "many fishes in the sea," but he throws it right back at her with the common-sense observation that "Each fisherman can wish" for exclusive access, wishing that " . . . every tide / were his alone to fish," meaning that it is not unreasonable to want fidelity in a relationship, choice C. Choice A, the idea that it is futile to expect faithfulness, is the opposite of the lover's actual point; he is arguing that all people desire fidelity, not that it is useless to expect it. The idea in choice B may or may not be true, but the differing standards for men is certainly not the first point in the third stanza. Choices D and E both reflect a serious misunderstanding of this poem; the fish are not literal, they are a metaphor.

51. E. This poem displays a marked difference in the tone of the two speakers' comments. The mistress opens with two in-your-face, direct questions and then follows with her own answer, the equivalent of "So what?" On the other hand, her lover is at first speechless, but when he replies, he becomes philosophical, "And with such luck and loss / I will content myself." Therefore, choice E is correct. Each of the other answer choices has at least one incorrect word. The mistress may indeed be biting (A), but her lover is not logical; rather, he is philosophical. The mistress may be mocking him (B), but the lover is not pleading with her. It is unclear if the mistress is acting out of spite (C), but her lover is certainly not forgiving. The mistress may, perhaps, be unconcerned about her unfaithfulness (D), but her lover is not overwhelmed; he gathers his thoughts and comes up with a zinger of a comeback to his mistress' smug questions and self-serving answers.

52. A. This poem is intentionally composed of very short words with the intended effect of giving it a rhythmic, staccato beat, choice A; this helps to propel the action, seemingly hurtling the reader toward the conclusion. (You can read the poem out loud and listen for the distinctive beat.) This technique is certainly not intended to distract from the content (B), nor is it used to streamline the meaning of the poem (whatever that means), as in choice C. The exclusive use of short words does not generate a tone of regret (D), nor does it rush the reader's judgment (E).

53. B. The metaphor of fish and fishing begins in the first stanza and continues in every stanza of dialogue; thus, it governs the entire poem, choice B. The fish represent the women that men woo; fishing represents the actions men take to lure and catch those women. All of the other answer choices use incorrect terminology. The poem is not a parody (A), which is a deliberately exaggerated imitation of a previous work that creates humorous effect. Choice C is incorrect because the poem is not an allegory, which is a work in which characters represent abstract ideas that are intended to present a moral story. The fish and fishing concepts are not a simple fable (D), which is a brief tale, frequently using animal characters, to convey a moral lesson. Choice E incorrectly uses the word "personification"; the fish are not given human characteristics.

54. D. The term "in medias res" literally means "in the middle of things" and refers to literary works that begin in the middle of the action. While it usually is employed in longer works, especially epic poetry, this short poem begins in the middle of a conversation and meets the basic definition of the term, choice D. Choice A is incorrect for two reasons: A syllogism is not a poetic convention in the first place, and the poem does not have a syllogism (an argument that draws a specific conclusion from general points), let alone an extended one. The remaining answer choices are indeed elements of poetry, but they are not poetic *conventions*. Literary conventions encompass the customary features of certain literary forms, such as the use of a chorus in Greek tragedy, the inclusion of an explicit moral in a fable, or the use of a particular rhyme scheme in a villanelle. Literary conventions are defining features of particular literary genres, such as novel, short story, ballad, sonnet, and play. The poem does have an *abab* rhyme scheme (B) and is written in iambic trimeter and tetrameter (C), and it does have a decent amount of imagery (E), but none of these are poetic conventions. Be sure to read the question very carefully to help eliminate wrong answer choices.

55. C. This correct answer is solidified by the action implied at the end of the poem: that the metaphorical fishermen's boats will eventually get caught in the outgoing tide ("Till tides of turning time may toss / Such fishers on the shelf") and then become stranded on a sandbar ("And when they stick on sands,"). At this point the marooned and humiliated fishermen, visible to all on shore ("That every man may see"), will become the object of the narrator's gloating as he will "laugh and clap my hands" at their folly, just as they apparently did to him, choice C. The narrator likely enjoys getting the last word (A), but the poem offers no evidence that he takes pride in it; that one single word makes the answer too strong. Choice B is off base; the last stanza does not address his mistress, nor the idea that the narrator seeks to accept her infidelity. Likewise, the last stanza does not address his wish to see her wronged (D). Choice E may look attractive, but it goes too far. The narrator does not plot revenge against those who laughed at him; that would require some form of action on his part, and he merely plans on passively waiting until those men suffer the same humiliation as he has; then he can enjoy a good laugh at their expense.

Section II: Free-Response Questions

Question 1: "The Trees Are Down" by Charlotte Mew

The following scoring guide explicitly explains how to earn up to 6 total points for a poetry analysis essay. Row A (thesis) can earn up to 1 point; Row B (evidence and commentary) can earn up to 4 points, and Row C (sophistication) can earn up to 1 point.

Row A: Thesis (0–1 point)	
Scoring Criteria	
0 points for any of the following:	**1 point for**
• Having no defendable thesis. • Only restating the prompt in the thesis. • Only summarizing the issue with no claim in the thesis. • Presenting a thesis that does not address the prompt.	• Addressing the prompt with a defendable thesis that presents an interpretation and may establish a line of reasoning.
Decision Rules and Scoring Notes	
Theses that do not earn this point	**Theses that do earn this point**
• Only restate the prompt. • Only offer an irrelevant generalized comment about the poem. • Simply describe the poem's features rather than making a defendable claim.	• Take a position on the prompt and provide a defendable interpretation of how the poet portrays the complex relationship between the speaker and the trees.
Additional Notes	
• The thesis may be one or more sentences anywhere in the essay. • A thesis that meets the criteria can be awarded the point whether or not the rest of the response successfully conveys that line of reasoning.	

Row B: Evidence AND Commentary (0–4 points)				
Scoring Criteria				
0 points for	**1 point for**	**2 points for**	**3 points for**	**4 points for**
• Simply repeating the thesis (if present). • **OR** restating provided information. • **OR** providing mostly irrelevant and/or incoherent examples.	• Summarizing the poem without reference to a thesis. • **OR** providing vague textual references. • **OR** providing textual references of questionable relevance. • **AND** providing little or no commentary.	• Making relevant textual references (direct quotes or paraphrases). • **AND** providing commentary but repeats, oversimplifies, or misinterprets the cited evidence or text.	• Making relevant textual references (direct quotes or paraphrases). • **AND** providing commentary that explains the logical relationship between textual examples and the thesis; however, commentary is uneven, limited, or incomplete.	• Making relevant textual references (direct quotes or paraphrases). • **AND** providing well-developed commentary that explicitly explains the relationship between the evidence and the thesis.

Decision Rules and Scoring Notes				
Typical responses that earn 0 points:	**Typical responses that earn 1 point:**	**Typical responses that earn 2 points:**	**Typical responses that earn 3 points:**	**Typical responses that earn 4 points:**
• Are unclear or fail to address the prompt. • May present mere opinion with no relevant textual references.	• Mention textual references, devices, or techniques with little or no analysis.	• Contain numerous inaccuracies or repetition in commentary. • Offer only simplistic explanations that do not strengthen the argument.	• Provide commentary that is not sufficiently developed or is too limited. • Assume or imply a connection to the thesis that is not consistently explicit.	• Provide commentary that uses significant details of the text to draw conclusions. • Integrate short excerpts throughout in order to support the thesis' interpretation.

Additional Notes

• Writing that suffers from grammatical and/or mechanical errors that interfere with communication cannot earn the fourth point in this row.

Row C: Sophistication (0–1 point)

Scoring Criteria	
0 points for	**1 point for**
• Not meeting the criteria for 1 point.	• Exhibiting sophistication of thought and/or advancing a complex literary argument.

Decision Rules and Scoring Notes	
Responses that do not earn this point:	**Responses that earn this point demonstrate one (or more) of the following:**
• Try to contextualize an interpretation, but make predominantly sweeping generalizations (*"Throughout all history . . ."* OR *"Everyone believes . . ."*). • Only hint at other possible interpretations (*"Some may think . . ."* OR *"Though the poem might be said to . . ."*). • Write one statement about a thematic interpretation of the poem without consistently maintaining that idea. • Oversimplify complexities in the poem. • Present complicated or complex sentences or language that is ineffective and detracts from the argument.	• Present a thesis that demands nuanced analysis of textual evidence and successfully prove it. • Illuminate the significance or relevance of an interpretation within a broader context. • Discuss alternative interpretations of a text. • Acknowledge and account for contradictions, ambiguities, and/or complexities within the text. • Provide relevant analogies to help better understand an interpretation. • Develop a prose style that is especially vivid, persuasive, resounding, or appropriate to the student's argument.

Additional Notes

• This point should be awarded only if the demonstration of sophistication or complex understanding is part of the argument, not merely a phrase or brief reference.

High-Scoring Essay

In the elegiac poem "The Trees Are Down," the speaker weaves a carefully-modulated tapestry, an homage to the trees that are coming down, as well as a revealing portrait of herself and her relationship to the trees. Mew provides a window into the speaker's wrenching, personal lamentation on the loss of the trees and she does it through exceptionally adroit use of figurative language, along with a plethora of intertwined poetic devices.

The melancholic tone is established immediately, "They are cutting down the great plane-trees," a very tidy introduction to a very chaotic scene. For the remainder of the opening stanza, the speaker is assailed by the horrific noise of the work; she does not need to look out her window to be reminded of "the grate of the saw, the swish of the branches as they fall, / The crash of the trunks," she knows that her beloved trees are being torn down and felled, one by one. She displays palpable disdain for the rough men doing the work, the ones with "loud common talk" and "loud common laughs" that rings in her ears, even louder than the sounds of the trees. In just the opening stanza, and without using any visual imagery whatsoever, the author has already painted a nuanced portrait of the trees, and the crew wrecking the trees, and her reaction to the trees destruction.

The second stanza opens promisingly with a recollection from a long-ago Spring, but the dreary tone returns immediately with the image of a dead rat. Once again, Mew signals the dismal tone through her choice of imagery. However, she manages to turn even the image of this "god-forsaken thing" into a life lesson for this speaker: in spring even a lowly rat deserves to be alive. This foreshadows the later revelation that the speaker feels that it is even more painful to lose her beloved trees in the springtime.

The third stanza is remarkable for its amazing change in the poetic form. The previous stanzas each had four lines, a form that will be repeated in the fourth stanza. However, the third stanza has eight lines, and most of the lines are extremely short, compared to the other stanzas. It seems reasonable to infer that Mew intended these lines to appear to be isolated, perhaps the form is meant to evoke the appearance of being trimmed down like the trees, winnowed down to the last limb, until all that remains is "just one bough . . . in the fine grey rain . . . lonely against the sky." This shift in form allows the reader to empathize with the dying trees, to feel some part of what the speaker is feeling.

The fourth stanza returns to the previous quatrain form, but the sad narrative continues. The speaker knows that a dead rat once "unmade" a day in her beloved Spring, and she carries that memory still; now she fears that with the terrible loss of the trees, "Half the Spring, for me, will have gone with them." The imagery is stark, the tone is plaintive; the reader is tempted to wail along with the speaker.

In the closing stanza, the speaker further laments the loss of her friends, "my heart has been struck with the hearts of the planes." The speaker has good reason to be grief-stricken; the trees have been there for "half my life . . . in the sun, in the rains . . . in the great gales that came over to them. . . ." And yet, after all that, it was man's greed that brought them down as "There was only a quiet rain when they were dying;" she regrets that they did not die a natural death.

In this poem, Mew displays her command of figurative language and form, which is so masterful, so powerful, that the reader wants to symbolically join in at the end, to enlist with the angel in crying out, "Hurt not the trees."

(666 words)

Analysis of High-Scoring Essay

This insightful essay begins with an introduction that is clearly on topic and hints at a perceptive understanding of the poem. The pleasing phrasing "the speaker weaves a carefully-modulated tapestry" addresses the prompt, but it does so without repeating it. The student accurately pinpoints the speaker's relationship to the trees as a "wrenching, personal lamentation on the loss of the trees." It earns a point in Row A for its defendable thesis that provides an interpretation of how the poet portrays the complex relationship between the speaker and the trees.

The first body paragraph explores the first stanza, paying particular attention to the poetic devices of tone and imagery. After clarifying the tone as melancholic and providing a quotation for support, the student describes it as a "tidy introduction to a very chaotic scene." While the word "tidy" can refer to neatness, it also refers to an uncluttered and systematic way of doing something, and it is in this sense that the word works well. Next, instead of using the typical bland phrasing, the student claims the speaker is "assailed by the horrific noise of the work" and supports that point with examples of the auditory imagery. The use of the negative word "assailed" helps establish the intensity of the speaker's emotion, and then further deepens the speaker's relationship to the trees by acknowledging that her trees are "beloved" and that she feels "palpable disdain" for the unsavory men who fell her treasured trees. The paragraph is not without errors, but they are minor, and it's easy to believe that the student would fix these simple boo-boos with a proofreading. Notice that the first sentence is a run-on, one that commonly appears when students quote complete sentences from a passage. The last sentence has a punctuation error, missing the necessary apostrophe in the possessive word "trees." A Reader will look past these minor mistakes, hoping they do not multiply in the remainder of the essay.

320

The next paragraph makes note of the initial promise of the speaker's old recollection of spring, but then the student establishes that the "dreary tone returns" and mentions the dead rat image. Most students will dwell on this sudden and disturbing visual image, but this student comprehends the speaker's purpose, and instead of dropping it with an "eww!" type of observation, connects the rat's untimely death to the speaker's later emotions over the loss of the trees. The idea that nothing deserves to die in spring is true to the poem.

The following body paragraph analyzes the next stanza and it includes some very astute observations about form in the poem. Many students will not know what to say about the poem's irregular form, but this student notices how the truncated lines perhaps resemble the "appearance of being trimmed down like the trees, winnowed down to the last limb." The student's phrasing and insight are both very pleasing.

The paragraph devoted to the fourth stanza notes that the speaker's connection between the dead rat and the trees is the way they both can "unmake" the spring. The difference is that the rat disturbed just one spring day in the speaker's past; the loss of the trees will unmake much more. The student's claim that the imagery is "stark" would be stronger with textual examples, but the accurate assertion of plaintive tone and the reader's corresponding empathy are powerful, compelling statements.

The final body paragraph explores the speaker's grief over losing the trees that have stood "half my life." Furthermore, the student points to man's greed as being the real culprit that has destroyed the trees; while this point could be better developed, it is significant; the Reader senses the student is simply running short of time.

The brief conclusion, only one sentence, seems at first to merely summarize, and yet it rises above with the phrase "so masterful, so powerful" while explaining that the reader wants to join the angel and cry out "Hurt not the trees." This poignant ending serves to reinforce the poem's theme. The strong use of evidence and commentary to support the thesis's interpretation deserves 4 points in Row B.

Overall, this essay deserves its high score. Its interpretation of the poem is valid, and its points are made with precision and panache. Clearly on topic, effectively organized, and well developed, the essay will be a pleasure for any Reader to score. The use of a prose style that is especially vivid and appropriate to the student's argument earns a point in Row C. The essay deserves an overall score of 6.

Medium-Low-Scoring Essay

Charlotte Mew's poem *The Trees Are Down* presents a sad, sorrowful situation: a stand of trees that the narrator loves is being cut down. The speaker's close relationship with the trees is evoked mainly through the use of poetic devices.

The poem opens with direct, naturalistic language describing the irritating noise emanating from the work; the sounds rise and then fall, "the grate of the saw, the swish of the branches as they fall / The crash of the trunks, the rustle of trodden leaves." The speaker also remarks disparagingly on "the loud common talk . . . above it all," which helps to establish the negative tone. Notice that the imagery in the first stanza is all sound imagery; there is no visual imagery yet.

The second stanza continues with the negativity by providing the speaker's memory of the image of "a large dead rat in the mud" The imagery has switched from sound to visual, but the tone is still very dark.

Next, the poem tries to combine the imagery from the first two stanzas by providing a visual description of the last falling tree and comparing that to the old memory of the image of a dead rat. This is where the speaker begins to use figurative language about death cancelling out the spring, such as "If an old dead rat / Did once, for a moment, unmake the Spring." This helps to establish the speaker's close relationship with the trees, as the reader begins to understand that she is mourning the trees as if they were lost friends.

The rest of the poem continues this theme, as the speaker praises the trees and disparages the men who chopped them down. She returns again and again to the idea that "Spring is unmade today." The speaker uses a lot of poetic devices towards the end, "my heart has been struck with the hearts of the planes," which further enhances the closeness of her relationship with the trees. The poem closes with more poetic language, a line that mirrors the opening of the poem, "an angel crying / Hurt not the trees."

(354 words)

Analysis of Medium-Low-Scoring Essay

This essay has some points in its favor; the writer seems to understand the poem and the relationship between the trees and the speaker, and presents ideas with plausible analysis.

The overly brief introduction is not terribly enticing to the Reader. It does pinpoint that the dramatic cutting of the trees in the poem is "a sad, sorrowful situation" in the first sentence, which is enough to earn a point in Row A. However, rather than offering insights, it leaves us with a simplistic restatement of the prompt in the second sentence. A Reader will likely frown at the student's attempt to handwrite in italics for two reasons: It looks silly and it is grammatically incorrect. Always use quotation marks to punctuate poem titles (unless the work is of epic length).

The first body paragraph explores the opening stanza's auditory imagery and claims that the poem uses "direct, naturalistic language" of the "irritating noise" as the trees are cut. The student's awareness that the sounds rise and fall is encouraging, but it would be more impressive if he or she developed the idea in more depth instead of simply copying a quotation and leaving it at that. The student is also accurate in noticing that the speaker's remarks are "disparaging" and provides a quotation to back up "the negative tone." Some may quibble with the student's idea that the entire stanza has only "sound imagery" and no "visual imagery," but, in all fairness, the auditory imagery does indeed dominate this stanza.

The next brief body paragraph that explores the second stanza suffers from a lack of development. It accurately notes continued negativity in the poem and adds the example of the dead rat, an example most students will comment on. However, instead of presenting insightful analysis of the speaker's point about the dead rat, the student merely tells us that the imagery has "switched from sound to visual" and that the "tone is still very dark" without any examples to prove the point or any analysis of its importance vis-à-vis the prompt. The student is trying hard, but seems to either have nothing to say or feels the constraints of time.

The following paragraph is more developed, but begins with the questionable assertion that the third stanza "tries to combine the imagery from the first two stanzas." Since the student's point about the first stanza was that it has only auditory imagery and the second switches to visual, the Reader is not sure if the student is trying to say that this new stanza provides both auditory and visual imagery. This initial confusion is cleared up as the student clarifies that the combined imagery deals with the last falling tree and the dead rat. Of course, it is not accurate to claim that "this is where the speaker begins to use figurative language," since the entire poem uses figurative language. However, the student does acknowledge that death cancels out spring, but does not demonstrate a strong understanding of the speaker's point about the rat and the trees. More than just the idea of death cancelling spring, the speaker laments that in the springtime month of May, all things, from lowly creatures to majestic trees, deserve to be alive. It enhances the speaker's point that the trees do not deserve to die, to be cut down, especially in spring.

The essay concludes with a brief discussion of "the rest of the poem," intimating that the student is running out of time. He or she simply points out that the speaker repeats the idea that "Spring is unmade." The student tells us that "the speaker uses a lot of poetic devices towards the end" but provides no examples of specific devices; instead, we are presented with a quotation and a bland comment and left to draw our own conclusions. Finally, the student asserts that the "poem closes with more poetic language" and that its end mirrors the opening biblical quotation. This is not a strong ending. It will earn 2 points in Row B; although the essay makes relevant textual references, the commentary is simplistic and does not strengthen the argument.

The essay's overall strengths lie in its plausible understanding of the poem and its adequate organization. But its weaknesses are apparent in its lack of development and weak wording. It does not qualify for a point in Row C. It should earn an overall score of 3.

Question 2: *Look Homeward, Angel* by Thomas Wolfe

The following scoring guide explicitly explains how to earn up to 6 total points for a prose analysis essay. Row A (thesis) can earn up to 1 point; Row B (evidence and commentary) can earn up to 4 points, and Row C (sophistication) can earn up to 1 point.

Row A: Thesis (0–1 point)	
Scoring Criteria	
0 points for any of the following:	**1 point for**
• Having no defendable thesis. • Only restating the prompt in the thesis. • Only summarizing the issue with no claim in the thesis. • Presenting a thesis that does not address the prompt.	• Addressing the prompt with a defendable thesis that presents an interpretation and may establish a line of reasoning.
Decision Rules and Scoring Notes	
Theses that do not earn this point	**Theses that do earn this point**
• Only restate the prompt. • Only offer an irrelevant generalized comment about the passage. • Simply describe the passage's features rather than making a defendable claim.	• Take a position on the prompt and provide a defendable interpretation of how Wolfe portrays the complex relationship between the characters.
Additional Notes	
• The thesis may be one or more sentences anywhere in the response. • A thesis that meets the criteria can be awarded the point whether or not the rest of the response successfully conveys that line of reasoning.	

Row B: Evidence AND Commentary (0–4 points)				
Scoring Criteria				
0 points for	**1 point for**	**2 points for**	**3 points for**	**4 points for**
• Simply repeating the thesis (if present). • **OR** restating provided information. • **OR** providing mostly irrelevant and/or incoherent examples.	• Summarizing the passage without reference to a thesis. • **OR** providing vague textual references. • **OR** providing textual references of questionable relevance. • **AND** providing little or no commentary.	• Making relevant textual references (direct quotes or paraphrases). • **AND** providing commentary but repeats, oversimplifies, or misinterprets the cited evidence or text.	• Making relevant textual references (direct quotes or paraphrases). • **AND** providing commentary that explains the logical relationship between textual examples and the thesis; however, commentary is uneven, limited, or incomplete.	• Making relevant textual references (direct quotes or paraphrases). • **AND** providing well-developed commentary that explicitly explains the relationship between the evidence and the thesis.

Decision Rules and Scoring Notes				
Typical responses that earn 0 points:	**Typical responses that earn 1 point:**	**Typical responses that earn 2 points:**	**Typical responses that earn 3 points:**	**Typical responses that earn 4 points:**
• Are unclear or fail to address the prompt. • May present mere opinion with no relevant textual references.	• Mention textual references, devices, or techniques with little or no analysis.	• Contain numerous inaccuracies or repetition in commentary. • Offer only simplistic explanations that do not strengthen the argument.	• Provide commentary that is not sufficiently developed, or is too limited. • Assume or imply a connection to the thesis that is not consistently explicit.	• Provide commentary that uses significant details of the text to draw conclusions. • Integrate short excerpts throughout in order to support the thesis' interpretation.

Additional Notes

• Writing that suffers from grammatical and/or mechanical errors that interfere with communication cannot earn the fourth point in this row.

Row C: Sophistication (0–1 point)

Scoring Criteria	
0 points for	**1 point for**
• Not meeting the criteria for 1 point.	• Exhibiting sophistication of thought and/or advancing a complex literary argument.

Decision Rules and Scoring Notes	
Responses that do not earn this point:	**Responses that earn this point demonstrate one (or more) of the following:**
• Try to contextualize an interpretation, but make predominantly sweeping generalizations (*"Throughout all history . . . "* OR *"Everyone believes . . . "*). • Only hint at other possible interpretations (*"Some may think . . . "* OR *"Though the passage might be said to . . . "*). • Write one statement about a thematic interpretation of the passage without consistently maintaining that idea. • Oversimplify complexities in the passage. • Present complicated or complex sentences or language that is ineffective and detracts from the argument.	• Present a thesis that demands nuanced analysis of textual evidence and successfully prove it. • Illuminate the significance or relevance of an interpretation within a broader context. • Discuss alternative interpretations of a text. • Acknowledge and account for contradictions, ambiguities, and/or complexities within the text. • Provide relevant analogies to help better understand an interpretation. • Develop a prose style that is especially vivid, persuasive, resounding, or appropriate to the student's argument.

Additional Notes

• This point should be awarded only if the demonstration of sophistication or complex understanding is part of the argument, not merely a phrase or brief reference.

High-Scoring Essay

In this excerpt from <u>Look Homeward Angel,</u> Thomas Wolfe introduces the reader to his two main characters, Oliver Gant, a businessman, and Eliza Pentland, a young woman of unknown provenance who turns out to be a book seller. The action and dialogue in the entire excerpt is devoted to establishing the nuances in the complex relationship that develops between these two characters; by the end, some facets of the relationship are revealed, and yet some remain concealed.

As the scene opens, these two meet for the first time, and their initial interaction is a bit awkward. Oliver is at rest, lying on the couch in his office, when he hears a woman's footfalls approaching. He does not wish to appear to be a slacker, and he wants to keep up appearances, so he hops up to dress. Unfortunately, Eliza bursts in just as Oliver is donning his jacket; she immediately ascertains that Oliver has, indeed, been lying on the couch and she makes a snarky comment, intimating that he has "nothing to do but lie around all day on a good easy sofa." This example of her quick mind and sharp tongue immediately helps to establish Eliza's perceptive character.

Also, some seemingly-minor details of Oliver's office help to lay the foundation for his personality. Oliver is the type of man who would have a nice "smooth leather sofa," even though he can afford only a "little office." He is a man of contradictions, who enjoys a "restoring peace," yet who negates it as "brooding over his great extended body." He is a man who can hear "bright piping noises in the Square," and yet he is not bothered by the noise; rather he contemplates comforting images of nature, of "the loamy black earth" and the "sudden young light of flowers" and "the beaded chill of beer." It appears that Oliver is not your typical business-oriented office worker. However, Oliver is apparently eager to keep up appearances, to maintain a public impression of prosperity and decorum. To this end, Oliver responds to Eliza's snarky opening line by putting on a show of propriety, exhibiting "a flourishing bow" and making the apparently false claim that "'I very rarely lie down in the daytime.'" These details indicate that, even though Oliver may not appear to be a huge success in the business world, he is keenly interested in how he is viewed, or at least, it seems, how he is viewed by Eliza.

Eliza on the other hand, appears to be quite unconcerned about presenting a glorified image of herself. This is established by her immediate and very long-winded commentary on her own past health problems; she does not hold back any details that might help her to maintain a demure, ladylike image in Oliver's eyes. She also provides details that help to establish her as a free-thinking and independent-minded young woman. Rather than deferring to the medical specialists of the day, she claims instead that "'Most of the time we think we're sick it's all in the mind,'" a very independent position in that era.

Eliza's character, and thus her relationship with Oliver, is further developed by the tone of her dialogue. Her lack of formal language skills, and her shirking of conventional norms, is repeatedly reinforced by her diction in phrases such as "'Pshaw! . . . There's nothing wrong with you . . .'" and "'I reckon I was convalescin',''' along with many others. The tone and detail presented in this dialogue establishes Eliza's social standing, her education (or lack thereof), and her outgoing personality. However, Oliver's personality is also defined by his reaction to her monologs, her off-topic interjections, and her breezy use of language. Rather than being put-off by Eliza's over-the-top personality, he seems perhaps to be smitten, responding "'You hit the nail on the head that time. A truer word was never spoken.'" Oliver's positive reaction to Eliza is heightened by Wolfe's point of view, as he reveals Oliver's thoughts. He sees Eliza as "a pippin," and looks at her "appreciatively," noting her physique and physical quirks. In the same paragraph, Wolfe switches to Eliza's mind, explaining the "interminable divagations" of her thought patterns. Oliver is intrigued by Eliza, but she seems only interested in her immediate purpose.

When Eliza finally states the purpose of her visit, both her vocal posture and her body language change abruptly. "'My name,'" she said portentously, with slow emphasis, "'is Eliza Pentland, and I represent the Larkin Publishing Company,'" A proclamation that she utters "proudly, with dignified gusto." This abrupt change in Eliza gives the author a chance to further develop Oliver's character, and thus, further explore his relationship to Eliza. Upon learning that Eliza is, in fact, a book seller, Oliver's immediate reaction is aghast, he thinks "Merciful God! A book-agent!"

However, the author finally tips his hand about the budding relationship between this oh-so-proper businessman and this over-the-top book seller. In spite of everything to the contrary, the excerpt ends with a telling detail, "He bought the books."

In this brief excerpt, the author successfully weaves together a quite nuanced portrait of these characters contrasting personalities, and even provides character development, through skillful use of tone, the characters' use of diction, and his selection of detail. The reader of the excerpt is left with a lingering curiosity, wondering where this relationship will lead and what lies in store for Oliver and Eliza in the chapters yet to come.

(910 words)

Analysis of High-Scoring Essay

This lengthy essay begins with a qualified promise. The two-sentence introduction addresses the prompt and characters acceptably, but leaves the reader with a somewhat vague thesis: that "some facets of the relationship are revealed, and yet some remain concealed." The initial phrase could be more specific; we'd love to know what kinds of "facets" are revealed, but the more one thinks about the student's wording, the more unclear the meaning becomes. However, the thesis does qualify for a point in Row A. The student's vague phrase about some facets of the relationship remaining concealed is finally explained at the end of the essay, when we discover the student wants to read on in the novel to see how Oliver and Eliza's relationship develops.

The first body paragraph explains the awkward nature of Oliver and Eliza's initial interaction. The paragraph is a bit heavy on plot synopsis, but also includes some analysis, such as mentioning that Oliver "does not wish to appear to be a slacker," and that Eliza, with her "snarky" comment, is perceptive enough to know that he had been resting on his office sofa. Although the student's diction is a bit informal, it is accurate and refreshing. The paragraph would be improved if the student were to address the prompt more; we see what happens in Oliver and Eliza's first meeting, but do not yet know *how* these details depict their relationship.

The next paragraph discusses Oliver's character and demonstrates good understanding of his contradictions. The student incorporates apt examples via direct quotations and textual references while analyzing them in a reasonable way. One wonders how this paragraph helps to analyze the relationship between Oliver and Eliza, but the Reader senses that the student is trying to develop character awareness before moving into analysis of their relationship. The second half of the paragraph, beginning with the transition "however," moves toward stronger analysis of the prompt and acknowledges that Oliver cares about Eliza's perception of him. The paragraph is well developed with strong attention to textual detail.

The following paragraph explores Eliza's character and contrasts her lack of pretention with Oliver's ostentatious show of faux dignity. The student includes accurate commentary about Eliza, noting how she is forceful, forward, and apparently does not desire to present a "demure, ladylike image in Oliver's eyes." The student presents Eliza's opinionated comment about illness being "all in the mind" to establish that she is "free-thinking and independent-minded." The paragraph would be improved if it provided more analysis of the prompt; the student accurately analyzes character, but he or she should spend more time exploring how the text depicts their relationship.

Fortunately, the subsequent paragraph is clearly on topic, presenting well-chosen examples that explore tone, diction, and detail as they develop Oliver and Eliza's relationship. Picking out Eliza's common language, replete with her grammatical errors, the student demonstrates that Eliza's diction and tone establish her low social standing but outgoing personality. The student notices how Oliver's reaction to Eliza's brusqueness actually hints that he is "perhaps . . . smitten," and backs this idea up with an exploration of Wolfe's point of view. This portion of the essay is very well done, clearly showing that the student understands how Wolfe is revealing the characters' relationship. The student even notices how Wolfe shifts the focus mid-paragraph from Oliver's mind to Eliza's and concludes that "Oliver is intrigued by Eliza" but she is only concerned with "her immediate purpose."

In the following paragraph we learn that that her purpose is selling books. The student astutely notices Eliza's change in posture and language as she becomes professional and how that shift helps further develop Oliver's character and his relationship with Eliza. The student presents Oliver's exclamation, "Merciful God! A book-agent!" as his being aghast, but other students might interpret this differently. The text does not confirm if he is pleased or not, and a Reader will give the student the benefit of the doubt.

The student's last body paragraph is brief, as is the end of the excerpt. Despite the student's claim that "the author finally tips his hand about the budding relationship" between the characters, he or she does not explicitly articulate what that tip of the hand means. Instead, we are left to infer they are growing closer with the closing quote from the text, "He bought the books."

The conclusion sums up the essay well and then adds the notion that readers must wonder where the relationship will lead and "what lies in store for Oliver and Eliza." Although some of the commentary is uneven, the overall explanation of the characters' complex relationship is significant enough to earn 4 points in Row B.

Overall, it's easy to praise this essay. It is very well developed, more so than most. The student's interpretation of the relationship between Oliver and Eliza is reasonable. Equally admirable is the way that the student effectively weaves textual examples with his or her analysis and utilizes sophisticated language. Such impressive word choices as "provenance," "nuances," and "propriety" elevate the student's diction. As commendable as the essay is, it could always be improved with attention to a few elements of composition. The organization sometimes lacks a clear focus on the prompt; the essay presents plenty of character analysis, but the essay would be better served if all paragraphs clearly explored how Wolfe depicts the relationship between the two characters. The essay has evidence of some sophisticated language and thought, but not enough throughout the essay to qualify for a point in Row C. While the ability to produce six healthy body paragraphs under timed pressure is admirable, one can only imagine what the student would do with a little more time to organize those paragraphs. It is possible some should be joined, and some edited to address the prompt more. These comments are a bit nit-picky, but only in the effort of helping students improve. In an actual AP reading, this student will be amply rewarded for what he or she does well, and this essay will, indeed, receive a high overall score of 5.

Low-Scoring Essay

You can tell that this passage is all about the relationship between the two characters because the opening line is "Then Oliver met Eliza." This proves that the passage is going to concentrate on their relationship, rather than something else.

The details that the author uses in the first paragraph establish that Oliver is somewhat lazy, sleeping on his couch at work, but he doesn't want to get caught at it, so he jumps up to put on his coat when he hears someone coming and it turns out to be Eliza and she wishes that she could have a nice easy office job too, so that she could "lie around all day on a good easy sofa." These details show that the two characters have a lot in common.

The dialogue that the author writes also tells a lot about the characters and their relationship. Oliver gets in only a couple of lines of dialogue in the third and fourth paragraphs, before Eliza cuts him off with her long soliloquy. This shows that the author wants us to see that Oliver is a milquetoast and that he is bowled over by the talkative Eliza. This dialogue tells us a lot about these characters and their relationship.

Finally, the tone of the passage also helps to show the character development. The tone starts out slow, with lazy Oliver sleeping on his couch, then the tone changes with Eliza's long soliloquy, then the tone changes again at the end, with Eliza's effective sales pitch and Oliver being forced into buying her books. This change in tone shows us a lot about their relationship.

(272 words)

Analysis of Low-Scoring Essay

This brief essay tries to address the prompt but does a less-than-adequate job of it. The student's first sentence has several strikes against it, including its improper pronoun as the first word. Beginning a sentence with "You can tell . . . " will never impress an AP Reader; the student continues this poor opening with the illogical idea that the passage's first sentence, in which Oliver and Eliza meet, guarantees that the passage "is all about the relationship." The student then repeats the same idea in the next sentence, beginning with another off-putting phrase that Readers never wish to encounter, "This proves that. . . ." This introduction basically says nothing and says it in weak language. Unfortunately, the essay does not have a defendable thesis that addresses the prompt. It will not earn a point in Row A.

The student next dives into a paragraph on "the details that the author uses." The first sentence, a long run-on, is packed with plot details and includes the questionable assertion that "Oliver is somewhat lazy." Instead of analyzing *how* such details depict the characters' relationship, the student merely dumps plot synopsis into one run-on sentence and then erroneously claims that "These details show that the two characters have a lot in common." The beginning of this sentence uses another phrase that is often derided by Readers; a writer should always try to avoid phrases such as "this proves that . . . " or "this shows that . . . " and avoid vague phrasing like "a lot."

The next paragraph claims that the dialogue "tells us a lot." The student identifies where in the passage Oliver speaks, namely in "the third and fourth paragraphs," but this information is neither necessary nor insightful. More astute writers will comment on the content of Oliver's dialogue instead of its position in the passage. The student accurately notices that Eliza cuts Oliver off, but erroneously classifies her dialogue as a soliloquy, which is yet another strike against the essay's accuracy. Too many strikes will always hurt the score. Although the student again relies on the clichéd phrase "this shows that . . . ," the insight that Oliver is a "milquetoast" who is "bowled over by the talkative Eliza" is an interesting thought. The Reader will reward this thinking while still wishing for more textual analysis and proof.

The last paragraph of the essay is devoted to tone, but it is apparent that the student needs more experience in assessing and addressing tone. After a bland first sentence that only tells us the tone "helps to show" character, the student declares that the tone "starts out slow," which is not an appropriate way to describe tone. The student notes the changes in tone (and again wrongly classifies Eliza's speech as a soliloquy), but provides no textual evidence or insightful analysis of *how* the tone helps depict their relationship. The Reader is left with the vacuous remark that the "change in tone shows us a lot about their relationship." The evidence and commentary should earn 2 points in Row B.

One can praise that the student tries to write on topic and that he or she does have an organizational scheme, albeit formulaic. However, the bland and hollow language, grammatical errors, inaccuracies in identification, and lack of adequate development of ideas and analysis all add up to a low score. The essay does not meet the criteria for a point in Row C. This student's writing does show promise and it will likely improve after addressing these weaknesses through additional practice. As written, the essay deserves an overall score of 2.

Question 3: How a Character Faces Danger

The following scoring guide explicitly explains how to earn up to 6 total points for a literary analysis essay. Row A (thesis) can earn up to 1 point; Row B (evidence and commentary) can earn up to 4 points, and Row C (sophistication) can earn up to 1 point.

Row A: Thesis (0–1 point)	
Scoring Criteria	
0 points for any of the following:	**1 point for**
• Having no defendable thesis. • Only restating the prompt in the thesis. • Only summarizing the issue with no claim in the thesis. • Presenting a thesis that does not address the prompt.	• Addressing the prompt with a defendable thesis that presents an interpretation and may establish a line of reasoning.
Decision Rules and Scoring Notes	
Theses that do not earn this point	**Theses that do earn this point**
• Only restate the prompt. • Only offer an irrelevant generalized comment about the chosen work.	• Take a position on the prompt and provide a defendable interpretation of how danger affects a character and adds to an interpretation of the chosen work as a whole.
Additional Notes	
• The thesis may be one or more sentences anywhere in the response. • A thesis that meets the criteria can be awarded the point whether or not the rest of the response successfully conveys that line of reasoning.	

Row B: Evidence AND Commentary (0–4 points)				
Scoring Criteria				
0 points for	**1 point for**	**2 points for**	**3 points for**	**4 points for**
• Simply repeating the thesis (if present). • **OR** restating provided information. • **OR** providing mostly irrelevant and/or incoherent examples.	• Summarizing the chosen work without reference to a thesis. • **OR** providing vague textual references. • **OR** providing textual references of questionable relevance. • **AND** providing little or no commentary.	• Making relevant textual references (direct quotes or paraphrases). • **AND** providing commentary but repeats, oversimplifies, or misinterprets the cited evidence or text.	• Making relevant textual references (direct quotes or paraphrases). • **AND** providing commentary that explains the logical relationship between textual examples and the thesis; however, commentary is uneven, limited, or incomplete.	• Making relevant textual references (direct quotes or paraphrases). • **AND** providing well-developed commentary that explicitly explains the relationship between the evidence and the thesis.
Decision Rules and Scoring Notes				
Typical responses that earn 0 points:	**Typical responses that earn 1 point:**	**Typical responses that earn 2 points:**	**Typical responses that earn 3 points:**	**Typical responses that earn 4 points:**
• Are unclear or fail to address the prompt. • May present mere opinion with no relevant textual references.	• Mention textual references, devices, or techniques with little or no analysis.	• Contain numerous inaccuracies or repetition in commentary. • Offer only simplistic explanations that do not strengthen the argument.	• Provide commentary that is not sufficiently developed or is too limited. • Assume or imply a connection to the thesis that is not consistently explicit.	• Provide commentary that uses significant details of the text to draw conclusions. • Integrate short excerpts throughout in order to support the thesis' interpretation.
Additional Notes				
• Writing that suffers from grammatical and/or mechanical errors that interfere with communication cannot earn the fourth point in this row.				

Row C: Sophistication (0–1 point)	
Scoring Criteria	
0 points for	**1 point for**
• Not meeting the criteria for 1 point.	• Exhibiting sophistication of thought and/or advancing a complex literary argument.
Decision Rules and Scoring Notes	
Responses that do not earn this point:	**Responses that earn this point demonstrate one (or more) of the following:**
• Try to contextualize an interpretation, but make predominantly sweeping generalizations (*"Throughout all history. . ."* OR *"Everyone believes . . ."*). • Only hint at other possible interpretations (*"Some may think . . ."* OR *"Though the work might be said to . . ."*). • Write one statement about a thematic interpretation of the chosen work without consistently maintaining that idea. • Oversimplify complexities in the chosen work. • Present complicated or complex sentences or language that is ineffective and detracts from the argument.	• Present a thesis that demands nuanced analysis of textual evidence and successfully prove it. • Illuminate the significance or relevance of an interpretation within a broader context. • Discuss alternative interpretations of a text. • Acknowledge and account for contradictions, ambiguities, and/or complexities within the text. • Provide relevant analogies to help better understand an interpretation. • Develop a prose style that is especially vivid, persuasive, resounding, or appropriate to the student's argument.
Additional Notes	
• This point should be awarded only if the demonstration of sophistication or complex understanding is part of the argument, not merely a phrase or brief reference.	

High-Scoring Essay

The way people react in the face of danger reveals a great deal about their character. Some confront danger head-on with courage, disregarding any possible negative outcomes. Some cringe from danger with cowardice, fearful of personal harm. Some ponder assorted possibilities and their repercussions before taking any action. Antigone, the title character in the play by Sophocles, proves to be the type of person who stares down danger as she defies the law of Creon, the King of Thebes, who had decreed that no enemy of the state could be buried after the recent uprising and that anyone doing so would be stoned to death. In the process of thumbing her nose at her uncle, the king, Antigone reveals that her loyalty is not to man's law but to a higher law, that of the gods. Antigone's actions symbolize that people should live in a way that honors what is morally right, even if it requires breaking man's laws.

The play begins assuming the audience knows the myth of Oedipus and his descendants. Necessary before beginning this play is the knowledge that his two sons, Polynices and Etcocles, died at each other's hand in the recent Theban uprising. Polynices had fought to overthrow the current regime, and Etcocles represented that regime as the King of Thebes. The first scene in <u>Antigone</u> immediately dives into the philosophical conundrum between the Greek concept of phusis, the universal laws of nature, and nomos, the specific laws of man. Antigone confronts her sister, Ismene with the fact that she will fearlessly defy Creon's law and bury their brother, obeying the greater laws of the gods. Ismene represents those who cower in the face of danger as she not only refuses to join Antigone but also reminds her that they are women, weaklings, who must submit to Creon's laws. Antigone, ever defiant and rebellious, refuses to agree to any voice of reason. She is hell-bent on burying Polynices and willing to face the danger her action will cause. It is interesting to note that Creon's decree demands that anyone defying his law be stoned to death within the city limits; the repercussions of this are universally morally important, as such a punishment would require all citizens to participate in the death sentence, surely a sin in the eyes of the gods. It anticipates the conflict citizens face when they are forced to choose to follow man's law over the gods' law.

This conflict is clarified by the chorus immediately before Antigone's next appearance. The famous choral ode that glorifies the wonders of man culminates by declaring that man will only become great when "he weaves in the laws of the land with the justice of the gods." Antigone enters, arrested by the sentry during the act of burying Polynices. Stoic and unrepentant, she accuses Creon of trying to override the gods' will and utters a dangerously daring slur as she tells Creon that "I've been accused of folly by a fool." Creon comes unglued at the thought that he has been defied, especially by a woman that he is related to, and insists that no one supports her action. Her stark reply is that the people would do so if they were not locked in fear of him. Clearly significant is the way she constantly values universal dignity for all.

Antigone's last appearance in the play occurs as she is led to a tomb, where Creon decides, in a policy change, that she will be walled in and left to starve to death instead of being stoned by the citizens. Perhaps he is beginning to question his ethics, but he simply claims this action will clean his hands and absolve him of any guilt. Antigone willingly faces death, vowing her reverence for the gods as she is escorted out. In the process Antigone shows us what consolation tragedy can bring: in the classic tragic hero, suffering and death can be met with such greatness of soul that it brings honor to all mankind.

The remaining action of the play is swift and horribly tragic; Antigone hangs herself; Haemon, her fiancé and Creon's son, kills himself, as does his mother, Creon's wife. All of these sudden deaths compel Creon to repent. Alas, this play is a tragedy and by definition intense suffering comes with the territory; however tragedy could have been avoided if Creon had learned earlier the lesson the messenger delivers, that of all the problems afflicting man, the worst is lack of judgment. The dangers that men like Creon pose to the wellbeing of society can be averted if all people act with moral judgment.

(771 words)

Analysis of High-Scoring Essay

This laudable essay deserves its high score because it is clearly on topic, well organized, highly developed, and well written. The introduction entices the Reader as it addresses the varying ways people react to danger; the student shows an admirable degree of style, using parallel construction and effective alliteration. The focus then narrows to Antigone and classifies her as the type who "stares down danger" as she defies Creon's law; this addresses the first part of the prompt that asks how the character responds to danger. This sentence is a bit cumbersome because it combines its first mention of the text, the author, and some brief plot information. If allowed time to edit, the student might clean this up, but under timed circumstances one cannot criticize too much. After the enjoyable phrasing about Antigone "thumbing her nose at the uncle," the student nails the remaining two parts of the topic. (1) Antigone reveals her obedience to higher, universal law, and (2) her actions symbolize the way all humans should live. The student is sophisticated enough to not repeat the phrasing of the prompt, and the reader will be grateful to not encounter trite phrases such as "this idea is significant to the work as a whole because. . . ." The quality of the thesis clearly deserves a point in Row A.

The first body paragraph is devoted to Antigone's initial scene with Ismene, her sister. Before analyzing that, though, the student acknowledges the background mythical information that is required before reading the play. While plot summary is not necessary, the essay would be hard to follow without this information. Then the student does an outstanding job of proving that he or she has not only read the play, but has also studied it intellectually. The addition of the "philosophical conundrum" between phusis and nomos is apropos to this play and to the student's thesis. The student briefly explains the two terms, perhaps anticipating that not all AP Readers will be familiar with them. The essay establishes that Antigone and Ismene have landed on opposite sides of this conflict, with Antigone defying man's law and Ismene supporting it. The discussion of the implications of a sentence of death by stoning is mature and relevant, especially as the student ties it to the thesis.

The next paragraph transitions to Antigone's second appearance in the play, but before analyzing her role, the student accurately reminds the Reader of the message of the choral ode that man will only be great when "he weaves in the laws of the land with the justice of the gods." It's admirable that the student can quote the play, especially in service of his or her analysis. The student emphasizes how Antigone reacts to danger, being "stoic and unrepentant," and provides ample evidence of her audacious attitude. The paragraph ends somewhat abruptly, but it does more than merely relate the plot; instead, it widens its focus to comment on the significance of the work as a whole.

The last body paragraph explores Antigone's final appearance in the play as she is led to the tomb where she will meet her tragic death. After commenting on Creon's policy change, the student addresses how facing danger affects Antigone; she maintains her reverence for the gods as she faces certain death. The paragraph finishes with a flourish, presenting the global idea that tragic heroes teach us about "greatness of soul that brings honor to all mankind." A Reader will be impressed with such sophistication in the student's thought and expression.

The final paragraph provides a thankfully swift summary of the action that occurs in the play after Antigone is escorted offstage; being an ancient tragedy, of course, people die in droves and Creon suffers. The student appropriately mentions the thematic statement from the messenger about bad judgment being the bane of mankind. The student finishes with an analogy between Creon and all people, reminding us that we need to "act with moral judgment." The evidence and commentary strongly support the thesis' interpretation of the work as a whole and deserve 4 points in Row B.

Overall, the essay is extremely pleasing. It does not fall into the trap of simply retelling the plot; rather, it uses the text very effectively to aid its analysis. The writing is sophisticated and the organization logical. The student clearly addresses the prompt throughout the essay and develops ideas with panache. The essay qualifies for a point in Row C because it successfully proves a demanding, nuanced thesis, and does so with sophisticated style throughout. A Reader will be gratified to reward this essay with a high overall score of 6.

Medium-Low-Scoring Essay

In William Golding's "Lord of the Flies," a group of British schoolboys, who are being evacuated because of the war, become stranded on a tropical island with no adult supervision. Naturally chaos ensues. They face danger daily, and the boys react in different manners. Some become primitive, some try to maintain their civilization. Of the latter group, Piggy stands out as the only one who continually tries to do the right thing. Piggy responds to danger with persistent logic which reveals his inner character and adds significance to the novel.

In the early part of the book, after the boys' plane was shot down, they begin to find each other and assemble on the beach. Piggy helps Ralph by being logical and offering logical suggestions. He helps make a list of the boys and reminds Ralph that, without any adults, they need to act properly as adults would want them to do. Piggy is the only logical one so far who thinks of the basic things they need to do. He also discovers the conch and knows how they can use it to call the others to order. It becomes a symbol of communication as they decide only the one who holds it can speak. Piggy is behind this organization and without his logical approach, they boys might not have gathered together in the first place.

Later, things get much worse as danger encroaches. They struggle to get food daily, and Jack's tribe of wild boys only wants to hunt feral pigs. Piggy and Ralph's group are responsible for building shelters, which is also a logical need, but Jack looks down on them for not being as important. At one time he even refuses to share food with Piggy and cracks one of the lenses in Piggy's glasses, which are a symbol of Piggy's intelligence. Half-blinded, Piggy doesn't face danger as logically as he did before when he could see clearly.

By the end of the book, Jack's tribe has gone bonkers and they kill Piggy when he tries to get his glasses back from them and begs for them to return to normalcy. Piggy's logic is sound, but he is made a martyr by the others.

This shows that people have to try hard to keep their senses in the face of danger. It can make us forget who we are and what's important in life.

(397 words)

Analysis of Medium-Low-Scoring Essay

This *Lord of the Flies* essay tries to address the prompt. The novel and the character Piggy are an appropriate choice (indeed, any major character in this novel would work well), but the student does not fully seize upon the opportunity the prompt offers.

The introductory paragraph jumps right in, citing the name of the novel and its author, while explaining the basic plot scenario: The boys are stranded on an island during the war. A discerning Reader will notice that the student placed the book title in quotations, instead of remembering to underline it (and *please* never try to slant your handwriting to make it "look" like italics; Readers chortle at that!). The student then tries to address the topic by mentioning that the boys "face danger daily," and that they react to it differently. While some "become primitive," others "try to maintain civilization." The student is not inaccurate, but the presentation so far is somewhat bland

and matter-of-fact. An exception is the statement that "Naturally chaos ensues," which elicits a true "Duh!" moment in the Reader's mind. Next, the student narrows the focus to Piggy's character, but somewhat erroneously claims he is the "only one who continually tries to do the right thing." A Reader might forgive this inaccurate phrasing, knowing Piggy is not alone in his attempts and that he, like the others, has lapses in his proper actions. Many students exaggerate by using absolutes in their phrasing when they should use qualified, nuanced statements. This student completes the introduction with an attempt to address all parts of the prompt: (1) Piggy responds to danger "with persistent logic," (2) his logic "reveals his inner character," and (3) apparently all of this "adds significance to the novel." We don't yet know what that purported significance is, but we can only hope the student will articulate it in the coming paragraphs. The student does present a thesis that begins in the introduction and concludes in the last paragraph; thus, it eventually earns a point in Row A.

The first body paragraph explores the beginning chapter of the novel, albeit with some factual inaccuracies. Again, a Reader might be willing to overlook the fact that the student implies actions occur in the wrong order; for example, in the text, Piggy and Ralph must find the conch shell before they can use it to call the boys together and then organize their names. The student repeats the idea that Piggy is logical four times in the paragraph, apparently thinking that overkill is impressive. The paragraph would be stronger if it were to address what the examples imply about Piggy's character and how they enhance the novel's overall meaning. As written, we only know that Piggy helps with logical ideas, and we are to assume these ideas relate to facing danger in some way.

The next paragraph opens with the student suddenly remembering to address danger, but the first sentence is banal, telling us only that "things get much worse as danger encroaches." The student mentions the daily need for food and then tells us Jack's boys only want to hunt. Apparently danger and hunting are connected in some way, but the student does not explain how. Next, we read a very brief allusion to the intense power struggle that develops in the novel. The language and grammar become sloppy; for example, when the student notes that "Piggy and Ralph's group are responsible for building shelters . . . but Jack looks down on them for not being as important," we are not sure if the pronoun "them" refers to the shelters or to Piggy and Ralph. Grammatically, the antecedent should be the shelters, but in the text it is more accurate that Jack's disdain is directed at Piggy and Ralph. This paragraph presents weak plot summary and scant analysis of the prompt. Mentioning that Piggy, half-blinded with cracked glasses, "doesn't face danger as logically as he did before" may be true, but it is hardly an impressive insight. Superficial, obvious commentary like this does not fare well.

The last body paragraph is quite undeveloped, with only two sentences. The Reader may smile when reading that the student's best word choice to describe Jack's tribe is "bonkers," but this opening sentence is merely more plot synopsis. The paragraph claims Piggy's "logic is sound," but that comes across as a feeble attempt to address the prompt and stay on topic. Insightful analysis, it is not. The evidence includes some relevant text examples, but the commentary oversimplifies the text and includes some inaccuracies; therefore, the essay earns 2 points in Row B.

The concluding paragraph is also very weak, with only two sentences; it falls into the trap that many students do. It attempts to discuss what significance Piggy's character has to the novel as a whole, but it's too little, too late, and far too simplistic. True, it addresses some universal idea, that we "have to try hard" when facing danger and can "forget who we are and what's important," but this commentary seems so bland, so timid. The text offers much more depth about the evil that lies hidden within civilized people, but the student does not go there. He or she only addresses the surface-level danger in the scenario—namely, basic survival—but ignores the deeper issues and insights about mankind that Golding presents so well.

Overall, the essay fails to develop apt textual examples and analyze them with insightful depth. It presents an oversimplified understanding of the work and fails to connect how Piggy's response to danger relates to his character and the work as a whole. It does not qualify for a point in Row C, and deserves an overall score of 3.

Scoring Worksheet

Use the following worksheet to arrive at a probable final AP score on Practice Exam 5. While it is sometimes difficult to be objective enough to score one's own essay, you can use the sample essay answers to approximate an essay score for yourself. Better yet, give your essays (along with the sample scored essays) to a friend or relative who you think is competent to score the essays.

Section I: Multiple-Choice Questions

$$\frac{}{\text{right answers}} = \frac{}{\text{multiple-choice raw score}}$$

$$\frac{}{\text{multiple-choice raw score}} \times 1.25 = \frac{}{\text{multiple-choice converted score}} \text{ (of possible 67.5)}$$

Section II: Free-Response Questions

$$\frac{}{\text{question 1 raw score}} + \frac{}{\text{question 2 raw score}} + \frac{}{\text{question 3 raw score}} = \frac{}{\text{essay raw score}}$$

$$\frac{}{\text{essay raw score}} \times 4.583 = \frac{}{\text{essay converted score}} \text{ (of possible 82.5)}$$

Final Score

$$\frac{}{\text{multiple-choice converted score}} + \frac{}{\text{essay converted score}} = \frac{}{\text{final converted score}} \text{ (of possible 150)}$$

Probable Final AP Score	
Final Converted Score	**Probable AP Score**
150–100	5
99–86	4
85–67	3
66–0	1 or 2

Chapter 12

Practice Exam 6

Section I: Multiple-Choice Questions

Time: 1 hour
55 questions

Directions: This section contains selections from two passages of prose and three poems, with questions on their content, style, and form. Read each selection carefully. Choose the best answer of the five choices.

For questions 1–11, read the following passage carefully before choosing your answers.

May in Ayemenem[1] is a hot, brooding month. The days are long and humid. The river shrinks and black crows gorge on the bright mangoes in still, dustgreen trees. Red bananas ripen. Jackfruits
(5) burst. Dissolute bluebottles hum vacuously in the fruity air. Then they stun themselves against clear windowpanes and die, fatly baffled in the sun.

The nights are clear, but suffused with sloth and sullen expectation.

(10) But by early June the southwest monsoon breaks and there are three months of wind and water with short spells of sharp, glittering sunshine that thrilled children snatch to play with. The countryside turns an immodest green. Boundaries
(15) blur as tapioca fences take root and bloom. Brick walls turn mossgreen. Pepper vines snake up electric poles. Wild creepers burst through laterite banks and spill across the flooded roads. Boats ply in the bazaars. And small fish appear in the
(20) puddles that fill the potholes on the highways.

It was raining when Rahel came back to Ayemenem. Slanting silver ropes slammed into loose earth, plowing it up like gunfire. The old house on the hill wore its steep, gabled roof pulled
(25) over its ears like a low hat. The walls, streaked with moss, had grown soft, and bulged a little with dampness that seeped up from the ground. The wild, overgrown garden was full of the whisper and scurry of small lives. In the
(30) undergrowth a rat snake wrapped itself against a glistening stone. Hopeful yellow bullfrogs cruised the scummy pond for mates. A drenched mongoose flashed across the leaf-strewn driveway.

The house itself looked empty. The doors and
(35) windows were locked. The front veranda bare. Unfurnished. But the skyblue Plymouth with chrome tailfins was still parked outside, and inside, Baby Kochamma was still alive.

She was Rahel's baby grandaunt, her
(40) grandfather's younger sister. Her name was really Navomi, Navomi Ipe, but everybody called her Baby. She became Baby Kochamma when she was old enough to be an aunt. Rahel hadn't come to see her, though. Neither niece nor baby grandaunt
(45) labored under any illusions on that account. Rahel had come to see her brother, Estha. They were two-egg twins. "Dizygotic" doctors called them. Born from separate but simultaneously fertilized eggs. Estha—Esthappen—was the older
(50) by eighteen minutes.

They never did look much like each other, Estha and Rahel, and even when they were thin-armed children, flat-chested, worm-ridden, and Elvis Presley-puffed, there was none of the usual
(55) "Who is who?" and "Which is which?" from oversmiling relatives or the Syrian Orthodox bishops who frequently visited the Ayemenem House for donations.

The confusion lay in a deeper, more secret
(60) place.

In those early amorphous years when memory had only just begun, when life was full of Beginnings and no Ends, and Everything was Forever, Esthappen and Rahel thought of
(65) themselves together as Me, and separately, individually, as We or Us. As though they were a rare breed of Siamese twins, physically separate, but with joint identities.

---

[1]**Ayemenem:** an area in southwestern India

(70) Now, these years later, Rahel has a memory of waking up one night giggling at Estha's funny dream.

She has other memories too that she has no right to have.

(75) She remembers, for instance (though she hadn't been there), what the Orangedrink Lemondrink Man did to Estha in Abhilash Talkies. She remembers the taste of the tomato sandwiches—*Estha's* sandwiches, that *Estha* ate—on the Madras Mail to Madras.

(80) And these are only the small things.

. . .

Anyway, now she thinks of Estha and Rahel as *Them*, because, separately, the two of them are no longer what *They* were or ever thought *They'd* be.

(85) Ever.

Their lives have a size and a shape now. Estha has his and Rahel hers.

Edges, Borders, Boundaries, Brinks, and Limits have appeared like a team of trolls on their (90) separate horizons. Short creatures with long shadows, patrolling the Blurry End. Gentle half-moons have gathered under their eyes and they are as old as Ammu[2] was when she died. Thirty-one.

(95) Not old.

Not young.

But a viable die-able age.

---

[2]**Ammu:** the twins' mother

1. The effect of the short subject-verb sentences "Red bananas ripen. Jackfruits burst" (lines 4–5) serves to

A. emphasize the intensity of the "hot, brooding month" (line 1)
B. hasten the pace of the overall narrative
C. contradict the monsoon imagery that follows
D. distract attention from the nearby crows and bluebottles
E. establish a scene of deteriorating vegetation

2. The alliteration in the single sentence of the second paragraph adds the effect of

A. creating suspense before the monsoon arrives
B. minimizing the imagery in the description
C. separating the description of the night from the rest of the narration
D. compounding the lethargy and sluggishness of the atmosphere
E. mimicking the sound of the snake in the fourth paragraph

3. In the context of the passage as a whole, the phrase "Boundaries blur" (lines 14–15) is ironic because

A. the monsoon makes everything grow at a dizzying pace
B. the alliteration links the words to the action of the sentence
C. the location has no boundaries in the first place
D. the narrator later informs us that boundaries have separated things
E. the separate images are not blurred at all

4. Which of the following clarifies a difference in the monsoon imagery between paragraphs three and four?

A. Paragraph three shows the beginning of the monsoon; paragraph four describes its end.
B. Paragraph three displays abundant natural growth; paragraph four stresses negative effects of the rain.
C. Paragraph three only employs visual imagery; paragraph four only employs auditory imagery.
D. Paragraph three depicts vigorous plant growth; paragraph four focuses more on humanity.
E. Paragraph three implies the present; paragraph four discusses the past.

5. The mention of the "skyblue Plymouth with chrome tailfins" (lines 36–37) suggests

A. the family wishes to show off their economic status
B. that the car no longer runs
C. the modernity of the family
D. a commitment to American culture
E. an incongruous yet stable detail in the family

6. Which of the following is implied about Rahel and Baby Kochamma's relationship?

A. They are estranged.
B. They will enjoy a family reunion.
C. They became bitter enemies.
D. They hardly endure each other.
E. They are disillusioned about familial relationships.

7. The ninth paragraph, which begins "In those early amorphous years . . . " (lines 61–68), suggests that

   A.   children struggle to find their own identity

   B.   the twins will indefinitely share their conjoined identity

   C.   the twins see themselves as an extension of each other

   D.   all twins share intertwined thoughts

   E.   children need someone they can relate to

8. The effect of capitalizing the nouns " . . . when life was full of Beginnings and no Ends, and Everything was Forever" (lines 62–64) is that it

   A.   changes the substance of the words

   B.   emphasizes the way children see the world as infinite

   C.   shows how limited a child's view really is

   D.   enlarges the twins' awareness

   E.   reduces the twins' separate identities

9. The point of view in the passage has the effect of

   A.   dwelling on minutiae related to the monsoon

   B.   diminishing the importance of understanding the character's motives

   C.   remaining distant until exploring one character's thoughts

   D.   exploring atmosphere before introducing character

   E.   establishing the importance of family

10. The nonlinear plot allows the narration to

   A.   develop characters over time

   B.   foreshadow conflicts the twins will face

   C.   jump in and out of Rahel's mind

   D.   explore abstract ideas

   E.   echo the disjointed processes of memory

11. The end of the passage implies that

   A.   Rahel and Estha no longer have anything in common

   B.   the twins will die an early death

   C.   Rahel and Estha's shared memories do not reflect reality

   D.   the twins now understand their role in the family

   E.   Rahel and Estha have attained separate identities

For questions 12–22, read the poem carefully before choosing your answers.

> Nuns fret not at their convent's narrow room;
> And hermits are contented with their cells;
> And students with their pensive citadels;
> Maids at the wheel, the weaver at his loom,
> Sit blithe and happy; bees that soar for bloom,   (5)
> High as the highest Peak of Furness-fells,[1]
> Will murmur by the hour in foxglove bells:
> In truth the prison, into which we doom
> Ourselves, no prison is: and hence for me,
> In sundry moods, 'twas pastime to be bound   (10)
> Within the Sonnet's scanty plot of ground;
> Pleased if some Souls (for such there needs must be)
> Who have felt the weight of too much liberty,
> Should find brief solace there, as I have found.

[1]**Furness-fells:** upland tracts of Furness, in the Lake District of northern England

12. The word "contented" (line 2) functions as the verb for hermits and which of the following subjects?

    A. "Nuns" (line 1)
    B. "students" (line 3)
    C. "Maids" (line 4)
    D. "weaver" (line 4)
    E. "bees" (line 5)

13. The phrase "pensive citadels" (line 3) can best be interpreted as which of the following?

    A. Melancholy fortress
    B. Monastery for self-contemplation
    C. Stronghold of higher education
    D. Fortress that commands
    E. Bastion of unhappy thinking

14. The most pervasive idea in the first half of the poem can be summarized as which one of the following?

    A. Nuns fret not.
    B. Hermits are satisfied.
    C. Students are pensive.
    D. Maids are happy.
    E. Most people are content with their position in life.

15. The prison in line 8 could confine all of the following EXCEPT

    A. nuns
    B. maids
    C. weavers
    D. bees
    E. Furness-fells

16. "In truth the prison, into which we doom / Ourselves, no prison is . . . " (lines 8–9) is an example of

    A. dissonance
    B. ambiguity
    C. caesura
    D. paradox
    E. euphemism

17. The poem's diction is notable for

    A. an abundance of descriptive adjectives
    B. unconventional contrasts
    C. a shift from positive connotations to negative ones
    D. using so many different descriptions of prisons
    E. several unusual prepositional phrases

18. The phrase "scanty plot of ground" (line 11) can be identified as which of the following figures of speech?

    A. Simile
    B. Apostrophe
    C. Juxtaposition
    D. Oxymoron
    E. Metaphor

19. Where has the speaker found "brief solace" (line 14)?

    A. "the highest Peak of Furness-fells" (line 6)
    B. "the prison, into which we doom / Ourselves" (lines 8–9)
    C. "no prison is: and hence for me" (line 9)
    D. "the Sonnet's scanty plot of ground" (line 11)
    E. "too much liberty" (line 13)

20. All of the following are related to the speaker's complex relationship with writing a sonnet EXCEPT

    A. "Will murmur by the hour" (line 7)
    B. "the prison, into which we doom / Ourselves" (lines 8–9)
    C. "In sundry moods" (line 10)
    D. "'twas pastime to be bound" (line 10)
    E. "scanty plot of ground" (line 11)

21. One irony of the speaker's praising the sonnet form so highly is that

    A. the speaker finds it merely a pastime now and then
    B. writing sonnets brings endless comfort
    C. some souls have too much liberty
    D. for poets, the sonnet form is a good exercise in restraint
    E. the speaker veers from the traditional sonnet formula

22. Which of the following identifies a potential logical objection to the speaker's argument?

    A. The speaker posits a false dilemma: Everyone is either trapped in a prison or it is not a prison at all.
    B. It draws a conclusion based on anecdotal evidence.
    C. The entire argument is based on the speaker's questionable assumptions.
    D. It uses circular logic, restating its opening point in other words.
    E. It asserts a causal relationship, but without considering correlation.

For questions 23–34, read the poem carefully before choosing your answers. The following was written by an American female poet during the colonial era.

The Prologue

To sing of Wars, of Captains, and of Kings,
Of Cities founded, Common-wealths begun,
For my mean Pen are too superior things;
Or how they all, or each their dates have run,
Let Poets and Historians set these forth.   (5)
My obscure lines shall not so dim their worth.

But when my wond'ring eyes and envious heart
Great Bartas'[1] sugar'd lines do but read o'er,
Fool, I do grudge the Muses did not part
'Twixt him and me that over-fluent store.   (10)
A Bartas can do what a Bartas will
But simple I according to my skill.

From School-boy's tongue no Rhet'ric we expect,
Nor yet a sweet Consort from broken strings,
Nor perfect beauty where's a main defect.   (15)
My foolish, broken, blemished Muse so sings,
And this to mend, alas, no Art is able,
'Cause Nature made it so irreparable.

Nor can I, like that fluent sweet-tongued Greek[2]
Who lisp'd at first, in future times speak plain.   (20)
By Art he gladly found what he did seek,
A full requital of his striving pain.
Art can do much, but this maxim's most sure:
A weak or wounded brain admits no cure.

I am obnoxious to each carping tongue   (25)
Who says my hand a needle better fits.
A Poet's Pen all scorn I should thus wrong,
For such despite they cast on female wits.
If what I do prove well, it won't advance,
They'll say it's stol'n, or else it was by chance.   (30)

But sure the antique Greeks were far more mild,
Else of our Sex, why feigned they those nine
And poesy made Calliope's own child?
So 'mongst the rest they placed the Arts divine,
But this weak knot they will full soon untie.   (35)
The Greeks did nought but play the fools and lie.

Let Greeks be Greeks, and Women what they are.
Men have precedency and still excel;
It is but vain unjustly to wage war.
Men can do best, and Women know it well.   (40)
Preeminence in all and each is yours;
Yet grant some small acknowledgement of ours.

---

[1]**Bartas:** Guillaume du Bartas, a French Protestant poet
[2]**sweet-tongued Greek:** an allusion to Demosthenes, the famous Athenian statesman who overcame a speech impediment to present his oratories in public

And oh ye high flown quills that soar the skies,
And ever with your prey still catch your praise,
If e'er you deign these lowly lines your eyes,   (45)
Give thyme or Parsley wreath, I ask no Bays.
This mean and unrefined ore of mine
Will make your glist'ring gold but more to shine.

23. The phrase "my mean Pen" in line 3 is most likely used as

  A. a metaphor for the speaker's anger that will be developed in the poem
  B. personification of the speaker's writing about the midpoint between two extremes
  C. an analogy that represents women's roles in society
  D. a metonymy of the speaker's poetry symbolizing that it is too modest, too inadequate for the task
  E. an understated antithesis to separate the speaker's poetry from men's poetry

24. Which of the following best summarizes the speaker's thoughts about her writing poetry on lofty subjects, such as "Wars . . . Captains . . . Kings . . . Cities . . . Common-wealths" (lines 1–2)?

  A. She is enthusiastic because she wants to make her mark in the world of poetry.
  B. She is fervent because these are well-known subjects.
  C. She is hesitant, but then she changes her mind.
  D. She declines because she feels that she is not up to the task.
  E. She refuses because these famous events have already been written about by historians.

25. In the second stanza, all of the following are involved in the speaker's discussion of the poet Bartas EXCEPT that

  A. she is so jealous of his talent that she vows to exceed his fame
  B. she reads Bartas' poetry with "wond'ring eyes and envious heart" (line 7)
  C. she concludes that the Muses greatly favored him
  D. she gives him credit for his greatness
  E. she is content to write her own simple poetry, using her own simple skills

26. Which of the following poetic techniques is used in line 17, "And this to mend, alas, no Art is able"?

  A. Allegory
  B. Allusion
  C. Aphorism
  D. Apostrophe
  E. Assonance

27. In the fifth stanza, the speaker's primary focus is to

  A. extol the virtues of her own poetry
  B. castigate and rebuke her critics
  C. commend the virtues of a "fluent sweet-tongued Greek"
  D. bemoan that "A weak or wounded brain admits no cure"
  E. admit that "my hand a needle better fits"

28. Within the context of the last stanza, what is the intended meaning underlying line 46, "Give thyme or Parsley wreath, I ask no Bays"?

  A. She is a woman, so a wreath made from garden herbs would be most appropriate.
  B. The word "Bays" is a metaphor; she just wants a small opening, she is not asking for a huge ocean bay.
  C. She is indicating that she poses no threat to male poets.
  D. She is not asking men to howl for her poetry, as if they were dogs baying at the moon.
  E. She is not asking for a bay window, a place of her own in which to write.

29. In which of the following does the speaker most defend female creativity and demand respect?

- **A.** "But simple I according to my skill" (line 12)
- **B.** "My foolish, broken, blemished Muse so sings" (line 16)
- **C.** "A Poet's Pen all scorn I should thus wrong" (line 27)
- **D.** "If what I do prove well, it won't advance" (line 29)
- **E.** "Yet grant some small acknowledgement of ours" (line 42)

30. Which stanza stands out from the others in its angry tone?

- **A.** First
- **B.** Third
- **C.** Fifth
- **D.** Seventh
- **E.** Eighth

31. Within context, the intended meaning of the word "obnoxious" in line 25 is most likely

- **A.** vulnerable, exposed
- **B.** insufferable, unspeakable
- **C.** defenseless, frail
- **D.** unbearable, intolerable
- **E.** feeble, unprotected

32. Each of the following contributes to the speaker's attitude of modesty EXCEPT

- **A.** "Let Poets and Historians set these forth" (line 5)
- **B.** "But simple I according to my skill" (line 12)
- **C.** "Who says my hand a needle better fits" (line 26)
- **D.** "Let Greeks be Greeks, and Women what they are" (line 37)
- **E.** "Give thyme or Parsley wreath, I ask no Bays" (line 46)

33. In the context of the seventh stanza, the effect of the word "yours" (line 41) can best be described as

- **A.** shifting the intended audience in an appeal for mercy
- **B.** directly speaking to men and thus appearing less threatening
- **C.** redirecting the focus from herself to others to gain humility
- **D.** mimicking men's poetry and attitude of self-importance
- **E.** disputing men's claim to superiority in all things

34. An ironic aspect of the speaker's overarching humility is that she

- **A.** is deferential to male poets because of their superior skill
- **B.** intimidates others from attempting to write
- **C.** reinforces traditional attitudes toward women
- **D.** writes poetry that is polished, multi-faceted, and quite eloquent
- **E.** finally modifies her attitude in the last stanza

For questions 35–46, read the passage carefully before choosing your answers.

The following excerpt takes place in the English countryside near the end of World War I, as two British soldiers, on leave from the front, help with the harvest.

At first Joe thought the job O.K. He was loading hay on the trucks, along with Albert, the corporal. The two men were pleasantly billeted in a cottage not far from the station: they were their own (5) masters, for Joe never thought of Albert as a master. And the little sidings of the tiny village station was as pleasant a place as you could wish for. On one side, beyond the line, stretched the woods: on the other, the near side, across a green (10) smooth field red houses were dotted among flowering apple trees. The weather being sunny, work being easy, Albert, a real good pal, what life could be better! After Flanders, it was heaven itself.

Albert, the corporal, was a clean-shaven, (15) shrewd-looking fellow of about forty. He seemed to think his one aim in life was to be full of fun and nonsense. In repose, his face looked a little withered, old. He was a very good pal to Joe, steady, decent and grave under all his 'mischief'; (20) for his mischief was only his laborious way of skirting his own *ennui*.

(25) Joe was much younger than Albert—only twenty-three. He was a tallish, quiet youth, pleasant looking. He was of a slightly better class than his corporal, more personable. Careful about his appearance, he shaved every day. "I haven't got much of a face," said Albert. "If I was to shave every day like you, Joe, I should have none."

(30) There was plenty of life in the little goods-yard: three porter youths, a continual come and go of farm wagons bringing hay, wagons with timber from the woods, coal carts loading at the trucks. The black coal seemed to make the place sleepier, (35) hotter. Round the big white gate the station-master's children played and his white chickens walked, whilst the stationmaster himself, a young man getting too fat, helped his wife to peg out the washing on the clothes line in the meadow.

(40) The great boat-shaped wagons came up from Playcross with the hay. At first the farm-men waggoned it. On the third day one of the land-girls[1] appeared with the first load, drawing to a standstill easily at the head of her two great (45) horses. She was a buxom girl, young, in linen overalls and gaiters. Her face was ruddy, she had large blue eyes.

"Now that's the waggoner for us, boys," said the corporal loudly.

(50) "Whoa!" she said to her horses; and then to the corporal: "Which boys do you mean?"

"We are the pick of the bunch. That's Joe, my pal. Don't you let on that my name's Albert," said the corporal to his private. "I'm the (55) corporal."

"And I'm Miss Stokes," said the land-girl coolly, "if that's all the boys you are."

"You know you couldn't want more, Miss Stokes," said Albert politely. Joe, who was bare-(60) headed, whose grey flannel sleeves were rolled up to the elbow, and whose shirt was open at the breast, looked modestly aside as if he had no part in the affair.

"Are you on this job regular, then?" said the (65) corporal to Miss Stokes.

"I don't know for sure," she said, pushing a piece of hair under her hat, and attending to her splendid horses.

"Oh, make it a certainty," said Albert.

(70) She did not reply. She turned and looked over the two men coolly. She was pretty, moderately blonde, with crisp hair, a good skin, and large blue eyes. She was strong, too, and the work went on leisurely and easily.

(75) "Now!" said the corporal, stopping as usual to look round, "pleasant company makes work a pleasure—don't hurry it, boys." He stood on the truck surveying the world. That was one of his great and absorbing occupations: to stand and (80) look out on things in general. Joe, also standing on the truck, also turned round to look what was to be seen. But he could not become blankly absorbed, as Albert could.

Miss Stokes watched the two men from under (85) her broad felt hat. She had seen hundreds of Alberts, khaki soldiers standing in loose attitudes, absorbed in watching nothing in particular. She had seen also a good many Joes, quiet, good-looking young soldiers with half-(90) averted faces. But there was something in the turn of Joe's head, and something in his quiet, tender-looking form, young and fresh—which attracted her eye. As she watched him closely from below, he turned as if he felt her, and his (95) dark-blue eye met her straight, light-blue gaze. He faltered and turned aside again and looked as if he were going to fall off the truck. A slight flush mounted under the girl's full, ruddy face. She liked him.

35. One can reasonably infer from the opening line, "At first Joe thought the job O.K.," that eventually

A. Albert will also come to find the work acceptable
B. the land-girl could make the job even more tolerable
C. Joe might come to change his opinion
D. the land-girl will possibly come between Joe and Albert
E. the job will become more tedious

36. All of the following are details of their pleasant billeting EXCEPT

A. " . . . in a cottage not far from the station" (lines 3–4)
B. " . . . they were their own masters" (lines 4–5)
C. " . . . red houses were dotted among flowering apple trees" (lines 10–11)
D. "The weather being sunny, work being easy" (lines 11–12)
E. "After Flanders" (line 13)

[1]**land-girls:** women who contributed to the war effort by doing "men's work" on the farms

37. The narrator's description of Albert suggests that he

A. is duplicitous
B. follows his intuition
C. is a man of principled integrity
D. values entertainment over duty
E. is not as free-spirited as he appears

38. Joe differs from Albert in that he is

A. the older of the two
B. more interested in appearances
C. the smaller of the two
D. more garrulous
E. from a slightly lower class

39. The overall atmosphere of the village can best be described as

A. lethargic because of the summer weather
B. enduring the effects of war rationing
C. congenial with social interactions among the neighbors
D. thriving despite the war
E. burgeoning with bustling wartime commerce

40. The manner in which Miss Stokes arrives on one of the "great boat-shaped wagons" (line 40) suggests that she

A. is commanding and bossy
B. cannot help with unloading the hay
C. cares for her horses more than the soldiers
D. will assert her higher social status
E. is robust but respectful

41. Miss Stokes' reply "Which boys do you mean?" (line 51) is understood to mean that she

A. expected help from more soldiers
B. is excited to meet the new soldiers and hopes there are more of them
C. is unimpressed by Albert's implied exaggeration
D. is confused about which of the many new "boys" Albert is referring to
E. intends to humiliate Albert and Joe by referring to them as mere "boys"

42. In their initial meeting with Miss Stokes, Albert attempts to be

A. teasing but easy-going
B. respectful and deferential
C. in charge of the operation
D. professionally militaristic
E. boastful and immodest

43. Miss Stokes' initial reaction to meeting Albert and Joe may be described as

A. discomfited and abashed
B. aloof and unimpressed
C. surprised and pleased
D. enthralled and intrigued
E. flirty and manipulative

44. The narrator's repetition of the word "She," which begins every sentence of the 14th paragraph (lines 70–74), has the effect of

A. making Miss Stokes a random villager
B. dismissing Miss Stokes' ability to control the wagon
C. enhancing Albert's fascination with Miss Stokes
D. stripping Miss Stokes of her identity
E. suggesting she is observing the soldiers surreptitiously

45. Which of the following is NOT a reasonable implication of Albert's penchant for observation?

A. He likes to see the big picture in life.
B. Surveying the world is his modus operandi.
C. His observation skills are superior to Joe's.
D. His absorption in observing is a ruse to keep him from having to work.
E. He and Joe would not have survived the war without his looking around so much.

46. The narrator intimates that "She liked him" because

A. Joe is so much different from Albert
B. Joe is quiet and young
C. she sees his vulnerability
D. she had seen so many like Joe before
E. Joe's loose attitude makes him an easy conquest

For questions 47–55, read the following poem carefully before choosing your answers.

Harvest Song

I am a reaper whose muscles set at sun-down. All my oats are cradled.
But I am too chilled, and too fatigued to bind them. And I hunger.

I crack a grain between my teeth. I do not taste it.
I have been in the fields all day. My throat is dry. I hunger.

My eyes are caked with dust of oat-fields at harvest-time.   (5)
I am a blind man who stares across the hills, seeking stack'd fields
    of other harvesters.

It would be good to see them . . . crook'd, split, and iron-ring'd handles
    of the scythes . . . It would be good to see them, dust-caked and
    blind. I hunger.

(Dusk is a strange fear'd sheath their blades are dull'd in.)
My throat is dry. And should I call, a cracked grain like the oats
    . . . eoho—

I fear to call. What should they hear me, and offer me their grain,   (10)
    oats, or wheat or corn? I have been in the fields all day. I fear
    I could not taste it. I fear knowledge of my hunger.

My ears are caked with dust of oat-fields at harvest-time.
I am a deaf man who strains to hear the calls of other harvesters whose
    throats are also dry.

It would be good to hear their songs . . . reapers of the sweet-stalked
    cane, cutters of the corn . . . even though their throats cracked, and
    the strangeness of their voices deafened me.

I hunger. My throat is dry. Now that the sun has set and I am chilled.
    I fear to call. (Eoho, my brothers!)

I am a reaper. (Eoho!) All my oats are cradled. But I am too fatigued   (15)
    to bind them. And I hunger. I crack a grain. It has no taste to
    it. My throat is dry . . .

O my brothers, I beat my palms, still soft, against the stubble of my
    harvesting. (You beat your soft palms, too.) My pain is sweet.
    Sweeter than the oats or wheat or corn. It will not bring me
    knowledge of my hunger.

47. The irony of the speaker's statement "I crack a grain between my teeth" (line 3) is that

   A. the imagery is as simplistic as the speaker's thoughts

   B. the speaker has been in the fields all day

   C. the speaker's gustatory sense is denied

   D. the speaker's throat is too dry to swallow

   E. other harvesters are able to enjoy the fruits of their labor

48. All of the following refer to the speaker's hunger EXCEPT

   A. "All my oats are cradled." (line 1)

   B. "I do not taste it." (line 3)

   C. "I am a blind man who stares" (line 6)

   D. "My ears are caked with dust of oat-fields at harvest-time." (line 11)

   E. "It would be good to hear their songs . . ." (line 13)

49. The purpose of the speaker's use of many simple sentences can best be described as

   A. minimizing the speaker's hunger

   B. contradicting the message in the complex sentences

   C. crystalizing the speaker's thoughts and actions

   D. establishing that the speaker has few needs

   E. reinforcing the simplicity of the speaker's work

50. The speaker's overall tone can best be described as

   A. complacent

   B. offended

   C. vindictive

   D. felicitous

   E. desolate

51. The speaker's hunger metaphorically represents

   A. food and rest

   B. an unfulfilled life

   C. communication with the other harvesters

   D. a universal need for ample nourishment

   E. the unheard songs of the harvesters

52. The implication of the title is ironic because

   A. the "Eoho" call is hardly a song

   B. the harvest is over, and the workers have no more need for song

   C. a harvest should be plentiful, but this one is not

   D. it implies bounty and celebration, but the speaker has none

   E. the other harvesters do not sing

53. The ironic effect of the imagery as a whole can best be described as one of

   A. contradicting the speaker's emotions

   B. bombarding one's visual sense

   C. establishing sensory overload

   D. releasing the speaker's anger

   E. having a lack of sensation

54. The predominance of negative connotations over positive ones has the effect of

   A. pinpointing the physical demands of the work

   B. enhancing the speaker's hunger

   C. turning the harvest into a dreaded event

   D. mocking the beauty of the crops

   E. expanding the ironic imagery

55. The prevailing technique in the poem is one of

   A. unconventional description

   B. presenting lush natural imagery

   C. a series of contradictory ideas

   D. balanced narrative about the harvest

   E. repeated pleas for help

IF YOU FINISH BEFORE TIME IS CALLED, CHECK YOUR WORK ON THIS SECTION ONLY. DO NOT WORK ON ANY OTHER SECTION IN THE TEST.

Section II: Free-Response Questions

Time: 2 hours

3 questions

Question 1

(Suggested time: 40 minutes. This question counts toward one-third of the total free-response section score.)

Directions: In the following poem, "Spring," by Edna St. Vincent Millay (1921), the speaker presents an unusual attitude about the arrival of spring. Read the poem carefully. Then, in a well-written essay, analyze how the use of poetic devices helps to convey the speaker's complex attitude toward the coming of spring.

In your response you should do the following:

- Respond to the prompt with a thesis that presents an interpretation and may establish a line of reasoning.
- Select and use evidence to develop and support your line of reasoning.
- Explain the relationship between the evidence and your thesis.
- Use appropriate grammar and punctuation in communicating your argument.

Spring

To what purpose, April, do you return again?
Beauty is not enough.
You can no longer quiet me with the redness
Of little leaves opening stickily.

I know what I know. (5)
The sun is hot on my neck as I observe
The spikes of the crocus.
The smell of the earth is good.

It is apparent that there is no death.
But what does that signify? (10)
Not only under ground are the brains of men
Eaten by maggots.

Life in itself
Is nothing,
An empty cup, a flight of uncarpeted stairs. (15)
It is not enough that yearly, down this hill,

April
Comes like an idiot, babbling and strewing flowers.

Question 2

(Suggested time: 40 minutes. This question counts toward one-third of the total free-response score.)

Directions: The following excerpt from Elizabeth Gaskell's 1851 novel, *Cranford,* describes life in the 1830s in a small English town, one that is mostly inhabited by women. Read the passage carefully. Then, in a well-written essay, analyze the literary elements and techniques that Gaskell employs to characterize the complex inhabitants of Cranford.

In your response you should do the following:

- Respond to the prompt with a thesis that presents an interpretation and may establish a line of reasoning.
- Select and use evidence to develop and support your line of reasoning.
- Explain the relationship between the evidence and your thesis.
- Use appropriate grammar and punctuation in communicating your argument.

In the first place, Cranford is in possession of the Amazons; all the holders of houses above a certain rent are women. If a married couple come to settle in the town, somehow the gentleman disappears; he is either fairly frightened to death by being the only man in the Cranford evening parties, or he is accounted for by being with his regiment, his ship, or closely engaged in business all the week in the great neighboring
(5) commercial town of Drumble, distant only twenty miles on the railroad. In short, whatever does become of the gentlemen, they are not at Cranford. What could they do if they were there? The surgeon has his round of thirty miles, and sleeps at Cranford; but every man cannot be a surgeon. For keeping the trim gardens full of choice flowers without a weed to speck them; for frightening away little boys who look wistfully at the said flowers through the railings; for rushing out at the geese that occasionally venture into the gardens if the
(10) gates are left open; for deciding all questions of literature and politics without troubling themselves with unnecessary reasons or arguments; for obtaining clear and correct knowledge of everybody's affairs in the parish; for keeping their neat maid-servants in admirable order; for kindness (somewhat dictatorial) to the poor, and real tender good offices to each other whenever they are in distress, the ladies of Cranford are quite sufficient. "A man," as one of them observed to me once, "is *so* in the way in the house!" Although the ladies
(15) of Cranford know all each other's proceedings, they are exceedingly indifferent to each other's opinions. Indeed, as each has her own individuality, not to say eccentricity, pretty strongly developed, nothing is so easy as verbal retaliation; but, somehow, good-will reigns among them to a considerable degree.

The Cranford ladies have only an occasional little quarrel, spirited out in a few peppery words and angry jerks of the head; just enough to prevent the even tenor of their lives from becoming too flat. Their dress is
(20) very independent of fashion; as they observe, "What does it signify how we dress here at Cranford, where everybody knows us?" And if they go from home, their reason is equally cogent, "What does it signify how we dress here, where nobody knows us?" The materials of their clothes are, in general, good and plain, and most of them are nearly as scrupulous as Miss Tyler, of cleanly memory; but I will answer for it, the last gigot, the last tight and scanty petticoat in wear in England, was seen in Cranford—and seen without a smile.
(25)   . . .

I imagine that a few of the gentlefolks of Cranford were poor, and had some difficulty in making both ends meet; but they were like the Spartans, and concealed their smart under a smiling face. We none of us spoke of money, because that subject savoured of commerce and trade, and though some might be poor, we were all aristocratic. The Cranfordians had that kindly *esprit de corps* which made them overlook all
(30) deficiencies in success when some among them tried to conceal their poverty. When Mrs. Forrester, for instance, gave a party in her baby-house of a dwelling, and the little maiden disturbed the ladies on the sofa by a request that she might get the tea-tray out from underneath, everyone took this novel proceeding as the most natural thing in the world, and talked on about household forms and ceremonies as if we all believed that our hostess had a regular servants' hall, second table, with housekeeper and steward, instead of the one
(35) little charity-school maiden, whose short ruddy arms could never have been strong enough to carry the tray upstairs, if she had not been assisted in private by her mistress, who now sat in state, pretending not to know what cakes were sent up, though she knew, and we knew, and she knew that we knew, and we knew that she knew that we knew, she had been busy all the morning making tea-bread and sponge-cakes.

Question 3

(Suggested time: 40 minutes. This question counts toward one-third of the total free-response section score.)

Directions: In many works of literature, a character's struggle to rise above injustice plays a major role. The struggle itself may become more significant and revealing than whether or not the character succeeds.

Either from your own reading or from the list below, choose a character from a work of fiction who struggles to rise above injustice. Then, in a well-written essay, analyze how the struggle affects the character and what the struggle adds to an interpretation of the work as a whole. Do not summarize the plot.

In your response you should do the following:

- Respond to the prompt with a thesis that presents an interpretation and may establish a line of reasoning.
- Select and use evidence to develop and support your line of reasoning.
- Explain the relationship between the evidence and your thesis.
- Use appropriate grammar and punctuation in communicating your argument.

1984

The Adventures of Huckleberry Finn

All the King's Men

All the Pretty Horses

Atonement

The Awakening

Beloved

Billy Budd

The Blind Assassin

The Bonesetter's Daughter

A Gathering of Old Men

The God of Small Things

The Grapes of Wrath

Invisible Man

Jane Eyre

The Jungle

King Lear

The Last of the Mohicans

A Lesson Before Dying

The Merchant of Venice

The Mill on the Floss

Native Son

No Country for Old Men

Oliver Twist

The Poisonwood Bible

Rosencrantz and Guildenstern Are Dead

Set This House on Fire

The Story of Edgar Sawtelle

Tess of the D'Urbervilles

Things Fall Apart

A Thousand Acres

A Thousand Splendid Suns

To Kill a Mockingbird

Uncle Tom's Cabin

The Underground Railroad

IF YOU FINISH BEFORE TIME IS CALLED, CHECK YOUR WORK ON THIS
SECTION ONLY. DO NOT WORK ON ANY OTHER SECTION IN THE TEST.

Answer Key

Section I: Multiple-Choice Questions

First Prose Passage	First Poem	Second Poem	Second Prose Passage	Third Poem
1. A	12. B	23. D	35. C	47. C
2. D	13. C	24. D	36. E	48. A
3. D	14. E	25. A	37. E	49. C
4. B	15. E	26. E	38. B	50. E
5. E	16. D	27. B	39. D	51. B
6. A	17. C	28. C	40. A	52. D
7. C	18. E	29. E	41. C	53. E
8. B	19. D	30. C	42. A	54. B
9. C	20. A	31. A	43. B	55. A
10. E	21. E	32. C	44. D	
11. E	22. C	33. B	45. E	
		34. D	46. C	

Answers and Explanations

Section I: Multiple-Choice Questions

First Prose Passage

The passage for these questions comes from The God of Small Things, *written by Arundhati Roy in 1997. The action takes place in a region in the southwest of India.*

1. **A.** The first few sentences of the passage establish that May is a long, hot, brooding, and humid month, which implies a lethargic and sluggish mood. The short subject-verb sentences emphasize the intensity of this listlessness, choice A, as if one does not even have enough energy to add an article or any modifiers to the sentence. Choice B is inaccurate because the two short sentences do not speed up the pace of the overall narrative in any substantial way; they are surrounded by longer sentences that slow the narrative. Choice C misinterprets the text. The ripening of the fruit foreshadows the upcoming rapid vegetation growth; it does not contradict the effects of the upcoming monsoon. Choice D is unreasonable; the effect of two truncated sentences cannot distract attention from the imagery in either a previous sentence (the crows) or a following sentence (the bluebottles). Choice E incorrectly claims the vegetation is deteriorating; instead, it is ripening and bursting. It will deteriorate in the future after it is overripe.

2. **D.** The second paragraph, only one isolated sentence, contains the alliterative phrase "suffused with sloth and sullen expectation." One cannot pronounce this phrase quickly; its slow pace increases the sluggishness of the first paragraph, choice D. The alliteration is not intended to create suspense (A). We know the monsoon will come; we just do not know exactly when it will arrive. Choice B makes no sense; it's hard to imagine how alliteration could ever minimize imagery. Choice C may initially seem inviting because the second paragraph does describe the night, and since the entire paragraph is one sentence it might make sense that it separates something from the rest of the narration. However, this response does not address this question about alliteration; it only mentions the night, which is not part of the alliterative phrase. Choice E might appeal to those who generically associate any alliterative "s" sounds with slithering or hissing snakes. That may sometimes be the case, but not in this passage. While a snake does appear in the fourth paragraph, the snake is simply wrapped around a "glistening stone" and not connected to the alliteration in the second paragraph.

349

3. D. In the third paragraph, the narrator describes the effects of the monsoon, one of which is that "Boundaries blur as tapioca fences take root and bloom." This visual fuzziness blurs the shapes of different plants together as if they were one. Ironically, the narrator later claims that "Boundaries . . . have appeared" between Rahel and Estha, thus separating them into individual entities, choice D. On the other hand, the speed with which plants grow during the monsoon is not ironic (A). Choice B is quite an unreasonable stretch; the two "b" sounds are not connected to the action, which deals with a tapioca fence forming roots. Choice C incorrectly asserts that the physical location originally had no boundaries in the first place, a notion that cannot be accurate. The image of boundaries in this part of the passage deals with the visual distinction between plants and trees; it does not deal with anything like boundaries between countries. Choice E is inaccurate for two reasons: It contradicts the passage, and it does not address the question about irony.

4. B. The imagery in the third paragraph visualizes growth in the natural habitat during the monsoon: "The countryside turns an immodest green," boundaries between plants disappear with growth, brick walls take on a green hue, "vines snake up electric poles," and wild creepers overflow. Nature is abundant. The fourth paragraph, however, does not present such visually pleasing images. The rain is now described as "slanting silver ropes" that plow the earth "like gunfire" as it slams down. The old house appears to pull its roof "over its ears like a low hat." The soft, moss-covered walls "bulged a little with dampness that seeped up from the ground." The garden is now "wild, overgrown." The pond is "scummy," the driveway is "leaf-strewn," and the mongoose is "drenched." The imagery has none of the vibrancy of the third paragraph. Therefore, choice B is correct. Choice A is simply wrong; the third paragraph does not limit itself to the beginning of the monsoon, nor does the fourth describe its end. Choice C incorrectly claims that the fourth paragraph only employs auditory imagery, but it also contains many examples of visual imagery. Choice D also falls apart in its description of the fourth paragraph, which does not focus more on humanity; it has ample imagery of the house, the walls, the garden, the snake, bullfrogs, and a mongoose, while it only mentions humanity once, in Rahel's arrival at the house. Choice E is tricky to some degree, but ultimately it is not accurate because it does not answer the question. It is true that the third paragraph is written in the present tense and describes the "three months of wind and water," while the fourth paragraph is written in the past tense. However, the question asks about the difference in the *imagery* of the two paragraphs, and the verb tense, past or present, does not address the imagery.

5. E. The "skyblue Plymouth with chrome tailfins" appears quite incongruous with the description of the green vegetation and dilapidated house, yet we also find that it "was still parked outside," which implies it has been there some time; apparently it has been a stable detail in the family, choice E. Most of the other answer choices have no evidence at all in the passage; we do not have any hint if the family wants to display its economic status (A), nor do we know if the car no longer runs (B), or if the family is modern (C). Choice D, claiming that the Plymouth suggests a commitment to American culture, is a huge stretch because the fact that the car is still parked in the yard does not demonstrate a commitment; it is just one of the many details of the scene.

6. A. It appears Rahel and Baby Kochamma are estranged, choice A; the passage informs us Rahel had come to the old house to see her brother, not her elderly grandaunt, and "Neither niece nor baby grandaunt labored under any illusions on that account." It is clear that these two do not care for each other, so it is unreasonable to think they will enjoy a family reunion (B). Also, since we do not know the cause of their estrangement, we cannot assume with any confidence that they became bitter enemies (C); this is too strong of a claim without any textual evidence. Choice D is too strong; we can reasonably assume that the two women are not close, but to claim that they hardly endure each other is not substantiated in the passage. Choice E is on equally thin ice; we simply do not know to what extent they may be disillusioned about familial relationships in general.

7. C. The paragraph in question explains how the twins "thought of themselves together as Me, and separately, individually, as We or Us. As though they were a rare breed of Siamese twins, physically separate, but with joint identities." These ideas emphasize that both of the twins envisioned themselves as an extension of the other, choice C. They do not, as yet, have separate identities. However, the paragraph has no suggestion that they struggle to find their own identity (A). Choice B is too strong because of the word "indefinitely"; a boundless time period is not suggested in this paragraph or in the passage. Choice D incorrectly uses the absolute term "all" to claim that twins share intertwined thoughts; we have no proof of that idea, and the paragraph limits its comments to Rahel and Estha only. Choice E posits yet another idea that sounds nice and that might be accurate in the real world; it's true that children are well-served when they can relate to someone, but that concept is not supported in this paragraph.

8. **B.** Children have a propensity to see the world in hyperbolic terms, and in this paragraph the twins are young enough to think that their current reality will last forever; capitalizing the words "Beginnings . . . Ends . . . Everything . . . [and] Forever" emphasizes this exaggerated way in which children view the world, choice B. Choice A is too vague to be the best choice; capitalizing words does not really change their substance, their actual meaning. Choice C contradicts the quotation. While children may naturally have a limited view of the world, this quotation claims the opposite; it states that the twins see the world as unending, as forever. Choice D is inaccurate because the effect of the quotation is not one of enlarging the twins' awareness; they already have hyperbolic awareness and the capitalization does not make it bigger. Choice E contradicts the passage and does not logically address the question; the effect of capitalization does not reduce their individual identities.

9. **C.** The third-person narrator in this excerpt initially remains in the distance, describing the scene without any particular slant, until the narration focuses in on Rahel's thoughts, choice C. We discover that years have passed as Rahel arrives at the old house and she recalls memories of her childhood; she also reveals that now she and Estha are grown and they have separate identities. Choice A is too limited; the point of view in the passage covers much more than just the monsoon. It's also an exaggeration to claim that the vivid description at the beginning of the passage "dwells on minutiae." Choice B is unreasonable; in this passage, the point of view helps readers begin to understand the character's motives; it does not diminish the importance of that. Choice D doesn't address the *effect* of the point of view. The passage does describe the atmosphere of the location before and during the monsoon and then introduces Rahel, but these details do not address the effect of the third-person point of view; they simply restate the passage's progression. Choice E, that the point of view establishes the importance of family, has no strong evidence in the passage. We can reasonably infer that Estha is the reason Rahel has returned to the old house, but other than that, we do not know how important family ties are to her.

10. **E.** The narrative sequence jumps around in time, from present to past, and then back to present. Because a large portion of the plot deals with Rahel's memories, this back-and-forth plot line effectively echoes the disjointed process of memory as children grow up, choice E. Choice A is not really evident in the passage; we do see that Rahel has aged and matured, just as anyone would, but that alone does not address the effect of the nonlinear plot. Choice B is unreasonable; we have no foreshadowing of any conflict the twins must face. Choice C is incorrect; the narration does not jump in and out of Rahel's mind. Rather, once the narration has explored her mind, it moves on, without returning to her thoughts. Choice D makes no sense; a plot deals with action, the sequence of events in a story; plot does not explore abstract ideas.

11. **E.** By the end of the passage, Rahel and Estha indeed have separate identities, choice E; in fact, "Their lives have a size and a shape now. Estha has his and Rahel hers." They now have "Edges, Borders, Boundaries . . . on their separate horizons." Choice A is too much of an absolute and is likely a contradiction; we do not know what Rahel and Estha still have in common at this point in their lives, but we do know that they will always share the commonality of being twins. Choice B misreads the text, which does not imply the twins will die. It simply states that they are the same age that their mother was when she died; they may be "a viable die-able age," but that does not imply an inevitable early death. Choice C goes too far; we have no evidence whether or not the twins' shared memories are accurate. Choice D is also too much of a stretch; the passage offers no information about the twins gaining an understanding about their role within the family.

First Poem

The poem for these questions, commonly called "Nuns Fret Not at Their Convent's Narrow Room," was written by William Wordsworth in 1806.

12. **B.** In the second line, the subject "hermits" is immediately followed by its verb "are contented," and in line 3, the same verb is understood: "students [are contented] with their pensive citadels," choice B. Choice A is incorrect because the subject "nuns" is immediately followed by its verb, "fret." Both "maids" (C) and "the weaver" (D) have the same verb, "sit," in line 5. The verb for the subject "bees" (E) is "will murmur" in line 7.

13. C. The word "citadel" usually refers to a strong fortress, such as a castle, that can be a place of safety; in the poem, the students are in a "pensive citadel" that serves as a stronghold for higher education, the university room in which they study, choice C. Choice A incorrectly uses the word "melancholy," perhaps assuming that test-takers might think it a synonym for pensive; instead, pensive refers to someone who is meditative and thoughtful. Choice B confuses the students' citadel with a religious monastery. Choice D makes no sense; a citadel can be another word for a fortress, but the students in this poem are hardly commanding. A bastion (E) is a synonym for a fortress or citadel, but the poem gives no indication that the students are unhappy; the word "pensive" has no such connotations.

14. E. Be sure to read this question carefully; it asks for the *most pervasive* idea in the first half of the poem, which means you must prioritize the answer choices. Indeed, all of the possible answer choices are in the poem, but the choice that is the most universal is the idea that the majority of people are content with their lot in life, choice E. This encompasses all of the specifics, such as nuns not fretting (A), hermits being satisfied (B), students being pensive (C), and maids being happy (D).

15. E. In this question, be sure to look for the one answer choice that does NOT have any connection to confinement. Once you arrive at the last answer choice, "Furness-fells" should jump out as the right answer, the correct exception. In the poem, "Furness-fells," choice E, merely refers to a mountainous area in the Lake District; it is not related in any way to the idea of the prison in line 8. All of the other answer choices are listed in the poem, and they could, indeed, be trapped in a prison of their own making, including nuns (A), maids (B), weavers (C), and even bees (D).

16. D. The paradoxical idea, choice D, that the prison we doom ourselves into is, in reality, not a prison at all, is a seemingly self-contradictory idea with some truth in it. When you extend it to the poem's meaning, it becomes a nifty conceit, claiming that poets can find a sort of artistic freedom within a self-imposed discipline, writing sonnets. The poem definitely has no examples of dissonance (A), which is a juxtaposition of jarring sounds that clash with each other. Ambiguity (B), the vagueness or uncertainty produced from words with multiple meanings, is also not evidenced in the poem; the words in the quotation are certain and unequivocal. The idea of caesura (C) cannot apply; it refers to a natural break in a line of poetry, usually achieved with a separation between phrases, but lines 8–9 have enjambment, not caesura. This is not an example of euphemism (E), which is the device of substituting a more agreeable term for something unpleasant. You can find definitions and examples of these terms in Chapter 5.

17. C. The diction in this poem is quite interesting. Notice how the speaker uses positive connotations when describing the imprisoned people in the first lines: They are "contented," "pensive," "blithe and happy." Even the bees have positive descriptions; they "soar for bloom" in beautiful locations and "murmur by the hour in foxglove bells." However, in the second half of the poem, the speaker switches to negative connotations, such as "bound," "scanty," "weight," and "brief solace." It becomes ironic when those imprisoned are described positively, while the poet and sonnet are described negatively, choice C. The poem does not have an abundance of descriptive adjectives, which makes choice A wrong. Additionally, the poem does not contain unusual contrasts (B); in fact, it does not include contrasts at all. Choice D might seem viable for a moment, but the different forms of prisons that the speaker describes do not make the diction particularly notable. Be sure you read the question carefully before you choose the best answer. Choice E can be eliminated because the poem contains no unusual prepositional phrases; each one is quite traditional, beginning with the preposition and ending a few words later with the object of the preposition. See, for example, "with their cells," "at the wheel," "for bloom," and "of ground," among others.

18. E. The phrase "scanty plot of ground" serves as a metaphor, choice E, for the limitations of the sonnet form; it may offer something to work with, some perhaps-fertile ground, but it is scarce and slight. The sonnet form metaphorically offers the poet a plot of ground to cultivate into a poem, but it's constrained and it's not much ground to work with. The phrase is not a simile (A) because no comparison is made; the metaphor is a complete substitution. An apostrophe (B) occurs when the speaker directly addresses someone or something that is not present; this poem has no such device. Choice C, juxtaposition, makes no sense because the phrase does not associate or contrast ideas. It is not an example of an oxymoron (D) because nothing is contradictory in the phrase.

19. D. The speaker found "brief solace" in writing sonnets, which are symbolically located in the metaphorical "scanty plot of ground," choice D. Choice A is incorrect because the highest peak of Furness-fells is the location bees might fly to; the speaker does not indicate he has visited the spot. Choice B makes no sense; the speaker does not find solace in the mental prison. Similarly, the speaker finds no solace in the fact that the prison isn't really a prison at all (C); rather, he found solace from writing sonnets. Choice E incorrectly attributes the phrase "too much liberty" to the speaker, when he instead uses it to refer to others who have felt the weight of too much freedom. Yes, he might have felt that emotion in the past, but not after writing sonnets.

20. **A.** Remember that in this question you are looking for the response that does NOT relate to the speaker's complex relationship with writing a sonnet. Choice A does not relate because the line describes bees as they feed on foxglove bells. Choice B does relate to the speaker's relationship because it connects him to others who have felt imprisoned; he breaks from it by writing sonnets. The phrase "in sundry moods" (C) refers to the conditions under which the speaker wrote sonnets. A "pastime" (D) refers to something one does for a diversion, for entertainment, and it fits the speaker's sonnet writing. The "scanty plot of ground" (E) refers to the sonnet form itself.

21. **E.** It is ironic that the speaker gives such high praise to the sonnet, even extolling the limitations of the form, claiming that "no prison is" found in the format, yet in spite of this, he still veers from the traditional sonnet formula, choice E. The irony is that in this sonnet, the volta, or shift, begins in line 8 and finishes in line 9, while usually line 8 is end-stopped and line 9 begins the volta. You should at least be aware that the traditional Italian (or Petrarchan) sonnet sets up the idea (or problem) in the first eight lines and resolves it in the final six lines. (The English or Shakespearean sonnet sets up the idea in the first twelve lines and resolves it in the final two.) The speaker also adds one other variant; line 13 has 11 syllables, not 10. It is not ironic that the speaker describes his writing of sonnets to be a pastime (A); after all, he did find solace in the writing. Choice B represents a misread of the poem. The speaker did not find endless comfort; he found only "brief solace." Choice C makes no sense; the speaker suggests that those souls (poets) who feel too much liberty should try writing the constrained sonnet; this idea does not address irony. Also, the fact that poets find the sonnet form a good exercise in restraint (D) is not ironic; the speaker's praise for the sonnet form includes the idea that this exercise is helpful to poets. If this question is difficult for you, remember to use your elimination techniques to dismiss inaccurate choices and improve your odds.

22. **C.** The speaker's argument may be open to objection or counterarguments because it is based entirely on unsubstantiated assumptions, choice C; every one of the speaker's specific examples that begin the poem can be called into question. Who knows whether or not nuns fret at their confinement? Hermits may not necessarily be happy in their isolation; students may become bored with their studies; maids and weavers are not necessarily happy and blithe as they work and toil. There is no evidence that any iota of this is actually true. Choice A mistakenly claims that the speaker posits a false dilemma, the feeling of being imprisoned or not, but this is not the case. Also, the speaker's argument is not based on anecdotal evidence (B); he divulges only his own experience of writing sonnets, but he offers no anecdotes about the experiences of others. The poem does not employ circular logic (D), in which an argument essentially restates its original assumption as if it is a conclusion, when in reality, it is just repetition. The poem does not assert a causal relationship, nor does it consider correlation (E); it does not address cause-and-effect logic at all.

Second Poem

The poem for these questions comes from "The Prologue" by Anne Bradstreet. The poem first appeared in 1650 in a British publication of her works, The Tenth Muse Lately Sprung Up in America. Bradstreet was the first poet from England's North American colonies to be published.

23. **D.** When the speaker refers to her "Pen," she provides an example of metonymy, choice D, a figure of speech in which a part stands in for the whole; thus, "my mean Pen" actually refers to her poetry, not just her specific writing utensil. Also, by calling it "mean," the speaker implies that her poetry is just too humble; it is inadequate to the task of composing works about such important historical events. She'll leave that task to the men. The reference to her pen is not a metaphor (A), nor does it refer to her anger in the poem. Choice B, labeling "my mean Pen" as personification, may seem plausible if one thinks of "mean" as a human attribute, such as being unkind; however, in this context the word is not intended to refer to any human trait. Additionally, the second idea in this answer that brings up the midpoint between two extremes

seems to have the mathematical definition of mean in mind, something akin to the average; but that is irrelevant to this poem. Choice C is inaccurate because the pen is not an analogy, nor is the figure of speech a reference to all women's roles in society. You can eliminate choice E because of the incorrect word "antithesis," which refers to a rhetorical device that uses parallel grammatical structures that seemingly contradict one another.

24. D. In the first stanza, the speaker presents a list of "important" subjects that she feels are appropriate for men's poetry, such as chronicling wars, great leaders, cities, and commonwealths. However, she herself declines to write about such subjects, claiming her pen (her poetry) is not up to the task and she will not "dim" the worth of what other (male) poets write of great historical events, choice D. You can immediately identify choice A as incorrect because of the word "enthusiastic," which totally contradicts the speaker's attitude. She may indeed want to make her mark in the world of poetry, but not by writing about the subjects in lines 1–2. Similarly, choice B is inaccurate because of the word "fervent," which is synonymous with enthusiastic; the speaker is not keen on writing about the subjects that men typically explore. Choice C begins with promise, although the word "hesitant" is too mild to describe the speaker's position; the answer goes on to contradict the poem; she does not change her mind about this. Choice E begins by correctly stating that she refuses, but her reason is not because historians have already written about such events; it is because she does not think her efforts would be judged as appropriate.

25. A. This question requires that you pinpoint what the speaker does NOT include in the discussion of Bartas; be sure to read the question carefully. Choice A is the correct exception, because in the second stanza, while the speaker may be jealous of Bartas' talent, she never vows to exceed his fame; rather, she vows to write according to her own skill, which she describes as "simple." All of the other answer choices definitely do appear in the second stanza; she does "read o'er" the famous French poet's "sugar'd lines" with "wond'ring eyes and envious heart" (B). Choice C is also evident; the muses have given Bartas an "over-fluent store" of talent. Choice D is also in this stanza; she gives Bartas credit when she claims "A Bartas can do what a Bartas will." Choice E is evidenced in the final line of the stanza, as she states she will write simply, according to her own skill.

26. E. Assonance involves the close placement of similar vowel sounds. Notice that although the words in line 17 are short, you can hear the assonance of the open, round vowel sounds with the many "a" sounds: "And this to mend, alas, no Art is able." It also has consonance with its multiple "s" sounds; these two devices combine to create a slow, soothing softness. Therefore, choice E is correct. Choice A, allegory, is incorrect; an allegory describes a type of work that uses characters to represent an abstract idea; it cannot be found in any single line of poetry. The poem uses many allusions (B) such as referring to Bartas, the muses, and Calliope, but the line in this question does not do so. An aphorism (C) is a brief statement that articulates a universal truth, which this line does not do. Apostrophe (D) is the technique of speaking to someone or something that is not present, and this also fails to describe the line in question.

27. B. In the fifth stanza, the speaker angrily rebuffs her critics, choice B, those men who condescendingly think she should only be doing womanly work with a needle in her hand instead of a pen, and who think that, if she ever possibly produced any good poetry, she must have done so by chance or theft. Choice A is incorrect because the speaker never extols or praises her own poetry; rather, she maintains a humble opinion of her own work throughout the poem. Choice C is misplaced; she does commend the virtues of a "fluent sweet-tongued Greek," which is an allusion to Demosthenes, the Greek who overcame a lisp and became a famous orator, but that is in the fourth stanza, not the fifth. Likewise, the line "A weak or wounded brain admits no cure" (D) is also in the fourth stanza; it refers to the idea that she's not entirely confident that art alone can fix her problem. Choice E contradicts her point; she refuses to accept that she should be relegated to the menial task of sewing something by hand instead of writing poetry.

28. C. Within the context of the last stanza, when the speaker claims "I ask no Bays," she is indicating that she has no desire for high acclaim such as a laurel bay wreath, the traditional award for the most accomplished (male) poets. She is trying to diminish any perceived threat that male poets may feel from this female poet, choice C, particularly by stating she would prefer a wreath made of thyme or parsley, herbs women traditionally use in the kitchen. Choice A is misguided and a bit deceptive; when you consider the context of the line within the whole stanza, you'll realize that she is trying to appease those men who might feel threatened by her poetry; it is too simplistic, too limited to suggest that a garden herb wreath would be more appropriate for her simply because she is a woman. Choice B goes astray thinking that "bays" is a metaphor in the first place, and then really goes off the deep end suggesting that she is referring to a body of water. Choice D likewise misses the mark completely, thinking that the noun "bays" refers to the verb meaning to bark or woof. Choice E is nearly as ludicrous, thinking she is referring to a bay window; this is a complete misread of the line in particular and of the poem in general. If you are focused, you should be able to eliminate choices B, D, and E very quickly!

29. **E.** Notice that the question asks you to prioritize which quotation *most* defends female creativity and *most* demands respect. In the last line of the seventh stanza, the speaker pleads with men to "Yet grant some small acknowledgement of ours" after she already defers that they have "Preeminence in all." The word "ours" is plural, referring to all female poets, not just herself, and the imperative verb "grant" is a demand for respect. Therefore, choice E is correct. Choice A seems to defend her personal poetic skill, calling it "simple," but it does not allude to all female poets, nor does it demand respect. Choice B refers to the way the speaker chastises her muse; it is irrelevant to this question. Choice C is a line in the poem with convoluted syntax, but it basically claims that her male critics, whether real or imaginary, have nothing but scorn for the idea of her writing poetry; it does not answer the question. Choice D simply states that any worthy poetry she may write won't advance, won't improve, men's opinions of her, since they will think she stole the verse or wrote it by pure luck.

30. **C.** The fifth stanza, choice C, stands out for its vitriolic tone; it angrily attacks those condescending men who feel women should only perform traditional women's work, like sewing, and it intimates that those critics are shortsighted in thinking she cannot ever write respectable poetry. The remaining stanzas are not nearly as angry in their tone. Consider what the other stanzas discuss: The first stanza (A) describes her admission that she is not worthy of writing about significant historical events. The third stanza (B) addresses having reasonable expectations for any person's talent. The seventh stanza (D) entreats men to acknowledge that women do have at least some degree of ability. The eighth stanza (E) suggests that her poetry will not compete with men's, but rather, will help theirs to shine more.

31. **A.** In its current usage, the word "obnoxious" usually refers to someone who is disgusting and repellant, but within the context of this poem it has a more archaic meaning; the speaker is suggesting that she is vulnerable and exposed, choice A, to those who, with carping tongues, criticize her desire to write poetry and contemptuously cast scorn "on female wits." It makes perfect sense that she is sensitive and susceptible to their criticisms. But she is not insufferable or unspeakable to them (B), nor is she defenseless (C) since she does defend herself, trying to prove that she is not as frail as they think. The adjectives "unbearable" and "intolerable" (D) fit the modern connotation of one who is obnoxious, but they do not apply to her intended meaning in this stanza. She may feel somewhat unprotected (E), but she is not feeble; she strongly defends her right to compose poetry.

32. **C.** For this question, you must identify the quotation that does NOT demonstrate her modesty. Choice C fits because it decries those who disparage her writing poetry, intimating that she should put a needle in her hand instead of a pen. Choice A states that the speaker modestly feels it is male poets and historians who would be better for setting forth the stories of important historical events. Choice B further demonstrates the speaker's modesty as she describes her poetry and skills as "simple." Choice D also shows a degree of unpretentiousness when she claims that women should be allowed to be what they are. Choice E also shows restraint as she only hopes for wreaths made of thyme or parsley, not the ceremonial laurel bays given to great male poets.

33. **B.** In the seventh stanza, the speaker personally addresses men, choice B, conceding that they are preeminent in all things and that women have to admit that "Men can do best." This effectively undermines any intimidation that some men may feel from her writing. Choice A is partially correct; the pronoun "yours" does shift the intended audience, but the shift is not even remotely an appeal for mercy. Choice C is mistaken in thinking the pronoun shift redirects the focus from herself to others; it merely speaks to a specific audience, and also it is not an effort to gain humility. Choice D is incorrect due to the use of the word "mimicking." The speaker is not trying to imitate men whatsoever, and she will not challenge men's attitude of self-importance, whether or not she agrees with it. Choice E contradicts the speaker's position in the seventh stanza; she does not rebut or dispute men's claim of superiority; rather, she reaffirms it.

34. **D.** The speaker's attitude throughout the poem is predominantly one of humility about her own poetic abilities. She insists that male poets are better at composing poems about important historical events; she

refers to her own skills as "simple"; she laments that men like Bartas were granted more talent than she has; she grants men "Preeminence in all." However, in an ironic twist, she writes so well! Notice that the poem is polished and eloquent: Its form and meter are perfect; it incorporates many effective poetic devices such as assonance, consonance, allusion, and metaphor; it reveals the speaker to be well educated and highly skilled. The speaker deserves to be judged by the same standards as male poets, but she ironically asks not to be. Therefore, choice D is correct. Choice A, the idea that she is deferential to male poets, is true, but it is not ironic; it is unfortunate and sad that she feels she must do so. Choice B contradicts the poem entirely; she never intimidates anyone from writing. Do not be fooled by choice C; it may be argued that the speaker possibly reinforces traditional attitudes toward women, but that fact is not ironic; like choice A, it is perhaps just sad. The idea in choice E is not substantiated in the last stanza; her attitude at the end is entirely consistent with her position throughout the poem, and she does not modify or change it.

Second Prose Passage

The passage for these questions comes from the short story "Monkey Nuts" written by D. H. Lawrence in 1919.

35. **C.** If *at first* Joe thought the job O.K, it is most reasonable to infer that he might alter his opinion at a later time. A young soldier's first impression about fieldwork after being in the war can indeed change. The passage offers no evidence that Albert will agree with Joe's opinion (A), either at the present or in the future. It is too much of a stretch to infer that Miss Stokes will make the job more tolerable (B); after all, we haven't met her yet and the job is already acceptable. We have no reason to believe it will become even more so. Also, since Miss Stokes has not been introduced at the beginning of the passage, it is unreasonable to infer she will come between Joe and Albert (D). Choice E, that the job will become more tedious, has no proof in the passage because Joe likes the job enough as is; it is not tedious.

36. **E.** The mere mention of Flanders, choice E, conjures up horrific images of the huge battles that were fought there in World War I, in which thousands of British servicemen lost their lives; this is certainly not a detail of their current pleasant situation. Now they are housed in an agreeable cottage (A) and the scenery has "red houses . . . dotted among flowering apple trees" (C). Additionally, the two soldiers feel they are in charge of their lives (B), and they are enjoying the sunny weather and easy workload (D).

37. **E.** Read carefully between the lines to understand Albert's character; he is not necessarily the happy-go-lucky man he initially appears to be, choice E. For example, he only "seemed" to have one goal in life, having fun; additionally, when he is restful, in repose, his face becomes a little withered and old. Furthermore, he is described as mischievous, but that rascally behavior is merely a ploy to dodge his ennui, his boredom, his tedium. Albert's description does not suggest that he is duplicitous (A); instead, he appears quite steady and trustworthy and is a good pal to Joe. The passage offers no evidence of Albert's intuitions or if he follows them (B). While Albert appears to be a good man, "steady" and "decent," we do not know the extent to which he is actually principled or a man of integrity (C). Choice D is questionable because its wording is too strong. Since we only know that he "*seemed* to think his one aim in life was to be full of fun," we cannot necessarily conclude that he values entertainment over duty. His being in the military implies that he did value doing his duty.

38. **B.** Joe is described as being pleasant looking, "Careful about his appearance," and that he shaves every day. Albert, on the other hand, is described as shrewd-looking and he claims that if he shaved every day he'd have no face left at all. Therefore, choice B is correct. The remaining answer choices all contradict the passage's description of Joe. He is 23 and Albert is 40, so he is not older (A). He is "tallish," so we have no indication that he is smaller than Albert (C). Joe is a "quiet youth," the opposite of being garrulous or chatty and effusive (D). Joe is of a "slightly better class than his corporal," not of a lower class (E).

39. **D.** Even though the war is raging in Europe, the local village seems to be thriving, choice D. We know the village has "plenty of life in the little goods-yard" with three youths serving as porters, a "continual come and go of farm wagons bringing hay," other wagons that deliver timber, and coal carts. The stationmaster's children play while the chickens walk about the yard, and he, "getting too fat," helps his wife hang the laundry. It's quite a bustling scene. Choice A is unreasonable; the village seems quite full of activity, not lethargy, and the weather is sunny. Choice B contradicts the atmosphere in the passage; we see nothing like the deprivation usually associated with wartime rationing. Choice C, that the neighbors demonstrate congenial social interactions, may seem reasonable until you think about it in more depth. We only have evidence of the stationmaster's family, no other neighbors, and while there is "plenty of life," we do not know how congenial or friendly it is, only that it is not dull, and we have no evidence of any social interactions. Choice E is too exaggerated; although the village is lively, that does not necessarily equate to bourgeoning or enlarging commerce.

40. **A.** Miss Stokes arrives on the scene doing what was then called "men's work," piloting one of the "great boat-shaped wagons" carrying the hay that will be loaded onto the trucks by the soldiers. She is clearly in charge, "drawing to a standstill easily at the head of her two great horses," and she later attends to them. Her appearance is healthy and vigorous, commanding the attention of Albert and Joe, while maintaining control of the conversation about how many "boys" are present to help her unload the hay. Therefore, choice A is correct. All indications point to her helping with the labor, because "She was strong, too, and the work went on . . . easily," which contradicts choice B. Choice C simply has not enough proof in the passage to be the best response; she does tend to her horses, but that does not imply she cares more for them than the soldiers. Choice D has no evidence in the passage whatsoever; we have no indication of her social status. Choice E is only partially correct; Miss Stokes is indeed hearty and robust, but she treats the men with the bare minimum of respect.

41. **C.** Notice the verbal sparring between Albert and Miss Stokes upon her arrival. The two soldiers are away from the war front, working in a countryside field when an attractive girl arrives with a wagonload of hay for them to unload. Albert jokes that "' . . . that's the waggoner for us, boys,'" even though only two men are present. She retorts, "'Which boys do you mean?'" as if his exaggeration of having multiple "boys" under his command is not amusing, choice C. Choice A is inaccurate because the passage gives no impression of what Miss Stokes expected at all; it is possible she may have wished for more help, but we cannot say she expected it. Choice B contradicts the passage; Miss Stokes shows no enthusiasm at meeting the soldiers and no hope for more to show up. The passage contains no hint that Miss Stokes is ever confused by Albert's comment (D). Choice E is too strong with the word "humiliate." The passage does not imply she intends to humiliate the men by calling them "boys," and they appear to take no offense.

42. **A.** Albert's initial comments to Miss Stokes are easy-going and mildly teasing, choice A. When she asks which boys he has in mind for the job, he replies "'We are the pick of the bunch,'" and tells Joe, loudly enough to be heard, "'Don't you let on that my name's Albert,'" clearly wanting her to know his name. She does not respond in kind and rebuffs him. Albert is definitely not deferential or submissive (B), and he announces "'I'm the corporal.'" He does not really try to be in charge of the operation (C), but simply muffs the initial meeting. Albert may be in the military as a corporal, but his demeanor is far from professional in this meeting (D). He is informal, even flirtatious. Albert's manner with Miss Stokes is hardly immodest or boastful (E).

43. **B.** While Albert toys with Miss Stokes in a playful way, she responds coolly, unimpressed with his playfulness, choice B. She is definitely not discomfited and abashed (A); she stands up for herself immediately, as if she is establishing her territory. The passage offers no evidence that she is surprised at their initial meeting (C), but one might describe her as pleased with Joe by the end of the passage, noting that "She liked him." In choice D, the adjective "enthralled" is too strong, but the word "intrigued" could apply to her feelings about Joe. Choice E is incorrect in that if anyone is flirty, it is Albert, not Miss Stokes, and she is not exactly manipulative.

44. **D.** When the narrator only refers to Miss Stokes as "she" in every sentence of the paragraph that describes her, it has the effect of dropping her identity and diminishing her individuality, choice D; she no longer has a name but is a mere entity. Choice A is too bland; Miss Stokes already has enough personality to be more than a random villager, although we do not yet know her origin. Choice B is unreasonable and contradicts the passage; Miss Stokes has already proven her prowess at controlling the wagon. Choice C is irrelevant; the repetition of "she" has nothing to do with any fascination Albert may have with her. Choice E is not evidenced in the paragraph in question; although she does watch Joe surreptitiously in the last paragraph, she does not do so in this one.

45. **E.** Be careful to focus on the word "NOT" in the question and remember that you are looking for the one answer choice that is unreasonable regarding Albert's observing the world. Notice how his behavior is presented. The three characters begin moving the hay, "leisurely and easily," when Albert stops *as usual* to look around." Then he tells them not to hurry and he surveys the world from the truck. Next, we are informed "That was one of his great and absorbing occupations: to stand and look out on things in general," as if it is his job to merely observe. It does reasonably follow, therefore, that he likes to see the big picture (A) and that such behavior is his modus operandi, his normal behavior (B). It is also reasonable to infer that his observational skills are superior to Joe's (C) because Joe looked around but "could not become blankly absorbed, as Albert could." Because he does this to stop for a moment and take a break from their work, it is indeed a ruse to avoid labor (D). However, choice E is the one unreasonable implication, stating as an absolute that he and Joe would not have survived the war without his observing, but we cannot jump to that conclusion, as we know nothing of their wartime experiences.

46. **C.** In the last paragraph, Miss Stokes watches the two men from under her hat brim. She has seen many soldiers like Albert and many like Joe, but notice that she decides she likes Joe when he senses her gaze and meets her eyes; this causes him to falter, turning again "as if he were going to fall off the truck." This moment brings a flush to her cheeks as she realizes she likes him. His vulnerability is something she must find attractive, choice C. The passage does not suggest that the reason she likes Joe is his difference from Albert (A), nor the fact that he is quiet and young (B). These traits do not come into play when she realizes her attraction to him. The fact that she has seen many like him before (D) does not connect with her suddenly liking him; if he reminds her of many others, why did she not like them, too? Joe does not have a loose attitude (E); this idea contradicts his quiet, thoughtful manner.

Third Poem

The poem for these questions comes from "Harvest Song," which was written by the African-American poet Jean Toomer and published in 1923.

47. **C.** The speaker states that he "crack[ed] a grain between my teeth," implying that he will taste the flavor of the grain; however, the remainder of the line contradicts this idea as he laments, "I do not taste it." The irony is that he cannot even taste the flavor of the grain he has just harvested; he cannot share the bounty. His gustatory sense is denied, choice C. Choice A is irrelevant; it may be accurate to state that the imagery of the grain and the speaker's thoughts are both simplistic, but that does necessarily make them ironic. Thus, this choice does not answer the question. Choice B is true to the facts of the poem, but the idea that he worked all day does not equate to irony. Choice D is unreasonable; it reads too much into the line "My throat is dry," and it erroneously concludes that he cannot swallow. The poem offers no support for this conclusion, and it is not ironic. Choice E has no evidence in the poem; we simply do not know whether or not other harvesters enjoy the fruits of their labor.

48. **A.** The speaker's hunger represents his existential emptiness of spirit and his lack of sensation, a hunger for something that does not physically exist and which cannot be directly sensed. But when he states that "All my oats are cradled," choice A, he is referring to the actual crop of oats that he has harvested, not to his own hunger. On the other hand, all of the other answer choices refer to the speaker's hunger in one way or another. Choice B clarifies that he cannot taste, and therefore he gets no satisfaction from the grain he has "crack[ed] between [his] teeth." Choice C acknowledges that he is a "blind man who stares," but the fact that he cannot see the other harvesters he seeks also tends to reinforce the idea of his loneliness and existential hunger. Choice D likewise corresponds to the implied meaning of hunger as it describes his ears that are so caked with dust that he becomes a deaf man. Choice E connects to his unachievable hunger in that he acknowledges "It would be good to hear their songs," but he cannot; "their voices deafened me."

49. **C.** The speaker's dominant use of short, declarative, simple sentences ultimately serves to condense, clarify, and crystalize the speaker's thoughts and actions, choice C: His oats are cradled; he hungers; he cannot taste; his throat is dry; he fears calling out; he cracks a grain; he is a reaper; his pain is sweet. Since the speaker is most often the subject in these abundant simple subject-predicate sentence patterns, the verbs that follow help to illuminate and clarify his persona. Choice A is wrong because it includes the word "minimizing," which inaccurately describes the effect of the simple sentences. Choice B is completely off base; all of the sentences in the poem point in the same direction; the simple sentences do not contradict the complex ones. Choice D makes little sense; the simple sentences do not establish that the speaker had few needs; rather, it appears that he has many unstated physical and spiritual needs, and also this answer choice does not address the question of the *purpose* of the simple sentences. Choice E erroneously equates simple sentences with simple work; rather, the reaper's tasks are complex and physically exhausting.

50. **E.** The speaker's tone can best be described as desolate or bleak, choice E, because he yearns for something intangible that he seemingly can never have. His tone is hardly complacent (A), which has positive connotations implying satisfaction. Choice B, offended, is just too strong; the field worker may possibly have sufficient reasons to be offended by his lot in life, but the poem offers no strong support for this far-fetched inference. Choice C is also too strong, too absolute; the speaker does not imply that he is vindictive; some readers may try to infer that he maliciously seeks revenge, but the speaker's words do not support the idea. Choice D offers a contradiction; the term "felicitous" refers to that which is positive, fortunate, even happy. Obviously, this does not fit the speaker's tone.

51. **B.** The speaker's hunger, which is mentioned often, represents something that he does not have and he cannot have: a fulfilling life. Choice B is the most comprehensive and inclusive; all other choices are too specific, too narrow, or too concrete. The speaker does not merely hunger for food and rest (A), nor does he merely hunger for communicating with the other harvesters (C). Choice D incorrectly focuses on only physical nourishment, food, which is too simplistic to describe the poem's complex metaphors. Choice E is likewise too narrow of an answer; the hunger metaphor stands for much more than just the unheard songs of the others.

52. **D.** This question requires you to understand the implication of the title and then explore *why* it is intended to be ironic. Examine each individual word of the title. *Harvest* has positive connotations; it refers to gathering the bounty of the ripened crops; it promises food for the future; it connotes richness and fulfillment. *Song* has an auditory meaning with a suggestion of melody, and when combined with *harvest,* implies a song of joy as one celebrates the completion of a natural cycle of growth. But ironically, neither word fits the actual content of the poem: The harvest has nothing positive to offer this speaker; the poem has no audible song, and the speaker feels no joy, choice D. Even the "eoho" call is parenthetical, not actual. Choice A correctly claims that this call is hardly a song, but this answer fails to address the irony of the word "harvest." Choice B makes little sense, especially for this question that asks about irony. It is true that the harvest is ending (but it is not necessarily "over") and the poem offers no support for the idea that the workers have no more need of song, nor if they ever did. Choice C goes too far out on a limb, connecting the negativity of the speaker's emotions to the quality of the harvest. We do not know how plentiful the harvest actually is, and this answer choice ignores the word "song" in the title. Choice E is unsupported in the poem; we do not know whether or not the other harvesters sing, and also this answer does not address irony.

53. **E.** This question asks about the ironic effect of the imagery as a whole, so begin by considering the overall effect that imagery usually produces: It describes the physical sensations of what one sees, tastes, touches, hears, and smells. The poem offers ample examples of imagery, but ironically, instead of arousing sensory perceptions, the speaker's senses are most often nullified, choice E. Although it is set in the fields during harvest, the poem does not evoke any images of color or nature; none of the predictable or expected lush intensity of a harvest is included. We simply know it is "sun-down," and the "oats are cradled." But the speaker cannot taste the grain; he cannot see the other harvesters; he cannot hear their calls. Even the speaker's being chilled and fatigued is only related as a semantic statement. The speaker can only feel an emptiness, a lack of sensation. Choice A is a reversal of this idea; the poem's imagery does not contradict the speaker's emotions; rather, it is consistent with them. Choice B incorrectly claims that the visual imagery bombards the reader, and it limits the scope to only the visual sense. Choice C completely misunderstands the imagery, claiming that it has the effect of sensory overload. Choice D attempts to make a connection between the imagery and the speaker's anger, but the imagery does not release any anger; rather, the speaker ends with the same feeling of hunger he began with. Additionally, all of these incorrect answer choices do not address *how* the overall effect of the imagery becomes ironic.

54. **B.** The speaker's hunger is much more than a physical hunger for food after a hard day in the fields; it is a symbolic hunger of spirit, a hunger of unfulfilled desires. The negativity of this void in the speaker is enhanced, choice B, by the intensity of the repeated negative connotations in the poem. Notice that the setting is at sun-down, and that the speaker refers to himself not as a harvester, but "a reaper," an image that connotes death. He is "chilled" and "fatigued." He cannot taste; his "throat is dry." His eyes and ears are "caked with dust," making him "a blind man" and "a deaf man." He fears calling out to others. Although the poem offers some isolated words that can have a positive connotation, such as the oats, corn, wheat, and grain, within context they too become negative as the speaker cannot experience them in a positive light. Collectively, they all enhance his intense existential hunger. The idea in choice A, how physically demanding the field work is, does not exist in the poem; the speaker never describes the actual work he has been doing all day. Choice C goes astray by suggesting that the harvest itself has become a dreaded event, another idea that is not supported in the poem. Choice D is incorrect for two reasons: The use of "mocking" is inaccurate, as is the statement that the crops are beautiful, which has no evidence in the poem. Choice E makes no sense, incorrectly trying to connect the negative connotations and the poem's ironic use of imagery.

55. **A.** This poem consistently uses unconventional description, choice A, in that the speaker's account deals more often with what he *cannot* experience than with what he can. The poem describes what the speaker cannot see, what he cannot hear, what he cannot taste, what he cannot feel. Choice B completely contradicts the poem; it presents sparse natural imagery, not lush imagery. Choice C likewise has no evidence in the poem; the negative hole in the speaker's emotion is emphasized, not contradicted. In choice D, the incorrect phrase *balanced narrative* does not accurately describe the technique used in the poem, which is hardly balanced and not a narrative at all. Remember that a narrative tells a story, and this poem is merely a series of statements. Choice E is completely unfounded; the speaker utters no pleas for help, let alone repeats any such pleas.

Section II: Free-Response Questions

Question 1: "Spring" by Edna Vincent Millay

The following scoring guide explicitly explains how to earn up to 6 total points for a poetry analysis essay. Row A (thesis) can earn up to 1 point; Row B (evidence and commentary) can earn up to 4 points, and Row C (sophistication) can earn up to 1 point.

Row A: Thesis (0–1 point)	
Scoring Criteria	
0 points for any of the following: • Having no defendable thesis. • Only restating the prompt in the thesis. • Only summarizing the issue with no claim in the thesis. • Presenting a thesis that does not address the prompt.	**1 point for** • Addressing the prompt with a defendable thesis that presents an interpretation and may establish a line of reasoning.
Decision Rules and Scoring Notes	
Theses that do not earn this point • Only restate the prompt. • Only offer an irrelevant generalized comment about the poem. • Simply describe the poem's features rather than making a defendable claim.	**Theses that do earn this point** • Take a position on the prompt and provide a defendable interpretation of how the poet portrays the speaker's complex attitude toward the coming of spring.
Additional Notes • The thesis may be one or more sentences anywhere in the essay. • A thesis that meets the criteria can be awarded the point whether or not the rest of the response successfully conveys that line of reasoning.	

Row B: Evidence AND Commentary (0–4 points)

Scoring Criteria

0 points for	1 point for	2 points for	3 points for	4 points for
• Simply repeating the thesis (if present). • **OR** restating provided information. • **OR** providing mostly irrelevant and/or incoherent examples.	• Summarizing the poem without reference to a thesis. • **OR** providing vague textual references. • **OR** providing textual references of questionable relevance. • **AND** providing little or no commentary.	• Making relevant textual references (direct quotes or paraphrases). • **AND** providing commentary but repeats, oversimplifies, or misinterprets the cited evidence or text.	• Making relevant textual references (direct quotes or paraphrases). • **AND** providing commentary that explains the logical relationship between textual examples and the thesis; however, commentary is uneven, limited, or incomplete.	• Making relevant textual references (direct quotes or paraphrases). • **AND** providing well-developed commentary that explicitly explains the relationship between the evidence and the thesis.

Decision Rules and Scoring Notes

Typical responses that earn 0 points:	Typical responses that earn 1 point:	Typical responses that earn 2 points:	Typical responses that earn 3 points:	Typical responses that earn 4 points:
• Are unclear or fail to address the prompt. • May present mere opinion with no relevant textual references.	• Mention textual references, devices, or techniques with little or no analysis.	• Contain numerous inaccuracies or repetition in commentary. • Offer only simplistic explanations that do not strengthen the argument.	• Provide commentary that is not sufficiently developed or is too limited. • Assume or imply a connection to the thesis that is not consistently explicit.	• Provide commentary that uses significant details of the text to draw conclusions. • Integrate short excerpts throughout in order to support the thesis' interpretation.

Additional Notes

• Writing that suffers from grammatical and/or mechanical errors that interfere with communication cannot earn the fourth point in this row.

Row C: Sophistication (0–1 point)	
Scoring Criteria	
0 points for	**1 point for**
• Not meeting the criteria for 1 point.	• Exhibiting sophistication of thought and/or advancing a complex literary argument.
Decision Rules and Scoring Notes	
Responses that do not earn this point:	**Responses that earn this point demonstrate one (or more) of the following:**
• Try to contextualize an interpretation, but make predominantly sweeping generalizations (*"Throughout all history . . . "* OR *"Everyone believes . . . "*). • Only hint at other possible interpretations (*"Some may think . . . "* OR *"Though the poem might be said to . . . "*). • Write one statement about a thematic interpretation of the poem without consistently maintaining that idea. • Oversimplify complexities in the poem. • Present complicated or complex sentences or language that is ineffective and detracts from the argument.	• Present a thesis that demands nuanced analysis of textual evidence and successfully prove it. • Illuminate the significance or relevance of an interpretation within a broader context. • Discuss alternative interpretations of a text. • Acknowledge and account for contradictions, ambiguities, and/or complexities within the text. • Provide relevant analogies to help better understand an interpretation. • Develop a prose style that is especially vivid, persuasive, resounding, or appropriate to the student's argument.
Additional Notes	
• This point should be awarded only if the demonstration of sophistication or complex understanding is part of the argument, not merely a phrase or brief reference.	

High-Scoring Essay

In the poem "Spring," the speaker displays a quite complex relationship with the coming of spring. Although she notices and appreciates the natural beauty of spring, she cannot reconcile the rebirth of the season with images of death. Millay combines traditional and jarring imagery, with an overall gloomy tone and an unusual poetic form to create a speaker who confronts April, not as a welcome month of resurgence, but as a babbling idiot.

The poem gets right to the point in the opening line as the speaker asks, "To what purpose, April, do you return again?" The tone is immediately confrontational, as the speaker demands that April justify its appearance. But then she answers her own question, indicating that natural splendor is insufficient to right her mood; stating, "Beauty is not enough," and letting spring know she sees right through its artifices. This establishes that, although she is forced to take note of the blooming spring around her, the season conceals something darker. Her complex attitude is revealed when one studies the intricacy of the imagery. Individual words and phrases in the first two stanzas such as "April," "Beauty," "quiet," "redness," "little leaves," "sun," "crocus," and "the earth is good," all appear to carry positive and traditional connotations of spring. However, that simple interpretation is deceiving. For example, the word "redness" implies the color of blood; the leaves are deliberately "little," and they are opening "stickily," which implies something unpleasant, not vibrant. The sun is not pleasantly warming; it is "hot" and the speaker observes the "spikes" of the crocus, as if those small, delicate, beautiful early-spring flowers are threatening. The speaker is almost mocking the customary notions of spring, making a reader wonder why she scorns the season so.

The next two stanzas help explain. Although on this sunny spring day everything is sprouting and growing and "there is no death," this thought seems to trigger something dark in the speaker's mind, plunging her ever deeper into her abyss. Her tone becomes more sarcastic as she challenges, "But what does that signify?" It is as if the speaker is unwilling to accept the actual growth and new life associated with spring because she is unable to forget those who have died. Perhaps she has war victims in mind, but in any case she slaps and shocks the reader with intense imagery of death, with "the brains of men eaten by maggots." She suggests nihilism, "Life in itself is nothing," and despair, "An empty cup, a flight of uncarpeted stairs." She is not going to let April arrive as if all's right with the world. However, the depressing tone and negative attitude have a purpose: she points out that it is *not only* the brains of men underground that are "eaten by maggots." This, coupled with the "empty cup" and "uncarpeted stairs" images implies that humanity needs to make something of the life they've been given; a life without substance "Is nothing." Therefore, it is up to mankind to fill their cup, to carpet their stairs, to keep the maggots at bay.

The poem concludes with the very same idea with which it began, that the natural beauty of spring is insufficient to soothe her inner torment. The opening states, "Beauty is not enough," and this thought is echoed at the end, "It is not enough. . . . " Finally, in the closing couplet, the author uses a most unusual poetic form, placing poor little April all alone on one line before mocking the month more, calling April an "idiot" who is merely "babbling and strewing flowers." The enjambment causes one to pause and take a deep breath before this final contemptuous blow to April is announced.

The reason this poem works so well is that it seems to be a bit off balance; the speaker's tone belies traditional notions of spring. The speaker's imagery acts like a double-edged sword, negatively modifying visions that should be welcome and beautiful. The poetic form at first appears traditional: four quatrains. But notice how the form falls apart at the end, as if the speaker's vitriol causes her to spit out lines in short bursts. The truncated lines "Life in itself / Is nothing," lead into the final couplet, where "April / Comes like an idiot, babbling and strewing flowers." All elements in the poem throw us off balance as we grasp the speaker's complex attitude, viewing spring in a new light.

(740 words)

Analysis of High-Scoring Essay

This astute student presents a strong interpretation of the poem "Spring," and it adroitly addresses the complexity of the speaker's attitude about the coming of spring. The introduction begins ably and on topic, identifying the speaker as one who confronts April, even as she is forced to respond to the natural beauty all around her. The quality of the thesis clearly deserves a point in Row A because it presents a defendable interpretation of the speaker's complex attitude about the coming of spring.

The first body paragraph is strongly developed and it addresses the first two stanzas extremely well. The student accurately identifies the speaker's tone as confrontational and demanding from the outset of the poem. Particularly pleasing is the way that the student analyzes the imagery. First, the student presents a healthy list of words and phrases that, when taken in isolation, "appear to carry positive and traditional connotations of spring," and then points out how this interpretation could be deceptive. The student details how the supposedly positive images were altered with unpleasant modifiers, noting that "the speaker is almost mocking the customary notions of spring." It is interesting that, instead of concluding the paragraph with an assertion, the student chooses to end the paragraph with a lingering question, wondering why the speaker is so disdainful; this works well. Additionally, the student's use of alliteration, " . . . she scorns the season so" reinforces the speaker's attitude, hissing out the "s" sounds.

The next paragraph explores the third and fourth stanzas with aplomb; it provides an explanation and an answer to the query posed in the previous paragraph. The student understands that the speaker sees the beauty and rebirth in the coming of spring, but points out that it "trigger[s] something dark in the speaker's mind." Boy, does it ever! The student also nails the speaker's tone as sarcastic and challenging, acknowledging that the speaker cannot reconcile spring's lush new growth with her thoughts of those who have died. The student, in passing, suggests the speaker may have World War I victims in mind, but does not pursue that avenue. Instead, the student jumps right to the disturbing image of maggots eating men's brains and then labels the speaker as nihilistic and despairing. The student nicely incorporates Robert Browning's "all's right with the world" quote into the essay's analysis. Then the student provides a strong interpretation of the poem and an understanding of the speaker's purpose: to imply that living people can be as hollow as the dead, leading empty lives without substance. The student supports this with convincing detail from the poem and sums up the poem's message with pleasing parallel construction: "it is up to mankind to fill their cup, to carpet their stairs, to keep the maggots at bay."

The last body paragraph analyzes the end of the poem, pointing out how it concludes by repeating the same thought it began with, the idea that beauty alone is not enough. Then the student focuses on the final couplet, noticing the "most unusual poetic form" of placing the word "April" as the only word in a line. The student's voice comes through distinctly, sympathizing with "poor little April all alone," before acknowledging that the speaker continues "mocking the month." The alliteration works well, as does the student's comment that the enjambment causes one to "pause and take a deep breath"; this is insightful and accurate.

The concluding paragraph is, thankfully, not just a stock summary, nor does it employ the all-too-common cliché lines, such as "So, as you can see. . . . " Instead, we are treated to more of the student's perceptive insights. The idea that the poem "seems to be a bit off balance" is supported by acknowledging the tone, the imagery, and the form. However, the student does not simply state that these elements are used in the poem; he or she analyzes them in greater detail. Especially effective is the student's look at how the poetic "form falls apart at the end," explaining that "the truncated lines lead into the final couplet." Again, the student's voice becomes vibrant and distinct, asserting that "the speaker's vitriol causes her to spit out lines in short bursts." Returning to the idea that the poem works because it is a bit off balance, the student claims that "all elements in the poem throw us off balance as we grasp the speaker's complex attitude" because the speaker's view of spring is so unconventional. This is certainly not a run-of-the-mill conclusion, and it leaves the Reader with food for thought. The textual evidence and commentary are both stellar, earning 4 points in Row B.

Overall, this excellent essay deserves a very high score because it is so well organized and well written. The ideas are sophisticated, as is the presentation, and the vocabulary is top-notch. Every paragraph is well developed and well organized. The student's interpretation of the poem is convincing, insightful, and thought-provoking. The student's prose style is vivid and appropriate to the essay's argument, earning a point in Row C. A Reader is likely to smile and gladly give the essay an overall score of 6.

Low-Scoring Essay

In her poem Spring, Edna St. Vincent-Millay tries to depict a speaker with a very complex attitude toward the coming of spring. This complex attitude is very evident throughout the poem. Because of its date, I think this poem might be more about the end of WWI than about the coming of spring.

The imagery is the first tip-off that the speaker is conflicted. It starts off with images of spring, "red little leaves" and "the earth is good," but then she gets all mixed up and starts babbling about weird stuff like maggots eating man's brains and "Life is nothing," before going back to pretty flowers in the last line. All of this mixed-up imagery shows that the speaker is very conflicted about the coming of spring.

The dismal tone of the poem is another clue that the speaker is conflicted. It starts right out with a dark tone when the speaker says "Beauty is not enough." The tone appears to get brighter for a while, with the speaker enjoying the beauty of spring, but then it gets dark again and it stays that way all the way to the end. This back & forth with the mostly-dark tone is another clue that the speaker is conflicted about the coming of spring.

Also, the unusual form of the poem contributes to the feeling of conflict. The poem starts out OK with a standard-looking form, four stanzas with four lines each. But then it gets weird at the end, with a final 2-line stanza that just seems to hang there like an afterthought or something. This unusual form also adds to the feeling of conflict or confusion in the speaker.

In conclusion, Edna St Vincent Millay depicts a very conflicted speaker here; she seems to like the spring flowers, but she keeps interrupting with negative images of death and stuff. You can see this conflicted attitude in the imagery, and in the tone, and in the odd form. As I said, I think this poem might really be more about the ending of WWI, than about the coming of spring.

(362 words)

Analysis of Low-Scoring Essay

The student does not begin this essay with much assurance, merely informing us that Millay "tries to depict a speaker with a very complex attitude," which makes one wonder if she succeeded. Apparently she did, for we learn that the complex attitude is evident throughout. The student ends with a personal opinion, stating that he or she thinks the poem is more about the end of World War I than the coming of spring, which is irrelevant. This idea seems as if the student is grasping at straws, taking the date in the prompt and making it fit, regardless of its connection. The introduction is somewhat on topic, but offers no analysis. Additionally, a Reader will wish that the student had punctuated the title of the poem; remember to place poem titles inside quotation marks. Because the thesis only restates the prompt and does not present a relevant interpretation, it does not earn a point in Row A.

Like many formulaic essays, this one opens with a body paragraph devoted to one poetic element, imagery. However, instead of analyzing how the imagery contributes to the speaker's complex attitude, the student merely asserts that the speaker is conflicted. The student provides two quotations from the beginning of the poem, but offers no analysis of them; they are simply labeled as "images of spring." Next, the student proceeds to tell us that "she gets all mixed up and starts babbling about weird stuff." Unfortunately, the student is the one who gets all mixed up, apparently unable to reconcile the image of maggots with "pretty flowers in the last line." Many students will fall into this trap of not knowing what to say, especially since the maggot imagery is so untraditional, or they may completely ignore the speaker's unusual imagery. The paragraph ends with a comment that essentially states "this shows that . . . " and repeats that the speaker is conflicted.

The next body paragraph purports to explore tone, labeling it as dismal and informing us that this is another clue to the speaker's confusion. Although the student inserts one quotation from the poem's second line, the entire paragraph merely summarizes the tone as shifting from bad to good and then back to bad. We get no more examples and certainly no analysis.

The final body paragraph claims the "unusual form of the poem contributes to the feeling of conflict." The student observes that Millay produces four quatrains (without using that technical term) and calls that an "OK . . . standard-looking form." But, just like the student's claim about imagery, we are simply informed that the form "gets weird" with its final couplet. Instead of analyzing *how* the couplet adds to the speaker's complex attitude, the student states that it "hang[s] there like an afterthought," and again claims it contributes to the "conflict or confusion in the speaker."

The conclusion does not benefit from the overly obvious opening phrase, and it continues to demonstrate that the student did not really grasp the speaker's complex attitude; instead, the student cannot reconcile the images of pretty "spring flowers" with the "negative images of death and stuff." The conclusion provides a mere summary and a repetition of the essay, including the off-topic remark about the poem being more about the ending of WWI than the coming of spring. Indeed, the speaker in the poem may possibly be alluding to the destruction of the war, but that is only one interpretation, and this student does not know how to process it. The evidence and commentary are sufficient enough to earn 2 points in Row B. The Reader gets text examples, but with scant analysis and misinterpretations of the evidence.

Ultimately, the student does not appear to grasp the intensity and complexity of the poem's message, and he or she oversimplifies it to a great degree. The essay fails to analyze how the poetic devices help to convey the speaker's complex attitude, offering insubstantial evidence and confused ideas. Its focus is repetitive and simplistic, as is its language. It does not qualify for a point in Row C. This essay deserves an overall score of 2 because it presents an incomplete understanding of the task required by the prompt.

Question 2: *Cranford* by Elizabeth Gaskell

The following scoring guide explicitly explains how to earn up to 6 total points for a prose analysis essay. Row A (thesis) can earn up to 1 point; Row B (evidence and commentary) can earn up to 4 points, and Row C (sophistication) can earn up to 1 point.

Row A: Thesis (0–1 point)

Scoring Criteria

0 points for any of the following:	1 point for
• Having no defendable thesis. • Only restating the prompt in the thesis. • Only summarizing the issue with no claim in the thesis. • Presenting a thesis that does not address the prompt.	• Addressing the prompt with a defendable thesis that presents an interpretation and may establish a line of reasoning.

Decision Rules and Scoring Notes

Theses that do not earn this point	Theses that do earn this point
• Only restate the prompt. • Only offer an irrelevant generalized comment about the passage. • Simply describe the passage's features rather than making a defendable claim.	• Take a position on the prompt and provide a defendable interpretation of how Gaskell portrays the complex characters of Cranford.

Additional Notes

• The thesis may be one or more sentences anywhere in the response.
• A thesis that meets the criteria can be awarded the point whether or not the rest of the response successfully conveys that line of reasoning.

Row B: Evidence AND Commentary (0–4 points)

Scoring Criteria

0 points for	1 point for	2 points for	3 points for	4 points for
• Simply repeating the thesis (if present). • **OR** restating provided information. • **OR** providing mostly irrelevant and/or incoherent examples.	• Summarizing the passage without reference to a thesis. • **OR** providing vague textual references. • **OR** providing textual references of questionable relevance. • **AND** providing little or no commentary.	• Making relevant textual references (direct quotes or paraphrases). • **AND** providing commentary but repeats, oversimplifies, or misinterprets the cited evidence or text.	• Making relevant textual references (direct quotes or paraphrases). • **AND** providing commentary that explains the logical relationship between textual examples and the thesis; however, commentary is uneven, limited, or incomplete.	• Making relevant textual references (direct quotes or paraphrases). • **AND** providing well-developed commentary that explicitly explains the relationship between the evidence and the thesis.

Decision Rules and Scoring Notes				
Typical responses that earn 0 points:	**Typical responses that earn 1 point:**	**Typical responses that earn 2 points:**	**Typical responses that earn 3 points:**	**Typical responses that earn 4 points:**
• Are unclear or fail to address the prompt. • May present mere opinion with no relevant textual references.	• Mention textual references, devices, or techniques with little or no analysis.	• Contain numerous inaccuracies or repetition in commentary. • Offer only simplistic explanations that do not strengthen the argument.	• Provide commentary that is not sufficiently developed, or is too limited. • Assume or imply a connection to the thesis that is not consistently explicit.	• Provide commentary that uses significant details of the text to draw conclusions. • Integrate short excerpts throughout in order to support the thesis' interpretation.

Additional Notes

• Writing that suffers from grammatical and/or mechanical errors that interfere with communication cannot earn the fourth point in this row.

Row C: Sophistication (0–1 point)

Scoring Criteria	
0 points for	**1 point for**
• Not meeting the criteria for 1 point.	• Exhibiting sophistication of thought and/or advancing a complex literary argument.

Decision Rules and Scoring Notes	
Responses that do not earn this point:	**Responses that earn this point demonstrate one (or more) of the following:**
• Try to contextualize an interpretation, but make predominantly sweeping generalizations (*"Throughout all history . . ."* OR *"Everyone believes . . ."*). • Only hint at other possible interpretations (*"Some may think . . ."* OR *"Though the passage might be said to . . ."*). • Write one statement about a thematic interpretation of the passage without consistently maintaining that idea. • Oversimplify complexities in the passage. • Present complicated or complex sentences or language that is ineffective and detracts from the argument.	• Present a thesis that demands nuanced analysis of textual evidence and successfully prove it. • Illuminate the significance or relevance of an interpretation within a broader context. • Discuss alternative interpretations of a text. • Acknowledge and account for contradictions, ambiguities, and/or complexities within the text. • Provide relevant analogies to help better understand an interpretation. • Develop a prose style that is especially vivid, persuasive, resounding, or appropriate to the student's argument.

Additional Notes

• This point should be awarded only if the demonstration of sophistication or complex understanding is part of the argument, not merely a phrase or brief reference.

Medium-Scoring Essay

An interesting intellectual exercise when reading fiction is to consider the date or era when the work was written and then compare it to the date or era when it is set. You will notice that different authors use widely divergent approaches to the concept of anachronism; some works that are set in the more distant past may seem quite contemporary, and yet other works that are set in the recent past may be filled with artifacts and anachronisms. It all depends on the author's choice of tone and their use of literary devices to develop their characters.

Elizabeth Gaskell's novel <u>Cranford</u> is of the later type. The novel was written in 1851 and it is set in the 1830s, a scarce two decades earlier, certainly in the realm of living memory, yet it is presented as being almost wholly anachronistic. The residents of Cranford, who are almost exclusively women, dress in archaic styles, speak in archaic diction, and dwell on archaic details. Gaskell makes it clear that the ladies dress in styles that are "very independent of fashion" and she makes good use of details such as the scrupulous Miss Tyler, who displayed "the last tight and scanty petticoat in wear in England, was seen in Cranford—and seen without a smile."

This last bit of comedic diction is part of a recurring pattern in this work; Gaskell uses humor effectively throughout the piece to help emphasize her larger points. She begins with a humorous hyperbolic overstatement right in the opening line, "In the first place, Cranford is in possession of the Amazons," a statement which is certain to get the attention of her readers, but which also serves to set the tone of the piece. She immediately continues with rapid-fire bon mots, such "somehow the gentleman disappears" and "whatever does become of the gentlemen, they are not at Cranford. What could they do if they were there?" By using this light tone, Gaskell entices her readers to enter her fictional world with a smile, to laugh along with her characters, not at them.

Gaskell makes skillful use of diction to help develop her complex characters. You may guffaw when you hear a description of a character uttering a line, such as "'A man,' as one of them observed to me once, 'is *so* in the way in the house!'" The intended function of the dialogue goes far deeper than the obvious comedic aspects; this line establishes that the character is independent, outspoken, and quite comfortable in her own skin. Gaskell's skillful use of diction and idiom tells her readers a great deal about the characters, much more than they would learn from simple description.

The details of everyday life in Cranford are also telling; Gaskell includes a multitude of elements, each distinct in its own right, but she intertwines the details to produce a tapestry wherein the whole is greater than the sums of its parts. She entrances us with her depictions of men who are "fairly frightened to death" and "trim gardens full of choice flowers without a weed to speck them" and "rushing out at the geese that occasionally venture into the gardens if the gates are left open" and that "The Cranfordians had that kindly *esprit de corps* which made them overlook all deficiencies in success" and on and on. Her readers devour these details and Gaskell uses this humor to develop her characters, to flesh out her setting, to make you believe in her little world, the fictional village of Cranford.

Overall, Gaskell shows equally deft talents for each literary device she chooses; whether it is a telling line of diction, a revealing instance of too-often-overlooked detail, or a humorous highlight that makes the reader chuckle, this author knows how to work her audience. But she hints that her readers may be in on the joke too, as is displayed in the amazingly long and wonderfully tongue-in-cheek closing sentence, which concludes with Mrs. Forrester " . . . pretending not to know what cakes were sent up, though she knew, and we knew, and she knew that we knew, and we knew that she knew that we knew, she had been busy all the morning making tea-bread and sponge-cakes." Bravo Ms. Gaskell!

(707 words)

Analysis of Medium-Scoring Essay

Introductions are tricky. The student who immediately begins the first sentence by stating the title, author, and relating the prompt will have produced a predictable and boring introduction; although it may fulfill the essential purpose of an introduction, it's still boring. But a student who can quickly grab the Reader's attention with a thought-provoking idea, even before weaving in the title, author, and prompt, usually fares better, at least in the Reader's first impression. However, a student who babbles without any insight and never gets around to the prompt will not impress the Reader at all. The introduction to this essay falls into that category. It, sadly, basically says nothing. The Reader has to stretch to find the thesis, but the student eventually addresses the prompt enough to earn a point in Row A by claiming that "Gaskell uses humor effectively throughout the piece to help emphasize her larger points," and " Gaskell makes skillful use of diction to help develop her complex characters."

The first body paragraph introduces the author and title while telling us Gaskell's novel "is of the later [sic] type," but by now the Reader has forgotten what that idea was and will be annoyed at having to go back and reread the introduction. Fortunately, the student basically repeats the idea, that the setting is anachronistic, but whether or not that is accurate or relevant to the prompt is yet to be seen. The paragraph picks up steam as it tries to prove the Cranford ladies' independence, yet a Reader will be unconvinced that the ladies' speech is archaic and that they dwell on archaic details. Textual evidence would certainly help, as would stronger analysis. It seems as if the student is trying to address Gaskell's diction and is trying to do it with stylistic parallel construction, but the student's content does not impress. The Reader ends up wondering what the student's point really is.

The next paragraph again is confusing; the imprecise phrase "last bit of comedic diction" leaves one wondering what the student is referring to; is it the quotation that ends the previous paragraph? If so, why begin discussing it in a new paragraph? In what way is it "part of a recurring pattern" of Gaskell making "larger points," aided by humor? Instead of providing a logical explanation and transition, the student oddly appears to use the first sentence of the excerpt as an example of the "last bit of comedic diction," which makes no sense. The student deserves credit for understanding that Gaskell is inviting readers to enter the fictional world of Cranford "with a smile, to laugh along with her characters." However, if the student's organizational scheme is trying to analyze Gaskell's use of humor in this paragraph, it is falling flat.

The following paragraph addresses diction and gets a smile from the Reader for accurately claiming one may "guffaw" at one of Gaskell's humorous phrases. The student also accurately identifies the character as independent and outspoken; however, the paragraph suddenly ends with a bland statement informing us that Gaskell's "skillful use of diction and idiom" enhances what we know about characters. It is a claim that needs more analysis and additional text examples to be persuasive.

The subsequent paragraph examines the details of life in Cranford, letting us know that they are "telling." The first sentence in this paragraph is overly long, 42 words, and unfortunately it essentially says nothing. This is a typical error by students who attempt to develop paragraphs without first clarifying what it is that they have to say. This student does then include several examples of details in the excerpt and claims they "entrance us" as we "devour these details" and buy into the fictional world of Cranford. The claim is hyperbolic, but well-meaning.

The conclusion begins with an adequate summary before moving on to the somewhat exaggerated claim that Gaskell "knows how to work her audience." Although including new examples in a conclusion is risky, the student's addition of the humorous last sentence of the excerpt seems appropriate for the claim that readers are "in on the joke." It's hard to predict whether AP Readers will applaud or grimace at the student's closing line ("Bravo Ms. Gaskell!"), but one has to appreciate this student's enthusiasm. The evidence and commentary are sufficient to warrant 3 points in Row B. The analysis is too uneven and limited to deserve more.

As a whole, the essay earns only a medium score. It's really not bad, but it's not great, either. It does not meet the criteria for a point in Row C. To earn a higher score this student should concentrate on clarity and brevity; too many sentences and phrases are vacuous. The overall organization is acceptable, but the development of ideas is no more than adequate. If this student were to work on explaining the logic that connects the text evidence with the student's analytical ideas, the essay would definitely improve. As it is, it should earn an overall score of 4.

Low-Scoring Essay

You can tell a lot about a character in a novel by his actions, but you can learn a lot more by paying attention to the how he is presented by the author, for example by how he talks, along with all of the myriad little details that the character himself might not even notice. This a good way to look at the characters in Cranford, a comedic novel by Elizabeth Gaskel, by examining their diction, their little tiny details, and maybe even their sense of humor.

In the opening line, the author immediately sets an offbeat tone about the town's odd inhabitants; she apparently implies that the old Greek gods are alive because, "Cranford is in possession of the Amazons!" This line is designed to grab the readers attention and it is followed by more reasons why the town's all-women inhabitants are so odd, "somehow the gentleman disappears," and "he is fairly frightened to death," and "A man is *so* in the way in the house!" All of these examples of the diction in the text point the same way, the characters are all odd, they do not have a sense of humor, and they really do not seem to like men at all.

The author also helps to develop her characters by her attention to a million little details, sometimes things that the character herself might not even notice. The shows up when she describes the characters "fashion sence," she says the ladies are "very independent of fashion" and she describes the characters discussing why they do not ever dress up, they do not care what they look like when they are away, and they certainly do not care about fashion here at home in Cranford. These details about their odd fashion sense, and their independence, help to flesh out the characters personalities.

The excerpt ends with a situation that is quite funny for the reader, even if it is quite uncomfortable to the characters, because they have no sence of humor. The ladies are having a tea party at a friend's house, but the house is very tiny and so they are physically uncomfortable. But the funny part is how the author shows us more about the characters personalities by their show down with the maid; apparently she is faking ignorance about the hidden cakes, but the characters know, and she knows they know, and etc., so now the characters are also socially uncomfortable too. This touch of comedic humor at the end helps to seal in our impressions of the various characters; these ladies are incapable of laughing at themselves, but the reader can enjoy laughing at them.

(442 words)

Analysis of Low-Scoring Essay

The first sentence of this weak essay fails to impress the Reader, with its double use of the bland phrase "a lot," and its unclear concept about "the myriad little details that the character himself might not even notice." Some people unthinkingly accept the cliché that actions speak louder than words, but this student appears to believe in the opposite, claiming that readers learn more about characters from the author's presentation and "how he talks." This comment is even more inaccurate since no male actually "talks" in this excerpt, and even the female dialogue is sparse. When the student claims "This is a good way to look at the characters," the improper pronoun "this" apparently refers to the entire first sentence. The thesis offers very little promise, nothing more than stating that by examining the characters' "diction, their little tiny details, and maybe even their sense of humor," we will have a "good way to look at the characters." However, the thesis is adequate enough to earn a point in Row A. Unfortunately, this introduction is barely on topic, and it offers no insight. The student does not punctuate the novel's title and even misspells the author's name, but an AP Reader will try to ignore that lack of precision.

The first body paragraph, unfortunately, continues this pattern by offering no analysis and including far too many errors. The first claim, that the "author sets an offbeat tone," is fairly accurate, but the student provides no evidence to back up the claim. This is immediately followed by the erroneous idea that the author is implying the Greek gods are alive. The student then strings together three quotations that supposedly establish the characters' oddness, but the Reader is left wondering how these quotations could possibly prove what the student intends. Simply stating that "these examples of the diction . . . point the same way" does not convince a Reader of the accuracy of the student's claim that the characters are offbeat. In addition, these quotations could appropriately be used to explore the prompt, but the student apparently missed Gaskell's dry and subtle humor. When the student states that the characters do not have a sense of humor, he or she is misunderstanding the excerpt and the prompt, in addition to contradicting the thesis.

Many students are guilty of using hyperbole as they try to make their point, but to claim the author develops characters with "a million little details" is laughable. Next, the student repeats the questionable introduction assertion that these details "might" not be noticed even by the characters in the first place. Whether or not that is true or relevant is unclear. Additionally, the student misuses the example of the "characters 'fashion sence' [sic]." Gaskell does not actually present any dialogue among the characters about their clothing, only two comical observations that may be apocryphal in the first place; therefore, the characters do not "discuss" their "odd fashion sence [sic]." The student has failed once again to appreciate or notice the author's subtle humor and diction.

Finally, the student's conclusion also goes astray; the introduction thesis hints that "maybe" one can examine the Cranford inhabitants via their sense of humor, but the first sentence of the last paragraph contradicts that idea by stating "they have no sence [sic] of humor." The student tries to explore the example of the tea party at Mrs. Forrester's home, first irrelevantly claiming that the ladies are "physically uncomfortable" in her "very tiny" home. The student misunderstands the tea party scene. Instead of comprehending Gaskell's gentle diction that informs us the Cranford ladies are actually quite forgiving of their neighbors who might not be as wealthy, and instead of understanding that the ladies gladly pretend not to notice what everyone obviously notices and ignores, the student misreads the scene and concludes that the characters are "socially uncomfortable" and "incapable of laughing at themselves." It's a bit sad to think that anyone who reads *Cranford* would actually be laughing at the characters. Despite the presence of relevant textual evidence, the misinterpreted evidence, inaccuracies in commentary, and oversimplification of ideas earns 2 points in Row B.

Overall, this student needs to concentrate on reading the passage more carefully and addressing the task more clearly. The prompt asks for an analysis of Gaskell's techniques, and this student simply does not fulfill that task. Additionally, the student's writing is riddled with misreadings and other errors such as run-on sentences, apostrophe errors, spelling mistakes, and inaccurate phrasing. It does not qualify for a point in Row C, making the overall score 3.

Question 3: A Character's Struggle to Rise above Injustice

The following scoring guide explicitly explains how to earn up to 6 total points for a literary analysis essay. Row A (thesis) can earn up to 1 point; Row B (evidence and commentary) can earn up to 4 points, and Row C (sophistication) can earn up to 1 point.

Row A: Thesis (0–1 point)	
Scoring Criteria	
0 points for any of the following:	**1 point for**
• Having no defendable thesis. • Only restating the prompt in the thesis. • Only summarizing the issue with no claim in the thesis. • Presenting a thesis that does not address the prompt.	• Addressing the prompt with a defendable thesis that presents an interpretation and may establish a line of reasoning.
Decision Rules and Scoring Notes	
Theses that do not earn this point	**Theses that do earn this point**
• Only restate the prompt. • Only offer an irrelevant generalized comment about the chosen work.	• Take a position on the prompt and provide a defendable interpretation of how a character's struggle to rise above injustice adds to an interpretation of the chosen work as a whole.
Additional Notes	
• The thesis may be one or more sentences anywhere in the response. • A thesis that meets the criteria can be awarded the point whether or not the rest of the response successfully conveys that line of reasoning.	

Row B: Evidence AND Commentary (0–4 points)				
Scoring Criteria				
0 points for	**1 point for**	**2 points for**	**3 points for**	**4 points for**
• Simply repeating the thesis (if present). • **OR** restating provided information. • **OR** providing mostly irrelevant and/or incoherent examples.	• Summarizing the chosen work without reference to a thesis. • **OR** providing vague textual references. • **OR** providing textual references of questionable relevance. • **AND** providing little or no commentary.	• Making relevant textual references (direct quotes or paraphrases). • **AND** providing commentary but repeats, oversimplifies, or misinterprets the cited evidence or text.	• Making relevant textual references (direct quotes or paraphrases). • **AND** providing commentary that explains the logical relationship between textual examples and the thesis; however, commentary is uneven, limited, or incomplete.	• Making relevant textual references (direct quotes or paraphrases). • **AND** providing well-developed commentary that explicitly explains the relationship between the evidence and the thesis.
Decision Rules and Scoring Notes				
Typical responses that earn 0 points:	**Typical responses that earn 1 point:**	**Typical responses that earn 2 points:**	**Typical responses that earn 3 points:**	**Typical responses that earn 4 points:**
• Are unclear or fail to address the prompt. • May present mere opinion with no relevant textual references.	• Mention textual references, devices, or techniques with little or no analysis.	• Contain numerous inaccuracies or repetition in commentary. • Offer only simplistic explanations that do not strengthen the argument.	• Provide commentary that is not sufficiently developed or is too limited. • Assume or imply a connection to the thesis that is not consistently explicit.	• Provide commentary that uses significant details of the text to draw conclusions. • Integrate short excerpts throughout in order to support the thesis' interpretation.

Additional Notes

• Writing that suffers from grammatical and/or mechanical errors that interfere with communication cannot earn the fourth point in this row.

Row C: Sophistication (0–1 point)

Scoring Criteria	
0 points for	**1 point for**
• Not meeting the criteria for 1 point.	• Exhibiting sophistication of thought and/or advancing a complex literary argument.

Decision Rules and Scoring Notes	
Responses that do not earn this point:	**Responses that earn this point demonstrate one (or more) of the following:**
• Try to contextualize an interpretation, but make predominantly sweeping generalizations (*"Throughout all history . . . "* OR *"Everyone believes . . . "*). • Only hint at other possible interpretations (*"Some may think . . . "* OR *"Though the work might be said to . . . "*). • Write one statement about a thematic interpretation of the chosen work without consistently maintaining that idea. • Oversimplify complexities in the chosen work. • Present complicated or complex sentences or language that is ineffective and detracts from the argument.	• Present a thesis that demands nuanced analysis of textual evidence and successfully prove it. • Illuminate the significance or relevance of an interpretation within a broader context. • Discuss alternative interpretations of a text. • Acknowledge and account for contradictions, ambiguities, and/or complexities within the text. • Provide relevant analogies to help better understand an interpretation. • Develop a prose style that is especially vivid, persuasive, resounding, or appropriate to the student's argument.

Additional Notes

• This point should be awarded only if the demonstration of sophistication or complex understanding is part of the argument, not merely a phrase or brief reference.

High-Scoring Essay

The truth can be elusive, but all people must constantly pursue it, protect it, and preserve it. Some truths are horrific, some enlightening, but it is an injustice to humanity when the truth is suppressed. In George Orwell's prescient novel <u>1984</u>, Winston Smith struggles to learn the truth and to preserve it, but his attempts are ultimately crushed by the unjust totalitarian state. As Winston struggles, we too struggle, terrified of the consequences that must follow when the truth is suppressed. This novel shouts out against the attacks on the truth in society, even more so today than when it was written in 1949.

The irony of Winston Smith's job in the novel's dystopian society cannot be overestimated: He works at the ludicrously titled Ministry of Truth, literally rewriting history and changing the facts of the past to coincide with the present claims of the Party. This injustice against the truth manifests itself in Winston's personal life as he dreams of the past, particularly his mother's disappearance and it makes him begin to wonder what is really true. While he dutifully exercises in front of the telescreen, as required of all citizens every morning, he wracks his brain, trying to remember details of his past. Then, he returns to work daily to rewrite facts and alter past articles, relentlessly changing the truth of history. However, it turns out that Winston does have some backbone; in an alcove in his apartment, above the all-seeing eye of Big Brother in the telescreen, he uses a secret diary to record true facts he has learned and his own rebellious thoughts, a crime unto itself. Apparently he values the truth so much that he'll even break the law to preserve it.

In time, Winston realizes that he no longer trusts anything the Party says; their propaganda is an injustice against him and against all others. As he struggles to remember the truth of his personal past and the facts of world history, he begins to comprehend the extent to which the Party secretly controls the minds of the populace, although he feels he is personally above brainwashing. Winston still wants to fight against this unjust and corrupt system and tries to do so inconspicuously. He begins a secret affair with Julia, a coworker in the Party, and in their intimate moments together, when they are not having sex, he voices lofty, rebellious thoughts that she barely shares. He is apparently a one-man army in the struggle against injustice at this point. Unfortunately he and Julia agree to meet with another supposed subversive, O'Brien, thinking he's on their side. But injustice pervades this society, so of course O'Brien has set them up and he turns in the lovers instead of helping their cause. In a nutshell, it all goes to Hell, as Julia betrays Winston during torture and he, in turn, betrays her. At the end of the novel, Winston is a beaten man, mindlessly repeating Big Brother's slogans and falling in line.

Winston's struggle and defeat symbolize the fear we should all have of losing access to the truth. The novel's extreme and effective examples of torture, both physical and mental, demonstrate that humans can and do cave in and begin believing that which they previously knew to be untrue. We always like to think that the hero can somehow overcome evil, and we constantly hope that Winston can escape the Party's grip. After all, historical and literary examples abound of such heroism leading to triumph. However, Orwell will not allow such a fairytale ending to happen. We struggle along with Winston and ultimately realize that totalitarian rule can kill the human spirit, just as it kills all semblance of the truth. That is a terrifying concept in this time of "alternative facts." Perhaps by vicariously living through Winston's travails, by persistently rooting for him in his struggles against unjust authority, we can become more aware and more diligent at protecting the truth in our own lives.

(663 words)

Analysis of High-Scoring Essay

This sophisticated essay persuasively analyzes Winston Smith's struggle to rise above injustice in the novel *1984*. The "injustice to humanity" he confronts is clarified as the government's suppression and distortion of the truth, its rewriting of history and deceptive use of mind control on its citizens. The student displays refined style, using parallel construction in the phrase " . . . pursue it, protect it, and preserve it," and in "As Winston struggles, we too struggle." The student directly addresses *how* the struggle adds to the meaning of the work as a whole, and he or she expands the topical and timely message of "fighting to preserve the truth" in today's society. It definitely deserves a point in Row A.

The body paragraphs begin by exploring the early part of the novel, adroitly noting the irony that Winston's job is at the Ministry of Truth, where his task is to search historical print sources and changes their facts to fit the Party's current positions. The student's analysis extends this injustice against the truth to Winston's personal life, as he wrestles to remember his past and clarify what is actually true in his life. Although Winston appears to follow the dictates of the Party, the student cleverly notes that he has "some backbone," and describes how he keeps a secret diary to write down accurate facts and to record his own rebellious thoughts. The purpose of this paragraph, to establish Winston's character within the novel's dystopian society, is fulfilled quite acceptably.

In the next paragraph, the student summarizes a great deal of the plot, but does so in the service of analysis. This novel has a great many scenes and the student does a decent job of condensing them in order to show how Winston's character develops. He "realizes that he no longer trusts anything." He "struggles to remember the truth." He "still wants to fight against" the injustice of the Party, which "pervades this society." It is challenging to provide ample plot information from this novel without lapsing into mere plot summary, and many students, perhaps overly excited at the novel's action, fall into that trap. But this student avoids being banal by inserting enough analytical phrases to stay focused on the prompt.

The conclusion of this essay propels it to a stellar score. We have already learned Winston's fate in the previous paragraph, and now the student, with a strong independent voice, condemns the suppression of truth in any society. Acknowledging the powerful persuasion of torture, the student understands that humans "can and do cave in." The student is perceptive to recognize how we all want the hero to overcome adversity, and even though some historical and literary examples may prove that to happen, Orwell could not permit "such a fairytale ending." Indeed, this novel would not have had such a huge international impact if Winston had somehow succeeded in his struggle to rise above injustice. Next, the student strongly condemns modern society's attack on the truth in "this time of 'alternative facts.'" The last sentence does not claim we can eliminate this injustice, but we can become "more aware and more diligent at protecting the truth." The Reader will thank the student for not summarizing the essay; the conclusion instead moves it forward with even more thoughtful commentary and contributes to earning 4 points in Row B.

If the essay's body paragraphs had the same force as the conclusion, it might earn a higher score, but the body paragraphs are a bit too plot-laden and they are not quite as strong in their analysis as the highest-scoring essay should display. It does not qualify for a point in Row C, and should earn an overall score of 5.

Low-Scoring Essay

Atticus Finch in <u>To Kill a Mockingbird</u> by Harper Lee struggles to defeat injustice in the small town of Macomb. He is a good man and a good lawyer who is assigned to defend Tom Robinson, an innocent black man accused of raping a white woman. As Atticus struggles to maintain his dignity and his family's safety during the trial, he also stands up to the town's racists and tries to change a few minds.

Atticus always stands up for what is right and fights against that which is wrong. When an angry mob wants to yank Tom Robinson out of jail and lynch him before the trial, he camps out in front of the door to confront the angry men and secure Tom's safety. He knows every person deserves the right to a fair trial and it would be an injustice if he did not stand up to the mob.

Atticus keeps his head high when others fight low. When the opposing attorney, Mr. Gilmer, resorts to any down-and-dirty means to convict Tom, including inciting the jury's inner racism, Atticus struggles to represent all that is good. He stands up tall and appeals to the jury's sense of what is right, what is just in this crazy case of injustice. Tom is convicted and the injustice continues, but that is not Atticus' fault.

Atticus Finch is a man we should all strive to be like. He tries to stand up to injustice and even though he loses the case, he is a symbol of those who fight for the right cause.

(262 words)

Analysis of Low-Scoring Essay

This essay, unfortunately, does not live up to its potential. *To Kill a Mockingbird* is an entirely appropriate choice for this prompt, which invites students to analyze a character who struggles to rise above injustice. A few Readers might quibble with this student's choice to discuss Atticus Finch, arguing that he does not technically struggle to rise above injustice, but rather, he struggles to maintain justice. However, most Readers will not bicker about this detail. The essay's introduction immediately names Atticus Finch, the novel's title, and the author before beginning to address the concepts in the prompt. Next, the student describes Atticus in somewhat understated terms; many will think he is much more than simply "a good man and a good lawyer." The student also mentions the struggle Atticus will face defending Tom Robinson. The introduction ends with the student's thesis: that Atticus struggles to maintain his dignity and his family's safety, that he stands up to racists, and that he tries to change a few minds. Some might question the student's choice to include Atticus' dignity and his family's safety as part of the struggle to rise above injustice. But in any case, this introduction fails to include any mention of what the struggle adds to the meaning of the work as a whole. However, it does earn a point in Row A for presenting a defendable thesis.

The first body paragraph presents the topic sentence that Atticus "always stands up for what is right and fights against that which is wrong." This idea is followed by one lone text example, the incident in which the angry mob tries to lynch Tom Robinson. The example is presented simplistically, without even explaining whether or not Atticus does manage to "secure Tom's safety." Of course, the Reader will know the outcome, and the student thankfully does not lapse into long-winded plot summary. However, the student just drops this one example and then sums up the paragraph, stretching to tie in the prompt by claiming "it would be an injustice if he did not stand up to the mob." This paragraph would be much more persuasive if it were to include additional textual evidence and more developed and insightful analysis.

The second body paragraph also begins with a topic sentence, this time stating that "Atticus keeps his head high when others fight low." But just like the preceding weak paragraph, this idea is followed with one single example from the textual trial itself. The student points out that Mr. Gilmer, the prosecuting attorney, "resorts to any down-and-dirty means" in his remarks and "incit[es] the jury's inner racism." That notion is countered by stating that Atticus "stands up tall" as he entreats the jury to see justice served. The jarring phrase "what is just in this crazy case of injustice" could certainly use some editing, but the student seems to be trying to address the prompt. The paragraph finishes simplistically, with the plot information that Atticus loses the case, but the student claims that it is not his fault. This is a greatly oversimplified analysis of such an important scene in the novel.

The conclusion is overly brief, with just two terse sentences, and it shows that the student is running out of steam. It does begin with a very reasonable notion, namely that Atticus Finch is a man "we should all strive to be like," and indeed, in the novel he is beyond admirable. The last sentence provides a decent summary, that he "stands up to injustice" and even though he loses, he is a symbol of those who do fight injustice. These ideas are valid, but they are not developed with any substance. Plus, the student never addresses what Atticus' struggle to rise above injustice adds to the work as a whole, which is half of the prompt, so at the end of the essay, we're left with an unfulfilled promise. These traits earn the essay 2 points in Row B.

The essay is certainly not all bad. It can be rewarded for proper use of some of the fundamentals of composition. It attempts to address the topic, although it does not discuss deeper issues of the prompt or the novel. It shows a viable organization, properly using a thesis, topic sentences, and a conclusion. The presentation is grammatically correct. However, the essay falls below par for several reasons and does not earn a point in Row C. The development of analytical ideas is slight and shallow. Each body paragraph needs more textual examples and much more examination of how the examples relate to the prompt. The failure to address deeper significance holds the essay back and unfortunately, the essay merely skims the surface of what is obvious: Atticus Finch is a "good man." This novel and this character present so much more depth that the student could have addressed. Each paragraph needs more thorough development; as it is, they average a paltry three sentences apiece. No writer can substantially prove a point with such skimpy and shallow development. The student's word choices could also be stronger; notice that all four paragraphs begin with the same word, "Atticus," and the phrase "stands up" appears five times in four short paragraphs. Some variety and sophistication in language usage would be appreciated and rewarded by the Reader. As written, this essay deserves an overall score of 3.

Scoring Worksheet

Use the following worksheet to arrive at a probable final AP score on Practice Exam 6. While it is sometimes difficult to be objective enough to score one's own essay, you can use the sample essay answers to approximate an essay score for yourself. Better yet, give your essays (along with the sample scored essays) to a friend or relative who you think is competent to score the essays.

Section I: Multiple-Choice Questions

$$\frac{}{\text{right answers}} = \frac{}{\text{multiple-choice raw score}}$$

$$\frac{}{\text{multiple-choice raw score}} \times 1.25 = \frac{}{\text{multiple-choice converted score}} \text{ (of possible 67.5)}$$

Section II: Free-Response Questions

$$\frac{}{\text{question 1 raw score}} + \frac{}{\text{question 2 raw score}} + \frac{}{\text{question 3 raw score}} = \frac{}{\text{essay raw score}}$$

$$\frac{}{\text{essay raw score}} \times 4.583 = \frac{}{\text{essay converted score}} \text{ (of possible 82.5)}$$

Final Score

$$\frac{}{\text{multiple-choice converted score}} + \frac{}{\text{essay converted score}} = \frac{}{\text{final converted score}} \text{ (of possible 150)}$$

Probable Final AP Score	
Final Converted Score	**Probable AP Score**
150–100	5
99–86	4
85–67	3
66–0	1 or 2